BENCHMARK SERIES

Microsoft® Excel

2016

Level 2

Jan Davidson

PARADIGM
EDUCATION SOLUTIONS

St. Paul

Senior Vice President	Linda Hein
Editor in Chief	Christine Hurney
Director of Production	Timothy W. Larson
Production Editor	Jen Weaverling
Cover and Text Designer	Valerie King
Copy Editors	Communicáto, Ltd.
Senior Design and Production Specialist	Jack Ross
Design and Production Specialist	PerfecType
Assistant Developmental Editors	Mamie Clark, Katie Werdick
Testers	Janet Blum, Fanshawe College; Traci Post
Instructional Support Writers	Janet Blum, Fanshawe College; Brienna McWade
Indexer	Terry Casey
Vice President Information Technology	Chuck Bratton
Digital Projects Manager	Tom Modl
Vice President Sales and Marketing	Scott Burns
Director of Marketing	Lara Weber McLellan

ISBN 978-0-76386-939-7 (print)
ISBN 978-0-76386-940-3 (digital)

© 2017 by Paradigm Publishing, Inc.
875 Montreal Way
St. Paul, MN 55102
Email: educate@emcp.com
Website: ParadigmCollege.com

Brief Contents

Contents

Preface

Benchmark Series: Microsoft® Excel 2016 is designed for students who want to learn how to use this powerful spreadsheet program to manipulate numerical data in resolving issues related to finances or others numbers-based information. After successfully completing a course using this textbook and digital courseware, students will be able to:

- Create and edit spreadsheets worksheets of varying complexity
- Format cells, columns, and rows as well as entire workbooks in a uniform, attractive style
- Analyze numerical data and project outcomes to make informed decisions
- Plan, research, create, revise, and publish worksheets and workbooks to meet specific communication needs
- Given a workplace scenario requiring a numbers-based solution, assess the information requirements and then prepare the materials that achieve the goal efficiently and effectively

In addition to mastering Excel skills, students will learn to import and export files between Excel and other programs in the Office 2016 suite. Upon completing the text, students can expect to be proficient in using Excel to organize, analyze, and present information.

Well-designed textbook pedagogy is important, but students learn technology skills through practice and problem solving. Technology provides opportunities for interactive learning as well as excellent ways to quickly and accurately assess student performance. To this end, this textbook is supported with SNAP 2016, Paradigm's web-based training and assessment learning management system. Details about SNAP as well as additional student courseware and instructor resources can be found on page xiv.

Achieving Proficiency in Excel 2016

Since its inception several Office versions ago, the *Benchmark Series* has served as a standard of excellence in software instruction. Elements of the *Benchmark Series* function individually and collectively to create an inviting, comprehensive learning environment that produces successful computer users. The following visual tour highlights the structure and features that comprise the highly popular *Benchmark* model.

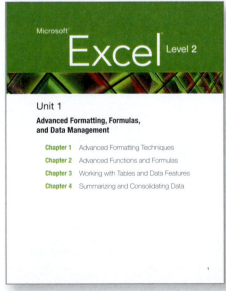

Unit Openers display the unit's four chapter titles. *Excel Level 2* contains two units; each unit concludes with a comprehensive unit performance assessment.

Student Textbook and eBook

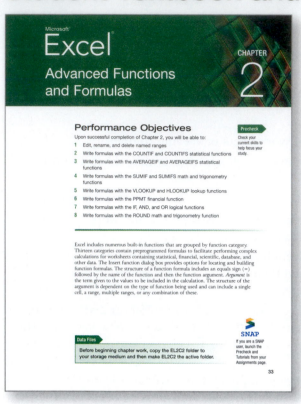

Chapter Openers present the performance objectives and an overview of the skills taught.

Precheck quizzes allow students to check their current skills before starting chapter work.

Data Files are provided for each chapter from the ebook. A prominent note reminds students to copy the appropriate chapter data folder and make it active.

Students with SNAP access are reminded to launch the Precheck quiz and chapter tutorials from their SNAP Assignments page.

Projects Build Skill Mastery within Realistic Context

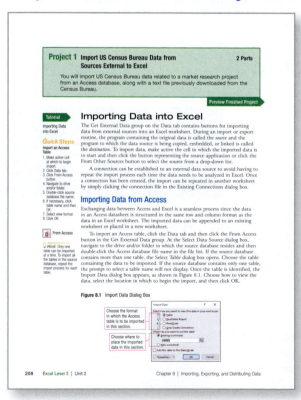

Multipart Projects provide a framework for instruction and practice on software features. A project overview identifies tasks to accomplish and key features to use in completing the work.

Preview Finished Project shows how the file will look after students complete the project.

Tutorials provide interactive, guided training and measured practice.

Quick Steps provide feature summaries for reference and review.

Hint margin notes offer useful tips on how to use features efficiently and effectively.

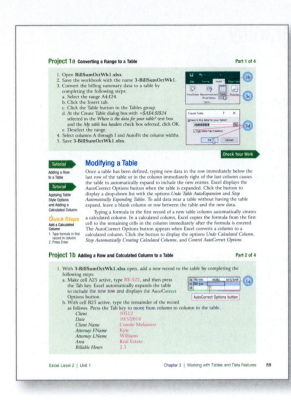

Step-by-Step Instructions guide students to the desired outcome for each project part. Screen captures illustrate what the screen should look like at key points.

Magenta Text identifies material to type.

Check Your Work allows students to confirm they have completed the project activity correctly.

Between project parts, the text presents instruction on the features and skills necessary to accomplish the next section of the project.

Typically, a file remains open throughout all parts of the project. Students save their work incrementally. At the end of the project, students save and then close the file.

Chapter Review Tools Reinforce Learning

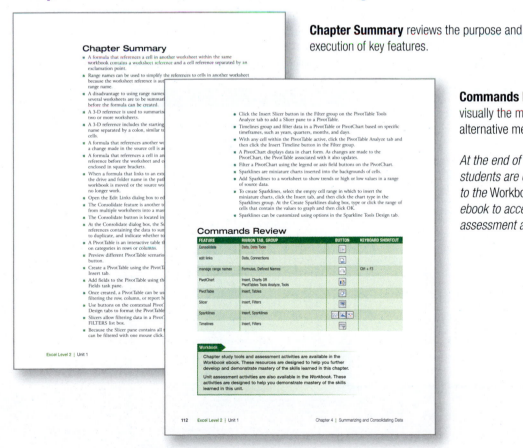

Chapter Summary reviews the purpose and execution of key features.

Commands Review summarizes visually the major features and alternative methods of access.

At the end of each chapter, students are encouraged to go to the Workbook *pages of the ebook to access study tools and assessment activities.*

Workbook eBook Activities Provide a Hierarchy of Learning Assessments

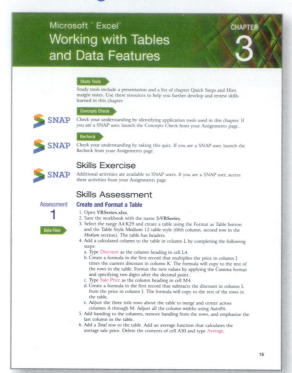

Study Tools are presentations with audio support and a list of chapter Quick Steps and Hint margin notes designed to help students further develop and review skills learned in the chapter.

Concepts Check is an objective completion exercise that allows students to assess their comprehension and recall of application features, terminology, and functions.

Recheck concept quizzes for each chapter enable students to check how their skills have improved after completing chapter work.

Skills Exercises are available to SNAP 2016 users. SNAP will automatically score student work, which is performed live in the application, and provide detailed feedback.

Skills Assessment exercises ask students to develop both standard and customized types of spreadsheets without how-to directions.

Visual Benchmark assessments test problem-solving skills and mastery of application features.

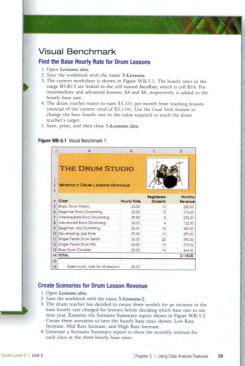

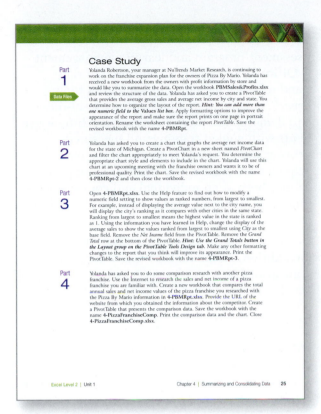

Case Study requires analyzing a workplace scenario and then planning and executing a multipart project.

Students search the web and/or use the program's Help feature to locate additional information required to complete the Case Study.

Unit Performance Assessments Deliver Cross-Disciplinary, Comprehensive Evaluation

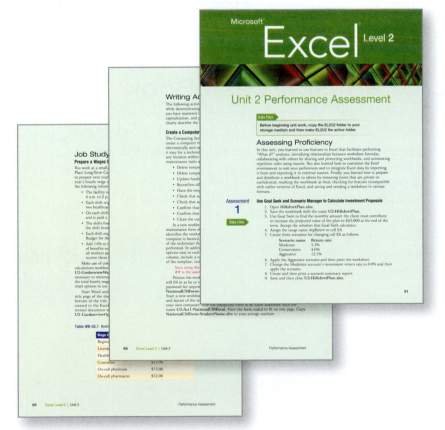

Assessing Proficiency exercises check mastery of features.

Writing Activities involve applying application skills in a communication context.

Internet Research projects reinforce research and information processing skills.

Job Study at the end of Unit 2 presents a capstone assessment requiring critical thinking and problem solving.

SNAP Training and Assessment

SNAP is a web-based training and assessment program and learning management system (LMS) for learning Microsoft Office 2016. SNAP is comprised of rich content, a sophisticated grade book, and robust scheduling and analytics tools. SNAP courseware supports the *Benchmark Series* content and delivers live-in-the-application assessments for students to demonstrate their skills mastery. Interactive tutorials increase skills-focused moments with guided training and measured practice. SNAP provides automatic scoring and detailed feedback on the many activities, exercises, and quizzes to help identify areas where additional support is needed, evaluating student performance both at an individual and course level. The *Benchmark Series* SNAP course content is also available to export into any LMS system that supports LTI tools.

Paradigm Education Solutions provides technical support for SNAP through 24-7 chat at ParadigmCollege.com. In addition, an online User Guide and other SNAP training tools for using SNAP are available.

Student eBook

The student ebook, available through SNAP or online at Paradigm.bookshelf.emcp.com, provides access to the *Benchmark Series* content from any device (desktop, tablet, and smartphone) anywhere, through a live Internet connection. The versatile ebook platform features dynamic navigation tools including a linked table of contents and the ability to jump to specific pages, search for terms, bookmark, highlight, and take notes. The ebook offers live links to the interactive content and resources that support the print textbook, including the student data files, Precheck and Recheck quizzes, and interactive tutorials. The *Workbook* pages of the ebook also provide access to presentations with audio support and to end-of-chapter Concept Check, Skills Assessment, Visual Benchmark, Case Study, and end-of-unit Performance Assessment activities.

Instructor eResources eBook

All instructor resources are available digitally through a web-based ebook at Paradigm.bookshelf.emcp.com. The instructor materials include these items:

- Planning resources, such as lesson plans, teaching hints, and sample course syllabi
- Presentation resources, such as PowerPoint slide shows with lecture notes
- Assessment resources, including live and annotated PDF model answers for chapter work and workbook activities, rubrics for evaluating student work, and chapter-based exam banks

Microsoft® Excel® Level 2

Unit 1

Advanced Formatting, Formulas, and Data Management

Microsoft® Excel®

Advanced Formatting Techniques

Performance Objectives

Precheck

Check your current skills to help focus your study.

Upon successful completion of Chapter 1, you will be able to:

1 Apply conditional formatting by entering parameters for a rule

2 Create and apply new rules for conditional formatting

3 Edit and delete conditional formatting rules

4 Apply conditional formatting using icon sets, data bars, and color scales

5 Apply conditional formatting using a formula

6 Apply conditional formatting using Quick Analysis

7 Apply fraction and scientific formatting

8 Apply special number formats

9 Create custom number formats

10 Modify text using the text functions PROPER, UPPER, LOWER, SUBSTITUTE, RIGHT, LEFT, MID, TRIM and CONCATENATE

11 Filter a worksheet using a custom AutoFilter

12 Filter and sort a worksheet using conditional formatting or cell attributes

Many worksheets can be formatted using the buttons available in the Font, Alignment, and Number groups on the Home tab of the ribbon, on the Mini toolbar, and with the Quick Analysis button. However, some situations require format categories that are not represented with buttons. Excel offers advanced formatting techniques to format specific values based on conditions. Conditional formatting changes allow for quick identification of any trends or highlight any values that may need to be investigated or monitored.

SNAP

If you are a SNAP user, launch the Precheck and Tutorials from your Assignments page.

Data Files

Before beginning chapter work, copy the EL2C1 folder to your storage medium and then make EL2C1 the active folder.

Working with a payroll worksheet, you will change the appearance of cells based on criteria related to pay rate and gross pay.

Preview Finished Project

Tutorial

Applying
Conditional
Formatting Using
Top/Bottom Rules

 Conditional
Formatting

Applying Conditional Formatting

Conditional formatting applies special formatting to those cells within a specified range that meet a specific condition. The formatting of the cells that do not meet the condition does not change. Changing the appearance of a cell based on a condition will quickly identify values that are high or low and makes it easier to spot trends. Formatting can be applied based on a specific value or a value that falls within a range or it can be applied by using a comparison operator, such as equal to (=), greater than (>), or less than (<). Conditional formats can also be based on dates, text entries, or duplicated values. Consider using conditional formatting to analyze a question, such as *Which store locations earned sales above their targets?* Using a different color to identify those stores that exceeded their target sales makes it easy to quickly identify the top performers.

Excel provides predefined conditional formatting rules that can be accessed from the Conditional Formatting button drop-list, as shown in Figure 1.1. Unique conditional formatting rules can also be created. Using options in the *Top/Bottom Rules* drop-down list, cells can be highlighted based on a top 10 or bottom 10 value or percent or by above average or below average values.

Figure 1.1 Conditional Formatting Button Drop-Down List

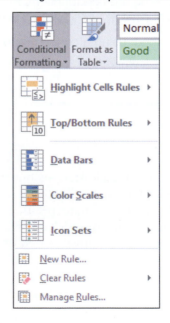

1. Open **VRPay-Oct20.xlsx**.
2. Save the workbook with the name **1-VRPay-Oct20.xlsx**.
3. Using conditional formatting, apply green fill with dark green text formatting to the pay rate values to identify employees whose pay rate is less than $10.50 by completing the following steps:
   a. Select the range L6:L23.
   b. Click the Conditional Formatting button in the Styles group on the Home tab.
   c. Point to *Highlight Cells Rules* and then click *Less Than* at the drop-down list.

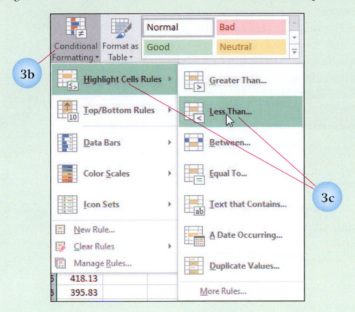

   d. At the Less Than dialog box with the text automatically selected in the *Format cells that are LESS THAN* text box, type 10.50.
   e. Click the *with* option box arrow and then click *Green Fill with Dark Green Text*.

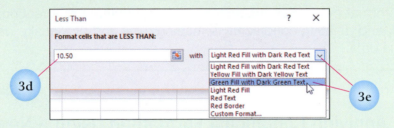

   f. Click OK.
   g. Click in any cell to deselect the range.
   h. Review the cells that have been conditionally formatted.
4. Save **1-VRPay-Oct20.xlsx**.

Check Your Work

1. With **1-VRPay-Oct20.xlsx** open, apply light red fill with dark red text conditional formatting to the gross pay values to identify employees who earned above average wages for the week by completing the following steps:

   a. Select the range M6:M23.

   b. Click the Conditional Formatting button in the Styles group on the Home tab.

   c. Point to *Top/Bottom Rules* and then click *Above Average* at the drop-down list.

   d. At the Above Average dialog box, with *Light Red Fill with Dark Red Text* selected in the *Format cells that are ABOVE AVERAGE* option box, click OK.

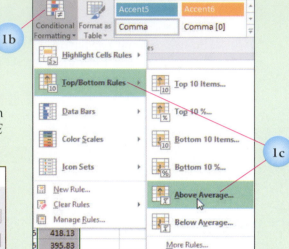

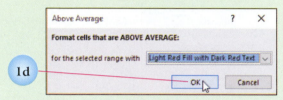

   e. Click in any cell to deselect the range.

   f. Review the cells that have been conditionally formatted.

2. Print the worksheet.

3. Save and then close **1-VRPay-Oct20.xlsx**.

Check Your Work

Project 2 Apply Conditional Formatting to Insurance Policy Data   6 Parts

You will format cells in an insurance claims worksheet by creating, editing, clearing, and deleting conditional formatting rules and by visually identifying trends within the data.

Preview Finished Project

Applying Conditional Formatting Using a New Rule

Cells are conditionally formatted based on rules. A rule defines the criterion by which cells are selected for formatting and includes the formatting attributes that are applied to cells that meet the criterion. The predefined rules that were applied in Project 1a and Project 1b used the feature without having to specify each component in the parameters for a rule. At the New Formatting Rule dialog box, shown in Figure 1.2, a custom conditional formatting rule can be created that defines all the parts of the criterion and the formatting. The *Edit the Rule Description* section of the dialog box varies depending on the active option in the *Select a Rule Type* list box.

Figure 1.2 New Formatting Rule Dialog Box

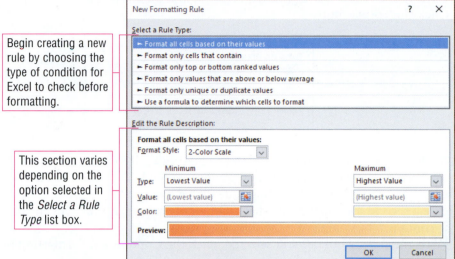

Begin creating a new rule by choosing the type of condition for Excel to check before formatting.

This section varies depending on the option selected in the *Select a Rule Type* list box.

Project 2a Applying Conditional Formatting Using a New Rule

Part 1 of 6

1. Open **ACInsce.xlsx**.
2. Save the workbook with the name **1-ACInsce**.
3. The owner of AllClaims Insurance Brokers is considering changing the discount plan for customers with no claims or with only one claim. The owner would like to see the names of customers who meet either of the two claim criteria formatted in color to provide a reference for how many customers this discount would affect. Create a formatting rule that changes the appearance of cells in the *Claims* column that contain *0* by completing the following steps:
   a. Select the range H4:H20.
   b. Click the Conditional Formatting button in the Styles group on the Home tab.
   c. Click *New Rule* at the drop-down list.
   d. At the New Formatting Rule dialog box, click *Format only cells that contain* in the *Select a Rule Type* list box.
   e. Click the second option box arrow (which displays *between*) in the *Format only cells with* section and then click *equal to* at the drop-down list.

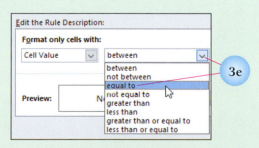

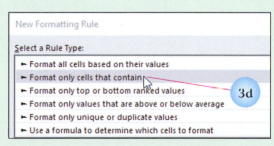

---

f. Click in the blank text box next to *equal to* and then type 0.
g. Click the Format button.

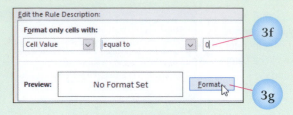

h. At the Format Cells dialog box with the Font tab selected, apply the Dark Red color (first option in the *Standard Colors* section), apply bold formatting, and then click OK.
i. Click OK at the New Formatting Rule dialog box.

4. Create a second formatting rule that changes the appearance of cells in the *Claims* column that contain *1* by completing the following steps:
   a. With the range H4:H20 still selected, click the Conditional Formatting button and then click *New Rule*.
   b. At the New Formatting Rule dialog box, click *Format only cells that contain* in the *Select a Rule Type* list box.
   c. Click the second option box arrow in the *Format only cells with* section (which displays *between*) and then click *equal to* at the drop-down list.
   d. Click in the blank text box next to *equal to* and then type *1*.
   e. Click the Format button.
   f. At the Format Cells dialog box with the Font tab selected, apply the Blue color (eighth option in the *Standard Colors* section), apply bold formatting, and then click OK.
   g. Click OK at the New Formatting Rule dialog box.

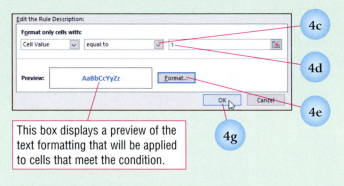

This box displays a preview of the text formatting that will be applied to cells that meet the condition.

Rating	Claims
1	0
1	0
2	1
2	1
5	3
4	2
2	1
5	2
5	2
8	4
5	3
6	3
1	0
3	2
5	3
2	1
1	0

Bold, dark red formatting has been applied to cells containing *0* and bold, blue formatting has been applied to cells containing *1*.

5. Click in any cell to deselect the range and review the conditionally formatted cells in the *Claims* column.
6. Save **1-ACInsce.xlsx**.

Check Your Work

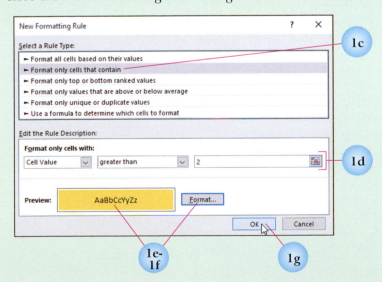

Editing and Deleting a Conditional Formatting Rule

To edit the comparison rule criteria and/or formatting options for a conditional formatting rule, open the Conditional Formatting Rules Manager dialog box. Click to select the rule to change and then click the Edit Rule button. At the Edit Formatting Rule dialog box, make the required changes and then click OK two times. By default, *Show formatting rules for* is set to *Current Selection* when the Conditional Formatting Rules Manager dialog box is opened. If necessary, click the option box arrow and then select *This Worksheet* to show all of the formatting rules in the current sheet.

To remove conditional formatting from a range, select the range, click the Conditional Formatting button in the Styles group on the Home tab, point to *Clear Rules* at the drop-down list, and then click either *Clear Rules from Selected Cells* or *Clear Rules from Entire Sheet*. Another way to remove conditional formatting is to select the range, click the Quick Analysis button, and then click the Clear Format button. Clicking the Delete button in the Conditional Formatting Rules Manager dialog box can also be used to remove a rule. Formatting applied to the cells by the deleted rule(s) will be removed.

Quick Steps

Edit a Formatting
Rule
1. Select range.
2. Click Conditional
   Formatting button.
3. Click *Manage Rules*.
4. Click a rule.
5. Click Edit Rule
   button.
6. Make changes.
7. Click OK twice.

Project 2b   Creating, Editing, and Deleting a Conditional Formatting Rule   Part 2 of 6

1. With **1-ACInsce.xlsx** open, create a new formatting rule to add a fill color to the cells in the *No. of Autos* column for those auto insurance policyholders who have more than two cars by completing the following steps:
   a. Select the range C4:C20.
   b. Click the Conditional Formatting button and then click *New Rule* at the drop-down list.
   c. Click *Format only cells that contain* in the *Select a Rule Type* list box.
   d. In the *Edit the Rule Description* section, change the parameters for the rule to format only cells with values greater than 2. (If necessary, refer to Project 2a, Steps 3e–3f, for assistance.)
   e. Click the Format button and then click the Fill tab at the Format Cells dialog box.
   f. Click the *Yellow* color (fourth column, bottom row in the *Background Color* palette) and then click OK.
   g. Click OK to close the New Formatting Rule dialog box.

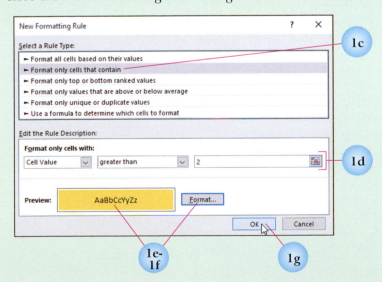

   h. Click in any cell to deselect the range.

2. After reviewing the formatted cells, it is decided that cells should be formatted for all policy holders with two or more cars. Edit the formatting rule by completing the following steps:

a. Select the range C4:C20.

b. Click the Conditional Formatting button and then click *Manage Rules* at the drop-down list.

c. Click *Cell Value > 2* in the Conditional Formatting Rules Manager dialog box to select the rule and then click the Edit Rule button.

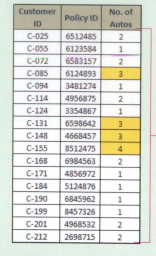

Customer ID	Policy ID	No. of Autos
C-025	6512485	2
C-055	6123584	1
C-072	6583157	2
C-085	6124893	3
C-094	3481274	1
C-114	4956875	2
C-124	3354867	1
C-131	6598642	3
C-148	4668457	3
C-155	8512475	4
C-168	6984563	2
C-171	4856972	1
C-184	5124876	1
C-190	6845962	1
C-199	8457326	1
C-201	4968532	2
C-212	2698715	2

Formatting has been applied to cell values greater than 2.

2c

d. Click the second option box arrow (which displays *greater than*) and then click *greater than or equal to* at the drop-down list.

e. Click OK.

f. Click OK to close the Conditional Formatting Rules Manager dialog box.

g. Click in any cell to deselect the range.

3. Save and print the worksheet.

4. To prepare for experimenting with another method of formatting the data, save the revised worksheet under a new name and then delete the formatting rule in the original worksheet by completing the following steps:

a. Save the workbook with the name **1-ACInsce-Autos2+**. Saving the workbook under a new name ensures that a copy of the workbook with the conditional formatting applied in this project is kept.

b. Close **1-ACInsce-Autos2+.xlsx**.

c. Open **1-ACInsce.xlsx**.

d. Click the Conditional Formatting button and then click *Manage Rules* at the drop-down list.

e. Click the *Show formatting rules for* option box arrow and then click *This Worksheet*.

f. Click *Cell Value >= 2* to select the rule and then click the Delete Rule button.

2d   2e

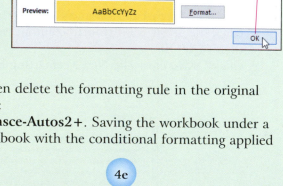

4e

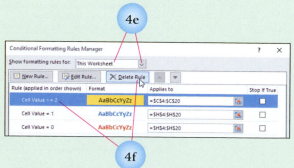

4f

g. Click OK to close the Conditional Formatting Rules Manager dialog box. Notice that the formatting has been removed from the cells in the number of autos column.

5. Save **1-ACInsce.xlsx**.

Check Your Work

Tutorial

Applying Conditional Formatting Using an Icon Set

Green Up Arrow

Red Down Arrow

Yellow Sideways Arrow

Ϙuick Steps

Apply Conditional Formatting Using an Icon Set
1. Select range.
2. Click Conditional Formatting button.
3. Point to *Icon Sets*.
4. Click icon set.
5. Deselect range.

Applying Conditional Formatting Using an Icon Set

Format a range of values using an icon set to categorize data into three to five categories. When this type of conditional formatting is applied, Excel places an icon in a cell to visually portray the value of the cell relative to the values of the other cells within the selected range. Using an icon set, similar data are categorized to easily identify high points, low points, or other trends. Icons are assigned to cells based on default threshold values for the selected range. For example, if the *3 Arrows (Colored)* icon set option is selected, icons are assigned as follows:

- Green up arrows for values greater than or equal to 67%
- Red down arrows for values less than 33%
- Yellow sideways arrows for values between 33% and 67%

The available icon sets, shown in Figure 1.3, are organized into four sections: *Directional*, *Shapes*, *Indicators*, and *Ratings*. Choose the icon set that best represents the number of different categories within the range and symbol type, such as directional colored arrows, traffic light shapes, flag indicators, star ratings, and so on. Modify the default threshold values or create unique icon sets by opening the Manage Rules dialog box and editing an existing rule or creating a new rule.

Figure 1.3 Conditional Formatting Icon Sets Gallery

Chapter 1 | Advanced Formatting Techniques

1. With **1-ACInsce.xlsx** open, select the range C4:C20.
2. Use an icon set to classify the number of automobiles into categories by completing the following steps:
   a. Click the Conditional Formatting button.
   b. Point to *Icon Sets*.
   c. Click *Red To Black* (first column, third row in the *Shapes* section) at the drop-down gallery.
   d. Click in any cell to deselect the range. Notice that Excel assigns an icon to each cell and that these icons correlate with the values of the cells. For example, all cells containing the value *1* have the same icon, all cells containing the value *2* have the same icon, and so on.
3. Save **1-ACInsce.xlsx**.

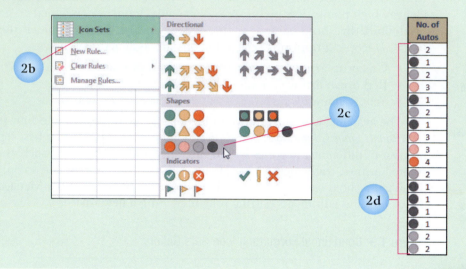

Check Your Work

Applying Conditional Formatting Using Data Bars and Color Scales

Excel also provides the ability to conditionally format cells using two-color scales, three-color scales, and data bars to provide visual guides for identifying distributions or variations within a range.

Use data bars to easily identify the highest and lowest values within a range. A data bar appears in the background of a cell and the length of the bar depends on the value within the cell. A cell with a higher value within the range displays a longer bar than a cell with a lower value. Excel offers six colors for data bars and each color is available in a gradient or solid fill.

Color scales format a range using a two-color or three-color palette. Excel provides 12 color scale gradients, half of which are two-color combinations and half of which are three-color combinations. The gradation of color applied to a cell illustrates its value relative to the rest of the range. Color scales are useful for reviewing the distribution of data. In a two-color scale, the shade applied to a cell represents either a higher or lower value within the range. In a three-color scale, the shade applied to a cell represents a higher, middle, or lower value within the range.

💡 *Hint* Be careful not to use too many icon sets, color scales, and/or data bars. Readers can quickly lose focus when too many items compete for their attention.

1. With **1-ACInsce.xlsx** open, apply gradient blue data bar formatting to the premium values to easily identify the higher and lower premiums by completing the following steps:
   a. Select the range I4:I20.
   b. Click the Conditional Formatting button in the Styles group on the Home tab.
   c. Point to *Data Bars* and then click *Blue Data Bar* (first option in the *Gradient Fill* section) at the drop-down gallery.
   d. Click in any cell to deselect the range. Notice that the lengths of the colored bars in the cells reflect various premium amounts, with longer bars representing higher premiums.

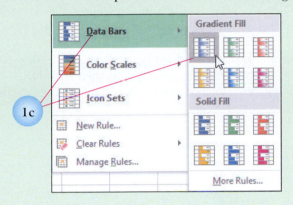

2. Save **1-ACInsce.xlsx**.

Check Your Work

Tutorial

Applying Conditional Formatting Using a Formula

Applying Conditional Formatting Using a Formula

Use conditional formatting and a formula to format a cell based on the value in another cell or using some logical test. At the New Formatting Rule dialog box, choose *Use a formula to determine which cells to format* in the *Select a Rule Type* list box. Enter a formula, such as an IF statement, to determine whether a cell will be formatted.

For example, in Project 2e, the premium values in column I of the insurance worksheet are formatted based on the rating values for the policies stored in column G. In this project, the IF statement allows a premium to be conditionally formatted if the rating value number for the policy is greater than 3. The IF function's logical test returns only a true or false result. The value in the rating cell is either greater than 3 (true) or not greater than 3 (false). Excel conditionally formats only those cells in the *Premium* column for which the conditional test returns a true result.

The formula that is entered into the New Formatting Rule dialog box in Project 2e is *=IF(G4:G20>3,TRUE,FALSE)*. Excel treats any formula entered for conditional formatting as an array formula, which means one rule needs to be added for the range G4:G20. In the first cell in the selected range (cell I4), Excel will perform the following test: *Is the value in G4 greater than 3?* In the first row, this test returns a false result, so Excel will not conditionally format the value in cell I4. Excel will apply bold formatting and the standard red font color to those cells in column I for which the test returns a true result based on the corresponding cell in column G.

1. With **1-ACInsce.xlsx** open, select the range I4:I20.
2. The owner of AllClaims Insurance Brokers would like the premiums for those clients with ratings higher than 3 to stand out in the worksheet. Conditionally format the premiums in column I using a formula that checks the ratings in column G by completing the following steps:
   a. Click the Conditional Formatting button and then click *New Rule* at the drop-down list.
   b. At the New Formatting Rule dialog box, click *Use a formula to determine which cells to format* in the *Select a Rule Type* list box.
   c. Click in the *Format values where this formula is true* text box in the *Edit the Rule Description* section of the New Formatting Rule dialog box and then type =if(g4:g20>3,true,false).
   d. Click the Format button.
   e. At the Format Cells dialog box, click the Font tab and apply the Red font color (second option in the *Standard Colors* section), apply bold formatting, and then click OK.
   f. Click OK to close the New Formatting Rule dialog box and apply the rule to the selected cells.

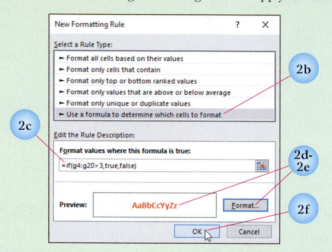

   g. Click in any cell to deselect the range. Notice that the cells in column I with bold formatting and the standard red font color are those for which the corresponding rating values in column G are greater than 3. For the most part, the higher ratings correspond to higher premiums, which are identified by the longer blue data bars.
3. Save **1-ACInsce.xlsx**.

G	H	I
Rating	Claims	Premium
1	0	1,875.00
1	0	995.00
2	1	1,575.00
2	1	2,250.00
5	3	2,150.00
4	2	2,345.00
2	1	1,168.00
5	2	3,247.00
5	2	2,948.00
8	4	4,177.00
5	3	2,110.00
6	3	1,845.00
1	0	995.00
3	2	1,550.00
5	3	2,150.00
2	1	2,025.00
1	0	1,140.00

Check Your Work

Tutorial

Applying
Conditional
Formatting Using
Quick Analysis

Quick Analysis

Applying Conditional Formatting Using Quick Analysis

Use the Quick Analysis button to quickly apply preset conditional formatting. After the data is selected, the Quick Analysis button appears near the fill handle at the bottom right corner of the selection and the options shown in Figure 1.4 become available. Use these options to quickly apply conditional formatting, create charts, add totals, create tables, and add Sparklines. With predefined conditional formatting rules, Excel can quickly analyze and format the data. If more options are required than those provided by the Quick Analysis button, access the rules from the Conditional Formatting button drop-down list.

Figure 1.4 Quick Analysis Button

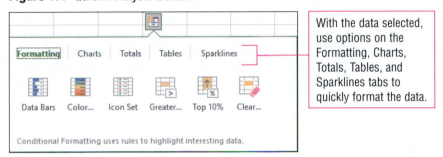

With the data selected, use options on the Formatting, Charts, Totals, Tables, and Sparklines tabs to quickly format the data.

Project 2f Apply Conditional Formatting Using Quick Analysis Based on a Value Comparison   Part 6 of 6

1. With **1-ACInsce.xlsx** open, apply conditional formatting to apply a light red fill with dark red text for the number of drivers over three by completing the following steps:
   a. Select the range F4:F20.
   b. Click the Quick Analysis button at the bottom right of the selected range.
   c. Click the Greater Than button on the Formatting tab.

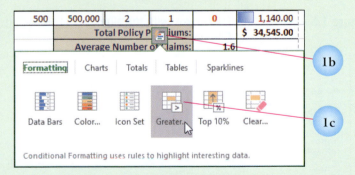

   d. At the Greater Than dialog box, with the text already selected in the *Format cells that are GREATER THAN* text box, type 3.
   e. With *Light Red Fill with Dark Red Text* selected, click OK.
   f. Review the cells that have been conditionally formatted. Notice that cells with values over 3 are formatted with a light red fill and dark red text.
2. Save, print and then close **1-ACInsce.xlsx**.

Check Your Work

Project 3 **Use Fraction and Scientific Formatting Options for a Tutor's Lesson Plan Worksheet** 1 Part

Using two lesson plan worksheets, you will format cells in a solution column to display the answers for a math tutor.

Preview Finished Project

Tutorial

Applying Fraction and Scientific Formatting

Tutorial

Review: Applying Number Formatting

Quick Steps

Apply Fraction Formatting
1. Select range.
2. Click Number group dialog box launcher.
3. Click *Fraction* in *Category* list box.
4. Click option in *Type* list box.
5. Click OK.
6. Deselect range.

Apply Scientific Formatting
1. Select range.
2. Click *Number Format* option box arrow.
3. Click *Scientific*.
4. Deselect range.

Applying Fraction and Scientific Formatting

Most worksheet values are formatted using the Accounting Number Format, Percent Style, or Comma Style buttons in the Number group on the Home tab. However, some worksheets contain values that require other number formats. When clicked, the *Number Format* option box arrow in the Number group on the Home tab displays a drop-down list with additional format options, including date, time, fraction, scientific, and text options.

Click *More Number Formats* at the Number Format drop-down list to open the Format Cells dialog box with the Number tab selected, as shown in Figure 1.5. At this dialog box, specify additional parameters for the number format categories. For example, with the *Fraction* category selected, choose the type of fraction to be displayed. The Format Cells dialog box with the Number tab active may also be opened by clicking the Number group dialog box launcher at the bottom right of the Number group on the Home tab.

Scientific formatting converts a number to exponential notation. Part of the number is replaced with E+n, where E means "exponent" and n represents the power. For example, the number *1,500,000.00* formatted in scientific number format displays as *1.50E+06*. In this example, *+06* means "Add six zeros to

Figure 1.5 Format Cells Dialog Box with the Number Tab Selected and *Fraction* Category Active

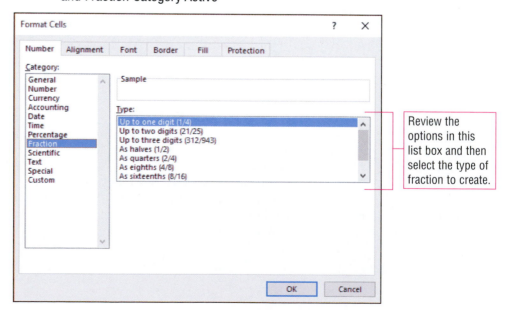

Review the options in this list box and then select the type of fraction to create.

the right of the number left of E and then move the decimal point six places to the right." Scientists, mathematicians, engineers, and statisticians often use exponential notation to write very large numbers and very small numbers in a more manageable way.

Project 3 Applying Fraction and Scientific Formatting

Part 1 of 1

1. Open **JTutor.xlsx**.
2. Save the workbook with the name **1-JTutor**.
3. Make Fractions the active worksheet by clicking the Fractions sheet tab.
4. Apply fraction formatting to the values in column D to create the solution column for the math tutor by completing the following steps:
   a. Select the range D11:D19.
   b. Click the Number group dialog box launcher in the Number group on the Home tab.
   c. At the Format Cells dialog box with the Number tab selected, click *Fraction* in the *Category* list box.
   d. Click *Up to two digits (21/25)* in the *Type* list box.

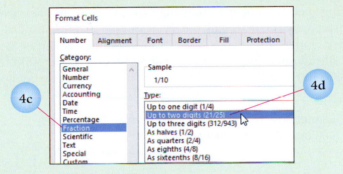

   e. Click OK.
   f. Click in any cell to deselect the range.
5. Save **1-JTutor**.
6. Print the worksheet.
7. Click the Exponents sheet tab.
8. Apply scientific formatting to the values in column D to create the solution column for the math tutor by completing the following steps:
   a. Select the range D11:D25.
   b. Click the *Number Format* option box arrow (which displays *Custom*) in the Number group on the Home tab and then click *Scientific* at the drop-down list.
   c. Click in any cell to deselect the range.
9. Print the worksheet.
10. Save and then close **1-JTutor.xlsx**.

Examples		Converted to Scientific Notation	
1,000,000,000		1.00E+09	
100,000,000		1.00E+08	
10,000,000		1.00E+07	
1,000,000		1.00E+06	
100,000		1.00E+05	Scientific
10,000		1.00E+04	formatting
1,000		1.00E+03	is applied
100		1.00E+02	to the range
10		1.00E+01	D11:D25 in
1		1.00E+00	Steps 8a–8c.
0.1		1.00E-01	
0.01		1.00E-02	
0.001		1.00E-03	
0.0001		1.00E-04	

Check Your Work

Preview Finished Project

Project 4 **Apply Advanced Formatting Options to a Products Worksheet** 2 Parts

You will update a products worksheet by formatting telephone numbers and creating a custom number format to add descriptive characters before and after values.

Applying Special Number Formatting

Quick Steps

Apply Special Number Formatting
1. Select range.
2. Click Number group dialog box launcher.
3. Click *Special* in *Category* list box.
4. Click option in *Type* list box.
5. Click OK.
6. Deselect range.

Excel provides special number formats that are specific to countries and languages at the Format Cells dialog box with the Number tab active. As shown in Figure 1.6, when *Special* is selected in the *Category* list box and *English (United States)* is selected in the *Locale (location)* option box, the *Type* list box includes *Zip Code, Zip Code + 4, Phone Number,* and *Social Security Number.* When the *English (Canadian)* option is selected in the *Locale (location)* option box, the *Type* list box includes *Phone Number* and *Social Insurance Number.*

Applying special number formatting can save time and keystrokes, as well as help to ensure consistent formatting. For example, if special social security number formatting is applied to a range, social security numbers can be typed into the range without hyphens because Excel will add them. Typing 000223456 will enter 000-22-3456 in the cell with social security number formatting applied.

Figure 1.6 Format Cells Dialog Box with the Number Tab Selected and the *Special* Category Active

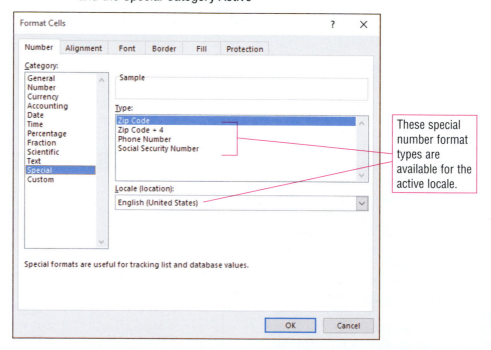

These special number format types are available for the active locale.

1. Open **Precision.xlsx**.
2. Save the workbook with the name **1-Precision**.
3. Format the range that will contain telephone numbers to include brackets around each area code and a hyphen between the first three and last four digits of each number by completing the following steps:
   a. Select the range C15:C20.
   b. Click the Number group dialog box launcher.
   c. At the Format Cells dialog box with the Number tab selected, click *Special* in the *Category* list box.
   d. Click *Phone Number* in the *Type* list box and make sure the *Locale (location)* option box is set to *English (United States)*.
   e. Click OK.
   f. Click in cell C15 to deselect the range and make the first cell to contain a telephone number the active cell.

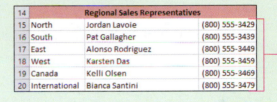

4. Type the telephone numbers for the sales representatives as follows:

   C15: 8005553429
   C16: 8005553439
   C17: 8005553449
   C18: 8005553459
   C19: 8005553469
   C20: 8005553479

14	Regional Sales Representatives		
15	North	Jordan Lavoie	(800) 555-3429
16	South	Pat Gallagher	(800) 555-3439
17	East	Alonso Rodriguez	(800) 555-3449
18	West	Karsten Das	(800) 555-3459
19	Canada	Kelli Olsen	(800) 555-3469
20	International	Bianca Santini	(800) 555-3479

5. Save **1-Precision.xlsx**.

Check Your Work

Tutorial

Creating a Custom
Number Format

Quick Steps

**Create a Custom
Number Format**
1. Select range.
2. Click Number group
   dialog box launcher.
3. Click *Custom* in
   Category list box.
4. Select *General* in
   Type text box.
5. Press Delete.
6. Type custom format
   code.
7. Click OK.
8. Deselect range.

Hint Custom
number formats are
stored in the workbook
in which they are
created.

Creating a Custom Number Format

Use a custom number format for a worksheet to enter values that do not conform to predefined number formats or values to which punctuation, text, or formatting such as color is to be added. For example, in Project 4b, a custom number format is created to automatically add two product category letters before each model number.

Formatting codes are used in custom formats to specify the type of formatting to apply. Type unique custom number format codes or select from a list of custom formats and modify the codes as necessary. Table 1.1 displays commonly used format codes along with examples of their uses.

Once a custom format has been created, it can be applied elsewhere within the workbook. To do this, open the Format Cells dialog box with the Number tab selected, select the *Custom* category, scroll down to the bottom of the *Type* list box, click to select the custom format code, and then click OK.

Text, numbers, and punctuation added as part of a custom number format are not saved as part of the cell value. In Project 4b, a custom number format that displays *PD-* in front of each model number is created. The value in cell A5 displays as *PD-1140*, but *1140* is the actual value that is stored. This is important to remember when searching for or filtering data.

Table 1.1 Examples of Custom Number Format Codes

Format Code	Description	Custom Number Format Example	Display Result
#	Represents a digit; type one for each number. Excel rounds numbers if necessary to fit the number of digits after the decimal point.	###.###	Typing *145.0068* displays *145.007*.
0	Also represents a digit. Excel rounds numbers to fit the number of digits after the decimal point but also fills in leading zeros.	000.00	Typing *50.45* displays *050.45*.
?	Rounds numbers to fit the number of digits after the decimal point but also aligns numbers vertically on the decimal point by adding spaces.	???.???	Typing *123.5, .8,* and *55.356* one below the other in a column aligns the numbers vertically on the decimal points.
"text"	Adds the characters between the quotation marks to the entry.	"Model No." ##	Typing *58* displays *Model No. 58*.
[color]	Applies the font color specified in square brackets to the cell entry.	[Blue]##.##	Typing *55.346* displays *55.35*.
;	Separates the positive value format from the negative value format.	[Blue];[Red]	Typing *25* displays as *25* and typing *-25* displays as *25*.

Project 4b Creating a Custom Number Format

Part 2 of 2

1. With **1-Precision.xlsx** open, select the range A5:A12.
2. Create a custom number format to insert *PD-* before each model number by completing the following steps:
   a. Click the Number group dialog box launcher.
   b. Click *Custom* in the *Category* list box in the Format Cells dialog box with the Number tab selected.
   c. Scroll down the list of custom formats in the *Type* list box and notice the various combinations of format codes for numbers, dates, and times.
   d. Select *General* in the *Type* text box, press the Delete key, and then type "PD-"####.
   e. Click OK.
   f. With the range A5:A12 still selected, click the Center button in the Alignment group on the Home tab.
   g. Click in any cell to deselect the range.

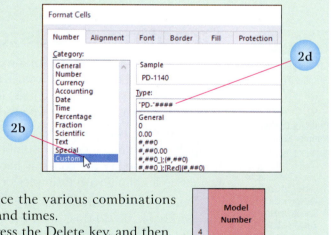

3. Create a custom number format to insert *lbs* after the weights in columns D and E by completing the following steps:
   a. Select the range D5:E12.
   b. Click the Number group dialog box launcher.
   c. Click *Custom* in the *Category* list box.
   d. Select *General* in the *Type* text box, press the Delete key, and then type ### "lbs". Make sure to include one space after ###.
   e. Click OK.
   f. Click in any cell to deselect the range.

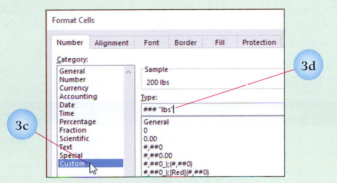

4. Save, print and then close **1-Precision.xlsx**.

Check Your Work

 Quick Steps

Delete a Custom Number Format
1. Click Number group dialog box launcher.
2. Click *Custom* in *Category* list box.
3. Click custom format code.
4. Press Delete.
5. Click OK.

To delete a custom number format, open the workbook where the custom format code was created, open the Format Cells dialog box with the Number tab selected, click *Custom* in the *Category* list box, scroll down the list of custom formats in the *Type* list box to the bottom of the list, click the custom format code that was added, and then click the Delete button. Deleting the formatting code also removes the custom formatting from any cells to which it was applied.

Project 5 Convert Text Using Text Functions in Various Worksheets   2 Parts

You will use text functions to modify a heading, convert state names to uppercase, and extract and combine data.

Preview Finished Project

Tutorial

Using Text Functions

A Text

Using Text Functions

Text can be formatted or modified using text functions. Insert a text function by typing it or by clicking the Text button in the Functions group on the Formulas tab and then selecting a function from the drop-down list. For example, use the LOWER and UPPER functions to convert text from uppercase to lowercase and vice versa. Text that has incorrect capitalization can be changed to title case using the PROPER function. New text can be substituted for existing text using the SUBSTITUTE function.

Use text functions to extract the data when only some of the characters in a cell need to be copied. Text can be extracted from the rightmost, leftmost, or middle of a string of characters using the RIGHT, LEFT, or MID functions, respectively. These three functions—along with the TRIM function, which removes extra spaces between characters—also can be used on data that has been imported or copied from another source. Table 1.2 provides more information about each text function.

Tutorial

Using the CONCATENATE Function

Use the CONCATENATE function to join the content of two or more cells, including text, numbers, or cell references. The formula used in Project 5b, =CONCATENATE(e6,f6,g6), joins the first letter of the first name, the first four letters of the last name, and the middle two digits of the social security number to create a new login. In a CONCATENATE formula, cell references are separated by commas and any spaces or characters (text, numbers, or symbols) added directly into the formula are enclosed in quotation marks.

Quick Steps

Use the SUBSTITUTE Function
1. Make cell active.
2. Type =substitute(.
3. Type source text cell address.
4. Type ,.
5. Type text to be changed within quotation marks.
6. Type ,.
7. Type replacement text within quotation marks.
8. Type).
9. Press Enter.

Use the UPPER Function
1. Make cell active.
2. Type =upper(.
3. Type source cell address.
   OR
   Type text to convert within quotation marks.
4. Type).
5. Press Enter.

Table 1.2 Examples of Text Functions

Text Function	Description	Example
=PROPER(text)	Capitalizes first letter of each word	=PROPER("annual budget") returns *Annual Budget* in formula cell OR A3 holds the *annual budget*; =PROPER(a3) entered in C3 causes C3 to display *Annual Budget*
=UPPER(text)	Converts text to uppercase	=UPPER("annual budget") returns *ANNUAL BUDGET* in formula cell OR A3 holds text *annual budget*; =UPPER(a3) entered in C3 causes C3 to display *ANNUAL BUDGET*
=LOWER(text)	Converts text to lowercase	=LOWER("ANNUAL BUDGET") returns *annual budget* in formula cell OR A3 holds text *ANNUAL BUDGET*; =LOWER(a3) entered in C3 causes C3 to display *annual budget*
=SUBSTITUTE(text)	Inserts new text in place of old text	A3 holds text *Annual Budget*; =SUBSTITUTE(a3,"Annual","2015") entered in C3 causes C3 to display *2015 Budget*
=RIGHT(text,num_chars)	Extracts requested number of characters, starting at rightmost character	=RIGHT("2015 Annual Budget",13) returns *Annual Budget* in formula cell OR A3 holds text *2015 Annual Budget*; =RIGHT(a3,13) entered in C3 causes C3 to display *Annual Budget*

continues

Table 1.2 Examples of Text Functions—*Continued*

Text Function	Description	Example
=LEFT(text,num_chars)	Extracts requested number of characters, starting at leftmost character	=LEFT("2015 Annual Budget",4) returns *2015* in formula cell OR A3 holds text *2015 Annual Budget*; =LEFT(a3,4) entered in C3 causes C3 to display *2015*
=MID(text,start-num, num-chars)	Extracts requested number of characters, starting at given position	=MID("2015 Annual Budget",6,13) returns *Annual Budget* in formula cell OR A3 holds text *2015 Annual Budget*; =MID(a3,6,13) entered in C3 causes C3 to display *Annual Budget*

Project 5a Converting Text Using the SUBSTITUTE, LOWER, and UPPER Text Functions   Part 1 of 2

1. Open **USIncomeStats.xlsx**.
2. Save the workbook with the name **1-USIncomeStats**.
3. The worksheet contains 2013 median income data downloaded from the US Census Bureau. Estimate 2018 median income values using a formula based on 2013 statistics. To begin, copy and substitute text at the top of the worksheet to create the layout for the 2018 data by completing the following steps:
   a. Click in cell A1, press Ctrl + C, click in cell F1, press Ctrl + V, click the Paste Options button, and then click the Keep Source Column Widths button in the *Paste* section of the drop-down gallery.

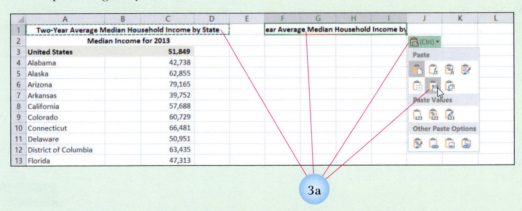

   b. Press the Esc key to remove the scrolling marquee from cell A1.
   c. Click in cell F2, click the Formulas tab, click the Text button in the Function Library group, and then click the *SUBSTITUTE* option.

d. With the insertion point positioned in the *Text* text box, type a2 and then press the Tab key.

e. Type 2013, press the Tab key, and then type 2018. Quotes are not needed around numbers in this formula.

f. Click OK.

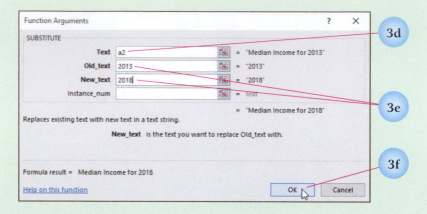

g. Merge and center cell F2 across the range F2:I2 and apply bold formatting.

4. Copy cell A3 and the state names below it to column F and then convert the text to lowercase and then uppercase by completing the following steps:

a. Make cell F3 active.

b. Type =lower(a3) and then press the Enter key. Excel returns the text *united states* in cell F3. Press Ctrl + Z to reverse this action.

c. Type =upper(a3) and then press the Enter key. Excel returns the text *UNITED STATES*.

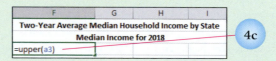

d. Make cell F3 active and then drag the fill handle into cell F54.

5. Enter the formula to estimate 2018 median income based on the 2013 data plus 7.3% by completing the following steps:

a. Make cell H3 active, type =c3+(c3*7.3%), and then press the Enter key.

b. Select cell H3 and apply the Comma format with no digits after the decimal point.

c. Drag the fill handle in cell H3 down into cell H54.

d. Deselect the range.

6. Select the range F3:H3, apply bold formatting, and then apply the Orange, Accent 6, Lighter 80% fill color (last column in second row of *Theme Colors* section). Deselect the range.

7. Save, print, and then close **1-USIncomeStats.xlsx**.

Check Your Work

Project 5b Extracting and Combining Text Using the RIGHT, LEFT, MID, TRIM, and CONCATENATE Functions

1. Open **VRCodes.xlsx**.
2. Save the workbook as **1-VRCodes**.
3. The Information Technology (IT) director wants to create new computer user names by extracting different parts of employees' personal information. A workbook has been created from various sources with the employees' first names, last names, and social security numbers (SSNs). The director notices that the SSNs include extra spaces. Use the TRIM function to remove the extra spaces between the characters so that only one space displays by completing the following steps:
   a. Make cell D6 active, type =trim(c6), and then press the Enter key.

Last Name	SSN	SSN	
Burkowski	000 25 548	=trim(c6)	3a

   b. Drag the fill handle in cell D6 into cell D14.
   c. Deselect the range.
4. Use the LEFT function to extract the first letter of the first name by completing the following steps:
   a. Make cell E6 active, type =left(a6,1), and then press the Enter key.

	First
SSN	Name
000 25 548	=left(a6,1)

4a

   b. Drag the fill handle in cell E6 into cell E14.
   c. Deselect the range.
5. Use the LEFT function to extract the first four letters of the last name by completing the following steps:
   a. Make cell F6 active, type =left(b6,4), and then press the Enter key.
   b. Drag the fill handle in cell F6 into cell F14.
   c. Deselect the range.
6. Extract the middle two digits of the SSN using the MID function by completing the following steps:
   a. Make cell G6 active, type =mid(d6,5,2), and then press the Enter key.

	First	Last		
SSN	Name	Name	SSN	6a
000 25 548	T		=mid(d6,5,2)	

   b. Drag the fill handle in cell G6 into cell G14.
   c. Deselect the range.
7. Use the CONCATENATE function to combine the extracted data to create the new employee logins by completing the following steps:
   a. Make cell H6 active, type =concatenate(e6,f6,g6), and then press the Enter key.
   b. Drag the fill handle in cell H6 down into cell H14.
   c. Deselect the range.
8. Use the RIGHT function to extract the date from the end of the text string in cell A2 by making cell B16 active, typing =right(a2,10), and then pressing the Enter key.
9. Save, print, and then close **1-VRCodes.xlsx**.

Check Your Work

Project 6 **Filter and Sort Data Based on Values, Icon Set,** **4 Parts**
and Font Colors in an Insurance Policy Workbook
and a Payroll Workbook

You will filter an insurance policy worksheet to show policies based on a range
of liability limits and by number of claims, filter policies based on the number of
automobiles, and filter and sort a payroll worksheet by font and cell colors.

Preview Finished Project

Tutorial

Filtering a
Worksheet
Using a Custom
AutoFilter

 Sort & Filter

Q̌uick Steps

Filter Using a Custom
AutoFilter
1. Select range.
2. Click Sort & Filter
   button.
3. Click *Filter*.
4. Deselect range.
5. Click filter arrow at
   top of column to be
   filtered.
6. Point to *Number*
   Filters.
7. Click filter category.
8. Enter criteria at
   Custom AutoFilter
   dialog box.
9. Click OK.

Filtering a Worksheet Using a Custom AutoFilter

The Custom AutoFilter feature is used to display only the rows that meet specific
criteria defined using the filter arrow at the top of each column. Rows that do not
meet the criteria are temporarily hidden from view. At the top of each column in
the selected range or table, click a filter arrow to display a drop-down list of all the
unique field values that exist within the column. To filter the values by more than
one criterion using a comparison operator, open the Custom AutoFilter dialog box,
shown in Figure 1.7. Use the ? and * wildcard characters in a custom filter. For
example, filter a list of products by a product number beginning with P by using *P**
as the criteria.

To display the Custom AutoFilter dialog box, select the range to filter and
then click the Sort & Filter button in the Editing group. Click *Filter* at the drop-
down list and then deselect the range. Click the filter arrow in the column that
contains the criteria. Point to *Number Filters* or *Text Filters* and then choose one of
the options at the drop-down list. The type of filter and options available depend
on the type of data in the column—for example, text or numbers.

Figure 1.7 Custom AutoFilter Dialog Box

Use the Custom AutoFilter
dialog box to specify two
criteria by which to filter
using either an *And* or an
Or statement.

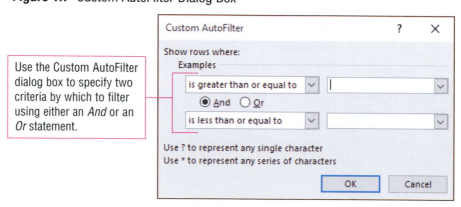

1. Open 1-**ACInsce.xlsx**.
2. Save the workbook with the name **1-ACInsce-LL**.
3. The owner of AllClaims Insurance Brokers wants to review policies with liability limits from $500,000 to $1,000,000 that have had more than one claim to determine if customers should increase their coverage. Filter the policy information to produce the list of policies that meet the owner's request by completing the following steps:
   a. Select the range A3:I20.
   b. Click the Sort & Filter button in the Editing group on the Home tab.
   c. Click *Filter* at the drop-down list. A filter arrow displays at the top of each column.
   d. Deselect the range.
   e. Click the filter arrow next to *Liability Limit* in cell E3.
   f. Point to *Number Filters* and then click *Between* at the drop-down list.
   g. At the Custom AutoFilter dialog box with the insertion point positioned in the blank text box next to *is greater than or equal to*, type 500000.
   h. Notice that *And* is the option selected between the criteria. This is correct, since the owner wants a list of policies with a liability limit greater than or equal to $500,000 *and* less than or equal to $1,000,000.
   i. Click in the blank text box next to *is less than or equal to* and type 1000000.
   j. Click OK to close the Custom AutoFilter dialog box. The range is filtered to display the rows for customers with liability limits from $500,000 to $1,000,000.
   k. Click the filter arrow next to *Claims* in cell H3.
   l. Point to *Number Filters* and then click *Greater Than* at the drop-down list.
   m. At the Custom AutoFilter dialog box with the insertion point positioned in the blank text box next to *is greater than*, type 1 and then click OK.
4. Print the filtered worksheet.
5. Save 1-**ACInsce-LL.xlsx**.

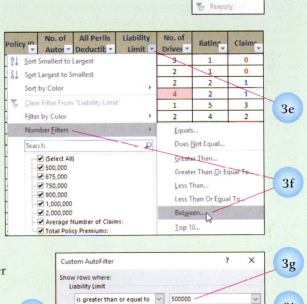

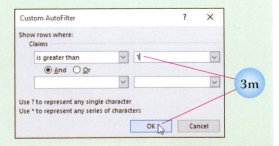

Check Your Work

Filtering and Sorting Data Using Conditional Formatting or Cell Attributes

💡 **Hint** If an error message about merged cells needing to be the same size appears when sorting, select the range to be sorted and do a custom sort.

A worksheet with cells that have been formatted manually or by conditional formatting to change the cell or font color can be filtered by color. In addition, a worksheet conditionally formatted using an icon set can be filtered using an icon.

To filter by color or icon, select the range, click the Sort & Filter button, click *Filter*, and then deselect the range. Click the filter arrow in the column to filter and then point to *Filter by Color* at the drop-down list. Depending on the formatting that has been applied, the list contains cell colors, font colors, or icon sets. Click the specific color or icon option to filter the column.

Quick Steps

Filter or Sort by Color or Icon Set
1. Select range.
2. Click Sort & Filter button.
3. Click *Filter*.
4. Deselect range.
5. Click filter arrow at top of column to be filtered.
6. Point to *Filter by Color* or *Sort by Color*.
7. Click a color or icon.

The filter drop-down list also contains a *Sort by Color* option to sort rows within a range or table by a specified cell color, font color, or cell icon. To sort by color, follow steps similar to those used to filter by color. For example, to sort a column by font color, point to *Sort by Color* from the column filter drop-down list and then click the specific font color. Excel sorts the column by placing cells with the specified font color at the top. The list does not sort itself within the different color groupings.

The shortcut menu can also be used to sort or filter data. To do this, right-click a cell that contains the color or icon to filter, point to *Filter*, and then click *Filter by Selected Cell's Color*, *Filter by Selected Cell's Font Color*, or *Filter by Selected Cell's Icon*.

Project 6b Clearing a Filter and Filtering by an Icon Set

Part 2 of 4

1. With **1-ACInsce-LL.xlsx** open, save the workbook as **1-ACInsce-1Auto**.
2. Remove the filter by completing the following steps:
   a. Click anywhere in the filtered list.
   b. Click the Sort & Filter button.
   c. Click *Clear* at the drop-down list.
3. Filter the worksheet to display the customers with coverage for only one automobile by completing the following steps:
   a. In Project 2c, the Red to Black icon set was applied to the data in column C. Note that the black circle icon represents the *1* data set. Click the filter arrow next to *No. of Autos* in cell C3.
   b. Point to *Filter by Color* at the drop-down list.
   c. Click the black circle icon in the *Filter by Cell Icon* list.
4. Print the filtered worksheet.
5. Save **1-ACInsce-1Auto**.

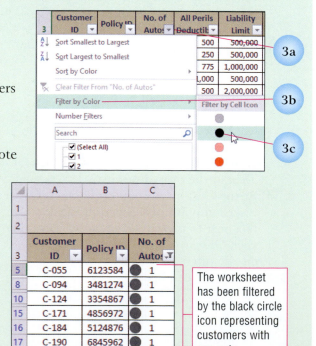

The worksheet has been filtered by the black circle icon representing customers with one auto.

Check Your Work

Project 6c Filtering by Font Color

1. With **1-ACInsce-1Auto** open, further filter the list to display the customers that have had zero claims. Recall that zero claims were conditionally formatted by applying a red font color and bold formatting to cells with values equal to zero. Filter the worksheet by the conditional formatting by completing the following steps:

   a. Right-click in cell H5 (or in any other cell in column H with a red font color).

   b. Point to *Filter* and then click *Filter by Selected Cell's Font Color* at the shortcut menu.

2. Print the filtered worksheet.

3. Save and then close **1-ACInsce-1Auto.xlsx**.

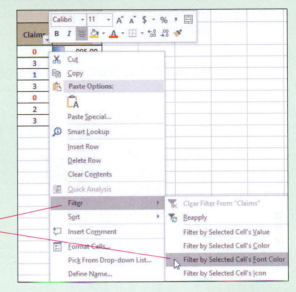

Check Your Work

Project 6d Sorting by Cell Color

1. Open **1-VRPay-Oct20.xlsx**.

2. Save the workbook with the name **1-VRPay-Oct20-Sorted**.

3. Sort the payroll worksheet in descending order by cell color by completing the following steps:

   a. Select the range A5:M23, click the Sort & Filter button in the Editing group on the Home tab, and then click *Filter* at the drop-down list.

   b. Deselect the range.

   c. Click the filter arrow next to *Gross Pay* in cell M5.

   d. Point to *Sort by Color* and then click the pink fill color box in the *Sort by Cell Color* section.

4. Print the sorted worksheet.

5. Save and then close **1-VRPay-Oct20-Sorted.xlsx**.

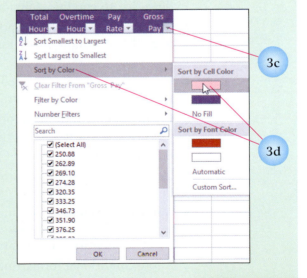

Check Your Work

Define a custom sort in a worksheet when more than one cell or font color is applied to a column. Select the range, click the Sort & Filter button in the Editing group on the Home tab, and then click *Custom Sort* at the drop-down list. At the Sort dialog box, shown in Figure 1.8, define the color by which to sort first and then add a level for each other color in the order in which the sorting is to occur. Select *Values*, *Cell Color*, *Font Color*, or *Cell Icon* from the *Sort On* drop-down list at the Sort dialog box. Figure 1.8 illustrates a sort definition for a column in which four cell icons have been used.

Figure 1.8 Sort Dialog Box with Four-Color Sort Defined

Cells will be sorted first by the black icon, then by the gray icon, then by the pink icon, and lastly by the red icon.

Chapter Summary

- Conditional formatting applies format changes to cells based on a condition; cells that meet the condition have the formatting applied, and cells that do not meet the condition remain unformatted.
- Conditional formats can be based on values, dates, text entries, or duplicated values.
- Use the *Highlight Cells Rules* option at the Conditional Formatting button drop-down list to conditionally format based on a value comparison.
- Use the *Top/Bottom Rules* option at the Conditional Formatting button drop-down list to conditionally format based on the top 10 or bottom 10 percentage or average values.
- Conditional formats are based on rules that specify a criterion by which cells are tested and the formatting attributes to apply to cells that meet the criterion.
- Create a new conditional formatting rule by selecting *New Rule* at the Conditional Formatting button drop-down list.
- Edit or delete a rule at the Conditional Formatting Rules Manager dialog box.
- Use the Quick Analysis button to quickly apply a predefined conditional format.
- Apply conditional formatting using data bars, color scales, or icon sets to add small bar charts, gradations of color, or icons, respectively, to cells to make it easier to identify certain data.
- Apply conditional formatting using a formula to apply formatting to a selected range of cells based on values in other cells. Excel treats any formula entered for conditional formatting as an array formula, which means one rule needs to be added for a selected range.

- An IF statement can be used to conditionally format those cells for which the conditional test returns a true result.
- Fraction formatting converts decimal values to fractions.
- To choose the type of fraction to create, open the Format Cells dialog box with the Number tab selected.
- Scientific formatting displays numbers in exponential notation, in which part of the number is replaced with E+n, where E stands for "exponent" and n represents the power.
- Excel provides special number formats that are specific to countries and languages to format entries such as telephone numbers and social security numbers.
- Custom number formats use formatting codes to specify the type of formatting to apply.
- A custom number format can be used to add text, numbers, or punctuation to a value entered into a cell.
- Convert text from lowercase to uppercase or from uppercase to lowercase using the UPPER and LOWER text functions.
- Replace existing text with new text using the SUBSTITUTE text function.
- Extract data from a cell based on its position in a cell using the RIGHT, LEFT, or MID text functions.
- Combine the content of two or more cells using the CONCATENATE text function.
- Display the Custom AutoFilter dialog box to filter values by more than one criterion using a comparison operator, such as greater than (>) or equal to (=).
- A worksheet with cells that have been formatted manually or by conditional formatting can be filtered by color or icon.
- To specify the order of the sorted colors, define a custom sort if the worksheet contains more than one cell color, font color, or cell icon.

Commands Review

FEATURE	RIBBON TAB, GROUP	BUTTON	KEYBOARD SHORTCUT
conditional formatting	Home, Styles Flashfill		
custom AutoFilter	Home, Editing		Ctrl + Shift + L
custom number format	Home, Number		Ctrl + 1
fraction formatting	Home, Number		Ctrl + 1
scientific formatting	Home, Number		Ctrl + 1
special number formatting	Home, Number		Ctrl + 1
text functions	Formulas, Function Library		

> **Workbook**
>
> Chapter study tools and assessment activities are available in the *Workbook* ebook. These resources are designed to help you further develop and demonstrate mastery of the skills learned in this chapter.

Microsoft® Excel®

Advanced Functions and Formulas

CHAPTER 2

Performance Objectives

Upon successful completion of Chapter 2, you will be able to:

1 Edit, rename, and delete named ranges

2 Write formulas with the COUNTIF and COUNTIFS statistical functions

3 Write formulas with the AVERAGEIF and AVERAGEIFS statistical functions

4 Write formulas with the SUMIF and SUMIFS math and trigonometry functions

5 Write formulas with the VLOOKUP and HLOOKUP lookup functions

6 Write formulas with the PPMT financial function

7 Write formulas with the IF, AND, and OR logical functions

8 Write formulas with the ROUND math and trigonometry function

Precheck

Check your current skills to help focus your study.

Excel includes numerous built-in functions that are grouped by function category. Thirteen categories contain preprogrammed formulas to facilitate performing complex calculations for worksheets containing statistical, financial, scientific, database, and other data. The Insert function dialog box provides options for locating and building function formulas. The structure of a function formula includes an equals sign (=) followed by the name of the function and then the function argument. *Argument* is the term given to the values to be included in the calculation. The structure of the argument is dependent on the type of function being used and can include a single cell, a range, multiple ranges, or any combination of these.

Data Files

Before beginning chapter work, copy the EL2C2 folder to your storage medium and then make EL2C2 the active folder.

SNAP

If you are a SNAP user, launch the Precheck and Tutorials from your Assignments page.

Project 1   Calculate Statistics and Sums Using   6 Parts
            Conditional Formulas for an Insurance Claims Worksheet

You will manage range names in an insurance claims worksheet and use the range names in statistical formulas that count, average, and sum based on single and multiple criteria.

Preview Finished Project

Managing Range Names

Tutorial

Managing Range Names

Tutorial

Review: Naming and Using a Range

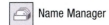 Name Manager

Quick Steps

Modify a Range Name Reference
1. Click Formulas tab.
2. Click Name Manager button.
3. Click range name.
4. Click Edit button.
5. Click in *Refers to* text box.
6. Modify range address.
7. Click OK.
8. Click Close.

Edit a Range Name
1. Click Formulas tab.
2. Click Name Manager button.
3. Click range name.
4. Click Edit button.
5. Type new range name in *Name* text box.
6. Click OK.
7. Click Close.

Hint The Formulas tab contains a Create from Selection button in the Defined Names group that can be used to automatically create range names for a list or table. Select the list or table and click the button. Excel uses the names in the top row or left-most column as the range names.

Recall from Level 1 that assigning a name to a cell or range of cells allows for referencing the source using a descriptive label, rather than the cell address or range address, when creating a formula, printing a worksheet, or navigating in a worksheet. Creating range names makes the task of managing complex formulas easier and helps others who may work in or edit a worksheet understand the purpose of a formula more quickly.

By default, the range that a range name applies to is referenced using absolute referencing. Later in this chapter, when creating a lookup formula, take advantage of the absolute referencing of a range name when including a group of cells in the formula that stay fixed when the formula is copied. A range name also includes the worksheet reference by default; therefore, typing the range name in the formula automatically references the correct worksheet. For example, assume that cell A3 in Sheet 2 has been named *ProductA* and cell A3 in Sheet 3 has been named *ProductB*. To add the two values, type the formula =*ProductA+ProductB* in the formula cell. Notice that the worksheet references do not need to be included.

The Name Manager dialog box, shown in Figure 2.1, is opened by clicking the Name Manager button in the Defined Names group on the Formulas tab. The Name Manager dialog box can be used to create, edit, and delete range names.

Figure 2.1 Name Manager Dialog Box

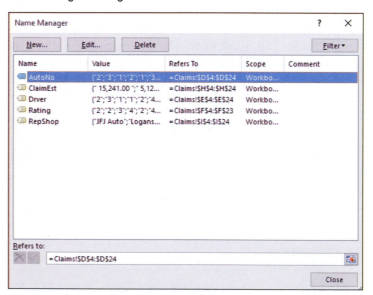

A range name can be edited by changing the name or modifying the range address associated with it. A range name can also be deleted, but extra caution should be used when doing so. Cells that include a deleted range name in the formula will display the error text *#NAME?* Also use the Name Manager dialog box to add new range names to a worksheet.

Project 1a Modifying and Deleting Range Names

Part 1 of 6

1. Open **ACOct18VehRpt.xlsx**.
2. Save the workbook with the name **2-ACOct18VehRpt**.
3. Named ranges have been created for the auto number, driver number, rating, claim estimate, and repair shop data. Modify the range name *Drver* by completing the following steps:
   a. Click the Formulas tab.
   b. Click the Name Manager button in the Defined Names group.
   c. Click *Drver* in the *Name* column and then click the Edit button.
   d. At the Edit Name dialog box with *Drver* selected in the *Name* text box, type DriverNo and then click OK.
4. Modify the references in the range named *Rating* to include cell F24 by completing following steps:
   a. Click *Rating* at the Name Manager dialog box and then click the Edit button.
   b. At the Edit Name dialog box, click right of the text in the *Refers to* text box (which displays *Claims!$F$4:$F:$23*), press the Backspace key, type 4, and then click OK.
5. Delete the range name *AutoNo* by completing the following steps:
   a. Click *AutoNo* at the Name Manager dialog box and then click the Delete button.
   b. Click OK.
6. Click the Close button.
7. Save **2-ACOct18VehRpt.xlsx**.

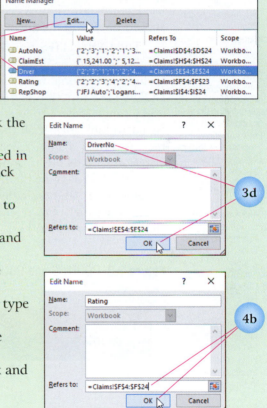

Tutorial

Review: Using Statistical Functions

Using Statistical Functions

Commonly used statistical functions include AVERAGE, MAX, and MIN. AVERAGE returns the arithmetic mean, MAX returns the largest value, and MIN returns the smallest value in the range. Other common functions, COUNT and COUNTA, return the number of cells based on what is contained in the cells. COUNT is used if the cells contain numbers or dates and COUNTA is used when the cells contain text or a combination of text and numbers. Excel provides additional AVERAGE and COUNT functions to find counts or averages for a range based on a criterion.

 Insert Function

Quick Steps

Create a COUNTIF Formula

1. Make cell active.
2. Click Insert Function button.
3. Change category to *Statistical*.
4. Select *COUNTIF*.
5. Click OK.
6. Enter range address or range name to select by in *Range* text box.
7. Enter condition expression or text in *Criteria* text box.
8. Click OK.

Create a COUNTIFS Formula

1. Make cell active.
2. Click Insert Function button.
3. Change category to *Statistical*.
4. Select *COUNTIFS*.
5. Click OK.
6. Enter range address or range name to select by in *Criteria_range1* text box.
7. Enter condition expression or text in *Criteria1* text box.
8. Enter range address or range name to select by in *Criteria_range2* text box.
9. Enter condition expression or text in *Criteria2* text box.
10. Continue adding criteria range expressions and criteria as needed.
11. Click OK.

Using Statistical Functions: COUNTIF and COUNTIFS

Use the COUNTIF function to count cells within a range that meet a single criterion or condition. For example, in a grades worksheet, use a COUNTIF function to count the number of students who achieved greater than 75%. The structure of a COUNTIF function is *=COUNTIF(range,criteria)*. The range is where to look for the data. The criteria defines a conditional test that must be passed (what to look for) in order for the cell to be counted. For the grades worksheet example, the function to count the cells of students who achieved greater than 75% is *=COUNTIF(grades,">75")*, assuming the range name *grades* has been defined. Notice that the syntax of the argument requires enclosing the criteria in quotation marks. If the Insert Function dialog box is used to create a formula, Excel adds the required syntax automatically. A cell reference may also be used as the criterion. A cell reference is not enclosed in quotation marks and should only contain the exact criterion.

The COUNTIFS function is used to count cells when more than one condition must be met. The formula uses the same structure as COUNTIF but includes additional ranges and criteria within the argument. The structure of a COUNTIFS function is *=COUNTIFS(range1,criteria1,range2,criteria2,. . .)*. For every range (where to look), there is a corresponding criteria or conditional test (what to look for). If all the conditions are met for each range, then the count increases by 1. Figure 2.2 shows a nursing education worksheet with a single-criterion COUNTIF to count the number of nurses (RNs) and a multiple-criteria COUNTIFS to count the number of RNs who are current with their professional development (PD) activities. The formulas shown in Figure 2.2 include range names for which *Title* references the entries in column D and *PDCurrent* references the entries in column H.

Figure 2.2 COUNTIF and COUNTIFS Formulas

Employee Number	Employee Last Name	Employee First Name	Title	Unit	Extension	Years Experience	PD Current?	Nursing Educational Statistical Summary	
FT02001	Santos	Susan	RN	Med/Surg	36415	30	Yes	Number of RNs	16
FT02002	Daniels	Jasmine	RN	Med/Surg	36415	27	No	Number of LPNs	12
FT02003	Walden	Virgina	RN	ICU	34211	22	No		
FT02004	Jaffe	Paul	LPN	CSRU	36418	24	Yes	RNs who are current with PD	9
FT02005	Salvatore	Terry	LPN	ICU	34211	22	Yes	LPNs who are current with PD	7
FT02006	Mander	Kaitlynn	RN	ICU	34211	24	Yes		
FT02007	Friesen	Jessica	LPN	ICU	34211	20	Yes	formula =COUNTIF(Title,"RN")	
FT02008	Lavigne	Gisele	RN	CSRU	36418	20	No		
FT02009	Gauthier	Jacqueline	RN	PreOp	32881	19	No		
FT02010	Williamson	Forman	RN	CSRU	36418	19	Yes		
FT02011	Orlowski	William	RN	Ortho	31198	22	No		
FT02012	Kadri	Ahmed	LPN	Ortho	31198	21	No		
FT02013	El-Hamid	Lianna	LPN	Med/Surg	36415	20	No		
FT02014	Vezina	Ursula	LPN	Ortho	31198	20	No		
FT02015	Adams	Sheila	LPN	Med/Surg	36415	25		formula =COUNTIFS(Title,"RN",PDCurrent,"Yes")	
FT02016	Jorgensen	Macy	RN	Med/Surg	36415	10	No		
FT02017	Pieterson	Eric	RN	ICU	34211	8	No		
FT02018	Keller	Douglas	RN	ICU	34211	10	No		
FT02019	Costa	Michael	RN	Ortho	31198	10	No		
FT02020	Li-Kee	Su-Lynn	LPN	PreOp	32881	8	No		
FT02021	Besterd	Mary	RN	PreOp	32881	7	Yes		

Department of Human Resources
Full-Time Nursing Education Worksheet

1. With **2-ACOct18VehRpt.xlsx** open, make cell L4 active.
2. Create a COUNTIF function to count the number of auto insurance claims for which A+ Paint & Body is the repair shop by completing the following steps:
   a. Click the Insert Function button in the Formula bar.
   b. At the Insert Function dialog box, click the *Or select a category* option box arrow and then click *Statistical* at the drop-down list. ***Note: Skip this step if Statistical is already selected as the category***.

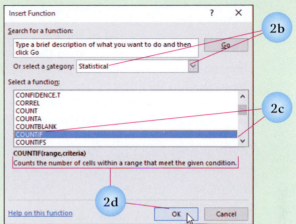

   c. Scroll down the *Select a function* list box and then click *COUNTIF*.
   d. Read the formula description below the function list box and then click OK.
   e. At the Function Arguments dialog box with the insertion point positioned in the *Range* text box, type repshop and then press the Tab key. Recall from Project 1a that a range name exists for the entries in column I. ***Note: If the dialog box is obscuring the view of the worksheet, drag the Function Arguments dialog box title bar left or right.***

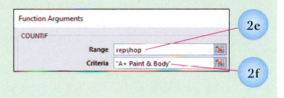

   f. With the insertion point positioned in the *Criteria* text box, type A+ Paint & Body and then press the Tab key. When the Tab key is pressed, Excel adds quotation marks around the criteria text.
   g. Click OK. Excel returns the value *3* in cell L4.
   h. Look at the formula in the Formula bar created by the Function Arguments dialog box: *=COUNTIF(RepShop,"A+ Paint & Body")*.
3. Make cell L5 active. The repair shop names are located in the range K4:K7. Use cell K5 as the cell reference for JFJ Auto by typing the formula =countif(repshop,k5) and then press the Enter key. (When entering a formula, type the cell references and range names in lowercase letters. Excel will automatically display uppercase letters once the formula has been entered.)

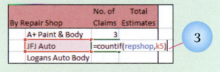

4. Use the fill handle to copy the formula in cell L5 into the range L6:L7. When completed, the COUNTIF formulas will be as follows:

   L6: *=COUNTIF(RepShop,K6)*
   L7: *=COUNTIF(RepShop,K7)*

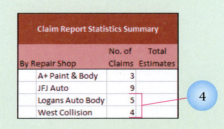

5. Save **2-ACOct18VehRpt.xlsx**.

Check Your Work

1. With **2-ACOct18VehRpt.xlsx** open, make cell L10 active.
2. Create a COUNTIFS function to count the number of auto insurance claims for which the repair shop is JFJ Auto and the claims estimate is greater than $5,000 by completing the following steps:

   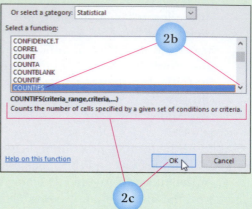

   a. Click the Insert Function button in the Formula bar.
   b. With *Statistical* selected in the *Or select a category* option box, scroll down the *Select a function* list box and then click *COUNTIFS*.
   c. Read the formula description below the function list box and then click OK.
   d. At the Function Arguments dialog box with the insertion point positioned in the *Criteria_range1* text box, type repshop and then press the Tab key. After the Tab key is pressed, a *Criteria_range2* text box is added to the dialog box.
   e. With the insertion point positioned in the *Criteria1* text box, type k10 as the cell reference for JFJ Auto and then press the Tab key. After the Tab key is pressed, a *Criteria2* text box is added to the dialog box.
   f. With the insertion point positioned in the *Criteria_range2* text box, type claimest and then press the Tab key. After the Tab key is pressed, a *Criteria_range3* text box is added to the dialog box.
   g. With the insertion point positioned in the *Criteria2* text box, type >5000 and then press the Tab key. When the Tab key is pressed, Excel adds quotation marks around the criteria text.
   h. Click OK. Excel returns the value *5* in cell L10.

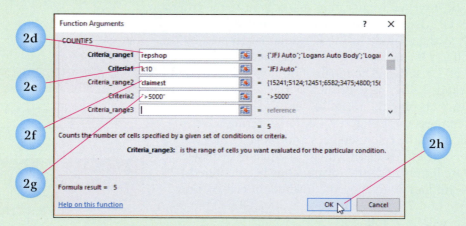

3. Look at the formula in the Formula bar created by the Function Arguments dialog box: *=COUNTIFS(RepShop,K10,ClaimEst,">5000")*.
4. In cell L13, enter a COUNTIFS formula to count the number of claims for which the repair shop is JFJ Auto and the rating is greater than 3 by using the Insert Function dialog box or by typing the following formula into the cell: =countifs(repshop,k13,rating,">3").

   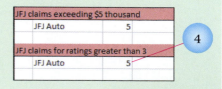

5. Save **2-ACOct18VehRpt.xlsx**.

Check Your Work

Using Statistical Functions: AVERAGEIF and AVERAGEIFS

The AVERAGEIF function is used to find the arithmetic mean of the cells within a specified range that meet a single criterion or condition. The structure of an AVERAGEIF function is *=AVERAGEIF(range,criteria,average_range)*. *Range* is the cells to be tested for the criterion or where to look for the data. *Criteria* is the conditional test that must be passed (what to look for). *Average_range* is the range containing the values to average. If *average_range* is omitted, the cells in the *range* are used to calculate the average. The AVERAGEIFS function is used to average cells that meet multiple criteria using the formula *=AVERAGEIFS(average_range,criteria_range1,criteria1,criteria_range2,criteria2,. . .)*. Notice that the *average_range* (what to actually average) is at the beginning of the formula. It is followed by pairs of ranges (where to look for the specific condition) and criteria (the conditions that must be met).

Figure 2.3 shows an executive management salary report for a hospital. Average salary statistics are shown below the salary data. In the first two rows of salary statistics, the average total salary is calculated for each of two hospital campuses. In the second two rows of salary statistics, the average total salary is calculated for each campus for executives hired before 2016. The formulas shown in Figure 2.3 include range names for which *Year* references the values in column E, *Campus* references the entries in column F, and *Total* references the values in column I.

Quick Steps

Create an AVERAGEIF Formula

1. Make cell active.
2. Click Insert Function button.
3. Change category to *Statistical*.
4. Select *AVERAGEIF*.
5. Click OK.
6. Enter range address or range name to select by in *Range* text box.
7. Enter condition expression or text in *Criteria* text box.
8. Enter range address or range name to average in *Average_range* text box.
9. Click OK.

Create an AVERAGEIFS Formula

1. Make cell active.
2. Click Insert Function button.
3. Change category to *Statistical*.
4. Select *AVERAGEIFS*.
5. Click OK.
6. Enter range address or range name to average in *Average_range* text box.
7. Enter range address or range name to select by in *Criteria_range1* text box.
8. Enter condition expression or text in *Criteria1* text box.
9. Enter range address or range name to select by in *Criteria_range2* text box.
10. Enter condition expression or text in *Criteria2* text box.
11. Continue adding criteria range expressions and criteria as needed.
12. Click OK.

Figure 2.3 AVERAGEIF and AVERAGEIFS Formulas

formula
=AVERAGEIFS(Total,Campus,"Sunnyside",Year,"<2016")

formula
=AVERAGEIF(Campus,"Portland",Total)

1. With **2-ACOct18VehRpt.xlsx** open, make cell M16 active.
2. Create an AVERAGEIF function to calculate the average auto insurance claim estimate for those claims with a rating of 1 by completing the following steps:
   a. Click the Insert Function button in the Formula bar.
   b. With *Statistical* selected in the *Or select a category* option box, click *AVERAGEIF* in the *Select a function* list box.
   c. Read the formula description below the function list box and then click OK.

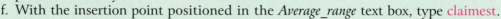

   d. At the Function Arguments dialog box with the insertion point positioned in the *Range* text box, type rating and then press the Tab key.
   e. With the insertion point positioned in the *Criteria* text box, type 1 and then press the Tab key.
   f. With the insertion point positioned in the *Average_range* text box, type claimest.
   g. Click OK. Excel returns the value *2691* in cell M16.

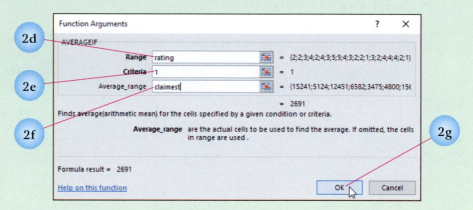

   h. Look at the formula in the Formula bar created by the Function Arguments dialog box: *=AVERAGEIF(Rating,1,ClaimEst)*.
3. Apply the Comma format with no digits after the decimal point to cell M16.
4. Make cell M17 active, type the formula =averageif(rating,2,claimest), and then press the Enter key.
5. Apply the Comma format with no digits after the decimal point to cell M17.
6. With cell M17 active, drag the fill handle into cell M20.
7. Edit the formulas in cells M18, M19, and M20 by changing the rating criterion values from *2* to *3*, *4*, and *5*, respectively. When completed, the AVERAGEIF formulas will be as follows:

    M18: *=AVERAGEIF(Rating,3,ClaimEst)*
    M19: *=AVERAGEIF(Rating,4,ClaimEst)*
    M20: *=AVERAGEIF(Rating,5,ClaimEst)*

By Rating	Avg. Est.
1	2,691
2	6,987
3	9,014
4	7,830
5	14,564

8. Save **2-ACOct18VehRpt.xlsx**.

Check Your Work

1. With **2-ACOct18VehRpt.xlsx** open, make cell M22 active.
2. Create an AVERAGEIFS function to calculate the average auto insurance claim estimate for those claims with a rating of 2 and a driver number of 1 by completing the following steps:
   a. Click the Insert Function button in the Formula bar.
   b. With *Statistical* selected in the *Or select a category* option box, click *AVERAGEIFS* in the *Select a function* list box.
   c. Read the formula description and then click OK.
   d. At the Function Arguments dialog box with the insertion point positioned in the *Average_range* text box, type claimest and then press the Tab key.
   e. Type rating in the *Criteria_range1* text box and then press the Tab key.
   f. Type 2 in the *Criteria1* text box and then press the Tab key.
   g. Type driverno in the *Criteria_range2* text box and then press the Tab key.
   h. Type 1 in the *Criteria2* text box.
   i. Click OK. Excel returns the value *6272.6667* in the cell.

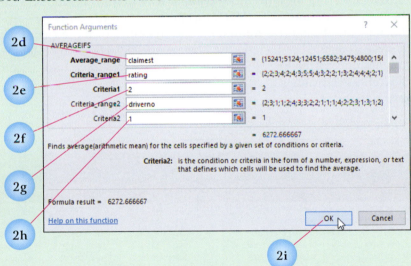

   j. Apply the Comma format with no digits after the decimal point to cell M22.
3. Copy the AVERAGEIFS formula in cell M22 and paste it into cell M23.
4. Edit the formula in cell M23 to change the rating criterion from *2* to *3*. When completed, the AVERAGEIFS formula will be *=AVERAGEIFS(ClaimEst,Rating,3,DriverNo,1)*.
5. Save **2-ACOct18VehRpt.xlsx**.

Check Your Work

Tutorial

Using Math and Trigonometry Functions: SUMIF and SUMIFS

 Math & Trig

Quick Steps

Create a SUMIF Formula
1. Make cell active.
2. Click Formulas tab.
3. Click Math & Trig button.
4. Scroll down and click *SUMIF*.
5. Enter range address or range name to select by in *Range* text box.
6. Enter condition expression or text in *Criteria* text box.
7. Enter range address or range name to add in *Sum_range* text box.
8. Click OK.

Using Math and Trigonometry Functions: SUMIF and SUMIFS

Excel provides several math and trigonometry functions, such as ABS to return the absolute value of a number, SQRT to find the square root of a number, and RAND to return a random number between 0 and 1, to name a few. At the Insert Function dialog box, change the *Or select a category* option to *Math & Trig* and scroll down the list of available functions.

Within the category of math and trigonometry functions, Excel includes SUMIF to add the cells within a range that meet a single criterion or condition and SUMIFS to add the cells within a range that meet multiple criteria or conditions. The structure of the SUMIF formula is *=SUMIF(range,criteria,sum_range)*, where *range* is where to look for the data, *criteria* is the conditional statement (the conditions that must be met or what to look for), and *sum_range* is the range containing the values to add. The SUMIFS function is used to add cells that meet multiple criteria using the formula *=SUMIFS(sum_range,criteria_range1,criteria1,criteria_range2,criteria2,...)*. Similar to the AVERAGEIFS function, the *sum_range* (what to actually sum) appears at the beginning of the formula. It is followed by pairs of ranges (where to look for the specific conditions), and criteria (the conditions that must be met).

Figure 2.4 shows how the SUMIF and SUMIFS formulas are used in the standard cost worksheet for examination room supplies at a medical clinic. Right of the clinic supplies inventory data, a SUMIF formula adds up the costs of items by supplier number. A SUMIFS formula adds up the costs by supplier number for items that require a minimum stock quantity of more than four. The formulas shown in Figure 2.4 include the range names *Supplier*, which references the entries in column C; *MinQty*, which references the values in column E; and *StdCost*, which references the values in column F.

Figure 2.4 SUMIF and SUMIFS Formulas

	A	B	C	D	E	F	G	H	I
1			North Shore Medical Clinic						
2			Clinic Supplies Inventory Units and Price						
3	Item	Unit	Supplier Number	Price	Minimum Stock Qty	Standard Cost		Exam Room Cost Analysis	
4	Sterile powder-free synthetic gloves, size Small	per 100	101	35.95	4	143.80		Cost by Supplier	
5	Sterile powder-free synthetic gloves, size Medium	per 100	101	35.95	8	287.60		Supplier Number 101	1,401.40
6	Sterile powder-free synthetic gloves, size Large	per 100	101	35.95	10	359.50		Supplier Number 155	364.33
7	Sterile powder-free latex gloves, size Small	per 100	101	16.25	4	65.00		Supplier Number 201	1,918.00
8	Sterile powder-free latex gloves, size Medium	per 100	101	16.25	8	130.00		Supplier Number 350	790.80
9	Sterile powder-free latex gloves, size Large	per 100	101	16.25	10	162.50			
10	Sterile powder-free vinyl gloves, size Small	per 100	101	11.50	4	46.00			
11	Sterile powder-free vinyl gloves, size Medium	per 100	101	11.50	8	92.00		Cost by Supplier with	
12	Sterile powder-free vinyl gloves, size Large	per 100	101	11.50	10	115.00		Minimum Qty over 4	
13	Disposable earloop mask	per 50	155	5.61	8	44.88		Supplier Number 101	1,146.60
14	Disposable patient gown	per dozen	155	7.90	16	126.40		Supplier Number 155	310.80
15	Disposable patient slippers	per dozen	155	4.27	16	68.32		Supplier Number 201	1,330.00
16	Cotton patient gown	per dozen	201	133.00	10	1,330.00		Supplier Number 350	659.00
17	Cotton patient robe	per dozen	201	147.00	4	588.00			
18	Disposable examination table paper	per roll	155	8.90	8	71.20			
19	Lab coat, size Small	each	350	32.95	4	131.80			
20	Lab coat, size Medium	each	350	32.95	8	263.60			
21	Lab coat, size Large	each	350	32.95	12	395.40			
22	Disposable shoe cover	per 300	155	37.75	1	37.75			
23	Disposable bouffant cap	per 100	155	7.89	2	15.78			
24	TOTAL STANDARD EXAM ROOM SUPPLIES COST:					4,474.53			

formula
=SUMIF(Supplier,"101",StdCost)

formula
=SUMIFS(StdCost,Supplier,"350",MinQty,">4")

Project 1f Creating SUMIF Formulas

Note: In Step 4, check with your instructor before printing to see if two copies of the worksheets for the projects in this chapter need to be printed: one as displayed and another displaying the cell formulas. Save the worksheet before displaying formulas (Ctrl + `) so that column widths can be adjusted as necessary and then close without saving the changes.

1. With **2-ACOct18VehRpt.xlsx** open, make cell M4 active.
2. Create a SUMIF function to add up the auto insurance claim estimates for those claims being repaired at A+ Paint & Body by completing the following steps:
   a. Click the Formulas tab.
   b. Click the Math & Trig button in the Function Library group.
   c. Scroll down the drop-down list and then click *SUMIF.*
   d. At the Function Arguments dialog box with the insertion point positioned in the *Range* text box, type repshop and then press the Tab key.
   e. Designate cell K4 as the cell reference for A+ Paint & Body by typing k4 in the *Criteria* text box and then press the Tab key.
   f. Type claimest in the *Sum_range* text box.
   g. Click OK. Excel returns the value *16656* in cell M4.

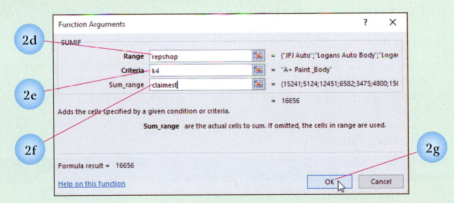

h. Apply the Comma format with no digits after the decimal point to cell M4.
3. Use the fill handle to copy the formula in cell M4 into the range M5:M7. When completed, the SUMIF formulas will be as follows:

   M5: *=SUMIF(RepShop,K5,ClaimEst)*
   M6: *=SUMIF(RepShop,K6,ClaimEst)*
   M7: *=SUMIF(RepShop,K7,ClaimEst)*
4. Save, print, and then close **2-ACOct18VehRpt.xlsx.**

Claim Report Statistics Summary		
	No. of	Total
By Repair Shop	Claims	Estimates
A+ Paint & Body	3	16,656
JFJ Auto	9	66,128
Logans Auto Body	5	51,990
West Collision	4	31,683

Check Your Work

Project 2 **Populate Cells by Looking Up Data in a Discount Table** 1 Part

You will use a lookup formula to automatically enter discounts for containers and then calculate net prices.

Preview Finished Project

Using Lookup Functions

Tutorial

Using Lookup Functions

 Lookup & Reference

The Lookup & Reference functions provide formulas for looking up values in a range. For example, in a grades worksheet, the final numerical score for a student can be looked up in a range of cells that contain the letter grades with corresponding numerical scores. The letter grade can be returned in the formula cell by looking up the student's score. Being able to look up a value automates data entry in large worksheets and, when used properly, can prevent inaccuracies caused by data entry errors.

Excel provides the VLOOKUP and HLOOKUP functions, which refer to vertical and horizontal lookups, respectively. The layout of the lookup range (referred to as a *lookup table*) determines whether to use VLOOKUP or HLOOKUP. VLOOKUP is used more commonly, since most lookup tables are arranged with comparison data in columns (which means Excel searches for the lookup value in a vertical order). HLOOKUP is used when the lookup range contains comparison data in rows (which means Excel searches for the lookup value in a horizontal order).

Using the VLOOKUP Function

The structure of a VLOOKUP formula is =*VLOOKUP(lookup_value,table_array,col_index_num,range_lookup)*. Table 2.1 explains all the parameters of a VLOOKUP argument.

The VLOOKUP function is easier to understand when explained using an example. In the worksheet shown in Figure 2.5, VLOOKUP is used to return the starting salary for new hires at a medical center. Each new hire is assigned a salary

Table 2.1 VLOOKUP Argument Parameters

Argument Parameter	Description
lookup_value	The value that Excel should search for in the lookup table. Enter a value or cell reference to a value.
table_array	The range address or range name for the lookup table that Excel should search for. Do not include column headers in the range. Use range names or absolute cell referencing.
col_index_num	The column number from the lookup table that contains the data to be placed in the formula cell.
range_lookup	Enter TRUE to instruct Excel to find an exact or approximate match for the lookup value. If this parameter is left out of the formula, Excel assumes TRUE, which means if an exact match is not found, Excel returns the value for the last category into which the known value fits. For the formula to work properly, the first column of the lookup table must be sorted in ascending order. Enter FALSE to instruct Excel to return only exact matches to the lookup value.

Create a VLOOKUP
Formula
1. Make cell active.
2. Click Formulas tab.
3. Click Lookup &
   Reference button.
4. Click *VLOOKUP*.
5. Enter cell address,
   range name, or value
   in *Lookup_value* text
   box.
6. Enter range or range
   name in *Table_array*
   text box.
7. Type column number
   to return values from
   in *Col_index_num*
   text box.
8. Type false or leave
   blank for TRUE in
   Range_lookup text
   box.
9. Click OK.

grid number depending on his or her education and years of work experience. This salary grid number determines the new hire's starting salary. The lookup table contains the grid numbers with the corresponding starting salaries. In column E, VLOOKUP formulas automatically insert the starting salary for each new employee based on his or her grid number in column D. In the formula shown in Figure 2.5, range names have been included. *Rating* references the values in column D and *grid* represents the lookup table in the range G4:H8.

Figure 2.5 VLOOKUP Example

	A	B	C	D	E	F	G	H
1	**HealthPlus Medical Center**							
2			New Hires for 2018				Reference Table	
3	Date of Hire	First Name	Last Name	Salary Grid Rating	Starting Salary		Salary Grid Rating	Starting Salary
4	10/5/2018	Joel	Adams	3	40,375		1	$ 34,675
5	10/8/2018	David	Bannerman	4	42,250		2	$ 36,750
6	10/15/2018	Jill	Williams	2	36,750		3	$ 40,375
7	10/15/2018	Kendall	Borman	1	34,675		4	$ 42,250
8	10/22/2018	Leigh	Wilcox	1	34,675		5	$ 46,175
9	10/23/2018	Vanessa	Lopez	4	42,250			
10	10/25/2018	Cory	Campbell	5	46,175			
11	10/26/2018	George	Sorrenti	2	36,750			
12	10/30/2018	Paula	Gorski	1	34,675			
13	10/31/2018	Kyla	Vanwyst	3	40,375			

The lookup table is named *grid*.

formula =VLOOKUP (Rating,grid,2)

The VLOOKUP formula populates the range E4:E13 by matching the salary grid rating number in column D with the corresponding salary grid rating number in the lookup table named *grid*.

Project 2 Creating a VLOOKUP Formula

Part 1 of 1

1. Open **PrecisionPrices.xlsx**.
2. Save the workbook with the name **2-PrecisionPrices**.
3. Create a VLOOKUP formula to find the correct discount value for each product by completing the following steps:
   a. Select the range H4:I8 and name it *DiscTable*.
   b. Make cell E4 active and then click the Formulas tab.
   c. Click the Lookup & Reference button in the Function Library group.
   d. Click *VLOOKUP* at the drop-down list.
   e. If necessary, drag the Function Arguments dialog box out of the way so that the first few rows of the product price list and discount table data can be seen.

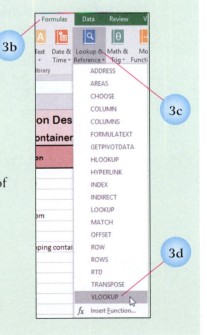

f. With the insertion point positioned in the *Lookup_value* text box, type c4 and then press the Tab key. Product discounts are categorized by letter codes. To find the correct discount, Excel needs to look for the matching category letter code for the product within the first column of the discount table. Notice that the letter codes in the discount table are listed in ascending order.

g. Type disctable in the *Table_array* text box and then press the Tab key. Using a range name for a reference table is a good idea, since the formula will be copied and absolute references are needed for the cells in the lookup table.

h. Type 2 in the *Col_index_num* text box and then press the Tab key. The discount percentage in column 2 of DiscTable will be placed in cell E4.

i. Type false in the *Range_lookup* text box.

j. Click OK. Entering *false* instructs Excel to return a value for exact matches only. Should a discount category be typed into a cell in column C for which no entry exists in the discount table, Excel will return *#N/A* in the formula cell; this is an alert that an error has occurred in the data entry.

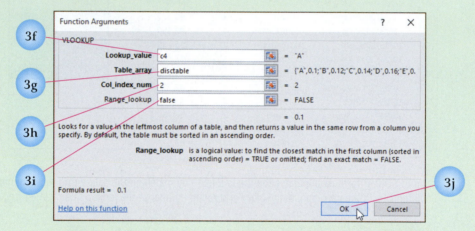

4. Look at the formula in the Formula bar:
   =VLOOKUP(C4,DiscTable,2,FALSE).
5. Apply the Percent format to cell E4.
6. Make cell F4 active, type the formula =d4-(d4*e4) to calculate the net price, and then press the Enter key.
7. Select the range E4:F4 and then drag the fill handle into row 21.
8. Deselect the range.
9. Print the worksheet.
10. Save and then close **2-PrecisionPrices.xlsx**.

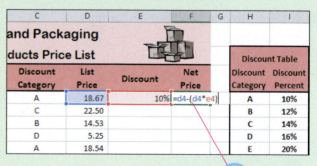

Check Your Work

Using the HLOOKUP Function

The HLOOKUP function uses the same argument parameters as the VLOOKUP function. Use HLOOKUP when the table being searched for a comparison value is arranged horizontally, like the one shown in the range J3:O4 in Figure 2.6. Excel searches across the table in the first row for a matching value and then returns to the formula cell the value from the same column.

The structure of an HLOOKUP formula is *=HLOOKUP(lookup_value,table_array,row_index_num,range_lookup)*. The argument parameters are similar to the VLOOKUP parameters described in Table 2.1 on page 44. Excel searches the first row of the table for the lookup value. When a match is found, Excel returns the value from the same column in the row number specified in the *row_index_num* argument.

Figure 2.6 HLOOKUP Example

formula
=HLOOKUP(F4,GradeTable,2)

	A	B	C	D	E	F	G	H	I	J	K	L	M	N	O
1	Math by Janelle Tutoring Service														
2	Student Progress Report														
3	Student Name	Test 1	Test 2	Test 3	Test 4	Total	Grade		Score	0	50	60	70	80	90
4	Dana Rosenthal	51	48	55	50	51.0	D		Grade	F	D	C	B	A	A+
5	Kelsey Williams	75	82	66	72	73.8	B								
6	Hilary Orbet	81	88	79	83	82.8	A								
7	Jose Alvarez	67	72	65	78	70.5	B								
8	Linden Porter	42	51	40	55	47.0	F								
9	Carl Quenneville	65	44	72	61	60.5	C								
10	Andrewa Desmond	55	48	60	50	53.3	D								
11	Kylie Winters	78	82	67	71	74.5	B								
12	Lindsay Cortez	82	78	85	88	83.3	A								

The lookup table is named *GradeTable*.

The HLOOKUP formula populates the range G4:G12 by looking up the total value in column F in the first row in the lookup table (GradeTable). The formula stops at the largest value in the table that is less than or equal to the lookup value. For example, looking for *62.3* would make Excel stop at *60*.

Project 3 **Analyze an Expansion Project Loan** **1 Part**

You will use a financial function to calculate the principal portion of an expansion loan payment for two lenders.

Preview Finished Project

Tutorial

Using the PPMT Financial Function

Tutorial

Review: Using Financial Functions

Financial

Using the PPMT Financial Function

Financial functions can be used to perform a variety of financial analyses, including loan amortizations, annuity payments, investment planning, depreciation, and so on. The PMT function is used to calculate a payment for a loan based on a constant interest rate and constant payments for a set period. Excel provides two related financial functions: PPMT, to calculate the principal portion of the loan payment, and IPMT, to calculate the interest portion.

Quick Steps

Create a PPMT Formula

1. Make cell active.
2. Click Formulas tab.
3. Click Financial button.
4. Click *PPMT*.
5. Enter value, cell address, or range name for interest rate in *Rate* text box.
6. Enter number representing payment to find principal for *Per* text box.
7. Enter value, cell address, or range name for total number of payments in *Nper* text box.
8. Enter value, cell address, or range name for amount borrowed in *Pv* text box.
9. Click OK.

Knowing the principal portion of a loan payment is useful in determining the amount of the payment being used to reduce the principal balance owed. The difference between the loan payment and the PPMT value represents the interest cost. The function returns the principal portion of a specific payment for a loan. For example, calculate the principal on the first payment, last payment, or any payment in between. The structure of a PPMT function is =*PPMT(rate,per,nper,pv,fv,type)*, where

- *rate* is the interest rate per period,
- *per* is the period for which to find the principal portion of the payment,
- *nper* is the number of payment periods,
- *pv* is the amount of money borrowed,
- *fv* is the balance at the end of the loan (if left blank, 0 is assumed), and
- *type* is either 0 (payment at end of period) or 1 (payment at beginning of period).

Make sure to be consistent with the units for the interest rate and payment periods. If the interest rate is divided by 12 for a monthly rate, the payment period should also be expressed monthly. For example, multiply the term by 12 if the amortization is entered in the worksheet in years.

Project 3 Calculating Principal Portions of Loan Payments Using the PPMT Function   Part 1 of 1

1. Open **DExpansion.xlsx**.
2. Save the workbook with the name **2-DExpansion.xlsx**.
3. Calculate the principal portion of the first loan payment for two loan proposals to fund a building expansion project by completing the following steps:
   a. Make cell C10 active.
   b. If necessary, click the Formulas tab.
   c. Click the Financial button in the Function Library group.
   d. Scroll down the drop-down list and then click *PPMT*.
   e. If necessary, move the Function Arguments dialog box to the right side of the screen so that all the values in column C can be seen.

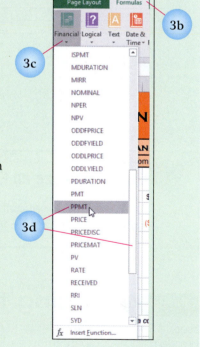

f. With the insertion point positioned in the *Rate* text box, type c4/12 and then press the Tab key. Since the interest rate is stated per annum (per year), dividing the rate by 12 calculates the monthly rate.

g. Type 1 in the *Per* text box to calculate the principal for the first loan payment and then press the Tab key.

h. Type c5*12 in the *Nper* text box and then press the Tab key. Since a loan payment is made each month, the number of payments is 12 times the amortization period.

i. Type c6 in the *Pv* text box.

j. Click OK. *Pv* refers to present value; in this example, it means the loan amount for which the payments are being calculated. It is positive because it represents cash received by the company. Excel returns the value *-1853.05* in cell C10. Payments are shown as negative numbers because they represent cash that is paid out. In this worksheet, negative numbers have been formatted to display in red and enclosed in parentheses.

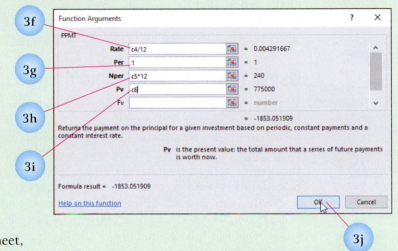

4. Copy and paste the formula from cell C10 into cell E10 and then press the Esc key to remove the scrolling marquee from cell C10.

5. Make cell C12 active, type =c8*12*c5, and then press the Enter key.

6. Copy and paste the formula from cell C12 into cell E12. Press the Esc key to remove the scrolling marquee from cell C12 and then AutoFit the width of column E. Notice that the loan from Dominion Trust is a better choice for Deering Industries, assuming the company can afford the higher monthly payments. Although the interest rate is higher than that for the Victory Trust loan, the shorter term means the loan will be repaid sooner and at a lesser total cost.

		Victory Trust
3		
4	Interest Rate	5.15%
5	Amortization	20
6	Loan Amount	$ 775,000
7		
8	Monthly Payment	($5,179.09)
9		
10	Monthly Principal Payment (1st payment)	($1,853.05)
11		
12	Total Loan Payments	=c8*12*c5

7. Print the worksheet.

8. Save and then close **2-DExpansion.xlsx**.

Check Your Work

Project 4 Calculate Benefit Costs Using Conditional Logic   2 Parts

You will create formulas to calculate the employee benefit costs for ViewRite using logical functions to test multiple conditions.

Preview Finished Project

Using and Nesting Logical Functions

Quick Steps

Create an IF Formula
1. Make cell active.
2. Click Formulas tab.
3. Click Logical button.
4. Click *IF*.
5. Type conditional test argument in *Logical_test* text box.
6. Press Tab.
7. Type argument in *Value_if_true* text box.
8. Press Tab.
9. Type argument in *Value_if_false* text box.
10. Click OK.

Using conditional logic in a formula requires Excel to perform a calculation based on the outcome of a logical or conditional test. One calculation is performed if the test proves true and another calculation is performed if the test proves false. For example, the following is an IF formula using named ranges that could be used to calculate a salesperson's bonus if his or her sales exceed a target: *=IF(Sales>Target,Bonus,0)*. Excel first tests the value in the cell named *Sales* to see if it is greater than the value in the cell named *Target*. If the condition proves true, Excel returns the value of the cell named *Bonus*. If the sales value is not greater than the target value, the condition proves false and Excel places a *0* in the cell. The structure of the IF statement is *=IF(logical_test,value_if_true,value_if_false)*.

Using the Nested IF Logical Function

When more than two outcomes are possible or a decision is based on more than one field, a nested IF statement is used. A nested IF function is one IF function inside another. The structure of a nested IF statement is *=IF(logical_test,value_if_true,IF(logical_test,value_if_true,value_if_false))*. Excel evaluates the first *logical_test*. If the answer is true, then depending on what is entered for the *value_if_true*, a calculation is performed and text or numbers are entered; or if the *value_if_true* is omitted, a 0 is entered. If the first *logical_test* is not true, then the next *logical_test* is evaluated and if the answer is true, the *value_if_true* is placed in the cell. Excel stops evaluating the formula once the *logical_test* has been answered as true. If the answer is never true, then depending on what is entered as the *value_if_false*, a calculation is performed and text or numbers are entered; if the *value_if_false* is omitted, a 0 is entered.

For example, assume that a company has three sales commission rates based on the level of sales achieved by the salesperson. If sales are less than $40,000, the salesperson earns a 5% commission; if sales are greater than or equal to $40,000 but less than $80,000, the salesperson earns a 7% commission; and if sales are greater than or equal to $80,000, the salesperson earns a 9% commission. Since there are three possible sales commission rates, a single IF function will not work. To correctly calculate the sales commission rate, two conditional tests must be done. The last level (or in this case, the third commission rate of 9%) is used for the *value_if_false*.

Consider the following formula: *=IF(Sales<40000,Sales*5%,IF(Sales<80000, Sales*7%,Sales*9%))*. This formula includes two IF functions. In the first IF function, the conditional test is to determine if the sales value is less than $40,000 (*Sales<40000*). If the test proves true (for example, sales are $25,000), then Excel calculates the sales times 5% and returns the result in the active cell. If the test is not true, then Excel reads the next section of the argument, which is the next IF function that includes the conditional test to determine if sales are less than $80,000 (*Sales<80000*). If this second conditional test proves true, then Excel calculates the sales times 7%. If the test proves false, Excel calculates the sales times 9%. Since these are the only three possible actions, the formula ends. While up to 64 IF functions can be nested, doing this would create a very complex formula. Consider using a VLOOKUP or HLOOKUP to test different conditions.

Tutorial

Using the Nested IF Logical Function

Tutorial

Review: Using Logical IF Functions

 Logical

💡 **Hint** If you type a nested IF function directly into a cell, Excel color-codes the parentheses for the different IF functions so you can keep track of the functions separately.

💡 **Hint** The number of right parentheses needed to end a nested IF statement equals the number of times IF appears in the formula.

Create an AND Formula
1. Make cell active OR nest formula in IF statement *Logical_ test* text box.
2. Type =and(or and(if nesting in IF statement.
3. Type first conditional test argument.
4. Type ,.
5. Type second conditional test argument.
6. Repeat Steps 4–5 for remaining conditions.
7. Type).

Create an OR Formula
1. Make cell active OR nest formula in IF statement *Logical_ test* text box.
2. Type =or(or or(if nesting in IF statement.
3. Type first conditional test argument.
4. Type ,.
5. Type second conditional test argument.
6. Repeat Steps 4–5 for remaining conditions.
7. Type).

Any function can be nested inside another function. For example, in the PPMT formula discussed in the previous section, Excel returns a negative value for the principal portion of the payment. The PPMT formula can be nested inside the ABS formula to have the principal payment displayed without a negative symbol. ABS is the function used to return the absolute value of a number (that is, the number without its sign). For example, *=ABS(PPMT(C4/12,1,C5*12,C6))* displays the payment calculated in Project 3 as $1,853.05 instead of -$1,853.05.

Using the ROUND Function

ROUND is another example of a function that can easily be nested with other functions. Excel uses the entire number stored in the cell and not just the visible number in any calculations. The function ROUND is used to modify the actual number of characters by rounding the value. The structure of this function is *=ROUND(number,num_digits)*. The *num_digits* number can be positive or negative. A positive number rounds the decimal value (the numbers right of the decimal point) to the designated number of places. A negative number rounds the numbers left of the decimal point to the nearest ones, tens, hundreds, and so on. Table 2.2 demonstrates how positive and negative *num_digits* are handled.

Table 2.2 Examples of Applying the ROUND Function

Example	Description	Result
=ROUND(1625.09,1)	Rounds *1625.09* to one digit past the decimal point.	*1625.1*
=ROUND(1625.1,0)	Rounds *1625.1* to zero digits past the decimal point.	*1625*
=ROUND(1625,-1)	Rounds *1625* to the nearest 10s value.	*1630*

When nesting the ROUND function, make sure that the original function is working before rounding the final result. In Project 4a, the nested IF AND formula used to calculate the pension contributions returns some values with three decimal places. The ROUND function will be added after the IF AND statement.

Using Logical Functions: Nested IF, AND, and OR

Other logical functions offered in Excel include AND and OR. These functions use Boolean logic to construct a conditional test in a formula to be either true or false. Table 2.3 describes how each function works to test a statement and also provides an example of each function.

Table 2.3 AND and OR Logical Functions

Logical Function	Description	Example
AND	Returns *TRUE* if all the conditions test true Returns *FALSE* if any of the conditions tests false	=AND(Sales>Target,NewClients>5) Returns *TRUE* if both test true Returns *FALSE* if Sales is greater than *Target* but NewClients is less than 5 Returns *FALSE* if Sales is less than Target but NewClients is greater than 5
OR	Returns *TRUE* if any of the conditions tests true Returns *FALSE* if all the conditions test false	=OR(Sales>Target,NewClients>5) Returns *TRUE* if Sales is greater than Target or NewClients is greater than 5 Returns *FALSE* only if Sales is not greater than Target and NewClients is not greater than 5

Project 4a Calculating Pension Costs Using Nested IF, AND, and ROUND Functions   Part 1 of 2

1. Open **VRSalCost.xlsx**.
2. Save the workbook with the name **2-VRSalCost**.
3. ViewRite contributes 5.575% of an employee's salary into a privately managed company retirement account if the employee works full time and earns more than $45,000 a year. Calculate the pension benefit costs for eligible employees by completing the following steps:
   a. Make cell H6 the active cell.
   b. Click the Formulas tab.
   c. Click the Logical button in the Function Library group and then click *IF* at the drop-down list.
   d. If necessary, drag the Function Arguments dialog box down until all of row 6 can be seen in the worksheet.
   e. With the insertion point positioned in the *Logical_test* text box, type and(c6="FT",g6>45000) and then press the Tab key. An AND function is required, since both conditions must be true for the company to contribute to the pension plan. The testing of the two conditions—being a full-time (FT) employee and having a salary over $45,000—are separated by a comma. *Note: Excel requires having quotation marks around text when it is used in a conditional test formula*.
   f. Type g6*5.575% in the *Value_if_true* text box and then press the Tab key.
   g. Type 0 in the *Value_if_false* text box and then click OK.

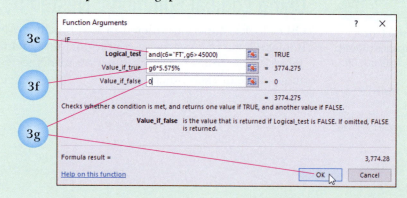

3e

3f

3g

Function Arguments

IF

Logical_test   and(c6="FT",g6>45000)   = TRUE

Value_if_true   g6*5.575%   = 3774.275

Value_if_false 0   = 0

= 3774.275

Checks whether a condition is met, and returns one value if TRUE, and another value if FALSE.

Value_if_false is the value that is returned if Logical_test is FALSE. If omitted, FALSE is returned.

Formula result =   3,774.28

Help on this function   OK   Cancel

h. Look at the formula *=IF(AND(C6="FT",G6>45000),G6*5.575%,0)* in the Formula bar. Notice that the AND function is nested within the IF function. Since both conditions for the first employee tested true, the pension cost is calculated.

4. With cell H6 selected, increase the number of digits after the display point to three. Use the ROUND function to round the pension amount to the nearest penny by completing the following steps:

a. Click right of the equals sign in the Formula bar.

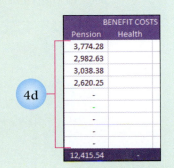

b. Type round(and then press the End key to move to the end of the formula.

c. Type ,2) and then press the Enter key.

d. Select cell H6, decrease the number of digits after the decimal point to two, and then copy the formula in cell H6 into the range H7:H14. Deselect the range. Notice that only the first four employees have pension benefit values. This is because they are the only employees who both work full time and earn over $45,000 a year in salary.

5. Save **2-VRSalCost.xlsx**.

Check Your Work

Project 4b Calculating Health and Dental Costs Using Nested IF and OR Functions   Part 2 of 2

1. With **2-VRSalCost.xlsx** open, make cell I6 the active cell.

2. ViewRite offers to pay the annual health premiums for employees not covered by other medical plans. The company pays $2,600 per year per employee for family coverage, $1,580 per year per employee for single coverage, and $0 per year if the employee declines coverage. Calculate the cost for each employee who chose to join the health plan by completing the following steps:

a. This formula requires a nested IF statement, since the result will be $2,600, $1,580, or 0 depending on the contents of cell D6. (An OR statement

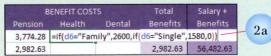

will not work for this formula, since two different health premiums are used.) In cell I6, type *=if(d6="Family",2600,if(d6="Single",1580,0))* and then press the Enter key. *Note: Recall that Excel requires the use of quotation marks around text entries within an IF function*.

b. Copy the formula in cell I6 into the range I7:I14. Notice the cells in column I for which no values are entered. In column D in the corresponding row, the text *Declined* displays. Excel returned a value of 0 in column I because the conditions *D6="Family"* and *D6="Single"* both proved false.

3. ViewRite has negotiated a flat fee with its dental benefit service provider. The company pays $1,750 per year for each employee, regardless of the type of coverage. However, the service provider requires ViewRite to report each person's coverage as *Family* or *Single* for audit purposes. The dental plan is optional and some employees have declined coverage. Calculate the cost of the dental plan by completing the following steps:

a. Make cell J6 the active cell.

b. If necessary, click the Formulas tab.

c. Click the Logical button and then click *IF* at the drop-down list.

d. If necessary, drag the Function Arguments dialog box down until all of row 6 can be seen in the worksheet.

e. With the insertion point positioned in the *Logical_test* text box, type or(e6="Family",e6="Single") and then press the Tab key. An OR function is appropriate for calculating this benefit, since either condition can be true for the company to contribute to the dental plan. The testing of the two conditions, being a family or being single, is separated by a comma.

f. Type 1750 in the *Value_if_true* text box and then press the Tab key.

g. Type 0 in the *Value_if_false* text box and then click OK.

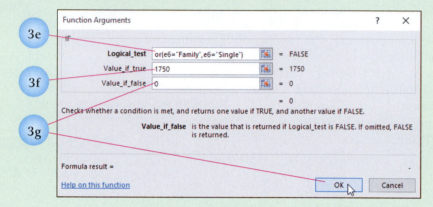

h. Look at the formula *=IF(OR(E6="Family", E6="Single"),1750,0)* in the Formula bar. Notice that the OR function is nested within the IF function. Since cell E6 contains neither *Family* nor *Single*, the OR statement tests false and *0* is returned in cell J6.

i. Copy the formula in cell J6 into the range J7:J14 and then deselect the range.

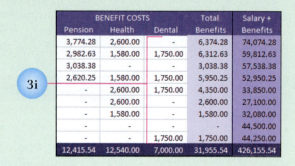

4. Save **2-VRSalCost.xlsx**.
5. Print and then close **2-VRSalCost.xlsx**.

Check Your Work

In this chapter, a small sampling of functions from the statistical, math and trigonometry, lookup, financial, and logical categories have been discussed. Excel provides more than 300 functions in 13 categories. To check on the availability of an existing preprogrammed function, open the Insert Function dialog box, type a description of the function in the *Search for a function* text box, and then click the Go button.

Chapter Summary

- Using range names in formulas makes it easier to manage complex formulas and helps others who work in, or edit a worksheet, to understand the purpose of a formula more quickly.

- Click the Name Manager button in the Defined Names group on the Formulas tab to open the Name Manager dialog box.

- Use options at the Name Manager dialog box to create, edit, or delete a range name or edit the cells that a range name references.

- The COUNTIF statistical function counts cells within a range that meet a single criterion or condition.

- The COUNTIFS statistical function counts cells within a range that meet multiple criteria or conditions.

- Find the arithmetic mean of a range of cells that meet a single criterion or condition using the statistical AVERAGEIF function.

- Use the AVERAGEIFS statistical function to find the arithmetic mean for a range that meet multiple criteria or conditions.

- The math function SUMIF adds cells within a range that meet a single criterion or condition.

- To add cells within a range based on multiple criteria or conditions, use the SUMIFS math function.

- The Lookup & Reference functions VLOOKUP and HLOOKUP look up data in a reference table and return in the formula cell a value from a column or row, respectively, in the lookup table.

- The PPMT financial function returns the principal portion of a specified loan payment within the term based on an interest rate, total number of payments, and loan amount.

- Using conditional logic in a formula requires Excel to perform a calculation based on the outcome of a logical or conditional test, in which one calculation is performed if the test proves true and another calculation is performed if the test proves false.

- A nested function is one function inside another function.

- Use the ROUND function to modify the number of characters by rounding the value.

- Use the AND logical function to test multiple conditions. Excel returns *TRUE* if all the conditions test true and *FALSE* if any of the conditions tests false.

- The OR logical function also tests multiple conditions. The function returns *TRUE* if any of the conditions tests true and *FALSE* if all the conditions test false.

Commands Review

FEATURE	RIBBON TAB, GROUP	BUTTON	KEYBOARD SHORTCUT
financial functions	Formulas, Function Library		
Insert Function dialog box	Formulas, Function Library		Shift + F3
logical functions	Formulas, Function Library		
lookup and reference functions	Formulas, Function Library		
math and trigonometry functions	Formulas, Function Library		
Name Manager dialog box	Formulas, Defined Names		Ctrl + F3
statistical functions accessed from More Functions button	Formulas, Function Library		

Workbook

Chapter study tools and assessment activities are available in the *Workbook* ebook. These resources are designed to help you further develop and demonstrate mastery of the skills learned in this chapter.

Microsoft®
Excel®

Working with Tables and Data Features

Performance Objectives

Upon successful completion of Chapter 3, you will be able to:

1 Create a table in a worksheet

2 Expand a table to include new rows and columns

3 Add a calculated column in a table

4 Format a table by applying table styles and table style options

5 Add a *Total* row to a table and formulas to sum cells

6 Sort and filter a table

7 Use Data Tools to split the contents of a cell into separate columns

8 Use Flash Fill to organize data from other sources

9 Remove duplicate records

10 Restrict data entry by creating validation criteria

11 Convert a table to a normal range

12 Create subtotals in groups of related data

13 Group and ungroup data

Precheck

Check your current skills to help focus your study.

A *table* is a range that can be managed separately from other rows and columns in a worksheet. Data in a table can be sorted, filtered, and totaled as a separate unit. A worksheet can contain more than one table, which allows managing multiple groups of data separately within the same workbook. In this chapter, you will learn how to use the table feature to manage a range. You will use tools to validate data, search for and remove duplicate records, and convert text to a table. You will also convert a table back to a normal range and use data tools such as grouping related records and calculating subtotals.

Data Files

Before beginning chapter work, copy the EL2C3 folder to your storage medium and then make EL2C3 the active folder.

SNAP

If you are a SNAP user, launch the Precheck and Tutorials from your Assignments page.

Project 1 Create and Modify a Table in a Billing Summary Worksheet

4 Parts

You will convert data in a billing summary worksheet to a table and then modify the table by applying table styles and sorting and filtering the data.

Preview Finished Project

Preview Finished Project

Tutorial

Formatting Data as a Table

Quick Steps

Create a Table
1. Select range.
2. Click Quick Analysis button.
3. Click Tables tab.
4. Click Table button.
5. Deselect range.

Table

Formatting Data as a Table

A table in Excel is similar in structure to a database. Columns are called *fields*. Each field is used to store a single unit of information about a person, place, or object. The first row of a table contains the column headings and is called the *field names row* or *header row*. Each column heading in the table should be unique. Below the field names, data is entered in rows called *records*. A record contains all the field values related to the single person, place, or object that is the topic of the table. No blank rows exist within the table, as shown in Figure 3.1.

To create a table in Excel, enter the data in the worksheet and then define the range as a table using the Table button in the Tables group on the Insert tab, the Format as Table button in the Styles group on the Home tab, or the Table button on the Tables tab in the Quick Analysis button at the bottom right of the selected range. Before converting a range to a table, delete any blank rows between the column headings and the data or within the data range.

Figure 3.1 Worksheet with the Range Formatted as a Table

The first row of a table contains field names and is called the *header row*.

	Stock No.	Title	Season No./Episode	Year Aired	Genre	DVD	Blu-ray	Download	Multiformat	Price	Current Discount
5	CV-1001	Once Upon a Time	S3 E22	2013-14	Drama	Yes	Yes	Yes	Yes	34.99	10%
6	CV-1002	Once Upon a Time	S4 E22	2014-15	Drama	Yes	Yes	Yes	Yes	39.99	
7	CV-1003	Once Upon a Time	S5 E22	2015-16	Drama	Yes	Yes	Yes	Yes	39.99	
8	CV-1004	The Big Bang Theory	S8 E24	2014-15	Comedy	Yes	Yes	Yes	Yes	28.99	7%
9	CV-1005	The Big Bang Theory	S9 E24	2015-16	Comedy	Yes	Yes	Yes	Yes	32.99	
10	CV-1006	Doctor Who	S8 E12	2014	Sci-Fi	Yes	Yes	No	No	69.99	7%
11	CV-1007	Modern Family	S4 E24	2012-13	Comedy	Yes	No	Yes	Yes	19.99	10%
12	CV-1008	Modern Family	S5 E24	2013-14	Comedy	Yes	No	Yes	Yes	19.99	10%
13	CV-1009	Modern Family	S6 E24	2014-15	Comedy	Yes	No	Yes	Yes	24.99	
14	CV-1010	Modern Family	S7 E24	2015-16	Comedy	Yes	No	Yes	Yes	24.99	
15	CV-1011	Gotham	S2 E22	2015-16	Drama	Yes	Yes	Yes	Yes	32.99	7%
16	CV-1012	Grey's Anatomy	S10 E24	2013-14	Drama	No	No	Yes	No	20.99	10%
17	CV-1013	Grey's Anatomy	S11 E25	2014-15	Drama	No	No	Yes	No	20.99	
18	CV-1014	Parks and Recreation	S6 E22	2013-14	Comedy	No	No	Yes	No	12.99	10%
19	CV-1015	Parks and Recreation	S7 E13	2014-15	Comedy	No	No	Yes	No	25.99	
20	CV-1016	NCIS	S11 E24	2013-14	Drama	Yes	Yes	Yes	Yes	30.99	10%
21	CV-1017	NCIS	S12 E24	2014-15	Drama	Yes	Yes	Yes	Yes	34.99	
22	CV-1018	NCIS	S13 E24	2015-16	Drama	Yes	Yes	Yes	Yes	49.99	
23	CV-1019	Grimm	S4 E22	2014-15	Supernatural	Yes	No	No	No	32.99	
24	CV-1020	Criminal Minds	S8 E24	2012-13	Thriller/Drama	No	Yes	Yes	Yes	19.99	10%
25	CV-1007	Modern Family	S4 E24	2012-13	Comedy	Yes	No	Yes	Yes	19.99	10%
26	CV-1022	Criminal Minds	S10 E23	2014-15	Thriller/Drama	No	Yes	Yes	Yes	24.99	
27	CV-1023	Criminal Minds	S11 E22	2015-16	Thriller/Drama	No	Yes	Yes	Yes	24.99	
28	CV-1024	Supernatural	S9 E23	2014-15	Horror	Yes	Yes	Yes	Yes	26.99	7%
29	CV-1025	Supernatural	S10 E23	2015-16	Horror	Yes	Yes	Yes	Yes	34.99	7%

ViewRite
TV Series Collection

A row in a table is called a *record*.

A column in a table contains a single unit of information for each record and is called a *field*.

1. Open **BillSumOctWk1.xlsx**.
2. Save the workbook with the name **3-BillSumOctWk1**.
3. Convert the billing summary data to a table by completing the following steps:
   a. Select the range A4:I24.
   b. Click the Insert tab.
   c. Click the Table button in the Tables group.
   d. At the Create Table dialog box with *=$A$4:$I$24* selected in the *Where is the data for your table?* text box and the *My table has headers* check box selected, click OK.
   e. Deselect the range.
4. Select columns A through I and AutoFit the column widths.
5. Save **3-BillSumOctWk1.xlsx**.

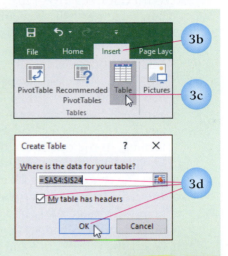

> Check Your Work

Modifying a Table

Once a table has been defined, typing new data in the row immediately below the last row of the table or in the column immediately right of the last column causes the table to automatically expand to include the new entries. Excel displays the AutoCorrect Options button when the table is expanded. Click the button to display a drop-down list with the options *Undo Table AutoExpansion* and *Stop Automatically Expanding Tables*. To add data near a table without having the table expand, leave a blank column or row between the table and the new data.

Typing a formula in the first record of a new table column automatically creates a calculated column. In a calculated column, Excel copies the formula from the first cell to the remaining cells in the column immediately after the formula is entered. The AutoCorrect Options button appears when Excel converts a column to a calculated column. Click the button to display the options *Undo Calculated Column*, *Stop Automatically Creating Calculated Columns*, and *Control AutoCorrect Options*.

1. With **3-BillSumOctWk1.xlsx** open, add a new record to the table by completing the following steps:
   a. Make cell A25 active, type RE-522, and then press the Tab key. Excel automatically expands the table to include the new row and displays the AutoCorrect Options button.
   b. With cell B25 active, type the remainder of the record as follows. Press the Tab key to move from column to column in the table.

24	RE-501	10384	10/5/2018
25	RE-522		
26			

   AutoCorrect Options button

Client	10512
Date	10/5/2018
Client Name	Connie Melanson
Attorney FName	Kyle
Attorney LName	Williams
Area	Real Estate
Billable Hours	2.5

c. With cell I25 active, type 175 and then press the Enter key. (If you press the Tab key, a new table row will be created.)

2. Add a calculated column to multiply the billable hours times rate by completing the following steps:

   a. Make cell J4 active, type Fees Due, and then press the Enter key. Excel automatically expands the table to include the new column.

   b With cell J5 active, type =h5*i5 and then press the Enter key. Excel creates a calculated column and copies the formula to the rest of the rows in the table.

   c. Double-click the column J boundary to AutoFit the column.

3. Adjust the centering and fill color of the titles across the top of the table by completing the following steps:

   a. Select the range A1:J1 and then click the Merge & Center button in the Alignment group on the Home tab two times.

   b. Select the range A2:J2 and press the F4 function key to repeat the command to merge and center row 2 across columns A through J.

   c. Select the range A3:J3 and press the F4 function key to repeat the command to merge and center row 3 across columns A through J.

4. Save **3-BillSumOctWk1.xlsx**.

Rate	Fees Due
185.00	1,248.75
185.00	601.25
175.00	918.75
200.00	850.00
200.00	650.00
190.00	522.50
200.00	1,000.00
175.00	918.75
175.00	743.75
190.00	617.50
200.00	900.00
200.00	750.00
200.00	900.00
185.00	971.25
175.00	918.75
200.00	850.00
200.00	750.00
175.00	918.75
175.00	612.50
190.00	855.00
175.00	437.50

2a
2b

Check Your Work

Applying Table Styles and Table Style Options

Quick Steps

Change the Table Style
1. Make table cell active.
2. If necessary, click Table Tools Design tab.
3. Click a style in Table Styles gallery.
   OR
1. Click More button in Table Styles gallery.
2. Click desired style at drop-down gallery.

Add a *Total* Row
1. Make table cell active.
2. If necessary, click Table Tools Design tab.
3. Click *Total Row* check box.
4. Click in cell in *Total* row.
5. Click down arrow.
6. Click function.

The contextual Table Tools Design tab, shown in Figure 3.2, contains options for formatting the table. Apply a different visual style to a table using the Table Styles gallery. Excel provides several table styles that are categorized by *Light*, *Medium*, and *Dark* color themes. By default, Excel bands the rows within the table, which means that even-numbered rows are formatted differently from odd-numbered rows. Banding rows or columns makes it easier to read data across a row or down a column in a large table. The banding can be removed from the rows and/or added to the columns. Insert check marks in the *First Column* and *Last Column* check boxes in the Table Style Options group to add emphasis to the first or last column in the table by formatting them differently from the rest of the table. Use the *Header Row* check box to show or hide the column headings in the table. Use the *Filter Button* check box to remove the filter arrows from the header row.

Adding a *Total* row to the table causes Excel to add the word *Total* in the leftmost cell of a new row at the bottom of the table. A Sum function is added automatically to the last numeric column in the table. Click in a cell in the *Total* row to display a down arrow that when clicked displays a pop-up list; a function formula can be selected from this list.

Figure 3.2 Table Tools Design Tab

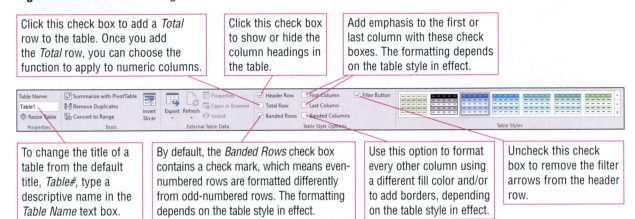

Click this check box to add a *Total* row to the table. Once you add the *Total* row, you can choose the function to apply to numeric columns.

Click this check box to show or hide the column headings in the table.

Add emphasis to the first or last column with these check boxes. The formatting depends on the table style in effect.

To change the title of a table from the default title, *Table#*, type a descriptive name in the *Table Name* text box.

By default, the *Banded Rows* check box contains a check mark, which means even-numbered rows are formatted differently from odd-numbered rows. The formatting depends on the table style in effect.

Use this option to format every other column using a different fill color and/or to add borders, depending on the table style in effect.

Uncheck this check box to remove the filter arrows from the header row.

Project 1c Formatting a Table and Adding a *Total* Row

1. With **3-BillSumOctWk1.xlsx** open, change the table style by completing the following steps:
   a. Click in any cell in the table to activate the table.
   b. Click the Table Tools Design tab.
   c. Click the More button in the Table Styles gallery.
   d. Click *Table Style Medium 15* at the drop-down gallery (first column, third row in the *Medium* section). Notice that the header row stays a dark blue and does not change to black.

2. Change the table style options to remove the row banding, insert column banding, and emphasize the first column by completing the following steps:
   a. Click the *Banded Rows* check box in the Table Style Options group on the Table Tools Design tab to remove the check mark. All the rows in the table are now formatted the same.
   b. Click the *Banded Columns* check box in the Table Style Options group to insert a check mark. Every other column in the table is now formatted differently.

   c. Click the *First Column* check box in the Table Style Options group to insert a check mark. Notice that a darker fill color and reverse font color are applied to the first column.
   d. Click the *Header Row* check box in the Table Style Options group to to remove the check mark. Notice that the first row of the table (the row containing the column headings) disappears and is replaced with empty cells. The row is also removed from the table range definition.
   e. Click the *Header Row* check box to insert a check mark and redisplay the column headings.
   f. Click in the *Table Name* text box in the Properties group, type OctWk1, and then press the Enter key to define the table title.

3. Add a *Total* row and add function formulas to numeric columns by completing the following steps:

a. Click the *Total Row* check box in the Table Style Options group to add a *Total* row to the bottom of the table. Excel formats row 26 as a *Total* row, adds the label *Total* in cell A26, and automatically creates a Sum function in cell J26.

b. In the *Billable Hours* column, make cell H26 active, click the down arrow that appears just right of the cell, and then click *Sum* at the pop-up list.

None	175.00	918.75
Average	200.00	850.00
Count		
Count Numbers	200.00	750.00
Max	175.00	918.75
Min		
Sum	175.00	612.50
StdDev	190.00	855.00
Var		
More Functions...	175.00	437.50
	16,935.00	

3b

The *Fees Due* column automatically sums when a *Total* row is added in Step 3a.

c. Make cell B26 active, click the down arrow that appears, and then click *Count* at the pop-up list.

19	CL-412	None	/5/2018	Hilary Schmidt	Toni	Sullivan	Corporate	5.25	175.00	918.75
20	IN-801	Average	/5/2018	Paul Sebastian	Rosa	Martinez	Insurance	4.25	200.00	850.00
21	EP-685	Count / Count Numbers	/5/2018	Frank Kinsela	Rosa	Martinez	Estate	3.75	200.00	750.00
22	CL-412	Max / Min	/5/2018	Hilary Schmidt	Toni	Sullivan	Corporate	5.25	175.00	918.75
23	CL-450	Sum	/5/2018	Henri Poissant	Toni	Sullivan	Corporate	3.50	175.00	612.50
24	RE-501	StdDev / Var	/5/2018	Jade Eckler	Kyle	Williams	Real Estate	4.50	190.00	855.00
25	RE-522	More Functions...	/5/2018	Connie Melanson	Kyle	Williams	Real Estate	2.50	175.00	437.50
26	Total							90.25		16,935.00

3c

4. Click the Page Layout tab and change the *Width* option to *1 page* in the Scale to Fit group.
5. Preview and then print the worksheet.
6. Save **3-BillSumOctWk1.xlsx**.

Check Your Work

Tutorial

Sorting a Table

Tutorial

Filtering a Table

Tutorial

Filtering a Table with a Slicer

Sorting and Filtering a Table

By default, Excel displays a filter arrow next to each label in the table header row. Click the filter arrow to display a drop-down list with the same sort and filter options used in Chapter 1.

A table can also be filtered using the Slicer feature. When a Slicer is added, a Slicer pane containing all the unique values for the specified field is opened. Click an option in the Slicer pane to immediately filter the table. Add several Slicer panes to filter by more than one field as needed.

To insert a Slicer pane, make any cell within the table active, click the Table Tools Design tab if necessary, and then click the Insert Slicer button in the Tools group. Excel opens the Insert Slicers dialog box, which contains a list of the fields in the table with a check box next to each field. Click to insert a check mark in the check box for each field to be filtered and then click OK. Click the option that the list is to be filtered on. Use the Shift and the Ctrl keys to select several adjacent and nonadjacent options respectively.

Quick Steps

Sort or Filter a Table
1. Click filter arrow.
2. Click sort or filter options.
3. Click OK.

Custom Sort a Table
1. Click Sort & Filter button.
2. Click *Custom Sort*.
3. Define sort levels.
4. Click OK.

1. With **3-BillSumOctWk1.xlsx** open, filter the table by the attorney's last name to print a list of billable hours for O'Donovan by completing the following steps:
   a. Click the filter arrow next to *Attorney LName* in cell F4.
   b. Click the *(Select All)* check box to remove the check mark.
   c. Click the *O'Donovan* check box to insert a check mark and then click OK. The table is filtered to display only those records with *O'Donovan* in the *Attorney LName* field. The Sum functions in columns H and J reflect the totals for the filtered records only.
   d. Print the filtered worksheet.
2. Redisplay all the records by clicking the *Attorney LName* filter arrow and then clicking *Clear Filter From "Attorney LName"* at the drop-down list.
3. Click the *Filter Button* check box in the Table Style Options group on the Table Tools Design tab to remove the check mark. Notice that the filter arrows disappear from the header row.
4. Filter the table using Slicers and the area of law by completing the following steps:
   a. With any cell active in the table, click the Insert Slicer button in the Tools group.
   b. At the Insert Slicers dialog box, click the *Area* check box to insert a check mark and then click OK. Excel inserts a Slicer pane in the worksheet with all the areas of law listed.
   c. If necessary, position the mouse pointer at the top of the Area Slicer pane until the pointer changes to a four-headed arrow and then drag the pane to an empty location right of the table.
   d. Click *Corporate* in the Area Slicer pane to filter the table. Excel filters the table by the *Corporate* area.
   e. Press and hold down the Ctrl key, click *Employment*, and then release the Ctrl key. Excel adds the *Employment* area to the filter.
5. Print the filtered worksheet.
6. Click the Clear Filter button at the top right of the Area Slicer pane to redisplay all the data.

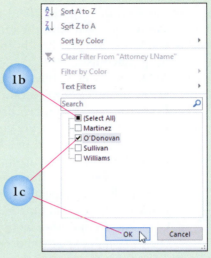

Area Slicer pane has filtered the table by *Corporate* and *Employment*

7. Click the Area Slicer pane and press the Delete key to delete the Slicer pane.

8. Use the Sort dialog box to sort the table first by the attorney's last name, then by the area of law, and then by the client name by completing the following steps:

a. With any cell within the table active, click the Home tab.

b. Click the Sort & Filter button in the Editing group and then click *Custom Sort* at the drop-down list.

c. At the Sort dialog box, click the *Sort by* option box arrow in the *Column* section and then click *Attorney LName* at the drop-down list. The default options for *Sort On* and *Order* are correct since the column values are to be sorted in ascending order.

d. Click the Add Level button.

e. Click the *Then by* option box arrow and then click *Area* at the drop-down list.

f. Click the Add Level button.

g. Click the second *Then by* option box arrow and then click *Client Name* at the drop-down list.

h. Click OK.

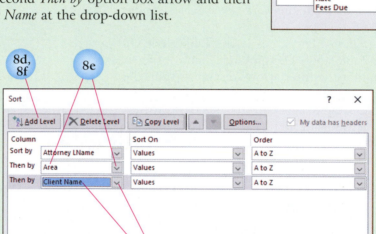

9. Print the sorted table.

10. Save and then close **3-BillSumOctWk1.xlsx**.

Check Your Work

Project 2 Use Data Tools to Split Data and Ensure Data Integrity in a Billing Summary Workbook for a Law Office

6 Parts

You will use Excel's data tools to split the client's first and last names into two columns, combine two columns, remove duplicate records, and restrict the type of data that can be entered into a field.

Preview Finished Project

Working with Data Tools

The Data Tools group on the Data tab, shown in Figure 3.3, includes useful features for working with data in tables.

Tutorial

Separating Data
Using Text to
Columns

Text to
Columns

Separating Data Using Text to Columns

A worksheet in which more than one field has been entered into the same column can be separated into multiple columns using the Text to Columns feature. For example, a column that has first and last names in the same cell can be split so the first name appears in one column and the last name appears in a separate column. Breaking up the data into separate columns better facilitates sorting and other data management tasks.

Before using the Text to Columns feature, insert the required number of blank columns to separate the data immediately right of the column to be split. Select the column to be split and then click the Text to Columns button to start the Convert Text to Columns Wizard. Work through the three dialog boxes of the wizard to separate the data.

Quick Steps

**Split Text into
Multiple Columns**
1. Insert blank
   column(s) next to
   source data.
2. Select data to be
   split.
3. Click Data tab.
4. Click Text to
   Columns button.
5. Click Next at first
   dialog box.
6. Select delimiter
   check box for
   character that
   separates data.
7. Click Next.
8. Click Finish.

Figure 3.3 Data Tools Group on the Data Tab

Project 2a Separating Client Names into Two Columns

Part 1 of 6

1. Open **3-BillSumOctWk1.xlsx**.
2. Save the workbook with the name **3-BillSumOctWk1-2**.
3. Click in any cell in the table and then redisplay the filter arrows by clicking the *Filter Button* check box in the Table Style Options group on the Table Tools Design tab.
4. Click the Home tab, click the Sort & Filter button in the Editing group, and then click *Clear* at the drop-down list to clear the existing sort criteria.
5. Create a custom sort to sort the table first by date (oldest to newest) and then by client (smallest to largest). Refer to Project 1d, Step 8, for assistance with this step.
6. Split the client first and last names in column D into two columns by completing the following steps:

   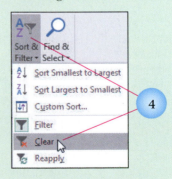

   a. Right-click column letter *E* at the top of the worksheet area and then click *Insert* at the shortcut menu to insert a blank column between the *Client Name* and *Attorney FName* columns in the table.
   b. Select the range D5:D25.
   c. Click the Data tab.
   d. Click the Text to Columns button in the Data Tools group.

e. At the Convert Text to Columns Wizard - Step 1 of 3 dialog box, with *Delimited* selected in the *Choose the file type that best describes your data* section, click Next.

f. In the *Delimiters* section of the Convert Text to Columns Wizard - Step 2 of 3 dialog box, click the *Space* check box to insert a check mark and then click Next. The *Data preview* section of the dialog box updates after the *Space* check box is clicked to show the names split into two columns.

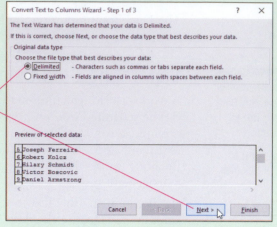

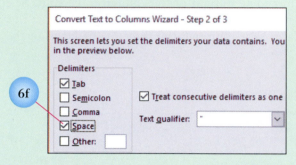

g. Click Finish at the last Convert Text to Columns Wizard dialog box to accept the default General data format for both columns.

h. Deselect the range.

7. Make cell D4 active, change the label to *Client FName*, and then AutoFit the column width.

8. Make cell E4 active, change the label to *Client LName*, and then AutoFit the column width.

9. Save **3-BillSumOctWk1-2.xlsx**.

Client first and last names are split into two columns in Steps 6a–6g.

Check Your Work

Tutorial

Populating Data Using Flash Fill

Populating Data Using Flash Fill

The Flash Fill feature extracts, joins, and inserts text, numbers, dates, and times. It is useful for organizing data that has been pasted or imported from other sources. Join all or extract parts of the contents of cells. Flash Fill analyzes adjacent columns while entering data, detects any patterns, and suggests how the rest of the column should be completed.

For example, in Project 2a, instead of using Text to Columns to split the client names into two columns, use Flash Fill. To do this, insert two new columns instead of one. Type the first name *Joseph* in column E, as shown in Figure 3.4. Press the Enter key and then type *R* to start the second name, *Robert*. Excel recognizes that the first word of the adjacent column D is to be extracted and suggests doing the same for the remaining cells in column E. Notice that the rest of the names are grayed out. Press the Enter key to accept the suggestion or continue typing to reject the suggestion. Repeat the process for the last name.

Quick Steps

Extract Data Using Flash Fill

1. Insert blank column(s) next to source data.
2. Type first record.
3. Press Enter.
4. Start typing second record.
5. When grayed-out text appears, press Enter.

Figure 3.4 Flash Fill for Project 2a

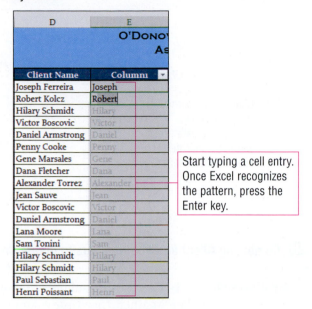

Start typing a cell entry. Once Excel recognizes the pattern, press the Enter key.

In Project 2b, the file and client numbers are joined to create the case code number. A few rows of data may need to be entered before Excel recognizes the pattern. Once the pattern is established, press the Enter key. Other methods for using Flash Fill are to click the Fill button in the Editing Group on the Home tab and then choose *Flash Fill* from the drop-down menu, to click the Flash Fill button in the Data Tools group on the Data Tab, or to press the keys Ctrl + E. The CONCATENATE function, discussed in Chapter 1, can also be used to join the contents of two or more cells.

 Flash Fill

Tutorial

Identifying and Removing Duplicate Records

Identifying and Removing Duplicate Records

Excel can compare records within a worksheet and automatically delete duplicate rows based on the columns selected that might contain duplicate values. All the columns are selected by default when the Remove Duplicates dialog box, shown in Figure 3.5, is opened. Click the Unselect All button to remove the check marks from all the columns, click the individual columns to compare, and then click OK. Excel automatically deletes the rows that contain duplicate values, and when the operation is completed, it displays a message with the number of rows that were removed from the worksheet or table and the number of unique values that remain.

Consider conditionally formatting duplicate values first to view the records that will be deleted. To do this, use the *Duplicate Values* option. Access this option by clicking the Conditional Formatting button in the Styles group on the Home tab and then pointing to *Highlight Cells Rules* at the Conditional Formatting drop-down list.

Excel includes the Remove Duplicates button in the Data Tools group on the Data tab and in the Tools group on the Table Tools Design tab. Click Undo to restore any duplicate rows removed by mistake.

Quick Steps

Remove Duplicate Rows
1. Select range or make cell active in table.
2. Click Data tab.
3. Click Remove Duplicates button.
4. Select columns to compare.
5. Click OK.
6. Click OK.

 Remove Duplicates

Figure 3.5 Remove Duplicates Dialog Box

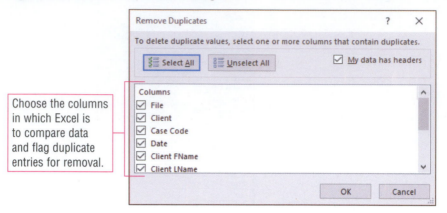

Choose the columns in which Excel is to compare data and flag duplicate entries for removal.

Project 2b Combining Client and File Numbers to Create Case Codes   Part 2 of 6

1. With **3-BillSumOctWk1-2.xlsx** open, combine the information in the *Client* and *File* columns to create the data in a new *Case Code* column by completing the following steps:
   a. Insert a column between the *Client* and *Date* columns in the table, change the column width to 13 characters, and then type Case Code in cell C4. In cell C5, type 10104-FL-325 and then press the Enter key. (This number is composed of the client number, a dash, and the file number.)
   b. In cell C6, type 1. Flash Fill recognizes the sequence and suggests how to fill the rest of the column.
   c. Press the Enter key to accept the suggestions. If Excel does not recognize the pattern right away, continue to type the client number, a dash, and then the file number or click the Flash Fill button in the Data Tools group on the Data tab.
2. Save **3-BillSumOctWk1-2.xlsx**.

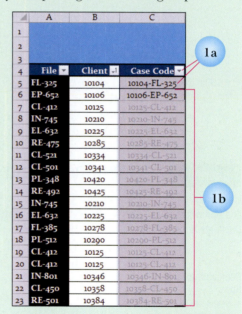

Check Your Work

1. With **3-BillSumOctWk1-2.xlsx** open, remove the duplicate rows in the billing summary table by completing the following steps:
   a. With any cell in the table active, click the Remove Duplicates button in the Data Tools group on the Data tab.
   b. At the Remove Duplicates dialog box with all the columns selected in the *Columns* list box, click the Unselect All button.
   c. In the billing summary table, only one record should be assigned per case code per date, since the attorneys record once per day the total hours spent on each case. (Records are duplicates if the same values exist in the two columns that store the case code number and date). Click the *Case Code* check box to insert a check mark.
   d. Click the *Date* check box to insert a check mark and then click OK.
   e. Click OK at the Microsoft Excel message box stating that a duplicate value was found and removed and 20 unique values remain.

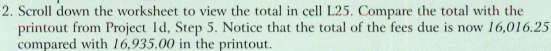

2. Scroll down the worksheet to view the total in cell L25. Compare the total with the printout from Project 1d, Step 5. Notice that the total of the fees due is now *16,016.25* compared with *16,935.00* in the printout.
3. Save **3-BillSumOctWk1-2.xlsx**.

Check Your Work

Validating Data Entry

Excel's data validation feature allows controlling the type of data that is accepted for entry in a cell. The type of data can be specified, along with parameters that validate whether the entry is within a certain range of acceptable values, dates, times, or text lengths. A list of values can also be set up that displays as a drop-down list when the cell is made active.

To do this, click the Data Validation button in the Data Tools group on the Data tab. At the Data Validation dialog box, shown in Figure 3.6, choose the type of data to be validated in the *Allow* option box on the Settings tab. Additional list or text boxes appear in the dialog box depending on the option chosen in the *Allow* drop-down list.

If a custom number format adds punctuation or text to the appearance of a cell, ignore the added characters when validating or restricting data entry. For example, a cell that contains the number *1234*, with a custom number format "PD-"####, and displays as *PD-1234* has a text length equal to four characters.

In addition to defining acceptable data entry parameters, there is the option of adding an input message and an error alert message to the range. Customized text can be added to define these messages.

Figure 3.6 Data Validation Dialog Box with Settings Tab Selected

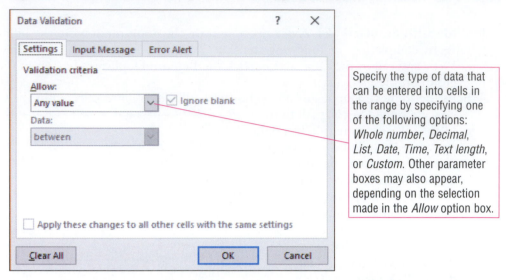

Specify the type of data that can be entered into cells in the range by specifying one of the following options: *Whole number*, *Decimal*, *List*, *Date*, *Time*, *Text length*, or *Custom*. Other parameter boxes may also appear, depending on the selection made in the *Allow* option box.

When a cell to which data validation rules apply is made active, an input message displays. This kind of message is informational in nature. An error alert message appears when incorrect data is entered in a cell. There are three styles of error alerts, and a description and example of each type is provided in Table 3.1. If an error alert message has not been defined, Excel displays the Stop error alert with this default error message: *The value you entered is not valid. A user has restricted values that can be entered into this cell.*

Table 3.1 Data Validation Error Alert Message Styles

Error Alert Icon	Error Alert Style	Description	Message Box Examples
(red X icon)	Stop	Prevents the data from being entered into the cell. The error alert message box provides three buttons to ensure that new data is entered.	Date is outside accepted range. ⊗ Please enter a date from October 1 to October 5, 2018. [Retry] [Cancel] [Help]
(yellow warning icon)	Warning	Does not prevent the data from being entered into the cell. The error alert message box provides four buttons below the prompt *Continue?*	Check number of hours ⚠ The hours you have entered are greater than 8. Continue? [Yes] [No] [Cancel] [Help]
(blue info icon)	Information	Does not prevent the data from being entered into the cell. The error alert message box provides three buttons below the error message.	Verify hours entered ⓘ The hours you have entered are outside the normal range. [OK] [Cancel] [Help]

1. With **3-BillSumOctWk1-2.xlsx** open, create a validation rule, input message, and error alert for dates in the billing summary worksheet by completing the following steps:
   a. Select the range D5:D24.
   b. Click the Data Validation button in the Data Tools group on the Data tab.
   c. With Settings the active tab in the Data Validation dialog box, click the *Allow* option box arrow (displays *Any value*) and then click *Date* at the drop-down list. Validation options are dependent on the *Allow* setting. When *Date* is chosen, Excel adds *Start date* and *End date* text boxes to the *Validation criteria* section.
   d. With *between* selected in the *Data* option box, click in the *Start date* text box and then type 10/1/2018.
   e. Click in the *End date* text box and then type 10/5/2018. (Since the billing summary worksheet is for the work week of October 1 to 5, 2018, entering this validation criteria will ensure that only dates between the start date and end date are accepted.)
   f. Click the Input Message tab.
   g. Click in the *Title* text box and then type Billing Date.
   h. Click in the *Input message* text box and then type This worksheet is for the week of October 1 to October 5 only.
   i. Click the Error Alert tab.
   j. With *Stop* selected in the *Style* option box, click in the *Title* text box and then type Date is outside accepted range.
   k. Click in the *Error message* text box and then type Please enter a date from October 1 to October 5, 2018.
   l. Click OK. Since the range is active for which the data validation rules apply, the input message box appears.
   m. Deselect the range.
2. Add a new record to the table to test the date validation rule by completing the following steps:
   a. Right-click row number *25* and then click *Insert* at the shortcut menu to insert a new row into the table.
   b. Make cell A25 active, type PL-348, and then press the Tab key.
   c. Type 10420 in the *Client* column and then press the Tab key.
   d. Type 10420-PL-348 and then press the Tab key. The input message title and text appear when the *Date* column is made active.
   e. Type 10/8/2018 and then press the Tab key. Since the date entered is invalid, the error alert message box appears.

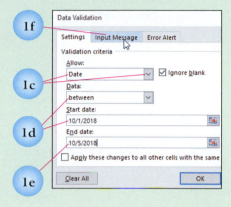

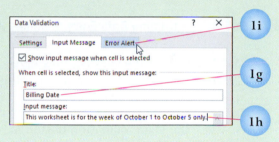

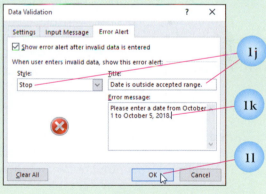

f. Click the Retry button.

g. Type 10/5/2018 and then press the Tab key.

h. Enter the data in the remaining fields as follows (pressing the Tab key to move from column to column and pressing the Enter key after the fees due calculation is done):

Client FName	Alexander
Client LName	Torrez
Attorney FName	Rosa
Attorney LName	Martinez
Area	Patent
Billable Hours	2.25
Rate	200.00

3. Save 3-BillSumOctWk1-2.xlsx.

Check Your Work

Project 2e Restricting Data Entry to Values within a List

Part 5 of 6

1. With **3-BillSumOctWk1-2.xlsx** open, create a list of values allowed in a cell by completing the following steps:

   a. Select the range K5:K25.

   b. Click the Data Validation button in the Data Tools group on the Data tab.

   c. If necessary, click the Settings tab.

   d. Click the *Allow* option box arrow and then click *List* at the drop-down list.

   e. Click in the *Source* text box and then type 175.00,185.00,190.00,200.00.

   f. Click OK.

   g. Deselect the range.

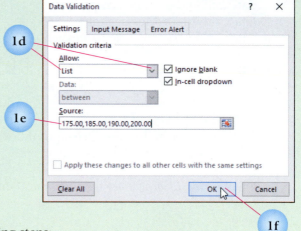

2. Add a new record to the table to test the rate validation list by completing the following steps:

   a. Right-click row number *26* and then click *Insert* at the shortcut menu to insert a new row in the table.

   b. Make cell A26 active and then type data in the fields as follows (pressing the Tab key to move from column to column):

File	IN-745
Client	10210
Case Code	10210-IN-745
Date	10/5/2018
Client FName	Victor
Client LName	Boscovic
Attorney FName	Rosa
Attorney LName	Martinez
Area	Insurance
Billable Hours	1.75

c. At the *Rate* field, the validation list becomes active and a down arrow appears to the right of the cell. Type 225.00 and then press the Tab key to test the validation rule. Since no error alert message was entered, the default message appears.

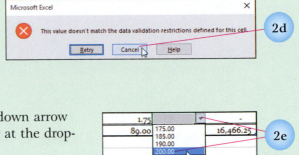

d. Click the Cancel button. The value is cleared from the field.

e. Make cell K26 the active cell, click the down arrow at the right side of the cell, click *200.00* at the drop-down list, and then press the Tab key.

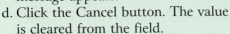

3. Save **3-BillSumOctWk1-2.xlsx**.

Project 2f Ensuring Data Entered Is a Specified Text Length Part 6 of 6

1. With **3-BillSumOctWk1-2.xlsx** open, create a validation rule to ensure that all client identification numbers are five characters (to be compatible with the firm's accounting system) by completing the following steps:
   a. Select the range B5:B26 and then click the Data Validation button in the Data Tools group on the Data tab.
   b. With the Settings tab active, click the *Allow* option box arrow and then click *Text length* at the drop-down list.
   c. Click the *Data* option box arrow and then click *equal to* at the drop-down list.
   d. Click in the *Length* text box and then type 5.
   e. Click OK.
   f. Deselect the range.

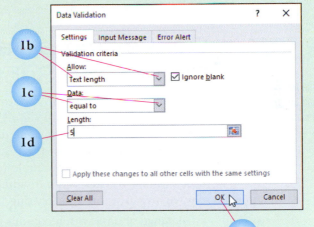

2. Add a new record to the table to test the client identification validation rule by completing the following steps:
   a. Right-click row number *27* and then click *Insert* at the shortcut menu.
   b. Make cell A27 active, type FL-325, and then press the Tab key.
   c. Type 1010411 in cell B27 and then press the Tab key. Since this value is greater than the number of characters allowed in the cell, the default error message appears.
   d. Click the Retry button.
   e. Delete the selected text, type 1010, and then press the Tab key. Since this value is less than the specified text length, the default error message appears again. (Using a Text Length validation rule ensures that all entries in the range have the same number of characters. This rule is useful for validating customer numbers, employee numbers, inventory numbers, or any other data that requires a consistent number of characters.)
   f. Click the Cancel button, type 10104, and then press the Tab key. Since this entry is five characters in length, Excel moves to the next field.

g. Enter the remaining fields as follows:

Case Code	10104-FL-325
Date	10/5/2018
Client FName	Joseph
Client LName	Ferreira
Attorney FName	Marty
Attorney LName	O'Donovan
Area	Divorce
Billable Hours	5.75
Rate	185.00

3. Save, print, and then close **3-BillSumOctWk1-2.xlsx**.

Check Your Work

Project 3 **Group and Subtotal Related Records
in a Billing Summary Workbook for a Law Office** **4 Parts**

You will convert the billing summary table to a normal range, sort the rows by the attorney names, and then add subtotals to display total fees due, a count of fees, and the average billable hours and fees due for each attorney.

Preview Finished Project

Tutorial

Converting a Table to a Normal Range and Subtotaling Related Data

 Subtotal

 Convert to Range

Quick Steps

Convert a Table to a Range
1. Make table cell active.
2. Click Table Tools Design tab.
3. Click Convert to Range button.
4. Click Yes.

Create a Subtotal
1. Select range.
2. Click Data tab.
3. Click Subtotal button.
4. Select field to group by in *At each change in* option box.
5. Select function in *Use function* option box.
6. Select field(s) to subtotal in *Add subtotal to* list box.
7. Click OK.

Converting a Table to a Normal Range and Subtotaling Related Data

A table can be converted to a normal range using the Convert to Range button in the Tools group on the Table Tools Design tab. Convert a table to a range to use the Subtotal feature or when the data no longer needs to be treated as a table, independent of the data in the rest of the worksheet. Remove some or all the table styles before converting the table to a range. Use the Clear button in the Table Styles gallery or click the individual options in the Table Style Options group to remove any unwanted formatting.

A range of data with a column that has multiple rows with the same field value can be grouped and subtotals can be created for each group automatically by using the Subtotal button in the Outline group on the Data tab. For example, a worksheet with multiple records with the same department name in a field can be grouped by department name and a subtotal of a numeric field can be calculated for each department. Choose from a list of functions for the subtotal, such as Average and Sum. Multiple subtotal values can also be created for the different groups. Before creating subtotals, sort the data by the fields in which the records are to be grouped. Remove any blank rows within the range that is to be grouped and subtotaled.

Excel displays a new row with a summary total when the field value for the specified subtotal column changes. A grand total is also automatically included at the bottom of the range. Excel displays the subtotals with buttons along the left side of the worksheet area. These buttons are used to show or hide the details for each group using the Outline feature. Excel can create an outline with up to eight levels.

Figure 3.7 illustrates the data that will be grouped and subtotaled in Project 3a; the data is displayed with the worksheet at level 2 of the outline. Figure 3.8 shows the same worksheet with two attorney groups expanded to show the detail records.

Figure 3.7 Worksheet with Subtotals by Attorney Last Name Displayed at Level 2 of Outline

outline level buttons

File	Client	Case Code	Date	Client FName	Client LName	Attorney FName	Attorney LName	Area	Billable Hours	Rate	Fees Due
							Martinez Total				7,450.00
							O'Donovan Total				3,885.00
							Sullivan Total				4,112.50
							Williams Total				2,432.50
							Grand Total				17,880.00

O'DONOVAN & SULLIVAN LAW ASSOCIATES
ASSOCIATE BILLING SUMMARY
OCTOBER 1 TO 5, 2018

Hide Detail button

Show Detail button

Figure 3.8 Worksheet with Subtotals by Attorney Last Name with Martinez and Sullivan Groups Expanded

O'DONOVAN & SULLIVAN LAW ASSOCIATES
ASSOCIATE BILLING SUMMARY
OCTOBER 1 TO 5, 2018

File	Client	Case Code	Date	Client FName	Client LName	Attorney FName	Attorney LName	Area	Billable Hours	Rate	Fees Due
IN-745	10210	10210-IN-745	10/2/2018	Victor	Boscovic	Rosa	Martinez	Insurance	4.25	200.00	850.00
IN-745	10210	10210-IN-745	10/4/2018	Victor	Boscovic	Rosa	Martinez	Insurance	4.50	200.00	900.00
IN-745	10210	10210-IN-745	10/5/2018	Victor	Boscovic	Rosa	Martinez	Insurance	1.75	200.00	350.00
EL-632	10225	10225-EL-632	10/2/2018	Daniel	Armstrong	Rosa	Martinez	Employment	3.25	200.00	650.00
EL-632	10225	10225-EL-632	10/4/2018	Daniel	Armstrong	Rosa	Martinez	Employment	4.50	200.00	900.00
PL-512	10290	10290-PL-512	10/4/2018	Sam	Tonini	Rosa	Martinez	Pension	3.75	200.00	750.00
IN-801	10346	10346-IN-801	10/5/2018	Paul	Sebastian	Rosa	Martinez	Insurance	4.25	200.00	850.00
PL-348	10420	10420-PL-348	10/3/2018	Alexander	Torrez	Rosa	Martinez	Patent	5.00	200.00	1,000.00
PL-348	10420	10420-PL-348	10/5/2018	Alexander	Torrez	Rosa	Martinez	Patent	2.25	200.00	450.00
EP-685	10495	10495-EP-685	10/5/2018	Frank	Kinsela	Rosa	Martinez	Estate	3.75	200.00	750.00
							Martinez Total				7,450.00
							O'Donovan Total				3,885.00
CL-412	10125	10125-CL-412	10/1/2018	Hilary	Schmidt	Toni	Sullivan	Corporate	5.25	175.00	918.75
CL-412	10125	10125-CL-412	10/5/2018	Hilary	Schmidt	Toni	Sullivan	Corporate	5.25	175.00	918.75
CL-521	10334	10334-CL-521	10/3/2018	Gene	Marsales	Toni	Sullivan	Corporate	4.25	175.00	743.75
CL-501	10341	10341-CL-501	10/3/2018	Dana	Fletcher	Toni	Sullivan	Employment	5.25	175.00	918.75
CL-450	10358	10358-CL-450	10/5/2018	Henri	Poissant	Toni	Sullivan	Corporate	3.50	175.00	612.50
							Sullivan Total				4,112.50
							Williams Total				2,432.50
							Grand Total				17,880.00

Project 3a Converting a Table to a Normal Range and Subtotaling Related Data   Part 1 of 4

1. Open **3-BillSumOctWk1-2.xlsx**.
2. Save the workbook with the name **3-BillSumOctWk1-3**.
3. Remove style options and convert the table to a normal range to group and subtotal the records by completing the following steps:
   a. Click in any cell in the table and then click the Table Tools Design tab.
   b. Click the *Total row* check box in the Table Style Options group to remove the *Total* row from the table. The Subtotal feature includes a grand total automatically, so the *Total* row is no longer needed.
   c. Click the *Banded Columns* check box in the Table Style Options group to remove the banded formatting.

d. Click the Convert to Range button in the Tools group.

e. Click Yes at the Microsoft Excel message box asking if you want to convert the table to a normal range.

f. Select columns A through L and AutoFit the column widths.

g. Deselect the columns.

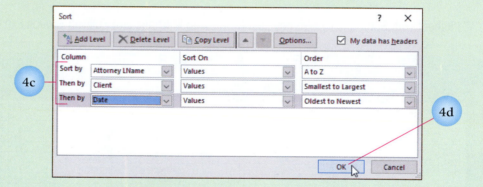

4. Sort the data by the fields to be subtotaled and grouped by completing the following steps:

a. Select the range A4:L27.

b. Click the Sort & Filter button in the Editing group on the Home tab and then click *Custom Sort* at the drop-down list.

c. At the Sort dialog box, define three levels to group and sort the records as follows:

Column	*Sort On*	*Order*
Attorney LName	Values	A to Z
Client	Values	Smallest to Largest
Date	Values	Oldest to Newest

d. Click OK.

5. Create a subtotal at each change in attorney last name by completing the following steps:

a. With the range A4:L27 still selected, click the Data tab.

b. Click the Subtotal button in the Outline group.

c. At the Subtotal dialog box, click the *At each change in* option box arrow (which displays *File*), scroll down the list, and then click *Attorney LName*.

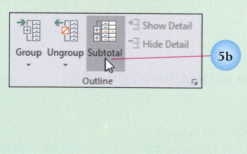

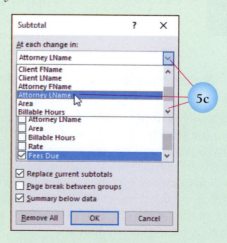

d. With *Use function* set to *Sum* and *Fees Due* selected in the *Add subtotal to* list box, click OK.

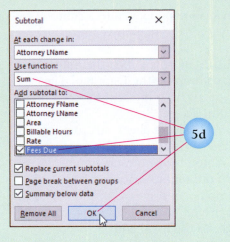

e. Deselect the range.
6. Double-click the column L boundry to AutoFit the column.
7. Print the worksheet.
8. Save **3-BillSumOctWk1-3.xlsx**.

Check Your Work

Project 3b Working with Outline Levels

Part 2 of 4

1. With **3-BillSumOctWk1-3.xlsx** open, show and hide levels in the outlined worksheet by completing the following steps:
   a. Click the level 1 button at the top left of the worksheet area below the Name text box. Excel collapses the worksheet to display only the grand total of the *Fees Due* column.
   b. Click the level 2 button to display the subtotals by attorney last names. Notice that a button with a plus symbol (+) displays next to each subtotal in the *Outline* section at the left side of the worksheet area. The button with the plus symbol is the Show Detail button and the button with the minus symbol (−) is the Hide Detail button. Compare your worksheet with the one shown in Figure 3.7 on page 75.
   c. Click the Show Detail button (which displays as a plus symbol) next to the row with the Martinez subtotal. The detail rows for the group of records for Martinez are displayed.
   d. Click the Show Detail button next to the row with the Sullivan subtotal.
   e. Compare your worksheet with the one shown in Figure 3.8 on page 75.
   f. Click the level 3 button to display all the detail rows.
2. Save **3-BillSumOctWk1-3.xlsx**.

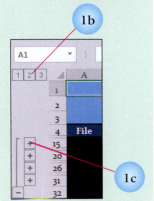

1. With **3-BillSumOctWk1-3.xlsx** open, add a subtotal to count the number of billable records for each attorney for the week by completing the following steps:
   a. Select the range A4:L32 and then click the Subtotal button in the Outline group on the Data tab. The Subtotal dialog box opens with the settings used for the subtotals created in Project 3a.
   b. Click the *Replace current subtotals* check box to remove the check mark. With this check box cleared, Excel adds another subtotal row to each group.
   c. Click the *Use function* option box arrow and then click *Count* at the drop-down list.
   d. With *Fees Due* still selected in the *Add subtotal to* list box, click OK. Excel adds a new subtotal row to each group with the count of records displayed.

2. Add a subtotal to calculate the average billable hours and average fees due for each attorney by completing the following steps:
   a. With the data range still selected, click the Subtotal button.
   b. Click the *Use function* option box arrow and then click *Average* at the drop-down list.
   c. Click the *Billable Hours* check box in the *Add subtotal to* list box to insert a check mark and then click OK. Excel adds a new subtotal row to each group with the average billable hours and average fees due for each attorney.
   d. Deselect the range.

Attorney LName	Area	Billable Hours	Rate	Fees Due
Martinez	Insurance	4.25	200.00	850.00
Martinez	Insurance	4.50	200.00	900.00
Martinez	Insurance	1.75	200.00	350.00
Martinez	Employment	3.25	200.00	650.00
Martinez	Employment	4.50	200.00	900.00
Martinez	Pension	3.75	200.00	750.00
Martinez	Insurance	4.25	200.00	850.00
Martinez	Patent	5.00	200.00	1,000.00
Martinez	Patent	2.25	200.00	450.00
Martinez	Estate	3.75	200.00	750.00
Martinez Average		3.73		745.00
Martinez Count				10
Martinez Total				7,450.00

The averages of the *Billable Hours* and *Fees Due* columns are added to the subtotals for all the attorneys in Steps 2a–2c. The data for the Martinez group is shown.

3. Save the revised workbook with the name **3-BillSumOctWk1-3c**.
4. Click the Page Layout tab and scale the height of the worksheet to 1 page.
5. Print the worksheet.
6. Save and then close **3-BillSumOctWk1-3c.xlsx**.

Check Your Work

Group

Ungroup

Grouping and Ungrouping Data

When a worksheet is outlined, use the Group and Ungroup buttons in the Outline group on the Data tab to individually manage collapsing and expanding groups of records at various levels. For example, in an outlined worksheet with detailed rows displayed, selecting a group of records and clicking the Ungroup button opens the Ungroup dialog box, shown in Figure 3.9. Clicking OK with *Rows* selected removes the group feature applied to the selection and removes the Hide Detail button so the records remain displayed at the outline level. Selecting records that have been ungrouped and clicking the Group button reattaches the group feature to the selection and redisplays the Hide Detail button.

Columns can also be grouped and ungrouped. The outline section with the level numbers and Show and Hide Detail buttons displays across the top of the worksheet area. For example, in a worksheet in which two columns are used to arrive at a formula, the source columns can be grouped and the details hidden so that only the formula column with the calculated results is displayed in an outlined worksheet.

Quick Steps

Group Data by Rows
1. Select range to be grouped within outlined worksheet.
2. Click Data tab.
3. Click Group button.
4. Click OK.

Ungroup Data by Rows
1. Select grouped range within outlined worksheet.
2. Click Data tab.
3. Click Ungroup button.
4. Click OK.

Figure 3.9 Ungroup Dialog Box

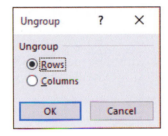

Project 3d Grouping and Ungrouping Data

Part 4 of 4

1. Open **3-BillSumOctWk1-3.xlsx**. Group client data within the Martinez attorney group by completing the following steps:
   a. Select the range A5:L7. These three rows contain billing information for client 10210.
   b. Click the Group button in the Outline group on the Data tab. (Make sure to click the button and not the button arrow.)
   c. At the Group dialog box with *Rows* selected, click OK. Excel adds a fourth outline level to the worksheet and a Hide Detail button below the last row of the grouped records in the Outline section.

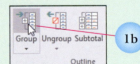

1b

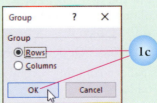

1c

d. Select the range A12:L13, click the Group button, and then click OK at the Group dialog box.

e. Deselect the range.

2. Experiment with the Hide Detail buttons in the Martinez group by hiding the detail for client 10210 and then hiding the detail for client 10420.

3. Redisplay the detail rows by clicking the Show Detail button for each client.

4. Select the range A5:L7, click the Ungroup button (make sure to click the button and not the button arrow), and then click OK at the Ungroup dialog box.

5. Select the range A12:L13, click the Ungroup button, and then click OK at the Ungroup dialog box.

6. Select the range A5:L14, click the Ungroup button, and then click OK at the Ungroup dialog box. Notice that the Hide Detail button is removed for the entire Martinez group.

7. Deselect the range and then click the level 2 button at the top of the outline section. Notice that the Martinez records do not collapse like the others, since they are no longer grouped.

8. Save the revised workbook with the name **3-BillSumOctWk1-3d**.

9. Print and then close **3-BillSumOctWk1-3d.xlsx**.

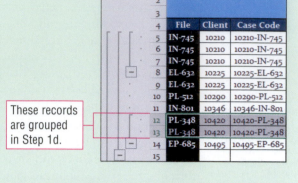

These records are grouped in Step 1d.

Check Your Work

Chapter Summary

- A table in Excel is a range of cells similar in structure to a database in which there are no blank rows and the first row of the range contains column headings.

- Define a range as a table using the Table button in the Tables group on the Insert tab.

- Columns in a table are called *fields* and rows are called *records*.

- The first row of a table contains the column headings and is called the *field names row* or *header row*.

- A table automatically expands to include data typed in a row or column immediately adjacent to a range that has been defined as a table.

- Typing a formula in the first record of a new column causes Excel to define the column as a calculated column and to automatically copy the formula to the remaining rows in the table.

- The contextual Table Tools Design tab contains options for formatting tables.

- The Table Styles gallery contains several options for changing the visual appearance of a table.

- Banding rows or columns formats every other row or column differently to make reading a large table easier.

- Add emphasis to the first column or last column in a table.

- The row containing field names in a table can be shown or hidden using the *Header Row* option in the Table Style Options group.

- Adding a *Total* row to a table causes Excel to add the word *Total* in the leftmost column and to create a Sum function in the last numeric column in the table. Additional functions can be added by clicking in a column in the *Total* row and selecting a function from the pop-up list.

- By default, Excel displays a filter arrow next to each label in the table header row. Use these arrows to filter and sort the table.

- Slicers are used to filter data in a table using a Slicer pane that contains all the items in the designated field.

- A column containing text that can be split can be separated into multiple columns using the Text to Columns feature. The Convert Text to Columns Wizard contains three dialog boxes that define how to split the data.

- Use Flash Fill to extract, join, and insert text, numbers, dates, and times.

- Use options at the Remove Duplicates dialog box to compare records within a worksheet and automatically delete rows that are duplicated.

- Data can be validated as it is being entered into a worksheet, and invalid data can be prevented from being stored or a warning can be issued stating that data has been entered that does not conform to the parameters.

- Define the validation criteria for a cell entry at the Settings tab in the Data Validation dialog box. Data can be allowed based on values, dates, times, and text lengths or restricted to values within a drop-down list.

- Define a message that pops up when a cell for which data is restricted becomes active at the Input Message tab in the Data Validation dialog box.

- Define the type of error alert to display and the content of the error message at the Error Alert tab in the Data Validation dialog box.

- Convert a table to a normal range to use the Subtotal feature or when a range of cells no longer needs to be treated independently from the rest of the worksheet.

- Sort a worksheet by column(s) to group data for subtotals before opening the Subtotals dialog box.

- The Subtotal button is in the Outline group on the Data tab.

- Excel adds a subtotal automatically at each change in content for the column specified as the subtotal field. A grand total is also automatically added to the bottom of the range.

- Display more than one subtotal row for a group to calculate multiple functions, such as Sum and Average.

- A subtotaled range is outlined and record details can be collapsed or expanded using the level number, Hide Detail, and Show Detail buttons.

- When a worksheet is outlined, use the Group and Ungroup buttons in the Outline group on the Data tab to manage the display of individual groups.

Commands Review

FEATURE	RIBBON TAB, GROUP	BUTTON	KEYBOARD SHORTCUT
convert table to range	Table Tools Design, Tools		
convert text to table	Data, Data Tools		
create table	Insert, Tables		Ctrl + T
Flash Fill	Home, Editing OR Data, Data Tools		Ctrl + E
group data	Data, Outline		Shift + Alt + Right Arrow key
remove duplicates	Data, Data Tools OR Table Tools Design, Tools		
sort and filter table	Home, Editing		
subtotals	Data, Outline		
table styles	Table Tools Design, Table Styles		
text to columns	Data, Data Tools		
Total row	Table Tools Design, Table Style Options		Ctrl + Shift + T
ungroup	Data, Outline		Shift + Alt + Left Arrow key
validate data	Data, Data Tools		

> **Workbook**
>
> Chapter study tools and assessment activities are available in the *Workbook* ebook. These resources are designed to help you further develop and demonstrate mastery of the skills learned in this chapter.

Microsoft®
Excel®

Summarizing and Consolidating Data

Performance Objectives

Precheck

Check your current skills to help focus your study.

Upon successful completion of Chapter 4, you will be able to:

1 Summarize data by creating formulas with range names that reference cells in other worksheets

2 Summarize data by creating 3-D references

3 Create formulas that link to cells in other worksheets or workbooks

4 Edit a link to a source workbook

5 Break a link to an external reference

6 Use the Consolidate feature to summarize data from multiple worksheets in a master worksheet

7 Create, edit, and format a PivotTable

8 Filter a PivotTable using Slicers

9 Filter a PivotTable using Timelines

10 Create and format a PivotChart

11 Create and format Sparklines

Data can be summarized by creating formulas that reference cells in other areas of the active worksheet or other worksheets within the same workbook or by linking to cells in other worksheets or workbooks. The Consolidate feature can also be used to summarize data from other worksheets or other workbooks into a master worksheet. Once the data has been summarized, consider presenting or analyzing the data by creating and formatting a PivotTable or PivotChart. Also consider creating Sparklines, which are miniature charts inserted into cells that reveal trends or other patterns in the data. Timelines allow the filtering of a PivotTable or PivotChart using a specified timeframe. In this chapter, you will learn how to summarize and filter data using a variety of methods and present visually summarized data for analysis.

SNAP

If you are a SNAP user, launch the Precheck and Tutorials from your Assignments page.

Data Files

Before beginning chapter work, copy the EL2C4 folder to your storage medium and then make EL2C4 the active folder.

Project 1 Calculate Park Attendance Totals

5 Parts

You will calculate total park attendance at three national parks by using data stored in separate worksheets and linking to a cell in another workbook. You will also edit a linked workbook and update the link in the destination file.

Preview Finished Project

Tutorial

Summarizing Data in Multiple Worksheets Using Range Names

Summarizing Data in Multiple Worksheets Using Range Names and 3-D References

Quick Steps

Sum Multiple Worksheets Using Range Names
1. Make formula cell active.
2. Type =sum(.
3. Type first range name.
4. Type comma ,.
5. Type second range name.
6. Type comma ,.
7. Continue typing range names separated by commas until finished.
8. Type).
9. Press Enter.

A workbook that has been organized with data in separate worksheets can be summarized by creating formulas that reference cells in other worksheets. When a formula is created that references a cell in the same worksheet, the sheet name does not need to be included in the reference. For example, the formula =A3+A4 causes Excel to add the value in cell A3 in the active worksheet to the value in cell A4 in the active worksheet. However, when a formula is created that references a cell in a different worksheet, the sheet name must be included in the formula.

Assume that Excel is to add the value in cell A3 that resides in Sheet2 to the value in cell A3 that resides in Sheet3 in the workbook. To do this, include the worksheet name in the formula by typing *=Sheet2!A3+Sheet3!A3* into the formula cell. This formula contains both worksheet references and cell references. The worksheet reference precedes the cell reference and is separated from the cell reference with an exclamation point. Without a worksheet reference, Excel assumes the cells are in the active worksheet.

A formula that references the same cell in a range that extends over two or more worksheets is often called a *3-D reference*. For a formula that includes a 3-D reference, the 3-D reference can be typed directly in a cell or entered using a point-and-click approach. Formulas that include 3-D references are sometimes referred to as *3-D formulas*.

As an alternative, consider using range names to simplify formulas that summarize data in multiple worksheets. Recall from Chapter 2 that a range name includes the worksheet reference by default; therefore, typing the range name in the formula automatically references the correct worksheet. Another advantage to using a range name is that the name can describe the worksheet with the source data. When using range names the two worksheets do not have to be made identical in organizational structure.

Project 1a Summarizing Data in Multiple Worksheets Using Range Names

Part 1 of 5

1. Open **MayEntries.xlsx**.
2. Save the workbook with the name **4-MayEntries**.
3. Click each sheet tab and review the data. Attendance data for each park is entered as a separate worksheet.

4. In the workbook, range names have already been created. Check each range name to find out what it references.

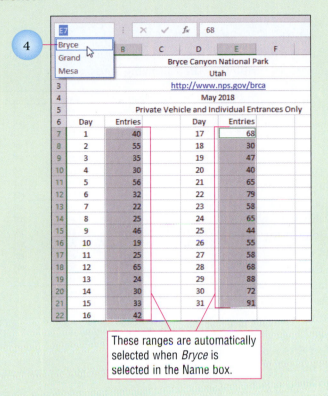

These ranges are automatically selected when *Bryce* is selected in the Name box.

5. Create a formula to add the total attendance for May at all three parks by completing the following steps:
   a. Click the AttendanceSummary tab to activate the worksheet.
   b. If necessary, make cell F7 active, type =sum(bryce,grand,mesa), and then press the Enter key. Notice that in a Sum formula, multiple range names are separated with commas. Excel returns the result *10460* in cell F7 of the AttendanceSummary worksheet.

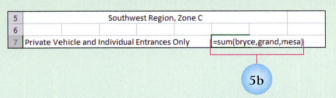

5b

   c. Apply the Comma format with no digits after the decimal point to cell F7.
6. Save and then close **4-MayEntries.xlsx**.

Check Your Work ▶

A disadvantage to using range names emerges when several worksheets need to be summarized because the range name references must be created in each worksheet. If several worksheets need to be summarized, a more efficient method is to use a 3-D reference. Generally, when using a 3-D reference, it is a good idea to set up the data in each worksheet in identical cells. In Project 1b, you will calculate the same attendance total for the three parks using a 3-D reference instead of range names.

Project 1b Summarizing Data in Multiple Worksheets Using a 3-D Reference Formula

1. Open **MayEntries.xlsx**.
2. Save the workbook with the name **4-3D-MayEntries**.
3. Calculate the attendance total for the three parks using a point-and-click approach to creating a 3-D reference by completing the following steps:
   a. In the AttendanceSummary worksheet, make cell F7 active and then type =sum(.
   b. Click the BryceCanyon sheet tab.
   c. Press and hold down the Shift key, click the MesaVerde sheet tab, and then release the Shift key. (Holding down the Shift key while clicking a sheet tab selects all the worksheets from the first sheet tab to the last sheet tab clicked.) Notice in the Formula bar that the formula reads =sum('BryceCanyon:MesaVerde'!
   d. With BryceCanyon the active worksheet, select the range B7:B22, press and hold down the Ctrl key, select the range E7:E21, and then release the Ctrl key.
   e. Type) and then press the Enter key. Excel returns the value *10460* in cell F7 in the AttendanceSummary worksheet.
   f. Apply the Comma format with no digits after the decimal point to cell F7.
4. With cell F7 the active cell, compare your formula with the one shown in Figure 4.1.
5. Save and then close **4-3D-MayEntries.xlsx**.

The three worksheets are grouped into the 3-D reference in Steps 3b and 3c.

Check Your Work

Figure 4.1 3-D Formula Created in Project 1b

This 3-D formula is created in Project 1b, Step 3, using a point-and-click approach.

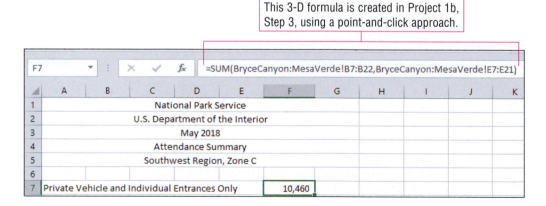

Chapter 4 | Summarizing and Consolidating Data

Summarizing Data by Linking to Ranges in Other Worksheets or Workbooks

Using a method similar to that used in Project 1a or Project 1b, data can be summarized in one workbook by linking to a cell, range, or range name in another worksheet or workbook. When data is linked, a change made in the source cell (the cell in which the original data is stored) is updated in any other cell to which the source cell has been linked. A link is established by creating a formula that references the source data. For example, entering the formula =*Sheet1!B10* into a cell in Sheet2 creates a link. The cell in Sheet2 displays the value in the source cell. If the data in cell B10 in Sheet1 is changed, the value in the linked cell in Sheet2 is also changed.

As an alternative to creating a formula, copy the source cell to the Clipboard task pane. Make the destination cell active, click the Paste button arrow in the Clipboard group, and then click the Paste Link button in the *Other Paste Options* section of the drop-down gallery. Excel creates the link formula using an absolute reference to the source cell.

Linking to a cell in another workbook incorporates external references and requires adding a workbook name reference to the formula. For example, linking to cell A3 in a sheet named *ProductA* in a workbook named *Sales* requires entering =*[Sales.xlsx]ProductA!A3* in the cell. Notice that the workbook reference is entered first in square brackets. The workbook in which the external reference is added is called the *destination workbook*. The workbook containing the data that is linked to the destination workbook is called the *source workbook*. In Project 1c, you will create a link to an external cell containing the attendance total for tour group entrances for the three parks.

The point-and-click approach to creating a linked external reference creates an absolute reference to the source cell. Delete the dollar symbols ($) in the cell reference if the formula is to be copied and the source cell needs to be relative. Note that the workbook and worksheet references remain absolute regardless.

Project 1c Summarizing Data by Linking to Another Workbook   **Part 3 of 5**

1. Open **4-MayEntries.xlsx**.
2. Open **MayGroupSales.xlsx**. This workbook contains tour group attendance data for the three national parks. Tour groups are charged a flat-rate entrance fee, so their attendance values represent bus capacities rather than the actual numbers of patrons on the buses.
3. Click the View tab, click the Arrange All button in the Window group, click *Vertical* in the *Arrange* section of the Arrange Windows dialog box, and then click OK.
4. In the worksheet created in Project 1a, create a linked external reference to the total attendance in the worksheet with the commercial tour vehicle attendance data by completing the following steps:
   a. Click in **4-MayEntries.xlsx** to make the workbook active. Make sure the active worksheet is AttendanceSummary.
   b. Make cell A9 active, type Commercial Tour Vehicles Only, and then press the Enter key.
   c. Make cell F9 active and then type =.

d. Click the **MayGroupSales.xlsx** title bar to activate the workbook and then click in cell F7. Notice that the formula being entered into the formula cell contains a workbook reference and a worksheet reference in front of the cell reference.

e. Press the Enter key.

f. Apply the Comma format with no digits after the decimal point to cell F9.

g. With cell F9 active, compare your worksheet with the 4-MayEntries worksheet shown below.

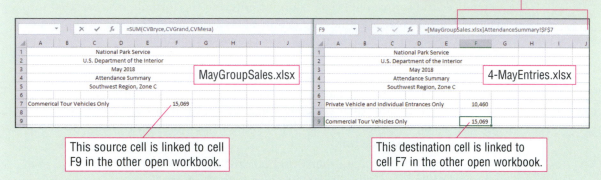

This formula contains the linked external reference created in Step 4.

MayGroupSales.xlsx

4-MayEntries.xlsx

This source cell is linked to cell F9 in the other open workbook.

This destination cell is linked to cell F7 in the other open workbook.

5. Click the Maximize button in the **4-MayEntries.xlsx** title bar.

6. Make cell A11 active, type Total Attendance, and then press the Enter key.

7. Make cell F11 active and then create a formula to add the values in cells F7 and F9.

8. Print the AttendanceSummary worksheet in **4-MayEntries.xlsx**. *Note: If you submit your work as hard copy, check with your instructor to see if you need to print two copies of the worksheet, with one copy displaying the cell formulas.*

9. Save and then close **4-MayEntries.xlsx**.

10. Close **MayGroupSales.xlsx**. Click Don't Save when prompted to save changes.

Check Your Work ▶

Maintaining External References

Quick Steps

Edit a Link to an External Reference
1. Open destination workbook.
2. Click Data tab.
3. Click Edit Links button.
4. Click link.
5. Click Change Source button.
6. Navigate to drive and/or folder.
7. Double-click source workbook file name.
8. Click Close button.
9. Save and close destination workbook.

 Edit Links

When linking to an external reference, Excel includes the drive and folder names in the path to the source workbook. If the source workbook is moved or the workbook name is changed, the link will no longer work. By default, when a workbook is opened with a linked external reference, the automatic updates feature is disabled and Excel displays a security warning message in the Message bar area above the workbook. From the message bar, the content can be enabled so that links can be updated.

Links can be edited or broken at the Edit Links dialog box, shown in Figure 4.2. The Edit Links button can be found in the Backstage area in the *Related Documents* section or in the Connections group on the Data tab. If more than one link is present in the workbook, begin by clicking the link to be changed in the *Source* list. Click the Change Source button to open the Change Source dialog box and navigate to the drive and/or folder in which the source workbook was moved or renamed. Click the Break Link button to permanently remove the linked reference and convert the linked cells to their existing values. Links cannot be restored using the Undo feature. If a broken link needs to be restored, the linked formula will have to be recreated.

Figure 4.2 Edit Links Dialog Box

Break a Link to an External Reference
1. Open destination workbook.
2. Click Data tab.
3. Click Edit Links button.
4. Click link.
5. Click Break Link button.
6. Click Break Links button.
7. Click Close button.
8. Save and close destination workbook.

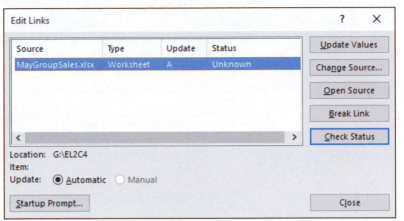

Project 1d Editing Source Data and Updating an External Link

1. Open **MayGroupSales.xlsx** and maximize the screen.
2. Save the workbook with the name **4-Source**.
3. Edit the attendance data value at each park by completing the following steps:
   a. Click the BryceCanyon sheet tab.
   b. Make cell B8 active and then change the value from *55* to *361*.
   c. Click the GrandCanyon sheet tab.
   d. Make cell B20 active and then change the value from *275* to *240*.
   e. Click the MesaVerde sheet tab.
   f. Make cell E21 active and then change the value from *312* to *406*.
4. Click the AttendanceSummary tab. Note that the updated value in cell F7 is *15,434*.
5. Save and then close **4-Source.xlsx**.
6. Open **4-MayEntries.xlsx**. Notice the security warning in the Message bar above the worksheet area that states that the automatic update of links has been disabled. Instruct Excel to allow automatic updates for this workbook (since you are sure the content is from a trusted source) by clicking the Enable Content button next to the message. *Note: If a Security Warning dialog box appears asking if you want to make the file a trusted document, click No.*

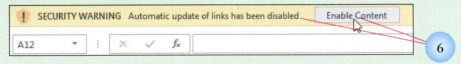

7. Edit the link to retrieve the data from the workbook you revised in Steps 2–5 by completing the following steps:
   a. Click the Data tab.
   b. Click the Edit Links button in the Connections group.

c. At the Edit Links dialog box, click the Change Source button.

d. If necessary, navigate to the EL2C4 folder. At the Change Source: MayGroupSales.xlsx dialog box, double-click **4-Source.xlsx** in the file list box. Excel returns to the Edit Links dialog box and updates the source workbook file name and path.

e. Click the Close button.

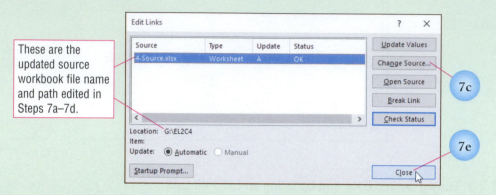

These are the updated source workbook file name and path edited in Steps 7a–7d.

8. Click in cell F9 in the AttendanceSummary worksheet to view the updated linked formula. Notice that the workbook reference in the formula is *[4-Source.xlsx]* and the drive and path are included in the formula. (Your drive and/or path may

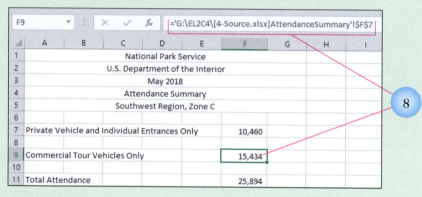

vary from the one shown. If the entire formula is not shown, click the Expand Formula bar down arrow to show the entire formula and then click the Collapse Formula bar up arrow to return the formula bar to one line.)

9. Print the AttendanceSummary worksheet.

10. Save and then close **4-MayEntries.xlsx**.

Check Your Work

Project 1e Removing a Linked External Reference

Part 5 of 5

1. Open **4-MayEntries.xlsx**.

2. At the Microsoft Excel message box that states that the workbook contains links to external sources, read the message text and then click the Update button to update the links. *Note: Depending on the system settings on the computer you are using, this message may not appear. Proceed to Step 3.*

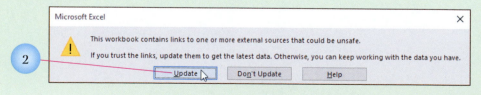

3. Remove the linked external reference to attendance values for commercial tour vehicles by completing the following steps:

a. With the Data tab active, click the Edit Links button in the Connections group.

b. Click the Break Link button at the Edit Links dialog box.

c. Click the Break Links button at the Microsoft Excel message box warning that breaking links permanently converts formulas and external references to their existing values and asking if you are sure you want to break the links.

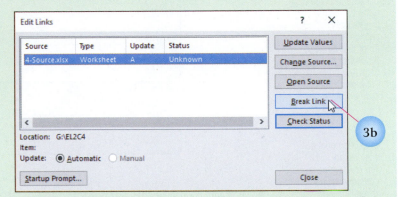

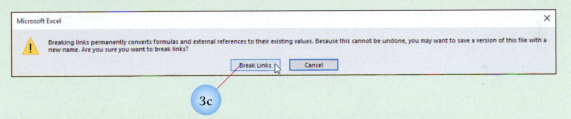

d. Click the Close button at the Edit Links dialog box with no links displayed.

4. In the AttendanceSummary worksheet with cell F9 active, look in the Formula bar. Notice that the linked formula has been replaced with the latest cell value, *15434*.

5. Save and then close **4-MayEntries.xlsx**.

6. Reopen **4-MayEntries.xlsx**. Notice that since the workbook no longer contains a link to an external reference, the security warning no longer appears in the Message bar.

7. Close **4-MayEntries.xlsx**. Click the Don't Save button if prompted to save changes.

Check Your Work

Project 2 Calculate Total Fees Billed by Three Dentists   1 Part

You will use the Consolidate feature to summarize the total dental fees billed by treatment category for three dentists.

Preview Finished Project

Tutorial

Summarizing Data Using the Consolidate Feature

 Consolidate

Summarizing Data Using the Consolidate Feature

The Consolidate feature is another tool that can be used to summarize data from multiple worksheets into a master worksheet. The worksheets can be located in the same workbook as the master worksheet or in a separate workbook. Open the Consolidate dialog box, shown in Figure 4.3, by clicking the Consolidate button in the Data Tools group on the Data tab.

Quick Steps

Consolidate Data

1. Make starting cell active.
2. Click Data tab.
3. Click Consolidate button.
4. If necessary, change function.
5. Enter first range in *Reference* text box.
6. Click Add button.
7. Enter next range in *Reference* text box.
8. Click Add button.
9. Repeat Steps 7–8 until all ranges have been added.
10. If necessary, click *Top row* and/or *Left column* check boxes.
11. If necessary, click *Create links to source data* check box.
12. Click OK.

Figure 4.3 Consolidate Dialog Box

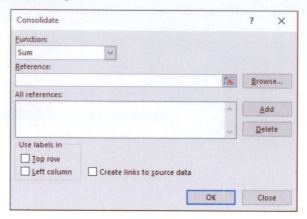

When the Consolidate dialog box opens, the Sum function is selected by default. Change to a different function, such as Count or Average, using the *Function* drop-down list. In the *Reference* text box, type the range name or use the Collapse Dialog button to navigate to the cells to be consolidated. If the cells are located in another workbook, use the Browse button to navigate to the drive and/or folder and locate the file name. Once the correct reference is inserted in the *Reference* text box, click the Add button. Continue adding references for all the units of data to be summarized.

In the *Use labels in* section, click to insert a check mark in the *Top row* or *Left column* check boxes to indicate where the labels are located in the source ranges. Insert a check mark in the *Create links to source data* check box to instruct Excel to update the data automatically when the source ranges change. Make sure enough empty cells are available to the right of and below the active cell when the Consolidate dialog box is opened, since Excel populates the rows and columns based on the size of the source data.

Project 2 Summarizing Data Using the Consolidate Feature

Part 1 of 1

1. Open **NADQ1Fees.xlsx**.
2. Save the workbook with the name **4-NADQ1Fees**.
3. The workbook is organized with the first quarter's fees for each of three dentists entered in separate worksheets. Range names have been defined for each dentist's first-quarter earnings. Review the workbook structure by completing the following steps:
   a. Click the Name box arrow and then click *Popovich* at the drop-down list. Excel makes the Popovich worksheet active and selects the range A2:E13.
   b. Deselect the range.
   c. Display the defined range for the range name *Vanket* and then deselect the range.
   d. Display the defined range for the range name *Jovanovic* and then deselect the range.
4. Use the Consolidate feature to total the fees billed by treatment category for each month by completing the following steps:
   a. Make FeeSummary the active worksheet.
   b. With cell A5 active, click the Data tab.
   c. Click the Consolidate button in the Data Tools group.

d. With *Sum* selected in the *Function* option box at the Consolidate dialog box and with the insertion point positioned in the *Reference* text box, type Popovich and then click the Add button.

e. With the text *Popovich* selected in the *Reference* text box, type Vanket and then click the Add button.

f. With the text *Vanket* selected in the *Reference* text box, type Jovanovic and then click the Add button.

g. Click the *Top row* and *Left column* check boxes in the *Use labels in* section to insert check marks in them.

h. Click OK.

5. Deselect the consolidated range in the FeeSummary worksheet.

6. AutoFit the width of each column in the FeeSummary worksheet.

7. Use the Format Painter to apply the formatting options for the column headings and the *Total* row from any of the three dentist worksheets to the FeeSummary worksheet.

8. Print the FeeSummary worksheet.

9. Save and then close **4-NADQ1Fees.xlsx**.

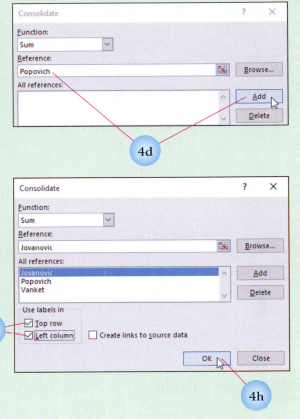

Check Your Work

Project 3   Analyze Fitness Equipment Sales Data in a PivotTable and PivotChart   8 Parts

You will create and edit a PivotTable and a PivotChart to analyze fitness equipment sales by region, product, manufacturer, and salesperson.

Preview Finished Project

Creating PivotTables

Quick Steps

Create a PivotTable
1. Select source range.
2. Click Insert tab.
3. Click PivotTable button.
4. Click OK.
5. Add fields as needed using PivotTable Fields task pane.
6. Modify and/or format as required.

A PivotTable is an interactive table that organizes and summarizes data based on fields (column headings) and records (rows). A numeric column is selected and then grouped by the rows and columns category; the data is summarized using a function such as Sum, Average, or Count. PivotTables are useful management tools, since they allow data to be analyzed in a variety of scenarios by filtering a row or column category and instantly seeing the change in results. The interactivity of a PivotTable allows a variety of scenarios to be examined with just a few mouse clicks. Create a PivotTable using the PivotTable button in the Tables group on the Insert tab.

 PivotTable

Before creating a PivotTable, examine the source data and determine the following elements:

- Which rows and columns will define how to format and group the data?
- Which numeric field contains the values to be grouped?
- Which summary function will be applied to the values? For example, should the values be summed, averaged, or counted?
- Should it be possible to filter the report as a whole, as well as by columns or rows?
- Should the PivotTable be beside the source data or in a new sheet?
- How many reports should be extracted from the PivotTable by filtering fields?

Tutorial

Creating, Modifying, and Filtering a Recommended PivotTable

 Recommended PivotTables

Creating a Recommended PivotTable

Use the Recommended PivotTables button to analyze the data and create different PivotTable previews to choose from. The PivotTable can then be edited and formatted further if required. (You will learn how to format a PivotTable in Project 3c.)

To have Excel analyze the data and create a PivotTable using a recommended view, select the source range, click the Insert tab, change the source data if required, and then click the Recommended PivotTables button in the Tables group. Click a PivotTable in the left panel of the Recommended PivotTables dialog box to preview it. Click OK to insert the selected PivotTable.

Tutorial

Building a PivotTable

Building a PivotTable

To build a PivotTable using the PivotTable button in the Tables group on the Insert tab, select the source range or make sure the active cell is positioned within the list range, click the Insert tab, and then click the PivotTable button in the Tables group. At the Create PivotTable dialog box, confirm that the source range is correct and then select whether to place the PivotTable in the existing worksheet or a new worksheet. Figure 4.4 presents the initial PivotTable and PivotTable Fields task pane, in which the report layout is defined. Each column or row heading in the source range becomes a field in the PivotTable Fields task pane list. A PivotTable can also be created by using the Blank button in the Tables tab on the Quick Analysis button.

Build a PivotTable by selecting fields in the PivotTable Fields task pane. Click the check box next to a field to insert a check mark and add it to the PivotTable. By default, non-numeric fields are added to the *Rows* box and numeric fields are added to the *Values* box in the layout section of the pane. Once a field has been added, move it to a different box by dragging the field header or clicking the field to display a shortcut menu. As each field is added, the PivotTable updates to show the results. Check and uncheck the various field check boxes to view the data in different scenarios. Figure 4.5 displays the PivotTable built in Project 3b.

Figure 4.4 PivotTable and PivotTable Fields Task Pane Used to Define Report Layout

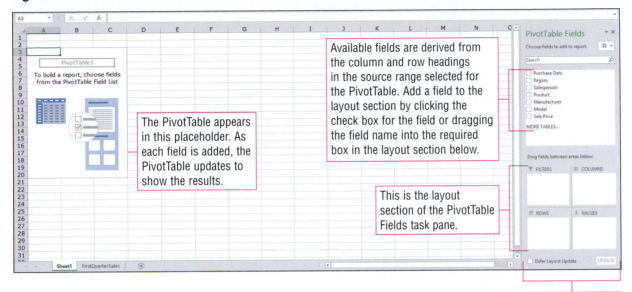

Available fields are derived from the column and row headings in the source range selected for the PivotTable. Add a field to the layout section by clicking the check box for the field or dragging the field name into the required box in the layout section below.

The PivotTable appears in this placeholder. As each field is added, the PivotTable updates to show the results.

This is the layout section of the PivotTable Fields task pane.

When a field is added to the report, Excel adds the header of the field to the corresponding list box in the layout section.

Project 3a Creating a PivotTable Using Recommended PivotTables

Part 1 of 8

1. Open **PF1stQSales.xlsx**.
2. Save the workbook with the name **4-PF1stQSales**.
3. Create a PivotTable to summarize the sale price by product by completing the following steps:
   a. A range has been defined to select the list data. Click the Name box arrow and then click *FirstQ* at the drop-down list.
   b. Click the Insert tab.
   c. Click the Recommended PivotTables button in the Tables group.
   d. Click the <u>Change Source Data</u> hyperlink at the bottom of the Recommended PivotTables dialog box to expand the range.

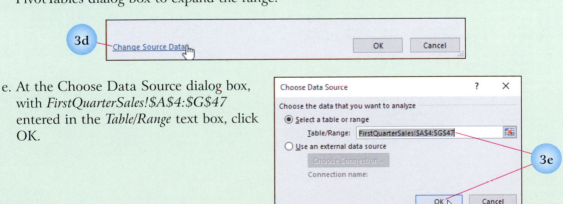

   e. At the Choose Data Source dialog box, with *FirstQuarterSales!$A$4:$G$47* entered in the *Table/Range* text box, click OK.

f. Click the second PivotTable scenario in the left column to select the *Sum of Sale Price by Product* PivotTable.

g. Click OK to insert the PivotTable in a new worksheet.

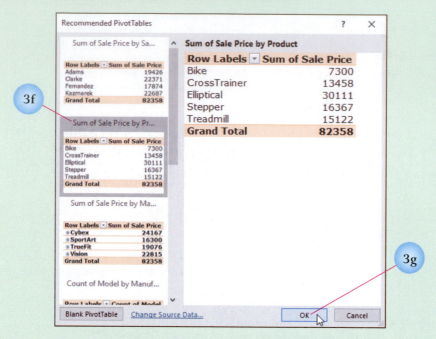

4. Apply the Comma format with no digits after the decimal point to the range B4:B9.
5. Rename the worksheet *PriceByProduct*.
6. Save **4-PF1stQSales.xlsx**.

Check Your Work

Figure 4.5 PivotTable for Project 3b

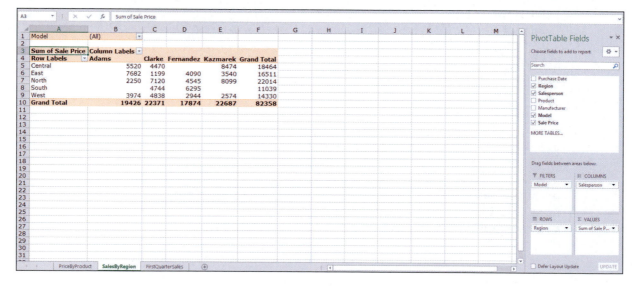

1. With **4-PF1stQSales.xlsx** open, make the FirstQuarterSales worksheet active. The FirstQ range should still be selected.
2. Create a PivotTable to summarize fitness equipment sales by region and salesperson, as shown in Figure 4.5, by completing the following steps:
   a. Click the Insert tab.
   b. Click the PivotTable button in the Tables group.
   c. At the Create PivotTable dialog box, with *FirstQuarterSales!$A$4:$G$47* entered in the *Table/Range* text box and *New Worksheet* selected for *Choose where you want the PivotTable report to be placed*, click OK.
   d. Click the *Region* check box in the PivotTable Fields task pane. *Region* is added to the *ROWS* list box in the layout section of the task pane and the report updates to show one row per region with a filter arrow at the top of the column and a *Grand Total* row automatically added to the bottom of the table. Since *Region* is a non-numeric field, Excel automatically places it in the *ROWS* list box.
   e. Click the *Salesperson* check box in the PivotTable Fields task pane. Excel automatically adds *Salesperson* to the *ROWS* list box in the layout section. (In the next step, you will correct the placement of the field to move it to the *COLUMNS* list box.)
   f. Click the *Salesperson* field header in the *ROWS* list box in the layout section and then click *Move to Column Labels* at the pop-up list. Notice that the layout of the report now displays one row per region and one column per salesperson. (In the next step, you will drag a field from the PivotTable Fields list into another list box in the layout section.)
   g. Position the mouse pointer over *Model* in the PivotTable Fields task pane, click and hold down the left mouse button, drag the field into the *FILTERS* list box in the layout section, and then release the mouse button. Notice that *Model* is added as a filter at the top left of the PivotTable in the range A1:B1.
   h. Click the *Sale Price* check box in the PivotTable Fields task pane. Since the field is numeric, Excel automatically adds it to the *VALUES* list box in the layout section and the report updates to show the Sum function applied to the grouped values in the PivotTable. Compare your results with the PivotTable shown in Figure 4.5.
3. Rename the worksheet *SalesByRegion*.
4. Save **4-PF1stQSales.xlsx**.

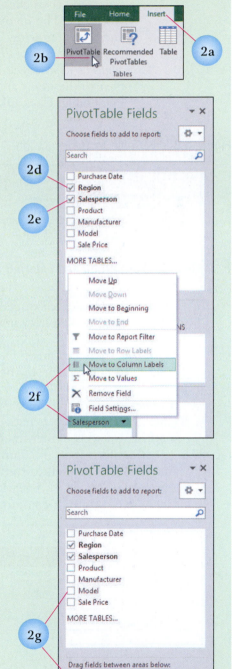

Check Your Work

When the active cell is positioned inside a PivotTable, the contextual PivotTable Tools Analyze and PivotTable Tools Design tabs become available. The features on the PivotTable Tools Design tab, shown in Figure 4.6, are similar to those on the Table Tools Design tab, which was discussed in Chapter 3.

To filter a PivotTable click the filter arrow on the Row Labels or the Column Labels, click the *(Select All)* check box to remove all the check marks next to the items and then click the check boxes for the items to show in the PivotTable. Click OK. The PivotTable filters the data to show the items that were checked and the filter arrow changes to indicate that a filter is applied. If a field has been placed in the *FILTERS* list box, click the filter arrow next to *(All)*, click the *Select Multiple Items* check box, click the *(All)* check box to remove all the check marks next to the items and then click the check boxes for the items to show in the PivotTable. Click OK.

Figure 4.6 PivotTable Tools Desgin Tab

Project 3c Formatting and Filtering a PivotTable

Part 3 of 8

1. With **4-PF1stQSales.xlsx** open and the SalesByRegion worksheet active, apply formatting options to the PivotTable to improve the report's appearance by completing the following steps:
   a. With the active cell positioned in the PivotTable, click the PivotTable Tools Design tab.
   b. Click the More button in the PivotTable Styles gallery.
   c. Click *Pivot Style Medium 2* at the drop-down gallery (second column, first row of the *Medium* section).
   d. Click the *Banded Rows* check box in the PivotTable Style Options group to insert a check mark. Excel adds border lines between the rows in the PivotTable. Recall from Chapter 3 that banding rows or columns adds a fill color or border style, depending on the style that has been applied to the PivotTable.
   e. Apply the Comma format with no digits after the decimal point to the range B5:F10.
   f. Change the width of columns B through F to 12 characters.

Formatting options are applied to the PivotTable in Steps 1a–1f.

   g. To stop Excel from using AutoFit to adjust the column widths after the cell content has been updated, right-click in the PivotTable and then click *PivotTable Options* at the shortcut menu. The PivotTable Options dialog box opens.

h. On the Layout & Format tab of the PivotTable Options dialog box, click the *Autofit column widths on update* check box to remove the check mark.

i. Click OK.

2. Filter the PivotTable to view sales for a group of product model numbers by completing the following steps:

a. Click the filter arrow next to *(All)* in cell B1.

b. Click the *Select Multiple Items* check box to insert a check mark and turn on the display of check boxes next to all the model numbers in the drop-down list.

c. Click the *(All)* check box to remove the check marks next to all the model numbers.

d. Click the check boxes for those model numbers that begin with *CX* to insert check marks. This selects all six models from Cybex.

e. Click OK.

f. Print the filtered PivotTable.

g. Click the filter arrow next to *(Multiple Items)* in cell B1, click the *(All)* check box to select all the model numbers in the drop-down list, and then click OK.

h. Experiment with the column labels and the row labels filter arrows to filter the PivotTable by region or salesperson.

i. Make sure all of the filters are cleared.

3. Save **4-PF1stQSales.xlsx**.

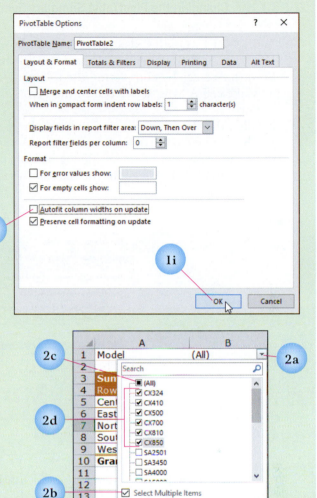

Check Your Work

Changing the PivotTable Summary Function

Field Settings

Quick Steps

Change the PivotTable Summary Function
1. Make any PivotTable cell active.
2. Click PivotTable Tools Analyze tab.
3. Click Field Settings button.
4. Click function.
5. Click OK.

By default, Excel uses the Sum function to summarize the numeric value added to a PivotTable. To change Sum to another function, click any numeric value within the PivotTable or click the cell containing *Sum of [Fieldname]* at the top left of the PivotTable. Click the PivotTable Tools Analyze tab and then click the Field Settings button in the Active Field group. This opens the Value Field Settings dialog box, where a function other than Sum can be chosen. Alternatively, right-click any numeric value within the PivotTable, point to *Summarize Values By* at the shortcut menu, and then click a function name.

1. With **4-PF1stQSales.xlsx** open, save the workbook with the name **4-PFAvg1stQSales**.
2. With the SalesByRegion worksheet active, change the function for the *SalePrice* field from Sum to Average by completing the following steps:
   a. Make cell A3 the active cell in the PivotTable. This cell contains the label *Sum of Sale Price*.
   b. Click the PivotTable Tools Analyze tab.
   c. Click the Field Settings button in the Active Field group.
   d. At the Value Field Settings dialog box with the Summarize Values By tab active, click *Average* in the *Summarize value field by* list box.
   e. Click OK.

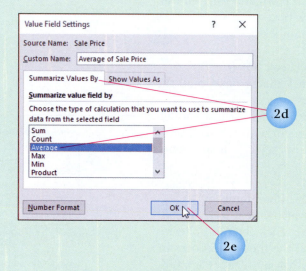

3. Change the page layout to landscape orientation and print the revised PivotTable.
4. Save and then close **4-PFAvg1stQSales.xlsx**.

Check Your Work

Tutorial

Filtering a
PivotTable Using
Slicers

 Insert Slicer

Quick Steps

Add a Slicer to a PivotTable
1. Make any cell within PivotTable active.
2. Click PivotTable Tools Analyze tab.
3. Click Insert Slicer button.
4. Click check box for specific field.
5. Click OK.

Filtering a PivotTable Using Slicers

Recall from Chapter 3 that *Slicers* allow you to filter without using a filter arrow. When Slicers are added to a PivotTable or PivotChart, a Slicer pane containing all the unique values for the specified field is added to the window.

To insert a Slicer pane, make any cell within the PivotTable active, click the PivotTable Tools Analyze tab, and then click the Insert Slicer button in the Filter group. Excel opens the Insert Slicers dialog box, which contains a list of the fields in the PivotTable with a check box next to each field. Click to insert a check mark in the check box for each field to which a Slicer pane is to be added and then click OK.

1. Open **4-PF1stQSales.xlsx**, make PriceByProduct the active worksheet and then display a Slicer pane for the manufacturer by completing the following steps:
   a. Make any cell active within the PivotTable.
   b. Add *Manufacturer* to the *FILTERS* list box and *Region* to the *COLUMNS* list box. (If necessary, refer to Project 3b, Steps 2e–2g for assistance.)
   c. Click the PivotTable Tools Analyze tab.
   d. Click the Insert Slicer button in the Filter group.
   e. At the Insert Slicers dialog box, click the *Manufacturer* check box to insert a check mark.
   f. Click OK. Excel inserts a Slicer pane in the worksheet with all the manufacturer names.
2. If necessary, position the mouse pointer at the top of the Manufacturer Slicer pane until the pointer changes to a four-headed arrow and then drag the pane into an empty area below the PivotTable.
3. Click *Vision* in the Manufacturer Slicer pane to filter the PivotTable. Excel filters the PivotTable by the Vision manufacturer. Notice that the *Manufacturer* filter arrow in cell B1 displays *Vision*.

PivotTable is filtered by the *Vision* manufacturer.

4. Click the Clear Filter button at the top right of the Manufacturer Slicer pane to redisplay all the data.
5. Add a second Slicer pane and filter by two fields by completing the following steps:
   a. If necessary, make any cell active within the PivotTable.
   b. Click the PivotTable Tools Analyze tab and then click the Insert Slicer button.
   c. At the Insert Slicers dialog box, click the *Region* check box to insert a check mark and then click OK.
   d. Drag the Region Slicer pane below the PivotTable next to the Manufacturer Slicer pane.

e. Click *West* in the Region Slicer pane to filter the PivotTable.

f. Click *Vision* in the Manufacturer Slicer pane to filter West region sales by the Vision manufacturer.

6. Print the filtered PivotTable.

7. Redisplay all the data and remove the two Slicer panes by completing the following steps:

a. Click the Clear Filter button at the top right of the Region Slicer pane.

b. Click the Clear Filter button at the top right of the Manufacturer Slicer pane.

c. Right-click the top of the Manufacturer Slicer pane and then click *Remove "Manufacturer"* at the shortcut menu.

d. Right-click the top of the Region Slicer pane and then click *Remove "Region"* at the shortcut menu.

8. Save **4-PF1stQSales.xlsx**.

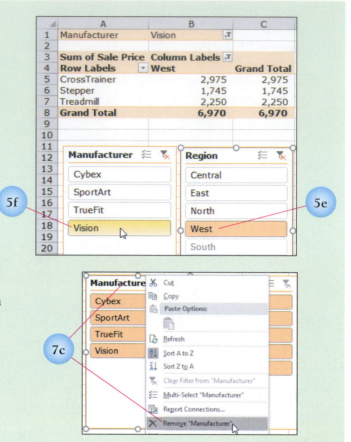

Check Your Work

A Slicer pane can be customized with buttons on the Slicer Tools Options tab. Click a Slicer pane to activate this tab. Click the tab to display customization options such as Slicer Styles. The height and width of the buttons in the Slicer pane and/or the height and width of the pane can also be changed with options on this tab.

Tutorial

Filtering a PivotTable Using a Timeline

 Insert Timeline

Quick Steps

Add a Timeline to a PivotTable
1. Make any cell within PivotTable active.
2. Click PivotTable Tools Analyze tab.
3. Click Insert Timeline button.
4. Click check box for field.
5. Click OK.
6. Select timeframe.

Filtering a PivotTable Using a Timeline

A Timeline groups and filters a PivotTable or PivotChart based on a specific timeframe. Select a field formatted as a date and a Timeline pane containing a timeline slicer is added to the PivotTable. The timeframe can be extended or shortened to instantly filter the data by the selected date range.

To insert a Timeline, make any cell within the PivotTable active, click the PivotTable Tools Analyze tab, and then click the Insert Timeline button in the Filter group. Excel opens the Insert Timelines dialog box and displays any field that contains data formatted as a date along with a check box next to it. Click to insert a check mark in the check box of any date field to which a Timeline pane is to be added and then click OK. More than one Timeline pane can be open but the data can only be filtered using one Timeline at a time. The PivotTable will display the data for the time period that is selected. Use the Time Level indicator at the upper right of the pane to change the time period to years, quarters, months, or days.

1. With **4-PF1stQSales.xlsx** open, make the SalesByRegion worksheet active. Display one Timeline for January and then another for February and March combined by completing the following steps:

   a. Make any cell active within the PivotTable.

   b. Click the PivotTable Tools Analyze tab.

   c. Click the Insert Timeline button in the Filter group. Excel displays an Insert Timelines dialog box with all the fields that have been formatted as dates.

   d. Click the check box next to *Purchase Date* in the Insert Timelines dialog box to insert a check mark.

   e. Click OK. Excel inserts a Timeline pane in the worksheet. The selection label displays *All Periods* to indicate that the PivotTable displays all periods.

2. If necessary, position the mouse pointer at the top of the Timeline pane until the pointer changes to a four-headed arrow and then drag the pane into an empty area below the PivotTable.

3. Click the left scroll arrow at the bottom of the Timeline pane, until JAN displays under 2018 and then click *JAN*. Excel filters the PivotTable by January. Notice that the selection label displays *Jan 2018*.

4. Click immediately right of the orange box on the Timeline to filter the PivotTable to include only the sales for February 2018. The selection label displays *Feb 2018*.

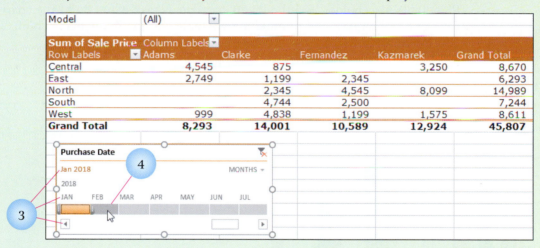

5. Position the mouse pointer over the orange box representing February, click and hold down the left mouse button, drag the mouse pointer into the orange box representing March, and then release the mouse button. The February timeframe is extended to include March. The selection label displays *Feb - Mar 2018* to indicate that the PivotTable has been filtered to include data for February and March.

6. Change the page layout to landscape orientation and print the filtered PivotTable.

7. Redisplay all the data and remove the Timeline pane by completing the following steps:

   a. Click the Clear Filter button at the top right of the Timeline pane.

   b. Right-click the top of the Timeline pane and then click *Remove Timeline* at the shortcut menu.

8. Save **4-PF1stQSales.xlsx**.

Check Your Work

Customize the Timeline pane with buttons on the Timeline Tools Options tab. Click a Timeline pane to activate the Timeline Tools Options tab. Click the tab to display customization options such as Timeline styles. The height and width of the buttons in the Timeline pane and/or the height and width of the pane can also be changed.

Creating a PivotChart

Tutorial

Creating a
PivotChart

 PivotChart

Quick Steps

Create a PivotChart from a PivotTable
1. Make cell active within PivotTable.
2. Click PivotTable Tools Analyze tab.
3. Click PivotChart button.
4. Select chart type.
5. Click OK.

A *PivotChart* visually displays data in chart form. As with a PivotTable, the data in a PivotChart is filtered to examine various scenarios between categories. As changes are made to the PivotChart, the PivotTable associated with it also updates. Figure 4.7 displays the PivotChart you will create in Project 3g.

In a worksheet that already contains a PivotTable, position the active cell anywhere in the PivotTable, click the PivotTable Tools Analyze tab, and then click the PivotChart button in the Tools group to create a chart from the existing summary data. The Insert Chart dialog box displays with a preview of the type of chart to create. Once the PivotChart has been generated, the PivotTable and PivotChart become connected. Making changes to the data by filtering in one causes the other to update with the same filter. For example, filtering the PivotChart by an individual salesperson name causes the PivotTable to filter by the same name.

If a PivotChart is created without a PivotTable, Excel displays a blank chart, a PivotTable placeholder, and the PivotChart Fields task pane. Build the chart using the same techniques used to build a PivotTable. As the PivotChart is built, Excel also builds a PivotTable that is connected to the PivotChart.

Figure 4.7 PivotChart for Project 3g

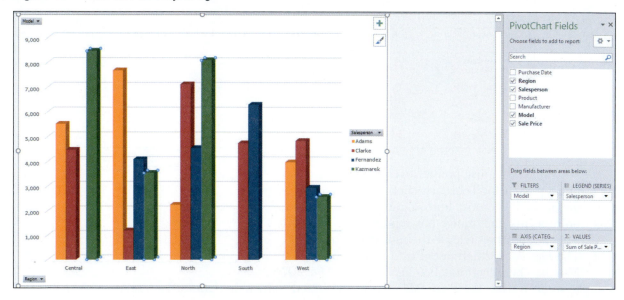

Create a PivotChart without an Existing PivotTable
1. Select range containing data for chart.
2. Click Insert tab.
3. Click PivotChart button arrow.
4. Click *PivotChart*.
5. Click OK.
6. Add fields as needed in PivotTable Fields task pane to build chart.
7. Modify and/or format as required.

 Move Chart

Before creating a PivotChart from scratch, examine the source data and determine the following:

- Which fields should display along the *x* (horizontal) axis? In other words, how should the data be compared when viewing the chart: by time period (such as months or years), by salesperson name, by department name, or by some other category?
- Which fields should display in the legend? In other words, how many data series (bars in a column chart) should be viewed in the chart: one for each region, product, salesperson, department, or some other category?
- Which numeric field contains the values to graph in the chart?

Use the Chart Elements button and the Chart Styles button at the upper right corner of the PivotChart to add or remove titles, labels, or other chart elements and to apply a style or color scheme to the PivotChart. To move the chart to a new sheet, use the Move Chart button in the Actions group on the PivotChart Tools Analyze tab.

Project 3g Creating a PivotChart

1. With **4-PF1stQSales.xlsx** open, make the SalesByRegion sheet active if necessary.
2. Create a PivotChart to visually present the data in the PivotTable by completing the following steps:
   a. If necessary, click in any cell within the PivotTable to activate the PivotTable contextual tabs.
   b. Click the PivotTable Tools Analyze tab.
   c. Click the PivotChart button in the Tools group.
   d. At the Insert Chart dialog box with *Column* selected in the left pane, click *3-D Clustered Column* (fourth option above preview) and then click OK.

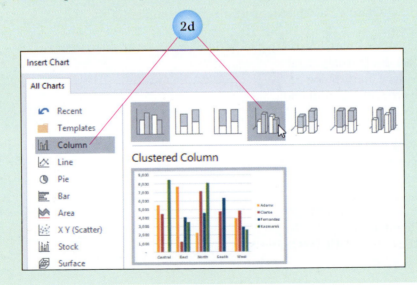

3. Filter the PivotChart to display sales for only one salesperson by completing the following steps:
   a. Click the Salesperson field button in the PivotChart. (This is the button above the salesperson names in the PivotChart legend.)
   b. Click the *(Select All)* check box to clear all the check boxes.
   c. Click the *Kazmarek* check box to insert a check mark.
   d. Click OK.
   e. Notice that the PivotTable behind the chart is also filtered to reflect the display of the chart. ***Note: If the chart is obscuring your view of the PivotTable, drag the PivotChart border to move it out of the way***.
   f. Click the Salesperson field button in the PivotChart and then click *Clear Filter From "Salesperson"*.

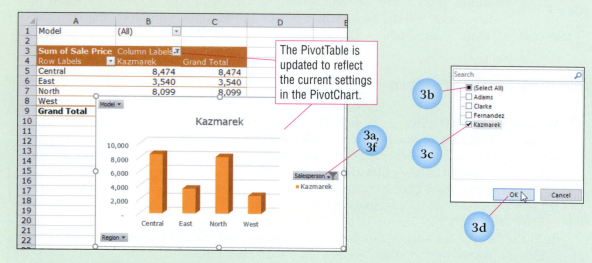

The PivotTable is updated to reflect the current settings in the PivotChart.

4. Move the PivotChart to a separate worksheet by completing the following steps:
   a. Click the Move Chart button in the Actions group on the PivotChart Tools Analyze tab.
   b. At the Move Chart dialog box, click the *New sheet* option and then type PivotChart in the *New sheet* text box.
   c. Click OK. Excel moves the PivotChart to a separate worksheet. Compare your PivotChart with the one shown in Figure 4.7 on page 104.
5. Print the PivotChart.
6. Save and then close **4-PF1stQSales.xlsx**.

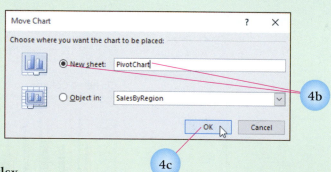

Check Your Work

1. Open **PF1stQSales**.
2. Save the workbook with the name **4-PFChart**.
3. Create a PivotChart to display the sales by manufacturer by region by completing the following steps:
   a. Select the named range *FirstQ* and then click the Insert tab.
   b. Click the PivotChart button arrow in the Charts group and then click *PivotChart* at the drop-down list.

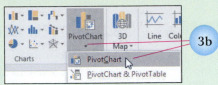

   c. At the Create PivotChart dialog box with *FirstQuarterSales!$A$4:$G$47* entered in the *Table/Range* text box and *New Worksheet* selected in the *Choose where you want the PivotChart to be placed* section, click OK.
   d. Excel displays a blank sheet with the PivotChart Fields task pane at the right side of the window. A PivotTable placeholder and chart placeholder appear in the worksheet area. As you build the PivotChart, notice that a PivotTable is created automatically.
   e. Click the *Manufacturer* check box in the PivotChart Fields task pane. Excel adds the field to the *AXIS (CATEGORIES)* list box in the layout section.
   f. Click the *Region* check box in the PivotChart Fields task pane. Excel adds the field below *Manufacturer* in the *AXIS (CATEGORIES)* list box in the layout section.
   g. Click the *Region* field header in the *AXIS (CATEGORIES)* list box and then click *Move to Legend Fields (Series)* at the pop-up list. Excel moves the field and updates the chart and PivotTable.
   h. Click the *Sale Price* check box in the PivotTable Fields task pane. Excel graphs the sum of the sale price values in the PivotChart and updates the PivotTable.
4. Point to the border of the PivotChart and then drag the PivotChart below the PivotTable.
5. Resize the chart to the approximate height and width of the chart shown below.
6. Experiment with the Chart Elements and Chart Styles buttons at the upper right corner of the chart. (See Level 1, Chapter 7 for more information on these buttons.)
7. Rename the sheet containing the PivotTable and PivotChart as *SummaryData*.
8. Print the PivotTable and PivotChart worksheet.
9. Save and then close **4-PFChart.xlsx**.

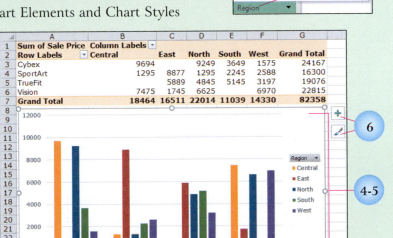

Project 4 Add Sparklines in a Worksheet to Show Trends   2 Parts

You will add and format Sparklines to identify trends in fees for dental services over the first quarter.

Preview Finished Project

Summarizing Data with Sparklines

Quick Steps

Create Sparklines
1. Select empty range in which to insert Sparklines.
2. Click Insert tab.
3. Click Line, Column, or Win/Loss in Sparklines group.
4. Type data range address or drag to select data range in *Data Range* text box.
5. Click OK.

Summarizing Data with Sparklines

Sparklines are miniature charts that are embedded into the background of cells. Entire charts exist in single cells. Since Sparklines can be placed directly next to the data set being represented, viewing them allows the quick determination of trends or patterns within the data. Consider using Sparklines to show high and low values within a range, as well as trends and other patterns. Figure 4.8 illustrates the three buttons in the Sparklines group used to create Sparkline charts: Line, Column, and Win/Loss.

Creating Sparklines

To create Sparklines, select the empty cell range in which to insert the miniature charts, click the Insert tab, and then click the Sparkline type in the Sparklines group, as shown in Figure 4.9. At the Create Sparklines dialog box, type or click the range of the cells that contain the data to graph in the *Data Range* text box and then click OK.

Figure 4.8 Line, Column, and Win/Loss Sparklines Added to a Worksheet

Use the Line or Column buttons to create Sparklines to show trends or patterns over a time period.

Since Sparklines are part of the background of a cell, text can be added to any cells that contain Sparklines.

Use the Win/Loss button to create Sparklines to show positive and negative values using bars. Notice that the bars are all the same height but that those quarters in which fees are lower than last year (negative percentages) show as red bars below the baseline.

Figure 4.9 Sparklines Group on the Insert Tab

1. Open **4-NADQ1Fees.xlsx**.
2. Save the workbook with the name **4-NADQ1Fees-4**.
3. Create Sparklines to illustrate the trends in categories of dental service fees during the first quarter by completing the following steps:
   a. With the FeeSummary worksheet active, select the range F6:F14.
   b. Click the Insert tab.
   c. Click the Line button in the Sparklines group.
   d. At the Create Sparklines dialog box with the insertion point positioned in the *Data Range* text box, type b6:d14.
   e. Click OK. Excel inserts miniature line charts within the cells.
4. Spend a few moments reviewing the Sparklines to determine what the charts indicate. Notice that the lines in cell F7 (*Cleanings and Fillings*) and cell F10 (*Porcelain Veneers*) slope downward and that the lines in cell F8 (*Teeth Whitening*) and cell F11 (*Crowns and Bridges*) have similar shapes. This shows that these dental services peaked in February and then began to decline.
5. Save **4-NADQ1Fees-4.xlsx**.

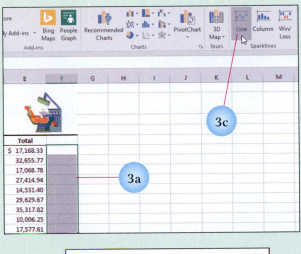

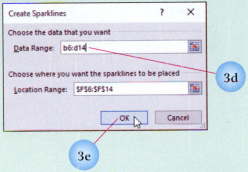

Check Your Work

Customizing Sparklines

Activate any Sparkline cell and the Sparkline Tools Design tab, shown in Figure 4.10, becomes visible. Click the Edit Data button to edit the range used to generate the Sparklines or instruct Excel how to graph hidden or empty cells in the data range. Use buttons in the Type group to change the chart type from Line to Column or Win/Loss. Click the check boxes in the Show group to show or hide data points in the chart or to show markers. Use options in the Style group to change the appearance of line and/or marker. Click the Axis button in the last group to customize the horizontal or vertical axis in the charts. Sparklines can be grouped, ungrouped, or cleared using the last three buttons on the tab.

Figure 4.10 Sparkline Tools Design Tab

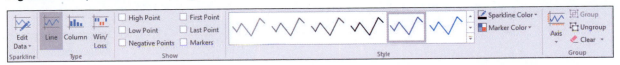

1. With **4-NADQ1Fees-4.xlsx** open, customize the Sparklines by completing the following steps:
   a. If necessary, click any Sparkline cell to activate the Sparkline Tools Design tab.
   b. Click the Sparkline Tools Design tab.
   c. Click the Sparkline Color button in the Style group and then click *Dark Red* (first option in the *Standard Colors* section) at the drop-down color palette.
   d. Click the *High Point* check box in the Show group to insert a check mark. Excel adds a marker at the highest point on each line graph.
   e. Click the *Markers* check box in the Show group to insert a check mark. Excel adds markers to all the other data points on each line.
   f. Click the Marker Color button in the Style group, point to *High Point*, and then click *Black, Text 1* (second column, first row in the *Theme Colors* section) at the drop-down color palette.

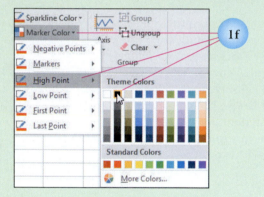

2. Widen the column and add a fill color to improve the appearance of the Sparklines by completing the following steps:
   a. Change the width of column F to 22 characters.
   b. Select the range F6:F14, click the Home tab, and then apply the Blue, Accent 1, Lighter 80% fill color (fifth column, second row in the *Theme Colors* section) to the selected cells.
   c. Click in any cell to deselect the range.
3. Make cell F5 active, type January to March Trends, and then, if necessary, format the title so it has the same formatting as the other titles in row 5.
4. Change the page layout to landscape orientation and then print the FeeSummary worksheet.
5. Save and then close **4-NADQ1Fees-4.xlsx**.

Check Your Work

	March	Total	January to March Trends
	$ 5,809.45	$ 17,168.33	
	9,406.42	32,655.77	
	5,731.19	17,068.78	
	9,719.33	27,414.94	
	4,171.52	14,531.40	
	9,418.07	29,629.67	
	14,185.13	35,317.82	
	3,814.69	10,006.25	
	8,333.21	17,577.61	
	$70,589.01	$201,370.57	

Chapter Summary

- A formula that references a cell in another worksheet within the same workbook contains a worksheet reference and a cell reference separated by an exclamation point.

- Range names can be used to simplify the references to cells in another worksheet because the worksheet reference is automatically included in the definition of the range name.

- A disadvantage to using range names to reference other worksheets emerges if several worksheets are to be summarized because each name has to be defined before the formula can be created.

- A 3-D reference is used to summarize the same cell in a range that extends over two or more worksheets.

- A 3-D reference includes the starting worksheet name and ending worksheet name separated by a colon, similar to the method used to define a range of cells.

- A formula that references another worksheet is linked to that worksheet, so that a change made in the source cell is automatically made in the other worksheet.

- A formula that references a cell in another workbook must include a workbook reference before the worksheet and cell references. The workbook reference is enclosed in square brackets.

- When a formula that links to an external reference is created, Excel includes the drive and folder name in the path to the source workbook. If the source workbook is moved or the source workbook file name is changed, the link will no longer work.

- Open the Edit Links dialog box to edit or remove a linked external reference.

- The Consolidate feature is another tool that can be used to summarize the data from multiple worksheets into a master worksheet.

- The Consolidate button is located in the Data Tools group on the Data tab.

- At the Consolidate dialog box, the Sum function is selected by default. Add the references containing the data to summarize, specify the location of the labels to duplicate, and indicate whether to create a link to the source data.

- A PivotTable is an interactive table that organizes and summarizes data based on categories in rows or columns.

- Preview different PivotTable scenarios with the Recommended PivotTables button.

- Create a PivotTable using the PivotTable button in the Tables group on the Insert tab.

- Add fields to the PivotTable using the field name check boxes in the PivotTable Fields task pane.

- Once created, a PivotTable can be used to view a variety of scenarios by filtering the row, column, or report headings.

- Use buttons on the contextual PivotTable Tools Analyze and PivotTable Tools Design tabs to format the PivotTable and/or edit the features used in it.

- Slicers allow filtering data in a PivotTable or PivotChart without using a filter arrow.

- Because the Slicer pane contains all the items in the designated field, the report can be filtered with one mouse click.

- Click the Insert Slicer button in the Filter group on the PivotTable Tools Analyze tab to add a Slicer pane to a PivotTable.
- Timelines group and filter data in a PivotTable or PivotChart based on specific timeframes, such as years, quarters, months, and days.
- With any cell within the PivotTable active, click the PivotTable Analyze tab and then click the Insert Timeline button in the Filter group.
- A PivotChart displays data in chart form. As changes are made to the PivotChart, the PivotTable associated with it also updates.
- Filter a PivotChart using the legend or axis field buttons on the PivotChart.
- Sparklines are miniature charts inserted into the backgrounds of cells.
- Add Sparklines to a worksheet to show trends or high or low values in a range of source data.
- To create Sparklines, select the empty cell range in which to insert the miniature charts, click the Insert tab, and then click the chart type in the Sparklines group. At the Create Sparklines dialog box, type or click the range of cells that contain the values to graph and then click OK.
- Sparklines can be customized using options in the Sparkline Tools Design tab.

Commands Review

FEATURE	RIBBON TAB, GROUP	BUTTON	KEYBOARD SHORTCUT
Consolidate	Data, Data Tools		
edit links	Data, Connections		
manage range names	Formulas, Defined Names		Ctrl + F3
PivotChart	Insert, Charts OR PivotTables Tools Analyze, Tools		
PivotTable	Insert, Tables		
Slicer	Insert, Filters		
Sparklines	Insert, Sparklines		
Timelines	Insert, Filters		

Microsoft Excel Level 2

Unit 2

Managing and Integrating Data and the Excel Environment

Microsoft® Excel®

Using Data Analysis Features

CHAPTER 5

Performance Objectives

Precheck

Check your current skills to help focus your study.

Upon successful completion of Chapter 5, you will be able to:

1 Convert data arranged in columns to rows and vice versa

2 Perform a mathematical operation during a paste routine

3 Populate cells using Goal Seek

4 Save and display various worksheet models using the Scenario Manager

5 Create a scenario summary report

6 Create a one-variable data table

7 Create a two-variable data table

8 Use auditing tools to view relationships between cells in formulas

9 Identify Excel error codes and troubleshoot formulas using formula auditing tools

10 Use the Circle Invalid Data feature

11 Use the Watch Window to track cells affected by key formulas

Excel's Paste Special dialog box includes several options for pasting copied data. Choose to paste attributes of a copied cell or alter the paste routine to perform a more complex operation. Apply a variety of *What-if Analysis* analysis tools to manage data and assist with decision-making and management tasks. Use formula-auditing tools to troubleshoot formulas or view dependencies between cells. By working through the projects in this chapter, you will learn about these tools and features available in Excel to assist with accurate data analysis.

SNAP

If you are a SNAP user, launch the Precheck and Tutorials from your Assignments page.

Data Files

Before beginning chapter work, copy the EL2C5 folder to your storage medium and then make EL2C5 the active folder.

Project 1 Analyze Data from a Request for Proposal

2 Parts

You will manipulate a worksheet containing vendor quotations for an enterprise resource-planning information system by copying and pasting using Paste Special options.

Preview Finished Project

Pasting Data Using Paste Special Options

Clicking the Paste button arrow opens the Paste drop-down gallery. This gallery contains many options for pasting copied data and is divided into three sections: *Paste*, *Paste Values*, and *Other Paste Options*. The Paste gallery includes a live preview of how the data will be pasted to assist in choosing the correct paste option. Click *Paste Special* at the bottom of the Paste gallery to open the Paste Special dialog box, shown in Figure 5.1. Use options at this dialog box to paste specific attributes of the source data, perform a mathematical operation in the destination range based on values in the source range, or carry out a more complex paste sequence.

Several options in the Paste Special dialog box are also available by clicking a button at the Paste drop-down gallery. For example, to copy a range of cells that has border formatting applied and paste the range without the borders, click the Paste button arrow and then click the No Borders button (first column, second row in the *Paste* section) at the drop-down gallery. This produces the same result as clicking the Paste button arrow, clicking *Paste Special* at the drop-down gallery, clicking *All except borders* in the *Paste* section of the Paste Special dialog box, and then clicking OK.

Figure 5.1 Paste Special Dialog Box

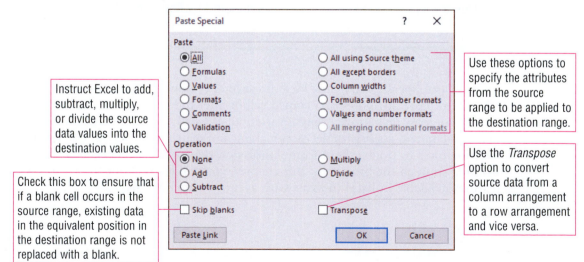

Transposing Data

Quick Steps

Transpose a Range
1. Select source range.
2. Click Copy button.
3. Click starting cell in destination range.
4. Click Paste button arrow.
5. Click Transpose button.

In some cases, the data in a worksheet is arranged in a way that is not suitable for performing the required analysis. For example, examine the worksheet shown in Figure 5.2. This is the worksheet used in Project 1. Notice that each company that submitted a proposal appears in a separate column, and the criteria for analysis (such as the cost of the hardware) are arranged in rows. At first glance, this layout may seem appropriate but consider that only those vendors that offer five-year contracts are to be examined. To use the filter feature on this data, the contract term needs to be displayed in a columnar format. Rearranging the data in this worksheet manually would be time consuming and risky due to the possibility of making errors. To avoid this, convert the columns to rows and the rows to columns using the Transpose button in the Paste button drop-down gallery or the Paste Special dialog box.

Figure 5.2 Project 1 Worksheet

	A	B	C	D	E	F
1		**Precision Design and Packaging**				
2		Enterprise Resource Planning (ERP) Information System				
3		Finance Department				
4		Request For Proposal (RFP) No. 385-XR-78				
5	Company	Westerveld Inc.	Kampson Ltd.	Jensen Systems	Core Solutions	NuTech Partners
6	Hardware	675,000	595,000	615,000	625,000	596,000
7	Software	212,000	281,000	267,000	250,000	292,000
8	Maintenance	22,500	21,675	20,750	23,450	26,432
9	Service Level	Same day	24 hours	24 hours	Same day	Same day
10	Term	5	4	5	5	4
11	Total Cost	909,500	897,675	902,750	898,450	914,432

Project 1a Converting Data from Rows to Columns   Part 1 of 2

1. Open **PreERP.xlsx**.
2. Save the workbook with the name **5-PreERP**.
3. Convert the worksheet to arrange the company names in rows and the criteria data in columns by completing the following steps:
   a. Select the range A5:F11.
   b. Click the Copy button.

c. Click in cell A13.

d. Click the Paste button arrow and then position the mouse over the Transpose button (third column, second row in the *Paste* section) at the drop-down gallery. A live preview shows how the copied data will be pasted. Click the Transpose button.

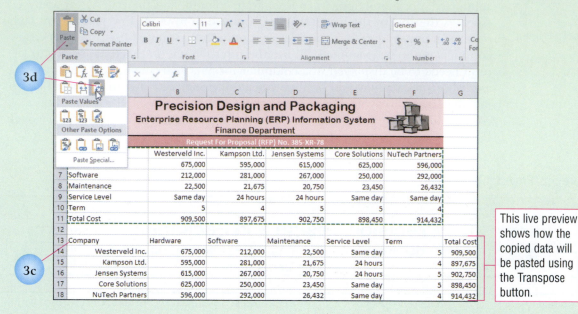

This live preview shows how the copied data will be pasted using the Transpose button.

e. Press the Esc key to remove the scrolling marquee from the source range and then click in any cell to deselect the range.

4. Delete rows 5 through 12.

5. Correct the merge and centering in rows 1 through 4 to extend the titles across columns A through G. If necessary, move or otherwise adjust the position of the picture at the right side of the worksheet after merging and centering.

6. Add a thick bottom border to cells A3 and A4.

7. Apply bold formatting to and center-align the labels in the range A5:G5.

8. Select the range A5:G10, turn on the Filter feature, and then click in any cell to deselect the range.

9. Click the filter arrow in cell F5 and then filter the worksheet to display only those vendors offering five-year contracts.

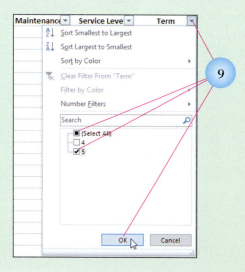

10. Click the filter arrow in cell E5 and then filter the remaining rows to display only those vendors offering same-day service.

Request For Proposal (RFP) No. 385-XR-78						
Company	Hardware	Software	Maintenance	Service Level	Term	Total C
Westerveld Inc.	675,000	212,000	22,500	Same day	5	909,500
Core Solutions	625,000	250,000	23,450	Same day	5	898,450

10

11. Print the filtered worksheet.
12. Turn off the Filter feature and then save **5-PreERP.xlsx**.

Check Your Work

Performing a Mathematical Operation While Pasting

Quick Steps

Perform a Mathematical Operation While Pasting
1. Select source range values.
2. Click Copy button.
3. Click starting cell in destination range.
4. Click Paste button arrow.
5. Click *Paste Special*.
6. Click mathematical operation.
7. Click OK.

A range of cells in a copied source range can be added to, subtracted from, multiplied by, or divided by the cells in the destination range. To do this, open the Paste Special dialog box and then select the mathematical operation to be performed. For example, in the worksheet for Project 1a, the values in the *Maintenance* column are the annual maintenance fees charged by the various vendors. To compare the fees across all the vendors, the maintenance value for the life cycle of the contract must be known.

In Project 1b, this calculation will be performed by copying and pasting using a multiply operation. Using this method makes it unnecessary to add a new column to the worksheet to show the maintenance fees for the entire term of the contract.

Project 1b Multiplying the Source Cells by the Destination Cells   **Part 2 of 2**

1. With **5-PreERP.xlsx** open, select the range F6:F10. These cells contain the terms for each company's individual contract.
2. Click the Copy button.
3. Paste the source range and instruct Excel to multiply the values when pasting by completing the following steps:
   a. Click in cell D6.
   b. Click the Paste button arrow and then click *Paste Special* at the drop-down gallery.

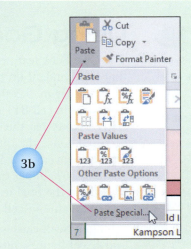

3b

c. Click *Multiply* in the *Operation* section of the Paste Special dialog box and then click OK.

d. Press the *Esc* key to remove the scrolling marquee from the source range and then click in any cell to deselect the range.

4. Print the worksheet.

5. Save and then close **5-PreERP.xlsx**.

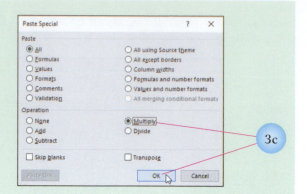

Check Your Work

Selecting Other Paste Special Options

A variety of options can be selected at the Paste Special dialog box. Click *Formulas* or *Values* to paste only the source formulas or displayed values, click *Formats* to paste only the formatting options from the source, and click *Validation* to paste a validation rule. Click *All using Source theme* to apply the theme from the source, click *All except borders* to paste everything but the borders from the source, and click *Column widths* to adjust the destination cells to the same column widths as the source. To paste formulas or values including the number formats from the source, click the *Formulas and number formats* option or the *Values and number formats* option.

Project 2 **Calculate a Target Test Score** **1 Part**

Using a grades worksheet, you will determine the score a student needs to earn on a final test to achieve a specified final average grade.

Preview Finished Project

Tutorial

Using Goal Seek to Populate a Cell

Quick Steps

Use Goal Seek to Return a Value

1. Make cell active.
2. Click Data tab.
3. Click What-If Analysis button.
4. Click *Goal Seek*.
5. Enter cell address in *Set cell* text box.
6. Enter target value in *To value* text box.
7. Enter dependent cell address in *By changing cell* text box.
8. Click OK.
9. Click OK or Cancel.

What-If Analysis

Using Goal Seek to Populate Cells

The Goal Seek feature calculates a value using a target to be achieved in another cell that is dependent on the cell that Goal Seek is to populate. For example, the worksheet shown in Figure 5.3 shows Whitney's grades on the first four tutoring assessments. The value in cell B11 (average grade) is the average of the five values in the range B5:B9. Note that the final test shows a grade of 0 even though the test has not yet occurred. Once the final test grade is entered, the value in cell B11 will update to reflect the average of all five scores. Suppose Whitney wants to achieve a final average grade of 76% in her tutoring assessments. Goal Seek will determine the score she needs to earn on the final test to achieve the 76% average. In Project 2, Goal Seek will return a value in cell B9 based on the target value of cell B11.

Goal Seek causes Excel to calculate in reverse. The ending value is specified and Excel figures out the input numbers that will achieve the result wanted. Note that the cell in which Excel is to calculate the target value must be referenced by a formula in the *Set cell* text box. Goal Seek is useful for any situation in which the wanted result is known but the value needed to get it is not.

Figure 5.3 Project 2 Worksheet

	A	B	C
1	**Math by Janelle Tutoring Service**		
2	**Student Assessment Report**		
3	Whitney Orlowicz		
4	**Assessments**	**100**	**Session**
5	Objective test	64.5	1
6	Performance test	72.0	6
7	Problem-solving test	83.5	10
8	Comprehensive test	78.5	15
9	Final test	0.0	20
10			
11	Average grade	59.7	

Use Goal Seek to determine the value needed in cell B9 for the final test to achieve the desired average grade in cell B11.

Project 2 Using Goal Seek to Return a Target Value

Part 1 of 1

1. Open **JTutorOrlowiczRpt.xlsx**.
2. Save the workbook with the name **5-JTutorOrlowiczRpt**.
3. Use Goal Seek to find the score Whitney needs to earn on the final test to achieve a 76% average grade by completing the following steps:
   a. Make cell B11 active.
   b. Click the Data tab.
   c. Click the What-If Analysis button in the Forecast group and then click *Goal Seek* at the drop-down list.
   d. If necessary, drag the Goal Seek dialog box so you can see all the values in column B.
   e. With *B11* already entered in the *Set cell* text box, click in the *To value* text box and then type 76.
   f. Press the Tab key and then type b9 in the *By changing cell* text box.
   g. Click OK.
   h. Click OK at the Goal Seek Status dialog box that shows Excel found a solution.

3c

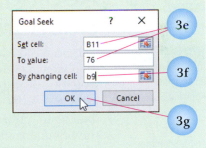
3e
3f
3g

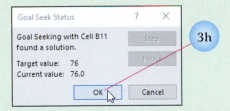
3h

4. Notice that Excel entered the value *81.5* in cell B9. This is the score Whitney must earn to achieve a final average grade of 76%.
5. Assume that Whitney wants to achieve a final average grade of 80%. Use Goal Seek to find the score she will need to earn on the final test to accomplish the new target by completing the following steps:
   a. Click the What-If Analysis button in the Forecast group and then click *Goal Seek* at the drop-down list.
   b. With *B11* already entered in the *Set cell* text box, click in the *To value* text box, type 80, and then press the Tab key.
   c. Type b9 in the *By changing cell* text box.
   d. Click OK.

e. Notice that the value entered in cell B9 is *101.5*. This is the score Whitney needs on the final test to earn an 80% average grade.

f. The final test is worth only 100, so Whitney will not be able to score 101.5. Restore the previous values in the report by clicking the Cancel button at the Goal Seek Status dialog box.

6. Save, print, and then close **5-JTutorOrlowiczRpt.xlsx**.

Check Your Work

Project 3 **Forecast a Budget Based on Various Inflation Rates**   **3 Parts**

You will determine how various rates of inflation impact a department's budget to determine the funding request to present to management to maintain service.

Preview Finished Project

Tutorial
Adding Scenarios

Tutorial
Editing and Applying Scenarios

Quick Steps

Add a Scenario
1. Click Data tab.
2. Click What-If Analysis button.
3. Click *Scenario Manager*.
4. Click Add button.
5. Type name in *Scenario name* text box.
6. Type or select variable cells in *Changing cells* text box.
7. Click OK.
8. Enter value for each changing cell.
9. Click OK.
10. Click Close button.

Adding, Editing, and Applying Scenarios

The Scenario Manager allows storing multiple sets of assumptions about data and then viewing how each set of assumptions affects the worksheet. Switch between scenarios to test the various inputs on the worksheet model. Save each scenario using a descriptive name, such as *BestCase* or *WorstCase*, to indicate the type of data assumptions stored in it. Generally, the first scenario created should contain the original values in the worksheet, since Excel replaces the content of each changing cell when a scenario is shown.

Examine the worksheet shown in Figure 5.4. In it, the Computing Services Department budget for the next year has been calculated based on projected percentage increases for various expense items. Assume that the department

Figure 5.4 Project 3 Worksheet

A	B	C	D
National Online Marketing Inc.			
Computing Services Department			
	Current budget	Projected increase	New budget
Wages and benefits	371,875	13,016	384,891
Computer supplies	150,350	2,255	152,605
Training and development	63,850	6,385	70,235
Other administrative costs	49,576	2,479	52,055
Total costs:	$ 635,651		$ 659,786

Hint Create a
range name for each
changing cell. This
allows a descriptive
reference next to the
input text box, rather
than a cell address,
when adding a
scenario.

manager has more than one projected increase for each expense item based on different inflation rates or vendor rate increases for next year. The manager can create and save various scenarios to view the impact on total costs that results from a combination of different forecasts.

Using the Scenario Manager dialog box, shown in Figure 5.5, create as many models as needed to test various what-if conditions. For example, two scenarios have been saved in the example shown in Figure 5.5: *LowInflation* and *HighInflation*. When a scenario is added, define which cells will change and then enter the data to be stored under the new scenario name.

Figure 5.5 Scenario Manager Dialog Box and Scenario Values Dialog Box

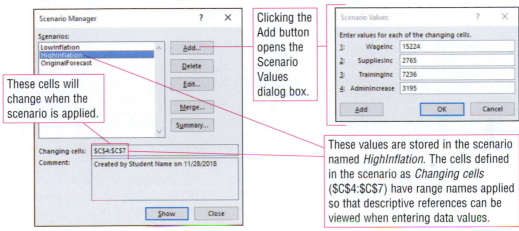

These cells will change when the scenario is applied.

Clicking the Add button opens the Scenario Values dialog box.

These values are stored in the scenario named *HighInflation*. The cells defined in the scenario as *Changing cells* ($C$4:$C$7) have range names applied so that descriptive references can be viewed when entering data values.

Project 3a   Adding Scenarios to a Worksheet Model

Part 1 of 3

1. Open **NationalBdgt.xlsx**.
2. Save the workbook with the name **5-NationalBdgt**.
3. View the range names already created in the worksheet by clicking the Name box arrow and then clicking *WageInc* at the drop-down list. Cell C4 becomes active. A range name has been created for each data cell in column C so that a descriptive label displays when scenarios are added in Steps 4 and 5.
4. Add a scenario with values assuming a low inflation rate for next year by completing the following steps:
   a. Click the Data tab.
   b. Click the What-If Analysis button in the Forecast group and then click *Scenario Manager* at the drop-down list.
   c. Click the Add button at the Scenario Manager dialog box.
   d. At the Add Scenario dialog box with the insertion point positioned in the *Scenario name* text box, type LowInflation and then press the Tab key.
   e. Type c4:c7 in the *Changing cells* text box.
   f. Click OK. (As an alternative, move the dialog box out of the way and select the cells that will change in the worksheet.)

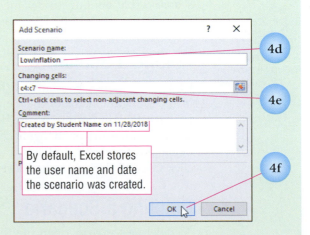

g. With the insertion point positioned in the
1: WageInc text box, type 12010 and then press
the Tab key.

h. Type 2150 and then press the Tab key.

i. Type 5276 and then press the Tab key.

j. Type 1998.

k. Click OK.

5. Add another scenario to the worksheet that assumes a
high inflation rate by completing the following steps:

a. Click the Add button at the Scenario Manager
dialog box.

b. Type HighInflation in the *Scenario name* text box
and then click OK. Notice that the *Changing cells*
text box already contains the range C4:C7.

c. At the Scenario Values dialog box, type the
following values into the text boxes indicated:

1: WageInc	15224
2: SuppliesInc	2765
3: TrainingInc	7236
4: AdminIncrease	3195

d. Click OK.

6. Add a third scenario, named *OriginalForecast*, that contains the original worksheet values by
completing the following steps:

a. Click the Add button at the Scenario Manager dialog box.

b. Type OriginalForecast in the *Scenario name* text box and then click OK.

c. At the Scenario Values dialog box, notice that the original values are already entered in
each text box. Click OK.

7. Click the Close button to close the Scenario Manager dialog box.

8. Save **5-NationalBdgt.xlsx**.

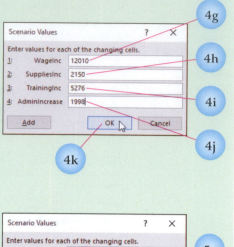

Applying a Scenario

Quick Steps

Apply a Scenario
1. Click Data tab.
2. Click What-If
   Analysis button.
3. Click *Scenario
   Manager* at drop-
   down list.
4. Click scenario name.
5. Click Show button.
6. Click Close button.

After creating the various scenarios to save with the worksheet, apply the values
stored in each scenario to the variable cells to view the effects on the worksheet
model. To do this, open the Scenario Manager dialog box, click the name of the
scenario that contains the values to be applied to the worksheet, and then click the
Show button. Click the Close button to close the Scenario Manager dialog box.

Editing a Scenario

Change the values associated with a scenario by opening the Scenario Manager dialog
box, clicking the name of the scenario that contains the values to be changed, and then
clicking the Edit button. At the Edit Scenario dialog box, make any changes to the
scenario name and/or changing cells and then click OK to open the Scenario Values
dialog box to edit the individual value associated with each changing cell. When done,
click OK and then click the Close button.

Deleting a Scenario

To delete a scenario, open the Scenario Manager dialog box, click the scenario to
be removed, and then click the Delete button. Click the Close button to close the
Scenario Manager dialog box.

1. With **5-NationalBdgt.xlsx** open, apply the scenario that assumes the low inflation rate by completing the following steps:
   a. With Data as the active tab, click the What-If Analysis button and then click *Scenario Manager* at the drop-down list.
   b. If necessary, drag the Scenario Manager dialog box so you can see all the values in column D.
   c. Click *LowInflation* in the *Scenarios* list box and then click the Show button. Excel changes the values in the range C4:C7 to the values stored within the scenario. Notice that based on the assumption of a low inflation rate, the total cost of the new budget shown in cell D8 is $657,085.

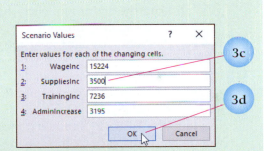

2. With the Scenario Manager dialog box still open, change the worksheet to display the scenario that assumes a high inflation rate by clicking *HighInflation* in the *Scenarios* list box and then clicking the Show button. Notice that in this high-inflation scenario, the total cost of the new budget is $664,071.

3. After reviewing the data, it is decided that the projected increase for computer supplies should be $3,500. Edit the HighInflation scenario by completing the following steps:
   a. With *HighInflation* selected in the *Scenarios* list box, click the Edit button.
   b. Click OK at the Edit Scenario dialog box.
   c. Select *2765* in the *SuppliesInc* text box and then type 3500.
   d. Click OK.

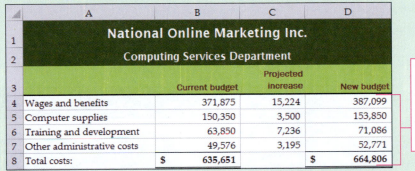

	A	B	C	D
1	National Online Marketing Inc.			
2	Computing Services Department			
3		Current budget	Projected increase	New budget
4	Wages and benefits	371,875	15,224	387,099
5	Computer supplies	150,350	3,500	153,850
6	Training and development	63,850	7,236	71,086
7	Other administrative costs	49,576	3,195	52,771
8	Total costs:	$ 635,651		$ 664,806

Excel displays the worksheet with the high inflation values applied and edited in Steps 2 and 3.

4. Show the worksheet with the data values from the OriginalForecast scenario.
5. Click the Close button to close the Scenario Manager dialog box.
6. Save **5-NationalBdgt.xlsx**.

Check Your Work

Generating a Scenario Summary Report

Create a scenario summary report to compare scenarios side by side in a worksheet or PivotTable. At the Scenario Summary dialog box, shown in Figure 5.6, enter in the *Result cells* text box the formula cell or cells that change when the data is applied in the various scenarios. Enter multiple cell addresses in this text box and use commas to separate them.

Figure 5.6 Scenario Summary Dialog Box

Enter the address of the cell containing the total or other formula results affected by the changing cells in each scenario. Enter multiple results cell addresses separated by commas.

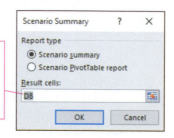

Project 3c Generating a Scenario Summary Report

Part 3 of 3

1. With **5-NationalBdgt.xlsx** open, display a scenario summary report by completing the following steps:
   a. With Data the active tab, click the What-If Analysis button and then click *Scenario Manager* at the drop-down list.
   b. Click the Summary button at the Scenario Manager dialog box.
   c. At the Scenario Summary dialog box, with the *Report type* set to *Scenario summary* and *Result cells* displaying the address *D8*, click OK.

2. Examine the Scenario Summary sheet added to the workbook. It displays each changing cell with the input for each scenario. Below the Changing Cells table, Excel displays the Result Cells, which provide the values that result from each scenario's input.
3. Print the Scenario Summary worksheet.
4. Save and then close **5-NationalBdgt.xlsx**.

In Step 2, Excel displays the Scenario Summary worksheet created in Step 1.

Scenario Summary		Current Values:	LowInflation	HighInflation	OriginalForecast
Changing Cells:					
	WageInc	13,016	12,010	15,224	13,016
	SuppliesInc	2,255	2,150	3,500	2,255
	TrainingInc	6,385	5,276	7,236	6,385
	AdminIncrease	2,479	1,998	3,195	2,479
Result Cells:					
	TotalNewCosts	$ 659,786	$ 657,085	$ 664,806	$ 659,786

Notes: Current Values column represents values of changing cells at time Scenario Summary Report was created. Changing cells for each scenario are highlighted in gray.

Check Your Work

<table>
<tr><td>Project 4</td><td>Compare the Effects of Various Inputs Related to Cost and Sales Pricing</td><td>2 Parts</td></tr>
</table>

Using one-variable and two-variable data tables, you will analyze the effects on the cost per unit and the selling price per unit of a manufactured container.

Preview Finished Project

Performing What-If Analysis Using Data Tables

The term *data table* refers to a range of cells that contains a series of input values. Excel calculates a formula substituting each input value in the data table range and places the result in the cell adjacent to the value. Either a one-variable or a two-variable data table can be created. A one-variable data table calculates a formula by modifying one input value in the formula. A two-variable data table calculates a formula substituting two input values. Using data tables provides a means of analyzing various outcomes in a calculation that occur as a result of changing a dependent value without creating multiple formulas.

Tutorial

Creating a
One-Variable
Data Table

 Data Table

Creating a One-Variable Data Table

Design a one-variable data table with the variable input data values in a series down a column or across a row. Examine the worksheet shown in Figure 5.7. Assume that management wants to calculate the effects on the cost per unit for a variety of production volumes given a standard set of costs per factory shift. The worksheet includes the total costs for direct materials, direct labor, and overhead.

The formula in cell B8 sums the three cost categories. Based on a standard production volume of 500,000 units, the cost per unit is $3.21, calculated by dividing the total cost by the production volume (cell B8 divided by cell B10). In the range E6:E12, the factory manager has input varying levels of production. The manager would like to see the change in the cost per unit for each level of production volume, assuming the costs remain the same. In Project 4a, a data table is used to show the various costs. This data table will manipulate one input value—production volume—so it is a one-variable data table.

Quick Steps

Create a One-Variable Data Table
1. Create variable data in column at right of worksheet.
2. Enter formula one row above and one cell right of variable data.
3. Select data range, including formula cell.
4. Click Data tab.
5. Click What-If Analysis button.
6. Click *Data Table*.
7. Type cell address for variable data in source formula in *Column input cell* text box.
8. Click OK.

Figure 5.7 Project 4a One-Variable Data Table

	A	B	C	D	E	F	G	H
1		**Precision Design and Packaging**						
2		**Cost Price Analysis**						
3		**"E" Container Bulk Cargo Box**						
4	Factory costs per shift				Variable unit production impact on cost			
5	Direct materials	$ 580,000						
6	Direct labor	880,552			425,000		In this area of the worksheet, calculate	
7	Overhead	145,350			450,000			
8	Total cost	$ 1,605,902			475,000		the change in cost per unit based	
9					500,000			
10	Standard production	500,000	units		525,000		on varying the production volume	
11					550,000			
12	Cost per unit	$ 3.21			575,000		using a data table.	

1. Open **PreEBoxCost.xlsx**.
2. Save the workbook with the name **5-PreEBoxCost**.
3. Calculate the cost per unit for seven different production levels using a one-variable data table by completing the following steps:
   a. In a data table, the formula for calculating the various outcomes must be placed in the cell in the first row above and one column right of the table values. The data table values have been entered in the range E6:E12; therefore, make cell F5 active.
   b. The formula that calculates the cost per unit is *=B8/B10*. This formula has already been entered in cell B12. Link to the source formula by typing =b12 and then pressing the Enter key.
   c. Select the range E5:F12.
   d. Click the Data tab.
   e. Click the What-If Analysis button in the Forecast group and then click *Data Table* at the drop-down list.

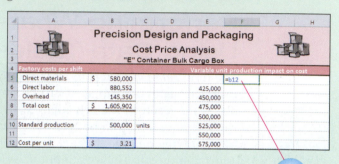

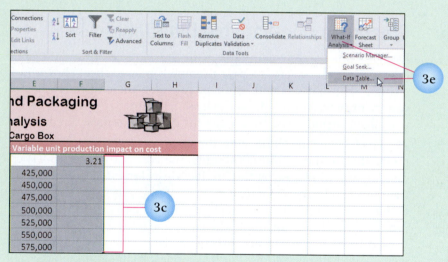

   f. At the Data Table dialog box, click in the *Column input cell* text box and then type b10.
   g. Click OK. At the Data Table dialog box, Excel needs to know which reference in the source formula is the address where the variable data is to be inserted. (The production volume is cell B10 in the source formula.)
   h. Click in any cell to deselect the range.
4. Print the worksheet.
5. Save and then close **5-PreEBoxCost.xlsx**.

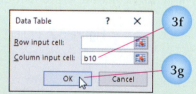

The data table calculates costs at all the production volumes. Notice that the costs are higher at lower volumes and decrease as the production volume increases.

Check Your Work

Creating a Two-Variable Data Table

A data table can substitute two variables in a source formula. To modify two input cells, design the data table with a column along the left containing one set of variable input values and a row along the top containing a second set of variable input values. In a two-variable data table, the source formula is placed at the top left cell in the table. In the worksheet shown in Figure 5.8, the source formula will be inserted in cell E5, which is the top left cell in the data table.

Quick Steps

Create a Two-Variable Data Table

1. Create variable data at right of worksheet with one input series in column and another in row across top of table.
2. Enter formula in top left cell of table.
3. Select data table range.
4. Click Data tab.
5. Click What-If Analysis button.
6. Click *Data Table*.
7. Type cell address for variable data in source formula in *Row input cell* text box.
8. Press Tab.
9. Type cell address for variable data in source formula in *Column input cell* text box.
10. Click OK.

Figure 5.8 Project 4b Two-Variable Data Table

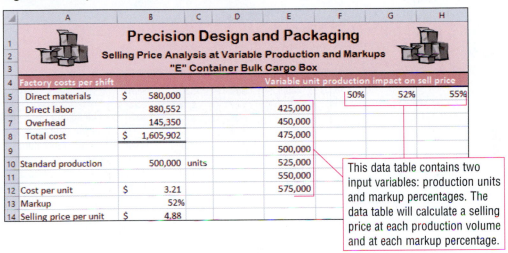

This data table contains two input variables: production units and markup percentages. The data table will calculate a selling price at each production volume and at each markup percentage.

Project 4b Creating a Two-Variable Data Table

Part 2 of 2

1. Open **PreEBoxSell.xlsx**.
2. Save the workbook with the name **5-PreEBoxSell**.
3. Calculate the selling price per unit for seven different production levels and three different markups using a two-variable data table by completing the following steps:
   a. In a two-variable data table, the source formula must be placed in the top left cell in the data table; therefore, make cell E5 active.
   b. Type =b14 and then press the Enter key. The formula that Excel is to use to create the data table is in cell B14. The selling price per unit, found in cell B14, is calculated by adding the cost per unit (cell B12) to the result of multiplying the cost per unit (cell B12) by the markup (cell B13).
   c. Select the range E5:H12.
   d. Click the Data tab.
   e. Click the What-If Analysis button in the Forecast group and then click *Data Table* at the drop-down list.

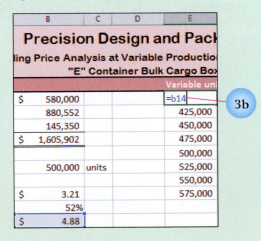

f. At the Data Table dialog box with the insertion point positioned in the *Row input cell* text box, type b13 and then press the Tab key. Excel needs to know which reference in the source formula is the address relating to the variable data in the first row of the data table. (The markup value is in cell B13 in the source formula.)

g. Type b10 in the *Column input cell* text box.

h. Click OK. As in Project 4a, Excel needs to know which reference relates to the production volume in the source formula.

i. Click in any cell to deselect the range.

4. Print the worksheet.

5. Save and then close **5-PreEBoxSell.xlsx**.

Variable unit production impact on sell price			
$ 4.88	50%	52%	55%
425,000	5.67	5.74	5.86
450,000	5.35	5.42	5.53
475,000	5.07	5.14	5.24
500,000	4.82	4.88	4.98
525,000	4.59	4.65	4.74
550,000	4.38	4.44	4.53
575,000	4.19	4.25	4.33

The selling price is calculated by the data table at each production volume and each percentage markup.

Check Your Work

Project 5 Audit a Worksheet to View and Troubleshoot Formulas

3 Parts

You will use buttons in the Formula Auditing group to view relationships between cells that comprise a formula, identify error codes in a worksheet, and troubleshoot errors using error checking tools.

Preview Finished Project

Tutorial

Using Auditing Tools

Using Auditing Tools

The Formula Auditing group on the Formulas tab, shown in Figure 5.9, contains options that are useful for viewing relationships between cells in formulas. Checking a formula for accuracy can be difficult when it is part of a complex sequence of operations. Opening a worksheet created by someone else can also present a challenge in understanding the relationships between sets of data. When Excel displays an error message in a cell, finding the source of the error can be made easier by viewing the relationships between the dependencies of cells.

Quick Steps

Trace Precedent Cells

1. Open worksheet.
2. Make cell active.
3. Click Formulas tab.
4. Click Trace
   Precedents button.
5. Continue clicking
   until all relationships
   are visible.

Trace Dependent Cells

1. Open worksheet.
2. Make cell active.
3. Click Formulas tab.
4. Click Trace
   Dependents button.
5. Continue clicking
   until all relationships
   are visible.

Figure 5.9 Formula Auditing Group on Formulas Tab

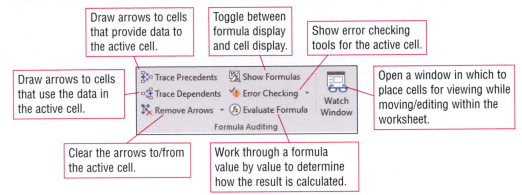

Draw arrows to cells that provide data to the active cell.

Toggle between formula display and cell display.

Show error checking tools for the active cell.

Draw arrows to cells that use the data in the active cell.

Open a window in which to place cells for viewing while moving/editing within the worksheet.

Clear the arrows to/from the active cell.

Work through a formula value by value to determine how the result is calculated.

Tracing Precedent and Dependent Cells

Precedent cells provide data to formula cells. For example, if cell B3 contains the formula =B1+B2, then cell B1 and cell B2 are precedent cells. Dependent cells contain formulas that refer to other cells. In the previous example, cell B3 is the dependent cell to cells B1 and B2, since cell B3 relies on the data from cells B1 and B2.

 Trace Precedents

Click in a cell and then click the Trace Precedents button to draw tracer arrows that show direct relationships to cell(s) that provide data to the active cell. Click the button a second time to show indirect relationships to cell(s) that provide data to the active cell at the next level. Continue clicking the button until no further arrows are drawn. Excel will sound a beep if the button is clicked and no more relationships exist.

 Trace Dependents

Click in a cell and then click the Trace Dependents button to draw tracer arrows that show direct relationships to other cell(s) in the worksheet that use the contents of the active cell. As with the Trace Precedents button, click a second time to show the next level of indirect relationships and continue clicking the button until no further tracer arrows are drawn.

 Remove Arrows

 Show Formulas

Excel draws blue tracer arrows if no error is detected in the active cell and red tracer arrows if an error is detected within the active cell.

Project 5a Viewing Relationships between Cells and Formulas   **Part 1 of 3**

1. Open **5-PreEBoxSell.xlsx**.
2. Display tracer arrows between cells to view the relationships between cells and formulas by completing the following steps:
   a. Make cell B8 active.
   b. Click the Formulas tab.
   c. Click the Trace Precedents button in the Formula Auditing group. Excel draws a blue tracer arrow that shows the cells that provide data to cell B8.
   d. Click the Remove Arrows button in the Formula Auditing group. The blue tracer arrow leading to cell B8 is cleared.
   e. Make cell B14 active.

This blue precedent arrow is drawn to cell B8 in Step 2c.

4	Factory costs per shift		
5	Direct materials	$	580,000
6	Direct labor		880,552
7	Overhead		145,350
8	Total cost	$	1,605,902

2a

f. Click the Trace Precedents button.

g. Click the Trace Precedents button a second time to show the next level of cells that provide data to cell B14.

h. Click the Trace Dependents button to view the cell(s) dependent on cell B14.

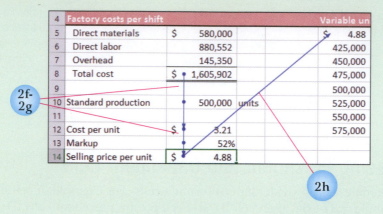

3. Click the Remove Arrows button in the Formula Auditing group to clear all the arrows.

4. Click the Show Formulas button in the Formula Auditing group to display the cell formulas. Click the Show Formulas button again to turn off the display of formulas.

5. Close **5-PreEBoxSell.xlsx**. Click the Don't Save button when prompted to save changes.

Troubleshooting Formulas

Quick Steps

Trace Errors
1. Click in cell containing error message.
2. Click Formulas tab.
3. Click arrow on Error Checking button.
4. Click *Trace Error*.

Hint Reference errors can also occur—for instance, when the formula uses correct syntax and logic but refers to the wrong data. These errors are difficult to find and only a thorough review and test of key figures will reveal their existence.

Formulas in Excel can contain various types of errors. Some errors are obvious because Excel displays an error message, such as *#VALUE!* Other errors occur without the display of an error message but are incorrect because the logic is flawed. For example, a formula could be entered in a cell that Excel does not flag as an error because the syntax is correct; however, the calculation could be incorrect for the data and the situation. Logic errors are difficult to find and require checking a worksheet by entering proof formulas or by manually checking the accuracy of each formula.

A proof formula is a formula entered outside the main worksheet area that checks key figures within the worksheet. For example, in a payroll worksheet, a proof formula to check the total net pay column could add the total net pay to the totals of all the deduction columns. The total displayed should be equal to the total gross pay amount in the worksheet.

Excel displays an error message code in a cell that is detected to have an error. Two types of error flags can occur. A green diagonal triangle in the upper left corner of a cell indicates an error condition. Activate the cell and an error checking button displays that can be used to access error checking tools. Errors can also be indicated with text entries, such as *#NAME?* Figure 5.10 displays a portion of the worksheet used in Project 5b to troubleshoot errors. Table 5.1 describes the three types of error codes displayed in Figure 5.10.

Figure 5.10 Project 5b Partial Worksheet

Precision Design and Packaging
Bulk Container 2018 Sales Target by Region
(in millions)

	Model Number	Description	Base	East	West	North	South	Total		Sales Target Assumptions	
4	PD-1140	Gaylord with lid	2.75	#NAME?	#N/A	2.81	2.80	#NAME?		East	1.50%
5	PD-2185	Premium Gaylord with lid	2 14	#VALUE!	#VALUE!	#VALUE!	#VALUE!	#VALUE!		West	#N/A
6	PD-1150	Gaylord bottom	2.33	#NAME?	#N/A	2.38	2.37	#NAME?		North	2.15%
7	PD-1155	Gaylord lid	1.85	#NAME?	#N/A	1.89	1.88	#NAME?		South	1.75%
8	PD-3695	Telescoping top and bottom	2.45	#NAME?	#N/A	2.50	2.49	#NAME?			
9	PD-3698	Telescoping bottom	2.96	#NAME?	#N/A	3.02	3.01	#NAME?			

Table 5.1 Types of Error Codes in Figure 5.10 Worksheet

Error Code	Description of Error Condition
#N/A	A required value for the formula is not available.
#NAME?	The formula contains an unrecognized entry.
#VALUE!	A value within the formula is of the wrong type or otherwise invalid.

Error Checking

Evaluate Formula

The Error Checking button in the Formula Auditing group can be used to help find the source of an error condition in a cell by displaying the Error Checking dialog box or drawing a red tracer arrow to locate the source cell that is contributing to the error. The Evaluate Formula button can be used to work through a formula value by value to determine where within the formula an error exists.

Project 5b Troubleshooting Formulas   Part 2 of 3

1. Open **PreSalesTrgt.xlsx**.
2. Save the workbook with the name **5-PreSalesTrgt**.
3. Solve the #N/A error by completing the following steps:
   a. Make cell E4 active.
   b. Point to the Trace Error button next to the cell and read the ScreenTip that displays below the button.
   c. Look in the Formula bar at the formula that has been entered into the cell. Notice that the formula includes a reference to a named cell. Tracer arrows will be used in the next step to locate the source of the named cell.

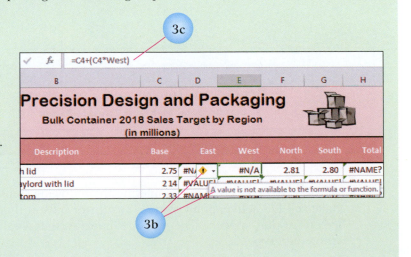

d. Click the Error Checking button arrow in the Formula Auditing group on the Formulas tab and then click *Trace Error* at the drop-down list.

e. Excel moves the active cell to K5 and draws a red tracer arrow from cell K5 to cell E4. Look in the Formula bar and notice that *#N/A* displays as the entry in cell K5. Also notice that the cell name *West* is displayed in the Name box. Since there is no value in the cell named *West*, which is cell K5, the dependent cell E4 was not able to calculate its formula.

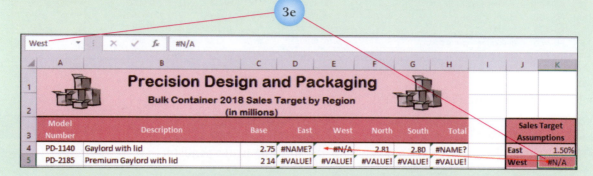

f. With cell K5 active, type 1.25% and then press the Enter key. The red tracer arrow changes to blue because the error is corrected and the #N/A error messages no longer display.

g. Click the Remove Arrows button to clear the blue tracer arrow and then right-align the entry in cell K5.

4. Solve the #NAME? error by completing the following steps:

a. Make cell D4 active, point to the Trace Error button that appears, and then read the ScreenTip that appears. The message indicates that the formula contains unrecognized text.

b. Look at the entry in the Formula bar: *=C4+(C4*East)*. Notice that the formula is the same as the one reviewed in Step 3c except that the named range is *East* instead of *West*. The formula appears to be valid.

c. Click the Name box arrow and view the range names in the drop-down list. Notice that the range name *East* is not in the list.

d. Click *North* at the Name box drop-down list. Cell K6 becomes the active cell. You know from this step and Step 3d that the named ranges should reference the percentage values within column K.

e. Make cell K4 active, type East in the Name box, and then press the Enter key. The #NAME? error is resolved.

5. Solve the #VALUE! error by completing the following steps:

a. Make cell D5 active, point to the Trace Error button that appears, and then read the ScreenTip that appears. The message indicates that a value within the formula is of the wrong data type.

b. Click the Trace Precedents button in the Formula Auditing group on the Formulas tab to display tracer arrows that show the source cells that provide data to cell D5. Two blue arrows appear, indicating that two cells provide the source values: cells K4 and C5.

c. Make cell K4 active and look at the entry in the Formula bar: *1.5%*. This value is valid.

d. Make cell C5 active and look at the entry in the Formula bar: *2 14*. Notice that there is a space instead of a decimal point between *2* and *1*.

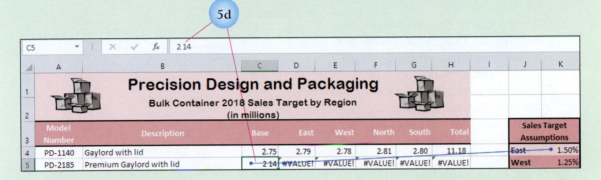

e. Click in the Formula bar and then edit the formula to delete the space between *2* and *1* and type a period (inserting a decimal point). Press the Enter key. The #VALUE! error is resolved.

f. Click the Remove Arrows button to clear the blue tracer arrows.

6. Save **5-PreSalesTrgt.xlsx**.

Check Your Work

Tutorial

Circling Invalid Data and Watching a Formula Cell

Circling Invalid Data

Recall from Chapter 3 that the data validation feature is used to restrict cell entries. If data validation rules are set up after data has been entered, existing values will not be tested against the new rules. In this situation, use the Circle Invalid Data feature, which draws red circles around the cells that do not conform to the new rule.

Watching a Formula Cell

 Watch Window

 Data Validation

In a large worksheet, a dependent cell may not always be visible while changes are being made to other cells that affect a formula. Open a Watch Window and add a dependent cell to it to view changes made to the cell as the worksheet is modified. Multiple cells can be added to the Watch Window to create a single window where cells affected by key formulas within a large worksheet can be tracked.

Consider assigning a name to a cell to be tracked using the Watch Window. At the Watch Window, the cell name will appear in the *Name* column and provide a descriptive reference to the entry being watched. Expand the width of the *Name* column if a range name is not entirely visible.

The Watch Window can be docked at the top, left, bottom, or right edge of the worksheet area by clicking the top edge of the window and dragging it to the edge of the screen. When the Watch Window is docked, Excel changes it to a Watch Window task pane.

Quick Steps

Circle Invalid Data
1. Open worksheet containing validation rules.
2. Click Data tab.
3. Click Data Validation button arrow.
4. Click *Circle Invalid Data*.

Watch a Formula Cell
1. Click Formulas tab.
2. Click Watch Window button.
3. Click Add Watch button.
4. Click in cell.
5. Click Add button.

1. With **5-PreSalesTrgt.xlsx** open, view the data validation rule in effect for column C by completing the following steps:

    a. If necessary, make active any cell containing a value in column C.

    b. Click the Data tab.

    c. Click the top of the Data Validation button in the Data Tools group. (Do not click the arrow on the button.) The Data Validation dialog box opens.

    d. Review the parameters for data entry in the Settings tab. Notice that the restriction is that values should be greater than or equal to 1.57.

    e. Click OK.

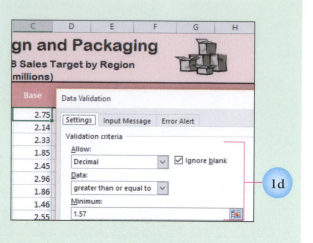

2. Click the Data Validation button arrow and then click *Circle Invalid Data* at the drop-down list. Three cells are circled in the worksheet: C11, C13, and C16.

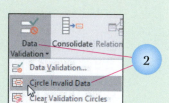

3. Watch the total in cell H22 update as the invalid data is corrected by completing the following steps:

    a. Make cell H22 active and then click the Formulas tab.

    b. Click the Watch Window button in the Formula Auditing group. A Watch Window opens.

    c. Click the Add Watch button in the Watch Window.

    d. At the Add Watch dialog box, move the dialog box out of the way if necessary to view cell H22. Notice that cell H22 is entered by default as the watch cell. Click the Add button.

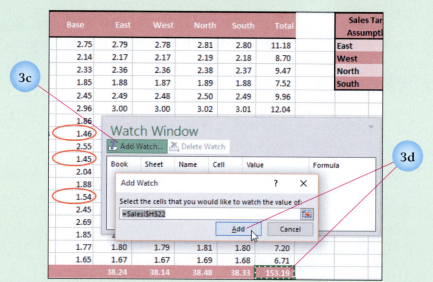

    e. Scroll up the worksheet if necessary until you can view cell C11. If necessary, drag the Watch Window to an out-of-the-way location in the worksheet.

    f. Make cell C11 active, type 1.58, and then press the Enter key. Notice that the red circle disappears because a value has been entered that conforms to the validation rule. Look at the value for cell H22 in the Watch Window. The new value is *153.67*.

g. Make cell C13 the active cell, type 1.61, and then press the Enter key. Look at the updated value for cell H22 in the Watch Window.

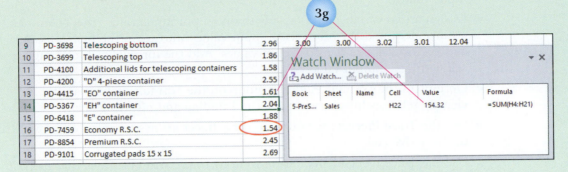

h. Make cell C16 active, type 1.57, and then press the Enter key.
i. Click the Watch Window button in the Formula Auditing group on the Formulas tab to close the Watch Window.
4. Print the worksheet.
5. Save and then close **5-PreSalesTrgt.xlsx**.

Check Your Work

Checking a worksheet for accuracy using auditing and error checking tools is an important skill to develop. Worksheets provide critical information to decision makers who rely on the validity of the data. After completing a worksheet, examine it carefully, to look for data entry mistakes, values that do not appear realistic, and other indications of potential errors that should be fixed.

Chapter Summary

- Open the Paste Special dialog box to paste attributes of the source cell(s) or perform a mathematical operation during the paste.
- Transposing data during a paste routine means that data arranged in columns is converted to rows and data arranged in rows is converted to columns.
- Click the Paste button arrow and then click *Paste Special* to access a gallery of pasting options.
- The Goal Seek feature returns a value in a cell based on a target value specified for another cell. The two cells must have a dependent relationship for Excel to calculate a value.
- Click the What-If Analysis button in the Forecast group on the Data tab to locate the Goal Seek, Scenario Manager, or Data Table command.
- Scenario Manager allows saving multiple sets of values for key cells in a worksheet. Switch between scenarios to view the effects of changing the input cells on one of the saved data sets for the worksheet.
- A scenario summary report presents the input data for each key cell in a scenario in tabular format; a results cell below each data set displays the value if the data set is applied.
- A data table is a range of cells that contains a series of input values; a calculated formula result is placed adjacent to each input value.
- A one-variable data table modifies one input value within a formula.

- A two-variable data table modifies two input values within a formula.

- Design a one-variable data table with the input values in a columnar arrangement and the formula cell one row above and one column right of the input values.

- Design a two-variable data table with one set of input values in a columnar arrangement and the other set of input values starting in the first column right and first row above the first set of values. Add the formula cell to the top left cell within the input table.

- Options in the Formula Auditing group on the Formulas tab are useful for viewing relationships between cells and finding and resolving errors.

- Use the Trace Precedents button to draw tracer arrows to cells that provide data to the active cell.

- Use the Trace Dependents button to draw tracer arrows to cells that use data from the active cell.

- Click the Trace Precedents or Trace Dependents button a second time to display an indirect set of relationship arrows at the next level.

- A logic error occurs when the formula is not correct for the data or situation.

- A reference error occurs when a formula points to the wrong data cell.

- Use proof formulas to test the accuracy of key figures in a worksheet. Proof formulas are entered outside the main worksheet area and double-checks key figures within the worksheet.

- Excel displays two types of error messages in a cell in which an error has been detected.

- A green diagonal triangle in the upper left corner of the cell indicates an error condition. Click the active cell and use the Trace Error button to access error checking options.

- Errors can also be indicated with text entries. For example, *#NAME?* means that the formula contains text that Excel cannot recognize.

- Other error codes include *#VALUE!*, which means a value within the formula is not valid, and *#N/A*, which means a value needed by the formula is not available.

- When a worksheet has data validation rules in force, data that existed before the rule was created is not tested. Use the Circle Invalid Data feature from the Data Validation button to place red circles around the cells that do not conform to the new rule.

- Open a Watch Window and add a dependent cell to it to view changes made to the cell as the worksheet is modified.

- After completing a worksheet, take time to examine the data carefully for entry errors and logic errors that can affect the results.

Commands Review

FEATURE	RIBBON TAB, GROUP	BUTTON
circle invalid data	Data, Data Tools	
data table	Data, Forecast	
Goal Seek dialog box	Data, Forecast	
Paste Special dialog box	Home, Clipboard	
remove tracer arrow	Formulas, Formula Auditing	
Scenario Manager	Data, Forecast	
trace dependent cell	Formulas, Formula Auditing	
trace error	Formulas, Formula Auditing	
trace precedent cell	Formulas, Formula Auditing	
transpose	Home, Clipboard	
Watch Window	Formulas, Formula Auditing	

Workbook

Chapter study tools and assessment activities are available in the *Workbook* ebook. These resources are designed to help you further develop and demonstrate mastery of the skills learned in this chapter.

Microsoft®

Excel

Protecting and Sharing Workbooks

CHAPTER 6

Performance Objectives

Precheck

Check your current skills to help focus your study.

Upon successful completion of Chapter 6, you will be able to:

1 Add information to a workbook's properties

2 Add comments to provide information to readers and collaborators

3 Share a workbook with other people and view other users who have the shared workbook open at the same time

4 Edit a shared workbook and resolve conflicts with changes

5 Print a history of changes made to a shared workbook

6 Stop sharing a workbook

7 Save and share a workbook using OneDrive and email

8 Protect cells within a worksheet to prevent changes

9 Protect and unprotect the structure of workbook

10 Require a password to open a workbook

11 Track changes made by individuals who share a workbook

12 Review and accept or reject tracked changes

In today's electronic business environment, collaborating with other people on an Excel workbook is becoming commonplace. Excel provides several features and tools that are useful for working in a collaborative environment. Adding information to a workbook's properties provides other users with descriptive information about the nature and purpose of the workbook. Attaching a comment to a cell allows adding questions or explanatory information when collaborating with others. Sharing a workbook, locking and unlocking worksheets and ranges, and tracking changes are all vital features for managing data that will be accessed by multiple individuals. By completing the projects in this chapter, you will learn how to use the collaborative tools in Excel.

SNAP

If you are a SNAP user, launch the Precheck and Tutorials from your Assignments page.

Data Files

Before beginning chapter work, copy the EL2C6 folder to your storage medium and then make EL2C6 the active folder.

Project 1   Add Workbook Properties and Insert Comments in a Car Rental Rates Workbook   2 Parts

You will add the author's name and other descriptive information in a workbook's properties and insert comments with explanatory information.

Preview Finished Project

Tutorial

Adding Workbook
Properties

Adding Workbook Properties

Workbook properties include information about the workbook, such as the author's name, the title, the subject, the category to which the workbook is related (such as finance), and general comments about the workbook. This information is added to the file at the Info backstage area, shown in Figure 6.1. The document information panel found in previous versions of Excel no longer exists in Excel 2016.

Some information is automatically added to a workbook's properties by Excel. For example, Excel maintains statistics such as the date the workbook was created, the date the workbook was last modified, and the name of the last person to save the workbook. Workbook properties are sometimes referred to as *metadata*—a term used to identify descriptive information about data.

To add an author's name or other descriptive information about a workbook, click the File tab. Excel displays the Info backstage area with the workbook's properties displayed at the right side of the screen. By default, when a new workbook is created, Excel inserts in the *Author* property box the name of the computer user (as defined when Microsoft Office is installed). To add another author or make a change to a workbook property (such as the title), click the mouse to open the text box next to the property's name. For example, click *Add a title* next to the Title property name. Type the appropriate title in the text box. Click outside the text box to end the entry. Properties that do not display with the message *Add a [property]* cannot be edited. Click the Show All Properties hyperlink at the bottom of the right section in the Info backstage area to add more properties.

Quick Steps

Add Information to Properties
1. Click File tab.
2. Click *Add a [property]* next to property name.
3. Type text.
4. Click outside property box.

Figure 6.1 Properties in the Info Backstage Area

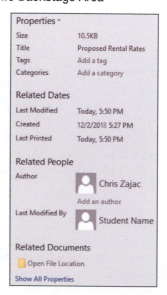

142   Excel Level 2 | Unit 2

Quick Steps

Add Advanced Properties
1. Click File tab.
2. Click Properties button.
3. Click *Advanced Properties.*
4. Add or edit properties as required.
5. Click OK.

To display the advanced properties shown in Figure 6.2, click the Properties button at the top of the right section in the Info backstage area and then click *Advanced Properties* at the drop-down list. Add other properties including, but not limited to, information regarding the date completed, the editor, and who checked the document.

Chapter 8 will discuss how to strip the metadata (including personal information) from a file if the information is not to be included when distributing a workbook outside your organization. However, having personal information available can be useful when browsing a list of files. The words *Authors*, *Size*, and *Date Modified* appear in a ScreenTip when the mouse pointer hovers over a workbook name in the Open dialog box. This information helps users to select the correct file.

Figure 6.2 Advanced Properties

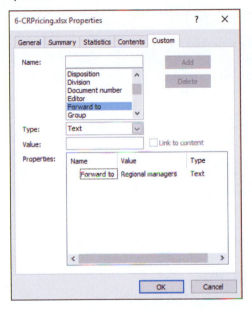

Project 1a Adding Workbook Properties

Part 1 of 2

1. Open **CRPricing.xlsx**.
2. Save the workbook with the name **6-CRPricing**.
3. Add an additional author's name, as well as a title, subject, and comments associated with the workbook, by completing the following steps:
   a. Click the File tab.
   b. At the Info backstage area, open an *Author* text box by clicking the *Add an author* text box below the current author's name in the *Related People* section.
   c. Type Chris Zajac. If the message *We couldn't find the person you were looking for* displays, ignore it.
   d. Click outside the *Author* text box to close it.
   e. Click *Add a title* in the *Title* text box, type Proposed Rental Rates, and then click outside the text box.

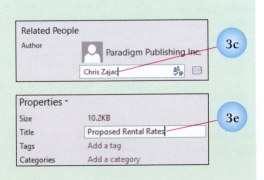

f. Click the <u>Show All Properties</u> hyperlink below the *Related Documents* section to display additional properties.

g. Click *Specify the subject* in the *Subject* text box, type Rental Rates for May 2018, and then click outside the text box.

h. Click *Add comments* in the *Comments* text box, type Proposed rental rates sent for review to regional managers., and then click outside the text box.

4. Right-click *Paradigm Publishing Inc.* next to the *Author* text box and then click *Remove Person* at the shortcut menu.

5. Click the <u>Show Fewer Properties</u> hyperlink at the bottom of the properties.

6. Compare your properties with those shown in Figure 6.1. Some of the dates may vary.

7. Add advanced properties by completing the following steps:

a. Click the Properties button above the workbook properties and then click *Advanced Properties* at the drop-down list.

b. Click the Custom tab.

c. Using the *Name* option box scroll bar, scroll down until *Forward to* appears in the list and then click this option.

d. Click in the *Value* text box, type Regional managers, and then click Add.

8. Compare your properties with those shown in Figure 6.2 and then click OK.

9. Save **6-CRPricing.xlsx**.

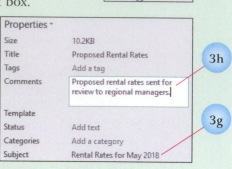
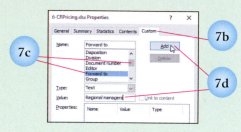
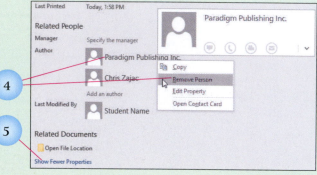

Tutorial

Inserting, Editing, and Printing Comments

Quick Steps

Insert a Comment
1. Make cell active.
2. Click Review tab.
3. Click New Comment button.
4. Type comment text.
5. Click in worksheet area outside comment box.

New Comment

Managing Comments

In Excel, a *comment* is a pop-up box containing text that displays when the mouse pointer hovers over the cell to which the comment is attached. Use comments to provide instructions, identify critical information, and add other explanatory information about a cell entry. Comments are also useful when collaborating with others to create or edit a worksheet. All the reviewers can use comments to add feedback and pose questions about cell entries and layout.

Inserting Comments

Insert a comment in an active cell by clicking the Review tab and then clicking the New Comment button in the Comments group. This displays a shaded box with the user's name inside. Type the comment text and then click in the worksheet area outside the comment box. Comments can also be inserted by right-clicking in a cell and then clicking *Insert Comment* at the shortcut menu.

Viewing Comments

A small, red, diagonal triangle appears in the upper right corner of a cell to alert the user that a comment exists. Hover the mouse pointer over a cell containing a comment and the comment box displays. Turn on the display of all comments by clicking the Show All Comments button in the Comments group on the Review tab. Navigate to cells containing comments by clicking the Next button or the Previous button in the Comments group on the Review tab.

Printing Comments

💡Hint Consider using the Next button to view the comments in a large worksheet to ensure you do not miss any cells with comments.

By default, comments do not print. If comments are to be printed with the worksheet, click the Page Layout tab, click the Page Setup group dialog box launcher, and then click the Sheet tab at the Page Setup dialog box. Click the *Comments* option box arrow and then click *At end of sheet* to print the comments on a separate page after the cell contents or *As displayed on sheet* to print the comments as they appear within the worksheet area.

Editing and Deleting Comments

To edit a comment, click in the cell containing the comment and then click the Edit Comment button in the Comments group on the Review tab. (The New Comment button changes to the Edit Comment button when the active cell contains a comment.) Edit a comment by right-clicking in the cell that contains it and then clicking *Edit Comment* at the shortcut menu. Insert or delete text as needed and then click in the worksheet area outside the comment box.

To delete a comment, click in the cell that contains the comment and then click the Delete button in the Comments group. A comment can also be deleted by right-clicking in the cell and then clicking *Delete Comment* at the shortcut menu.

⏱️Quick Steps

Copy and Paste Comments
1. Select source cell containing comment.
2. Click Copy button.
3. Click destination cell(s).
4. Click Paste button arrow.
5. Click *Paste Special.*
6. Click *Comments.*
7. Click OK.

Copying and Pasting Comments

A comment that has been added to a cell can be copied and pasted to one or more cells. After copying the source cell, click in the destination cell and then open the Paste Special dialog box. Click *Comments* in the *Paste* section and then click OK.

Project 1b   Inserting, Editing, Pasting, Viewing, and Deleting Comments   **Part 2 of 2**

1. With **6-CRPricing.xlsx** open, insert comments by completing the following steps:
   a. Make cell C10 active.
   b. Click the Review tab and then click the New Comment button in the Comments group. A tan shaded box with a green arrow pointing to cell C10 appears. The current user name (followed by a colon) is inserted in bold text at the top of the comment box. The insertion point is positioned at the left edge of the box on the second line.
   c. Type Most competitors charge 175.00 for weekend rentals of luxury vehicles.
   d. Click in the worksheet area outside the comment box. A small, red, diagonal triangle appears in the upper right corner of cell C10, indicating that a comment exists for the cell.

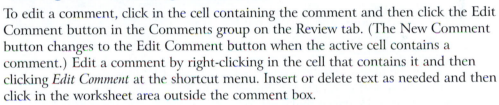
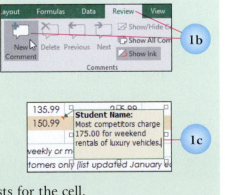

---

e. Right-click in cell F8 and then click *Insert Comment* at the shortcut menu.

f. Type Consider reducing the discount for minivans to 18%. and then click in the worksheet area outside the comment box.

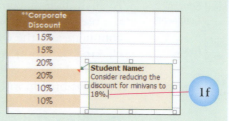

g. Right-click in cell F9, click *Insert Comment* at the shortcut menu, type Last year this discount was 12%., and then click in the worksheet area outside the comment box.

h. Right-click in cell F9, click *Copy* at the shortcut menu, right-click in cell F10, point to *Paste Special*, and then click *Paste Special* at the shortcut menu.

i. At the Paste Special dialog box, click the *Comments* option in the *Paste* section and then click OK.

j. Press the Esc key to remove the scrolling marquee from cell F9.

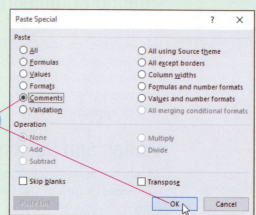

2. View comments by completing the following steps:

a. Hover the mouse pointer over cell C10. The comment box pops up and displays the comment text.

b. Hover the mouse pointer over cells F8, F9, and F10 (one after the other) to review the comments in these cells.

c. Press Ctrl + Home to make cell A1 active.

d. Click the Next button in the Comments group on the Review tab. Excel displays the comment box in cell F8.

e. Click the Next button to display the comment box in cell F9.

f. Click the Next button to display the comment box in cell C10.

g. Click the Next button to display the comment box in cell F10.

h. Click the Show All Comments button in the Comments group on the Review tab. All the comment boxes display in the worksheet area.

Clicking the Show All Comments button in Step 2h displays all the comments in the worksheet.

i. Click the Show All Comments button again to turn off the display of all the comments.

3. Edit and delete a comment by completing the following steps:

a. Right-click cell in C10 and then click *Edit Comment* at the shortcut menu. The comment box pops up with the insertion point positioned at the end of the existing comment text.

b. Change *175.00* to *185.99* by moving the insertion point and then typing and deleting text as required.

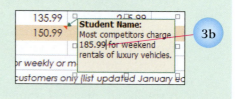

c. Click in the worksheet area outside the comment box.

d. Make cell F10 the active cell and then click the Edit Comment button in the Comments group on the Review tab.

e. Change *12%* to *15%* and then click in the worksheet area outside the comment box.

f. Right-click in cell F8 and then click *Delete Comment* at the shortcut menu.

g. Click in cell F9 and then click the Delete button in the Comments group on the Review tab.

4. Print the comments at the end of the worksheet by completing the following steps:

a. Click the File tab and then click the *Print* option.

b. At the Print backstage area, click the <u>Page Setup</u> hyperlink at the bottom of the *Settings* section.

c. At the Page Setup dialog box, click the Sheet tab.

d. Click the *Comments* option box arrow in the *Print* section and then click *At end of sheet* to print the comments on a separate sheet at the end of the document.

e. Click OK.

5. Print only the comments by printing only page 2.

6. Save and close **6-CRPricing.xlsx**.

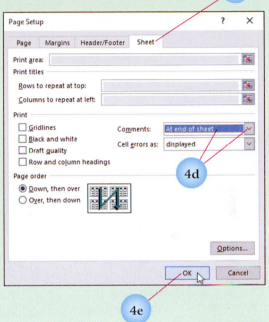

Check Your Work

Project 2 **Sharing a Proposed Rental Increase Workbook**   **7 Parts**

You will share the workbook with other users for editing and viewing.

Preview Finished Project

Tutorial

Sharing a Workbook

Sharing and Unsharing a Workbook

A workbook may need to be circulated among several people so they can review, add, delete, or edit data. Excel provides a number of options for collaborating in these ways. One method is to share a workbook. A shared workbook can be saved to a network folder that is accessible by the other individuals who need the file. Excel tracks each person's changes and displays a prompt if two people have the file open at the same time and attempt to make changes to the same data.

 Share Workbook

To share a workbook, click the Review tab and then click the Share Workbook button in the Changes group. At the Share Workbook dialog box with the Editing tab selected, as shown in Figure 6.3, click the *Allow changes by more than one user at the same time* check box.

Figure 6.3 Share Workbook Dialog Box with Editing Tab Selected

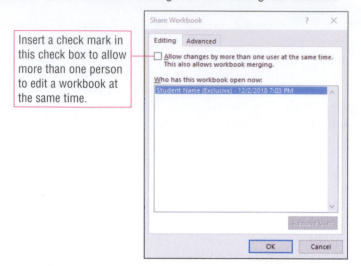

Insert a check mark in this check box to allow more than one person to edit a workbook at the same time.

Quick Steps

Share a Workbook
1. Open workbook.
2. Click Review tab.
3. Click Share Workbook button.
4. Click *Allow changes by more than one user at the same time* check box.
5. Click OK to close Share Workbook dialog box.
6. Click OK to continue.

💡 **Hint** To instruct Excel not to display the Resolve Conflicts dialog box, open the Share Workbook dialog box, click the Advanced tab, and then select *The changes being saved win* in the *Conflicting changes between users* section.

Click the Advanced tab in the Share Workbook dialog box to display settings for sharing the workbook, as shown in Figure 6.4. A shared workbook should be saved to a network folder that is designated as a shared folder and is accessible to the other users. The network administrator is usually the person who creates a folder on a server designated with the read/write access rights for multiple accounts (referred to as a *network share*); the administrator can assist with navigating to and saving to a network share. All the individuals with access to the shared network folder will have full access to the shared workbook.

One drawback of using a shared workbook is that it cannot support all of Excel's features. To use a feature that is unavailable or to make a change to a feature that is not allowed, the shared access needs to be removed. Project 3 demonstrates how to protect a worksheet by locking and unlocking it and the cells within it for editing before sharing the workbook. Protecting a worksheet can prevent cells from accidentally being deleted or modified.

Figure 6.4 Share Workbook Dialog Box with Advanced Tab Selected

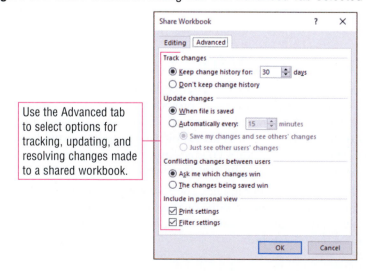

Use the Advanced tab to select options for tracking, updating, and resolving changes made to a shared workbook.

1. Open **6-CRPricing.xlsx** and save it with the name **6-CRPricingShared**.
2. Assume that you are Chris Zajac, regional manager of CutRate Car Rentals. You want to get feedback from another manager on the proposed rental rates. Share the workbook so that the other manager can make changes directly to the file by completing the following steps:
   a. If necessary, click the Review tab.
   b. Click the Share Workbook button in the Changes group.
   c. At the Share Workbook dialog box with the Editing tab selected, click the *Allow changes by more than one user at the same time* check box to insert a check mark.
   d. Click OK.
   e. At the Microsoft Excel message box stating that the workbook will now be saved and asking if you want to continue, click OK.
3. Notice that Excel adds *[Shared]* in the Title bar next to the workbook file name to indicate the workbook's status.
4. Close **6-CRPricingShared.xlsx**.

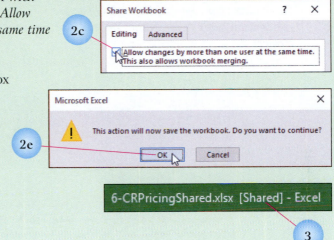

Changing the User Name and Viewing Users

When a workbook is shared, Excel tracks the names of the users that edit it. User name information is entered when Microsoft Office is installed. Change the user name associated with Excel by opening the Excel Options dialog box, selecting the existing text in the *User name* text box, typing the new user name, and then clicking OK. To view other users of a shared workbook, click the Review tab and then click the Share Workbook button. All reviewers will be listed in the *Who has this workbook open now* list box.

Opening Multiple Instances of Excel

When multiple workbooks are opened in Excel 2016, they are opened within the same instance of the program. Excel does not open a new copy of the program every time a new workbook is opened. Although working within the same instance of the program saves the computer's resources, at times multiple instances may need to be opened. To do this, press and hold down the Alt key and then right-click the Excel icon in the taskbar. Continue to hold down the Alt key as you left-click *Excel 2016* at the shortcut menu. Release the Alt key and then click Yes to answer the question *Do you want to start a new instance of Excel?*

Project 2b Changing the User Name and Editing a Shared Workbook

1. At a blank Excel screen, change the user name on the computer to simulate an environment in which another manager is opening the shared workbook from a network share location by completing the following steps:
   a. Click the File tab.
   b. Click *Options*.
   c. At the Excel Options dialog box with *General* selected in the left pane, make a note of the existing entry in the *User name* text box in the *Personalize your copy of Microsoft Office* section, if the entry is a name other than your own. **Note: You will restore the original user name in Project 4c.**
   d. Select the current entry in the *User name* text box and then type Aaron Rubin.
   e. Click OK.

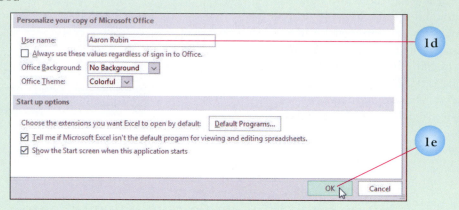

2. Open **6-CRPricingShared.xlsx**.
3. Make the following changes to the proposed rental rates:
   a. Make cell F5 active and then change the entry from *15%* to *12%*.
   b. Make cell B10 active and then change the entry from *85.99* to *95.99*.
   c. Make cell D10 active and then change the entry from *299.99* to *325.99*.
4. Save **6-CRPricingShared.xlsx**.

Check Your Work

Project 2c Viewing Other Users of a Shared Workbook

1. Open a new instance of Excel by completing the following steps:
   a. Press and hold down the Alt key and then right-click the Excel icon on the taskbar.
   b. Continue to hold down the Alt key as you left-click *Excel 2016* at the shortcut menu.
   c. Release the Alt key and then click Yes to answer the question *Do you want to start a new instance of Excel?* **Note: You are opening another copy of Excel to simulate an environment in which multiple copies of the shared workbook are open. You will also change the user name to continue the simulation using a different identity.**

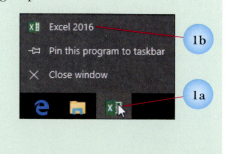

2. Click the <u>Open Other Workbooks</u> hyperlink at the bottom of the *Recent* section.
3. Click *Options* to open the Excel Options dialog box and then change the user name in the new copy of Excel to *Chris Zajac*. (Refer to Steps 1a–1d of Project 2b for assistance with this step.)
4. In the new copy of Excel, open **6-CRPricingShared.xlsx**.
5. View the names of the other users sharing the workbook by completing the following steps:
    a. Click the Review tab.
    b. Click the Share Workbook button in the Changes group.
    c. At the Share Workbook dialog box with the Editing tab selected, look at the names in the *Who has this workbook open now* list box.
    d. Click OK.
6. Leave both copies of Excel open for the next project.

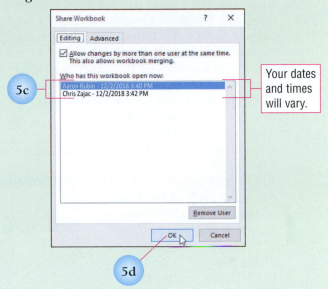

Resolving Conflicts in a Shared Workbook

Tutorial

Resolving Conflicts in a Shared Workbook

Quick Steps

Resolving Conflicts in a Shared Workbook
1. Open shared workbook.
2. Make edits.
3. Click Save button.
4. Click Accept Mine or Accept Other button at each conflict.
5. Click OK.

When two users have copies of a shared workbook open and each user makes a change to the same cell, Excel prompts the second user to resolve the conflict by displaying the Resolve Conflicts dialog box, shown in Figure 6.5, when the second user saves the workbook. The cell address, original entry, and revised entry are shown for each user. By clicking the Accept Mine button, the second user saves his or her change. By clicking the Accept Other button, the second user removes his or her change and restores the cell to the entry made by the other user. To avoid being prompted at each individual cell that has a conflict, click the Accept All Mine button or the Accept All Others button.

Figure 6.5 Resolve Conflicts Dialog Box

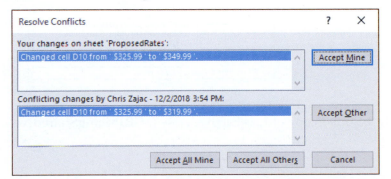

1. With **6-CRPricingShared.xlsx** open, assume that you are Chris Zajac and that you want to make a change to a proposed rental rate that will conflict with a change made by Aaron Rubin. Complete the following steps:
   a. Make sure the second copy of Excel you opened for Project 2c (in which you viewed the users with the shared workbook open) is active.
   b. Make cell D10 the active cell and then change *325.99* to *319.99*.
   c. Save **6-CRPricingShared.xlsx**.
2. Aaron Rubin has decided to change the weekly luxury rate again. Switch to the other copy of Excel to edit the worksheet and resolve the conflict by completing the following steps:
   a. Click the Excel icon on the taskbar and then click the other copy of the shared workbook to make it active.
   b. Make cell D10 active and change the entry to *349.99*.
   c. Click the Save button. Since this change conflicts with the change made by Chris Zajac in Step 1b, Excel prompts the second user (Aaron Rubin) with the Resolve Conflicts dialog box.
   d. Click the Accept Other button to restore the cell to the value entered by Chris Zajac.

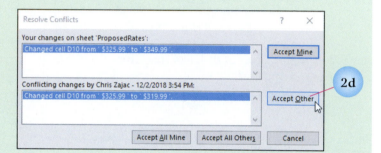

   e. At the Microsoft Excel message box stating that the workbook has been updated with changes saved by other users, click OK.

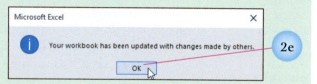

3. Notice that cell D10 is displayed with a colored border, indicating that a change has been made. Hover the mouse pointer over cell D10 to view the pop-up box with the name, date, and time the cell change was saved, along with the original and revised entries.

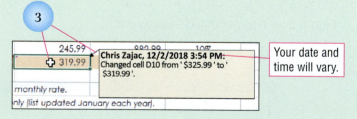

Your date and time will vary.

4. Exit the active copy of Excel.
5. With the other copy of Excel active, close **6-CRPricingShared.xlsx**.

Check Your Work

Printing a History Sheet and Removing Shared Workbook Access

Before changing the status of a shared workbook to an exclusive workbook, consider printing the change history so there is a record of the edits made by all the users who worked on the file. To do this, click the Review tab, click the Track Changes button, and then click *Highlight Changes* at the drop-down list. At the Highlight Changes dialog box, shown in Figure 6.6, change the *When* option to *All*, remove the check marks from the *Who* and *Where* check boxes, click the *List changes on a new sheet* check box to insert a check mark, and then click OK.

By default when track changes is active, Excel displays a colored border around each changed cell. When the mouse pointer rests over a cell with a colored border, Excel displays the cell's change history in a pop-up box. Remove the check mark from the *Highlight changes on screen* check box to not highlight changed cells in the worksheet. Print the history sheet before saving the document because this sheet is not saved with the workbook.

To stop sharing a workbook, open the workbook, click the Review tab, and then click the Share Workbook button. At the Share Workbook dialog box with the Editing tab selected, remove the check mark from the *Allow changes by more than one user at the same time* check box and then click OK. Excel displays a message with the information that changing the workbook to exclusive status will erase all the change history in the workbook and prevent users who might have the workbook open from saving their changes. Consider copying and pasting the cells in the history sheet to a new workbook and saving the history as a separate file because the history sheet will not be saved with the workbook.

Track Changes

Quick Steps

Print a History Sheet
1. Open shared workbook.
2. Click Review tab.
3. Click Track Changes button.
4. Click *Highlight Changes*.
5. Change *When* to *All*.
6. If necessary, clear *Who* check box.
7. If necessary, remove check mark from *Where* check box.
8. Click *List changes on a new sheet* check box.
9. Click OK.
10. Print history sheet.

Stop Sharing a Workbook
1. Open shared workbook.
2. Click Review tab.
3. Click Share Workbook button.
4. Remove check mark from *Allow changes by more than one user at the same time* check box.
5. Click OK.
6. Click Yes.

Hint Before changing the status of a workbook from shared to exclusive, make sure no one else is currently editing the workbook. Once shared access is removed, users that have the file open will not be able to save their changes.

Figure 6.6 Highlight Changes Dialog Box

Change this option to *All* to include in the history sheet changes made by all the users who accessed the shared workbook.

This option is selected by default, causing a colored border to display around each changed cell. Resting the mouse pointer over a highlighted cell causes a pop-up box to display with the change history.

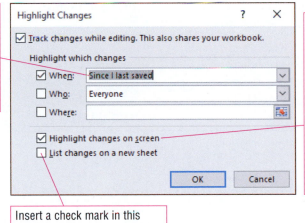

Insert a check mark in this check box to create a sheet named *History* in the workbook that includes a list of changes made by each user.

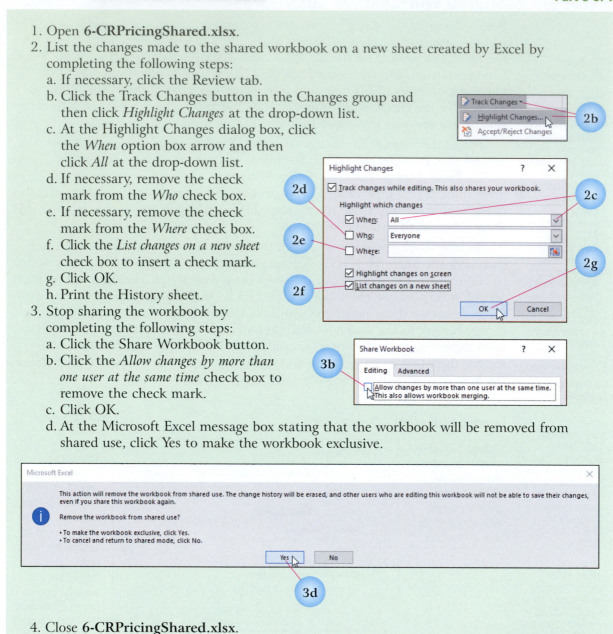

1. Open **6-CRPricingShared.xlsx**.
2. List the changes made to the shared workbook on a new sheet created by Excel by completing the following steps:
   a. If necessary, click the Review tab.
   b. Click the Track Changes button in the Changes group and then click *Highlight Changes* at the drop-down list.
   c. At the Highlight Changes dialog box, click the *When* option box arrow and then click *All* at the drop-down list.
   d. If necessary, remove the check mark from the *Who* check box.
   e. If necessary, remove the check mark from the *Where* check box.
   f. Click the *List changes on a new sheet* check box to insert a check mark.
   g. Click OK.
   h. Print the History sheet.
3. Stop sharing the workbook by completing the following steps:
   a. Click the Share Workbook button.
   b. Click the *Allow changes by more than one user at the same time* check box to remove the check mark.
   c. Click OK.
   d. At the Microsoft Excel message box stating that the workbook will be removed from shared use, click Yes to make the workbook exclusive.

4. Close **6-CRPricingShared.xlsx**.

Check Your Work

Tutorial

Sharing a
Workbook on
OneDrive

Sharing a Workbook on OneDrive

Another way to share a workbook is by using OneDrive. This Microsoft feature allows saving and sharing documents in a storage location on the Internet. Save a workbook to OneDrive and then access the file from any other location that has Internet access. Windows 10 automatically connects to your OneDrive account when you sign in and will sync the contents of your OneDrive with a folder on your computer. Instructions for saving a document to OneDrive are provided on the next page; however, OneDrive is constantly changing, so the steps may vary.

Quick Steps

Save a Workbook to OneDrive

1. Open workbook.
2. Click Share button.
3. Click Save to Cloud button.
4. Click OneDrive, if necessary.
5. Click OneDrive.
6. If necessary, select desired folder name.
7. Click Save button.

Hint If you have access to Microsoft SharePoint, a server application that allows you to share and collaborate on documents, you can save your workbook to a SharePoint library for others to view and/or edit.

After the workbook is saved to OneDrive, invite people to share it using the Share panel at the right side of the screen. When multiple people edit the workbook on OneDrive, multiple versions of the same file do not need to be managed. Users that are signed in to their Microsoft accounts may access the Excel Online application to edit a workbook shared with OneDrive. Note that not all of Excel's features are available with the online application.

Saving a workbook to OneDrive requires having a Microsoft or Hotmail account. If you do not already have a user name and password, sign up for a free account at login.live.com by clicking the Sign up now button.

To save a workbook to OneDrive, click the *Share* button in the upper right corner of the workbook then click the Save to Cloud button in the Share panel. The Save As backstage area displays. At the Save As backstage area with *OneDrive - Personal* selected in the *Places* section, click the *OneDrive - Personal* folder in the *Folders* section. At the Save As dialog box, choose the destination folder within OneDrive, type the file name, and then click Save. After a file is saved to OneDrive, a Share panel appears.

In the *Invite People* section, shown in Figure 6.7, type the names or email addresses of the people that are to view and/or edit the workbook or click the Address Book icon right of the *Type names or e-mail addresses* text box and choose people from your contacts. The option box right of the Address Book icon offers

Figure 6.7 Share Panel

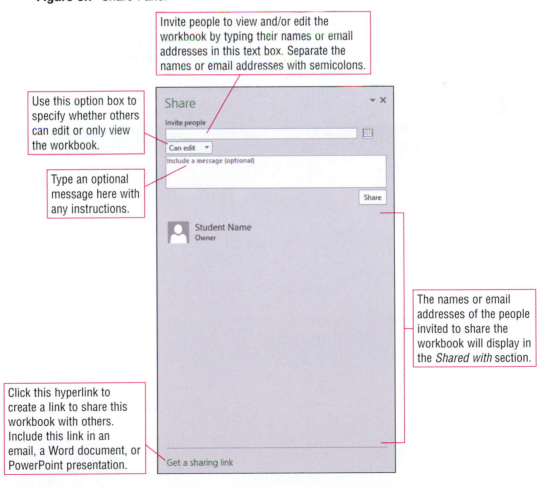

Invite people to view and/or edit the workbook by typing their names or email addresses in this text box. Separate the names or email addresses with semicolons.

Use this option box to specify whether others can edit or only view the workbook.

Type an optional message here with any instructions.

The names or email addresses of the people invited to share the workbook will display in the *Shared with* section.

Click this hyperlink to create a link to share this workbook with others. Include this link in an email, a Word document, or PowerPoint presentation.

the options *Can edit* and *Can view*. If people are allowed to view the workbook but are not allowed to make changes to it, make sure that this option is changed from the default *Can edit* to *Can view*. Separate invitations must be sent if certain people are invited to edit and others only to view. After typing a personal message, click the Share button. Emails are sent to the people that have been invited and their names or email addresses appear in the *Shared with* section.

A workbook can also be emailed to others at the Share backstage area. To do this, obtain a sharing link at the bottom of the Share panel or at the Share backstage area. Place the sharing link in a Word document or PowerPoint presentation and use it as a hyperlink to the workbook saved on OneDrive.

To stop sharing a workbook with someone, right-click the person's name in the *Shared with* section and then click *Remove User* at the shortcut menu. To remove the sharing link, click the Disable Link button at the Share backstage area.

Quick Steps

Share a Workbook
Saved on OneDrive
1. Type names or addresses in *Invite people* text box in Share panel.
2. Choose *Can edit* or *Can view* option.
3. Type optional message.
4. Click Share button.

Project 2f Optional: Saving and Sharing a Workbook Using OneDrive

Part 6 of 7

Note: Complete this project only if you have a Microsoft account.

1. Open **6-CRPricingShared.xlsx** and save the workbook to your OneDrive by completing the following steps. *Note: If you have already saved your work to your OneDrive, skip to Step 2.*

   a. Click the Share button in the upper right corner of the screen.

   b. Click the Save to Cloud button. At the Save As backstage area, click *OneDrive - Personal* in the *Places* section. *Note: OneDrive is constantly changing, so these steps may vary.*

   c. Click *OneDrive - Personal* in the *Folders* section. At the Save As dialog box, navigate to the appropriate folder and then click Save. The worksheet displays with the Share panel open.

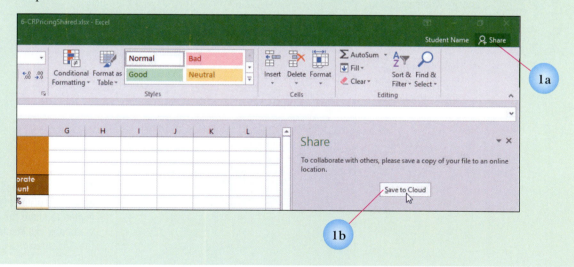

2. To invite people to share the workbook, complete the following steps:

a. In the Share panel, click in the *Invite people* text box and then type the email address of your instructor or a classmate. If necessary click outside the *Invite people* text box to close the message box stating that no suggestions were found.

b. Click the option box arrow for the option box containing the text *Can edit* and then click *Can view*.

c. Click in the text box containing *Include a message (optional)* and type Please review proposed rate changes.

d. Click the Share button. An email is sent to the person that has been invited and his or her name displays in the Share panel.

3. Check with your instructor or classmate to see if he or she received the email with the hyperlink to the workbook.

4. Stop sharing the workbook with your instructor or classmate by right-clicking his or her name or email address in the Share panel and then clicking *Remove User* at the shortcut menu.

5. Save and close **6-CRPricingShared.xlsx**.

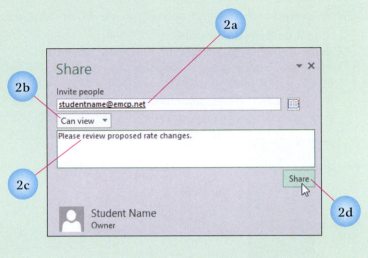

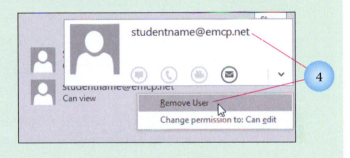

Sending a Workbook via Email

A workbook can be sent to others as a file attached to an email message. Attach the workbook using the email program's file attachment feature or initiate the message using Excel. To do this, click the File tab and then click the *Share* option. At the Share backstage area with *Email* selected in the *Share* section, click the Send as Attachment button in the *Email* section. The default email program, Microsoft Outlook, launches an email message window with the workbook file already attached and the file name inserted in the *Subject* text box. Type the recipient's email address in the *To* text box, type the message text in the message window, and then click the Send button. The message is moved to Outlook's Outbox folder and then sent to the recipient.

The *Email* section of the Share backstage area also contains buttons to attach the workbook to an email message as a portable document format (PDF) file or as an XML paper specification (XPS) file instead of the default workbook file format. In addition to being sent as an attachment, a workbook can be sent via a link in an email or as an Internet fax.

Note: Complete this project only if you use Microsoft Outlook as your email provider.

1. Open **CRFinalPrices.xlsx**.
2. Save the workbook with the name **6-CRFinalPrices**.
3. Send the workbook as a file attached to an email message by completing the following steps:
   a. Click the File tab and then click the *Share* option.
   b. Click *Email* in the *Share* section and then click the Send as Attachment button in the *Email* section.

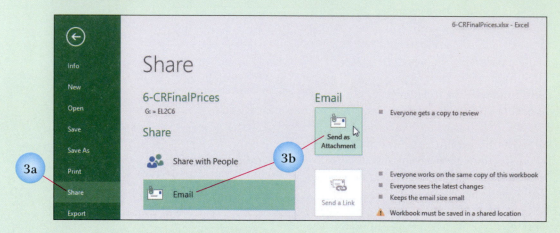

   c. With the insertion point positioned in the *To* text box at the message window, type your email address.
   d. Click in the message window and then type the following text: Here are the new rental rates that are effective May 1st. Please ensure that everyone is using these rates for any rentals after April 30th. Target revenues are on the second sheet. *Note: the "st" and "th" ordinals for the dates will automatically be formatted as superscript.*
   e. Click the Send button. The message is sent and the message window closes.

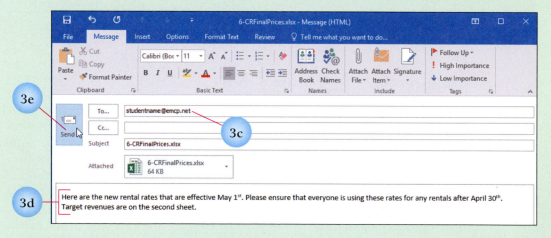

4. Open Outlook.
5. Check the inbox for the new message and then open and view the message. *Note: Depending on your email server, you may need to wait a few seconds for the message to be processed.*
6. Close the message and then exit Outlook.
7. Close **6-CRFinalPrices.xlsx**.

Project 3 **Lock and Unlock a Workbook, Worksheet, and Ranges in a Car Rental Rates Workbook** **4 Parts**

You will protect a worksheet, unlock ranges, prevent changes to the structure of a workbook, and then add a password to open a workbook.

 Format

 Protect Sheet

Quick Steps

Protect a Worksheet
1. Open workbook.
2. Activate sheet.
3. Click Review tab.
4. Click Protect Sheet button.
5. Type password.
6. Choose allowable actions.
7. Click OK.
8. Retype password if entered in Step 5.
9. Click OK.

Unlock a Cell
1. Select cell(s) to be unlocked.
2. Click Home tab.
3. Click Format button.
4. Click *Lock Cell*.
5. Deselect cell(s).

Protecting and Unprotecting Worksheets

Protecting a worksheet prevents other users from accidentally deleting or modifying cells that should not be changed. By default, when a worksheet is protected, each cell in it is locked. This means that no one can insert, delete, or modify the content. In most cases, some of the cells within a worksheet contain data that other users are able to change. Therefore, in a collaborative environment, protecting a worksheet generally involves two steps:

1. Clear the lock attribute on those cells that are allowed to be edited.
2. Protect the worksheet.

To clear the lock attribute from the cells that are allowed to be modified, select the cells to be unlocked, click the Home tab, and then click the Format button in the Cells group. Click *Lock Cell* in the *Protection* section of the drop-down list to turn off the lock attribute. To turn on worksheet protection, click the Review tab and then click the Protect Sheet button in the Changes group. At the Protect Sheet dialog box, shown in Figure 6.8, select the actions to be allowed and then click OK. A password can be assigned to unprotect the sheet. Be cautious if a password is added, since the worksheet cannot be unprotected if the password is forgotten. If necessary, write down the password and store it in a secure location.

Figure 6.8 Protect Sheet Dialog Box

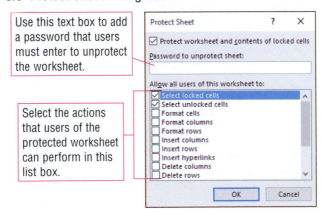

Use this text box to add a password that users must enter to unprotect the worksheet.

Select the actions that users of the protected worksheet can perform in this list box.

1. Open **6-CRFinalPrices.xlsx**.
2. Protect the entire FinalPrices worksheet by completing the following steps:
   a. Make sure FinalPrices is the active sheet.
   b. Click the Review tab.
   c. Click the Protect Sheet button in the Changes group.
   d. At the Protect Sheet dialog box with the insertion point positioned in the *Password to unprotect sheet* text box, type eL2-C6 and then click OK.

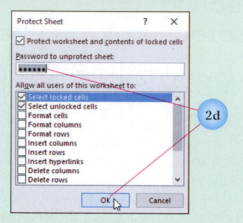

   e. At the Confirm Password dialog box with the insertion point positioned in the *Reenter password to proceed* text box, type eL2-C6 and then click OK.
   f. Make any cell active in the FinalPrices sheet and attempt to delete the data or type new data. Since the entire worksheet is now protected, all the cells are locked. A Microsoft Excel message appears stating that the cell or chart trying to be changed is on a protected worksheet. Click OK.

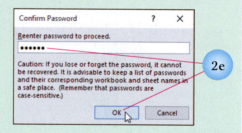

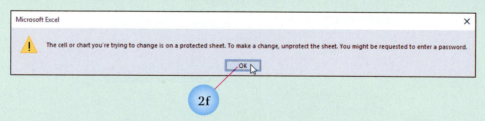

3. Notice that the Protect Sheet button changes to the Unprotect Sheet button when a worksheet has been protected.
4. Save **6-CRFinalPrices.xlsx**.

1. With **6-CRFinalPrices.xlsx** open, make TargetRevenue the active sheet.
2. Unlock the weekday target rental data cells for editing by completing the following steps:
   a. Select the range C5:C10.
   b. Click the Home tab.
   c. Click the Format button in the Cells group.
   d. At the Format button drop-down list, look at the icon next to *Lock Cell* in the *Protection* section. The highlighted icon indicates that the lock attribute is turned on.

   > A highlighted icon indicates that the lock attribute is active.

   2d

Protection
Protect Sheet...
Lock Cell
Format Cells...

   e. Click *Lock Cell* at the Format button drop-down list to turn the lock attribute off for the selected range.

   2f

Protection
Protect Sheet...
Lock Cell
Format Cells...

   > A nonhighlighted icon indicates that the lock attribute is not active.

   f. Click in any cell within the range C5:C10 and then click the Format button in the Cells group. Look at the icon next to *Lock Cell* in the drop-down list. The icon is no longer highlighted, which indicates that the cell is unlocked.
   g. Click within the worksheet area to close the drop-down list.
3. Unlock the remaining target rental ranges for editing by completing the following steps:
   a. Select the range F5:F10, press and hold down the Ctrl key, select the ranges I5:I10 and L5:L10, and then release the Ctrl key.
   b. Press the F4 function key to repeat the command to unlock the cells or click the Format button in the Cells group and then click *Lock Cell* at the drop-down list.
   c. Click in any cell to deselect the ranges.
4. Protect the TargetRevenue worksheet by completing the following steps:
   a. Click the Review tab.
   b. Click the Protect Sheet button in the Changes group.
   c. Type eL2-C6 in the *Password to unprotect sheet* text box.
   d. Click OK.
   e. Type eL2-C6 in the *Reenter password to proceed* text box.
   f. Click OK.
5. Save **6-CRFinalPrices.xlsx**.
6. Test the worksheet protection applied to the TargetRevenue sheet by completing the following steps:
   a. Make cell B8 active and then press the Delete key.
   b. Click OK at the Microsoft Office Excel message box stating that the protected cell cannot be changed.
   c. Make cell C8 active and then press the Delete key. Since cell C8 is unlocked, its contents are deleted and its dependent cells are updated.
   d. Click the Undo button on the Quick Access Toolbar to restore the contents of cell C8.
7. Save and then close **6-CRFinalPrices.xlsx**.

   6c

	Category	Weekday (Mo to Th)	Target Rentals	Target Revenue
4				
5	Compact	$ 36	675	$ 24,293
6	Mid-size	38.99	880	34,311
7	Full-size	40.99	425	17,421
8	Minivan	75.99		-
9	SUV	89.99	198	17,818
10	Luxury	99.99	86	8,599
11	**TOTAL**		Weekday:	$ 102,442

Unprotect Sheet

When a worksheet has protection turned on, the Protect Sheet button in the Changes group on the Review tab turns into the Unprotect Sheet button. To remove worksheet protection, click the Unprotect Sheet button or click the Unprotect hyperlink in the Info backstage area in the *Protect Workbook* section. If a password was entered when the worksheet was protected, the Unprotect Sheet dialog box appears, as shown in Figure 6.9. Type the password and then press the Enter key or click OK.

Figure 6.9 Unprotect Sheet Dialog Box

Tutorial

Protecting and
Unprotecting the
Structure of a
Workbook

 Protect
Workbook

Quick Steps

Protect the Workbook Structure
1. Open workbook.
2. Click Review tab.
3. Click Protect Workbook button.
4. Type password.
5. Click OK.
6. Retype password if entered at Step 4.
7. Click OK.

Protecting and Unprotecting the Structure of a Workbook

Use the Protect Workbook button in the Changes group on the Review tab to prevent changes to the structure of a workbook, such as inserting a new sheet, deleting a sheet, or unhiding a hidden worksheet. At the Protect Structure and Windows dialog box, shown in Figure 6.10, turn on protection for the workbook's windows. Click the *Windows* check box to prevent a user from resizing or changing the positions of the windows in the workbook. As with protecting a worksheet, enter an optional password that will protect the workbook.

Figure 6.10 Protect Structure and Windows Dialog Box

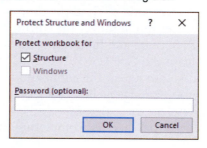

Project 3c Protecting the Structure of a Workbook

Part 3 of 4

1. Open **6-CRFinalPrices.xlsx**.
2. Protect the workbook structure by completing the following steps:
   a. If necessary, click the Review tab.
   b. Click the Protect Workbook button in the Changes group.
   c. At the Protect Structure and Windows dialog box with the insertion point positioned in the *Password (optional)* text box type eL2-C6.
   d. Click OK.
   e. At the Confirm Password dialog box with the insertion point positioned in the *Reenter password to proceed* text box type eL2-C6.
   f. Click OK.

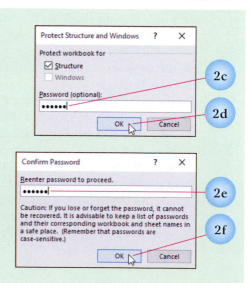

3. To test the workbook protection, attempt to insert a new worksheet by completing the following steps:
   a. Right-click the TargetRevenue sheet tab.
   b. Look at the shortcut menu. Notice that all the options related to managing worksheets are dimmed, which means they are unavailable.
   c. Click within the worksheet area to close the shortcut menu.
4. Save **6-CRFinalPrices.xlsx**.

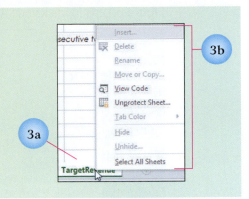

Unprotecting a Workbook

When the structure of a workbook has been protected, the Protect Workbook button in the Changes group on the Review tab displays with a gray shaded background. To remove workbook protection, click the Protect Workbook button. If a password was entered when the workbook was protected, the Unprotect Workbook dialog box appears, shown in Figure 6.11. Type the password and then press the Enter key or click OK.

Figure 6.11 Unprotect Workbook Dialog Box

Tutorial

Adding a Password to Open a Workbook

Protect Workbook

Quick Steps

Add a Workbook Password
1. Open workbook.
2. Click File tab.
3. Click Protect Workbook button.
4. Click *Encrypt with Password*.
5. Type password.
6. Click OK.
7. Retype password if entered in Step 5.
8. Click OK.
9. Save workbook.

Adding and Removing a Password to Open a Workbook

Prevent unauthorized access to Excel data by requiring a password to open a workbook. The password to open a workbook is encrypted. In an *encrypted password*, the plain text that is typed is converted into a scrambled format called *ciphertext*, which prevents unauthorized users from retrieving the password. To add an encrypted password to an open workbook, click the File tab. At the Info backstage area, shown in Figure 6.12, click the Protect Workbook button in *Protect Workbook* section. Click *Encrypt with Password* at the drop-down list to open the Encrypt Document dialog box, shown in Figure 6.13. Save the workbook after typing and confirming the password.

When creating a password, it is good practice to use a combination of four types of characters: uppercase letters, lowercase letters, symbols, and numbers. A password constructed using these elements is considered secure and more difficult to crack. Note that if the password is forgotten, the workbook cannot be opened. If necessary, write down the password and store it in a secure location.

Figure 6.12 Info Backstage Area with Protect Workbook Drop-Down List

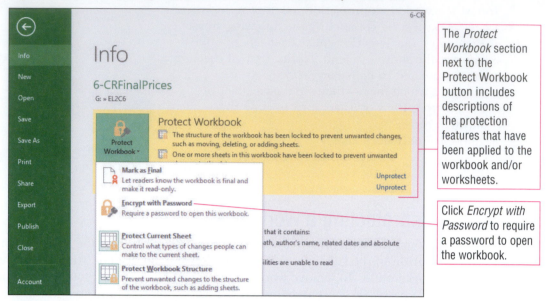

The *Protect Workbook* section next to the Protect Workbook button includes descriptions of the protection features that have been applied to the workbook and/or worksheets.

Click *Encrypt with Password* to require a password to open the workbook.

Figure 6.13 Encrypt Document Dialog Box

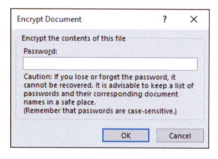

Project 3d Adding a Password to Open a Workbook

Part 4 of 4

1. With **6-CRFinalPrices.xlsx** open, add a password to open the workbook by completing the following steps:
   a. Click the File tab. The backstage area opens with the *Info* option selected.
   b. Read the information in the *Protect Workbook* section. Since this protection features have already been applied to this workbook, the existing features are described and a hyperlink is provided to unprotect each protected worksheet. In a workbook with no pre-existing protection, the *Permissions* section displays the text *Control what types of changes people can make to this workbook.*
   c. Click the Protect Workbook button.

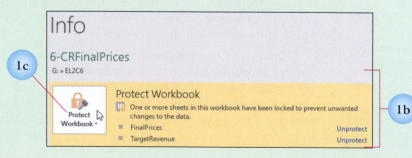

d. Click *Encrypt with Password* at the drop-down list.
e. At the Encrypt Document dialog box with the
   insertion point positioned in the *Password* text box,
   type eL2-C6.
f. Click OK.

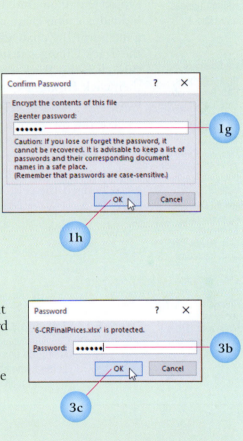

g. At the Confirm Password dialog box with
   the insertion point positioned in the *Reenter
   password* text box, type eL2-C6.
h. Click OK.
i. Notice that Excel has added to the first line of
   the *Protect Workbook* section next to the Protect
   Workbook button the text *A password is required
   to open this workbook*.
j. Click the Back button to return to the
   worksheet.
2. Save and then close **6-CRFinalPrices.xlsx**.
3. Test the password security on the workbook by
   completing the following steps:
   a. Open **6-CRFinalPrices.xlsx**.
   b. At the Password dialog box with the insertion point
      positioned in the *Password* text box, type a password
      that is incorrect for the file.
   c. Click OK.
   d. At the Microsoft Excel message box stating that the
      password is not correct, click OK.
   e. Open **6-CRFinalPrices.xlsx**.
   f. Type eL2-C6 in the *Password* text box.
   g. Click OK.
4. Close **6-CRFinalPrices.xlsx**.

To remove a password from a workbook, open the workbook using the
password. At the Info backstage area, click the Protect Workbook button in the
Protect Workbook section. Click *Encrypt with Password* at the drop-down list to open
the Encrypt Document dialog box. Delete the password, click OK, and then save
the workbook.

Project 4 Track and Resolve Changes Made to a Monthly Revenue Workbook

3 Parts

You will begin tracking changes made to a workbook, view changes made by two users, and then accept and reject changes.

Preview Finished Project

Tutorial

Tracking Changes in a Workbook

Tracking Changes in a Workbook

Project 2 demonstrated that Excel automatically tracks the changes made by individuals who share a workbook. The history sheet created in Project 2e displays a record of the changes and can be printed. If a workbook is not shared, turn on the Track Changes feature and Excel will automatically share the workbook. To do this, click the Track Changes button in the Changes group on the Review tab and then click *Highlight Changes* at the drop-down list. At the Highlight Changes dialog box, click the *Track changes while editing* check box and then click OK.

For the owner of a shared workbook, it is good practice to review the worksheet with all the changed cells highlighted. Figure 6.14 displays the worksheet edited in Project 4 with all the changes highlighted. Hover the mouse pointer over a highlighted cell and a pop-up box displays the name of the person who changed the cell, along with the date, time, original entry, and revised entry.

Quick Steps

Track Changes
1. Open workbook.
2. Click Review tab.
3. Click Track Changes button.
4. Click *Highlight Changes*.
5. Click *Track changes while editing* check box.
6. Click OK twice.

Highlight Changes
1. Open tracked workbook.
2. Click Review tab.
3. Click Track Changes button.
4. Click *Highlight Changes*.
5. Change *When* to *Not yet reviewed*.
6. Make sure *Who* is set to *Everyone*.
7. Click OK.

Figure 6.14 Project 4 Worksheet with Changes Highlighted

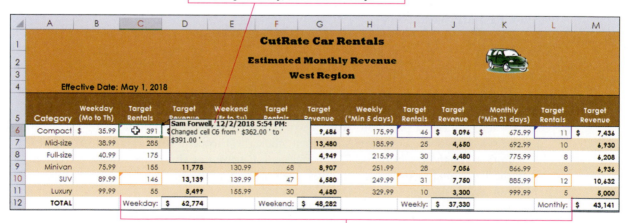

A pop-up box displays the name of the person who changed the cell, plus the date, time, original entry, and revised entry.

In a shared workbook, changed cells are displayed with colored borders for easy identification. Each person's changes are identified with a different color.

Accepting and Rejecting Tracked Changes

Quick Steps

Accept and Reject Changes
1. Open tracked workbook.
2. Click Review tab.
3. Click Track Changes button.
4. Click *Accept/Reject Changes*.
5. Make sure *When* is set to *Not yet reviewed*.
6. Make sure *Who* is set to *Everyone*.
7. Click OK.
8. Click Accept or Reject button at each change.

In addition to displaying and reviewing the worksheet with all the changes highlighted, changes can be navigated to and accepted or rejected individually. To do this, click the Track Changes button in the Changes group on the Review tab and then click *Accept/Reject Changes* at the drop-down list. At the Select Changes to Accept or Reject dialog box, shown in Figure 6.15, define which changes are to be reviewed and then click OK.

Excel navigates to the first changed cell and displays the Accept or Reject Changes dialog box, shown in Figure 6.16. Review the information in the dialog box and click the Accept button or the Reject button. If a change is accepted, the cell is updated to reflect the new value. If a change is rejected, the cell is restored to its original value. After each changed cell has been reviewed, the colored border is removed. The Accept or Reject Changes dialog box also provides an Accept All button and a Reject All button, which can be used to make a global review decision. Be careful when accepting and rejecting changes because Undo is not available after the cells have been reviewed.

Figure 6.15 Select Changes to Accept or Reject Dialog Box

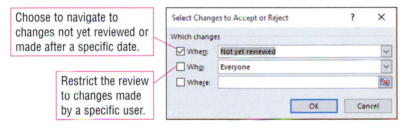

Choose to navigate to changes not yet reviewed or made after a specific date.

Restrict the review to changes made by a specific user.

Figure 6.16 Accept or Reject Changes Dialog Box

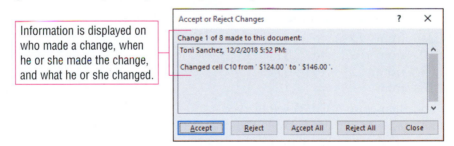

Information is displayed on who made a change, when he or she made the change, and what he or she changed.

Project 4a **Tracking Changes in a Workbook**   **Part 1 of 3**

1. Open **CRWestReg.xlsx**.
2. Save the workbook with the name **6-CRWestReg**.
3. Begin tracking changes by completing the following steps:
   a. If necessary, click the Review tab.
   b. Click the Track Changes button in the Changes group.
   c. Click *Highlight Changes* at the drop-down list.

d. At the Highlight Changes dialog box, click the *Track changes while editing* check box to insert a check mark. Notice that turning on the Track Changes feature automatically shares the workbook.

e. With the *When* option set to *All* and the *Who* option set to *Everyone* by default, click OK.

f. At the Microsoft Excel message box stating that this action will now save the workbook, click OK to continue.

4. Close **6-CRWestReg.xlsx**.

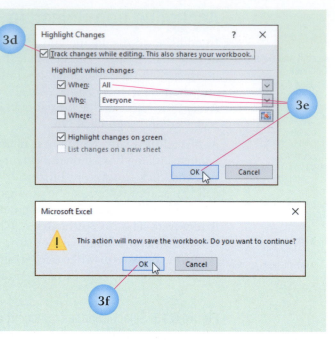

Project 4b Editing a Tracked Workbook

Part 2 of 3

1. Assume that you are Toni Sanchez, the SUV rental manager for the West region at CutRate Car Rentals. You have been asked to edit the target rental values for SUVs. At a blank Excel window, change the user name to *Toni Sanchez*. (Refer to Project 2b, Step 1 for assistance with changing the user name.) You will return to the original user name in Project 4c.

2. Open **6-CRWestReg.xlsx**.

3. Edit the cells that contain the SUV target data as follows:

C10	from	124	to	146
F10	from	22	to	47
I10	from	22	to	31
L10	from	8	to	12

4. Save and then close **6-CRWestReg.xlsx**.

5. Assume that you are Sam Forwell, the compact rental manager for the West region at CutRate Car Rentals. You have been asked to edit the target rental values for compact cars. At a blank Excel window, change the user name to *Sam Forwell*.

6. Open **6-CRWestReg.xlsx**.

7. Edit the cells that contain the compact target data as follows:

C6	from	362	to	391
F6	from	165	to	173
I6	from	33	to	46
L6	from	15	to	11

8. Save and then close **6-CRWestReg.xlsx**.

Check Your Work

1. Assume that you are the operations manager for the West region at CutRate Car Rentals. You decide to review the changes made by Toni Sanchez and Sam Forwell. At a blank Excel window, change the user name back to the original user name for the computer you are using.
2. Open **6-CRWestReg.xlsx**.
3. Highlight all the cells with changes that have not yet been reviewed by completing the following steps:
   a. Click the Track Changes button in the Changes group on the Review tab.
   b. Click *Highlight Changes* at the drop-down list.
   c. At the Highlight Changes dialog box, click the *When* option box arrow and then click *Not yet reviewed* at the drop-down list.
   d. With *Who* set to *Everyone* by default, click OK.

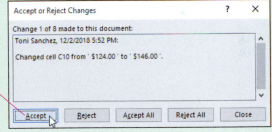

4. Navigate through the worksheet and accept and reject changes by completing the following steps:
   a. Press the keys Ctrl + Home to make cell A1 active.
   b. Click the Track Changes button and then click *Accept/Reject Changes* at the drop-down list.
   c. At the Select Changes to Accept or Reject dialog box with *When* set to *Not yet reviewed* and *Who* set to *Everyone*, click OK.
   d. Excel moves the active cell to cell C10, where the first change was made, and displays the Accept or Reject Changes dialog box. Click the Accept button to leave the value *$146.00* in cell C10.

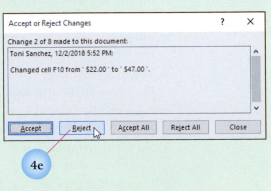

   e. Excel makes cell F10 the active cell. Click the Reject button to restore cell F10 to the original value of *$22.00*. **Note: *If necessary, drag the Accept or Reject Changes dialog box out of the way to see the cell being reviewed in the worksheet area.***
   f. Respond to the remaining changes to the cells as follows:

I10:	Accept
L10:	Accept
C6:	Reject
F6:	Accept
I6:	Reject
L6:	Accept

5. Save the worksheet.
6. Print and then close **6-CRWestReg.xlsx**.

Check Your Work

Turning Off Track Changes

Quick Steps

Turn Off Track Changes
1. Open tracked workbook.
2. Click Review tab.
3. Click *Highlight Changes*.
4. Click *Track changes while editing* check box to remove check mark.
5. Click OK.
6. Click Yes.

When tracking the changes made to a workbook is no longer necessary, click the Track Changes button and then click *Highlight Changes* at the drop-down list. At the Highlight Changes dialog box, click the *Track changes while editing* check box to remove the check mark and then click OK. Excel displays the warning message that the workbook will no longer be shared and that the change history will be erased. Click Yes to complete the action.

If some of the changes made to a workbook have not been reviewed, consider printing a copy of the history sheet before turning off the Track Changes feature. (Refer to Project 2e, Step 2 for assistance with printing a history sheet.)

Excel provides several methods for sharing data and collaborating with other users. The method chosen depends on factors such as the availability of a network share folder, the need to protect ranges or otherwise restrict access to sensitive data, and the resources available by the users who will receive the data. Chapter 8 explores other features to consider when distributing a workbook, such as restricting access and removing personal information.

Chapter Summary

- Workbook properties include descriptive information about the workbook, such as the author's name and the workbook title, subject, category, or comments.
- Display the Info backstage area to add information to a workbook's properties.
- Workbook properties are sometimes referred to as *metadata*.
- When Microsoft Office is installed, a user name is defined for the computer. Excel automatically inserts this name in the *Author* property box when a new workbook is created.
- A comment is a pop-up box that displays text when the cell pointer is hovering over the cell to which the comment is attached.
- Comments are useful for adding explanatory notes, descriptions, or questions about cell entries when a workbook is being created, edited, or shared with other reviewers.
- Insert, edit, view, or delete a comment using buttons in the Comments group on the Review tab. Copy and paste comment text to another cell using the Paste Special dialog box.
- Sharing a workbook generally involves turning on the sharing feature and saving the workbook to a folder on a networked server that is accessible to other users.
- When a workbook is shared, Excel automatically tracks the changes made by all the individuals who access the file.
- Turn on the sharing feature using the Share Workbook button in the Changes group on the Review tab.
- View the names of other users who have a shared workbook open at the Share Workbook dialog box.
- Change the user name associated with Excel at the Excel Options dialog box.
- When two users have copies of a shared workbook open at the same time and each user makes a change to the same cell, the Resolve Conflicts dialog box displays when the second user saves the workbook.

- At the Resolve Conflicts dialog box, the second user can choose to accept the change he or she made or to restore the cell to the entry made by the last person to save the file.
- Print a history sheet to provide a detailed record of all the changes made to a shared workbook before removing shared access to the workbook.
- When a shared workbook is changed to an exclusive workbook, all the change history is removed from the file.
- Save a shared workbook to a folder in your storage location on OneDrive, where you can retrieve it from any location with Internet access.
- Invite people to edit or view the workbooks saved to your OneDrive folders.
- A workbook can be sent to others as a file attached to an email using the Share backstage area. The workbook can be provided in the default Excel (.xlsx) format, as a portable document format (PDF) file, or as an XML paper specification (XPS) file.
- Protect an entire worksheet to prevent other users from accidentally inserting or deleting data.
- Protect a worksheet using the Protect Sheet button in the Changes group on the Review tab.
- By default, each cell in a worksheet has a lock attribute that activates when the worksheet is protected.
- To allow editing of individual cells in a protected worksheet, select the cells and turn off the lock attribute before protecting the worksheet.
- Add a password to unprotect a worksheet.
- Use the Protect Workbook button in the Changes group on the Review tab to prevent changes to the structure of a workbook, such as inserting, deleting, renaming, or otherwise managing worksheets within it.
- Prevent unauthorized access to an Excel workbook by requiring a password to open it. The plain text of the password is encrypted, which prevents unauthorized users from retrieving it.
- Add a password at the Info backstage area by clicking the Protect Workbook button and then clicking *Encrypt with Password*. Save the workbook after typing and confirming the password.
- Turn on or off the Track Changes feature or display changes in a shared workbook at the Highlight Changes dialog box.
- Use the Accept/Reject Changes feature to navigate to each changed cell in a worksheet and then accept or reject the revision.

Commands Review

FEATURE	RIBBON TAB, GROUP/OPTION	BUTTON	KEYBOARD SHORTCUT
accept/reject changes	Review, Changes		
add comment	Review, Comments		Shift + F2
add password	File, *Info*		
advanced properties	File, *Info*	Properties ▾	
change user name	File, *Options*		
delete comment	Review, Comments		
edit comment	Review, Comments		
highlight changes	Review, Changes		
paste copied comment	Home, Clipboard		Ctrl + Alt + V
protect workbook	Review, Changes		
protect worksheet	Review, Changes		
share workbook	Review, Changes		
track changes	Review, Changes		
unlock cells	Home, Format		

Workbook

Chapter study tools and assessment activities are available in the *Workbook* ebook. These resources are designed to help you further develop and demonstrate mastery of the skills learned in this chapter.

Microsoft®

Excel®

Automating Repetitive Tasks and Customizing Excel

Performance Objectives

Upon successful completion of Chapter 7, you will be able to:

1 Record, run, and edit a macro

2 Save a workbook containing macros as a macro-enabled workbook

3 Assign a macro to a keyboard shortcut

4 Customize the display options for Excel

5 Minimize the ribbon

6 Customize the ribbon by creating a custom tab and adding buttons

7 Customize the Quick Access Toolbar by adding and removing buttons for frequently used commands

8 Create and apply custom views

9 Create and use templates

10 Customize save options to AutoRecover files

Automating and customizing the Excel environment to accommodate preferences can increase efficiency. For example, create a macro if the same task is being frequently repeated to save time and ensure consistency. Add a button for a frequently used command to the Quick Access Toolbar to provide single-click access to it. Other ways to customize Excel include creating a custom template, ribbon tab, or view and modifying display and save options. By completing the projects in this chapter, you will learn how to effectively automate and customize the Excel environment.

SNAP

If you are a SNAP user, launch the Precheck and Tutorials from your Assignments page.

Data Files

Before beginning chapter work, copy the EL2C7 folder to your storage medium and then make EL2C7 the active folder.

Project 1 **Create Macros in a New Workbook** **4 Parts**

You will create, run, edit, and delete macros to automate tasks; assign a macro to a shortcut key; and then store frequently used macros in a macro workbook.

Automating Tasks Using Macros

A macro is a series of instructions stored in sequence that can be recalled and carried out whenever the need arises. Consider creating a macro to perform the same task repeatedly without variation. Saving the instructions for a task in a macro not only saves time, but it also ensures that the steps are performed consistently every time. This can prevent errors in data entry, formatting, or other worksheet tasks.

Tutorial

Creating a Macro

Creating a Macro

Before recording a new macro, take a few moments to plan the steps. Also consider if it is necessary to specify which cell must be active when the macro is run. For example, will the first step in the macro involve making a specific cell active? If so, position the active cell using a shortcut key or Go To command during the recording.

Quick Steps

Create a Macro
1. Click View tab.
2. Click Macros button arrow.
3. Click *Record Macro*.
4. Type macro name.
5. Click in *Description* text box and type description text.
6. Click OK.
7. Perform required actions.
8. Click Stop Recording button.

To create a macro, begin by turning on the macro recorder, which opens the Record Macro dialog box, as shown in Figure 7.1. Identify the macro by assigning a unique name to the steps that will be saved. A macro name must begin with a letter and can be a combination of letters, numbers, and underscore characters. A macro name cannot include spaces; use the underscore character to separate the words in a macro name. Also use the Record Macro dialog box to choose the location in which the macro is saved. By default, Excel saves the macro within the current workbook.

 Macros

A macro can be assigned to a shortcut key combination, which allows the user to run the macro more quickly by pressing the Ctrl key plus the chosen lowercase or uppercase letter. Enter a description of the purpose of a macro to

Figure 7.1 Record Macro Dialog Box

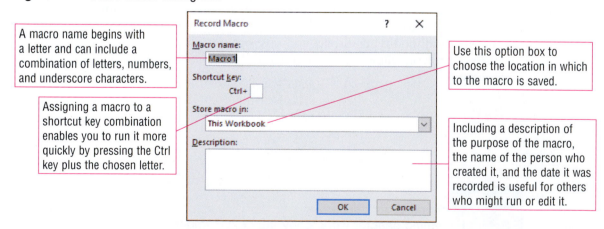

Hint When a macro is being recorded, the mouse clicks for select tabs within the ribbon are not saved.

Stop Recording

Quick Steps

Save a Macro-Enabled Workbook
1. Click File tab.
2. Click *Save As*.
3. Click *Browse*.
4. Navigate to appropriate folder.
5. Type file name in *File name* text box.
6. Click *Save as type* list arrow.
7. Click *Excel Macro-Enabled Workbook (*.xlsm)*.
8. Click Save.

provide information to other users who might use or edit it. In a macro workbook that will be shared, also consider entering the creator's name and the creation date into the description box for reference purposes. Click OK when finished identifying the macro and the recorder will begin saving the text and/or steps that are performed. Do not be concerned with making typing mistakes or canceling a dialog box while recording a macro. Correct mistakes as they happen since only the result is saved. After completing the tasks to be saved, click the Stop Recording button on the Status bar to end the recording.

Saving Workbooks Containing Macros

When a macro is created in Excel, the commands are written and saved in a language called *Microsoft Visual Basic for Applications (VBA)*. A workbook that contains a macro should be saved using the macro-enabled file format (.xlsm). The default XML-based file format (.xlsx) cannot store the macro code. The macro recorder used when creating a macro converts the actions to VBA statements behind the scenes. View and edit the VBA code or create macros from scratch by using the VBA Editor in Microsoft Visual Basic for Applications, which can be opened through the Macros dialog box. Project 1d looks at the VBA statements created when the AcctgDocumentation macro was recorded and edits an instruction.

To save a new or existing workbook as a macro-enabled workbook, perform one of the following actions:

- *New workbook.* Click the Save button on the Quick Access Toolbar or click the File tab and then click the *Save As* option. At the Save As backstage area, click the *Browse* option to display the Save As dialog box and navigate to the appropriate folder. Type the file name and then change the *Save as type* option to *Excel Macro-Enabled Workbook (*.xlsm)*. Click the Save button.

- *Existing workbook.* Click the File tab and then click the *Save As* option. At the Save As backstage area, click the *Browse* option to display the Save As dialog box and navigate to the appropriate folder. Type the file name and then change the *Save as type* option to *Excel Macro-Enabled Workbook (*.xlsm)*. Click the Save button.

Project 1a Creating a Macro and Saving a Workbook as a Macro-Enabled Workbook   **Part 1 of 4**

1. You work in the Accounting Department at a large company. The company has a documentation standard for all Excel workbooks that requires each worksheet to show the department name, author's name, creation date, and revision history. To standardize the documentation, you decide to create a macro that will insert row labels for this data. Begin by opening a new blank workbook.
2. Create the documentation macro by completing the following steps:
   a. Make cell C4 the active cell and then click the View tab.
      (Making a cell other than A1 active to move the active cell to the top left cell in the worksheet during the macro.)
   b. Click the Macros button arrow in the Macros group.
   c. Click *Record Macro* at the drop-down list.

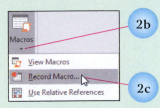

---

d. At the Record Macro dialog box with the insertion point positioned in the *Macro name* text box, type AcctgDocumentation.

e. Click in the *Description* text box and then type Accounting Department documentation macro. Created by [Student Name] on [Date]. Substitute your name for *[Student Name]* and the current date for *[Date]*.

f. Click OK. The macro recorder is now turned on, as indicated by the Stop Recording button in the Status bar (which displays as a gray square next to *Ready*).

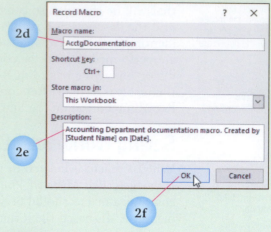

g. Press Ctrl + Home to move the active cell to cell A1. Including this command in the macro ensures that the documentation will begin at cell A1 in every workbook.

h. Type Accounting Department and then press the Enter key.

i. With cell A2 active, type Author and then press the Enter key.

j. With cell A3 active, type Date created and then press the Enter key.

k. With cell A4 active, type Revision history and then press the Enter key three times to leave two blank rows before the start of the worksheet.

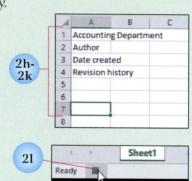

l. Click the Stop Recording button at the left side of the Status bar, next to *Ready*.

3. Save the workbook as a macro-enabled workbook by completing the following steps:

a. Click the Save button on the Quick Access Toolbar.

b. At the Save As backstage area, click the *Browse* option.

c. At the Save As dialog box, navigate to the EL2C7 folder in the Navigation pane and then double-click the *EL2C7* folder that displays in the Content pane.

d. Click in the *File name* text box and then type 7-Macros.

e. Click the *Save as type* option box, scroll up or down the pop-up list, and then click *Excel Macro-Enabled Workbook (*.xlsm)*.

f. Click the Save button.

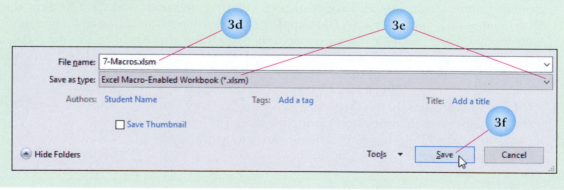

Tutorial

Running a Macro

Running a Macro

Running a macro is sometimes referred to as *playing a macro*. Since a macro is a series of recorded tasks, running a macro involves instructing Excel to *play back* the recorded tasks. Think of a macro as a video. When the video is played, the same thing happens every time.

Öuick Steps
Run a Macro
1. Click View tab.
2. Click Macros button.
3. Double-click macro name.

To run (play) a macro, view the list of macros by clicking the Macros button in the Macros group on the View tab. This opens the Macro dialog box, shown in Figure 7.2. Click the name of the macro to run and then click the Run button or double-click the name of the macro in the *Macro name* list box.

Figure 7.2 Macro Dialog Box

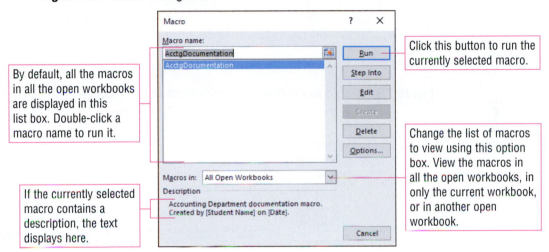

By default, all the macros in all the open workbooks are displayed in this list box. Double-click a macro name to run it.

Click this button to run the currently selected macro.

Change the list of macros to view using this option box. View the macros in all the open workbooks, in only the current workbook, or in another open workbook.

If the currently selected macro contains a description, the text displays here.

Project 1b Running a Macro

Part 2 of 4

1. With **7-Macros.xlsm** open, run the AcctgDocumentation macro to test that it works correctly by completing the following steps:
   a. Select the range A1:A4 and then press the Delete key to erase the cell contents.
   b. To test the Ctrl + Home command in the macro, make sure cell that A1 is not active when the macro begins playing. Click in any cell in the worksheet other than cell A1 to deselect the range.
   c. Click the Macros button in the Macros group on the View tab. Make sure to click the button and not the button arrow.
   d. At the Macro dialog box with *AcctgDocumentation* already selected in the *Macro name* list box, click the Run button.
2. Save and then close **7-Macros.xlsm**.

Assigning a Macro to a Shortcut Key

Quick Steps

Assign a Macro to a Shortcut Key
1. Click View tab.
2. Click Macros button arrow.
3. Click *Record Macro*.
4. Type macro name.
5. Click in *Shortcut key* text box.
6. Type a letter.
7. Click in *Description* text box.
8. Type description text.
9. Click OK.
10. Perform actions.
11. Click Stop Recording button.

When a macro is being recorded, it can be assigned to a Ctrl key combination. A macro assigned to a keyboard shortcut can be run without displaying the Macro dialog box. To create a keyboard shortcut, choose any lowercase or uppercase letter. Excel distinguishes the case of the letter when typing it in the *Shortcut key* text box at the Record Macro dialog box. For example, if an uppercase O is typed, Excel defines the shortcut key as *Ctrl + Shift + O*, as shown in Figure 7.3.

If an Excel feature is already assigned to the chosen key combination, the macro will override the feature. For example, pressing Ctrl + p in Excel causes the Print backstage area to display. If a macro is assigned to Ctrl + p, using this keyboard shortcut will run the new macro instead of displaying the Print backstage area box. View a list of Excel-assigned keyboard shortcuts in Help by typing *keyboard shortcuts* in the *Tell me* text box. Click *Get Help on "keyboard shortcuts"*. Scroll and then choose *Keyboard shortcuts in Excel 2016 for Windows* in the results list.

Figure 7.3 Record Macro Dialog Box with Shortcut Key Assigned

Record Macro

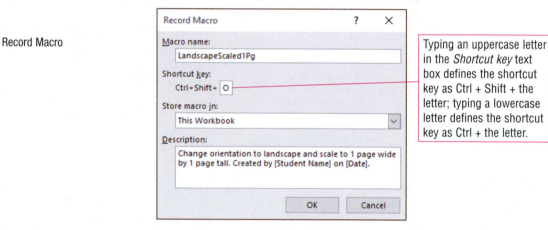

Typing an uppercase letter in the *Shortcut key* text box defines the shortcut key as Ctrl + Shift + the letter; typing a lowercase letter defines the shortcut key as Ctrl + the letter.

Project 1c Creating and Running a Macro Using a Shortcut Key   Part 3 of 4

1. Open **7-Macros.xlsm**.
2. When opening any workbook that contains a macro, the default security setting is *Disable all macros with notification*. This causes a security warning to appear in the message bar (between the ribbon and the formula bar) stating that macros have been disabled. Enable the macros in the workbook by clicking the Enable Content button.

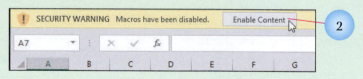

3. Create a macro that changes the print options for a worksheet and assign it to a keyboard shortcut by completing the following steps:

a. Once the recording of a macro has stopped in an Excel session, the Stop Recording button in the Status bar changes to the Record New Macro button. Click the Record New Macro button at the left side of the Status bar next to *Ready*. (If you exited Excel before starting this project, start a new macro by clicking the View tab, clicking the Macros button arrow, and then clicking *Record Macro*.)

b. Type LandscapeScaled1Pg in the *Macro name* text box.

c. Click in the *Shortcut key* text box, press and hold down the Shift key, type the letter O, and then release the Shift key.

d. Click in the *Description* text box and then type Change orientation to landscape and scale to 1 page wide by 1 page tall. Created by [Student Name] on [Date]. Substitute your name for *[Student Name]* and the current date for *[Date]*.

e. Click OK.

f. Click the Page Layout tab.

g. Click the Page Setup dialog box launcher at the bottom right of the Page Setup group.

h. At the Page Setup dialog box with the Page tab selected, click *Landscape* in the *Orientation* section.

i. Click *Fit to* in the *Scaling* section to scale the printout to 1 page wide by 1 page tall.

j. Click OK.

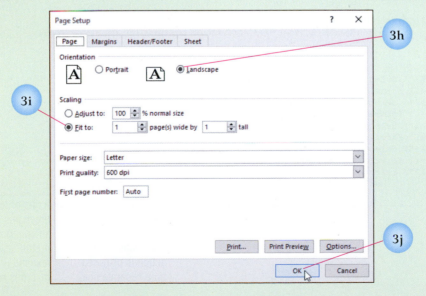

k. Click the Stop Recording button.

4. Press Ctrl + N to open a new blank workbook.
5. Press Ctrl + Shift + O to run the macro LandscapeScaled1Pg.
6. Type your name in cell A1, press the Enter key, and then press Ctrl + F2 to display the worksheet in the Print backstage area. Notice in the Print Preview that the page orientation is landscape. Review the options in the Settings category. Notice that *Landscape Orientation* and *Fit Sheet on One Page* have been selected by the macro.
7. Click the Back button to return to the worksheet and then close the workbook. Click Don't Save when prompted to save changes.
8. Save **7-Macros.xlsm**.

Editing a Macro

Tutorial

Editing a Macro

Quick Steps

Edit a Macro
1. Open workbook containing macro.
2. Click View tab.
3. Click Macros button.
4. Click macro name.
5. Click Edit button.
6. Make changes in VBA code window.
7. Click Save button.
8. Click File.
9. Click *Close and Return to Microsoft Excel*.

The actions performed while a macro is being recorded are stored in VBA code. Each macro is saved as a separate module within a VBAProject for the workbook. A module can be described as a receptacle for the macro instructions. Figure 7.4 displays the window containing the VBA code module for the macro created in Project 1a.

Use the module to edit a macro if the change needed is easy to decipher within the VBA statements. If several changes to a macro are required or if you do not feel comfortable with the VBA code, re-record the macro. When a new macro has been recorded and is being saved with the same name as an existing macro, Excel prompts the user to replace the existing macro. Save the re-recorded macro by overwriting the original macro.

Figure 7.4 Microsoft Visual Basic for Applications Window for Project 1a AcctgDocumentation Macro

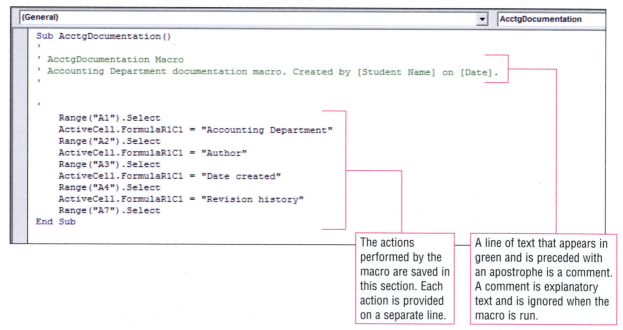

180 Excel Level 2 | Unit 2

Chapter 7 | Automating Repetitive Tasks and Customizing Excel

1. With **7-Macros.xlsm** open, edit the AcctgDocumentation macro to leave only one blank row after the last entry by completing the following steps:
   a. If necessary, click the View tab.
   b. Click the Macros button in the Macros group.
   c. At the Macro dialog box with *AcctgDocumentation* already selected in the *Macro name* list box, click the Edit button. A Microsoft Visual Basic for Applications window opens with the program code displayed for 7-Macros.xlsm - [Module1 (Code)].

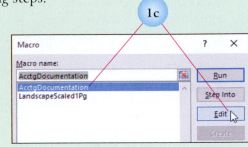

   d. Read the statements between the *Sub* and *End Sub* statements. *Sub* indicates the beginning of the procedure and *End Sub* indicates the end of the procedure. A procedure is a set of VBA statements that perform actions. The name of the procedure appears after the opening *Sub* statement and is the macro name. Each line beginning with a single apostrophe (') is a comment. A comment is used in programming to insert explanatory text that describes the logic or purpose of a statement. A statement that begins with an apostrophe is ignored when the macro is run. The commands that are executed when the macro is run are the indented lines of text below the comments.
   e. The last statement before *End Sub* reads *Range("A7").Select*. This is the last action in the macro and it makes cell A7 active. Notice that the entry two lines above this final action reads *Range("A4").Select*. To edit the macro to leave only one blank row, change the address in the last statement from *A7* to *A6*. To do this, position the mouse pointer between the *A* and the *7* and then click the left mouse button. Press the Delete key and then type 6.

```
(General)                                                              AcctgDocumentation

    Sub AcctgDocumentation()
    '
    ' AcctgDocumentation Macro
    ' Accounting Department documentation macro. Created by [Student Name] on [Date].
    '

    '
        Range("A1").Select
        ActiveCell.FormulaR1C1 = "Accounting Department"
        Range("A2").Select
        ActiveCell.FormulaR1C1 = "Author"
        Range("A3").Select
        ActiveCell.FormulaR1C1 = "Date created"
        Range("A4").Select
        ActiveCell.FormulaR1C1 = "Revision history"
        Range("A6").Select
    End Sub
```

1e

   f. Click the Save button on the toolbar.

1f

Microsoft Visual Basic for Applications - 7-Macros.xlsm - [Module1 (Code)]
File   Edit   View   Insert   Format   Debug   Run   Tools   Add-Ins   Window
Project - VBAProject
(General)
Sub AcctgDocumentation()

2. Click File and then click *Close and Return to Microsoft Excel*.

3. Test the edited macro to make sure that only one blank row is left before the active cell by completing the following steps:

   a. Select the range A1:A4 and then press the Delete key.

   b. Make any cell other than cell A1 active.

   c. Click the Macros button in the Macros group on the View tab. Make sure to click the button and not the button arrow.

   d. At the Macro dialog box, double-click *AcctgDocumentation* in the *Macro name* list box.

4. Save and then close **7-Macros.xlsm**.

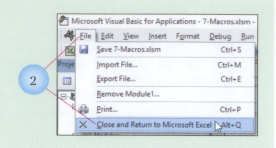

Deleting a Macro

Quick Steps

Delete a Macro
1. Open Macro dialog box.
2. Click macro name.
3. Click Delete button.
4. Click Yes.

If a macro is no longer needed, delete it in the Macro dialog box. Open the Macro dialog box, select the macro name in the *Macro name* list box, and then click the Delete button.

Managing Macros

By default, a macro is stored within the workbook that is active when it is recorded. When the workbook is closed, the macros within it are no longer available. For example, if the file 7-Macros.xlsm is closed, the AcctgDocumentation macro will not be available in a new workbook. To continue using the macros, leave the workbook that contains them open, since by default, the Macro dialog box displays the macros for all the open workbooks in the *Macro name* list box.

Consider creating a macros workbook with a set of standard macros, similar to the macros workbook created in Projects 1a through 1d. Open this workbook when working in Excel and the macros stored within it will be available for all the files that are created or edited during the Excel session. Create one macros workbook and copy it to other computers so a set of standard macros can be distributed to others for use.

Project 2 Customize the Excel Work Environment for Noranda Sportsplex   7 Parts

You will customize the Excel environment by minimizing the ribbon, changing display options, importing and exporting custom settings for the Quick Access Toolbar and ribbon, creating a custom ribbon tab, adding buttons to the Quick Access Toolbar to make features more accessible, and then creating custom views.

Preview Finished Project

Changing Display Options

The Excel Options dialog box contains many options for customizing the environment to suit the user's needs. As shown in Figure 7.5, Excel groups options that affect the display by those that are global settings, those that affect the entire workbook, and those that affect only the active worksheet. Changes to workbook and/or worksheet display options are saved with the workbook.

Quick Steps

**Change Display
Options**
1. Click File tab.
2. Click *Options*.
3. Click *Advanced* in left pane.
4. Change display options as required.
5. Click OK.

Collapse the
Ribbon

Ribbon Display
Options

Quick Steps

Minimize the Ribbon
Press Ctrl + F1.
OR
1. Click Ribbon Display Options button.
2. Click Show Tabs.
OR
Click Collapse the Ribbon button.

Minimizing the Ribbon

When working with a large worksheet, it may be easier to work with the ribbon minimized, which creates more space within the work area. Figure 7.6 shows the worksheet for Project 2a with the customized display options and minimized ribbon.

One way to minimize the ribbon is to click the Collapse the Ribbon button. With the ribbon minimized, clicking a tab temporarily redisplays it to allow selecting a feature. After the feature has been selected, the ribbon returns to the minimized state. Press Ctrl + F1 or double-click the ribbon to toggle it on or off.

Another way to minimize the ribbon is to click the Ribbon Display Options button, which remains in the upper right corner of the screen. Options under this button allow for the quick auto-hiding of the ribbon (including tabs and commands), the showing of the ribbon tabs only (commands are hidden), or the redisplaying of the ribbon tabs and commands.

Figure 7.5 Excel Options Dialog Box with Display Options Shown

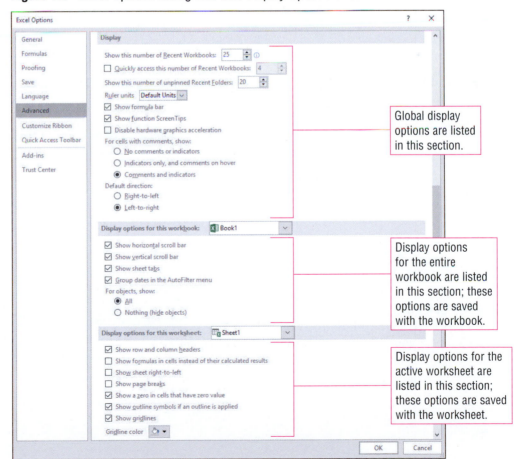

1. Open **NWinterSch.xlsx**.
2. Save the workbook with the name **7-NWinterSch**.
3. Turn off the display of the Formula bar (since no formulas exist in the workbook), turn off the display of sheet tabs (since only one sheet exists in the workbook), and turn off the display of row and column headers and gridlines by completing the following steps:
   a. Click the File tab.
   b. Click *Options*.
   c. Click *Advanced* in the left pane.
   d. Scroll down the Excel Options dialog box to the *Display* section and then click the *Show formula bar* check box to remove the check mark.

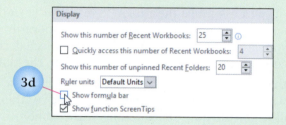

   e. Scroll down to the *Display options for this workbook* section and then click the *Show sheet tabs* check box to remove the check mark.

   f. Scroll down to the *Display options for this worksheet* section and then click the *Show row and column headers* check box to remove the check mark.
   g. Click the *Show gridlines* check box to remove the check mark.

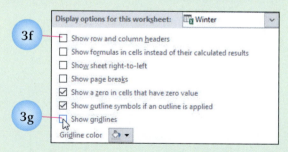

   h. Click OK.
4. Press Ctrl + F1 to hide the ribbon.
5. Compare your screen with the one shown in Figure 7.6.
6. Save and then close **7-NWinterSch.xlsx**.

Figure 7.6 Project 2a Worksheet with Customized Display Options and Minimized Ribbon

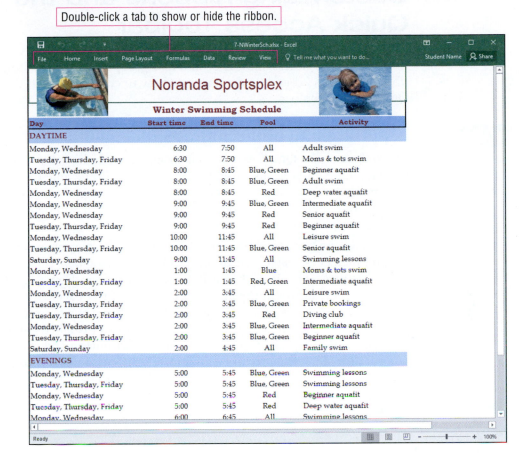

Double-click a tab to show or hide the ribbon.

Project 2b Restoring Default Display Options

1. Press Ctrl + N to open a new blank workbook.
2. Notice that the workbook and worksheet display options that were changed in Project 2a are restored to the default options. The Formula bar remains hidden (since this is a global display option) and the ribbon remains minimized (since the display of the ribbon is a toggle on/off option).
3. Open **7-NWinterSch.xlsx**.
4. Notice that the sheet tabs, row and column headers, and gridlines are hidden (since these display option settings are saved with the workbook).
5. Close **7-NWinterSch.xlsx** without saving it.
6. Click the Ribbon Display Options button next to the Minimize button in the upper right corner of the screen and then click *Show Tabs and Commands* at the drop-down list.
7. Redisplay the Formula bar by completing the following steps:
   a. Open the Excel Options dialog box.
   b. Click *Advanced* in the left pane.
   c. Scroll down the Excel Options dialog box to the *Display* section, click the *Show formula bar* check box to insert a check mark, and then click OK.
8. Close the workbook without saving it.

Customizing Ribbons and the Quick Access Toolbar

When working with Excel, a user may prefer to access frequently used features from the Quick Access Toolbar or in a new group within an existing or new ribbon. Projects 2d and 2e demonstrate how to customize both the ribbon and the Quick Access Toolbar.

Tutorial

Exporting and Importing Customizations

Exporting and Importing Customizations

The ribbon or the Quick Access Toolbar may already have been customized on the computers in your institution's computer lab. To be able to restore these customizations after making changes in the upcoming projects, Project 2c will demonstrate how to save (export) them and Project 2f will demonstrate how to reinstall (import) them.

To save the current ribbon and Quick Access Toolbar settings, click the File tab and then click *Options*. At the Excel Options dialog box, click *Customize Ribbon* in the left pane. The dialog box will display as shown in Figure 7.7. Click the Import/Export button in the lower right corner of the Excel Options dialog box. Click *Export all customizations* to save the file with the custom settings. Use this file to reinstall the saved settings in Project 2f or to install customized settings on a different computer. Click the Import/Export button and then click *Import customization file*. Locate the file and reinstall the customized settings.

Project 2c Exporting Customizations

Part 3 of 7

1. Press Ctrl + N to open a new blank workbook.
2. Save the current ribbon and Quick Access Toolbar settings to the desktop by completing the following steps:
   a. Click the File tab and then click *Options*.
   b. Click *Customize Ribbon* in the left pane of the Excel Options dialog box.
   c. Click the Import/Export button at the bottom right of the Excel Options dialog box.
   d. Click *Export all customizations* at the drop-down list.
   e. Click *Desktop* in the *This PC* list in the left panel of the File Save dialog box.
   f. Change the file name to **7-ExcelCustomizations** and then click Save. The file is saved as **7-ExcelCustomizations.exportedUI**.
   g. Click OK.
   h. Close the workbook. Click Don't Save if prompted to save changes.

Tutorial

Customizing the Ribbon

Customizing the Ribbon

To customize the ribbon by adding a new tab, group, or button, click the File tab and then click *Options*. At the Excel Options dialog box, click *Customize Ribbon* in the left pane. The dialog box will display as shown in Figure 7.7.

The commands shown in the left list box are dependent on the current option in the *Choose commands from* option box. Click the *Choose commands from* option box arrow (displays *Popular Commands*) to select from a variety of options, such as

Figure 7.7 Excel Options Dialog Box with *Customize Ribbon* Selected

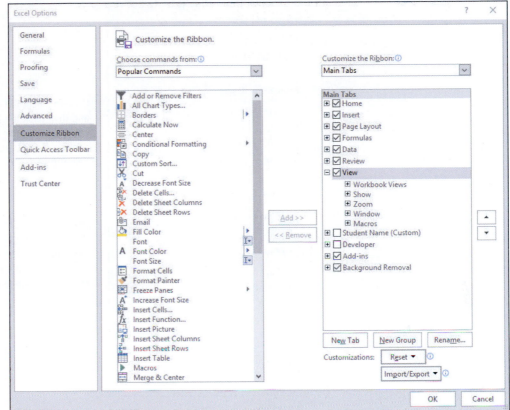

Hint To save the mouse clicks used when switching tabs and choosing options from drop-down lists, create a custom tab with buttons used on a regular basis.

Quick Steps

Create a New Tab and Group

1. Click File tab.
2. Click *Options*.
3. Click *Customize Ribbon* in left pane.
4. Click tab name to precede new tab.
5. Click New Tab button.

Add a New Group to an Existing Tab

1. Click File tab.
2. Click *Options*.
3. Click *Customize Ribbon* in left pane.
4. Click tab name on which to add new group.
5. Click New Group button.

Add a Button to a Group

1. Click File tab.
2. Click *Options*.
3. Click *Customize Ribbon* in left pane.
4. Click group name in which to insert new button.
5. Change *Choose commands from* to command list.
6. Click command.
7. Click Add button.

Commands Not In the Ribbon and *All Commands*. The tabs shown in the right list box are dependent on the current option in the *Customize the Ribbon* option box. Click the *Customize the Ribbon* option box arrow (displays *Main Tabs*) to select *All Tabs*, *Main Tabs*, or *Tool Tabs*.

Create a new group in an existing tab and add buttons within the new group, or create a new tab, create a new group within the tab, and then add buttons to the new group.

Creating a New Tab In the *Main Tabs* list box, click the tab name that is to appear before the new tab when it is positioned and then click the New Tab button below the *Main Tabs* list box. This inserts a new tab in the list box along with a new group below the new tab, as shown in Figure 7.8. If the wrong tab name was selected before clicking the *New Tab* button, the new tab can be moved up or down the list box. Click *New Tab (Custom)* and then click the Move Up button or Move Down button at the right side of the dialog box.

Adding Buttons to a Group Click the group name within the tab, click the desired command in the list box at the left, and then click the Add button that displays between the two list boxes. Remove commands in a similar manner: click the command to be removed from the tab group and then click the Remove button between the two list boxes.

Renaming a Tab, Group, or Command Click the tab name in the *Main Tabs* list box and then click the Rename button below the *Main Tabs* list box. At the Rename dialog box, type the name for the tab and then press the Enter key or

Figure 7.8 New Tab and Group Created in the Customize Ribbon Pane at the Excel Options Dialog Box

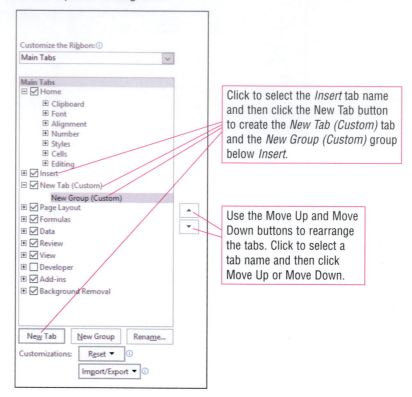

Click to select the *Insert* tab name and then click the New Tab button to create the *New Tab (Custom)* tab and the *New Group (Custom)* group below *Insert*.

Use the Move Up and Move Down buttons to rearrange the tabs. Click to select a tab name and then click Move Up or Move Down.

Quick Steps

Rename a Tab or Group
1. Click File tab.
2. Click *Options*.
3. Click *Customize Ribbon* in left pane.
4. Click tab or group to be renamed.
5. Click Rename button.
6. Type new name.
7. Click OK.

click OK. Display the Rename dialog box by right-clicking the tab name and then clicking *Rename* at the shortcut menu.

Complete similar steps to rename a group or command. The Rename dialog box for a group or command name contains a *Symbol* list box as well as the *Display name* text box. Type the new name for the group in the *Display name* text box and then press the Enter key or click OK. Using symbols helps to identify new buttons.

Project 2d Customizing the Ribbon

Part 4 of 7

1. Open **NationalJE.xlsx**.
2. Save the workbook with the name **7-NationalJE**.
3. Customize the ribbon by adding a new tab and two new groups within the tab by completing the following steps. *Note: The ribbon will be reset to its original settings in Project 2f.*
   a. Click the File tab and then click *Options*.
   b. Click *Customize Ribbon* in the left pane of the Excel Options dialog box.

c. Click *Insert* in the *Main Tabs* list box at the right of the dialog box.

d. Click the New Tab button below the list box. (This inserts a new tab below the Insert tab and a new group below the new tab.)

e. With *New Group (Custom)* selected below *New Tab (Custom)*, click the New Group button below the list box. (This inserts another new group on the new tab.)

4. Rename the tab and the groups by completing the following steps:

a. Click to select *New Tab (Custom)* in the *Main Tabs* list box.

b. Click the Rename button below the list box.

c. At the Rename dialog box, type your first and last names and then click OK.

d. Click to select the first *New Group (Custom)* group name that displays below the new tab.

e. Click the Rename button.

f. At the Rename dialog box, type Borders in the *Display name* text box and then click OK. (The Rename dialog box for a group or button displays symbols in addition to the *Display name* text box. You will apply a symbol to a button in a later step.)

g. Right-click the *New Group (Custom)* group name below *Borders (Custom)* and then click *Rename* at the shortcut menu.

h. At the Rename dialog box, type Statistics in the *Display name* and then click OK.

5. Add buttons to the *Borders (Custom)* group by completing the following steps:

a. Click to select *Borders (Custom)* in the *Main Tabs* list box.

b. Click the *Choose commands from* option box arrow (displays *Popular Commands*) and then click *All Commands* at the drop-down list.

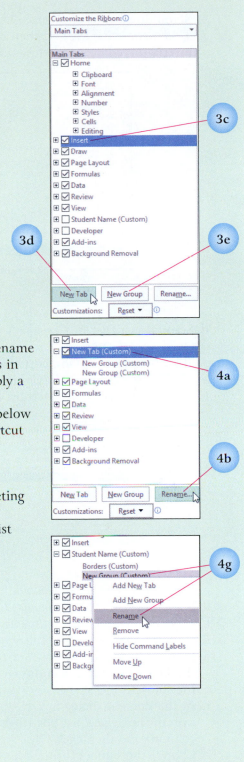

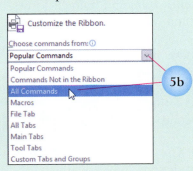

c. Scroll down the *All Commands* list box (the commands display alphabetically), click *Thick Bottom Border*, and then click the Add button between the two list boxes. (This inserts the command below the *Borders (Custom)* group name.)

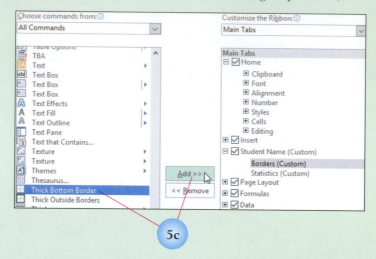

5c

d. Scroll down the *All Commands* list box, click *Top and Double Bottom Border*, and then click the Add button.
6. Add buttons to the *Statistics (Custom)* group by completing the following steps:
   a. Click to select *Statistics (Custom)* in the *Main Tabs* list box.
   b. Scroll up the *All Commands* list box, click *Average*, and then click the Add button.

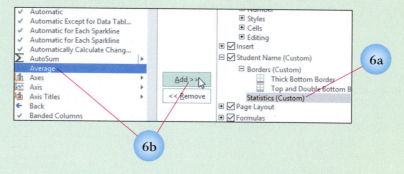

6a

6b

c. Scroll down the *All Commands* list box, click *Max*, and then click the Add button.
d. Scroll down the *All Commands* list box, click *Min*, and then click the Add button.
7. Change the symbol for the Average, Max, and Min buttons by completing the following steps:
   a. Right-click *Average* below *Statistics (Custom)* in the *Main Tabs* list box and then click *Rename* at the shortcut menu.
   b. At the Rename dialog box, click the calculator icon in the *Symbol* list box (fifth row, second column) and then click OK.
   c. Change the symbol for the *Max* and the *Min* buttons to the calculator symbol by completing actions similar to those in Step 7b.

7b

8. Click OK to close the Excel Options dialog box.
9. Use buttons on the custom tab to format and add formulas to the worksheet by completing the following steps:

a. Make cell A3 the active cell, click the custom tab labeled with your name, and then click the Thick Bottom Border button in the Borders group.

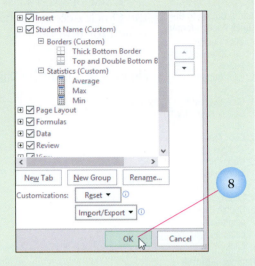

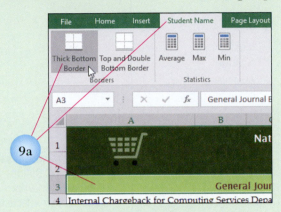

b. Select the range B6:H6 and then click the Thick Bottom Border button in the Borders group.
c. Make cell D18 the active cell and then click the Top and Double Bottom Border button in the Borders group.
d. Make cell D20 the active cell and then click the Average button in the Statistics group.
e. With the range D7:D19 selected in the formula *=AVERAGE(D7:D19)*, drag to select the range D7:D17 and then press the Enter key.
f. With cell D21 active, click the Max button in the Statistics group, drag to select the range D7:D17, and then press the Enter key.
g. With cell D22 active, click the Min button in the Statistics group, drag to select the range D7:D17, and then press the Enter key.
10. Save **7-NationalJE.xlsx**.
11. In a new Word document, insert a screenshot of the worksheet showing the custom tab by using either the Print Screen with Paste or the Screenshot feature (Insert tab, Screenshot button in Illustrations group). Type your name a few lines below the screenshot.
12. Save the Microsoft Word document with the name **7-NationalJE**.
13. Print **7-NationalJE.docx** and then exit Word.
14. Print and then close **7-NationalJE.xlsx**.

Check Your Work

Tutorial

Customizing the
Quick Access
Toolbar

 Customize
Quick Access
Toolbar

Customizing the Quick Access Toolbar

Click the Customize Quick Access Toolbar button at the right side of the Quick Access Toolbar to open the Customize Quick Access Toolbar drop-down list, as shown in Figure 7.9. Click *More Commands* at the drop-down list to open the Excel Options dialog box with *Quick Access Toolbar* selected in the left pane, as shown in Figure 7.10. Change the list of commands shown in the left list box by clicking the *Choose commands from* option box arrow and then clicking the appropriate category. Scroll down the list box to locate the command and then double-click the command name to add it to the Quick Access Toolbar.

Quick Steps

Add a Button to the Quick Access Toolbar

1. Click Customize Quick Access Toolbar button.
2. Click button.

OR

1. Click Customize Quick Access Toolbar button.
2. Click *More Commands*.
3. Click *Choose commands from* option box arrow.
4. Click category.
5. Double-click command in commands list box.
6. Click OK.

Remove a Button from the Quick Access Toolbar

1. Click Customize Quick Access Toolbar button.
2. Click command.

OR

1. Click Customize Quick Access Toolbar button.
2. Click *More Commands*.
3. Click command in right list box.
4. Click Remove button.
5. Click OK.

A few of Excel's less popular features are available only by adding buttons to the Quick Access Toolbar. If a feature is not available in any tab on the ribbon, search for it in the *All Commands* list box.

Figure 7.9 Customize Quick Access Toolbar Drop-Down List

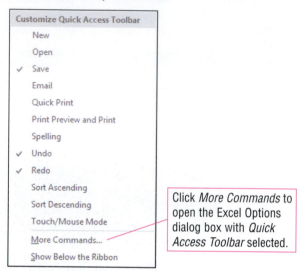

Click *More Commands* to open the Excel Options dialog box with *Quick Access Toolbar* selected.

Figure 7.10 Excel Options Dialog Box with *Quick Access Toolbar* Selected

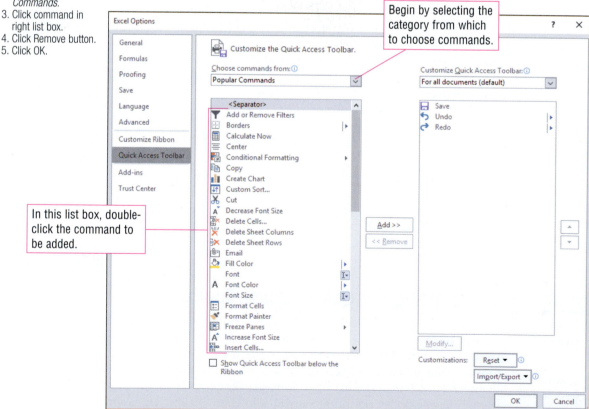

Begin by selecting the category from which to choose commands.

In this list box, double-click the command to be added.

1. Press Ctrl + N to open a new blank workbook and then add the Print Preview and Print and Sort commands to the Quick Access Toolbar by completing the following steps. *Note: You will reset the Quick Access Toolbar to the original settings in Project 2f.*

   a. Click the Customize Quick Access Toolbar button at the right side of the Quick Access Toolbar.

   b. Click *Print Preview and Print* at the drop-down list. The Print Preview and Print button is added to the end of the Quick Access Toolbar. *Note: Skip to Step 1d if the Print Preview and Print button already appears on your Quick Access Toolbar.*

   c. Click the Customize Quick Access Toolbar button.

   d. Click *More Commands* at the drop-down list.

   e. At the Excel Options dialog box with *Quick Access Toolbar* selected in the left pane, click the *Choose commands from* option box arrow and then click *All Commands*.

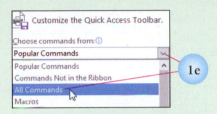

   f. Scroll down the *All Commands* list box and then double-click the second *Sort* option, which displays the ScreenTip *Data Tab | Sort & Filter | Sort...(SortDialog)*. *Note: The commands are organized in alphabetical order; you will need to scroll far down the list to find this option.*

   g. Click OK. The Sort button is added to the end of the Quick Access Toolbar.

2. Type your name in cell A1, press the Enter key, and then click the Print Preview and Print button on the Quick Access Toolbar to display the Print backstage area.

3. Press Esc to close the Print backstage area.

4. Click the Sort button on the Quick Access Toolbar to open the Sort dialog box.

5. Click the Cancel button at the Sort dialog box.

6. Close the workbook. Click the Don't Save button when prompted to save changes.

Delete a button from the Quick Access Toolbar by clicking the Customize Quick Access Toolbar button and then clicking the command at the drop-down list. If the command is not in the drop-down list, click the *More Commands* option. At the Excel Options dialog box, double-click the command in the right list box.

Resetting the Ribbons and the Quick Access Toolbar

Restore the original ribbons and Quick Access Toolbar that came with Excel 2016 by clicking the Reset button below the *Main Tabs* list box in the Excel Options dialog box with *Customize Ribbon* selected. Clicking the Reset button displays two options: *Reset only selected Ribbon tab* and *Reset all customizations*. Click *Reset all customizations* to restore the ribbons and Quick Access Toolbar to their original settings and then click Yes at the message box that displays the question *Delete all Ribbon and Quick Access Toolbar customizations for this program?* To remove a tab that was created previously, right-click the tab and then click *Customize the Ribbon*. Right-click the tab in the *Main Tabs* list box and then click *Remove*.

To restore the ribbons and Quick Access Toolbar to your institution's original settings, import the settings exported in Project 2c. Click the Import/Export button in the lower right corner of the Excel Options dialog box and then click *Import customization file*. Locate the file and reinstall the customized settings.

Project 2f Importing Ribbon and Quick Access Toolbar Customizations   **Part 6 of 7**

1. Import the ribbon and Quick Access Toolbar customizations you saved in Project 2c to reset your institution's original settings by completing the following steps:
   a. Press Ctrl + N to open a new blank workbook.
   b. Click the File tab and then click *Options*.
   c. Click *Customize Ribbon* in the left pane of the Excel Options dialog box.
   d. Click the Import/Export button at the bottom right of the Excel Options dialog box.
   e. Click *Import customization file* at the drop-down list.
   f. Click *Desktop* in the *This PC* list in the left panel of the File Open dialog box.
   g. Click **7-ExcelCustomizations.exportedUI**.
   h. Click Open.
   i. Click Yes at the message asking if you want to replace all the existing ribbon and Quick Access Toolbar customizations for this program.
   j. Click OK.
2. Close the workbook. Click Don't Save if prompted to save changes.

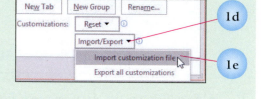

Tutorial

Creating and Applying a Custom View

Quick Steps
Create a Custom View
1. Change display and print settings as desired.
2. Click View tab.
3. Click Custom Views.
4. Click Add button.
5. Type name for view.
6. Choose *Include in view* options.
7. Click OK.

Custom Views

Creating and Applying a Custom View

A custom view saves display and print settings for the active worksheet. These settings can involve column widths, row heights, hidden rows and/or columns, filter settings, cell selections, windows settings, page layout options, and print areas. Create multiple custom views for the same worksheet and access stored views using the Custom Views dialog box. In Project 2g, three custom views are created that store display settings, hidden rows, and a row height for a swimming schedule. Switch between views to show different portions of the worksheet, such as only the daytime swimming activities.

Begin creating a custom view by applying the required settings to the active worksheet, clicking the cell to be active, and displaying the rows and columns to be shown on the screen. When finished, click the View tab, click the Custom Views button in the Workbook Views group, click the Add button, type a name for the custom view, and then click OK.

Quick Steps

Apply a Custom View
1. Click View tab.
2. Click Custom Views button.
3. Click view name.
4. Click Show button.

💡 **Hint** A custom view cannot be used in a worksheet with a table.

Change a worksheet to display the settings for a custom view by opening the Custom Views dialog box, selecting the view name in the *Views* list box, and then clicking the Show button. Another method is to double-click the view name. If a worksheet is active other than the one in which the view was created, Excel will switch to the worksheet the view applies to. A custom view can be applied only to the worksheet in which it was created.

If a custom view is no longer required, delete it by opening the Custom Views dialog box, selecting the custom view name in the *Views* list box, and then clicking the Delete button.

Project 2g Creating and Applying Custom Views   Part 7 of 7

1. Open **7-NWinterSch.xlsx**.
2. Save the workbook, name it **7-NWinterSch-CV**, and redisplay the row and column headers in the worksheet. Refer to Project 2b for assistance with this step.
3. Create a custom view with display settings for all the swimming sessions by completing the following steps:
   a. Select rows 4 through 37, click the Format button in the Cells group on the Home tab, click *Row Height* at the drop-down list, type **20** in the *Row height* text box at the Row Height dialog box, and then click OK.
   b. Press Ctrl + Home.
   c. Click the View tab.
   d. Click the Custom Views button in the Workbook Views group.
   e. Click the Add button at the Custom Views dialog box.
   f. With the insertion point positioned in the *Name* text box at the Add View dialog box, type **AllSessions**.
   g. Make sure that the *Print settings* and *Hidden rows, columns and filter settings* check boxes contain check marks and then click OK.
4. Create a second custom view to display the daytime swimming activities and hide the evening activities by completing the following steps:
   a. Select rows 24 through 37 and then press Ctrl + 9 to hide the rows.
   b. Press Ctrl + Home.
   c. Click the View tab and then click the Custom Views button in the Workbook Views group.
   d. At the Custom Views dialog box, click the Add button.
   e. At the Add View dialog box, type **DaytimeSessions** in the *Name* text box.
   f. Make sure that the *Print settings* and *Hidden rows, columns and filter settings* check boxes contain check marks and then click OK.
5. Click the Custom Views button in the Workbook Views group.
6. With *AllSessions* selected in the *Views* list box, click the Show button to apply the custom view.

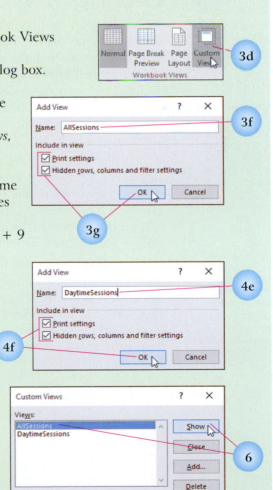

7. Create a third custom view to show only the evening swimming sessions by completing the following steps:
   a. Select rows 4 through 23 and hide the rows by completing a step similar to Step 4a.
   b. Create a custom view named *EveningSessions* by completing steps similar to Steps 4b–4f.
8. Click the Custom Views button and then double-click *DaytimeSessions* in the *Views* list box at the Custom Views dialog box.
9. Show the *EveningSessions* custom view.
10. Show the *AllSessions* custom view.
11. Save and then close **7-NWinterSch-CV.xlsx**.

Check Your Work

Project 3 **Save a Workbook as a Template for Noranda Sportsplex**   **2 Parts**

You will modify an existing workbook and then save the revised version as a template.

Preview Finished Project

Tutorial

Saving a
Workbook as
a Template

Saving a Workbook as a Template

A template is a workbook that contains standard text, formulas, and formatting. Cell entries are created and formatted for all the data that does not change. Cells that will contain variable information have formatting applied but are left empty, since they will be filled in when the template is used to generate a worksheet. Examples of worksheets that are well suited to templates include invoices, purchase orders, time cards, and expense forms. These types of worksheets are usually filled in with the same kinds of data but the data itself varies.

Several templates have already been created and are installed with Excel or can be installed after they are downloaded. To use a template to create a worksheet, first check the New backstage area to see if the template already exists. Another option is to search online for templates using categories such as *Budget*, *Invoice*, *Calendars*, and *Expenses*. Once a topic has been selected in the *Suggested Searches* section of the New backstage area, either download one of the templates shown or choose another topic from the Category task pane.

If none of the existing templates meet your needs, create a custom template. To do this, create a workbook that contains all the standard data, formulas, and formatting. Leave the cells empty for any information that is variable but format those cells as required. Save the workbook as a template at the Save As dialog box by changing the *Save as type* option to *Excel Template (*.xltx)*. Before saving the worksheet as a template, consider protecting it by locking all the cells except those that will hold variable data.

Quick Steps

Save a Workbook as a Template
1. Open workbook.
2. Make changes.
3. Click File tab.
4. Click *Save As*.
5. Click *Browse*.
6. Change *Save as type* to *Excel Template (*.xltx)*.
7. Type file name.
8. Click Save button.

Hint If the template workbook contains macros, change the *Save as type* option to *Excel Macro-Enabled Template (*.xltm)*.

1. Open **7-NWinterSch.xlsx**.
2. Redisplay the row and column headers in the worksheet. Refer to Project 2b for assistance with this step.
3. Assume that you work at the Noranda Sportsplex, which publishes swimming schedules on a continual basis. The days and times the pool operates never change but the activities and assigned pools often change. You decide to modify this workbook and then save it as a template to be reused whenever the schedule changes. To begin, make the following changes to the worksheet:
   a. Clear the cell contents for the ranges D5:E23 and D25:E37.
   b. Make cell A2 the active cell and then delete *Winter* in *Winter Swimming Schedule* so that the subtitle reads *Swimming Schedule*.
   c. Insert a new row between rows 2 and 3 and merge and center the cells in the new row to match the subtitle. (This will be used later to enter the timeframe for the new schedule.)

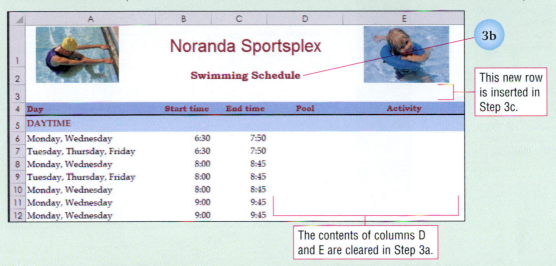

3b — This new row is inserted in Step 3c.

The contents of columns D and E are cleared in Step 3a.

   d. Select and turn off the lock attribute for cell A3 and for the ranges D6:E24 and D26:E38. Deselect the range.
   e. Protect the worksheet. Do not assign a password to unprotect it.
4. Save the revised workbook as a template by completing the following steps:
   a. Click the File tab.
   b. Click *Save As*.
   c. Click the *Browse* option.
   d. Click *Save as type* and then click *Excel Template (*.xltx)* at the pop-up list.
   e. Select the current text in the *File name* text box and then type SwimSchTemplate-StudentName, substituting your name for *StudentName*.
   f. Click the Save button.

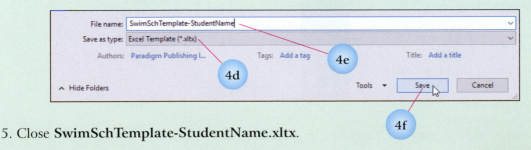

4d   4e   4f

5. Close **SwimSchTemplate-StudentName.xltx**.

Check Your Work

Using a Custom Template

Quick Steps

Use a Custom Template
1. Click File tab.
2. Click *New*.
3. Click *PERSONAL*.
4. Double-click template.

Delete a Custom Template
1. Click File tab.
2. Click *Open*.
3. Click *Computer*.
4. Click Browse button.
5. Navigate to [c:]\ Users*username*\ Documents\Custom Office Templates.
6. Right-click template name.
7. Click *Delete*.
8. Click Cancel.

💡 **Hint** By default, custom template workbook files are stored in the path [c:]\Users*username*\ Documents\Custom Office Templates.

To use a template that you created, click the File tab and then click *New*. At the New backstage area, click *PERSONAL*. This opens the PERSONAL template section, as shown in Figure 7.11. Double-click the name of the template to open it. A workbook (.xlsx) opens with the name of the template followed by a *1*. Save the document with a more descriptive name. In Project 3b, you will create a new workbook using the template created in Project 3a, add information for the Winter 2018 schedule, and then save the workbook as 7-SwimSchWinter2018.xlsx.

Figure 7.11 New Backstage Area with *PERSONAL* Template Section Selected

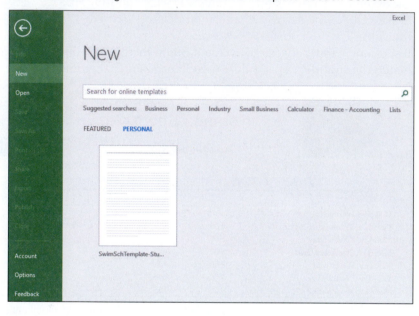

Project 3b Using a Custom Template

1. At a blank Excel screen, open the template created in Project 3a by completing the following steps:
   a. Click the File tab.
   b. Click *New*.
   c. At the New backstage area, click *PERSONAL*.
   d. In the PERSONAL template section, double-click *SwimSchTemplate-StudentName.xltx.* (Your template will have your name in place of *StudentName.*)

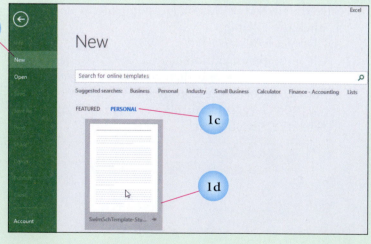

2. Look at the workbook name in the title bar. Notice that Excel has added *1* to the end of the name.
3. Make cell A3 the active cell and then type Winter 2018.

Deleting a Custom Template

To delete a custom template, use the Open dialog box to navigate to [c:]\Users\ *username*\Documents\Custom Office Templates. Right-click the name of the template to be deleted and then click *Delete* at the shortcut menu. Click Cancel to close the Open dialog box.

Project 4   **Managing Excel's Save Options**   **2 Parts**

You will review Excel's current save options, modify the AutoRecover options, and then recover an unsaved workbook.

Preview Finished Project

Customizing Save Options

The AutoRecover feature saves versions of your work at a specified time interval. This will be beneficial in case changes are not saved or Excel closes unexpectedly (such as during a power outage). When Excel restarts, the opening screen displays a *Recovered* section above the Recent list. Click the Show Recovered Files hyperlink and the Document Recovery task pane opens with a list of workbooks for which AutoRecover files exist.

By default, Excel's AutoRecover feature is turned on and will automatically save AutoRecover information every 10 minutes. The time interval can be adjusted to suit the user's needs. Keep in mind that data loss can still occur with AutoRecover turned on. For example, suppose the time interval is set at 20 minutes and a power outage occurs 15 minutes after an AutoSave. When Excel restarts, the recovered file will not contain the last 15 minutes of work if the workbook was not saved manually.

In conjunction with AutoRecover, Excel provides the AutoSave feature, which keeps the last version of a workbook saved in a temporary file. If a workbook is closed without saving or an earlier version of the file is wanted, the autosaved version can be recovered. At the bottom of the *Recent* option list, click the Recover Unsaved Workbooks button to view a list of autosaved files.

Open the Excel Options dialog box and select *Save* in the left pane to view and/or change the AutoRecover and AutoSave options.

Project 4a Customizing Save Options

1. At a blank Excel screen, click the File tab and then click *Options* to open the Excel Options dialog box.
2. Click *Save* in the left pane of the Excel Options dialog box.
3. Note the current settings for *Save AutoRecover information every [ ] minutes* and *Keep the last autosaved version if I close without saving*. By default, both check boxes should be checked and the time interval should be 10 minutes; however, the settings may have been changed on the computer you are using. If that is the case, write down the options so you can restore the program to its original state once you have finished this project.
4. If necessary, insert check marks in the two check boxes to turn on the AutoRecover and AutoSave features.
5. Select the current value in the *Save AutoRecover information every [ ] minutes* measurement box and then type 2 to change the time interval to 2 minutes.
6. Click OK.

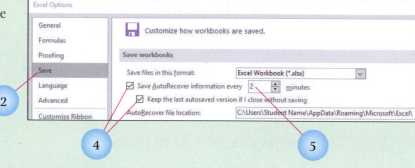

Project 4b Recovering a Workbook

1. Open **7-NationalJE.xlsx**.
2. Save the workbook with the name **7-NationalJE-4**.
3. Note the system time in the bottom right corner of the screen. You will use this time to make sure that more than two minutes elapse before you interrupt the Excel session.
4. Make the following changes to the worksheet:
   a. Select the range A7:A17 and apply the standard dark red font color (first color in the *Standard Colors* section of the drop-down color palette).
   b. Select the range E7:E17 and apply the standard dark red font color.
   c. Delete rows 20 through 22 to remove the data from the workbook.

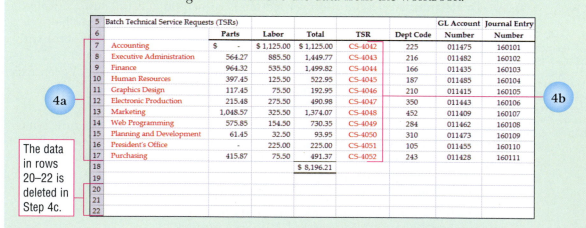

The data in rows 20–22 is deleted in Step 4c.

5. Make sure more than two minutes has elapsed since you checked the system time in Step 3. If necessary, wait until you are sure an AutoRecover file has been saved.

6. Press Alt + Ctrl + Delete.

7. At the Windows screen, select *Task Manager*.

8. At the Task Manager dialog box, click *Microsoft Excel (32 bit)* in the task list box and then click the End task button.

9. Close the Task Manager dialog box.

10. Restart Microsoft Excel. At the opening screen, click the Show Recovered Files hyperlink in the *Recovered* section. Two files are available: the original version of the file used in this project and the AutoRecovered version.

11. Point to the first file in the Document Recovery task pane. A ScreenTip displays stating that the first file is the AutoRecover version.

12. Point to the second file in the Document Recovery task pane. A ScreenTip displays stating that the second file is the original workbook.

13. Click the first file in the Document Recovery task pane. Notice that the edited version of the file appears. Look at the additional information displayed next to the file name in the Title bar. Excel includes *(version 1)* and *[Autosaved]* in the file name. Notice also that the autosaved file has the file extension *.xlsb*.

14. Double-click *Recovered* next to *Ready* in the task bar at the bottom of the screen to redisplay the Document Recovery task pane.

15. Click the second file in the Document Recovery task pane. Notice that the original workbook opens and the message *[Last saved by user]* is added to the file name in the Title bar.

16. Close both workbooks. Click Save when prompted to save changes and then click *Save* at the Save As dialog box to accept the default name *7-NationalJE-4 (Autosaved).xlsx*.

17. Open the Excel Options dialog box. The time interval changed back to 10 minutes when you clicked *End task* in Project 4b, Step 8. If necessary, restore the Save options to the settings you wrote down in Project 4a. Close the Excel Options dialog box.

Check Your Work

The Save options at the Excel Options dialog box also allow changing the drive and/or folder in which to store AutoRecovered files, as well as the default file location for all new workbooks.

At the Recent backstage area, click the Recover Unsaved Workbooks button at the bottom of the *Recent* option list to view a list of autosaved files.

Chapter Summary

- Create a macro for a task that is repeated frequently and for which the steps do not vary.

- To begin recording a new macro, click the View tab, click the Macros button arrow in the Macros group, and then click *Record Macro*.

- At the Record Macro dialog box, assign the macro a name, an optional shortcut key, and a description.

- Click OK to turn on the macro recorder and close the Record Macro dialog box. All the commands and keystrokes will be recorded until the Stop Recording button is clicked.

- Workbooks that contain macros are saved in the Excel Macro-Enabled Workbook (*.xlsm) file format.

- Run a macro by opening the Macro dialog box and double-clicking the macro name.

- Run a macro assigned to a shortcut key by pressing Ctrl + the assigned letter.

- Excel differentiates the case of the letter typed in the *Shortcut key* text box at the Record Macro dialog box. An uppercase letter is assigned with the shortcut key Ctrl + Shift + the assigned letter.

- If a macro and an Excel feature are both assigned to the same shortcut key, the macro overrides the feature.

- The instructions for a macro are recorded in Visual Basic for Applications (VBA) program code. To edit a macro, open the Macro dialog box, click the macro name to be edited, and then click the Edit button. A Microsoft Visual Basic for Applications window opens, displaying a code module in which the program code for the macro can be edited.

- After editing the macro, save the changes, click File, and then click *Close and Return to Microsoft Excel*.

- An alternative to editing a macro in VBA is recording a new macro and then saving it with the same name to replace the existing macro.

- Delete a macro at the Macro dialog box.

- Macros are stored in the workbook in which they are created. When the Macro dialog box is open, all the macros from all the open workbooks are accessible. Therefore, to use a macro stored in another workbook, open that workbook first.

- Another option for making macros accessible to other workbooks is to create a macros workbook with a set of standard macros and then open the macros workbook when working in Excel.

- Display options in Excel are grouped as global display options, options that affect the current workbook, and options that affect only the active worksheet.

- Customized workbook and worksheet display options are saved with the file.

- Minimize the ribbon to provide more space in the work area when working with a large worksheet. Clicking a tab temporarily redisplays the ribbon to allow a feature to be selected.

- To customize the ribbon, open the Excel Options dialog box and then click *Customize Ribbon* in the left pane.

- Customize the ribbon by creating a new tab, creating a new group within the new tab, and/or adding buttons within the new group.

- Create a new tab by clicking the tab name that will precede the new tab and then clicking the New Tab button. A new group is automatically added with the new tab.

- Add buttons to a group by clicking the group name, selecting the desired command in the commands list box, and then clicking the Add button between the two list boxes.

- Rename a tab by selecting the tab name, clicking the Rename button, typing a new name, and then pressing the Enter key or clicking OK. Rename a group or command using a similar process.

- Add buttons to or delete buttons from the Quick Access Toolbar using the Customize Quick Access Toolbar button. Locate a command to add by opening the Excel Options dialog box with *Quick Access Toolbar* selected.

- Export and import customizations to save and restore previous settings on the ribbon(s) and Quick Access Toolbar.

- A custom view saves display and print settings so they can be applied to a worksheet when needed.

- Multiple custom views can be created for the same worksheet at the Custom Views dialog box. Open this dialog box by clicking the Custom Views button in the Workbook Views group on the View tab.

- A template is a workbook that contains standard text, formatting, and formulas.

- Create a custom template from an existing workbook by selecting *Excel template (*.xltx)* in the *Save as type* option box at the Save As dialog box.

- To use a custom template, open the New backstage area, click *PERSONAL* to display the templates, and then double-click the custom template name.

- By default, Excel's AutoRecover feature saves an open file every 10 minutes. If an Excel session is unexpectedly terminated or a file is closed without saving, the file can be recovered at the Document Recovery task pane.

- The AutoSave feature saves the last version of a workbook in a temporary file. If a workbook is closed without saving or an earlier version is wanted, the autosaved version can be recovered using the Recover Unsaved Workbooks button.

Commands Review

FEATURE	RIBBON TAB, GROUP/OPTION	BUTTON	KEYBOARD SHORTCUT
customize display options	File, *Options*		
customize Quick Access Toolbar	File, *Options*		
customize ribbons	File, *Options*		
customize save options	File, *Options*		
customize view	View, Workbook Views		
delete macro	View, Macros		Alt + F8
edit macro	View, Macros		Alt + F8
minimize ribbon			Ctrl + F1
record macro	View, Macros	OR	
ribbon display options			Ctrl + F1
save as macro-enabled workbook	File, *Save As*		F12
use custom template	File, *New*		

Microsoft® Excel®

CHAPTER 8

Importing, Exporting, and Distributing Data

Performance Objectives

Upon successful completion of Chapter 8, you will be able to:

1 Import data from an Access table and text file

2 Append data from an Excel worksheet to an Access table

3 Embed and link data in an Excel worksheet to a Word document

4 Copy and paste data in an Excel worksheet to a PowerPoint presentation

5 Export data as a text file

6 Check for accessibilities issues

7 Scan and remove private or confidential information from a workbook

8 Mark a workbook as final

9 Check a workbook for features incompatible with earlier versions of Excel

10 View Trust Center settings

11 Save an Excel workbook as a PDF or XPS file

12 Save an Excel worksheet as a web page

Precheck

Check your current skills to help focus your study.

Exchanging data between programs by importing or exporting eliminates duplication of effort and reduces the likelihood of data errors or missed entries, which could occur if the data was retyped. One of the advantages of working with a suite of programs such as Microsoft Word, Excel, Access, and PowerPoint is being able to easily integrate data from one program to another. In this chapter, you will learn how to bring data into an Excel worksheet from external sources and how to export data in a worksheet to other programs. You will also learn how to use features that allow distributing Excel data using a variety of methods.

SNAP

If you are a SNAP user, launch the Precheck and Tutorials from your Assignments page.

Data Files

Before beginning chapter work, copy the EL2C8 folder to your storage medium and then make EL2C8 the active folder.

You will import US Census Bureau data related to a market research project from an Access database, along with a text file previously downloaded from the Census Bureau.

Preview Finished Project

Importing Data into Excel

Tutorial

Importing Data
into Excel

Quick Steps

Import an Access Table

1. Make active cell at which to begin import.
2. Click Data tab.
3. Click From Access button.
4. Navigate to drive and/or folder.
5. Double-click source database file name.
6. If necessary, click table name and then OK.
7. Select view format.
8. Click OK.

From Access

Hint Only one table can be imported at a time. To import all the tables in the source database, repeat the import process for each table.

The Get External Data group on the Data tab contains buttons for importing data from external sources into an Excel worksheet. During an import or export routine, the program containing the original data is called the *source* and the program to which the data source is being copied, embedded, or linked is called the *destination*. To import data, make active the cell in which the imported data is to start and then click the button representing the source application or click the From Other Sources button to select the source from a drop-down list.

A connection can be established to an external data source to avoid having to repeat the import process each time the data needs to be analyzed in Excel. Once a connection has been created, the import can be repeated in another worksheet by simply clicking the connection file in the Existing Connections dialog box.

Importing Data from Access

Exchanging data between Access and Excel is a seamless process since the data in an Access datasheet is structured in the same row and column format as the data in an Excel worksheet. The imported data can be appended to an existing worksheet or placed in a new worksheet.

To import an Access table, click the Data tab and then click the From Access button in the Get External Data group. At the Select Data Source dialog box, navigate to the drive and/or folder in which the source database resides and then double-click the Access database file name in the file list. If the source database contains more than one table, the Select Table dialog box opens. Choose the table containing the data to be imported. If the source database contains only one table, the prompt to select a table name will not display. Once the table is identified, the Import Data dialog box appears, as shown in Figure 8.1. Choose how to view the data, select the location in which to begin the import, and then click OK.

Figure 8.1 Import Data Dialog Box

Choose the format in which the Access table is to be imported in this section.

Choose where to place the imported data in this section.

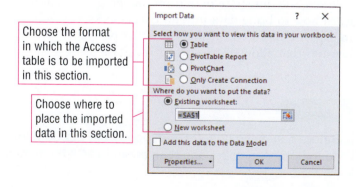

Project 1a Importing Data from an Access Database

1. Open **NuTrendsCensus.xlsx**.
2. Save the workbook with the name **8-NuTrendsCensus**.
3. Import four years of US state population estimates, which have been compiled by the US Census Bureau and stored in an Access database, and append the data to an existing worksheet by completing the following steps:
   a. With PopulationEstimates the active worksheet, make cell A5 active.
   b. Click the Data tab.
   c. Click the From Access button in the Get External Data group.

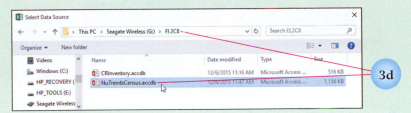

   d. At the Select Data Source dialog box, navigate to the EL2C8 folder on your storage medium and then double-click **NuTrendsCensus.accdb**.

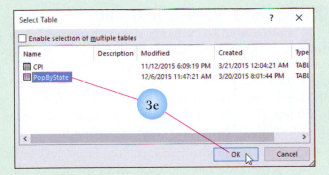

   e. Since the source database contains more than one table, the Select Table dialog box appears. Click *PopByState* in the *Name* column and then click OK.

   f. At the Import Data dialog box with *Table* selected in the *Select how you want to view this data in your workbook* section and the cell reference *=$A$5* in the *Existing worksheet* text box in the *Where do you want to put the data?* section, click OK.

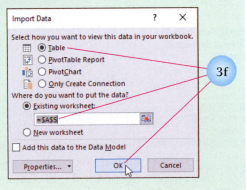

4. Scroll down through the imported table data. Notice that the data is formatted as a table with filter arrows.

5. With the Table Tools Design tab active, make the following changes to the worksheet:
   a. Remove the filter arrows.
   b. Change the table style to Table Style Medium 1 (first column, first row in the *Medium* section).
   c. Make the Home tab active and apply the Comma format with no digits after the decimal point to the range C6:F57.
   d. Adjust the width of columns C through F to 15 characters.
   e. Center-align the labels in the range C5:F5.

	A	B	C	D	E	F
1				NuTrends Market Research		
2				US Population Estimates by State		
3						
4	*Source: US Census Bureau*					
5	ID	State	July2014	July 2013	July 2012	July2011
6	1	Alabama	4,849,377.00	4,833,722.00	4,817,528.00	4,802,740.00
7	2	Alaska	736,732.00	735,132.00	730,307.00	722,718.00
8	3	Arizona	6,731,484.00	6,626,624.00	6,551,149.00	6,482,505.00
9	4	Arkansas	2,966,369.00	2,959,373.00	2,949,828.00	2,937,979.00
10	5	California	38,802,500.00	38,332,521.00	37,999,878.00	37,691,912.00

5a-5e

6. Print the PopulationEstimates worksheet scaled to fit one page in width and height and centered horizontally between the left and right margins.
7. Save **8-NuTrendsCensus.xlsx**.

Check Your Work

Importing Data from a Text File

Hint Most programs can export data in a text file. To use data from a program that is not compatible with Excel, check the program's export options for a text file format.

 From Text

Quick Steps

Import Data from a Comma Separated Text File
1. Make active cell at which to begin import.
2. Click Data tab.
3. Click From Text button.
4. Double-click .csv file name.
5. Click Next.
6. Click *Comma* check box.
7. Click Next.
8. Click Finish.
9. Click OK.

A text file is often used to exchange data between different programs because the file format is recognized by nearly all applications. Text files contain no formatting and consist only of letters, numbers, punctuation symbols, and a few control characters. Two commonly used text file formats separate fields with tabs (delimited file format) or commas (comma separated file format). The text file used in Project 1b is shown in a Notepad window in Figure 8.2. If necessary, view and edit a text file in Notepad before importing it.

To import a text file into Excel, use the From Text button in the Get External Data group on the Data tab and then select the source file at the Import Text File dialog box. Excel displays in the file list any file in the active folder that ends with the file extension *.prn, .txt,* or *.csv.* Once the source file is selected, Excel begins the Text Import Wizard, which will guide the user through the import process using three dialog boxes.

Non-native files including but not limited to web pages, extensible markup language (XML) files, text files, and data sources can also be opened directly in Excel. To open a non-native file directly in Excel, click the File tab and then click the *Open* option. Click the file location and then click the *Browse* option to display the Open dialog box. Navigate to the specific folder and then click the *File Type* option box to display a drop-down list of all the different file types that can be opened in Excel. Click the specific file type and then double-click the file name. If the exact file type is not known, select *All Files (*.*)* to display all the available files. Save the file as an Excel workbook, or if changes were made, resave it as a text file (but note that some features might be lost).

Figure 8.2 Project 1b Text File Content

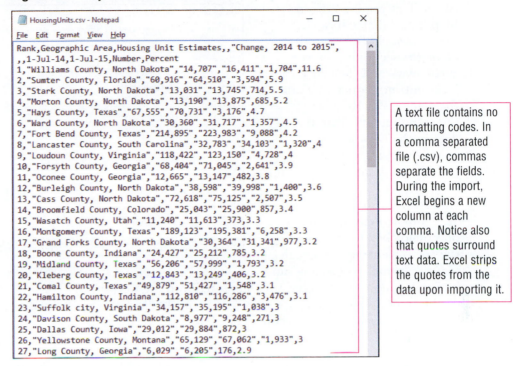

A text file contains no formatting codes. In a comma separated file (.csv), commas separate the fields. During the import, Excel begins a new column at each comma. Notice also that quotes surround text data. Excel strips the quotes from the data upon importing it.

Project 1b Importing Data from a Comma Separated Text File

Part 2 of 2

1. With **8-NuTrendsCensus.xlsx** open, make HousingUnitData the active worksheet.
2. Import statistics related to the top-growing US counties based on changes in housing units, which have been downloaded from the US Census Bureau website and saved in a text file, by completing the following steps:
   a. Make cell A6 active.
   b. Click the Data tab.
   c. Click the From Text button in the Get External Data group.
   d. At the Import Text File dialog box, navigate to the EL2C8 folder on your storage medium, and then double-click *HousingUnits.csv* in the file list.
   e. At the Text Import Wizard - Step 1 of 3 dialog box, with *Delimited* selected in the *Original data type* section, click the *My data has headers* check box to insert a check mark and then click the Next button. Notice that the preview window in the lower half of the dialog box displays a sample of the data in the source text file. Delimited files use commas or tabs as separators, while fixed-width files use spaces.

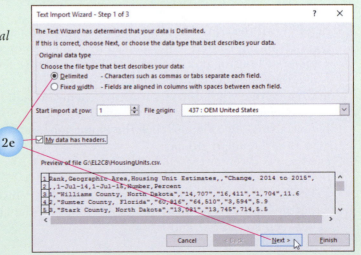

f. At the Text Import Wizard - Step 2 of 3 dialog box, click the *Comma* check box in the *Delimiters* section to insert a check mark and then click the Next button. Notice that after the comma is selected as the delimiter character, the data in the *Data preview* section updates to show the imported data arranged in columns.

g. Click the Finish button at the Text Import Wizard - Step 3 of 3 dialog box to import all the columns using the default *General* format. Formatting can be applied after the data has been imported into the worksheet.

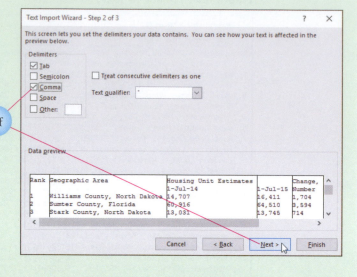

h. At the Import Data dialog box with =$A$6 in the *Existing worksheet* text box in the *Where do you want to put the data?* section, click OK.

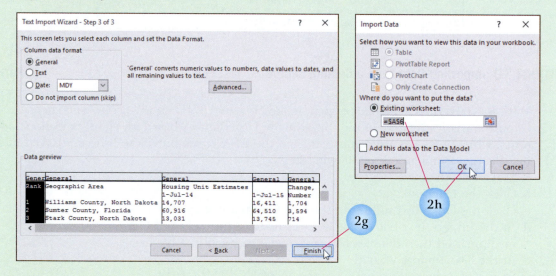

3. Scroll down the worksheet and view the imported data. The text file contains the top 100 counties in the United States ranked by change in housing units from 2014 to 2015. The number of housing units and the percentage change are included for each county.

4. Make the following changes to the data:

a. Change the width of column A to 5 characters and the width of columns C, D, and E to 14 characters.

b. Select the range C6:D6, click the Home tab, and then click the Merge & Center button in the Alignment group.

c. Merge and center the range E6:F6.

d. Right-align the data in cell E7.

e. Scroll to the bottom of the list. Using the Wrap Text, Merge and Center, and Format buttons in the Alignment and Cells groups on the Home tab, adjust the notes so they fit between columns A and F.

5. Center the HousingUnitData worksheet between the left and right margins, change the left and right margins to 0.5 inch, and then print it.
6. Save and then close **8-NuTrendsCensus.xlsx**.
7. The workbook **8-NuTrendsCensus** required two worksheets. If only one worksheet is required in a workbook, open the .csv file directly in Excel by completing the following steps:
   a. Click the File tab and then click the *Open* option. At the Open backstage area, click your OneDrive or *Computer* to locate the data files.
   b. Click the *Browse* option and then navigate to the EL2C8 folder on your storage medium.
   c. Click the *File Type* option box and then click *Text Files (*.prn, *.txt, *.csv)*.
   d. Double-click **HousingUnits.csv** in the file list.
8. Close the workbook without saving.

Check Your Work

Project 2   Export Data from Excel to Various Applications   6 Parts

You will copy and paste data related to car inventory from an Excel worksheet to integrate with an Access database, Word report, and PowerPoint presentation. You will also save a worksheet as a comma separated text file for use in a non-Microsoft program.

Preview Finished Project

Exporting Data from Excel

Excel data can be exported for use in other programs by copying the cells to the Clipboard task pane and then pasting them into the destination file. Another option for exporting is to save the worksheet as a separate file in another file format.

Quick Steps

Append Excel Data to an Access Table

1. Select cells.
2. Click Copy button.
3. Start Access.
4. Open database.
5. Open table in Datasheet view.
6. Click Paste button arrow.
7. Click *Paste Append*.
8. Click Yes.
9. Deselect pasted range.

To use Excel data in Word, PowerPoint, or Access, use the copy and paste method, since the programs within the Microsoft Office suite are designed for integration. To export Excel data for use in another program, open the Save As dialog box and then change the *Save as type* option to the desired file format. If the file format for the destination program does not appear in the *Save as type* list, try copying and pasting the data or go to the Microsoft Office Online website and search for a file format converter that can be downloaded and installed.

Another way to save the current worksheet in a different file format is to click the File tab and then click the *Export* option at the backstage area. At the Export backstage area, click *Change File Type* in the center section. In the *Change File Type* section at the right, click the desired file format in the *Workbook File Types* or *Other File Types* section and then click the Save As button. If necessary, navigate to the desired drive and/or folder in the Save As dialog box. Type the file name and then click the Save button.

Tutorial

Copying and Pasting Data into Access

Copying and Pasting Data into Access

Data in an Excel worksheet can be copied and pasted into an Access table datasheet, query, or form using the Clipboard task pane. Before pasting data into a table datasheet, make sure that the column structures in the two programs match. If the Access datasheet already contains records, choose to replace the existing records or append the Excel data to the end of the table. To export Excel data to an

Access database that does not have an existing table in which to receive the data, perform an import routine from Access. To do this, start Access, open the database, click the External Data tab, and then click the Import Excel spreadsheet button.

Project 2a   Copying and Pasting Excel Data into an Access Datasheet Part 1 of 6

1. Open **CRInventory.xlsx**.
2. Copy and paste the rows in the Inventory worksheet to the bottom of an Access table by completing the following steps:
   a. Make sure Inventory is the active worksheet.
   b. Select the range A5:G33 and then click the Copy button in the Clipboard group on the Home tab.
   c. Start Microsoft Access 2016.
   d. At the Access 2016 opening screen, click the *Open Other Files* option.
   e. At the Open backstage area, click the *Browse* option. At the open dialog box, navigate to the EL2C8 folder on your storage medium and then double-click ***CRInventory.accdb***. If a security warning message displays below the ribbon stating that active content has been disabled, click the Enable Content button.
   f. Double-click *CarInventory* in the Tables group in the Navigation pane at the left side of the Access window. This opens the CarInventory table in Datasheet view. Notice that the structure of the columns in the datasheet is the same as in the source worksheet in Excel.
   g. With the table open in Datasheet view, click the Paste button arrow in the Clipboard group and then click *Paste Append* at the drop-down list.

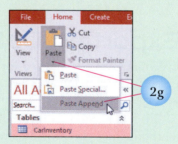

   h. At the Microsoft Access message box stating that you are about to paste 29 records and asking if you are sure, click Yes.

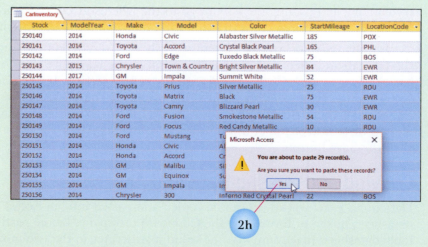

   i. Click in any cell within the datasheet to deselect the pasted records.

3. Print the Access datasheet in landscape orientation by completing the following steps:
   a. Click the File tab, click the *Print* option, and then click Print Preview.
   b. Click the Landscape button in the Page Layout group on the Print Preview tab.
   c. Click the Page Setup button in the Page Layout group.
   d. At the Page Setup dialog box with the Print Options tab selected, change the top and bottom margins to 0.5 inch. The left and right margins should already be set to 1 inch. Click OK.
   e. Click the Print button in the Print group and then click OK at the Print dialog box.
   f. Click the Close Print Preview button in the Close Preview group.
4. Click the Close button in the upper right corner to close Access.
5. Click in any cell to deselect the range in the Inventory worksheet and then press the Esc key to remove the scrolling marquee.
6. Leave the **CRInventory.xlsx** workbook open for the next project.

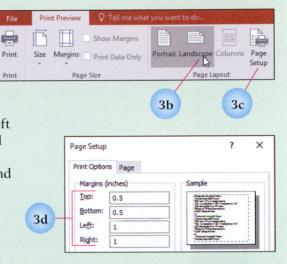

Check Your Work

Copying and Pasting Data into Word

Tutorial

Copying and Pasting Data into Word

Word allows the user to copy and paste Excel data, copy and embed Excel data as an object, or copy and link Excel data as an object using a process similar to the one in Project 2a. Use the copy and paste method if the data being brought into the Word document will not likely be updated or require editing after the source cells are pasted into the Word document. Copy and embed the data to be able to edit it in Word using Excel's editing tools and features. Copy and link the data if the information being pasted into the Word document may need to be updated because a change will likely be made in the source file.

Quick Steps

Embed Excel Data into a Word Document
1. Select cells.
2. Click Copy button.
3. Open Word document.
4. Position insertion point.
5. Click Paste button arrow.
6. Click *Paste Special*.
7. Click *Microsoft Excel Worksheet Object*.
8. Click OK.

Link Excel Data to a Word Document
1. Select cells.
2. Click Copy button.
3. Open Word document.
4. Position insertion point.
5. Click Paste button arrow.
6. Click *Paste Special*.
7. Click *Microsoft Excel Worksheet Object*.
8. Click *Paste link*.
9. Click OK.

Embedding Excel Data into a Word Document To embed copied Excel data in a Word document, open the document, move the insertion point to the location at which to insert the copied Excel data, and then open the Paste Special dialog box. At the Paste Special dialog box, click *Microsoft Excel Worksheet Object* in the *As* list box and then click OK.

To edit an embedded Excel object in Word, double-click the embedded cells to open them for editing in a worksheet. Word's ribbon is temporarily replaced with Excel's ribbon. Click outside the embedded object to restore Word's ribbon and close the worksheet object in Word.

Linking Excel Data to a Word Document When Excel data is linked to a Word document, the source data exists only in Excel. Word places a shortcut to the source data file name and range in the document. When a Word document is opened that contains one or more links, Word prompts the user to update the links. Since the data resides only in the Excel workbook, be careful not to move or rename the original workbook that contains the original data. If this happens, the link in the Word document will no longer work.

To paste copied Excel data as a link in a Word document, open the document, move the insertion point to the location at which to link the cells, open the Paste Special dialog box, click *Microsoft Excel Worksheet Object* in the *As* list box, click *Paste link*, and then click OK.

1. With **CRInventory.xlsx** open, copy and embed the data in the CarCosts worksheet to a Word document by completing the following steps:
   a. Make CarCosts the active worksheet.
   b. Select the range A4:F9.
   c. Click the Copy button in the Clipboard group.
   d. Start Microsoft Word 2016.
   e. Open **CRCarRpt.docx** from the EL2C8 folder on your storage medium. If a security warning displays in the message bar below the ribbon stating that the document is in Protected View, click the Enable Editing button.
   f. Save the document with the name **8-CRCarRpt**.
   g. Press Ctrl + End to move the insertion point to the end of the document.
   h. Click the Paste button arrow in the Clipboard group and then click *Paste Special* at the drop-down list.
   i. At the Paste Special dialog box click *Microsoft Excel Worksheet Object* in the *As* list box and then click OK.
2. Save **8-CRCarRpt.docx**.
3. When Paste Special is used, the copied cells are embedded as an object in the Word document. Edit the embedded object using Excel's editing tools by completing the following steps:
   a. Double-click in any cell in the embedded worksheet object. The object is surrounded with a border and Excel's column and row headers appear. Word's ribbon is temporarily replaced with Excel's ribbon.
   b. Select the range B4:F4 and then click the Center button in the Alignment group.

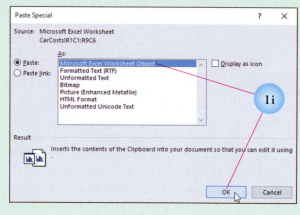

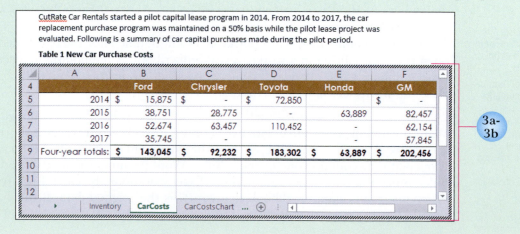

CutRate Car Rentals started a pilot capital lease program in 2014. From 2014 to 2017, the car replacement purchase program was maintained on a 50% basis while the pilot lease project was evaluated. Following is a summary of car capital purchases made during the pilot period.

Table 1 New Car Purchase Costs

	A	B Ford	C Chrysler	D Toyota	E Honda	F GM
4						
5	2014	$ 15,875	$ -	$ 72,850		$ -
6	2015	38,751	28,775	-	63,889	82,457
7	2016	52,674	63,457	110,452	-	62,154
8	2017	35,745	-		-	57,845
9	Four-year totals:	$ 143,045	$ 92,232	$ 183,302	$ 63,889	$ 202,456
10						
11						
12						

Inventory | **CarCosts** | CarCostsChart

c. Click in the document outside the embedded object to close the object and restore Word's ribbon. Excel becomes the active application.
4. Double-click Word in the taskbar. Save and then print **8-CRCarRpt.docx**.
5. Close Word.
6. Click in any cell to deselect the range in the CarCosts worksheet and leave the **CRInventory.xlsx** workbook open for the next project.

Check Your Work

Project 2c Linking Excel Data in a Word Document

Part 3 of 6

1. With **CRInventory.xlsx** open, copy and link the data in the CarCosts worksheet to a Word document by completing the following steps:
   a. With CarCosts the active worksheet, select the range A4:F9 and then click the Copy button.
   b. Start Microsoft Word 2016.
   c. Open **CRCarRpt.docx**.
   d. Save the document with the name **8-CRCarRptLinked**.
   e. Press Ctrl + End to move the insertion point to the end of the document.
   f. Click the Paste button arrow and then click *Paste Special* at the drop-down list.
   g. At the Paste Special dialog box, click *Microsoft Excel Worksheet Object* in the *As* list box and then click the *Paste link* option.
   h. Click OK.

   1g

   Paste Special   ? ×

   Source: Microsoft Excel Worksheet
            CarCosts!R4C1:R9C6

              As:
   ○ Paste: Microsoft Excel Worksheet Object ∧   ☐ Display as icon
   ⦿ Paste link: Formatted Text (RTF)
              Unformatted Text
              Picture (Windows Metafile)
              Bitmap
              Word Hyperlink
              HTML Format
              Unformatted Unicode Text   ∨

   Result
           [icons] Inserts the contents of the Clipboard as a picture.
                    Paste Link creates a shortcut to the source file. Changes to the source file will be reflected in your document.

                                        OK   Cancel

   1h

2. Save and then close **8-CRCarRptLinked.docx**. When data is linked, it exists only in the source program. In the destination document, Word inserts a shortcut to the source range. Edit the source range and view the update to the Word document by completing the following steps:
   a. Click the button on the taskbar representing the Excel workbook **CRInventory.xlsx**.
   b. With CarCosts the active worksheet, press the Esc key to remove the scrolling marquee (if necessary) and then click in any cell to deselect the copied range.
   c. Make cell E5 active, type 85000, and then press the Enter key.
   d. Click the button on the taskbar representing Word.
   e. Open **8-CRCarRptLinked.docx**.
   f. At the Microsoft Word message box asking whether to update the document with data from the linked files, click Yes.

Microsoft Word   ×

  ⚠ This document contains links that may refer to other files. Do you want to update this document with the data from the linked files?

      Show Help >>

                            2f

                              Yes   No

3. Notice that the data inserted in the Excel worksheet is also shown in the linked Word document.
4. Save and then print **8-CRCarRptLinked.docx**.
5. Exit Word.
6. With CarCosts the active worksheet in **CRInventory.xlsx**, delete the content of cell E5 and leave the workbook open for a later project.

Check Your Work

Breaking a Link to an Excel Object

Quick Steps

Break a Link to an Excel Object
1. Open Word document.
2. Right-click linked object.
3. Point to *Linked Worksheet Object*.
4. Click *Links*.
5. Click Break Link button.
6. Click Yes.
7. Save document.

If the Excel data in a Word document no longer needs to be linked, the connection between the source and destination files can be broken. Breaking the link means that the data in the Word document will no longer be connected to the data in the Excel workbook. If a change is made to the original data in Excel, the Word document will not reflect the update. Once the link to the document is broken, the prompt to update the object each time the Word document is opened will no longer appear.

To break a link, open the Word document, right-click the linked object, point to *Linked Worksheet Object,* and then click *Links* at the shortcut menu. This opens the Links dialog box. If more than one linked object exists in the document, click the source object for the link to be broken and then click the Break Link button. At the message box that appears, click Yes to confirm that the link is to be broken.

Project 2d Breaking a Link

Part 4 of 6

1. Start Word and open **8-CRCarRptLinked.docx**.
2. At the message asking whether to update the links, click No.
3. Break the link between the Excel workbook and the linked object by completing the following steps:
   a. Right-click the linked Excel worksheet object.
   b. Point to *Linked Worksheet Object* and then click *Links* at the shortcut menu.
   c. At the Links dialog box with the linked object file name selected in the *Source file* list box, click the Break Link button.

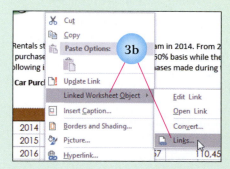
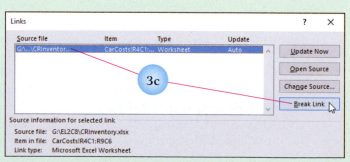

   d. At the Microsoft Word dialog box asking for confirmation to break the selected link, click Yes.
4. Save **8-CRCarRptLinked.docx** and then exit Word.

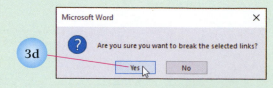

Check Your Work

Copying and Pasting Data into PowerPoint

As they can with Word, users can copy and paste, copy and embed, or copy and link Excel data into slides in a PowerPoint presentation. Charts are often incorporated into presentations to visually depict numerical data in a graph format that is easy to understand. Although tables and charts can be created in PowerPoint slides, users may prefer to use Excel to create these items and then copy and paste them into PowerPoint. In the Office 2016 suite, the charting system is fully integrated within Word, Excel, and PowerPoint. A chart inserted in a Word document or PowerPoint presentation is created as an embedded object and the source data used to generate the chart is stored in an Excel worksheet. The Excel worksheet containing the source data becomes part of the document or presentation file.

Since the chart feature is fully integrated within Word, Excel, and PowerPoint, a chart in a PowerPoint presentation can be edited using the same techniques for editing a chart in Excel. Clicking a chart in a PowerPoint slide causes the contextual Chart Tools Design and Chart Tools Format tabs to become active with the same groups and buttons available as in Excel. Three buttons—Chart Elements, Chart Styles, and Chart Filter—are also available for editing.

Quick Steps

Embed Excel Data in a PowerPoint Presentation
1. Select cells.
2. Click Copy button.
3. Open PowerPoint presentation.
4. Make slide active.
5. Click Paste button arrow.
6. Click *Paste Special.*
7. Make sure *Microsoft Excel Worksheet Object* is selected in *As* list box.
8. Click OK.

Project 2e Embedding Excel Data into a PowerPoint Presentation

Part 5 of 6

1. With **CRInventory.xlsx** open, copy and embed the chart from the CarCostsChart worksheet in a PowerPoint slide by completing the following steps:
   a. Make CarCostsChart the active worksheet.
   b. Click the Home tab and then click the Copy button.
   c. Start Microsoft PowerPoint 2016.
   d. Open **CRCarRpt.pptx**.
   e. Save the presentation with the name **8-CRCarRpt**.
   f. Click Slide 3 in the slide thumbnails pane.
   g. Click in the *Click to add text* placeholder and then click the Paste button in the Clipboard group. Since all charts are embedded by default, it is not necessary to use Paste Special.
2. Change the chart colors by clicking the Chart Styles button and then clicking the Color tab. Click the *Color 2* option (second option in the *Colorful* section of the color palette).

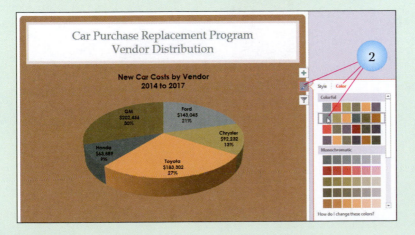

3. Copy the table used to generate the chart in the CarCosts worksheet and embed it in the next slide by completing the following steps:

   a. Click Slide 4 in the slide thumbnails pane.

   b. Click the button on the taskbar representing the Excel workbook **CRInventory.xlsx**.

   c. Make CarCosts the active worksheet, select the range A1:F9, and then click the Copy button.

   d. Click the button on the taskbar representing the PowerPoint presentation **8-CRCarRpt.pptx**.

   e. Click the Paste button arrow and then click *Paste Special* at the drop-down list.

   f. With *Microsoft Excel Worksheet Object* selected in the *As* list box, click OK.

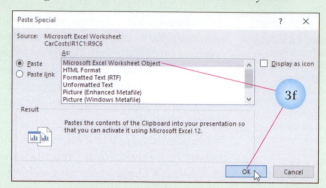

4. Resize and position the embedded table to the approximate height, width, and position shown at the right.

5. Click the File tab and then click the *Print* option. At the Print backstage area, click the button in the *Settings* category that reads *Full Page Slides* and then click *4 Slides Horizontal* at the drop-down list. Click the Print button.

6. Save **8-CRCarRpt.pptx** and then exit PowerPoint.

7. Press the Esc key to remove the scrolling marquee and then click in any cell to deselect the range in the CarCosts worksheet. Leave the **CRInventory.xlsx** workbook open for the next project.

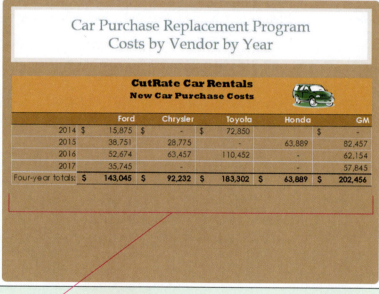

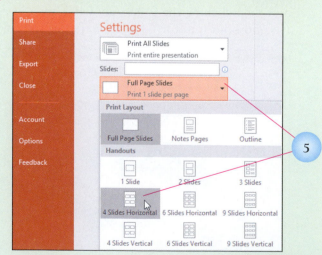

Exporting a Worksheet as a Text File

To exchange Excel data with someone who cannot import a Microsoft Excel worksheet or cannot copy and paste using the Clipboard task pane, save the data as a text file. Excel provides several text file options, including file formats suitable for computers that use the Apple operating system (Macintosh computers), as shown in Table 8.1. To save a worksheet as a text file, open the Save As dialog box and then change the file type to the correct option. Type a file name for the text file and then click the Save button. Click OK at the message box stating that only the active worksheet will be saved and then click Yes at the next message box to confirm saving the data as a text file.

Another way to save the current worksheet in a text file format is to click the File tab and then click the *Export* option. At the Export backstage area, click *Change File Type*. In the *Change File Type* section at the right, click *Text (Tab delimited) (*.txt)*, *CSV (Comma delimited) (*.csv)*, or *Formatted Text (Space delimited) (*.prn)* in the *Other File Types* section and then click the Save As button. If necessary, navigate to the appropriate drive and/or folder in the Save As dialog box. Type the file name and then click the Save button.

Quick Steps

Export a Worksheet as a Text File

1. Make sheet active.
2. Click File tab.
3. Click *Export* option.
4. Click *Change File Type.*
5. Click text file type in *Other File Types* section.
6. Click Save As button.
7. If necessary, navigate to drive and/or folder.
8. Type file name.
9. Click Save button.
10. Click OK.
11. Click Yes.

Hint Why are there so many text file formats? Although all systems support text files, there are differences across platforms. For example, the Apple operating system (used by Macintosh computers) denotes the end of a line in a text file with a carriage return character, Unix uses a linefeed character, and MS-DOS inserts both a linefeed and a carriage return character code at the end of each line.

Table 8.1 Supported Text File Formats for Exporting

Text File Format	File Extension
text (tab delimited)	.txt
unicode text	.txt
CSV (comma delimited)	.csv
formatted text (space delimited)	.prn
text (Apple)	.txt
text (MS-DOS)	.txt
CSV (Apple)	.csv
CSV (MS-DOS)	.csv

Project 2f Exporting a Worksheet as a Text File   Part 6 of 6

1. With **CRInventory.xlsx** open, export the Inventory worksheet data as a text file by completing the following steps:
   a. Make Inventory the active worksheet.
   b. Click the File tab and then click the *Export* option.

c. Click *Change File Type* at the Export backstage area.

d. Click *CSV (Comma delimited) (*.csv)* in the *Other File Types* section.

e. Click the Save As button.

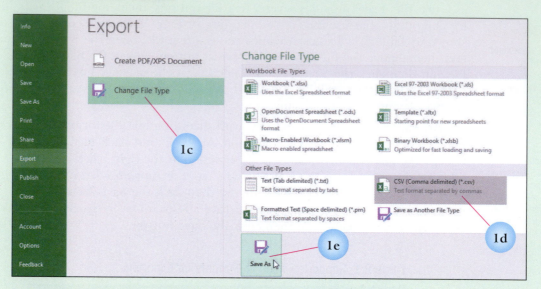

f. Type 8-CRInventory in the *File name* text box.

g. Click the Save button.

h. Click OK to save only the active sheet at the Microsoft Excel message box stating that the selected file type does not support workbooks that contain multiple sheets.

i. Click the Yes button to save the workbook in this format at the next message box stating that **8-CRInventory.csv** may contain features that are not compatible with CSV (comma delimited).

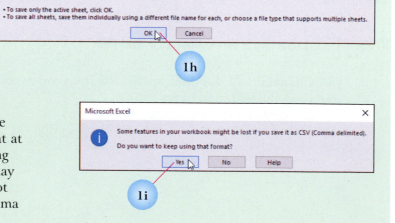

2. Close **8-CRInventory.csv**. Click Don't Save when prompted to save changes. (The file does not need to be saved because no changes have been made since the file type was changed.)
3. Open Notepad and view the text file created in Step 1 by completing the following steps:
   a. Click the Start button. At the Start screen, start typing *notepad*. When *Notepad* appears in the *Best match* area, press the Enter key. (Depending on your operating system, these steps may vary.)
   b. Click File on the Notepad Menu bar and then click *Open*.
   c. Navigate to the EL2C8 folder on your storage medium.

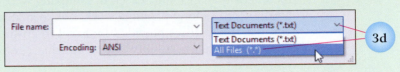

3d

   d. Click the *File type* option box arrow (which displays *Text Documents (*.txt)*) and then click *All Files (*.*)* at the drop-down list.
   e. Double-click **8-CRInventory.csv**.
   f. If necessary, scroll down to view all the data in the text file. Notice that commas have been inserted between the items of data previously arranged in columns.
4. Click File on the Notepad Menu bar and then click *Print*. Click the Print button at the Print dialog box.
5. Exit Notepad.

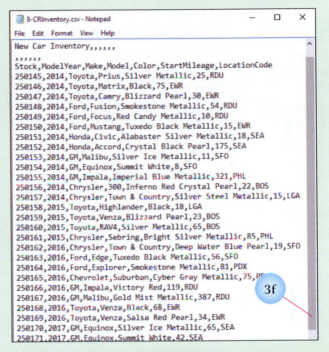

3f

Check Your Work

Project 3 Prepare a First Quarter Sales Workbook for Distribution   5 Parts

You will check for and fix any accessibility issues, remove confidential information from a workbook, and mark the workbook as final to prepare it for distribution. In another workbook, you will check for compatibility issues with earlier versions of Excel before sending the workbook to someone who uses Excel 2003. You will also explore the default settings in the Trust Center.

Preview Finished Project

Preparing a Workbook for Distribution

In today's workplace, individuals often work as part of a team both within and outside of an organization. Excel workbooks are frequently exchanged between coworkers via email message attachments; saving to a shared network folder, document management server, or company website; or other means of electronic distribution. Before making a workbook available for others to open, view, and edit, use the features provided by Excel to ensure that the workbook can be read by people with accessibility issues and that confidentiality will be protected and maintained.

Tutorial

Checking for
Accessibility
Issues

 Check for
Issues

 Check
Accessibility

Quick Steps
Check Accessibility
1. Click File tab.
2. Click Check for Issues button.
3. Click *Check Accessibility*.
4. Click issue.
5. Follow steps to fix issue.

Checking for Accessibility Issues

Before distributing a workbook, be sure to determine whether any features may make it difficult for someone with an accessibility issue to read the workbook. After opening the file, run the Accessibility Checker by clicking the File tab. Click the Check for Issues button and then click *Check Accessibility* in the drop-down list. There are three levels of errors; a description and example of each are provided in Table 8.2.

Excel displays the worksheet with the Accessibility Checker task pane on the right side of the screen listing the inspection results, shown in Figure 8.3. The flagged object or cell, including the name of the sheet in which it is located, is listed under the relevant issue (*Error*) and problem (*Missing Alt Text*). Click a problem and Excel selects the issue if possible. For example, objects like the table in Figure 8.3 are selected but sheet tabs are not. The options *Why Fix* and *How to Fix* appear in the *Additional Information* section at the bottom of the Accessibility Checker task pane. Follow the instructions and once an issue has been corrected, it will disappear from the Inspection Results.

Table 8.2 Accessiblity Issues

Accessibility Issue	Description	Example
Error	Workbook will be very difficult if not impossible for people with accessibility issues to understand.	Each object must have alternative text. Examples of objects are pictures, charts, tables, and shapes without text.
Warning	Workbook will be difficult in some cases for people with accessibility issues to understand.	Sheet tabs are named. Remove split or merged cells.
Tip	Workbook can be understood by people with accessibility issues but making changes might make it better organized and easier to understand.	Closed captions are included for inserted audio and video.

Figure 8.3 Accessiblity Checker Task Pane with Inspection Results Shown

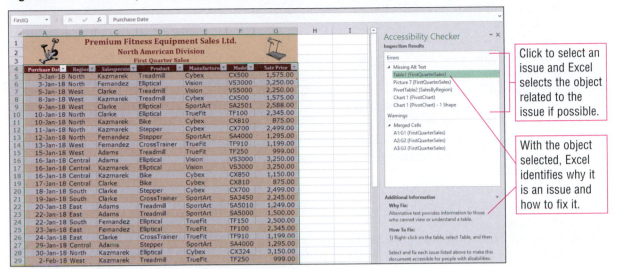

Click to select an issue and Excel selects the object related to the issue if possible.

With the object selected, Excel identifies why it is an issue and how to fix it.

Project 3a Inspecting a Workbook for Accessibility Issues

Part 1 of 5

1. Open **PF1stQSales.xlsx**.
2. Save the workbook with the name **8-PF1stQSales**.
3. Examine the workbook for accessibility issues by completing the following steps:
   a. Click the File tab.
   b. Click the Check for Issues button in the *Inspect Workbook* section at the Info backstage area and then click *Check Accessibility*.
   c. Read the inspection results in the Accessibility Checker task pane.
4. Correct the *Errors* in the *Inspection Results* by completing the following steps:
   a. Click *Table1 (FirstQuarterSales)* under *Missing Alt Text*. The table in the FirstQuarterSales worksheet is selected.
   b. Use the scroll bar to scroll through the details in the *Additional Information* section of the Accessibility Checker task pane to find out how to fix the error.
   c. Right-click in the table in the worksheet, point to the *Table* option, and then click *Alternative Text* at the drop-down list.

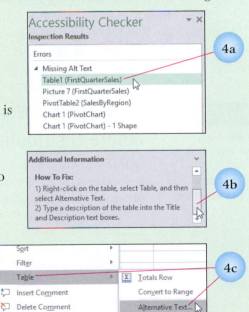

d. At the Alternative Text dialog box, click in the *Title* text box and then type First Quarter Sales Data.

e. Click in the *Description* text box and type First quarter sales data for the North American division.

f. Click OK. The issue is removed from the *Errors* list in the *Inspections Results*.

g. Click *Picture 7 (FirstQuarterSales)* under *Missing Alt Text*. The picture left of the title in row 1 in the FirstQuarterSales worksheet is selected.

h. Use the scroll bar to scroll through the details in the *Additional Information* section to find out how to fix the problem.

i. Right-click the object, click *Format Picture*, and then click the Size & Properties icon in the Format Picture task pane.

j. Click *Alt Text* in the list, click in the *Title* text box, type Company Logo, click in the *Description* text box, and then type Company Logo.

k. Click the Format Picture task pane Close button. The issue is removed from the *Errors* list in the *Inspections Results*.

5. Correct the three remaining issues in the *Errors* section by completing steps similar to Steps 4a–4f or 4g–4k. Enter appropriate alternative text for the title and description. After clicking the issue in the *Errors* section if the object is not selected, click the object directly. The last error (*Chart 1 (PivotChart) - 1 Shape*) is the yellow down arrow shape at the top of the PivotChart on the PivotChart tab.

6. Close the Accessibility Checker task pane by clicking the Accessibility Checker task pane Close button.

7. Close the Format Shape task pane by clicking the Format Shape task pane Close button.

8. Save **8-PF1stQSales.xlsx**.

Tutorial

Inspecting a Workbook

Inspect Document

Inspecting a Workbook and Removing Information before Distributing It

Before distributing a workbook electronically, consider using the Document Inspector to scan the workbook for personal data and hidden information that others should not view. Recall from Chapter 6 that a workbook's properties (sometimes referred to as *metadata*) include information that is tracked automatically by Excel, such as the names of the individuals that have accessed and edited a workbook. If a workbook will be sent electronically by email or made available on a server or other website, consider whether the recipients should be able to look at all of this hidden information.

If any of this sensitive or hidden information should remain confidential, remove it before distributing the file. To do this, click the File tab. At the Info backstage area, click the Check for Issues button in the *Inspect Workbook* section and then click *Inspect Document* at the drop-down list. This opens the Document Inspector dialog box, shown in Figure 8.4. By default, all the check boxes are selected. Clear the check boxes for those items that are not to be scanned or removed and then click the Inspect button.

Use the Document
Inspector to Remove
Private Information
1. Open workbook.
2. Click File tab.
3. Click Check for
   Issues button.
4. Click *Inspect
   Document.*
5. Clear check boxes
   for those items not
   to be scanned and
   removed.
6. Click Inspect button.
7. Click Remove All
   button in sections to
   be removed.
8. Click Close button.

Before removing sensitive data, save a copy of the original file that retains all the content using password protection or other security measures to limit access. In addition, use the Document Inspector to reveal the presence of headers, footers, hidden items, or other invisible data in a workbook created by someone else.

The Document Inspector scans the workbook to look for all the checked items. When the scan is completed, a dialog box like the one in Figure 8.5 appears. Excel displays check marks in the sections for which no items were found and red exclamation marks in the sections for which items were found. Click the Remove All button in the section that contains content to be removed. Click OK when finished and then distribute the workbook as needed.

Figure 8.4 Document Inspector Dialog Box

Click to remove the check marks from the check boxes next to those items that are not to be scanned or removed from the workbook before distributing it.

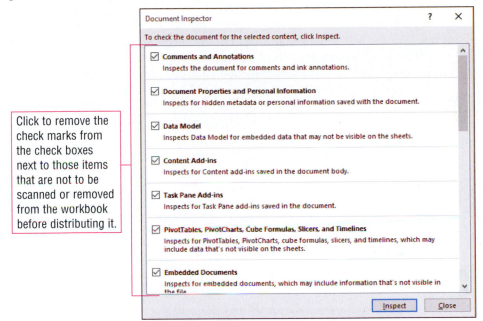

Figure 8.5 Document Inspector Dialog Box with Inspection Results Shown

Red exclamation marks indicate items that were found by scanning the workbook. Read the message about each item and then click the Remove All button next to the item to remove it.

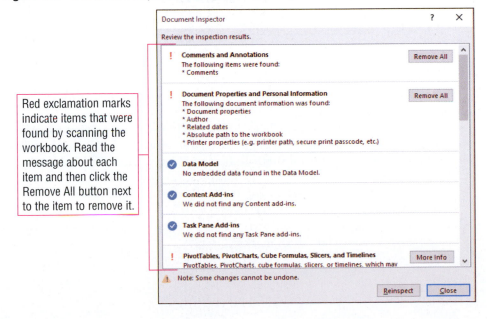

1. With **8-PF1stQSales.xlsx** open, examine the workbook for private and other confidential information by completing the following steps:

    a. Click the File tab.

    b. Read the property information in the fields in the *Properties* section at the right side of the screen.

    c. Click the Properties button and then click *Advanced Properties* at the drop-down list.

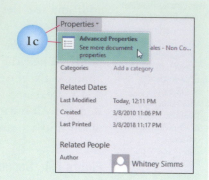

    d. Click the Custom tab in the 8-PF1stQSales.xlsx Properties dialog box.

    e. Position the mouse pointer on the right column boundary for the *Value* column in the *Properties* list box until the pointer changes to a left-and-right-pointing arrow with a vertical line in the middle and then drag the column width to the right until all the text in the column can be read.

    f. Notice that the extra information added to the workbook properties contains names and other data that should perhaps remain confidential.

    g. Click OK.

    h. Press the Esc key or click the Back button.

    i. Click the FirstQuarterSales tab, click the Review tab, and then click the Show All Comments button in the Comments group.

    j. Read the comment displayed in the worksheet area.

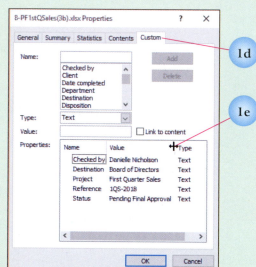

Manufacturer	Model	Sale Price
Cybex	CX500	1,575.00
Vision	VS3000	3,250.00
Vision	VS5000	2,250.00
Cybex	CX500	1,575.00
SportArt	SA2501	2,588.00

Whitney Simms:
Price increase expected next year.

2. Use the Document Inspector to scan the workbook for other confidential information by completing the following steps:

    a. Click the File tab, click the Check for Issues button in the *Inspect Workbook* section at the Info backstage area, and then click *Inspect Document* at the drop-down list.

    b. At the message box stating that the file contains changes that have not been saved, click Yes to save the file now.

    c. At the Document Inspector dialog box with all the check boxes selected, click the Inspect button to look for all the items.

    d. Read the messages in the first two sections of the Document Inspector dialog box, which display with red exclamation marks.

e. Click the Remove All button in the *Document Properties and Personal Information* section. Excel deletes the metadata and the section now displays with a check mark, indicating the information has been removed.

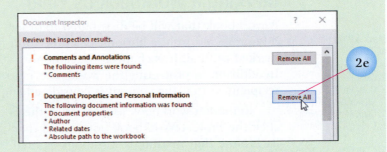

f. Scroll down and read the message for the *PivotTables, PivotCharts, Cub Formulas, Slicers, and Timelines* section. The PivotTable and PivotChart will not be altered.

g. Scroll down further and notice that the inspection results indicate that a header and three hidden rows were found. Review these items but do not click the Remove All buttons. Click the Close button to close the Document Inspector dialog box.

3. Display the worksheet in Page Layout view and view the header.

4. Look at the row numbers in the worksheet area. Notice that after row 10, the next row number is 14. Select row numbers 10 and 14, right-click the selected rows, and then click *Unhide* at the shortcut menu to display rows 11 through 13.

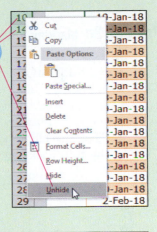

5. Click in any cell to deselect the range. Review the information in the rows that were hidden.

6. You decide that the rows that were initially hidden should remain displayed but you want to prevent reviewers of the workbook from seeing the header and comments. Use the Document Inspector to remove these items by completing the following steps:

a. Click the File tab, click the Check for Issues button, click *Inspect Document* at the drop-down list, and then click the Yes button to save the changes to the workbook.

b. Remove the check marks from all the check boxes except those next to the sections *Comments and Annotations* and *Headers and Footers*.

c. Click the Inspect button.

d. Click the Remove All button in the *Comments and Annotations* section.

e. Click the Remove All button in the *Headers and Footers* section.

f. Click the Close button.

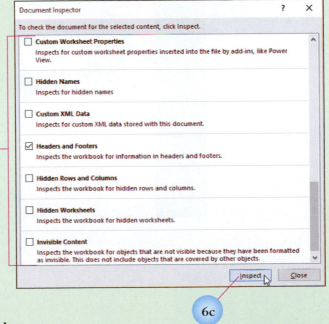

7. Notice that the comments and header have been deleted from the worksheet. Switch back to Normal view.

8. Click the Show All Comments button in the Comments group on the Review tab to turn off the feature.

9. Save and then close **8-PF1stQSales.xlsx**.

Check Your Work

Marking a Workbook as Final

Quick Steps

Mark a Workbook as Final
1. Open workbook.
2. Click File tab.
3. Click Protect Workbook button.
4. Click *Mark as Final*.
5. Click OK two times.

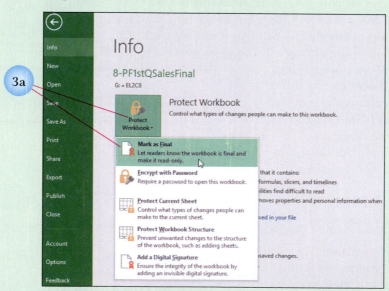

Mark as Final

A workbook that will be distributed to others can be marked as final, which means it is protected from additions, deletions, and modifications. When a workbook is marked as final, it is changed to read-only and the status property is set to *Final*. In addition to protecting the workbook, marking it as final also indicates to the recipient(s) that the content is considered complete.

To mark a workbook as final, click the File tab. At the Info backstage area, click the Protect Workbook button and then click *Mark as Final* at the drop-down list. (Note that marking a workbook as final is not as secure as using password-protected, locked ranges.)

A workbook marked as final displays with the ribbon minimized and a message above the Formula bar that informs the user that the author has marked the workbook as final to discourage editing. Click the Edit Anyway button in the message bar to remove the Mark as Final feature, redisplay the ribbon, and allow changes to be made to the workbook.

Project 3c Marking a Workbook as Final

Part 3 of 5

1. Open **8-PF1stQSales.xlsx**.
2. Save the workbook with the name **8-PF1stQSalesFinal**.
3. Mark the workbook as final to prevent changes from being made and set the Status property to *Final* by completing the following steps:
   a. Click the File tab, click the Protect Workbook button in the *Protect Workbook* section of the Info backstage area, and then click *Mark as Final*.

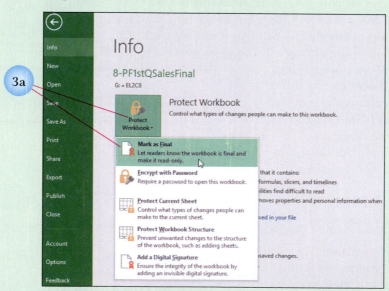

   b. Click OK at the message box stating that the workbook will be marked as final and then saved.

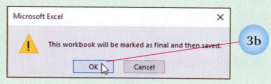

c. Click OK at the second message box stating that the workbook has been marked as final to indicate that editing is complete and this is the final version of the file. *Note: If this message box does not appear, it has been turned off by a previous user who clicked the Don't show this message again check box.*

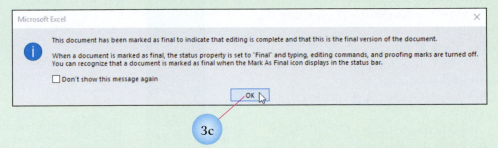

4. Click the File tab and notice that the *Protect Workbook* section of the Info backstage area displays in yellow and with a message stating that the workbook has been marked as final. Click the Back button and notice the addition of *[Read-Only]* next to the file name in the Title bar.
5. The ribbon is minimized and a marked as final message displays above the Formula bar, indicating that the workbook has been marked as final to discourage editing. Additionally, a *Marked as Final* icon displays in the Status bar next to *Ready*.

The ribbon is minimized and a marked as final message displays, as described in Step 5.

6. Make any cell active and attempt to insert or delete text in the cell. Since the workbook is now read-only, the cell cannot be opened to edit or delete the contents.
7. Close **8-PF1stQSalesFinal.xlsx**.

Using the Compatibility Checker

Quick Steps

Check a Workbook for Compatibility
1. Open workbook.
2. Click File tab.
3. Click Check for Issues button.
4. Click *Check Compatibility*.
5. Read information in *Summary* list box.
6. Click *Copy to New Sheet* button.
   OR
   Click Close.

Check Compatibility

If a workbook will be exchanged with other individuals who do not have Excel 2007, Excel 2010, Excel 2013, or Excel 2016, the workbook can be saved in an Excel 97-2003 file format. When a file is saved in an earlier version's file format, Excel automatically does a compatibility check and provides prompts about loss of functionality or fidelity. If preferred, use the Compatibility Checker feature before saving the workbook to identify in advance the areas of the worksheet that may need changes before saving to maintain backward compatibility.

If an issue in the *Summary* list box at the Microsoft Excel - Compatibility Checker dialog box displays a Fix hyperlink, click Fix to resolve the problem. To get more information about a loss of functionality or fidelity, click the Help hyperlink next to the issue. To return to the worksheet with the cells selected that are problematic for earlier Excel versions, click the Find hyperlink next to the issue.

1. Open **CRBuyLeaseAnalysis.xlsx**.
2. Run the Compatibility Checker to scan the workbook before saving it in an earlier Excel file format by completing the following steps:
   a. Click the File tab.
   b. Click the Check for Issues button in the Info backstage area.
   c. Click *Check Compatibility* at the drop-down list.
   d. At the Microsoft Excel - Compatibility Checker dialog box, read the information in the *Summary* box in the *Significant loss of functionality* section.
   e. Scroll down and read the information in the *Minor loss of fidelity* section.
   f. Scroll back up to the top of the *Summary* box.
   g. Click the Copy to New Sheet button.
3. At the Compatibility Report sheet, read the information in the box with the hyperlink NewCar'!D13:D16 and then click the hyperlink. The NewCar worksheet becomes active with those cells selected that have conditional formatting applied that is not supported in the earlier version of Excel (the range D13:D16).
4. Make the Compatibility Report sheet active and then print the worksheet with the worksheet scaled to *Fit Sheet on One Page*.
5. Save the revised workbook with the name **8-CRBuyLeaseAnalysisCompChk**.
6. Make NewCar the active worksheet and deselect the range.
7. To save the workbook in an earlier version of Excel, click the File tab, click the *Export* option, click *Change File Type*, click *Excel 97-2003 Workbook (*.xls)* in the *Workbook File Types* section, and then click the Save As button. Click the Save button at the Save As dialog box to accept the default file name. Click the Continue button at the Compatibility Checker dialog box.
8. Close **8-CRBuyLeaseAnalysisCompChk.xls**.

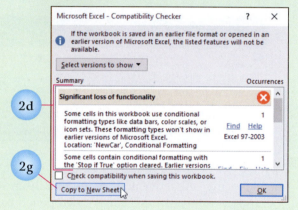

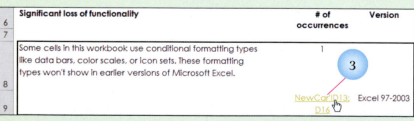

Check Your Work

Tutorial

Viewing Trust
Center Settings

ⓞuick Steps

**View Trust
Center Settings**
1. Click File tab.
2. Click *Options*.
3. Click *Trust Center* in
   left pane.
4. Click Trust Center
   Settings button.
5. Click desired trust
   center category in
   left pane.
6. View and/or modify
   options.
7. Click OK two times.

💡 **Hint** Changing
the macro security
setting in Excel does
not affect the macro
security setting in other
Microsoft programs,
such as Word and
Access.

Viewing Trust Center Settings

In Excel, the Trust Center is responsible for blocking unsafe content when a workbook is opened. Recall the security warning that sometimes appears in the message bar when a workbook is opened. That warning is generated by the Trust Center and it can be closed by clicking the Enable Content button. The Trust Center also allows the user to view and/or modify the security options that protect the computer from malicious content.

The Trust Center maintains a Trusted Locations list of locations from which content can be considered trusted. When a location is added to the Trusted Locations list, Excel treats any files opened from that location as safe. A workbook opened from a trusted location does not cause a security warning to display in the message bar and none of its content will be blocked.

If a workbook contains macros, the Trust Center checks for a valid and current digital signature from an entity in the Trusted Publishers list before enabling them. The Trusted Publishers list is maintained by the user on the computer being used. To add a publisher to the list, enable content from that publisher and then click the option *Trust all content from this publisher*.

Depending on the active macro security setting, if the Trust Center cannot match the digital signature information with an entity in the Trusted Publishers list or the macro does not contain a digital signature, a security warning displays in the message bar. The default macro security setting is *Disable all macros with notification*. Table 8.3 describes the four macro security settings. In some cases, the user may decide to change the default macro security setting. This can be done at the Trust Center dialog box. The Trust Center will be explored in Project 3e.

Table 8.3 Macro Security Settings for Workbooks Not Opened from Trusted Locations

Macro Setting	Description
Disable all macros without notification	All macros are disabled; security alerts do not appear.
Disable all macros with notification	All macros are disabled; security alerts appear with the option to enable content if the source of the file is trusted. This is the default setting.
Disable all macros except digitally signed macros	A macro that does not contain a digital signature is disabled; security alerts do not appear. If the macro is digitally signed by a publisher in the Trusted Publishers list, the macro is allowed to run. If the macro is digitally signed by a publisher not in the Trusted Publishers list, a security alert appears.
Enable all macros (not recommended, potentially dangerous code can run)	All macros are allowed; security alerts do not appear.

1. To explore the settings in the Trust Center, complete the following steps:
   a. Click the File tab and then click *Options*.
   b. Click *Trust Center* in the left pane of the Excel Options dialog box.
   c. Click the Trust Center Settings button in the *Microsoft Excel Trust Center* section.

   d. At the Trust Center dialog box, click *Macro Settings* in the left pane.
   e. Review the options in the *Macro Settings* section. Note which option is active on the computer you are using. The default option is *Disable all macros with notification*.
   Note: The security setting on the computer you are using may be different from the default option. Do not change the security setting without your instructor's permission.
   f. Click *Trusted Publishers* in the left pane. If any publishers have been added to the list on the computer you are using, their names will appear in the list box. If the list box is empty, no trusted publishers have been added.

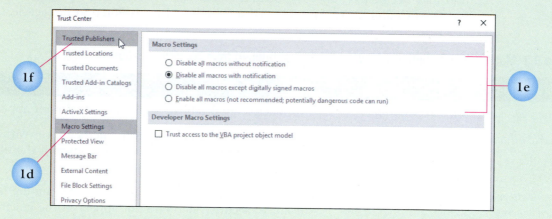

   g. Click *Trusted Locations* in the left pane. Review the paths and descriptions of the folders in the Trusted Locations list. By default, Excel adds the folder created upon installation that contains the templates provided by Microsoft. Additional folders that have been added by a system administrator or network administrator may also appear.
   h. Click OK to close the Trust Center dialog box.
2. Click OK to close the Excel Options dialog box.

Project 4 **Distributing a First Quarter Sales Workbook** **3 Parts**

You will publish a workbook as a PDF file and an XPS file. You will also publish a worksheet as a web page.

Preview Finished Project

Distributing Workbooks

Many organizations that need to make files accessible to several users create a document management server or network share folder from which users can retrieve files. Recall from Chapter 6 that if these resources are not available, a workbook can be sent by attaching it to an email message. The workbook can be attached using the email program's file attachment feature or by initiating the email attachment feature directly from Excel.

A popular method of distributing content over the Internet is to publish a workbook as a PDF or XPS file. A workbook can also be published as a web page to make the content available on the Internet.

Publishing a Workbook as a PDF File

Tutorial

Publishing a Workbook as a PDF or XPS File

Quick Steps

Publish a Workbook as a PDF File
1. Open workbook.
2. Click File tab.
3. Click *Export.*
4. Click Create PDF/XPS button.
5. Click Publish button.

💡 **Hint** Publish a multi-sheet workbook as a multi-page PDF file by clicking the Options button in the Publish as PDF or XPS dialog box and then clicking *Entire workbook in the Publish what* section of the Options dialog box.

Publishing a workbook as a PDF file involves saving it in a fixed-layout format known as *portable document format.* The PDF standard was developed by Adobe and has become a popular format for sharing files with people outside an organization. Creating a PDF file of a workbook ensures that it will look the same on most computers, with all the fonts, formatting, and images preserved. The recipient of the file does not have to have Microsoft Excel on his or her computer to read the file.

To open and view a PDF file, the recipient must have Adobe Reader on his or her computer. The reader is a free application available from Adobe and can be downloaded and installed if the computer being used does not already have it installed. (Go to http://adobe.com and click *Adobe Reader DC* to download and install the latest version of the software.)

A PDF file can also be opened with Word 2016. It converts a PDF to an editable file, converting any formulas to values and any charts to objects. The file may not look exactly like the original PDF file, however.

1. Open **8-PF1stQSales.xlsx**.
2. Publish the workbook as a PDF file by completing the following steps:
   a. Click the File tab.
   b. Click the *Export* option.
   c. With *Create PDF/XPS Document* selected in the Export backstage area, click the Create PDF/XPS button.

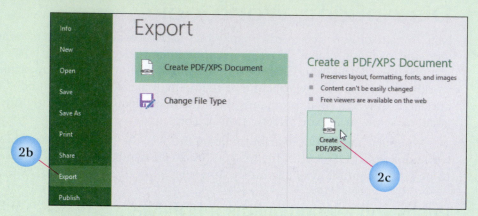

   d. Insert a check mark in the *Open file after publishing* check box at the bottom of the Publish as PDF or XPS dialog box.
   e. Click the Options button and then click the *Entire workbook* option in the *Publish what* section of the Options dialog box. This will create a PDF with three pages. Click OK.
   f. With *PDF(*.pdf)* in the *Save as type* option box and *8-PF1stQSales.pdf* in the *File name* text box, click the Publish button.

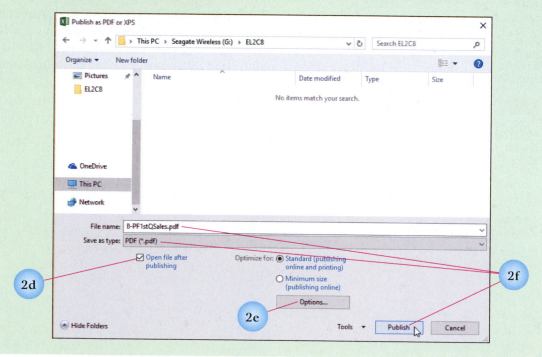

3. An Adobe Reader (or Adobe Acrobat) application window opens with the published workbook displayed. Notice that the workbook has retained all the Excel formatting and other visual features and contains three pages.

Premium Fitness Equipment Sales Ltd.
North American Division
First Quarter Sales

Purchase Date	Region	Salesperson	Product	Manufacturer	Model	Sale Price
3-Jan-18	North	Kazmarek	Treadmill	Cybex	CX500	1,575.00
3-Jan-18	North	Fernandez	Elliptical	Vision	VS3000	3,250.00
5-Jan-18	West	Clarke	Treadmill	Vision	VS5000	2,250.00
8-Jan-18	West	Kazmarek	Treadmill	Cybex	CX500	1,575.00
9-Jan-18	West	Clarke	Elliptical	SportArt	SA2501	2,588.00
10-Jan-18	North	Clarke	Elliptical	TrueFit	TF100	2,345.00
10-Jan-18	North	Kazmarek	Bike	Cybex	CX810	875.00

③

4. Close the Adobe application window.
5. Return to Excel and leave **8-PF1stQSales.xlsx** open for the next project.

Check Your Work

Publishing a Workbook as an XPS File

Quick Steps

Publish a Workbook as an XPS File
1. Open workbook.
2. Click File tab.
3. Click *Export*.
4. Click Create PDF/XPS button.
5. Click *Save as type* option box.
6. Click *XPS Document (*.xps)*.
7. Click Publish button.

XPS stands for *XML paper specification,* which is another fixed-layout format that has all the same advantages as PDF. XPS was developed by Microsoft with the Office 2007 suite. Similar to PDF files, which require Adobe Reader DC for viewing, XPS files require the XPS viewer. The viewer is provided by Microsoft and is packaged with Windows 10, Windows 8, Windows 7, and Windows Vista. However, to view an XPS file using Windows XP, the viewer application may need to be downloaded. (Go to www.microsoft.com and search using the phrase "View and Generate XPS" to locate the download page.)

Project 4b Publishing a Worksheet as an XPS File   **Part 2 of 3**

1. With **8-PF1stQSales.xlsx** open, publish the FirstQuarterSales worksheet as an XPS file by completing the following steps:
   a. Click the File tab.
   b. Click the *Export* option.
   c. With the *Create PDF/XPS Document* option in the Export backstage area selected, click the Create PDF/XPS button.
   d. At the Publish as PDF or XPS dialog box, click the *Save as type* option box below the *File name* text box and then click *XPS Document (*.xps)* at the drop-down list.

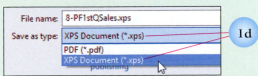

1d

e. With a check mark in the *Open file after publishing* check box and *8-PF1stQSales.xps* in the *File name* text box, click the Publish button.

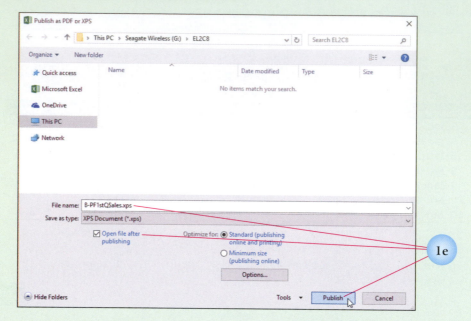

2. The XPS Viewer application window opens with the published worksheet displayed. ***Note: Choose the XPS Viewer application if a dialog box opens asking which application to view the file with.*** Notice that like the PDF file, the XPS file has retained all the Excel formatting and other visual features.

3. Close the XPS Viewer application window.

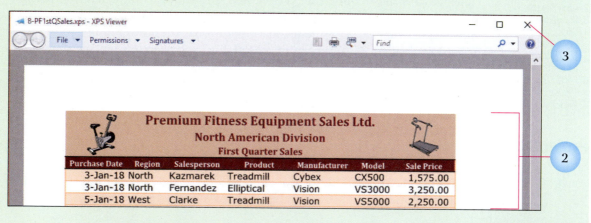

4. Leave **8-PF1stQSales.xlsx** open for the next project.

Check Your Work

Publishing a Worksheet as a Web Page

Quick Steps

Publish a Worksheet as a Web Page

1. Open workbook.
2. Click File tab.
3. Click *Export*.
4. Click *Change File Type*.
5. Click *Save as Another File Type* option.
6. Click Save As button.
7. Click *Save as type* option box.
8. Click *Single File Web Page (*.mht; *.mhtml).*
9. If necessary, change drive, folder, and/or file name.
10. Click Change Title button, type title, and then click OK.
11. Click Publish button.
12. Set options.
13. Click Publish.

Hint Not all browsers support the single file (.mht) web page format. If the page will not be viewed in Internet Explorer, consider using the traditional .htm or .html web page format.

Publish a worksheet as a single web page by changing the *Save as type* option to *Single File Web Page (*.mht; *.mhtml).* In this format, all the data in the worksheet, including graphics and other supplemental data, is saved in a single file that can be uploaded to a web server. Alternatively, publish the worksheet in the traditional hypertext markup language (html) file format for web pages by changing the *Save as type* option to *Web Page (*.htm; *.html).* In the *html* option, Excel creates additional files for supplemental data and saves them in a subfolder.

When a web page option is chosen at the *Save as type* list, the Save As dialog box changes, as shown in Figure 8.6. At this dialog box, specify whether to publish the entire workbook or only the active sheet. Click the Change Title button to add a title to the web page. The page title displays in the Title bar of the browser window and on the Internet Explorer tab when the page is viewed online. Click the Publish button and the Publish as Web Page dialog box appears, as shown in Figure 8.7, providing additional options.

Figure 8.6 Save As Dialog Box with File Type Changed to *Single File Web Page (*.mht; *.mhtml)*

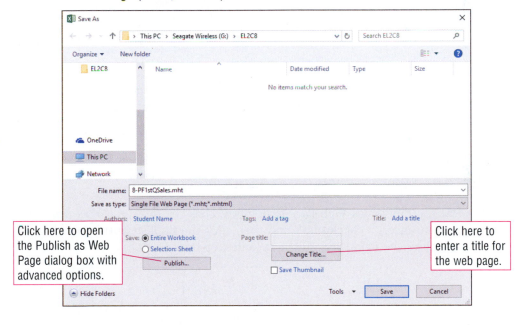

Click here to open the Publish as Web Page dialog box with advanced options.

Click here to enter a title for the web page.

Figure 8.7 Publish as Web Page Dialog Box

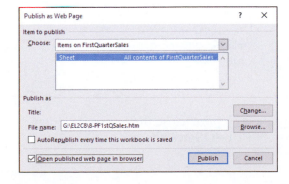

1. With **8-PF1stQSales.xlsx** open, publish the worksheet as a single file web page by completing the following steps:
   a. Click the File tab.
   b. Click the *Export* option.
   c. Click the *Change File Type* option and then click the *Save as Another File Type* option in the *Other File Types* section.
   d. Click the Save As button.
   e. Click the *Save as type* option box and then click *Single File Web Page (*.mht; *.mhtml)* at the drop-down list.
   f. Click the Change Title button.
   g. At the Enter Text dialog box, type Premium Fitness Equipment Sales Ltd. 1st Q Sales in the *Page title* text box and then click OK.
   h. Click the Publish button.

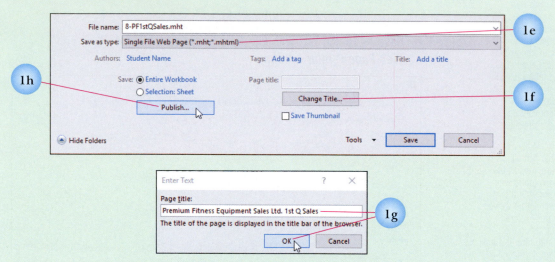

   i. At the Publish as Web Page dialog box, click the *Open published web page in browser* check box to insert a check mark and then click the Publish button. (This automatically displays the worksheet in the default web browser.)

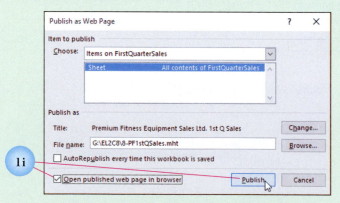

2. After viewing the web page, close the browser window.
3. Save and close **8-PF1stQSales.xlsx**.

Check Your Work

Chapter Summary

- The Get External Data group on the Data tab contains buttons for importing data into an Excel worksheet from an external source such as Access, the web, or a text file.

- Only one Access table can be imported at a time.

- Text files are often used to exchange data between different programs because the file format is recognized by nearly all applications.

- In a text file, the data between fields is generally separated with a tab character or a comma.

- The Text Import Wizard guides the user through the process of importing a text file through three dialog boxes, in which the source file is defined as delimited and the delimiter character is selected.

- Data in an Excel worksheet can be copied and pasted or copied and appended to an existing Access table.

- Worksheet data can be embedded or linked to a Word document. Embedding inserts a copy of the source data in the Word document and allows the object to be edited using Excel's tools within the Word environment. Linking the object inserts a shortcut to the Excel workbook from which the source data is retrieved.

- Breaking a link involves removing the connection between the source program and destination program. This means that the object is no longer updated in the destination file when the source data changes.

- Embed and link objects to slides in a PowerPoint presentation using the same techniques used to embed cells in or link cells to a Word document.

- In Office 2016, the charting tools are fully integrated. A chart copied and pasted from Excel to a PowerPoint presentation or Word document is embedded by default.

- To exchange Excel data with someone who cannot import an Excel worksheet or cannot copy and paste using the Clipboard task pane, save the data as a text file.

- Excel provides several text file formats to accommodate differences across operating systems, which configure text files using various end-of-line character codes.

- Before distributing a workbook for others to open, view, and edit, use Excel features to ensure the file can be read by individuals with accessibility issues and that confidentiality is being protected and maintained.

- Run the Accessibility Checker to see if there are any problems that will make the workbook difficult to understand for a person with accessibilities issues.

- The Document Inspector feature scans a workbook for personal or hidden information to be reviewed and removed if necessary before distributing it.

- After a workbook has been inspected, Excel displays a red exclamation mark in each section in which Excel detected a requested item. Click the Remove All button to delete all such items from the workbook.

- Marking a workbook as final changes it to a read-only file and sets the status property as *Final*.

- Run the Compatibility Checker before saving a workbook in an earlier version of Excel to identify areas of the worksheet that may need changes to maintain backward compatibility.

- The results of the compatibility check can be copied to a new worksheet for easy referencing and documentation purposes.

- View and modify security options at Excel's Trust Center to block unsafe content when a workbook is opened.
- Saving a workbook in a fixed-layout format such as PDF or XPS preserves all the Excel formatting and layout features.
- Adobe Reader or Word 2016 is required to open and view a workbook saved as a PDF file.
- The XPS Viewer is provided with Windows 10 and Windows 8, Windows 7, and Windows Vista.
- Adobe Reader and the XPS viewer can be downloaded for free from the Adobe and Microsoft websites, respectively.
- Open the Save As dialog box and change the *Save as type* option to either *Single File Web Page* or *Web Page* to publish the current worksheet as a web page.

Commands Review

FEATURE	RIBBON TAB, GROUP/OPTION	BUTTON, OPTION	KEYBOARD SHORTCUT
Accessibility Checker	File, *Info*, Check for Issues		
Compatibility Checker	File, *Info*, Check for Issues		
copy	Home, Clipboard		Ctrl + C
Document Inspector	File, *Info*		
import from Access table	Data, Get External Data		
import from text file	Data, Get External Data		
mark workbook as final	File, *Info*		
Paste Special	Home, Clipboard	, *Paste Special*	Ctrl + Alt + V
save as	File, *Save As*		F12
save as PDF/XPS	File, Export OR File, *Save As*		F12
save as web page	File, Export OR File, *Save As*		F12

Index

Consolidate button, 91
Consolidate dialog box, 91–92
Consolidate feature,
    summarizing data using, 83,
    91–93
Convert Text to Columns
    Wizard, 65–66
Convert to Range button, 74
copying
    to Access, 213–215
    comments, 145–147
    to PowerPoint, 217–218
    to Word, 213–215
COUNTA function, 35
COUNT function, 35
COUNTIF function, 36–37
COUNTIFS function, 36, 38
Create Sparklines dialog box,
    108, 109
CSV file format, 219
Custom AutoFilter dialog box,
    26–27
Custom AutoFilter feature,
    filtering worksheet using,
    26–27
Customize Quick Access
    Toolbar button, 191
customizing
    creating and applying custom
        view, 194–196
    display options, 183–185
    exporting and importing, 186
    macros, 174–182
    Quick Access Toolbar, 191–193
    ribbon, 183–184, 186–191
    save options, 199–201
    Sparklines, 109–110
custom number format,
    creating, 19–20
Custom Sort, 30
custom view, creating and
    applying, 194–196
Custom View button, 194
Custom View dialog box, 194,
    195

D
data
    circling invalid data, 135–137
    converting, from rows to
        columns, 117–119
    Data Tools group, 65–74

exporting, 211–221
    to Access, 211–213
    breaking link to Excel
        object, 216
    to PowerPoint, 217–218
    as text file, 219–221
    to Word, 213–216
filtering and sorting, using
    conditional formatting or
    cell attributes, 28–30
Flash Fill, 66–67
formatting as table, 58–62
Goal Seek to find target
    value, 121–122
grouping and ungrouping,
    79–80
importing, 206–211
    from Access, 206–208
    from text file, 208–211
maintaining external
    references for, 88–91
pasting, using Paste Special
    options, 116–120
PivotCharts, 104–107
PivotTables, 93–104
restricting data entry, 71–72
separating, using Text to
    Columns, 65–66
source, 206
subtotaling related data, 74–77
summarizing
    with consolidate feature,
        91–93
    linking to ranges in other
        worksheets/workbooks,
        87–88
    in multiple worksheets
        using range names and
        3-D references, 84–86
    with Sparklines, 108–110
transposing, 117–119
validating data entry, 69–74
what-if analysis
    with data tables, 127–130
    with Scenario Manager,
        122–126
data bars, conditional
    formatting using, 12–13
Data tab, 65, 67, 206
data table
    defined, 127
    one-variable data table,
        127–128

two-variable data table,
    129–130
Data Tools group, 65–74
    combining client and file
        numbers to create case
        codes, 68
    convert text to columns, 65–66
    overview, 65
    populating data using flash
        fill, 66–67
    removing duplicate records,
        67–69
    validating and restricting data
        entry, 69–74
data validation
    circling invalid data, 135–137
    ensuring data entered in
        specified text length, 73–74
    error alert message, 69–70
    input message, 69–70
    restricting data entry to dates
        within range, 71–72
    restricting data entry to
        values within list, 72–73
Data Validation button, 69, 135
Data Validation dialog box,
    69–70
Defined Names group, 34
Delete button, 145
deleting
    comments, 145–147
    conditional formatting rules,
        9–11
    custom number format, 21
    custom template, 199
    macro, 182
    range name, 35
    Scenario Manager, 124
delimited file format, 208
dependent cell, tracing, 131
destination, 207
destination workbook, 87
Directional icon set, 11–12
Disable Link button, 156
display options
    customizing, 183–185
    restoring default, 185
distribution of workbooks/
    worksheets
    checking accessibility issues,
        222–224
    compatibility checker, 229–230
    marking as final, 228–229

function formula
  argument in, 33
  creating name range, 34–35
  editing and deleting range
    name, 34–35
  structure of, 33
functions
  changing in PivotTable,
    99–100
  Lookup & Reference
    functions, 44–47
  math and trigonometry
    functions, 42–43
  nested functions, 50–54
  search for, 54
  Sum function, 60, 92
  text functions, 21–25

G

Get External Data group, 206,
  208
Goal Seek, 120–122
Gradient Fill section, 12–13
Green Up Arrow, 11
group
  adding button to, 187
  renaming, 187–188
Group button, 79–80

H

header row, 58
  formatting, 60
health and dental costs
  calculating using nested IF
    and OR functions, 53–54
Hide Detail button, 74–75, 79
Highlight Cells Rules option, 4, 5
Highlight Changes dialog box,
  153
HLOOKUP function, 44, 47
Hotmail account, 155

I

icon set
  conditional formatting using,
    11–12
  filtering by, 28
IF function, nested, 50–54
IF statement

conditional formatting using,
  13–14
  structure of, 50
Import Data dialog box, 206
importing customizations, 186
importing data, 206–211
  from Access, 206–208
  from text file, 208–211
Import Text File dialog box, 208
Indicators icon set, 11–12
Info backstage area, 142
Information error alert message,
  70
input message, 69–70
Insert Function button, 36
Insert Function dialog box, 36,
  37
inserting comments, 144–147
Insert Slicer button, 62–64, 100
Insert tab, 93, 108
Insert Timeline button, 102
Inspect Document button, 224
Invite People option, 155
IPMT function, 47

K

keyboard shortcut, creating and
  running macro to, 178–180

L

LEFT text function, 22–23, 25
Line button, 108
linking Excel data to Word
  document, 215–216
  breaking link, 216
Links dialog box, 216
loan payments, calculating
  principal portion of, 48–49
Logical button, 50
logical functions
  AND functions, 51–54
  IF function, 50–54
  nested functions, 50–54
  OR functions, 51–54
  ROUND function, 51
logic errors, 132
Lookup & Reference button, 45
  HLOOKUP function, 44, 47
  VLOOKUP function, 44–46
Lookup & Reference functions,
  44–47

lookup table, 44
lookup_value, 44
LOWER text function, 21–22,
  23–24

M

Macro dialog box, 177
macros, 174–182
  assigning to shortcut key,
    178–180
  creating, 174–176
  defined, 174
  deleting, 182
  editing, 180–182
  macro workbook creation,
    182
  naming, 174
  playing a, 177
  running, 177
  saving workbooks containing,
    175–176
  standard, 182
Macros button, 174
Mark as Final button, 228
marking workbook as final,
  228–229
mathematical operations,
  performing while pasting,
  119–120
math functions, 42–43
Math & Trig button, 42, 43
MAX function, 35
metadata
  defined, 142
  removing, 224–227
Microsoft account, 155
Microsoft Visual Basic for
  Applications (VBA), 175
MID text function, 22–23, 25
MIN function, 35
minimizing the ribbon, 183–184
module, 180
Move Chart button, 105
Move Down button, 187
Move Up button, 187

N

#N/A error, 133
#NAME? error, 132, 133
Name Manager button, 34

Name Manager dialog box, 34–35
name range
  creating, 34–35
  editing and deleting, 34–35
nested functions, 50–54
network share, 148
New Comment button, 144
New Formatting Rule dialog box, 6–8, 13
New Tab button, 187
Next button, 145
Notepad, 210
Number Format option box, 16
number formats
  custom, 19–21
  fraction and scientific, 16–17
  special, 18–19

O

OneDrive, shared workbooks on, 154–157
one-variable data table, 127–128
Options dialog box, 186–187
OR logical function, 51–54
Outline feature, 74–75, 77
Outline group, 79

P

Page Layout tab, 145
password
  adding and removing to workbook, 163–165
  elements of good password, 163
  encrypted, 163
  to unprotect worksheet, 159
Paste button, 116
Paste Special dialog box, 116, 119, 145, 146, 215
Paste Special options
  converting data from rows to columns, 117–119
  performing mathematical operations while pasting, 119–120
  selecting other, 120
  transposing data, 117–119
pasting

to Access, 213–215
comments, 145–147
to PowerPoint, 217–218
using Paste Special options, 116–120
to Word, 213–214
PDF document, publishing workbook as, 222–235
pensions costs, calculating using nested IF, AND and ROUND functions, 52–53
personal information, removing from workbook before publishing, 224–227
PivotChart button, 104
PivotCharts, 104–107
  creating, 104–107
  creating using PivotTable, 104–106
  defined, 104
  overview of, 104–105
  from scratch, 105, 107
PivotTable button, 93
PivotTables, 93–104
  changing Sum function in, 99–100
  creating with PivotTable button, 94–97
  defined, 93
  filtering
    overview, 98–99
    using Slicers, 100–102
    using Timelines, 102–104
  formatting, 98–99
  making PivotChart from, 104–106
  overview, 93–95
  using Recommended PivotTables to create, 94–96
PivotTable Tools Analyze tab, 98, 100, 104
PivotTable Tools Design tab, 98
playing a macro, 177
PMT function, 47
portable document format (PDF), 235–237
#, in custom number format code, 20
PowerPoint
  copying and pasting worksheet data to, 217–218
  embedding Excel data in, 217–219

precedent cell, tracing, 131
Previous button, 145
principal portion of loan payment, 48–49
printing
  change history of shared workbook, 153–154
  comments, 145–147
proof formula, 132
PROPER text function, 21–22
properties, adding to workbook, 142–144
Properties button, 143
protecting
  workbook, 162–163
  worksheets, 159–162
Protect Sheet button, 159, 161
Protect Sheet dialog box, 159–160
Protect Structure and Windows dialog box, 162
Protect Workbook button, 162
Publish as Web Page dialog box, 237

Q

? (question mark)
  in custom filter, 26
  in custom number format code, 20
Quick Access Toolbar
  adding commands to, 193
  customizing, 191–193
  importing customizations, 194
  removing buttons from, 193
  resetting to original setting, 193–194
Quick Analysis button, 9, 15

R

range
  converting table to normal range, 74
  converting table to range and creating subtotals, 74–77
  converting to table, 58–59
  restricting data entry to dates within range, 71–72
range_lookup, 44

AVERAGEIFS function, 39, 41

COUNTA function, 35

COUNT function, 35

COUNTIF function, 36–37

COUNTIFS function, 36, 38

MAX function, 35

MIN function, 35

Stop error alert message, 70

Stop Recording button, 175

SUBSTITUTE text function, 21–22, 23–24

Subtotal button, 74

subtotals

    converting table to range and creating subtotals, 74–77

    modifying, 78

    overview, 74

Sum function, 60

    changing in PivotTable, 99–100

SUMIF function, 42–43

SUMIFS function, 42

summarizing data

    with consolidate feature, 91–93

    by linking to ranges in other worksheets/workbooks, 87–88

    in multiple worksheets using range names and 3-D references, 84–86

    with Sparklines, 108–110

T

tab

    creating new, 187

    renaming, 187–188

table_array, 44

Table button, 58

tables

    adding row and calculated column to, 59–60

    automatic expansion of, 59

    banding rows and columns, 60

    converting, range to table, 58–59

    converting table to range and creating subtotals, 74–77

    converting to normal range, 74–77

copying and pasting data from Access to, 211–213

creating, 58–59

defined, 57

field names row in, 58

fields in, 58

filtering, 62–64

formatting table and adding *Total* row, 61–62

header row in, 58

importing

    from Access, 208–210

modifying, 59–60

PivotTables, 93–104

records in, 58

sorting, 62–64

style options for, 60–61

subtotaling related data, 74–77

Table Styles gallery, 60

Table Tools Design tab, 60–61, 67, 74

target value, Goal Seek to find, 121–122

template

    deleting custom template, 199

    saving workbook as, 196–199

    using custom template, 198–199

text

    converting to columns, 65–66

    converting using text functions, 23–24

    extracting and combining using text functions, 25

Text button, 21

text file

    exporting worksheets as, 221–223

    importing data from, 208–211

text functions, 21–25

    converting text using, 23–24

    extracting and combining text using, 25

Text Import Wizard, 208–210

"text" in custom number format code, 20

text #NAME? error message, 35

Text to Columns button, 65

3 Arrows (Colored) icon set, 11–12

3-D formulas, 84

3-D references

    defined, 84

    summarize data in multiple worksheet using, 86

Time Level indicator, 102

timelines, filtering PivotTables using, 102–104

Timeline Tools Options tab, 104

Tip (accessibility issue), 222

Title property name, 142

Top/Bottom Rules list, formatting cell based on, 4, 6

Total row, 60–62

Trace Dependents button, 131

Trace Precedents button, 131

track changes, 166–170

    accepting and rejecting changes, 167–168

    editing, 168

    highlighting and reviewing changes, 169

    turning off, 170

Track Changes button, 153, 166

Transpose button, 117

transposing data, 117–119

trigonometry functions, 42–43

TRIM text function, 22, 25

troubleshooting formulas, 132–135

TRUE, 44

Trust Center settings, 231–232

Trusted Locations list, 231–232

Trusted Publishers, 231

two-variable data table, 129–130

U

Undo feature, 88

Ungroup button, 79–80

Ungroup dialog box, 79–80

unicode text, 221

Unprotected Sheet dialog box, 161–162

unprotecting

    workbook, 162–163

    worksheet, 159–162

Unprotect Sheet button, 161

Unprotect Workbook dialog box, 163

UPPER text function, 21–22, 23–24
user name, changing, 149, 150

V

value comparison, formatting cells based on, 4, 15
#VALUE! error, 132, 133
Value Field Setting dialog box, 99–100
viewing, comments, 145–147
Visual Basic for Applications (VBA), 175, 180
VLOOKUP function, 44–46

W

Warning (accessibility issue), 224
Warning error alert message, 70
Watch Window button, 135
website, publishing worksheet as web page, 237–238
what-if analysis
   creating assumptions with Scenario Manager, 122–126
   with data tables, 127–130
   Goal Seek to find target value, 120–122
What-If Analysis button, 120
wildcard characters, in custom filter, 26
Win/Loss button, 108
Word document
   breaking link to Excel document, 216
   copying and pasting worksheet data to, 213–214
   embedding Excel data into, 214–215
   linking Excel data to, 215–216
workbooks
   changing user name, 149, 150
   creating macro workbook, 182
   destination, 87
   distributing, 233–238
      checking accessibility issues, 222–224

compatibility checker, 229–230
   marking as final, 228–229
   preparing for, 222–230
   publishing as PDF document, 233–235
   publishing as XPS document, 235–236
   removing information before, 224–227
opening multiple instances of Excel, 149
passwords, adding and removing, 163–165
properties, adding, 142–144
protecting and unprotecting structure of, 162–163
recovering, 200–201
saving as template, 196–199
saving containing macros, 175–176
sending by email, 157–158
sharing, 147–158
   changing user name, 149, 150
   on OneDrive, 154–157
   opening multiple instances of Excel, 149
   overview of, 147–149
   printing history sheet, 153–154
   removing shared workbook access, 153–154
   resolving conflicts in, 151–152
   sending by email, 157–158
   viewing other users of, 150–151
source, 87
summarizing data by linking ranges in another workbook or worksheet, 87–88
tracking changes, 166–170
   accepting and rejecting changes, 167–168
   editing, 168
   highlighting and reviewing changes, 169
   turning off, 170
worksheets
comments, managing, 144–147

converting range to table, 58–59
custom view for, 194–196
distributing, as web page, 237–238
exporting, 211–221
   breaking link to Excel object, 216
   copying and pasting worksheet data to
      Access, 211–213
      PowerPoint, 217–218
      Word, 213–216
   as text file, 219–221
filtering, using Custom AutoFilter, 26–27
importing data, 206–211
   from Access, 206–208
   from text file, 208–211
protecting and unprotecting, 159–162
range name and worksheet references, 34
summarizing data
   Consolidate feature, 91–93
   by linking ranges in another workbook, 87–88
   in multiple worksheets using range names and 3-D references, 84–86
worksheet reference, 84

X

XML paper specification, 235
XPS document, publishing workbook as, 235–236

Y

Yellow Sideways Arrow, 11

Z

0 (zero), in custom number format code, 20

Eleventh Edition

ILLUSTRATED GUIDE TO FOOD PREPARATION

Margaret McWilliams, Ph.D., R.D.
Professor Emeritus
California State University, Los Angeles

PEARSON

Boston Columbus Indianapolis New York San Francisco Upper Saddle River Amsterdam
Cape Town Dubai London Madrid Milan Munich Paris Montreal Toronto Delhi
Mexico City São Paulo Sydney Hong Kong Seoul Singapore Taipei Tokyo

Editorial Director: Vernon Anthony
Senior Acquisitions Editor: William Lawrensen
Editorial Assistant: Lara Dimmick
Director of Marketing: David Gesell
Senior Marketing Manager: Thomas Hayward
Assistant Marketing Manager: Alicia Wozniak
Senior Marketing Assistant: Les Roberts
Production Manager: Holly Shufeldt
Senior Art Director: Jayne Conte
Cover Designer: Bruce Kenselaar
Cover Art: Shutterstock
Full-Service Project Management and Composition: Integra Software Services Pvt. Ltd.
Printer/Binder: Edwards Brothers
Cover Printer: Lehigh-Phoenix Color Corp.

Photo credits: All photos courtesy of Plycon Press, unless otherwise noted.

Credits and acknowledgments borrowed from other sources and reproduced, with permission, in this textbook appear on the appropriate page within text.

Many of the designations by manufacturers and sellers to distinguish their products are claimed as trademarks. Where those designations appear in this book, and the publisher was aware of a trademark claim, the designations have been printed in initial caps or all caps.

Library of Congress Cataloging-in-Publication Data
McWilliams, Margaret.
Illustrated guide to food preparation / Margaret McWilliams.—11th ed.
    p. cm.
  Includes index.
  ISBN-13: 978-0-13-273875-0 (alk. paper)
  ISBN-10: 0-13-273875-9 (alk. paper)
  1. Cooking—Laboratory manuals.   I. Title.
  TX663.M25 2013
  641.5078—dc23

                                        2011048705

6 7 8 9 10 V0ZV 15

ISBN 10:   0-13-273875-9
ISBN 13: 978-0-13-273875-0

Dedication

*This edition is dedicated to the memory of Paul Peterson,
photographer and engineer extraordinaire.*

Contents

Preface

Welcome to the foods laboratory, where you will find intellectual rewards and dining pleasures, too. Not only will you be learning about the distinctive properties and characteristics of a wide range of ingredients, but you will also be developing the skills and knowledge needed to create delicious and nourishing dishes. An additional bonus is the pleasure of eating many of these tasty creations.

Illustrated Guide to Food Preparation is a unique book that combines scientific and aesthetic principles with the realities of working with food in the laboratory. Some experiments are presented for the entire class to do, while other laboratory sessions provide opportunities to explore various techniques and ingredients to enhance experiences with food. Numerous photographs have been included to help illustrate the techniques used in making the various types of food included in this book.

Because of the increasing recognition of the importance of locally grown foods, phytochemicals, and weight control as public health and safety concerns, emphasis has been given to preparation of vegetables and fruits in appetizing, tempting ways. Recipes are tailored to minimize calories while creating tempting and appealing dishes.

Basic laboratory techniques presented in Chapter 1 are designed to promote personal safety and food safety. Standards for working in the laboratory successfully to produce and evaluate quality products are also included. Subsequent chapters have been written to each be independent so they may be studied in a different sequence if preferred by your professor.

Chapters 2 through 4 feature plant foods and their preparation, cooked and raw in a variety of dishes, including their extensive use in salads. Sugar cookery introduces carbohydrates in Chapter 5. The behavior of starch in cereals and various food products (Chapter 6) is demonstrated by the recipes that are included. Protein-rich foods—milk and milk products, eggs, and meats and various alternatives—are the subjects in Chapters 7 through 9, respectively. Baked products in Chapters 10 through 12 include breads, cakes and cookies, and pies. A chapter on beverages completes the menu. Food preservation using heat (canning), freezing, and added sugar and/or acid is surveyed in Chapter 14. Meal management that emphasizes nutrition, the new MyPlate program, and optimizes the quality of food and its service is the topic of Chapter 15.

While you are preparing and evaluating the various recipes that illustrate important principles, you will doubtless find some dishes that will remain among your personal favorites. The good news is that you can put this book on a convenient shelf in your kitchen and continue to prepare these dishes whenever you like, even many years after you have completed this course. These recipes can be the springboard for a lifetime of eating pleasure. They will help extend your creativity with food while subtly reinforcing applications of science.

Former students have often returned to tell me that they still are preparing many of these recipes that they first made in class. They report that although some pages have spatters acquired when recipes were being prepared, this book is still being used long after they have graduated. I hope you will find similar pleasure in learning about food and its preparation. May you enjoy good food (but not too much of it) throughout your professional career and personal life.

Margaret McWilliams
Redondo Beach, California

Acknowledgments

It is a pleasure to thank Pat Chavez for her artistic and creative help during our days doing photo shoots. And kudos also go to her for her countless hours of proofreading to help keep gremlins off the printed page and out of the recipes.

ILLUSTRATED GUIDE TO FOOD PREPARATION

CHAPTER 1

Laboratory Basics

Welcome to the foods laboratory! Here you will develop laboratory skills while also increasing your knowledge of food and how to prepare tempting and satisfying products. There is much to learn about both the preparation and the evaluation of the foods you have prepared. Be sure to let your head, as well as your appetite, participate throughout each lab.

SAFE FOOD HANDLING

Objectives

1. To develop safe and sanitary habits of food handling.
2. To promote professional standards in the laboratory.

Food safety, although an unglamorous topic, is essential to your work in the foods lab and any time you are preparing food. A lapse in your attention to this subject can result in a variety of illnesses that can lead to considerable discomfort and even death (yours or those who have eaten your food). Because of the importance of good safety practices whenever food is involved, you will want to establish good personal habits when handling food. Be sure to develop and always practice the following habits:

*   Cover hair or tie it back before entering the lab.
*   Wash hands thoroughly with hot water and soap before handling food.
*   Be sure to turn away from food and cover your mouth and nose when sneezing and/or coughing.
*   Wash hands with hot water and soap any time you have blown your nose, coughed, sneezed, touched your hair or mouth, or have been to the bathroom.
*   Use only clean spoons for tasting. Place tasting spoons in the sink or other designated area and do not reuse them. Never use your fingers for tasting food.
*   Maintain a clean kitchen and avoid contaminating food while preparing it.
*   Keep protein-containing foods chilled or sufficiently hot to minimize risk from bacteria.

KEY CONCEPTS

1. Food has the potential for making people ill unless it is handled with careful attention to sanitation and temperature control.

2. Each person preparing or otherwise handling food must assume individual responsibility for personal habits to avoid contaminating the food.

3. Safety needs to be a primary concern when working in food preparation, particularly when heat, sharp instruments, and/or machines are being used.

4. Accurate measurements are important when preparing food products.

5. Various temperatures can be used in cooking foods, depending upon the food being heated, the results desired, and the cooking medium.

   a. Water may be heated to *lukewarm*, *scalding*, *simmering*, or *boiling* to cook foods.
   b. The addition of sugar or salt to cooking water has the potential for altering the temperature at which boiling takes place, but foods that do not *ionize* or dissolve as very small molecules do not have a significant effect.
   c. Oil can be heated to very high temperatures when frying foods because oil does not boil at frying temperatures.

- Always use serving silver to transfer samples from the serving table to your taste plate. Never use your personal silver to obtain samples from the display or serving table.

- Wash dishes in a dishwasher or in very hot water with plenty of soap. Rinse thoroughly with scalding water.

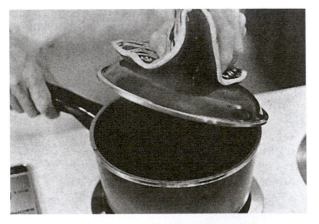

LABORATORY FUNDAMENTALS

Precautions with Heat

Hot pads adequate for protecting the hands from any hot pan or hot food should always be available near the range for instant use. To avoid steam burns, which can result when a lid is removed from a pan containing steam and boiling water, tilt the lid to direct the escaping steam away from the body. This is an important precaution because steam burns can be serious. If a burn does happen, immediately put ice wrapped in a paper towel or cloth on the burned area very briefly, but do not freeze the skin.

Hot pans require particular attention to avoid damaging kitchen counters. Any pan that has been used for frying, deep-fat frying, or pan broiling will be much hotter than the boiling point of water. These pans and skillets should remain on the range, be placed on special metal trivets, or be moved to a metal surface to cool. Under no circumstance should they be placed immediately on synthetic surfaces such as vinyl or Formica. The heat will scar the counter surface badly. On the other hand, pans that have been used to boil vegetables or to cook other water-containing items can safely be put on most surfaces commonly used for kitchen counters. The temperature of pans containing water will not cause scarring of the counter.

Pans should always have something in them when they are being heated on the range. Empty pans will be become dangerously hot very quickly, causing warping and possibly creating a fire hazard, too. When using a double boiler, always be certain that there is water remaining in the lower unit. For prolonged heating, it will be necessary to check the level occasionally and to add more water if the level has dropped greatly. Proper water level in a double boiler is usually about an inch, but the actual level recommended will vary with the design of the unit. The upper pan should not be in contact with the water in the lower pan. Usually, the water should be maintained at a gentle boil, but stirred custard can be prepared better by maintaining the water at simmering.

Be sure pan handles do not extend over another burner or over the edge of the range. For safety, form the habit of holding the handle of a pan with a hot pad whenever the food is being stirred. This practice helps to avoid the possibility of tipping the pan off the burner or of being burned by a hot handle. A wooden spoon is a useful utensil for stirring foods while they are cooking. The spoon feels comfortable in the hand, and the handle does not get hot as the food heats.

Before beginning to heat an oven, always pull out the rack to its extended position and press down to be sure the rack is locked properly into its slides so that it will not tip down when food is placed on it. This should be done as the first step in preparing any baked item. This is also the time to change the location of the rack if it is not in the correct position. Be sure to check the locking of the rack when the rack is in the desired position.

Broiler pans will vary in design, but they basically will be made to provide some means of protecting the fat and drippings from the very intense heat of the broiler unit. The pans should be used in the manner specified by the manufacturer. This will keep the fat from igniting when meat is being broiled. Aluminum foil should not be used to line the rack; it will allow pockets of fat to accumulate on the rack. Because the rack is so close to the heat, there is a likelihood that the fat may ignite and start a broiler fire.

Deep-Fat Frying

For deep-fat frying, oil should be heated just long enough to bring it to 190°C (375°F), the temperature best suited to frying doughnuts and most other foods. A deep-fat frying thermometer is useful to monitor temperature during frying. Vegetable oils, such as corn or canola oil, are suitable choices for deep-fat frying because of their high smoke points. They can be used several times if they are heated just to the frying temperature and then held at the desired temperature only until frying is completed. Long heating periods cause the fat molecules to begin to break down to release free fatty acids, glycerol, and eventually, acrolein. This breakdown will cause the smoke point of the oil to begin to drop toward the temperature needed for frying. These breakdown products are detrimental to the flavor of fried foods, and acrolein irritates the eyes.

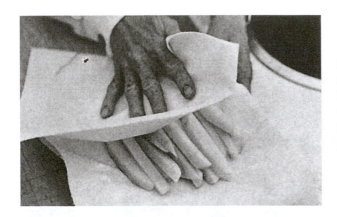

One of the concerns in deep-fat frying is the splattering that can occur. Temperatures used in deep-fat frying are considerably hotter than the temperature of boiling water. If water happens to come in contact with the hot fat, the water will splatter and can cause burns and greasy counters. These problems can be avoided by blotting foods with paper towels before placing them in the hot fat.

Use a slotted spoon or a pair of tongs to place the food in the hot oil when the oil has reached the correct temperature. This eliminates the risk of fingers coming in contact with the hot oil and minimizes splashing of hot oil.

For the maximum useful life, fats used for frying should be strained through cheesecloth after each use to remove extraneous particles that may have remained in the fat after the food was removed. Straining should be done after the fat is cool. Because oils are the preferred choice for deep-fat frying, there is no problem that the fat will be too hard to pour before it is cool enough to handle safely. An empty coffee can or other can with a tightly fitting plastic lid is ideal for storing the strained fat.

Cutting Techniques

Attention needs to be directed in the laboratory at all times toward personal safety as well as high standards of food preparation. Selection of the proper equipment can make many operations easier and faster. Chopping can be done with the aid of a French chef's knife. This type of knife is identified by its large blade, the recessed handle (which permits the fingers to grasp the handle without hitting the knuckles on the chopping board), and the linear, rather than curved, cutting edge. The tip of the blade is held in contact with the cutting board continually by gentle pressure from the left hand. The right hand moves the handle up and down to accomplish the chopping motion. For safety and maintenance of good cutting edges, store knives in a rack or sheath.

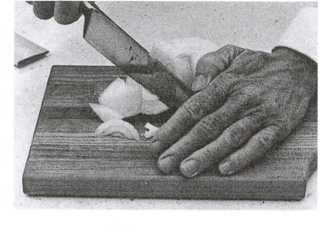

A utility knife can be used for numerous small cutting operations in the kitchen. Always cut on a cutting board. Avoid holding food in the hand while cutting, and be sure not to cut toward the thumb. The regular use of a cutting board will do much to reduce accidents caused by improper use of knives. The cutting board needs to be scrubbed thoroughly after each use. This practice avoids the possibility of spreading food-borne illnesses when foods come in contact with unclean surfaces.

Kitchen shears are useful for a wide number of purposes, ranging from cutting up poultry to snipping the green tops of scallions and parsley. These shears need to be washed thoroughly after each use. They can be washed well in a dishwasher or by hand.

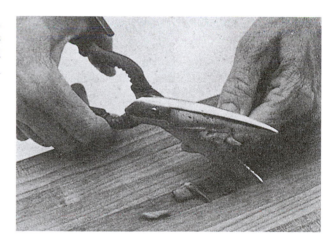

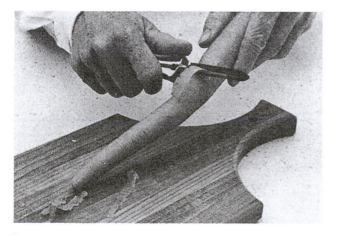

A vegetable peeler provides a quick means of paring potatoes, carrots, and other vegetables. Operate by using long strokes directed away from the body. This device can also be used to prepare thin slices of potatoes for potato chips and for making the thin, center slices needed for making carrot curls.

Mixers

For best results with electric mixers, read the manufacturer's directions carefully before using. The beater blades should be inserted with the mixer unplugged and the switch turned to OFF. This dual insurance will certainly avoid the possibility of having the blades begin to spin while they are still in the hand. Although seemingly redundant, both measures provide increased protection against the possibility of kitchen accidents.

The best results with a mixer are achieved when the mixer is set on the right bowl adjustment (small or large bowl). Check this before starting the mixer. Also check to be sure that the blades have been locked securely in the correct position. Use only the bowls designed for the mixer.

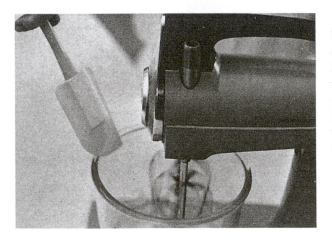

Nothing more substantial than a rubber spatula should be used to scrape the bowl when conventional mixers are in operation. Absolutely nothing metallic should be in the bowl. Even a rubber spatula cannot be used to scrape the bowl when a mixer with hypocycloidal action is used; the irregular path of the beaters makes it impossible to avoid having the spatula being caught in the mixer. For the safest operation with any type of mixer, *turn off the mixer* before scraping the sides of the bowl.

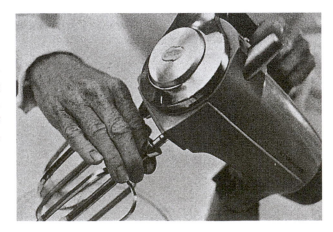

Remove the beater blades according to the manufacturer's directions after turning off the mixer and unplugging it. In removing blades from the type of mixer illustrated, twist the handle at the top of the mixer to release the blades from the locked position. After they are released, they will slide easily from the mixer head.

MEASURING TECHNIQUES

Objectives

1. To know the equivalents of measures used in food preparation.
2. To measure liquids, solids, and dry ingredients accurately using recommended techniques.

Success in food preparation begins with accurate measurements. Careless measurements result in products with ratios of ingredients different from the tested recipes, which leads to disappointing products. The techniques required are not difficult, but they do need to be studied and used. The recommended techniques and the appropriate utensils for measuring liquid and dry ingredients are presented below. Practice them throughout the term. Soon they will become a valuable habit.

Equivalent measures are essential to know when altering recipes. The equivalent measures in the table can be memorized quickly; this knowledge saves time and avoids mistakes when preparing recipes.

Equivalent Measures

1 Tablespoon (Tbsp)	= 3 teaspoons (tsp)
2 Tbsp	= 1 fluid ounce (fl oz)
4 Tbsp	= 1/4 cup (c)
8 fl oz	= 1 c
16 Tbsp	= 1 c
2 c	= 1 pint (pt)
4 c	= 2 pt = 1 quart (qt)
16 oz	= 1 pound (lb)

Dry Ingredients

Flour

To measure flour (either cake or all-purpose), it should be sifted once before measuring. The sifting process helps to lighten the flour enough to allow sufficiently accurate measurement by volume. This sifting can be done with a sifter or a strainer directly onto wax paper. Let the flour fall lightly on the paper. Sift only once before measuring. Recipes are based on measures of sifted flour.

Lightly spoon the flour into the appropriate graduated measuring cup. Be careful not to pack flour at this point, and avoid bumping the cup or jarring it in any way that would cause the flour to become more compact. The graduated measuring cups (also called Mary Ann cups) are appropriate for measuring all ingredients except liquids. These cups are designed so that the ingredients can be scraped off to give a level measure. This provides important accuracy in food preparation. Remember, this technique is used to help standardize flour measurements. The goal is not to see how much flour can be packed into the cup.

Without packing the flour, use a spatula to scrape off the extra flour that extends above the top of the cup. Be sure to use the straight portion of the metal blade of the spatula. Avoid the area of the blade that angles in toward the handle. Also avoid the curved area at the end of the blade.

Brown Sugar

Brown sugar presents a slightly different problem in measuring than is posed by other dry ingredients. A graduated measuring cup still is the utensil of choice. However, the sugar is packed lightly into the cup until the cup is overflowing. A spatula is used to level the measure. When properly measured, brown sugar will be packed just firmly enough to hold the shape of the container when it is turned out after measurement is completed. This packing technique provides adequately consistent measures.

Other Dry Ingredients

Sugar, cornmeal, rice, and other dry ingredients can be measured simply by spooning them directly into the appropriate graduated measuring cup. The greatest accuracy is achieved by using as few of the cups as possible. For example, greater accuracy probably will be achieved by measuring 3/4 cup of rice using a 1/2 cup and a 1/4 cup measure rather than by simply filling the 1/4 cup measure three times.

Measuring of dry ingredients always is completed by leveling the heaping cup with the straight portion of the blade of a metal spatula.

Smaller Amounts

When dry ingredients are needed in amounts less than 1/4 cup, graduated measuring spoons are used in place of the graduated measuring cups. Most measuring spoon sets consist of a tablespoon, a teaspoon, a half teaspoon, and a quarter teaspoon. Smaller amounts can only be estimated. The appropriate spoon is heaped more than full with the ingredient to be measured, and then a spatula is used to level the measure.

Solid Fats

Solid shortenings, butter, margarine, and lard may be measured using the marks on the wrappers encasing them or by using graduated measuring cups. For accuracy, the fat should be pressed firmly into the cup so that any air pockets are eliminated.

After the appropriate graduated measuring cup has been packed full of fat, a spatula is used to level the measure. Care should be taken to be certain that only the straight portion of the blade is being used to level the fat.

Liquids

A glass measuring cup is the appropriate device for measuring liquids. The cup should be placed on a flat, level surface to facilitate accurate measurement. The ingredient should be poured in the cup only to the appropriate mark. The reading should be made by bending over so that the eye is even with the desired level in the cup. This avoids the distortion that occurs when the measure is taken by looking down on the cup. Glass measuring cups are suitable only for measuring liquids, because it is not possible to level other types of ingredients accurately in the cup. The extra space above the cup measure in a glass cup is designed to prevent spills while lifting the cup from the counter to the mixing bowl.

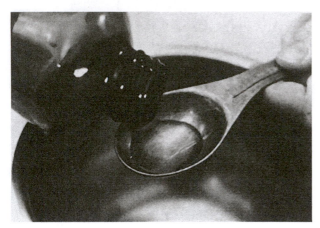

Liquid ingredients in amounts less than a fourth of a cup are measured with graduated measuring spoons. Ingredients should be measured over an empty bowl or over the container holding the ingredient. Measurements are not made over a bowl containing other ingredients because of the possibility of spilling extra amounts into the product. Liquids should be poured slowly to avoid overflowing the measure.

TEMPERATURES USED IN COOKING

Objectives

1. To know how water and oil look at selected temperatures used in food preparation.
2. To become aware of the different temperatures used in food preparation, as influenced by cooking media and equipment.
3. To determine the influence of added ingredients on the boiling point of water.

LABORATORY EXPERIMENT

1. Place a thermometer in a 1-quart saucepan containing 2 cups water. Heat the water to a boil. In the table, record the appearance of the water at each temperature.

Temperature	Appearance
104°F or 40°C (Lukewarm)	
149°F or 65°C (Scalding)	
180–211°F or 82–99°C (Simmering)	
212°F or 100°C (Boiling)	

2. Place 1 cup water in the bottom of a double boiler and 1 cup water in the top portion. Heat until the water in the top of the double boiler comes to a constant temperature. Note the highest temperature reached in the upper unit.

_____ °F or _____ °C

Place 1 cup water in a steamer. Put the steamer basket in position and cover the assembled unit. Heat the water until it boils and the steamer is well filled with steam. Barely lift the cover enough to insert a thermometer into the steam-filled upper chamber. Quickly note the temperature.

_____ °F or _____ °C

3. In a 1-quart saucepan, place 2 cups water. Mark the water level with a wax-marking pencil. Heat the water to boiling. When the water boils actively throughout the pan, note the temperature. By tablespoons, add the ingredient assigned, as indicated in the table. After each addition, be sure that the liquid has returned to an active boil before reading the temperature. As the water level drops below the mark in the pan, add water to maintain the original volume. Record results in the table.

Amount	Ingredient Added			
	Salt	Sugar	Corn Meal	Gelatin[1]
1 Tbsp				
2 Tbsp				
3 Tbsp				
4 Tbsp				

[1]Hydrate gelatin (1 envelope in 1/4 c water) before using.

4. Heat 1 cup salad oil in a 1-quart saucepan and complete the table. Place the pan and oil on a cool surface unit of the range to cool.

Temperature	Appearance of Oil
212°F or 100°C	
375°F or 190°C	

VOCABULARY

Lukewarm

Scalding

Simmering

Boiling

Atmospheric pressure

Vapor pressure

True solution

Ionize

Colloidal dispersion

Coarse suspension

CHAPTER 2

Vegetables

Vegetables are gaining considerable prestige as their nutritional merits and health benefits, such as possibly helping to prevent cancer, are being touted. They are so important that there is an ongoing national campaign urging everyone to eat "5-a-day" (five servings of vegetables and fruits). This chapter is designed to help you learn how to prepare vegetables in a variety of ways.

The range of suitable recipes is very wide; those appearing in this chapter are merely an introduction to what you might wish to try on your own. Examples of boiling, steaming, broiling, baking, stir-frying, and deep-fat frying are included. Try such simple ideas as boiling or steaming a vegetable, then serving it with one of the sauces in this chapter. You also may wish to experiment with different combinations of vegetables, in addition to some of the recipes presented here. Also, consider using raw or cooked vegetables in salads (see Chapter 4 for some ideas). Let your creativity with vegetables take over.

PIGMENTS AND TEXTURE

Objectives

1. To identify the color changes that pigments undergo when heated in (a) an acidic medium and (b) an alkaline medium.
2. To determine the effect on texture when vegetables are boiled in an (a) acidic medium and (b) alkaline medium.

KEY CONCEPTS

1. Color and texture of vegetables are optimized by minimizing cooking time and controlling pH of the water.

2. Selection of the method of preparing cooked vegetables (boiling, steaming, sautéing, stir-frying, deep-fat frying, microwaving, broiling, or baking) is determined by considering such factors as the type of vegetable being prepared, time and equipment that are available, and dietary requirements or preferences.

3. Potatoes vary in their cooking properties according to their comparative sugar and starch content.
   a. Waxy potatoes are relatively high in sugar and low in starch.
   b. Non-waxy (mealy) potatoes are higher in starch and lower in sugar than waxy potatoes.

4. Legumes of many types are available to provide inexpensive, healthful sources of protein; dried beans require an extended soaking period and slow cooking to produce the desired tenderness.

Pigments

Although many specific compounds contribute to the pigmentation of fruits and vegetables, these substances can be categorized into chlorophylls, carotenoids, and flavonoids. The chlorophylls include chlorophyll a and chlorophyll b; the carotenoids are the compounds contributing various bright colors in the yellow, orange, and red range; the flavonoids range from white to reds and blues. These pigments are modified in some cases by the medium to which they are exposed. Thus, there is a need to know what the pigment change may be in an acid versus an alkaline medium.

Chlorophyll *a* is a rather strong blue-green color, as can be seen in the flowers of broccoli. *Chlorophyll b* is also green, but it has a bit of yellow overtone to the color. Most green vegetables contain both of these forms of chlorophyll. In an alkaline medium, such as is provided by adding some soda to the cooking water, the green color will be intensified. However, on the acid side of neutral, as can be illustrated by adding lemon juice or vinegar to water, the green color of chlorophyll changes to the olive-green color of pheophytin. This color generally is considered less desirable than the green of chlorophyll. Thus, it can be concluded that it is wise to cook green vegetables in an uncovered pan to aid in the escape of volatile acids that might otherwise promote the development of pheophytin during cooking. The other factor that can cause the formation of pheophytin is prolonged cooking. This can be minimized by placing the vegetables in boiling water to shorten cooking time and by cutting them into relatively small pieces that will tenderize quickly.

Carotenoids include a range of compounds in the yellow through orange and red color range. The carotenes, which are nutritionally significant as being precursors of vitamin A, range from yellow through orange and are dominant in carrots and other orange-colored vegetables. Lycopene provides the red color in tomatoes; the xanthophylls are still different shades of yellow and orange, such as can be found in corn. All members of the carotenoids are stable pigments, remaining essentially the same color in either an acid or an alkaline medium. Vegetables colored by carotenoids can be boiled with a cover without harming the color.

The **flavonoids** include **anthoxanthins** and **anthocyanins,** two chemically related types of pigments with very different colors. The *anthoxanthins* are bleached or colorless in an acidic medium. A good example of anthoxanthins is provided by cauliflower. In an acidic medium, this pigment bleaches to a desirable white. In an alkaline medium, anthoxanthins become an unappealing yellow, as illustrated in the cooking of cauliflower in an alkaline medium created by the addition of soda. Boiling with a cover does not harm vegetables colored by anthoxanthins.

Anthocyanins give the reds and purples found in a few fruits, red cabbage, and beets. Red cabbage provides the most useful illustration of the pigment changes that develop when anthocyanins are subjected to acidic and alkaline media. In acid, anthocyanin will become a reddish color reminiscent of the color reaction of litmus paper, but in an alkaline medium, the anthocyanins change to blue, a reaction also paralleling litmus paper. The color in red cabbage can even evolve to almost a deep green in an alkaline medium because the yellow of the anthoxanthins, when superimposed on the blue of anthocyanins, gives the overall impression of green.

In summary, an acidic cooking medium promotes the change in color of chlorophyll from green to an undesirable olive green, the flavonoids (both anthoxanthins and anthocyanins) will be a satisfactory color, and the carotenoids will not be influenced significantly by acid. In an alkaline medium, anthoxanthins develop a yellow color and anthocyanins shift to blue. Chlorophyll becomes a bright green color in alkali; carotenoids are unchanged. Thus, the changes in the flavonoids are detrimental, while the change in chlorophyll is acceptable from an aesthetic standpoint.

	Color Pigment in	
	Acid	Alkali
Chlorophyll	Olive green	Bright green
Carotenoid	Orange	Orange
Anthoxanthin	White	Yellowish
Anthocyanin	Reddish	Bluish

Texture

The addition of lemon juice or vinegar greatly retards the softening of cellulose, making it extremely difficult to cook vegetables to the correct degree of doneness. If lemon juice or other flavoring substance of acidic reaction is to be used, this needs to be added after the vegetable is tender. In an alkaline medium, the cellulose will soften very rapidly, leading quickly to a very mushy texture. In addition, there will be excessive loss of thiamin in an alkaline cooking medium. This nutritional aspect is of special concern when cooking dried legumes because these vegetables are excellent sources of this B vitamin when properly prepared.

The influence of acidic and alkaline cooking media on vegetable pigments and on texture can be demonstrated by cooking vegetables, selected to represent the various types of pigments, in a vinegar-containing solution and in a soda-containing solution.

LABORATORY EXPERIMENT

Acidic and Alkaline Cooking Media

Method:

1	stalk broccoli
1/4	head cauliflower
1/4	head red cabbage
1	large carrot

1. Wash each of the vegetables; pare the carrot and cut each vegetable in half.
2. Prepare four 1-quart saucepans, each containing 2 cups boiling water and 1/4 cups vinegar.
3. Place half a carrot in one of the pans and note the time. Place half the red cabbage in another of the pans and note the time. Similarly, place half the cauliflower and half the broccoli in the remaining two pans, noting the time when each is started.
4. Prepare four 1-quart saucepans, each containing 2 cups boiling water and 2 tablespoons baking soda.

5. Place each of the remaining vegetables in one of these pans, noting the time when each is started.
6. Boil each of the vegetables without a cover on the pan until the vegetable tests tender when pierced with a fork. Note the elapsed time required to reach this point, and record in the table.
7. Remove the vegetable and place on a serving plate. Complete the table on pigments and texture.

Pigment	Vegetable Used	Color[1]		Cooking Time/Texture[2]	
		Acid	Alkali	Acid	Alkali
Chlorophyll					
Carotenoid					
Anthoxanthin					
Anthocyanin					

[1]Mark an asterisk (*) beside each acidic and alkaline color reaction that is pleasing to the eye. (Ignore the texture and look only at color for this decision.) For vegetables having the best color in an alkaline medium, it is preferable to cook them without using a lid on the pan so that volatile organic acids can escape. If a vegetable looks best in an acidic medium, it is wise to consider cooking it with the cover on the pan.
[2]What generalization can be drawn about the rate of cooking in acid versus the rate in alkali?

PREPARING VEGETABLES

Objectives

1. To identify criteria significant in selecting and buying vegetables.
2. To outline the procedures that can be used in preparing vegetables for cooking.
3. To demonstrate appropriate procedures for boiling, steaming, broiling, baking, sautéing, stir-frying, and deep-fat frying fresh vegetables.
4. To identify appropriate cooking methods to use for various fresh vegetables.
5. To evaluate the quality of preparation of fresh vegetables.
6. To determine the effect of various sauces on the palatability of selected fresh vegetables.

Selection

Fresh vegetables cannot be prepared so that they are of higher quality than they were when purchased. Therefore, it is important to select and buy vegetables that have a plump, unblemished, and crisp quality. In most instances, they should be placed in the hydrator drawer and refrigerated promptly. Potatoes, onions (except green onions), and winter squash should be stored in a cool, dry bin, but should not be refrigerated.

Preparation for Cooking

Before cooking, vegetables should be washed thoroughly. In the case of leafy vegetables, such as spinach, this task is done most easily by immersing them in a sinkful of water and changing the rinse water as many times as necessary. A firm scrubbing with a vegetable brush is useful in preparing potatoes and other vegetables with dirt-retaining skins. A stream of cold water from the faucet is the most efficient way of removing dirt from fresh vegetables.

The final form in which the vegetable is to be served should be considered at this time. If a head of cauliflower is to be served whole with a cheese sauce over it, the only preparation remaining to be done before cooking is the removal of any leaves or blemishes and a trimming of the core to remove the woody center portion. On the other hand, if cabbage wedges are the plan, the head of cabbage should be cut into wedges before cooking to help reduce cooking time and improve color and flavor.

Carrots, parsnips, and other vegetables with an outer skin ordinarily are pared before being cooked. An exception to this is beets, which are boiled with their skins on to help retain their highly soluble pigment. Extraneous parts of the vegetable, including the ends of string beans and the woody lower stalk of broccoli, are removed with a sharp knife. Then the vegetable is cut into the desired pieces.

Boiling

Boiling is a method suitable for preparing almost all vegetables. This method is done most efficiently by placing a saucepan containing the desired amount of salted water on the range, covering it with a tightly fitted lid, and preheating the water to a boil while quickly preparing the vegetable. By placing the vegetable in boiling water, the actual cooking time is minimized. This helps to retain optimum color and flavor in the vegetable. Long cooking is detrimental to green colors, nutritive value, and sulfur-containing flavoring compounds in vegetables.

The two main concerns in boiling vegetables are (1) the amount of water and (2) the use of a lid. For vegetables with mild flavors, the flavor will be retained at its maximum by using just enough water to boil over the vegetables and using a lid on the pan. Vegetables with strong flavors can be made more palatable by using an additional half inch of water to dilute the flavor and avoiding the use of a lid so that the volatile flavor compounds can escape into the air.

Green vegetables will have a more pleasing color if they are cooked without a lid, because the lid traps volatile organic acids in the pan and increases the likelihood of changing chlorophyll to the less desirable compound, pheophytin.

If either the flavor or color of a vegetable will be harmed by covering the pan, it is recommended that the lid not be used. The most important single concern in vegetable preparation is palatability. When vegetables are tempting,

Figure 2.1
Cabbage wedges can be trimmed to leave just enough of the tough core to hold the wedge together during cooking.

enough of them will be consumed to provide the nutrients available from them. Highly nourishing but unappetizing vegetables probably will not be consumed and are therefore wasted.

Obviously, some vegetables present a conflict in logic. Peas, for example, are mild flavored, thus suggesting that a lid should be used; the chlorophyll would be harmed by the use of the lid. The recommendation in such cases is to boil without using a lid. If there is no reason for boiling the vegetable uncovered, a lid should be used.

In all cases, vegetables should be boiled just until they are tender enough to be cut with a fork. A very tender vegetable has less interesting texture, and the color and flavor will be less appealing.

A guide for boiling a number of fresh vegetables is presented in the table. Canned vegetables require only reheating until they are hot throughout. Frozen vegetables should be cooked according to directions on the package. Specific suggestions for boiling spinach, globe artichokes, boiling onions, cabbage, carrots, and broccoli follow.

Guide for Boiling Fresh Vegetables

Vegetable	Size	Amount of Water	Use of Lid	Time (min)
Artichokes, globe	Whole	1 inch	Yes	40–60
Artichokes, Jerusalem	Whole	To cover	Yes	25–35
Asparagus	Spears	To base of tips	No	7
Beans, green	1 inch	To cover	No	20
Beans, lima	Shelled	To cover	No	30
Beets	Whole	To cover	Yes	35–60
Beet greens	Leaves	Clinging to leaves	Until wilted	10
Broccoli stalks	Split	To base of flower	No	7
Brussels sprouts	Whole	1/2 inch above vegetable	No	15
Cabbage	Wedges	1/2 inch above vegetable	No	7
Carrots	Strips	To cover	Yes	12
Cauliflower	Whole	1/2 inch above vegetable	No	20–30
Cauliflower	Flowerets	1/2 inch above vegetable	No	10
Corn	On cob	To cover	Yes	6
Okra	Sliced	To cover	No	12
Onions, boiling	Whole	1/2 inch above vegetable	No	15–20
Parsnips	Quartered strips	1/2 inch above vegetable	No	10–15
Peas	Shelled	To cover	No	10
Potatoes	Halves	To cover	Yes	20
Rutabagas	Diced	1/2 inch above vegetable	No	25
Spinach	Leaves	Clinging to leaves	Until wilted	5–8
Squash, summer	Sliced	1 inch	No	5
Squash, winter	2-inch cubes	1 inch	Yes	20
Sweet potatoes	Quarters	To cover	Yes	20
Turnips	Sliced	1/2 inch above vegetable	No	18
Zucchini	1 inch slice	1 inch	No	5

Figure 2.2
Brussels sprouts grow closely packed along a tall vertical stalk.

Specific Examples of Preparing Boiled Vegetables

Spinach   Fresh spinach requires careful washing. Deep veins in the leaves shelter sand and dirt that cling to the spinach as it comes from the field. The easiest and most efficient way to ensure thorough washing is to immerse the leaves in a sink full of water and dousing them up and down several times. While holding the leaves to one side, drain the water from the sink, and rinse away the sand and other sediment. Replace the sink stopper, and fill the sink with water again. Agitate the leaves in the water to help loosen clinging dirt and sand; again the water is drained from the sink. Repeat this process until there is no sediment remaining in the sink when the water is drained out. At this point, examine the leaves, and remove the roots and longer stems.

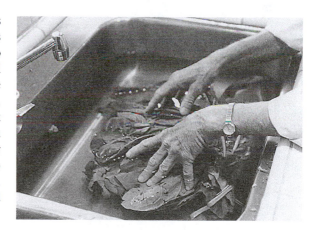

For boiled spinach, the washed leaves are placed in a large pan. No water is added to the pan because there will be enough moisture present from the water clinging to the leaves to prevent burning. The lid is placed on the pan at first to help trap steam in the pan and wilt the leaves to a smaller volume in the bottom of the pan. When the leaves have wilted down into the cooking water that has collected from the leaves, the lid is removed.

Boiling is continued just until the spinach is tender, usually in a matter of only about 3 to 5 minutes after the spinach wilts. Because there is a limited amount of water in the bottom of the pan, more uniform cooking is achieved by using a spoon or cooking fork to turn the spinach in the pan so that all of the spinach is in the water during part of the cooking period. To serve spinach, drain it thoroughly in a colander before adding desired seasonings.

Globe Artichokes   Globe artichokes are dramatic to serve and are well suited to a menu when last-minute touches would be a burden. Preparation begins by allowing a stream of water to run hard between the petals to remove any trapped dirt. Turn the artichoke upside down to allow the rinse water to run out. Repeat the washing and draining process several times to ensure all dirt and sand have been removed. Cut the stem off at the base of the flower, being careful to make a straight cut so that the artichoke will sit up straight on the plate when it is served. As is true with all cutting, a cutting board should be used to prevent dulling the knife on a hard surface.

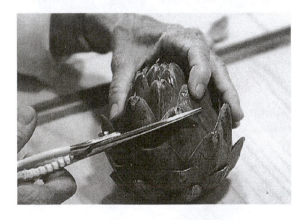

Artichokes will be easier to eat and more attractive when the sharp points on the petals are cut off. This can be done quickly using a pair of kitchen shears. Simply cut straight across the upper portion of each petal.

Artichokes require a long cooking period, often as long as 45 to 60 minutes, to tenderize the heart (base) of the vegetable. The most practical way to cook this vegetable is to place it in a pan containing approximately 3/4 inch of salted water. If desired, garlic salt and a teaspoon of olive oil may be added to the water to brighten the flavor. A lid is placed on the pan to trap the steam and help in cooking the petals, which extend above the water level. Artichokes are boiled gently until the base of the vegetable can be pricked easily with a cooking fork. Invert the artichoke to drain it before serving.

Artichokes can be served either hot or cold. It is eaten by removing a petal, dipping the base of the petal in melted butter or other sauce, and then scraping the small amount of meat at the base from the petal with the teeth. There is only a small amount of meat in each petal. This process is repeated until the center of the artichoke is reached. Then the choke is removed and set aside. Additional butter or sauce may be added to the heart, which is revealed. The heart is the principal edible part of this vegetable.

Boiling Onions Boiling onions are an example of a strong-flavored vegetable whose acceptance can be promoted by good preparation techniques. The strong flavor can be minimized by using enough water to cover the onions a half inch above the top to help dilute the onion flavor. Volatile flavoring compounds can be reduced by cooking them without a lid, thus allowing these substances to escape. After being washed, the onions are boiled uncovered until the centers can be penetrated easily with a fork. After draining, the boiled onions are placed on a cutting board and the root end is cut off. Then the onion can be squeezed out of the husk-like outer skins and the stem end trimmed.

Cabbage Cabbage is a vegetable that can be very attractive when properly prepared. One good way is to prepare wedges and then boil them. Wedges are cut from the washed head with a sharp knife. Care should be taken to ensure that the wedge contains a portion of the core because it holds the wedge intact during boiling. To help keep cooking time short, the tough core can be trimmed so that it is only about a quarter of an inch thick along its length. This trimming should be done on a cutting board, being careful to avoid releasing any of the cabbage leaves from the core.

For both optimum color and flavor, it is important to cook cabbage as short a time as possible. This is accomplished by dropping the wedges into salted water that is boiling actively and maintaining the active boil until the cabbage is done. Cabbage and related vegetables have a strong flavor that can be improved by the use of excess water to dilute the flavor. The flavor is reduced also by boiling cabbage and other sulfur-containing vegetables without a cover just until they are tender enough to be cut easily with a fork. It is better to cook cabbage just until barely tender rather than until it is quite limp because the flavor intensifies with longer cooking.

A short cooking time is important for the color as well as the flavor of cabbage. Chlorophyll will change to pheophytin when it is heated more than 7 minutes. This change to an olive-green color will make cabbage less inviting to diners. Thus, cabbage and related vegetables will be most palatable when cooked a very short time in an uncovered pan containing an excess of water.

Carrots   Carrots can add variety to menus while also contributing a potential source of vitamin A. Whether served raw or cooked, they require thorough scrubbing. Their appearance will be enhanced by paring, too. This can be done quickly using a vegetable peeler. After paring, carrots may be left whole or cut into shapes that will complement the other foods they are being served with. Use a sharp knife and a cutting board to cut them into strips or slices, being careful to make the pieces uniform in size.

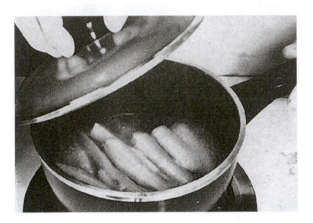

Carrots are a mild-flavored vegetables that needs to be cooked carefully to retain as much flavor as possible. This goal is achieved by boiling them just until they are tender in a covered pan with just enough salted, boiling water to barely cover the carrots; their color will not be impaired by trapping volatile acids in the pan. By having the water boiling when the carrots are added, the actual cooking time will be kept to a minimum. This is useful in promoting optimum retention of the nutrients and flavor.

Broccoli   The best broccoli will have a bluish-green color to the flowers. It requires thorough washing, some trimming, and cutting before cooking. The stalk is somewhat woody and tough, but softening during cooking can be hastened by cutting off the more woody portions of the stalk and then slitting the remaining stalk lengthwise almost to the point where the flowers begin. The stalk may be split in halves or quarters, depending on its size to reduce the time required to tenderize it, thus helping to finish cooking the vegetable before the green chlorophyll has been converted to the less attractive olive-green color of pheophytin.

Steaming

Vegetables can be cooked in a device known as a steamer. In this method, water is boiled actively in a lower container, and the vegetable is placed on a rack suspended in the steam above the water. The entire device is covered with a lid to trap the steam. Any vegetables that are suited to boiling can also be steamed. Preparation is begun by bringing the water to a boil in the lower portion of the steamer. The vegetable then is placed on the rack, and the lid is replaced on the steamer. A large volume of steam should be maintained in the steamer throughout the steaming period. Steaming will take longer than boiling. This method is good for retaining water-soluble vitamins despite the fact that the cooking period is lengthened. Chlorophyll, however, will undergo an undesirable color change with this method unless the pieces of vegetable are small enough to steam quickly.

Broiling

Broil vegetables, such as tomato slices, mushroom caps, eggplant slices, or zucchini slices, by arranging them on a broiler pan, sprinkling them liberally with buttered crumbs, and broiling them about 3 inches from the heat source until pleasingly browned and heated throughout. Thick slices may need to be broiled at a distance of 4 inches or more to allow time for the vegetable to cook before the surface becomes too brown. If a vegetable, such as boiling onions or green peppers, is to be broiled, the vegetable should be parboiled (boiled until almost fork tender) before being placed in the broiler for the broiling and final browning process. The parboiling softens the vegetable, and the broiling quickly finishes the cooking process and adds a pleasing appearance.

A few vegetables have a tender enough structure so that they will be appetizing and appealing when they are broiled. Fresh tomatoes and mushrooms are vegetables that often are broiled. Broiling, like stir-frying, avoids the loss of water-soluble vitamins. To prepare vegetables for broiling, wash them well. Tomatoes ordinarily are cut in half. A coating of buttered bread crumbs or Parmesan cheese is optional, but will add to the eye appeal of the finished vegetable. The tomatoes are arranged on the broiler pan and then placed in the broiler with the upper surface of the tomatoes approximately 3 inches from the heat source.

It is not necessary to turn vegetables when they are being broiled, but it is important to watch them carefully to avoid burning them. The intense heat will brown them quite quickly. Vegetables should be removed from the broiler as soon as they are attractive in appearance and have been heated through.

Baking

Winter squash and potatoes, both sweet and Irish, are the vegetables most commonly baked. The well-scrubbed vegetables are pricked with a fork to create steam vents before they are placed on a rack in the middle of the oven and baked at 375 to 425°F. They are done when a fork can be inserted easily. If desired, the vegetable may be placed on aluminum foil or in a shallow pan to protect the oven.

Oven Roasting

Oven roasting is done by lightly coating pieces of vegetables with oil and selected herbs and seasonings before roasting them uncovered in a hot oven (375 to 425°F) and stirring occasionally for about an hour until tender and pleasingly browned.

Sautéing

Sautéing is a suitable method for very tender or thinly sliced vegetables, such as thin slices of raw potato. To sauté, melt enough butter or margarine or use enough salad oil to cover the bottom of a skillet. Add the sliced vegetables and fry at medium heat until pleasingly browned on the bottom of the vegetable slices. Turn with a spatula and brown the other side. If still raw in the center, they may need to be turned more than once. Continue frying until the interior is tender. The heat should be controlled throughout the cooking period to avoid excessive splattering or any smoking of the fat. When tender and pleasing in appearance, remove from the skillet, salt, and serve.

Stir-Frying

Vegetables to be stir-fried are cut into very thin strips unless they are a vegetable, such as zucchini, that will become tender very quickly. Stir-frying is a method of cookery developed in Oriental cuisines. A wok is the preferred utensil for stir-frying because only a small portion of the bottom becomes very hot when heated.

The vegetable is added to the wok (containing a little cooking oil in the bottom) and stirred frequently to slide the browned, fried portions up the sides and bring uncooked portions down into the hot oil. This is a very rapid cooking process, one that requires careful attention and stirring to be successful. As soon as all of the vegetable has been fried just to the point of tenderness, the vegetable is served. If a less tender vegetable is being stir-fried, the heat may be reduced a bit after the initial browning of the vegetable, and the vegetable steamed with a cover just long enough to finish tenderizing the food. This method of vegetable cookery is excellent because it is so quick that flavor, color, and nutritive value are retained at maximum levels.

Deep-Fat Frying

Vegetables sometimes are deep-fat fried. This cooking method affords additional variety in the preparation of vegetables, but its use probably should be kept to a minimum because of the higher fat content of vegetables prepared in this way. For optimum quality of deep-fat fried vegetables, the pieces should be approximately 1/4 to 1/2 inch thick. While the pieces of vegetable are being cut, oil should be preheated in a deep-fat fryer or in a saucepan on a controlled heat unit to a temperature of 375°F. The vegetable pieces should be dried thoroughly on paper towels before being transferred to the hot fat. If desired, the vegetables can be dipped in flour or in a batter before frying. This use of a batter is demonstrated in the making of the Japanese dish called tempura. Vegetables are fried until golden brown and tender. They should be drained well on paper towels, salted, and then served quickly.

Figure 2.3
This Chinese chef is deep-fat frying batter-dipped vegetables in her wok.

Microwaving

Vegetables to be cooked in a microwave oven are heated more quickly when cut into small pieces than when prepared whole. Place the washed vegetables in a glass dish, with the slower cooking portions (stalks or cores) arranged toward the edge of the container. For most vegetables, the addition of about half a cup of water improves the quality of the finished product. The dish of vegetables should be covered, either with its own lid or with plastic wrap, to trap steam around the vegetables. During the heating period, the pieces should be stirred occasionally to facilitate uniform heating.

Because vegetables will continue to soften during the standing time after they are removed from the oven, a slightly crisp end product is the recommended degree of doneness when the vegetables are removed from the microwave oven. The time required to reach this state varies with the type of vegetable and the amount being prepared. A standing time of 3 minutes, with the vegetable covered, is recommended to aid in distributing the heat. Suggested guidelines for microwaving vegetables are presented in the table.

Microwave Cookery of Vegetables[1]

Vegetable	Piece Size	Amount	Water Added (c)	Time (min) (high)	Procedure
Artichokes	Whole	1	1/4	8	Cover; rotate after 8 min
		4	1	15	Cover; rotate after 8 min
Asparagus	spears	8	1/4	7	Cover; tips toward center of dish
	2"	1/2 lb	1/4	7	Cover; stir after 3 min
frozen	spears	10 oz	0	9	Cover; rearrange after 5 min
Beans, green	1–2"	1 lb	3/4	15	Cover; stir after 8 min
frozen		10 oz	1/4	9	Cover; stir after 5 min
Beets	whole	4 med	To cover	20	Cover; rearrange after 10 min
Broccoli	split stalks	1 bunch	1/4	12	Cover; flowerets in center
	1"	1 lb	1/2	9	Cover; stir after 5 min
frozen	chopped	10 oz	1/8	9	Cover; stir after 5 min
Brussels sprouts	whole	1/2 lb	1/4	5	Cover; stir after 3 min
frozen	whole	10 oz	1/8	8	Cover; stir after 4 min
Cabbage	shredded	1 small	1/4	9	Cover; stir after 5 min
Carrots	thin slices	4 med	1/2	12	Cover; stir after 6 min
Cauliflower	floweret	1 small head	1/2	13	Cover; stir after 7 min
	whole	1 small head	1/2	14	Cover; turn over after 7 min
frozen	floweret	10 oz	1/8	8	Cover; stir after 4 min
Corn	cob	2 ears	1/4	4	Cover; rearrange after 4 min
	kernels	1 c	1/2	5	Cover; stir after 3 min
frozen	kernels	10 oz	1/8	5	Cover; stir after 3 min
Eggplant	1" cubes (peeled)	3 c	1/8	6	Cover; stir after 3 min
Onions	quartered	4 med	1/2	11	Cover; rearrange after 6 min
Parsnips	sticks	2	1/4	7	Cover; stir after 4 min
Peas	shelled	1 lb	1/4	10	Cover; stir after 5 min
frozen	shelled	10 oz	1/8	6	Cover; stir after 3 min
Potatoes	whole	1	0	5	Pierce before cooking; turn after 3 min
Spinach	leaves	1 lb	0	7	Cover to trap water clinging to leaves; stir after 4 min
frozen	leaves	10 oz	1/8	8	Cover; stir after 4 min
Squash					
summer	sliced	1 lb	1/8	10	Cover; stir after 5 min
winter	half	1	0	8	Scrape out seeds, place cut side down; cover with wax paper
frozen	pureé	10 oz	0	6	Cover; stir after 3 min
Turnips	1" cubes	2 med	1/4	10	Cover; stir after 5 min

[1]Times are approximate. Glass casserole dishes or plates and plastic wrap are recommended. Plastic wrap or bag should be slightly loose or slit.

RECIPES

Artichoke with Garlic Butter

Time: 1 hour

1. Cut off stem at base so that artichoke sits up straight.
2. Use kitchen shears to trim off the sharp point on each petal.
3. Place artichokes in deep pan containing oil and garlic salt in 1 inch of water.
4. Cover and bring to a boil before reducing heat to maintain simmering until the bottom(s) of the artichoke(s) are moderately tender when tested with a fork.
5. Melt butter and stir in garlic salt shortly before serving.
6. Drain by inverting each artichoke and serve with individual small bowls of garlic butter for dipping (and a plate to hold the stripped petals and the choke).

(Serves two)

2	artichokes
1 tsp	olive oil
1/2 tsp	garlic salt
1 Tbsp	butter
1/8 tsp	garlic salt

(Serves four)

4	artichokes
1 tsp	olive oil
1/2 tsp	garlic salt
2 Tbsp	butter
1/4 tsp	garlic salt

Carnival Green Beans

Total Time: 20 minutes

1. Bring water to boil; add beans and boil until just tender (about 8 minutes).
2. While beans are boiling, melt margarine in saucepan; stir in mustard, flour, salt, and pepper.
3. Blend egg yolks and milk; add to roux (a cooking mixture of flour and fat), stirring constantly.
4. Heat mixture (while stirring constantly) until mixture thickens slightly. Be careful to avoid boiling the mixture.
5. Stir in lemon juice.
6. Drain beans well. Pour sauce over beans, and garnish with pimiento.

(Serves two)

1/2 lb	green beans
1-1/2 tsp	margarine or butter
1/4 tsp	dry mustard
1/2 tsp	flour
	pinch of salt
	pinch of black pepper
1	egg yolk, beaten
6 Tbsp	milk
1 tsp	lemon juice
2 tsp	chopped pimiento

(Serves four)

1 lb	green beans
1 Tbsp	margarine or butter
1/2 tsp	dry mustard
1 tsp	flour
1/4 tsp	salt
1/4 tsp	black pepper
2	egg yolks, beaten
2/3 c	Milk
1-1/2 tsp	lemon juice
1 Tbsp	chopped pimiento

Figure 2.4
Vegetables afford a variety of colors, textures, and flavors that can be combined in medleys enhanced with fresh basil or other flavorful ingredients.

Green Bean Casserole Deluxe

Total Time: 25 minutes

Baking: 375°F oven for 15 minutes

1. Preheat oven.
2. Boil beans according to package directions and drain well.
3. In a skillet, sauté onion and mushrooms in margarine to golden brown. Remove from heat.
4. Stir flour into onions and mushrooms until blended.
5. Add milk while stirring.
6. Return sauce to heat and stir constantly until mixture boils.
7. Remove from heat and add cheese, soy sauce, Worcestershire sauce, and water chestnuts.
8. Mix the drained beans with the sauce and place in casserole.
9. Garnish with almonds.
10. Bake 15 minutes at 375°F.

(Serves two)

1/2	package frozen green beans
1 Tbsp	margarine or butter
1 Tbsp	chopped onion
2 Tbsp	canned mushrooms, drained
1 tsp	flour
1/3 c	milk
2 Tbsp	grated cheddar cheese
1/4 tsp	soy sauce
1/4 tsp	Worcestershire sauce
1/4 c	water chestnuts, drained and sliced
1 Tbsp	slivered almonds

(Serves four)

1	package frozen green beans
2 Tbsp	margarine or butter
2 Tbsp	chopped onion
1/4 c	canned mushrooms, drained
2 tsp	flour
2/3 c	milk
1/4 c	grated cheddar cheese
1/2 tsp	soy sauce
1/2 tsp	Worcestershire sauce
1/2 c	water chestnuts, drained and sliced
2 Tbsp	slivered almonds

Polish Beets in Sour Cream (by Mary Kramer)

Total Time: 10 minutes

1. Grate beets on coarse grater.
2. Melt margarine.
3. Add flour and stir.
4. Remove from heat; add vinegar, salt, and sugar, and stir in grated beets.
5. Stir while simmering mixture for 5 minutes.
6. Remove from heat.
7. Stir in sour cream quickly, and serve immediately to avoid curdling sour cream.

(Serves two)

3	cooked beets
1 Tbsp	margarine or butter
1-1/2 tsp	flour
1-1/2 tsp	vinegar
	pinch of salt
1-1/2 tsp	sugar
1/4 c	sour cream

(Serves four)

6	cooked beets
2 Tbsp	margarine or butter
1 Tbsp	flour
1 Tbsp	vinegar
1/8 tsp	salt
1 Tbsp	sugar
1/2 c	sour cream

Broccoli Broil

Total Time: 15 minutes

1. Boil broccoli.
2. While broccoli is boiling for 3 minutes, lightly sauté onion in margarine in a 1-quart saucepan.
3. Remove saucepan from heat and stir flour and seasonings into onion and margarine.
4. Add bouillon cube and milk gradually, stirring constantly.
5. Return to heat and bring to a boil, stirring constantly. Remove from heat and add all but 2 tablespoons of cheese.
6. Drain broccoli and arrange in casserole.
7. Pour sauce over broccoli. Sprinkle remaining cheese and paprika over top.
8. Broil until lightly browned.

(Serves two)

1 c	broccoli flowerets
1-1/2 tsp	chopped onion
2 tsp	margarine or butter
1-1/2 tsp	flour
1/4 tsp	dry mustard
1/8 tsp	marjoram
	pinch of pepper
1/2	chicken bouillon cube
1/2 c	milk
3 Tbsp	grated Parmesan cheese
	paprika to garnish

(Serves four)

2 c	broccoli flowerets
1 Tbsp	chopped onion
1-1/2 Tbsp	margarine or butter
1 Tbsp	flour
1/2 tsp	dry mustard
1/4 tsp	marjoram
	dash of pepper
1	chicken bouillon cube
1 c	milk
1/3 c	grated Parmesan cheese
	paprika to garnish

Broccoli Salad Chinoise

Total Time: 30 minutes

1. Combine garlic, oils, soy sauce, salt, lime juice, vinegar, and ginger root to make marinade.
2. Clean mushrooms, slice in 1/4-inch slices, and add to marinade, stirring to coat. Chill.
3. Wash broccoli, cut into bite-sized flowerets, and steam until barely tender. Chill broccoli.
4. Combine broccoli with mushrooms to coat the broccoli and mushrooms with the marinade.
5. Spoon broccoli and mushrooms from marinade. Serve topped with a garnish of toasted, slivered almonds. Serve on greens or in a serving bowl.

(Serves two)

1/2 clove	garlic, crushed
1-1/3 Tbsp	walnut oil
1 tsp	sesame oil
1 tsp	soy sauce
1/4 tsp	salt
2 tsp	lime juice
1-1/3 Tbsp	rice vinegar
1/2 tsp	minced ginger root
1 Tbsp	almonds, slivered, toasted salad greens (optional)
3	mushrooms, medium
1/2 bunch	broccoli

(Serves four)

1 clove	garlic, crushed
2-2/3 Tbsp	walnut oil
2 tsp	sesame oil
2 tsp	soy sauce
1/2 tsp	salt
1-1/3 Tbsp	lime juice
2-2/3 Tbsp	rice vinegar
1 tsp	minced ginger root
6	mushrooms, medium
1 bunch	broccoli
2 Tbsp	almonds, slivered, toasted salad greens (optional)

Broccoli Soup

Total Time: 15 minutes

1. In a large saucepan, melt margarine. Sauté green pepper and onion just until translucent.
2. Add broccoli and water and boil until broccoli is tender.
3. Place in blender and whirl until smooth.
4. Add cream; stir in just enough milk to thin to consistency of a cream soup.
5. Add curry powder and salt and pepper to taste.
6. Reheat quickly to serving temperature and serve with dollop of sour cream and chopped parsley as garnish.

(Serves two)

1 Tbsp	margarine or butter
1 Tbsp	chopped green pepper
1-1/2 Tbsp	chopped onion
1 c	chopped broccoli
1/3 c	water
1/3 c	light cream
~1/4 c	milk
1/4 tsp	curry powder
	salt and pepper to taste
2 Tbsp	sour cream
1 tsp	chopped parsley

(Serves four)

2 Tbsp	margarine or butter
2 Tbsp	chopped green pepper
3 Tbsp	chopped onion
2 c	chopped broccoli
2/3 c	water
2/3 c	light cream
~1/2 c	milk
1/2 tsp	curry powder
	salt and pepper to taste
1/4 c	sour cream
2 tsp	chopped parsley

Sweet-Sour Red Cabbage

Total Time: 15 to 25 minutes

1. Wash, pare, core, and slice the apples into thin slices.
2. Combine the ingredients in a skillet or wok.
3. Cover and simmer over low heat, stirring occasionally. Continue to cook until desired tenderness is reached (approximately 8 minutes for crisp cabbage and 15 minutes for more tender cabbage).

(Serves two)

1	medium Pippin (or other tart apple)
1 Tbsp	salad oil
2 c	shredded red cabbage
2 Tbsp	brown sugar
2 Tbsp	vinegar
3/4 tsp	salt
2 Tbsp	water

(Serves four)

2	medium Pippins (or other tart apple)
2 Tbsp	salad oil
4 c	shredded red cabbage
1/4 c	brown sugar
1/4 c	vinegar
1-1/2 tsp	salt
1/4 c	water

Vegetarian Cabbage Rolls

Total Time: 35 minutes
Baking Time: 350°F oven for 25 minutes

1. Preheat oven.
2. Boil cabbage leaves for 3 minutes; drain.
3. Sauté bean sprouts and mushrooms in margarine until golden brown, stirring frequently.
4. Remove from heat and stir in remaining ingredients, except the tomato sauce and half the cheese.
5. Divide mixture onto cabbage leaves; roll and secure with toothpicks.
6. Place in casserole; top with tomato sauce and then sprinkle remaining cheese on top.
7. Bake at 350°F for 25 minutes.
8. Remove toothpicks and serve.

(Serves two)

4	cabbage leaves
1/4 lb	chopped bean sprouts
1/8 lb	mushrooms, chopped
1-1/2 Tbsp	margarine or butter
6 Tbsp	wheat germ
2 Tbsp	water chestnuts, drained and chopped
1/4 c	almonds, slivered
2-1/2 Tbsp	minced parsley
1/2 tsp	crumbled marjoram leaves
1/8 tsp	salt
6 Tbsp	grated Parmesan cheese
1/2 c	tomato sauce

(Serves four)

8	cabbage leaves
1/2 lb	chopped bean sprouts
1/4 lb	mushrooms, chopped
3 Tbsp	margarine or butter
3/4 c	wheat germ
1/4 c	water chestnuts, drained and chopped
1/2 c	almonds, slivered
1/3 c	minced parsley
1 tsp	crumbled marjoram leaves
1/4 tsp	salt
3/4 c	grated Parmesan cheese
1 c	tomato sauce

Dutch Cabbage

Total Time: 10 minutes

1. Fry bacon. Drain on paper towels, saving drippings in frying pan.
2. In a saucepan, combine flour, sugar, and salt. While stirring, slowly add water, followed by vinegar and egg. Stir until smooth.
3. Heat over a low heat, stirring constantly; continue heating until thick enough to coat spoon. Set aside.
4. Add cabbage and celery to frying pan containing bacon drippings; stir-fry until cabbage is just tender.
5. Add crumbled bacon, pepper, and sauce; toss and serve.

(Serves two)

1	slice bacon
1 Tbsp	flour
2 Tbsp	sugar
1/8 tsp	salt
1 c	water
1/2	egg
1/4 c	vinegar
1/2	cabbage, small head, shredded
1/4 c	celery, diced
	pinch of pepper

(Serves four)

2	slices bacon
2 Tbsp	flour
1/4 c	sugar
1/2 tsp	salt
1 c	water
1	egg
1/4 c	vinegar
1	cabbage, small head, shredded
1/2 c	celery, diced
1/8 tsp	pepper

Kaldomar (Cabbage Rolls)

Total Time: 1 hour and 20 minutes
Baking: 375°F oven for 1 hour

1. Preheat oven.
2. Boil cabbage for 10 minutes.
3. While cabbage is boiling, combine the meat, rice, egg, onion, salt, allspice, and milk.
4. Form meat mixture into balls and wrap in cabbage leaves, securing with toothpick.
5. Melt margarine in frying pan and brown each cabbage roll.
6. Place browned rolls in casserole.
7. Add water and onion soup mix to drippings; pour over cabbage rolls.
8. Bake at 375°F for 1 hour.
9. Remove toothpicks and serve.

(Serves two)

4	large cabbage leaves
1/2 lb	ground beef
3/4 c	boiled rice (barely tender)
1/2	egg
1/2	onion, minced
1/4 tsp	salt
1/2 tsp	allspice
1/4 c	milk
1 Tbsp	margarine or butter
1/4 c	water
1 Tbsp	dry onion soup mix

(Serves four)

8	large cabbage leaves
1 lb	ground beef
1-1/2 c	boiled rice (barely tender)
1	egg
1	onion, minced
1/2 tsp	salt
1 tsp	allspice
1/2 c	milk
2 Tbsp	margarine or butter
1/2 c	water
2 Tbsp	dry onion soup mix

Cabbage Supreme

Total Time: 15 minutes

1. Melt margarine in skillet.
2. Stir in garlic powder, water, and cabbage.
3. Cover and steam gently for 5 minutes.
4. In a small bowl, stir together sour cream, sugar, vinegar, and salt.
5. Stir into the cabbage and continue to heat just until the added ingredients are heated through.
6. Serve immediately, garnished with the sesame seeds.

(Serves two)

1-1/2 tsp	margarine or butter
2 c	cabbage, finely shredded
2 Tbsp	water
1/8 tsp	garlic powder
2 Tbsp	sour cream
1/2 tsp	sugar
1-1/2 tsp	vinegar
1/4 tsp	salt
1/8 tsp	sesame seeds, toasted

(Serves four)

1 Tbsp	margarine or butter
4 c	cabbage, finely shredded
3 Tbsp	water
1/4 tsp	garlic powder
1/4 c	sour cream
1 tsp	sugar
1 Tbsp	vinegar
1/2 tsp	salt
1/4 tsp	sesame seeds, toasted

Ginger Carrots

Total Time: 12 minutes

1. Wash and pare carrots. Cut in sticks (approximately 2 inches long and 1/3 inch in diameter).
2. Bring enough salted water to a boil to just cover the carrots.
3. Add the carrots to the boiling water, cover the pan, and boil until just fork tender (approximately 10 minutes).
4. While carrots are boiling, stir together the sugar, cornstarch, and salt.
5. Gradually stir in the orange juice.
6. In a saucepan, heat the sauce, while stirring continuously. Bring the sauce to a boil and continue to boil 1 minute.
7. Remove from the heat, and stir in the margarine, ginger, and lemon rind.
8. Drain the carrots thoroughly before pouring the sauce over them.
9. Toss in the sauce until carrots are coated with the sauce.
10. Serve immediately.

(Serves two)

3	small carrots
1 tsp	sugar
1/2 tsp	cornstarch
1/8 tsp	salt
1/8 tsp	grated fresh ginger
2 Tbsp	orange juice
1/8 tsp	grated lemon rind
1 tsp	margarine or butter

(Serves four)

6	small carrots
2 tsp	sugar
1 tsp	cornstarch
1/4 tsp	salt
1/4 tsp	grated fresh ginger
1/4 c	orange juice
1/4 tsp	grated lemon rind
2 tsp	margarine or butter

Carrot Puff

Total Time: 75 minutes
Baking: 350°F for 40 minutes and then 10 minutes

1. Preheat oven.
2. Peel carrots, cut in half, and cook in boiling water until tender.
3. Drain; cool in ice water; drain again.
4. Place cooled carrots, flour, vanilla, eggs, nutmeg, cayenne, curry powder, and butter (melted, but not hot) in blender.
5. Purée in blender until completely smooth, scraping sides as needed.
6. Bake in preheated oven at 350°F for 40 minutes before sprinkling nuts on top. Then bake 10 more minutes.

(Serves two)

1/2 lb	carrots (4 medium)
1-1/2 Tbsp	flour
1/2 tsp	vanilla
2	eggs
2 Tbsp	butter, melted
	pinch of nutmeg
	dash of cayenne
1/8 tsp	curry powder
2 Tbsp	coarsely chopped pecans

(Serves four)

1 lb	carrots (4 medium)
3 Tbsp	flour
1 tsp	vanilla
3	eggs
1/4 c	butter, melted
	dash of nutmeg
1/8 tsp	cayenne
1/4 tsp	curry powder
1/4 c	coarsely chopped pecans

Frosted Cauliflower

Total Time: 20 minutes (small); 25 minutes (large)
Baking: 375°F oven for 10 minutes

1. Preheat oven.
2. Trim off the leaves and stalk of the head.
3. Wash thoroughly under cold, running water.
4. Bring the salted water to a boil and add the cauliflower.
5. Boil actively, uncovered, until the cauliflower is barely able to be penetrated with a fork (approximately 12 to 15 minutes).
6. Drain thoroughly before placing on a sheet of foil in a shallow baking dish.
7. Thoroughly mix the mayonnaise and mustard before spreading over the upper surface of the cauliflower.
8. Sprinkle the grated cheese on top.
9. Bake at 375°F until cheese melts and topping bubbles (about 10 minutes).

(Serves two)

1/2	head cauliflower
1/2 tsp	salt
	water to cover cauliflower
1/4 c	mayonnaise or creamy salad dressing
1 tsp	prepared mustard
1/3 c	grated sharp cheddar cheese

(Serves four)

1	head cauliflower
1 tsp	salt
	water to cover cauliflower
1/2 c	mayonnaise or creamy salad dressing
2 tsp	prepared mustard
2/3 c	grated sharp cheddar cheese

Celery Orientale

Total Time: 5 minutes

1. Wash celery thoroughly; cut diagonal slices 1/4" thick. Wash, drain, and slice mushrooms.
2. In a wok or frying pan, melt the margarine.
3. Add the celery and stir-fry with constant stirring just until celery is slightly tender.
4. Add the mushrooms and almonds.
5. Continue to stir-fry, stirring constantly until the mushrooms are somewhat transparent and the almonds begin to brown.

(Serves two)

3	large outer stalks of celery
1 Tbsp	margarine or butter
1/2 c	sliced fresh mushrooms
2 Tbsp	chopped, blanched almonds

(Serves four)

6	large outer stalks of celery
2 Tbsp	margarine or butter
1 c	sliced fresh mushrooms
1/4 c	chopped, blanched almonds

Chiles Rellenos

Total Time: 30 minutes
Frying Temperature: 375°F

1. Begin preheating oil to 375°F.
2. Place tomato sauce and seasonings in 1-quart, covered saucepan and simmer 10 minutes.
3. Stuff chiles with cheese.
4. Beat egg yolks to foam and set aside.
5. Beat egg whites until peaks just bend over.
6. Fold egg yolks (which have been sprinkled with the flour) into the egg whites.
7. Dip chiles individually into the foam to coat thoroughly.
8. Carefully slip individual chiles into the hot fat and fry until golden brown.
9. Drain on paper towels before serving, topped with tomato sauce.

(Serves two)

	oil for deep-fat frying
1/2 c	tomato sauce
1 Tbsp	diced onion
1/8 tsp	oregano
	salt and pepper to taste
1/2 can	small Ortega chiles, drained
1/4 c	grated Monterey Jack cheese
2	eggs, separated
1/2 Tbsp	flour

(Serves four)

	oil for deep-fat frying
1 c	tomato sauce
2 Tbsp	diced onion
1/4 tsp	oregano
	salt and pepper to taste
1 can	small Ortega chiles, drained
1/2 c	grated Monterey Jack cheese
4	eggs, separated
1 Tbsp	flour

Eggplant Italianate

Total Time: 15 minutes (small); 17 minutes (large)
Baking: 450°F oven for 10 to 12 minutes

1. Preheat oven.
2. Dip eggplant in butter and then in cracker crumbs.
3. Place on jelly roll pan lined with aluminum foil.
4. Salt lightly.
5. Spoon tomato sauce over each slice; sprinkle lightly with oregano and top with mushrooms and cheese.
6. Bake at 450°F until tender (approximately 10 to 12 minutes).

(Serves two)

1/2	medium eggplant, pared and cut in 1/2-inch slices
1/4 c	melted margarine or butter
1/3 c	fine cracker crumbs
	dash of salt
1/2 c	tomato sauce
1/8 tsp	powdered oregano
1 Tbsp	canned, sliced mushrooms
1/2 c	grated mozzarella cheese

(Serves four)

1	medium eggplant, pared and cut in 1/2-inch slices
1/2 c	melted margarine or butter
2/3 c	fine cracker crumbs
1/8 tsp	salt
1 c	tomato sauce
1/4 tsp	powdered oregano
2 Tbsp	canned, sliced mushrooms
1 c	grated mozzarella cheese

Mushroom Appetizer

Total Time: 30 minutes
Baking: 350°F oven for 15 to 20 minutes

1. Preheat oven.
2. Boil onion in 1/2 cup water until tender; drain.
3. Combine all ingredients thoroughly and spread in baking dish (loaf pan for small recipe; 9 × 9-inch pan for large recipe).
4. Bake at 350°F until set (about 15 minutes for small and 20 minutes for large recipe).
5. Cut in 1-inch squares; serve hot.

(Serves two)

1/4	chopped onion
2	eggs, well beaten
2 Tbsp	dry bread crumbs
1/4 tsp	salt
	dash of pepper
	dash of paprika
	dash of oregano
1	drop of Tabasco sauce
4 oz	grated sharp cheddar cheese
6 oz	jar marinated mushrooms, drained, finely chopped

(Serves four)

1/2	chopped onion
4	eggs, well beaten
1/4 c	dry bread crumbs
1/2 tsp	salt
1/8 tsp	pepper
1/8 tsp	paprika
1/8 tsp	oregano
3	drops of Tabasco sauce
8 oz	grated sharp cheddar cheese
12 oz	two 6-oz jars marinated mushrooms, drained, finely chopped

Piñon-Stuffed Mushrooms

Total Time: 20 minutes
Baking: 425°F oven for 10 to 12 minutes

1. Preheat oven.
2. Thaw spinach in microwave oven and drain thoroughly.
3. Clean mushrooms, removing stems.
4. Chop stems; sauté stems with onion and garlic for 2 minutes.
5. Add spinach to stems and heat to evaporate the liquid.
6. Stir in crumbs, nuts, and seasonings.
7. Fill top of each mushroom with mixture; dust with Parmesan cheese.
8. Bake at 425°F about 10 minutes until mushrooms are tender.

(Serves two)

1/4	package frozen chopped spinach
2	large mushrooms
1 Tbsp	chopped onion
1/2	clove garlic, minced
2 tsp	olive oil
1 Tbsp	grated Parmesan cheese
1 Tbsp	dry bread crumbs
2 Tbsp	piñon nuts
1/8 tsp	dry oregano
1/8 tsp	dry basil

(Serves four)

1/2	package frozen chopped spinach
4	large mushrooms
2 Tbsp	chopped onion
1	clove garlic, minced
1-1/2 Tbsp	olive oil
2 Tbsp	grated Parmesan cheese
2 Tbsp	dry bread crumbs
1/4 c	piñon nuts
1/4 tsp	dry oregano
1/4 tsp	dry basil

Quiche Florentine

Total Time: 40 minutes
Baking: 350°F oven for 25 minutes

1. Preheat oven.
2. Cook spinach and squeeze out water thoroughly.
3. Beat eggs until light; add milk, cream, and cheese.
4. Purée spinach and add to above mixture. Add salt and pepper.
5. Pour into quiche pan lined with baked pastry.
6. Bake at 350°F until filling no longer shakes when moved (approximately 25 minutes).
7. Serve while hot.

(Serves two)

2	baked tart shells (see Pastry)
1/2 lb	fresh spinach
1-1/2	eggs
1/2 c	cream
2 Tbsp	milk
1/6 lb	grated Gruyere cheese
1/4 tsp	salt
	dash of pepper

(Serves four)

1	baked 10-inch shell in quiche pan (see Pastry)
1 lb	fresh spinach
3	eggs
1 c	cream
1/4 c	milk
1/3 lb	grated Gruyere cheese
1/2 tsp	salt
1/8 tsp	pepper

Spanish Spinach

Total Time: 10 minutes

1. Wash spinach thoroughly and drain well.
2. In a skillet, cook bacon until crisp; remove and crumble.
3. Pour off all but 1 Tbsp drippings.
4. Add remaining ingredients.
5. Stir constantly while sautéing over medium heat until spinach is wilted and hot.
6. Sprinkle with crumbled bacon.

(Serves two)

1	bunch fresh spinach
2	slices bacon
2 Tbsp	sliced pimiento-stuffed olives
1/8 tsp	garlic powder
1/2 tsp	grated lemon peel
1-1/2 tsp	lemon juice

(Serves fourv)

2	bunches fresh spinach
4	slices bacon
1/4 c	sliced pimiento-stuffed olives
1/4 tsp	garlic powder
1 tsp	grated lemon peel
3 tsp	lemon juice

Spinach Sauté (by Mary Kramer)

Total Time: 10 minutes

1. Break off stems and any blemished leaves.
2. Rinse leaves thoroughly in several changes of water until clean; drain well.
3. In a skillet, melt the butter, then add the oil.
4. Sauté onion and garlic for 5 minutes.
5. Add the spinach, a handful at a time, and stir-fry until wilted.
6. In a bowl, combine lemon juice, sour cream, salt, and pepper.
7. Drain off any liquid in the skillet.
8. Stir the sour cream mixture throughout the spinach.
9. Heat just to serving temperature and serve immediately. Avoid boiling the sour cream.

(Serves two)

1	bunch spinach
1 Tbsp	margarine or butter
1 Tbsp	salad oil
1/4 c	chopped onion
1/2	clove garlic, minced
1-1/2 tsp	lemon juice
1/4 c	sour cream
1/8 tsp	salt
1/8 tsp	pepper

(Serves four)

2	bunches spinach
2 Tbsp	margarine or butter
2 Tbsp	salad oil
1/2 c	chopped onion
1	clove garlic, minced
1 Tbsp	lemon juice
1/2 c	sour cream
1/4 tsp	salt
1/4 tsp	pepper

Spanakopita (Greek Spinach Pie)

Total Time: 1 hour 15 minutes
Baking: 300°F oven for 1 hour

1. Preheat oven.
2. Clean, chop, and blanch spinach; drain very thoroughly.
3. Sauté onion until tender.
4. Combine all ingredients except filo dough and margarine.
5. Melt butter.
6. In a greased baking dish (8 × 8 inches for small recipe; 13 × 9 inches for large recipe), layer 8 filo sheets, brushing each with melted margarine.
7. Spread spinach mixture over dough.
8. Layer another 8 sheets of filo dough, brushing each with melted margarine.
9. Score with parallel diagonal lines at 2-inch intervals.
10. Bake 1 hour at 300°F until golden brown.
11. Cut in squares to serve.

(Serves four)

1 lb	spinach
1 Tbsp	margarine or butter
1/3 c	chopped green onion
1 Tbsp	chopped parsley
1 tsp	dill weed
1/4 lb	crumbled feta cheese
1/8 lb	grated Romano cheese
3	eggs, beaten
16	half-sheets filo dough
1/8 lb	margarine or butter

(Serves eight)

2 lb	spinach
2 Tbsp	margarine or butter
2/3 c	chopped green onion
2 Tbsp	chopped parsley
2 tsp	dill weed
1/2 lb	crumbled feta cheese
1/4 lb	grated Romano cheese
7	eggs, beaten
16	sheets filo dough
1/4 lb	margarine or butter

Okra Delight

Total Time: 35 minutes

1. Sauté onions in olive oil until golden.
2. Stir in okra (uncut), tomatoes, salt, and pepper. Cover and simmer 25 minutes.
3. Microwave bacon until crisp; crumble into coarse pieces.
4. Add shrimp and bacon to tomato mixture.
5. Simmer 4 minutes.
6. Serve over rice.

(Serves two)

1/2	Spanish onion, sliced and halved
1/2 Tbsp	olive oil
5	small okra (leave whole)
1 c	stewed tomatoes
1/8 tsp	salt
1/4 tsp	coarse grind pepper
2	strips bacon
1/4 lb	raw shrimp, shelled
1 c	cooked rice

(Serves four)

1	Spanish onion, sliced and halved
1 Tbsp	olive oil
10	small okra (leave whole)
2 c	stewed tomatoes
1/4 tsp	salt
1/2 tsp	coarse grind pepper
4	strips bacon
1/2 lb	raw shrimp, shelled
2 c	cooked rice

Herbed Pearl Onions

Total Time: 40 minutes
Baking: 350°F for 30 minutes

1. Preheat oven.
2. Blanch unpeeled onions for 3 minutes.
3. Cut stem end and peel.
4. Melt butter in small saucepan and remove from heat. Stir in flour and milk. Heat with constant stirring until sauce thickens and comes to boil.
5. Add seasonings and onions and stir just to mix.
6. Put onions in shallow baking dish; pour sauce over onions and sprinkle cheese on top.
7. Bake at 350°F until lightly browned and very hot.

(Serves two)

9 oz	(1/2 package) pearl onions
1 Tbsp	butter
1 Tbsp	flour
1/2 c	milk
1/4 tsp	salt
1/4 tsp	dry thyme
1/4 tsp	garlic powder
	freshly ground pepper to taste (optional)
1 Tbsp	grated Parmesan cheese

(Serves four)

18 oz	(1 package) pearl onions
2 Tbsp	butter
2 Tbsp	flour
1 c	milk
1/2 tsp	salt
1/2 tsp	dry thyme
1/2 tsp	garlic powder
	freshly ground pepper to taste (optional)
2 Tbsp	grated Parmesan cheese

Ratatouille

Total Time: 70 minutes
Baking: 350°F for 50 minutes

1. Preheat oven.
2. Sauté onions, peppers, and garlic in oil for 4 minutes. Set aside.
3. In a bowl, combine cheese, basil, oregano, salt, and pepper. Set aside.
4. Arrange one-half of vegetables in a layer in a shallow baking pan.
5. Arrange one-half of onion mixture on the vegetables; add a layer of one-half of the cheese mixture.
6. Repeat layering.
7. Bake (covered) at 350°F for 40 minutes and then 10 minutes uncovered.

(Serves two)

1/2 c	sliced onion
1/2 c	red bell pepper strips
1/2 c	yellow bell pepper strips
1	garlic clove, minced
1 Tbsp	olive oil
1/4 c	grated Parmesan cheese
2 tsp	dry basil
2 tsp	dry oregano
	dash of salt
1/8 tsp	pepper
1 c	sliced zucchini
3/4 lb	tomatoes, sliced
1/2	small eggplant cut in slices 1/4-inch thick

(Serves four)

1 c	sliced onion
1 c	red bell pepper strips
1 c	yellow bell pepper strips
2	garlic clove, minced
2 Tbsp	olive oil
1/2 c	grated Parmesan cheese
4 tsp	dry basil
4 tsp	dry oregano
1/4 tsp	salt
1/4 tsp	pepper
2 c	sliced zucchini
1-1/2 lb	tomatoes, sliced
1	small eggplant cut in slices 1/4-inch thick

Chinese Snow Pea Stir-Fry

Total Time: 15 minutes

1. Wash snow peas and cut away stems and tails.
2. Clean mushrooms, and slice into vertical pieces 1/8-inch thick.
3. Heat olive oil slightly in a shallow skillet before adding the pea pods, mushrooms, and drained water chestnuts.
4. Sauté quickly while stirring frequently until mushrooms are somewhat translucent.
5. Quickly stir in soy sauce and serve.

(Serves two)

1/8 lb	snow peas
1/8 lb	mushrooms
2 tsp	olive oil
1 Tbsp	sliced canned water chestnuts
2 tsp	soy sauce

(Serves four)

1/4 lb	snow peas
1/4 lb	mushrooms
1 Tbsp	olive oil
2 Tbsp	canned sliced water chestnuts
4 tsp	soy sauce

Spaghetti Squash Salad

Total Time: 30 minutes

1. Cut squash in half lengthwise; remove seeds and microwave in 1/4 cup water until tender (10 to 15 minutes).
2. Scrape strands from shell; chill.
3. Slice radishes, basil, and onions thinly; cube tomatoes; cut cheese and salami in julienne strips.
4. Combine all ingredients and toss.

Figure 2.5
Spaghetti squash earned its name from the way its pulp separates into spaghetti-like strands after cooking.

(Serves two)

1/2	small spaghetti squash
2	radishes
2	leaves fresh basil
2	green onions
1	Roma tomato
1 oz	provolone cheese
1 oz	salami
1 oz	crumbled feta cheese with herbs
2 Tbsp	green bell pepper, diced
2 Tbsp	red pepper, diced
1/4 c	alfalfa sprouts
1 Tbsp	Italian dressing
	salt and pepper to taste

(Serves four)

1	small spaghetti squash
4	radishes
4	leaves fresh basil
4	green onions
2	Roma tomatoes
2 oz	provolone cheese
2 oz	salami
2 oz	crumbled feta cheese with herbs
1/4 c	green bell pepper, diced
1/4 c	red pepper, diced
1/2 c	alfalfa sprouts
2 Tbsp	Italian dressing
	salt and pepper to taste

Stuffed Tomatoes Provençale

Total Time: 1 hour
Baking: 375°F 30 to 40 minutes

1. Preheat oven.
2. Prepare rice according to package directions.
3. Remove a thin slice from the top of each tomato.
4. Carefully remove interior to leave shell 1/2" thick.
5. Chop flesh of tomato and drain off the liquid.
6. Sauté onion and garlic in oil.
7. Combine rice, onion mixture, vinegar, olives, salt, and pepper.
8. Stuff tomato shells with mixture and top with basil leaf and tomato slice.
9. Place on foil on baking sheet and bake in 375°F oven about 30 minutes until tomato is very hot, but not mushy.

(Serves two)

1/2 c	uncooked rice
2	large tomatoes
1/4 c	red onion, diced
1/2	clove garlic, minced
2 tsp	olive oil
2	Kalamata olives
1/2 tsp	balsamic vinegar
2	basil leaves

(Serves four)

1 c	uncooked rice
4	large tomatoes
1/2 c	red onion, diced
1	clove garlic, minced
1 Tbsp	olive oil
4	Kalamata olives
1 tsp	balsamic vinegar
4	basil leaves

Zucchini Sauté (by Mary Kramer)

Total Time: 7 minutes

1. Wash zucchini thoroughly and cut off stem.
2. Grate zucchini coarsely.
3. In a skillet, sauté onion and garlic in the oil for 2 minutes.
4. Add tomatoes and heat to boiling.
5. Stir in the zucchini, salt, and pepper.
6. Heat quickly just to boiling point. (Cooking beyond this point will cause zucchini to be very watery.)
7. Serve, garnished with Parmesan cheese.

(Serves two)

2	zucchini, coarsely grated
1 Tbsp	salad oil
1/2	onion, chopped
1/2	clove garlic, minced
1	fresh tomato, peeled and diced
1/4 tsp	seasoned salt
1/4 tsp	seasoned pepper
	Parmesan cheese

(Serves four)

4	zucchini, coarsely grated
2 Tbsp	salad oil
1	onion, chopped
1	clove garlic, minced
2	fresh tomatoes, peeled and diced
1/2 tsp	seasoned salt
1/2 tsp	seasoned pepper
	Parmesan cheese

Zesty Zucchini

Total Time: 7 minutes

1. Stir-fry zucchini and onions in oil until just tender.
2. Stir in remaining ingredients.
3. Serve immediately.

(Serves two)

2	medium zucchini squash, cut in 1/8" slices
1 Tbsp	onion, minced
1 Tbsp	olive oil
1/4 c	chopped parsley
1/8 tsp	grated lemon peel
1 tsp	lemon juice

(Serves four)

4	medium zucchini squash, cut in 1/8" slices
2 Tbsp	onion, minced
2 Tbsp	olive oil
1/2 c	chopped parsley
1/4 tsp	grated lemon peel
2 tsp	lemon juice

Figure 2.6
Zucchini blossoms sometimes are cooked and served with the squash.

SAUCES FOR VEGETABLES

Lemon Sauce

Total Time: 1 minute

1. Melt margarine or butter.
2. Stir in lemon juice; serve over well-drained boiled vegetables, such as carrots or broccoli.

(Serves two)

1 Tbsp	margarine or butter
2 tsp	lemon juice

(Serves four)

3 Tbsp	margarine or butter
2 Tbsp	lemon juice

Cream Sauce

Total Time: 5 minutes

1. Melt margarine or butter.
2. Remove from heat and stir in flour and salt.
3. Gradually add milk while stirring constantly to avoid lumps.
4. Return to heat. Heat to a rolling boil, stirring constantly.

(Serves two)

1 tsp	margarine or butter
1 tsp	flour
	pinch salt
1/4 c	milk

(Serves four)

2 tsp	margarine or butter
2 tsp	flour
1/8 tsp	salt
1/2 c	milk

Cheese Sauce

Total Time: 7 minutes

1. Make the cream sauce as described above.
2. Add grated cheese.
3. Reheat sauce over low heat, if necessary, to melt the cheese.
4. Serve immediately over well-drained boiled vegetables or use in casserole recipes. Avoid heating sauce to boiling or holding at serving temperature for more than 5 minutes. Excessive heat will toughen the cheese and may cause fat separation.
5. If fat does separate, stir in just enough milk to reunite the sauce.

Figure 2.7
Cheese sauce adds color and nutrients to steamed broccoli.

(Serves two)

1/4 c	cream sauce (see previous recipe)
3 Tbsp	grated sharp cheddar cheese

(Serves four)

1/2 c	cream sauce (see previous recipe)
1/3 c	grated sharp cheddar cheese

Sweet-Sour Sauce

Total Time: 5 minutes

1. Melt margarine or butter.
2. Remove from heat and stir in cornstarch, sugar, and salt. Gradually stir in white vinegar.
3. Return to heat. Heat to boiling, while stirring constantly.
4. When sauce becomes clear and thick, pour over well-drained boiled vegetables.

(Serves two)

1 tsp	margarine or butter
1/2 tsp	cornstarch
1/2 tsp	sugar
	pinch salt
1/4 c	white vinegar

(Serves four)

1 Tbsp	margarine or butter
1-1/2 tsp	cornstarch
1-1/2 tsp	sugar
	pinch salt
1/2 c	white vinegar

Hollandaise Sauce

Total Time: 10 minutes

1. Cream margarine or butter until soft.
2. Carefully stir in well-beaten egg yolk.
3. Slowly add hot water while stirring.
4. Cook over hot but not boiling water, and stir constantly until sauce thickens.
5. Remove from heat and gradually stir in lemon juice.
6. Serve over well-drained boiled vegetables.

(Serves two)

2 Tbsp	margarine or butter
1	egg yolk
2 Tbsp	hot water
1 tsp	lemon juice

(Serves four)

1/4 c	margarine or butter
2	egg yolks
1/4 c	hot water
2 tsp	lemon juice

Jiffy Hollandaise Sauce

Total Time: 5 minutes

1. Combine sour cream, mayonnaise, mustard, and lemon juice.
2. Stir while heating to serving temperature over low heat.

(Serves two)

2 Tbsp	dairy sour cream
2 Tbsp	mayonnaise
1/4 tsp	prepared mustard
1/2 tsp	lemon juice

(Serves four)

1/4 c	dairy sour cream
1/4 c	mayonnaise
1/2 tsp	prepared mustard
1 tsp	lemon juice

Roquefort Vegetable Dip

Total Time: 5 minutes
(To accompany a tray of raw vegetables as an
appetizer.)

1. In a bowl, mash cheese with fork.
2. Add mayonnaise and sour cream gradually, blending until smooth.
3. Add remaining ingredients and blend completely.
4. Store in refrigerator in tightly covered container.
5. Serve in a bowl on an attractive tray, surrounded by carrot sticks, radish roses, turnip slices, cauliflowerets, celery curls, zucchini slices, or other crisp, raw vegetables.

(Serves two)

1/8 lb	Roquefort, bleu, or Gorgonzola cheese
1/4 c	mayonnaise
1/4 c	sour cream
1 Tbsp	lemon juice
1 Tbsp	chopped parsley
1 Tbsp	chopped green onion tops
	dash of curry powder
	dash of Worcestershire sauce
	dash of season salt
	dash of garlic powder
1/8 tsp	coarsely ground black pepper
	dash of cayenne
	assorted raw vegetables for dipping

(Serves four)

1/4 lb	Roquefort, bleu, or Gorgonzola cheese
1/2 c	mayonnaise
1/2 c	sour cream
2 Tbsp	lemon juice
2 Tbsp	chopped parsley
2 Tbsp	chopped green onion tops
1/8 tsp	curry powder
1/8 tsp	Worcestershire sauce
1/8 tsp	season salt
1/8 tsp	garlic powder
1/4 tsp	coarsely ground black pepper
1/8 tsp	cayenne
	assorted raw vegetables for dipping

POTATOES

Objectives

1. To demonstrate the cooking qualities of waxy and non-waxy (mealy) potatoes in selected potato dishes.

2. To prepare and evaluate the quality of potato products.

Potatoes of different varieties are available in various parts of the country. Basically, potatoes may be classified as waxy or non-waxy. Usually, those that are round in shape will tend to be waxy, whereas the long flat ones tend to be non-waxy. A **waxy potato** is one that is comparatively high in sugar and low in starch. A **non-waxy (mealy) potato** is just the reverse—that is, it is high in starch and low in sugar.

   The storage temperature as well as the variety will influence the waxy nature of a potato. Storage at close to room temperature promotes starch content, while temperatures below 45°F favor more sugar formation. Optimum storage for potatoes is approximately 60°F. At this temperature, the basic starch to sugar ratio of a variety will be maintained. Russets provide a classic example of non-waxy potatoes, and Red Triumphs are a familiar example of waxy potatoes.

The higher starch content of the non-waxy potatoes makes them desirable for mashed potatoes, French fries, and baked potatoes. The best choice for making boiled potatoes, potato salads, and scalloped potatoes is the waxy potato with the higher sugar content.

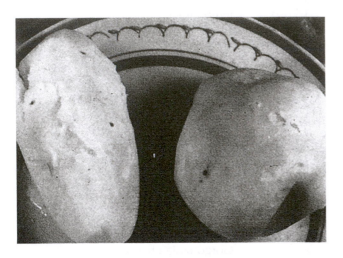

Boiling Potatoes

Boiled potatoes should retain a distinct outline even after cooking is completed. A waxy potato will be the better choice for boiling and for use in any potato recipe in which distinct pieces of potato are desired. Scalloped potatoes, potato salad, and au gratin potatoes are examples of potato preparations in which the distinct outline of the waxy potato is preferred to the less distinct and sloughed off exterior that develops when non-waxy potatoes are used. The non-waxy (mealy) potato is on the left in the figure; the waxy potato is on the right.

Frying Potatoes

French-fried potatoes should be tender in the center without being too dark on the exterior. The browning on the exterior of frying potatoes is the result of chemical change in the sugar. A potato that is high in sugar, specifically a waxy potato (right side of dish), will brown so readily that it may become almost burned on the outside before the interior is cooked. A non-waxy potato (left side of figure) is a better choice for frying because its lower sugar content means that it will take a longer time for the potato to become the desired brown on the exterior. This slower browning allows time for the potato to be cooked on the inside.

Mashing Potatoes

For mashing, a light and fluffy character is considered best. The fluffiness is provided by having a high starch content because the starch will swell during the gelatinization process. The preferred type of potato for mashing is the non-waxy potato (left side of figure) because it has a higher starch content than the waxy potato (right side of plate). Waxy potatoes will become rather gummy, pasty, and often darker in color than non-waxy potatoes when they are mashed.

Baking Potatoes

Non-waxy potatoes (left side of figure) are best suited to baking because the finished product should have a somewhat fluffy character. This texture is provided by a potato high in starch. Waxy potatoes (right) will be rather gummy and soggy when baked.

Summary on Potato Selection

Russets or non-waxy potatoes are preferred for mashing, baking, and frying because of their higher starch content. Red Triumphs or other varieties of waxy potatoes are the potato type of choice for boiling or for use in recipes requiring a potato that will hold its shape well. When practical, it is wise to stock the type of potato needed for specific preparations. When only a few potatoes will be consumed, it may be more practical to purchase an all-purpose potato such as a White Rose. All-purpose potatoes are not as desirable as the correct type of potato, but they can be used satisfactorily for any recipe.

RECIPES

To determine the best type of potato to use for each of the following preparations, prepare each recipe using waxy and non-waxy potatoes. Identify and record the characteristics of each in the evaluation table and indicate the preferred type of potato for each recipe. Compare your findings with the preceding discussion.

Boiled Potatoes

Total Time: 22 minutes

1. Pare potatoes.
2. Place them in a pan containing enough boiling water to just cover the potatoes. Add salt.
3. Cover and boil until easily penetrated with fork.
4. Drain and serve.

(Serves two)

2	potatoes
1/2 tsp	salt

(Serves four)

4	potatoes
1 tsp	salt

French-Fried Potatoes

Total Time: 20 minutes
Frying Temperature: 375°F

1. Begin preheating oil to 375°F.
2. Pare potatoes. Cut lengthwise into strips.
3. Blot dry with paper towels.
4. Place in wire basket and fry in deep fat that has been preheated to 375°F.
5. Fry until golden brown and tender in the middle.
6. Drain on paper towels.
7. Salt and serve.

(Serves two)

2	potatoes
	salad oil

(Serves four)

4	potatoes
	salad oil

Mashed Potatoes

Total Time: 25 minutes

1. Pare potatoes, cut in quarters, and boil in salted water (to cover the potatoes) until tender.
2. Drain the potatoes.
3. With a potato masher or electric mixer (on low speed), mash the potatoes.
4. After adding margarine or butter and sufficient warm milk, whip the potatoes until light and fluffy.
5. Add more salt and pepper, if desired.
6. Serve immediately.

(Serves two)

2	potatoes
	nonfat milk
2 tsp	margarine or butter

(Serves four)

4	potatoes
	nonfat milk
4 tsp	margarine or butter

Baked Potatoes

Total Time: 1 hour
Baking: 425°F oven for 1 hour

1. Preheat oven.
2. Under running water, scrub potatoes vigorously with a vegetable brush.
3. Grease potatoes with margarine or butter, place on aluminum foil, and bake in a 425°F oven for about 1 hour.
4. After 30 minutes, perforate skins with a fork to release steam.
5. When done, cut an X in the potato and squeeze potato partially open, using both hands.
6. Drop a dollop of margarine, butter, or sour cream in the X on each potato.

(Serves two)

2	potatoes
	margarine, butter, or sour cream

(Serves four)

4	potatoes
	margarine, butter, or sour cream

Evaluation of Types of Potatoes in Recipes[1]

Recipe	Type Preferred	Appearance and Palatability	
		Waxy	Non-waxy
Boiled			
French-fried			
Mashed			
Baked			

[1]The Red Triumph is a typical example of a waxy potato; the Russet is an example of a mealy or non-waxy potato. Storage temperatures of approximately 45°F promote the waxy character of a potato and temperatures between 60 and 70°F promote non-waxy character.

Scalloped Potatoes

Total Time: 1-1/4 hours (small); 1-1/2 hours (large)
Baking: 350°F oven for 60 to 75 minutes

1. Preheat oven.
2. Slice pared potatoes very thin.
3. In a 1-quart saucepan, melt the margarine or butter; remove from heat.
4. Stir in the flour and salt.
5. Gradually stir in the milk.
6. Return to heat. Heat to boiling, stirring constantly.
7. Place one-third of the potatoes in a casserole; pour one-third of the sauce over them. Repeat the layers, ending with a layer of the white sauce.
8. Bake with a cover in a 350°F oven for 1 hour.
9. Uncover and continue baking until surface is browned (about 15 minutes).

Figure 2.8
Potatoes Anna, a variation of scalloped potatoes, is framed by broccoli, boiling onions, and cherry tomatoes.

(Serves two)

2	waxy potatoes
1 Tbsp	margarine or butter
1 Tbsp	flour
1/4 tsp	salt
1 c	milk
	covered casserole dish, 2-cup capacity

(Serves four)

4	waxy potatoes
2 Tbsp	margarine or butter
2 Tbsp	flour
1/2 tsp	salt
2 c	milk
	covered casserole dish, 1-quart capacity

Note: For variety, chopped green peppers, pimiento, or onion may be added. Flavor can be varied by adding a dash of curry, pepper, or garlic powder. Scalloped potatoes may be assembled in a casserole, covered, and microwaved on high for 9 to 10 minutes (small recipe) or 18 to 20 minutes (large recipe), with the potatoes being stirred when half the time has elapsed. A standing time of 5 minutes after the microwaving period is necessary to complete the cooking.

Au Gratin Potatoes

Total Time: 1-1/4 hours (small); 1-1/2 hours (large)
Baking: 350°F oven for 60 to 75 minutes

1. Preheat oven.
2. Prepare the recipe for scalloped potatoes, but add grated sharp cheese to the white sauce before placing the layers in the dish.
3. Assemble and bake as described above.

(Serves two)

	scalloped potatoes (from previous recipe)
2/3 c	grated sharp cheddar cheese

(Serves four)

	scalloped potatoes (from previous recipe)
1-1/3 c	grated sharp cheddar cheese

Hash Brown Potatoes

Total Time: 30 minutes

1. Wash, pare, and grate potatoes.
2. Place them in a skillet containing 1/6 inch of hot salad oil.
3. Heat on medium high heat until the bottom side is crisp and golden brown.
4. Turn the entire mass in pancake fashion to brown the second side.
5. Cook until the second side is also golden brown and crisp.
6. Entire cooking time is approximately 25 minutes. Salt and serve.

	non-waxy potatoes
	salad oil

Stuffed Baked Potatoes

Total Time: 1 hour and 10 minutes
Baking: 425°F oven for 1 hour

1. Preheat oven.
2. Wash and grease potatoes before baking (about 1 hour at 425°F).
3. When potatoes are easily pierced with a fork, use a paring knife to cut a slice off most of the length of the upper surface of each potato.
4. Scoop the potato pulp into a bowl.
5. Prepare the pulp as for mashed potatoes.
6. Spoon the mashed potato back into the potato shells lightly.
7. If desired, place stuffed potatoes briefly under broiler to brown slightly.

non-waxy potatoes
milk
margarine or butter

Note: Variations may be created by adding crumbled fried bacon, grated cheese, or chopped chives to the mashed filling. A pastry tube can be used to add a more decorative appearance when the potatoes are being stuffed.

LEGUMES

Objectives

1. To identify the characteristics of various members of the **legume** family.

2. To demonstrate the use of legumes in providing interesting, relatively low-cost, protein-rich main dishes.

Basic Legume Cookery

Legume	Cups of Water/Cup of Dry Legumes	Soaking Time	Cooking Time (hours)
Split peas	4	1/2 hour	1
Pinto beans	4	None	2
Lentils	6	None	1
Navy beans	3	Boil 2 min, soak 1 hour	2
Pink beans	3	Boil 2 min, soak 1 hour	1
Great northern beans	3	Boil 2 min, soak 1 hour	3
Blackeye peas	4	Overnight or boil 2 min, soak 1 hour	1-1/2
Red kidney beans	4	Overnight	2
Garbanzos	4	Overnight	1/2
Lima beans	3	Boil 2 min, soak 1 hour	1-1/2

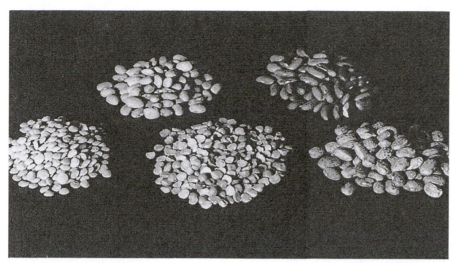

Figure 2.9
Legumes (front row, left to right): lentils, split peas, pinto beans; (back row) pink beans and kidney beans.

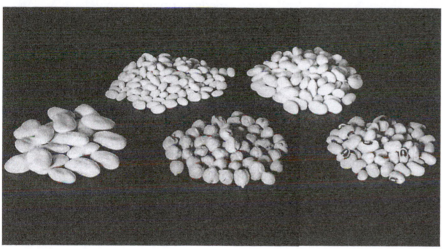

Figure 2.10
Legumes (front row, left to right): lima beans, garbanzos, black-eyed peas; (back row) navy beans and great northern beans.

RECIPES

El Rancho Pinto Beans

Total Time: 2 hours

1. Wash beans.
2. Add water and heat to boiling.
3. Reduce heat to simmering and simmer the beans for 1 hour.
4. Lightly fry the bacon and drain it.
5. Cut it up into small pieces and mix with the other ingredients.
6. Stir into the beans and continue simmering for another hour. Add water as needed. Use a cover throughout the cooking period.

(Serves two)

1/2 c	pinto beans, dry
2 c	water
3	strips bacon
1	small onion, chopped
1/4 c	tomato sauce
1/4 tsp	salt

(Serves four)

1 c	pinto beans, dry
4 c	water
6	strips bacon
1	medium onion, chopped
1	small can tomato sauce
1/2 tsp	salt

Sweet and Sour Baked Beans (by Paul Peterson)

Total Time: 1-1/2 hours
Baking: 350°F for 1 hour

1. Preheat oven.
2. Microwave or fry bacon until crisp.
3. Remove bacon and crumble it.
4. Sauté rings of onion in drippings until tender.
5. Stir in sugar, mustard, garlic powder, salt, and vinegar; simmer 20 minutes.
6. Combine in a casserole with the drained butter, lima, and kidney beans, and the baked beans with their sauce.
7. Bake at 350°F for 1 hour.

(Small recipe)

4	slices bacon
2	onions, sliced into rings
1/4 c	brown sugar
1/2 tsp	dry mustard
1/4 tsp	garlic powder
1/2 tsp	salt
1/4 c	cider vinegar
1	15 oz can butter beans
1	8 oz can lima beans
1	8 oz can red kidney beans
1	8 oz can baked beans

(Large recipe)

8	slices bacon
4	onions, sliced into rings
1/2 c	brown sugar
1 tsp	dry mustard
1/2 tsp	garlic powder
1 tsp	salt
1/2 c	cider vinegar
2	15 oz can butter beans
1	1 lb can lima beans
1	1 lb can red kidney beans
1	1 lb can baked beans

Pork Chops in Northern Beans

Total Time: 3 hours
Baking: 350°F for 1 hour

1. Preheat oven.
2. Wash beans.
3. Cover with the water, heat to boiling, boil 2 minutes, and then let the beans stand in the covered pan for 1 hour.
4. Continue cooking the beans at a simmer until they are tender.
5. Drain well.
6. Combine all of the remaining ingredients except the pork chops and pour over the beans, which have been placed in a casserole.
7. In a skillet, brown the pork chops and arrange on top of the beans.
8. Bake for 1 hour at 350°F.

(Serves two)

3/4 c	great northern beans, dry
1-1/2 c	water
1	small can tomato sauce
1	small onion, chopped
2 Tbsp	catsup
1/8 tsp	dry mustard
1 Tbsp	brown sugar
1 Tbsp	molasses
2	pork chops

(Serves four)

1-1/2 c	great northern beans, dry
3 c	water
1	medium can tomato sauce
1	medium onion, chopped
1/4 c	catsup
1/4 tsp	dry mustard
2 Tbsp	brown sugar
2 Tbsp	molasses
4	pork chops

Chili Black-Eyed Peas

Total Time: 3 hours and 45 minutes
Baking: 350°F for 45 minutes

1. Preheat oven.
2. Wash peas.
3. Put peas and water in a covered saucepan.
4. Heat to boiling and cook for 2 minutes.
5. Let the peas stand for 1 hour, then continue cooking until tender (approximately 1-1/2 hours).
6. Mix all the remaining ingredients except the cheese, and pour over the peas in a casserole.
7. Bake at 350°F for 45 minutes.
8. Sprinkle grated cheese generously over the top of the dish and return to the oven just long enough to melt the cheese.

(Serves two)

1/2 c	Black-eyed peas, dry
2 c	water
1	small onion, chopped
1/2	green pepper, chopped
1/2	No. 2 can stewed tomatoes
1/8 tsp	garlic powder
1-1/2 tsp	Worcestershire sauce
1/2 tsp	chili powder
1/2	bay leaf
1/4 tsp	salt
1/2 c	grated cheddar cheese

(Serves four)

1 c	Black-eyed peas, dry
4 c	water
1	medium onion, chopped
1	green pepper, chopped
1	No. 2 can stewed tomatoes
1/4 tsp	garlic powder
1 Tbsp	Worcestershire sauce
1 tsp	chili powder
1	bay leaf
1/2 tsp	salt
1 c	grated cheddar cheese

Pork Hocks and Lima Bean Stew

Total Time: 3 hours

1. Put hocks and water in large kettle.
2. Add salt, pepper, garlic, bay leaf, onion, and cloves.
3. Cover and bring to a boil.
4. Reduce heat and simmer 1-1/2 hours.
5. Meanwhile, rinse beans.
6. Heat beans and water to boiling in a large saucepan; boil 2 minutes.
7. Remove from heat, cover and let soak 1 hour.
8. Drain.
9. Add beans to hocks and continue to simmer 1 hour.
10. Add carrots and simmer 30 minutes more, or until meat and vegetables are tender.
11. Discard bay leaf.
12. Skin hocks with a sharp knife. Arrange with beans and carrots on hot platter.

(Serves two)

2	fresh pork hocks
3 c	water
3/4 tsp	salt
	dash pepper
1	garlic clove, crushed
1	small bay leaf
1/2	medium-size onion, pared and quartered
3	whole cloves
1/3 lb	dry lima beans
1-3/4 c	water
2	carrots, pared and cut into chunks

(Serves four)

4	fresh pork hocks
1-1/2 qt	water
1-1/2 tsp	salt
1/4 tsp	pepper
2	garlic cloves, crushed
1	bay leaf
1	medium-size onion, pared and quartered
6	whole cloves
2/3 lb	dry lima beans
3-1/2 c	water
4	carrots, pared and cut into chunks

Figure 2.11
Pork hocks and lima bean stew (see above recipe) is a hearty recipe particularly well suited to winter weather.

Kidney Bean Salad

Total Time: Overnight soaking plus 3 hours

1. Wash beans and soak them overnight.
2. Simmer until tender (about 2 hours).
3. Drain and chill.
4. Mix the beans with the remaining ingredients.
5. Cover tightly and refrigerate for at least an hour to blend the flavors.

(Serves two)

1/2 c	kidney beans
1-1/2 c	water
1/4 c	celery, chopped
1/2	green pepper, chopped
1/2	small onion, chopped
1	egg, hard cooked
1/4 c	pickle relish
2 Tbsp	mayonnaise

(Serves four)

1 c	kidney beans
3 c	water
1/2 c	celery, chopped
1	green pepper, chopped
1	small onion, chopped
2	eggs, hard cooked
1/2 c	pickle relish
1/4 c	mayonnaise

Split Pea Soup

Total Time: 1-1/2 hours

1. Soak peas in the water in a saucepan for 30 minutes.
2. Add remaining ingredients.
3. Cover and simmer for 1 hour or until the peas are soft enough to be pressed through a sieve easily.
4. Strain.
5. Salt to taste.
6. Serve piping hot. Reheat, if necessary, after straining.

(Serves two)

1/2 c	split peas, dry
2 c	water
1/4 c	celery, chopped
1/2	carrot, chopped
1 Tbsp	onion, chopped
1/8 tsp	thyme
piece	bay leaf
	ham bone

(Serves four)

1 c	split peas, dry
4 c	water
1/2 c	celery, chopped
1	carrot, chopped
1/2	medium onion, chopped
1/4 tsp	thyme
1	bay leaf
	ham bone

Lentil Soup

Total Time: 1 hour and 20 minutes

1. Wash lentils.
2. Cover with the water and simmer for 1 hour or until tender enough to be puréed easily.
3. Add the remaining ingredients to the puréed lentils.
4. Simmer, covered, for 20 minutes.
5. Serve piping hot.

(Serves two)

1/2 c	lentils, dry
3 c	water
1/4 c	ham tidbits
2 Tbsp	carrot slices
1 tsp	dehydrated onion
	dash salt

(Serves four)

1 c	lentils, dry
6 c	water
1/2 c	ham tidbits
1/4 c	carrot slices
2 tsp	dehydrated onion
1/8 tsp	salt

Baked Beans

Total Time: 4 hours
Baking: 350°F oven for 3 hours

1. Preheat oven.
2. Wash beans.
3. Cover with water and heat to boiling.
4. Reduce heat and simmer until tender (about 1 hour).
5. Drain, but save the cooking liquid.
6. Mix the remaining ingredients with the beans and place in a casserole. Add enough of the cooking liquid to cover the beans completely.
7. Cover and bake in a 350°F oven for 3 hours. Add more cooking liquid if needed.

(Serves two)

1/2 c	navy beans, dry
1-1/2 c	water
1/2 c	tomato sauce
1/4 c	catsup
2 Tbsp	molasses
1/2 tsp	dry mustard
1/4 c	brown sugar
1	small onion, chopped
piece	bay leaf
1/4 tsp	salt
3	strips bacon, cut up

(Serves four)

1 c	navy beans, dry
3 c	water
1 c	tomato sauce
1/2 c	catsup
1/4 c	molasses
1 tsp	dry mustard
1/2 c	brown sugar
1	medium onion, chopped
1	bay leaf
1/2 tsp	salt
6	strips bacon, cut up

Evaluation of Laboratory Products—Vegetables

Recipe	Notes on Color, Texture, Flavor, or Other Qualities	Comments or Suggestions for Making or Using this Product in the Future

VOCABULARY

Chlorophyll

Carotenoid

Flavonoid

Anthoxanthin

Anthocyanin

Legume

Waxy potato

Non-waxy potato

CHAPTER 3

Fruits

Key Concepts   Recipes
Cooking Fruits   Vocabulary

Fruits often are eaten raw to take advantage of their beautiful colors and delightful flavors. They also find their way into a variety of recipes, especially for desserts, where their sweetness enhances the pleasure of eating. Whether cooked or raw, fruits always enliven a meal or snack.

Preparation of all fruits needs to begin with careful washing to ensure that microorganisms and contaminants that may have found their way onto the fresh produce have been removed. Clean appearance is no guarantee that microorganisms are not present. Assume that fruit may have been harvested under somewhat unsanitary conditions, and you will be careful to even wash bananas in their skins before serving them.

As a general rule, prepare fruit close to the time that it will be served. Cut surfaces of fruit release juices, causing fruit to become a bit shriveled while standing, especially if sugar has been added. Two other cautions are (1) avoid having fresh pineapple in contact with meat or gelatin for more than a few minutes and (2) be careful about combining various colors of fruit juice lest you discover a new way to make a muddy-looking beverage.

COOKING FRUITS

Objectives

1. To demonstrate the control of osmotic pressure to enhance the quality of cooked fruits.
2. To determine cooking qualities of selected varieties of a fruit.
3. To illustrate the range of ways in which fruits can be prepared.

Applesauce and coddled apples illustrate the use of osmotic pressure to achieve the desired texture when preparing fruits. In applesauce, the fruit is simmered in water. This situation causes water to flow into the cells and tends to rupture the cell walls, resulting in the desired mushy texture. Sugar is then stirred in simply for flavor. Coddled apples are simmered in a sugar syrup that is approximately comparable to the sugar concentration in the cells in the apple. This concentration of sugar draws only a little water into the cell (just enough to give a plump appearance). If the syrup becomes too concentrated from evaporation during simmering, the apples will shrivel because of loss of water from the cells.

KEY CONCEPTS

1. Osmotic pressure can be created in systems consisting of fruit and a sugar solution by altering the sugar concentration to draw water in or out of cells.

2. When more than one variety of a fruit is available (apples and pears, for example), select the variety that is best suited to the intended preparation.

Figure 3.1
Among the several varieties of apples usually available in markets are: (left to right) Red Delicious, Golden Delicious, Granny Smith, Fuji, and Gala.

Frequently, it is necessary to make a decision between two or more varieties of a fruit. Each variety has certain characteristics that suit it better for one type of preparation than for another. This is illustrated clearly by preparing applesauce, coddled apples, baked apples, and apple dumplings from three or more varieties of apples. Delicious, Rome Beauty, and Pippin are three varieties that are recommended for comparison because of their distinctly different cooking characteristics.

RECIPES

Applesauce

Total Time: 15 minutes

1. Wash, pare, and quarter apples. Remove all traces of the core.
2. Place in a 1-quart saucepan and add just enough water to cover the bottom of the pan.
3. Simmer in a covered pan until the apples are tender (approximately 10 minutes).
4. Press the apples through a strainer or whirl in a blender to make a purée. Stir in sugar, and garnish with cinnamon, if desired.

(Serves two)

2	apples
2 Tbsp	sugar
	cinnamon
	(optional)

(Serves four)

4	apples
1/4 c	sugar
	cinnamon (optional)

Note: Apples may be placed in a covered casserole containing 1/4 cup water and microwaved on high, allowing 1-1/2 minutes per apple or until very tender.

Coddled Apples

Total Time: 15 minutes

1. Wash and core apples.
2. Cut doughnut-like slices 1/4" thick horizontally.
3. Cover slices with water to prevent discoloration before they are cooked.
4. In a 1-quart saucepan, stir together the sugar and water, and note the liquid level. Use a skillet for the large recipe.
5. Heat to a high simmer.
6. Add several apple slices and continue simmering until slices are tender (about 10 minutes).
7. Add water as necessary to maintain the original liquid level.
8. When slices are tender, remove them from the syrup with a slotted spoon.
9. Serve as a dessert or as a meat accompaniment.

(Serves two)

2	apples
2 c	sugar
1 c	water

(Serves four)

(If desired, the large recipe may be prepared in a skillet.)

4	apples
2 c	sugar
1 c	water

Baked Apples

Total Time: 1 hour
Baking: 375°F for 45 to 60 minutes

1. Preheat oven.
2. Wash and core apples, being careful to remove all of woody cellulose around the seeds.
3. Peel a strip of skin 1/4" wide around the equator of the apples and place apples in a casserole dish.
4. Combine the remaining ingredients and stuff into the center of each apple.
5. Pour 1 cup water into the bottom of the casserole dish. Cover, and bake at 375°F until tender (45 to 60 minutes).
6. Baste every 15 minutes.

(Serves two)

2	apples
2 Tbsp	brown sugar
1/4 tsp	cinnamon
1/2 tsp	butter
1 Tbsp	raisins

(Serves four)

4	apples
1/4 c	brown sugar
1/2 tsp	cinnamon
1 tsp	butter
2 Tbsp	raisins

Note: Apples may be placed in a covered casserole containing 2 Tbsp water per apple and microwaved on high, allowing 2 minutes per apple.

Evaluation of Apple Varieties

	Appearance and Flavor		
Type of Apple	**Sauce**	**Coddled**	**Baked**
Delicious			
Rome Beauty			
Pippin			

Apple Dumplings

Total Time: 1 hour
Baking: 400°F for 40 minutes

1. Preheat oven.
2. Combine sugar, water, cinnamon, food coloring, and margarine or butter in a 1-quart saucepan and boil for 2 minutes.
3. Wash, pare, and core apples.
4. Mix the flour and salt.
5. With a pastry blender, cut in the shortening to the size of rice grains.
6. While tossing the flour mixture with a fork, slowly add the water.
7. Press together with a fork until dough is in a ball.
8. Roll out on pastry cloth to make a 1/8″ thick rectangle 6-1/2″ × 13″ × (13″ × 13″ when serving four). Cut squares 6-1/2″ on a side.
9. Place one apple in the middle of each square.
10. Stuff center of each apple with raisins.
11. Sprinkle each apple generously with sugar and cinnamon.
12. Lightly moisten the edges of a square of dough.
13. Bring up the four corners and pinch them together on top of the apple.
14. Pinch the sides of the dough together.
15. Repeat for each apple.
16. Place in a rectangular cake pan, being sure that apples are at least an inch apart.
17. Pour the syrup over each of the dumplings. Bake at 400°F for 40 minutes, or until dumplings are browned and apples are done.

(Serves two)

1/2 c	sugar
3/4 c	water
1/8 tsp	cinnamon
2	drops red food coloring
1 Tbsp	margarine or butter
2	apples, medium size

Dough (Bisquick may be substituted for dough):

1 c	flour
1/2 tsp	salt
1/3 c	shortening
2-2/3 Tbsp	water
1 Tbsp	raisins
	sugar
	cinnamon

(Serves four)

1 c	sugar
1-1/2 c	water
1/4 tsp	cinnamon
4	drops red food coloring
2 Tbsp	margarine or butter
4	apples, medium size

Dough (Bisquick may be substituted for dough):

2 c	flour
1 tsp	salt
2/3 c	shortening
1/3 c	water
2 Tbsp	raisins
	sugar
	cinnamon

Strawberry Consommé

Total Time: 20 minutes

1. Wash, remove caps, and slice strawberries.
2. Simmer strawberries, rhubarb, cinnamon, sugar, and water for 5 minutes.
3. Strain juice.
4. Add burgundy and soda water to strained juice.
5. Serve either hot or cold with a dollop of sour cream on each serving.

(Serves two)

1 c	strawberries
1 c	fresh rhubarb (or 8 oz frozen rhubarb)
1-1/2"	stick of cinnamon
1/2 c	sugar
1 c	water
1/4 c	burgundy
1/4 c	soda water
2 Tbsp	sour cream

(Serves four)

2 c	strawberries
2 c	fresh rhubarb (or 8 oz frozen rhubarb)
3"	stick of cinnamon
1 c	sugar
2 c	water
1/2 c	burgundy
1/2 c	soda water
1/4 c	sour cream

Fruit Cobbler

Total Time: 45 minutes
Baking: 400°F for 30 minutes

(Serves four)

3/4 c	sugar
1 Tbsp	cornstarch
2-1/2 c	canned fruit and juice

Dough:

1 c	flour
1-1/2 tsp	baking powder
1 Tbsp	sugar
1/2 tsp	salt
3 Tbsp	shortening
6 Tbsp	milk
	sugar
	cinnamon, if desired

1. Preheat oven.
2. Stir the sugar and cornstarch together, and gradually add the canned fruit and juice to make a smooth mixture.
3. Pour into casserole dish and place in 400°F oven to heat while making the dough.
4. Mix the dry ingredients together.
5. Cut in the shortening to the size of rice grains.
6. Add the milk all at once, and stir with a fork until all the ingredients are moistened.
7. Drop from a spoon onto the hot fruit.
8. Sprinkle lightly with sugar and cinnamon, if desired.
9. Bake 30 minutes at 400°F until surface is golden brown.

(Serves two)

6 Tbsp	sugar
1-1/2 tsp	cornstarch
1-1/4 c	canned fruit and juice

Dough:

1/2 c	flour
3/4 tsp	baking powder
1-1/2 tsp	sugar
1/4 tsp	salt
4 tsp	shortening
3 Tbsp	milk
	sugar
	cinnamon, if desired

Figure 3.2
Peach cobbler is a quick and pleasing dessert that may be made with either fresh or canned fruit.

Broiled Grapefruit

Total Time: 10 minutes

1. Cut grapefruit in half. Carefully cut around the circumference of the pulp and separate each section from the membranes.
2. Sprinkle brown sugar over each half.
3. Place on broiler pan, and broil with the upper surface about 3″ from the heat. Watch continuously.
4. Remove from the broiler when the sugar is bubbly and brown.
5. Serve hot.

(Serves two)

1	grapefruit
1 Tbsp	brown sugar

(Serves four)

2	grapefruit
2 Tbsp	brown sugar

Blueberry Coffee Cake

Total Time: 50 minutes (small); 60 minutes (large)
Baking: 350°F oven for 35 to 40 minutes

1. Preheat oven.
2. Cream the sugar and shortening until light and fluffy.
3. Beat in the well-beaten egg.
4. Sift the dry ingredients together.
5. Add one-third of the dry ingredients to the creamed mixture, and stir.
6. Add one-half of the milk, and stir.
7. Repeat with the remaining thirds of dry ingredients alternately with the other half of the milk.
8. Pour into a well-greased pan (8″ × 8″ for the small recipe, 8″ × 12″ for the large).
9. Put blueberries over the surface of the batter.
10. Combine brown sugar, flour, cinnamon, and melted butter in a small bowl.
11. Sprinkle over the blueberries.
12. Bake at 350°F 35 to 40 minutes until a toothpick inserted in the center comes out clean.

(Serves two)

1/4 c	sugar
1/4 c	shortening
1/2	egg
1 c	flour
1 tsp	baking powder
1/8 tsp	salt
1/4 c	milk
1 c	blueberries, well drained

Topping:

1/4 c	brown sugar
1/4 c	flour
1/4 tsp	cinnamon
1 Tbsp	margarine or butter, melted

(Serves four)

1/2 c	sugar
1/2 c	shortening
1	egg
2 c	flour
2 tsp	baking powder
1/4 tsp	salt
1/2 c	milk
2 c	blueberries, well drained

Topping:

1/2 c	brown sugar
1/2 c	flour
1/2 tsp	cinnamon
2 Tbsp	margarine or butter, melted

Swedish Fruit Soup

Total Time: 50 minutes

1. Put apricots, prunes, and water in a saucepan and soak 1/2 hour.
2. In a small bowl, stir the cornstarch and sugar together.
3. Add this mixture, the cinnamon, and lemon to the fruit.
4. Stir while heating to simmering.
5. Simmer, covered, 8 to 10 minutes, stirring occasionally.
6. Add the raisins and currants, and simmer, covered, an additional 5 minutes.

(Serves two)

1/4 c	dried apricots
1/4 c	dried prunes
2 c	water
10	cinnamon stick
1	slice lemon
1 Tbsp	cornstarch
1/3 c	sugar
1 Tbsp	raisins
1 Tbsp	golden raisins
2 tsp	dried currants

(Serves four)

1/2 c	dried apricots
1/2 c	dried prunes
4 c	water
20	cinnamon stick
2	slices lemon
2 Tbsp	cornstarch
2/3 c	sugar
2 Tbsp	raisins
2 Tbsp	golden raisins
1 Tbsp	dried currants

Note: Traditionally, fruit soup is served chilled as a dessert. It is also a treat when served warm.

Banana Nut Bread

Total Time: 1 hour
Baking: 350°F oven for 40 to 45 minutes

1. Preheat oven.
2. Cream margarine or butter with sugar until light.
3. Beat in the egg.
4. Sift the dry ingredients together.
5. Combine milk with banana pulp.
6. Add a third of the dry ingredients to the fat–egg mixture and blend.
7. Stir in half of the banana–milk blend.
8. Add a third of the dry ingredients; blend.
9. Stir in the remaining liquid.
10. Add the final third of the dry ingredients and the chopped nuts; blend.
11. Grease loaf pan(s), 8-1/2" × 4-1/2". Pour in the batter.
12. Bake in preheated oven at 350°F 40 to 45 minutes until toothpick inserted in center comes out clean.
13. Cut the loaf loose from the edges of the pan, remove from the pan, and cool on a cooling rack.

(Serves two)

6 Tbsp	margarine or butter
3/4 c	sugar
1	egg, beaten
1-1/2 c	sifted all-purpose flour
1 tsp	baking powder
1/4 tsp	salt
1/4 tsp	soda
2 Tbsp	milk
6 Tbsp	mashed ripe banana
1/2 c	chopped walnuts

(Serves four)

3/4 c	margarine or butter
1-1/2 c	sugar
2	eggs, beaten
3 c	sifted all-purpose flour
2 tsp	baking powder
1/2 tsp	salt
1/2 tsp	soda
1/4 c	milk
3/4 c	mashed ripe banana
1 c	chopped walnuts

Riz à l'Amande

Total Time: 1 hour

1. Combine rice, milk, and sugar in saucepan and heat to boiling while stirring.
2. Immediately reduce heat to simmering and simmer until milk is absorbed (25 minutes), stirring frequently to avoid scorching.
3. Remove from heat and stir in cream sherry. Chill in a shallow dish while beating cream.
4. Beat cream until stiff, being careful not to beat until it turns to butter.
5. Fold the whipped cream and chopped almonds into the rice. Spoon into sherbet dishes and chill in refrigerator.
6. Prepare raspberry sauce by draining the syrup from the thawed raspberries and stirring this syrup gradually into the cornstarch.
7. Heat the raspberry–cornstarch mixture to a boil while stirring constantly. Boil 3 minutes.
8. Stir in the raspberries and chill.
9. Spoon some of the chilled sauce over each dish of pudding.

(Serves two)

1/4 c	uncooked rice
3/4 c	milk
1/4 c	sugar
1 Tbsp	cream sherry
1/2 c	whipping cream
1/4 c	chopped, toasted almonds
1	10 oz package frozen raspberries, thawed
1-1/2 tsp	cornstarch

(Serves four)

1/2 c	uncooked rice
1-1/2 c	milk
1/2 c	sugar
2 Tbsp	cream sherry
1 c	whipping cream
1/2 c	chopped, toasted almonds
2	10 oz packages frozen raspberries, thawed
1 Tbsp	cornstarch

Quick Lemon Pie

Total Time: 50 minutes
Baking: 350°F oven 10 minutes for crust and
15 minutes for meringue

1. Preheat oven.
2. Melt margarine or butter and stir in crumbs and sugar.
3. Pack firmly across the bottom and sides of tart pans.
4. Bake at 350°F for 10 minutes. Cool.
5. Beat yolks and stir in the milk, juice, and rind until dispersed uniformly. Pour into graham cracker crusts.
6. Beat egg whites until foamy; add cream of tartar and gradually add the sugar. Continue beating on the electric mixer until peaks just bend over.
7. Spread meringue on tarts, being sure to seal to edges of the crust.
8. Bake at 350°F for 12 to 15 minutes until a pleasing golden brown.
9. Cool at room temperature for 15 minutes before refrigerating.

(Serves two)

3 Tbsp	margarine or butter
3/4 c	graham cracker crumbs (9 crackers)
1 Tbsp	sugar
2	eggs, separated
1/2	can-sweetened condensed milk
1/4 c	lemon juice
	grated rind of 1 lemon
1/4 tsp	cream of tartar
1/4 c	sugar

(Serves four)

1/3 c	margarine or butter
1-1/2 c	graham cracker crumbs (9 crackers)
2 Tbsp	sugar
3	eggs, separated
1	can-sweetened condensed milk
1/2 c	lemon juice
	grated rind of 2 lemons
1/2 tsp	cream of tartar
6 Tbsp	sugar

Cherries Jubilee

Total Time: 10 minutes

1. In a chafing dish, melt red currant jelly.
2. Blend cornstarch with cherry juice until perfectly smooth.
3. Combine the starch slurry with the jelly, stirring rather vigorously while heating to boiling.
4. Add the spices, rinds, and cherries and continue heating until cherries are warmed through.
5. Warm kirsch in a very small pan before pouring it onto the hot cherry sauce. Immediately ignite with a long match without stirring the kirsch.
6. Spoon flaming cherries jubilee over a scoop of vanilla ice cream.

Figure 3.3
Cherries just picked from the tree are a highlight of summer, whether eaten fresh or in a pie or other treat.
(Courtesy of Brian Jung.)

(Serves two)

1/3 c	red currant jelly
1 c	canned dark sweet (Bing) cherries and their juice
1 tsp	cornstarch
	dash cinnamon
	dash ground cloves
	dash allspice
1/4 tsp	grated lemon rind
1 tsp	grated orange rind
2 Tbsp	kirsch (cherry brandy)
1/3 qt	vanilla ice cream

(Serves four)

2/3 c	red currant jelly
2 c	canned dark sweet (Bing) cherries and their juice
2 tsp	cornstarch
1/4 tsp	cinnamon
1/4 tsp	ground cloves
1/4 tsp	allspice
1/2 tsp	grated lemon rind
2 tsp	grated orange rind
1/4 c	kirsch (cherry brandy)
2/3 qt	vanilla ice cream

Prune Banana Cake

Total Time: 75 minutes
Baking: in 350°F oven for 30 minutes

1. Preheat oven.
2. Simmer prunes 10 minutes.
3. Prepare 8″ round cake pan(s) by lining bottom with layer of wax paper that just fits circle.
4. Sift dry ingredients together in mixing bowl.
5. Add shortening, milk, vanilla, and mashed banana and beat at medium speed on electric mixer for 2 minutes.
6. Add egg and beat 2 more minutes.
7. Add pitted chopped prunes and nuts.
8. Bake at 350°F until toothpick inserted in center comes out clean (30 minutes).
9. Cool on cooling rack.
10. Prepare icing by beating butter, cream, lemon juice, rind, and powdered sugar together until light and fluffy.

(One layer)

1/2 c	cooked prunes
1 c	sifted all-purpose flour
3/4 tsp	baking powder
1/2 tsp	soda
1/2 tsp	salt
2/3 c	sugar
1/4 c	shortening
2 Tbsp	milk
1/2 tsp	vanilla
1-1/2	bananas (1/2 cup mashed)
1	egg
1/4 c	chopped walnuts

Icing:

2 Tbsp	margarine or butter
1 Tbsp	cream or milk
1-1/2 tsp	lemon juice
1 tsp	grated lemon rind
1-1/2 c	powdered sugar

(Two layers)

1 c	cooked prunes
2 c	sifted all-purpose flour
1-1/2 tsp	baking powder
1 tsp	soda
1 tsp	salt
1-1/3 c	sugar
1/2 c	shortening
1/4 c	milk
1 tsp	vanilla
3	bananas (1/2 cup mashed)
2	eggs
1/2 c	chopped walnuts

Icing:

1/4 c	margarine or butter
2 Tbsp	cream or milk
3 tsp	lemon juice
2 tsp	grated lemon rind
3 c	powdered sugar

Fried Peaches

Total Time: 15 minutes

1. Peel and cut peaches in half.
2. Melt the margarine or butter and add the peach halves stuffed with brown sugar.
3. Sauté gently until tender.

(Serves two)

2	fresh peaches or 4 canned peach halves, drained
1 Tbsp	margarine or butter
4 tsp	brown sugar

(Serves four)

4	fresh peaches or 8 canned peach halves, drained
2 Tbsp	margarine or butter
3 Tbsp	brown sugar

Note: These are delicious as an accompaniment to ham and other meats or as a dessert topped with stirred custard or ice cream.

Stewed Dried Fruit

Total Time: 15 to 40 minutes

1. Wash dried fruit well.
2. Cover the fruit with water and simmer in a covered saucepan until fruit is tender.

dried fruit
water to cover

Note: The length of time required to tenderize the fruit varies with the size of the piece and the amount of cut surface. When done, they are plump, lustrous, and easily cut. Suggested cooking times for dried fruits are as follows: prunes, 35 minutes; apricots, 30 minutes; peaches, 35 minutes; figs, 35 minutes; and raisins, 10 minutes.

Poached Pears

Total Time: 15 minutes

1. Place the first four ingredients in a saucepan and bring to a boil.
2. Peel, halve, and core the pears.
3. Place them in the syrup.
4. Simmer gently until tender (approximately 15 minutes).
5. Chill and serve in sherbet glasses with a dollop of sour cream and a sprinkle of cinnamon.

(Serves two)

3 c	water
1 c	sugar
1″	stick cinnamon
1 tsp	vanilla extract
2	pears
1 Tbsp	sour cream
	cinnamon

(Serves four)

4 c	water
1-1/3 c	sugar
2″	stick cinnamon
1-1/2 tsp	vanilla extract
4	pears
2 Tbsp	sour cream
	cinnamon

Cherry Crunch Pie

Total Time: 50 minutes
Baking: 275°F oven for 35 minutes

1. Preheat oven.
2. Roll graham crackers into crumbs, blend in the sugar and margarine or butter.
3. Press all but one-fourth of the mixture into a 9"-pie plate (use individual pie plates for small recipe).
4. Chill in refrigerator while preparing filling.
5. Mix sugar and cornstarch together in a 1-quart saucepan.
6. Stir in the cherries and heat to boiling, stirring constantly.
7. Remove from the heat; add almond extract, and enough red coloring to turn the filling a bright red.
8. Pour into the chilled crust.
9. In the small bowl, beat the whites to the foamy stage, using an electric mixer.
10. Add the cream of tartar, and gradually add the sugar while beating on high.
11. Beat until the peaks just bend over.
12. Spread the meringue on the pie and sprinkle the remaining crumbs over the surface of the meringue.
13. Bake in a 275°F oven for 35 minutes.

(Serves two)

7	graham crackers
3 Tbsp	sugar
2 Tbsp	margarine or butter, melted
6 Tbsp	sugar
1-1/3 Tbsp	cornstarch
1 c	pie cherries, canned (drained)
1/8 tsp	almond extract
	red food coloring (optional)
1	egg white
	pinch cream of tartar
2 Tbsp	sugar

(Serves four)

15	graham crackers
6 Tbsp	sugar
1/4 c	margarine or butter, melted
3/4 c	sugar
2-2/3 Tbsp	cornstarch
1	No. 2 pie cherries, canned (drained)
1/4 tsp	almond extract
	red food coloring (optional)
3	egg whites
1/4 tsp	cream of tartar
6 Tbsp	sugar

Versatile Lemon-Orange Curd

Total Time: 25 minutes

1. Place all ingredients in the top of a double boiler over hot (not boiling) water.
2. Stir constantly while cooking until thickened (about 15 minutes).
3. Chill thoroughly.
4. Pour over chilled fruit in parfait or sherbet glasses.

(Serves two)

2	eggs, well beaten
1 c	sugar
2 Tbsp	lemon juice
2 Tbsp	orange juice
1-1/2 tsp	grated lemon peel
1-1/2 tsp	grated orange peel
2 Tbsp	margarine or butter

(Serves four)

4	eggs, well beaten
2 c	sugar
1/4 c	lemon juice
1/4 c	orange juice
1 Tbsp	grated lemon peel
1 Tbsp	grated orange peel
1/2 c	margarine or butter

Note: Versatile Lemon-Orange Curd is well suited to serving with fresh fruits.

Minted Tangerine Filling for Meringues

Total Time: 30 minutes

1. In a small saucepan, combine sugar, cornstarch, and salt.
2. With a wooden spoon, stir in the tangerine juice.
3. Cook over medium heat, stirring constantly, until thickened and clear.
4. Remove from heat. Stir in peel and extract.
5. Cool in refrigerator or at room temperature.
6. Meanwhile, place tangerine pieces in meringue shells.
7. Spoon glaze over fruit.
8. Chill until serving time.

(Serves two)

1/4 c	sugar
2 tsp	cornstarch
	few grains salt
1/2 c	fresh-squeezed tangerine juice
1-1/2 tsp	fresh-grated tangerine peel
1	drop mint extract
1	tangerine, peeled, seeded, cut in bite-sized pieces
or	
1/2 c	canned mandarin oranges, drained
2	baked meringue shells
	mint sprigs or orange cartwheels

(Serves four)

1/2 c	sugar
1/4 c	cornstarch
	dash salt
1 c	fresh-squeezed tangerine juice
3 tsp	fresh-grated tangerine peel
2	drops mint extract
2	tangerines, peeled, seeded, cut in bite-size pieces
or	
1 c	canned mandarin oranges, drained
4	baked meringue shells
	mint sprigs or orange cartwheels

Strawberries à La Mascarpone

Total Time: 10 minutes

1. Add honey to mascarpone and stir just until blended. Chill until 10 minutes before serving.
2. Wash strawberries, leaving tops and stems (if present). Drain on paper towel before arranging for service with the mascarpone.
3. Serve mascarpone as a dollop if **berries** are served in individual bowls or in a bowl for dipping.

(Small recipe)

1/3 c	mascarpone
1 Tbsp	honey
	fresh strawberries

(Large recipe)

1 c	mascarpone
1/4 c	honey
	fresh strawberries

Figure 3.4
Fresh fruit kabobs are a healthy and refreshing snack, particularly on a warm early summer day when fresh fruits abound.

Orange-Grape Punch

Total Time: 35 minutes
Baking: in 325°F oven for 30 minutes

1. Preheat oven.
2. Stud whole oranges with 10 cloves each; place on baking sheet.
3. Bake for 30 minutes until juices begin to run.
4. Cut oranges in half and place in a heat-proof bowl.
5. Sprinkle with brown sugar.
6. Meanwhile, heat grape juice and water to simmering.
7. Stir into punch bowl along with orange juice.
8. Serve piping hot.

(Makes 3 cups)

1	medium orange
10	whole cloves
2 Tbsp	firmly packed brown sugar
2 c	grape juice
2/3 c	boiling water
2/3 c	orange juice

(Makes 1-1/2 quarts)

3	medium oranges
30	whole cloves
1/3 c	firmly packed brown sugar
4 c	grape juice
1-1/3 c	boiling water
1-1/3 c	orange juice

Pears Delicious

Total Time: 35 minutes
Baking: in 325°F oven for 25 minutes

1. Preheat oven.
2. Place pears cut side up in buttered shallow baking dish.
3. Sprinkle walnuts in hollow of each pear.
4. Pour water, corn syrup, and lemon juice over pears.
5. Combine margarine or butter, brown sugar, flour, and ground ginger with fork until crumbly and sprinkle over pears.
6. Bake at 325°F until pears are tender (about 25 minutes).
7. Spoon sauce over hot pears to serve.

(Serves two)

2	pears, pared and cored
2-1/2 Tbsp	chopped walnuts
2-1/2 Tbsp	water
1-1/2 Tbsp	light corn syrup
3/4 tsp	lemon juice
1-1/2 Tbsp	margarine or butter
2-1/2 Tbsp	brown sugar
1 tsp	flour
1/8 tsp	ground ginger

(Serves four)

4	pears, pared and cored
1/3 c	chopped walnuts
1/3 c	water
1/3 c	light corn syrup
1-1/2 Tbsp	lemon juice
3 Tbsp	margarine or butter
1/3 c	brown sugar
2 tsp	flour
1/4 tsp	ground ginger

Figure 3.5
Among the different varieties of pears often available in markets are Red Bartlett, Bartlett, Bosc, and d'Anjou.

Grapes Suzette

Total Time: 35 minutes

1. Wash **grapes** and stem them.
2. In a heatproof baking dish, stir the grapes and sour cream to coat the grapes.
3. Sprinkle brown sugar over the mixture.
4. Broil until brown sugar bubbles.
5. Serve immediately.

(Serves two)

1/4 lb	seedless grapes
2 Tbsp	sour cream
1 Tbsp	brown sugar

(Serves four)

1/2 lb	seedless grapes
1/4 c	sour cream
2 Tbsp	brown sugar

Evaluation of Laboratory Products—Fruits

Recipe	Notes on Color, Texture, Flavor, or Other Qualities	Comments or Suggestions for Making or Using this Product in the Future

VOCABULARY

Berries

Citrus fruits

Drupes

Grapes

Melons

Pomes

Tropical and subtropical fruits

Browning

Osmosis

CHAPTER 4

Salads and Salad Dressings

CARE OF GREENS

Objectives

1. To illustrate the effect of varying storage conditions on the quality of greens.
2. To prepare high-quality, attractive salads.
3. To demonstrate the influence of ingredients and method of formation on the stability of emulsions.

This chapter discusses various aspects of storing and preparing greens and other ingredients in salads. It also includes preparation of emulsions, as demonstrated in making salad dressings.

HANDLING

Various external conditions influence the flow of water into and out of cells. Greens are categorized as **succulents**; they will be crisp when conditions draw water into the cell, but limp when water is withdrawn. To illustrate the effect of storage conditions on them, store lettuce according to the various conditions indicated in the chart. Record the results.

Effects of Varying Storage Conditions

Storage Condition	Description of Lettuce Leaf	Explanation
Uncovered on counter, room temperature, 24 hours		
Ice water, refrigerated, 24 hours		
Saltwater (1 tsp/c of water), refrigerated, 24 hours		
Tightly covered container, refrigerated, 24 hours		

KEY CONCEPTS

1. Refrigerated storage in a closed area helps salad greens stay crisp by retaining water in their cells.

2. Ingredients for salads need to be washed thoroughly to ensure cleanliness and food safety. Careful draining and/or drying will avoid diluting salad dressings and reducing their flavor accents.

3. Salad dressing should be added to greens just before serving because unfavorable osmotic pressure due to salts in the dressing draws water from the cells.

4. When hot, gelatin and water form a *sol* which transforms into a *gel* when the concentration of gelatin is adequate and the temperature is cold enough.

5. Refrigerated storage until serving time is needed to maintain a gel that will hold its shape when served.

Lettuce Cups

To remove attractive lettuce leaf cups from a head of lettuce, first cut out the core of the lettuce head with a sharp knife. Hold the lettuce under cold running water so that the hole resulting from removal of the core is filled with cold water. Let the water stand briefly in the head of lettuce. As the head begins to relax a bit, gently force the leaves apart. Place leaves on paper toweling or on a towel. Refrigerate in the hydrator drawer until ready to plate the salad.

Radish Roses

Radish roses are a quick, colorful garnish. Wash radishes thoroughly; cut off the root and the stem (unless the leaves are attractive). Cut deeply from the root end in an X or other desired shape, being sure that the segments thus created are fairly thin. Place in a bowl of water to cover. Chill in refrigerator at least 30 minutes.

Figure 4.1
To open up, radish roses require chilling in water after the cuts have been made.

RECIPES

Spring Salad

Total Time: 10 minutes

1. Wash basil leaves, drain, and arrange a bed of leaves on each salad plate.
2. Cut onion into slices 1/8" thick and place one whole slice on each bed of greens.
3. Slice tomato into slices 1/3" thick and arrange one on each onion slice.
4. Top each salad with one slice of cheese and garnish with a fresh basil leaf.
5. Combine lemon juice, vinegar, and olive oil before drizzling over each salad.

(Serves two)

1/2	bunch fresh basil or other greens
1/2	Maui or other white onion
1/2	large tomato
2	slices mozzarella cheese
1 tsp	lemon juice
1 Tbsp	rice wine vinegar
1 Tbsp	olive oil

(Serves four)

1	bunch fresh basil or other greens
1	Maui or other white onion
1	large tomato
4	slices mozzarella cheese
2 tsp	lemon juice
2 Tbsp	rice wine vinegar
2 Tbsp	olive oil

Cauliflower Caper

Total Time: 30 minutes

1. Break cauliflower into flowerets and boil in salted water until just tender (about 5 minutes). Drain and chill.
2. Combine mayonnaise, sour cream, mustard, lemon juice, and salt.
3. Toss cauliflower with dressing to coat completely. Chill.
4. Arrange on lettuce cups and garnish with red pepper strips and chopped cilantro.

(Serves two)

1/4	head cauliflower
3 Tbsp	Mayonnaise
1 Tbsp	sour cream
2 tsp	Dijon mustard
1/2 tsp	lemon juice
	pinch of salt
2	lettuce cups
1/8	red bell pepper
3	sprigs cilantro

(Serves four)

1/2	head cauliflower
6 Tbsp	mayonnaise
2 Tbsp	sour cream
4 tsp	Dijon mustard
1 tsp	lemon juice
1/8 tsp	salt
4	lettuce cups
1/4	red bell pepper
6	sprigs cilantro

Vegetable and Canadian Bacon Salad

Total Time: 20 minutes

1. Caramelize walnuts in melted butter and sugar in a hot skillet.
2. Blanch asparagus and snap peas in boiling water 1 minute. Drain.
3. Wash and dice the bell pepper.
4. Clean mushrooms and slice.
5. Wash cherry tomatoes and cut in half.
6. Wash radicchio and Belgian endive before separating leaves.
7. Sauté Canadian bacon briefly to heat.
8. Toss asparagus, peas, tomatoes, mushrooms, bell pepper, oil, vinegar, avocado, salt, and pepper thoroughly.
9. Arrange radicchio cup and endive on individual salad plates before filling cup with salad mixture.
10. Garnish with Canadian bacon and glazed walnuts.

(Serves two)

1-1/2 oz	walnuts
2 tsp	butter or margarine
2 Tbsp	sugar
6	asparagus spears in 1" pieces
2 oz	sugar snap peas
1/4	yellow bell pepper
3	small mushrooms
4	cherry tomatoes
2	leaves radicchio
4	leaves Belgian endive
2 oz	Canadian bacon, cubed
2 Tbsp	walnut oil
1 Tbsp	rice wine vinegar
1/2	avocado, diced
	salt and pepper

(Serves four)

3 oz	walnuts
4 tsp	butter or margarine
4 Tbsp	sugar
12	asparagus spears in 1" pieces
1/4 lb	sugar snap peas
1/2	yellow bell pepper
6	small mushrooms
8	cherry tomatoes
4	leaves radicchio
8	leaves Belgian endive
1/4 lb	Canadian bacon, cubed
1/4 c	walnut oil
2 Tbsp	rice wine vinegar
1	avocado, diced
	salt and pepper

Curried Cranberry Chicken Salad

Total Time: 15 minutes

1. Cut chicken into bite-sized cubes.
2. Cut apple into 1/4" chunks.
3. Slice celery and onions thinly.
4. Combine mayonnaise, lime juice, and curry powder completely.
5. Add all ingredients and stir to coat all portions of salad.
6. Serve on greens, if desired.

(Serves two)

1 c	cooked chicken breast
1/2	Delicious apple
1/2	celery stalk
1	green onion
1/3 c	mayonnaise
1 tsp	lime juice
3/8 tsp	curry powder
1/3 c	dried cranberries
2 Tbsp	chopped pecans salad greens (optional)

(Serves four)

2 c	cooked chicken breast
1	Delicious apple
1	celery stalk
2	green onions
2/3 c	mayonnaise
2 tsp	lime juice
3/4 tsp	curry powder
2/3 c	dried cranberries
1/4 c	chopped pecans salad greens (optional)

Harvest Salad

Total Time: 15 minutes

1. Clean and thinly slice mushrooms, radishes, and celery.
2. Cut tomatoes and chicken into bite-sized chunks.
3. Tear lettuce into bite-sized pieces.
4. Combine all ingredients and toss.

(Serves two)

2	mushrooms
2	radishes
1	stalk celery
2	Roma tomatoes
3 oz	cooked chicken breast
3	leaves Bibb lettuce
1/4	roasted yellow bell pepper, diced
1/4	roasted green bell pepper, diced
1-1/2 oz	pepper cheese, diced
3 Tbsp	champagne dressing
	salt and pepper

(Serves four)

4	mushrooms
4	radishes
2	stalks celery
4	Roma tomatoes
6 oz	cooked chicken breast
6	leaves Bibb lettuce
1/2	roasted yellow bell pepper, diced
1/2	roasted green bell pepper, diced
3 oz	pepper cheese, diced
6 Tbsp	champagne dressing
	salt and pepper

Note: To roast bell peppers, heat under broiler or over gas flame until skin pops and blackens a bit, being sure to turn frequently so that all portions are singed by the broiler heat. Remove from the broiler and immediately cover with damp paper towel. When cool enough to handle easily, pull off the singed skin; carefully wash off any trace of the skin. Remove stem and seeds before dicing or slicing.

Chicken Salad á la Greco

Total Time: 15 minutes

1. Wash romaine leaves and cut into shreds 1/2" thick.
2. Wash and cut tomatoes in pieces.
3. Put romaine, tomato, onion, olives, chicken, and cheese in bowl.
4. Combine lemon juice, olive oil, oregano, and parsley.
5. Toss salad ingredients with dressing, salt, and pepper.

(Serves two)

3	leaves romaine
1	Roma tomato
1/2	red onion, coarsely chopped
1/4 c	pitted Kalamata olives
1 c	cooked chicken breast, cubed
2 oz	crumbled feta cheese (with basil and sun-dried tomatoes)
1 Tbsp	lemon juice
1/4 c	olive oil
1-1/4 tsp	chopped fresh oregano
1-1/4 tsp	chopped fresh parsley salt and pepper

(Serves four)

6	leaves romaine
2	Roma tomatoes
1	red onion, coarsely chopped
1/2 c	pitted Kalamata olives
2 c	cooked chicken breast, cubed
4 oz	crumbled feta cheese (with basil and sun-dried tomatoes)
2 Tbsp	lemon juice
1/2 c	olive oil
1 Tbsp	chopped fresh oregano
1 Tbsp	chopped fresh parsley salt and pepper

Salad Wraps

Total Time: 30 minutes

1. With mixer, beat cream cheese to spreadable consistency.
2. Chop garlic finely.
3. Finely chop red onion, olives, tomatoes, lettuce, and parsley. Stir and blot dry with paper towels.
4. Spread tortilla thickly with cream cheese and a light layer of mustard.
5. Cover tortilla with slices of meat.
6. Add generous layer of mixed vegetables.
7. Roll tortilla into a tight log, beginning from far side and being sure to retain the vegetables within the roll. Wrap the roll carefully in aluminum foil and chill thoroughly.
8. Remove from foil. Slice into pinwheels 1" thick. Secure each with a colored toothpick or place against each other on a serving platter.

(Small recipe)

8 oz	cream cheese
1	garlic clove
1/2	red onion
2 Tbsp	chopped black olives
1/4	head lettuce or romaine
3	Roma tomatoes, seeded
1/2	bunch parsley (stems removed)
3	extra large flour tortillas
1 Tbsp	Dijon mustard
4 oz	thinly sliced turkey
4 oz	thinly sliced salami

(Large recipe)

1 lb	cream cheese
2	garlic cloves
1	red onion
1/4 c	chopped black olives
1/2	head lettuce or romaine
6	Roma tomatoes, seeded
1	bunch parsley (stems removed)
6	extra large flour tortillas
2 Tbsp	Dijon mustard
8 oz	thinly sliced turkey
8 oz	thinly sliced salami

Note: These wraps are a colorful, flavorful appetizer that can be prepared a day ahead, if desired.

Mixed Greens with Beef and Gorgonzola Salad

Total Time: 20 minutes

1. Wash and blot dry greens.
2. Thinly slice onion and mushrooms.
3. Toast pecans at 350°F.
4. Sauté beef until heated through. Cut into slices 3/8″ thick.
5. Combine all ingredients and toss with dressing. Serve immediately.

(Serves two)

1-1/4 c	mixed greens
1/4	small red onion
2	mushrooms
2 Tbsp	pecans
1/2	beef tenderloin (1″ thick)
1 Tbsp	crumbled Gorgonzola cheese
	salt and pepper
1 Tbsp	balsamic vinegar
2 Tbsp	olive oil

(Serves four)

2-1/2 c	mixed greens
1/2	small red onion
4	mushrooms
1/4 c	pecans
1	beef tenderloin (1″ thick)
2 Tbsp	crumbled Gorgonzola cheese
	salt and pepper
2 Tbsp	balsamic vinegar
1/4 c	olive oil

Potato Salad with Tuna, Snap Peas, and Tomatoes

Total Time: 30 minutes

1. Boil potatoes with skins on until tender. Drain. Cut into cubes.
2. Cut off both ends of each sugar snap pea pod before blanching in boiling, salted water for 30 seconds.
3. Thoroughly drain tuna; break into chunks.
4. Stir potatoes, peas, tuna, vinegar, mustard, lemon juice, lemon zest, olive oil, pepper, and chives together to coat vegetables.
5. Serve on bed of arugula garnished with tomatoes.

(Serves two)

1/2 lb	small Red Triumph potatoes
1/8 lb	sugar snap peas
3 oz	canned tuna (white, solid, water pack)
1-1/2 tsp	white wine vinegar
1/2 tsp	Dijon mustard
1 tsp	lemon juice
1/4 tsp	lemon zest
2-1/2 Tbsp	olive oil
	ground pepper
3 Tbsp	chives, minced
1 c	arugula, stemmed
2	ripe plum tomatoes (in wedges)

(Serves four)

1 lb	small Red Triumph potatoes
1/4 lb	sugar snap peas
6-1/2 oz	can tuna (white, solid, water pack)
1 Tbsp	white wine vinegar
1 tsp	Dijon mustard
2 tsp	lemon juice
1/4 tsp	lemon zest
1/4 c	olive oil
	ground pepper
1/3 c	chives, minced
2 c	arugula, stemmed
4	ripe plum tomatoes (in wedges)

Pasta Salad Primavera

Total Time: 1 hour

1. Boil broccoli florets, peas, and pea pods 3 minutes. Drain.
2. Mix together mustard, olive oil, vinegar, scallions, garlic, tomato, and cooked vegetables.
3. Marinate 45 minutes.
4. Meanwhile, cook pasta according to package directions to al dente. Drain thoroughly.
5. Toss pasta lightly with vegetables.

(Serves two)

1/4 c	broccoli florets
1/4 c	peas
1/2 c	sugar snap peas
2 Tbsp	Dijon mustard
1/4 c	olive oil
2 Tbsp	red wine vinegar
1	scallion, thinly sliced
1/2	garlic clove, minced
1/2	tomato, seeded and chopped
1 c	uncooked penne or other pasta of choice

(Serves four)

1/2 c	broccoli florets
1/2 c	peas
1 c	sugar snap peas
1/4 c	Dijon mustard
1/2 c	olive oil
1/4 c	red wine vinegar
2	scallions, thinly sliced
1	garlic clove, minced
1	tomato, seeded and chopped
2 c	uncooked penne or other pasta of choice

Kashi Vegetable Salad

Total Time: 50 minutes

1. Boil kashi, covered, until water is absorbed. Spread in shallow baking pan and chill briefly in freezer.
2. Meanwhile, combine all vegetables in large serving bowl.
3. Combine oil, soy sauce, vinegar, and mustard in small bowl.
4. Add kashi to vegetables and toss entire mixture with the dressing. Chill until served.

(Serves two)

1/2 c	uncooked kashi or bulgur
1 c	water
1/4 c	sliced mushrooms
2 Tbsp	diced green pepper
2 Tbsp	diced red pepper
2 Tbsp	diced water chestnuts
2 Tbsp	chopped parsley
2 Tbsp	diced green onions
2 Tbsp	diced, seeded tomato
1/4 c	olive oil
1/4 c	soy sauce
1-1/2 Tbsp	red wine vinegar
1 tsp	Dijon mustard

(Serves four)

1 c	uncooked kashi or bulgur
2 c	water
1/2 c	sliced mushrooms
1/4 c	diced green pepper
1/4 c	diced red pepper
1/4 c	diced water chestnuts
1/4 c	chopped parsley
1/4 c	diced green onions
1/4 c	diced, seeded tomato
1/2 c	olive oil
1/2 c	soy sauce
3 Tbsp	red wine vinegar
2 tsp	Dijon mustard

Raw Spinach Salad

Total Time: 20 minutes

1. Fry the bacon until it is crisp.
2. Drain on paper towel, and crumble into small pieces. Save the drippings for the dressing.
3. Thoroughly wash the spinach and drain it well.
4. Tear into bite-sized pieces, discarding the stems.
5. Warm the drippings and stir in the vinegar.
6. Stir and pour sparingly over the spinach. Toss the spinach.
7. Top with chopped egg and crumbled bacon.
8. Serve at once.

(Serves two)	
2	strips bacon
1/2	bunch fresh spinach
1	egg, hard cooked
1 Tbsp	vinegar

(Serves four)

4	strips bacon
1	bunch fresh spinach
2	eggs, hard cooked
2 Tbsp	vinegar

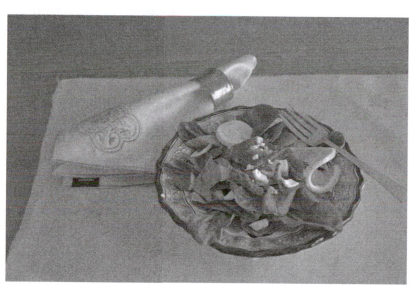

Figure 4.2
Raw spinach salad accented with hard-cooked egg and crisp bacon bits adds pleasing color, flavor, and nutrients to a meal.

Frozen Fruit Salad

Total Time: At least 2 hours

1. With an electric mixer, whip the cream until stiff.
2. Drain the fruit cocktail or cut fruit into small cubes.
3. Add the other ingredients.
4. Stir well and pour into individual salad molds or larger mold.
5. Cover tightly with aluminum foil.
6. Freeze.

(Serves two)

1/2 c	whipping cream, well chilled
1/2 c	fruit cocktail, drained (or fresh fruit)
2 Tbsp	mayonnaise
1	banana, sliced
1/4 c	salad marshmallows
1 Tbsp	sugar

(Serves four)

1 c	whipping cream, well chilled
1 c	fruit cocktail, drained (or fresh fruit)
1/4 c	mayonnaise
2	bananas, sliced
1/2 c	salad marshmallows
2 Tbsp	sugar

Note: When whipping cream, foam formation will be aided by using cream that has been chilled well. Also be sure to whip the cream until it piles well, but be careful not to whip it enough to break the emulsion and form butter.

Tossed Salad

Total Time: 10 minutes

1. Wash and drain lettuce well; tear into bite-sized pieces.
2. In a bowl, combine all ingredients except carrots.
3. Add dressing. Toss lightly.
4. Garnish with carrot curls.

(Serves two)

1/4	head lettuce or other lettuce
1	stalk celery
1/4 c	artichoke hearts
1	hard-cooked egg
6	cherry tomatoes
1 Tbsp	bacon bits
	black olives, pitted
	croutons
	Italian dressing
	carrot curls

(Serves four)

1/2	head lettuce or other lettuce
2	stalks celery
1/2 c	artichoke hearts
2	hard-cooked eggs
12	cherry tomatoes
2 Tbsp	bacon bits
	black olives, pitted
	croutons
	Italian dressing
	carrot curls

Note: Carrot curls are made by first paring large carrots with a vegetable peeler, and then using the peeler to peel off thin slices running the length of the carrot. These slices are wrapped in a curl around the index finger of the left hand and secured with a toothpick. Place in the refrigerator in a bowl of ice water. Chill until just prior to serving. Remove toothpicks, and use curls as a garnish.

Mixed Bean Salad

Total Time: 12 hours

1. Drain the beans well.
2. Put them in a large mixing bowl.
3. Add the other ingredients and mix everything well.
4. Cover tightly, and refrigerate overnight, stirring one or two times.
5. Just before serving, stir again thoroughly, and then remove the marinade.

(Serves four)

8-3/4 oz	Blue Lake green beans, canned
8-3/4 oz	garbanzo beans, canned
8-3/4 oz	wax beans, canned
8-3/4 oz	kidney beans, canned
5 Tbsp	diced green pepper
1	small onion, thinly sliced
1/2 c	red wine vinegar
1/4 c	salad oil
2 Tbsp	sugar
1/2 tsp	salt
1/2 tsp	black pepper, coarsely ground

(Serves eight)

1 lb	Blue Lake green beans, canned
1 lb	garbanzo beans, canned
1 lb	wax beans, canned
1 lb	kidney beans, canned
10 Tbsp	diced green pepper
1	medium onion, thinly sliced
1 c	red wine vinegar
1/2 c	salad oil
1/4 c	sugar
1 tsp	salt
1 tsp	black pepper, coarsely ground

Figure 4.3
Mixed bean salad not only provides a slightly sharp flavor to a meal, but it also is a good source of plant protein.

Hot Potato Salad

Total Time: 25 minutes

1. Boil unpeeled, but washed, potatoes in salted water (1 teaspoon salt/quart water) until tender.
2. Fry the bacon crisp, drain on paper towel, and crumble it.
3. Leave 1 teaspoon bacon drippings in the frying pan.
4. Stir in flour, and gradually stir in the vinegar and water.
5. Heat to boiling, while stirring constantly.
6. Add chopped onion and dry mustard to this dressing.
7. Peel and dice the hot potatoes.
8. Coat with dressing, and serve. Reheat, if necessary.

(Serves two)

2	medium Red Triumph (waxy) potatoes
3	slices bacon
1 tsp	flour
3 Tbsp	vinegar
3 Tbsp	water
1/4	medium onion
1/8 tsp	dry mustard

(Serves four)

4	medium Red Triumph (waxy) potatoes
6	slices bacon
2 tsp	flour
6 Tbsp	vinegar
6 Tbsp	water
1/2	medium onion
1/4 tsp	dry mustard

Potato Salad

Total Time: At least 2-1/2 hours

1. Boil unpeeled, but washed, potatoes in salted water (1 teaspoon salt/quart water) until tender.
2. Peel and cube the potatoes.
3. Stir in the remaining ingredients. If necessary, add more salt.
4. Chill for at least 2 hours (preferably overnight) before serving.

(Serves two)

2	medium Red Triumph (waxy) potatoes
2	hard-cooked eggs, chopped
1/2	medium onion, minced
1/2 tsp	celery seed
1/4 c	mayonnaise
1 tsp	prepared mustard
2 Tbsp	pickle relish

(Serves four)

4	medium Red Triumph (waxy) potatoes
4	hard-cooked eggs, chopped
1	medium onion, minced
1 tsp	celery seed
1/2 c	mayonnaise
2 tsp	prepared mustard
1/4 c	pickle relish

Figure 4.4
Potato salad is a summertime favorite, but for safety it is important to store it in the refrigerator.

Seafood Medley

Total Time: 30 minutes

1. Blend all ingredients thoroughly (except lettuce and lemon).
2. Chill and serve on lettuce leaves, using lemon cartwheels or quarters for garnish.

(Serves two)

1/2 c	lobster
1/2 c	crab
1/3 c	celery, chopped
1 Tbsp	lemon juice
1/8 tsp	curry powder
1	hard-cooked egg, chopped
3 Tbsp	mayonnaise
2	leaves Bibb lettuce
1/2	lemon

(Serves four)

1 c	lobster
1 c	crab
2/3 c	celery, chopped
2 Tbsp	lemon juice
1/4 tsp	curry powder
2	hard-cooked eggs, chopped
6 Tbsp	mayonnaise
4	leaves Bibb lettuce
1	lemon

Confetti Salad

Total Time: 2 hours

1. Thoroughly mix the gelatin with the boiling water; stir until no particles of gelatin can be seen.
2. Add the ice and stir slowly until the mixture begins to thicken perceptibly.
3. Remove any remaining ice, then stir in the vegetables.
4. Chill until congealed in mold.
5. To serve, unmold by dipping mold quickly in warm water, shaking to loosen, and then inverting onto the serving plate.
6. Garnish with greens.

(Serves two)

1	small package lime gelatin
1 c	boiling water
1/2	tray of ice cubes
1 c	finely grated cabbage
1/2 c	minced celery
1 c	grated carrots
	greens for serving

(Serves four)

1	large package lime gelatin
2 c	boiling water
1	tray of ice cubes
2 c	finely grated cabbage
1 c	minced celery
2 c	grated carrots
	greens for serving

Caesar Salad

Total Time: 10 minutes

1. Thoroughly wash romaine and blot dry with paper towels. Break into bite-sized pieces and drop in a wooden salad bowl that has been rubbed with a cut clove of garlic.
2. Lightly coddle egg by placing it in boiling water, removing the pan from the heat, and allowing the egg to sit in the water for 2 minutes.
3. Meanwhile, in a separate bowl, mash the anchovy in a spoonful of oil before adding the rest of the oil and the coddled egg. Blend together well and pour over greens in bowl.
4. Toss romaine until all leaves are coated with the dressing.
5. Squeeze lemon over the salad.
6. Garnish with Parmesan cheese, coarsely ground black pepper, and salad croutons. Serve immediately.

(Serves two)

1	clove of garlic
1/2	head of romaine
1	egg
1	anchovy fillet
1/4 c	salad oil (olive oil suggested)
1/2	lemon wrapped in square of cheesecloth
1/4 tsp	season salt
	coarsely ground black pepper
	Parmesan cheese, grated
1/2 c	garlic-flavored croutons

(Serves four)

1	clove of garlic
1	head of romaine
2	eggs
2	anchovy fillets
1/2 c	salad oil (olive oil suggested)
1	lemon wrapped in square of cheesecloth
1/2 tsp	season salt
	coarsely ground black pepper
	Parmesan cheese, grated
1 c	garlic-flavored croutons

Figure 4.5
Caesar salad is a salad classic that stays crisp because of the sturdy structure of romaine, the green traditionally used to make it.

Grapefruit and Avocado Salad

Total Time: 10 minutes

1. With a sharp knife, peel the rind and membrane surrounding the flesh of the grapefruit, leaving the meat of the fruit completely exposed.
2. Run the knife blade along one side of a membrane and back out along the other side of the grapefruit section. This releases the section from the membranes.
3. Repeat until all sections have been removed.
4. Pare the avocado and slice into thin slices lengthwise.
5. On a leaf of lettuce, alternate grapefruit segments and avocado slices.
6. Garnish with pomegranate seeds.

(Serves two)

1	grapefruit
1/2	avocado
	pomegranate seeds, if desired
2	lettuce cups

(Serves four)

2	grapefruit
1	avocado
	pomegranate seeds, if desired
4	lettuce cups

Hot Turkey Salad

Total Time: 40 minutes
Baking: in 325°F oven for 25 minutes

1. Blend all of the ingredients except the potato chips together in a casserole dish.
2. Sprinkle potato chips on top.
3. Bake uncovered in 325°F oven until salad is heated throughout and the cheese is melted (about 25 minutes).
4. Serve immediately.

(Serves two)

1 c	roasted turkey, diced
1 c	celery, diced
2 Tbsp	blanched, slivered almonds
2-1/2 Tbsp	diced green pepper
2 tsp	diced pimiento
1/4	medium onion, minced
1/4 tsp	salt
2-1/2 tsp	lemon juice
1/4 c	salad dressing or mayonnaise
1/4 c	grated Swiss cheese
1/4 c	crushed potato chips

(Serves four)

2 c	roasted turkey, diced
2-1/4 c	celery, diced
1/4 c	blanched, slivered almonds
1/3 c	diced green pepper
1-1/2 Tbsp	diced pimiento
1/2	medium onion, minced
1/2 tsp	salt
1-1/2 Tbsp	lemon juice
1/2 c	salad dressing or mayonnaise
1/2 c	grated Swiss cheese
1/2 c	crushed potato chips

Cole Slaw

Total Time: 10 minutes

1. Combine all of the ingredients and mix gently until all pieces are coated with the dressing.

(Serves two)

1 c	shredded cabbage
1/2 c	grated carrots
1 1/2 tsp	sugar
1 1/2 tsp	salad oil
1 Tbsp	vinegar
1 tsp	Horseradish

(Serves four)

2 c	shredded cabbage
1 c	grated carrots
1 Tbsp	sugar
1 Tbsp	salad oil
2 Tbsp	vinegar
2 tsp	Horseradish

Figure 4.6
Cole slaw is a familiar cabbage salad that often is made with varied additional ingredients.

Macaroni Salad

Total Time: 45 minutes

1. Boil the macaroni in salted water just until easily cut. Drain thoroughly and chill in a shallow dish in the refrigerator.
2. Combine all ingredients except the paprika, being sure to coat all the pieces with the dressing.
3. If time permits, chill a couple of hours to help flavors blend.
4. Serve on greens. Garnish with paprika.

(Serves two)

1/2 c	uncooked macaroni
2	strips bacon, fried and crumbled
1 Tbsp	minced onion
1 tsp	lemon juice
2 Tbsp	chopped green pepper
2 Tbsp	chopped stuffed olives
1/4 c	chopped celery
1	hard-cooked egg, chopped
1/4 c	mayonnaise or salad dressing paprika

(Serves four)

1 c	uncooked macaroni
4	strips bacon, fried and crumbled
2 Tbsp	minced onion
2 tsp	lemon juice
1/4 c	chopped green pepper
1/4 c	chopped stuffed olives
1/2 c	chopped celery
2	hard-cooked eggs, chopped
1/2 c	mayonnaise or salad dressing paprika

Cashew Chicken Salad

Total Time: 30 minutes plus chilling

1. Stir-fry the chicken in the oil about 4 minutes, turning frequently.
2. Add pineapple and salt; continue to fry 5 minutes.
3. Transfer to a refrigerator bowl and chill until 10 minutes before serving.
4. Add the remaining ingredients, stir, and serve garnished with some of the black olives and green onion tops.

(Serves two)

1-1/2 tsp	cooking oil
1	whole chicken breast, boned, skinned, and cut into bite-sized pieces
1/4 c	diced pineapple, drained
1/2 c	chopped celery
1/2 c	bean sprouts, drained
1/4 c	diced water chestnuts or jicama
1/8 tsp	curry powder
2-1/2 Tbsp	sour cream
2-1/2 Tbsp	mayonnaise
1/4 c	cashews
1/4 c	green onions, thinly sliced (including tops)
1/4 c	black olives, sliced

(Serves four)

1 Tbsp	cooking oil
2	whole chicken breasts, boned, skinned, and cut into bite-sized pieces
1/2 c	diced pineapple, drained
1 c	chopped celery
1 c	bean sprouts, drained
1/2 c	diced water chestnuts or jicama
1/4 tsp	curry powder
1/3 c	sour cream
1/3 c	mayonnaise
1/2 c	cashews
1/2 c	green onions, thinly sliced (including tops)
1/2 c	black olives, sliced

GELATIN SALADS

Flavored ***gelatin*** is used to make many molded salads, but some, such as tomato aspic, are made with unflavored gelatin. Either type of gelatin needs to be dissolved completely; otherwise, rubbery or chewy areas result. Flavored gelatin has been ground to a fairly fine powder and is dispersed with sugar or a sweetener to make dispersion of the gelatin quite easy. However, unflavored gelatin should be hydrated in cold water (1/4 cup cold water to 1 envelope of unflavored gelatin) until no dry particles of gelatin remain before the hot liquid is added to dissolve the gelatin. Failure to do this initial step makes it much harder to dissolve the gelatin in the hot liquid.

RECIPES

Apricot Salad

Total Time: 1 hour

1. In the appropriate pan, dissolve the gelatin in the boiling water. Stir continuously across all portions of the container until no granules of gelatin can be seen.
2. Add ice cubes and stir until gelatin begins to congeal. Remove pieces of ice.
3. Add the salad marshmallows and the drained fruits.
4. Chill in refrigerator while preparing the topping.
5. Blend the sugar, flour, egg, and apricot juice together and cook over boiling water until mixture thickens.
6. Remove from heat and add margarine or butter.
7. Cool in freezer.
8. Beat the whipping cream until stiff.
9. Fold the cooked mixture into the whipped cream, and then spread on the congealed gelatin.
10. Garnish with pecans.

(Use loaf pan)

1	small package orange-flavored gelatin
1 c	water, boiling
1/2	tray of ice cubes
1/3 c	salad marshmallows
1-3/4 c	canned apricot halves, drained
1 c	canned pineapple chunks, drained

Topping:

1/4 c	sugar
1-1/2 tsp	flour
1/2	egg, beaten
1/4 c	apricot juice
1 Tbsp	margarine or butter
1/2 c	whipping cream pecans for garnishing

(Use 8" × 8" pan)

1	large package orange-flavored gelatin
2 c	water, boiling
1	tray of ice cubes
2/3 c	salad marshmallows
3-1/2 c	canned apricot halves, drained
2 c	canned pineapple chunks, drained

Topping:

1/2 c	sugar
1 Tbsp	flour
1	egg, beaten
1/2 c	apricot juice
2 Tbsp	margarine or butter
1 c	whipping cream pecans for garnishing

Note: Pieces of fruit and other ingredients to be incorporated in gelatin salads are added when the gelatin begins to congeal. If they are added earlier, they will float to the top of the salad rather than being distributed uniformly.

Molded Strawberry Salad

Total Time: At least 2 hours

1. Pour boiling water over gelatin and stir until gelatin is dissolved completely.
2. Add frozen strawberries.
3. Stir occasionally and break up the block of berries as it thaws.
4. When berries are thawed completely, add the sliced banana and chopped pecans.
5. Pour into individual salad molds and refrigerate.
6. Garnish with the sour cream when the salad is served.

(Serves two)

1	3 oz package strawberry gelatin
1 c	boiling water
10 oz	frozen strawberries
1	banana
2 Tbsp	pecans, chopped
1/2 c	sour cream

(Serves four)

1	6 oz package strawberry gelatin
2 c	boiling water
20 oz	frozen strawberries
2	bananas
1/4 c	pecans, chopped
1 c	sour cream

Crab-Tomato Aspic Salad

Total Time: 3 hours

1. Hydrate gelatin in cold water.
2. Simmer tomato juice, celery salt, bay leaf, lemon juice, and onion 15 minutes.
3. Strain tomato mixture before stirring in the gelatin. Stir until all traces of gelatin particles are gone.
4. Chill until starting to thicken; immediately stir in celery and crab.
5. Pour into individual molds or one large ring or other shaped mold.
6. Chill until ready to unmold and serve.

(Serves three)

1	envelope unflavored gelatin
1/4 c	cold water
1 c	tomato juice
1/4 tsp	celery salt
1/2	bay leaf
1 Tbsp	lemon juice
1/2	medium onion, sliced
1/4 c	diced celery
3 oz	canned or fresh crab

(Serves six)

2	envelopes unflavored gelatin
1/2 c	cold water
2 c	tomato juice
1/2 tsp	celery salt
1	bay leaf
2 Tbsp	lemon juice
1	medium onion, sliced
1/2 c	diced celery
6 oz	canned or fresh crab

Sparkling Salad

Total Time: ~3 hours

1. Dissolve the gelatin completely in the boiling water.
2. Cool to room temperature.
3. Stir in the ginger ale, drained fruits, and banana.
4. Pour into molds and chill until firm.

(Makes four individual molds)

1		small package lemon-flavored gelatin
1 c		boiling water
1 c		ginger ale
1-1/4 c		pineapple chunks[1]
1/2 c		mandarin oranges, canned
1		sliced banana

(Makes eight individual molds)

1		large package lemon-flavored gelatin
2 c		boiling water
2 c		ginger ale
2-1/2 c		pineapple chunks[1]
1 c		mandarin oranges, canned
2		sliced bananas

[1]Use canned pineapple. Frozen or fresh pineapple will cause gelatin to remain fluid because of the action of the enzyme *bromelain* in these products.

Molded Black Cherry Salad

Total Time: 2 hours

1. Thoroughly mix the gelatin with the boiling liquid[1]; stir until no particles of gelatin can be seen.
2. Add the ice and stir slowly until the mixture begins to thicken perceptibly.
3. Remove any remaining ice and then stir in the other ingredients.
4. Chill until congealed in individual or ring molds.
5. To serve, unmold by dipping mold quickly in warm water, shaking to loosen, and then inverting onto the serving plate.
6. Garnish with greens.

[1]Note: If there is too little juice to provide the necessary liquid, water should be added to the correct measure.

(Serves four)

1		small package black cherry gelatin
1 c		boiling juice drained from the cherries[1]
1/2		tray of ice cubes
1/2		can pitted black cherries, drained
1/2 c		chopped celery
1/2 c		chopped pecans or walnuts to garnish

(Serves eight)

1		large package black cherry gelatin
2 c		boiling juice from the cherries[1]
1		tray of ice cubes
1		can pitted black cherries, drained
1 c		chopped celery
1 c		chopped pecans or walnuts to garnish

Sunshine Molded Salad

Total Time: 2 hours

1. Thoroughly mix the gelatin with the boiling juice; stir until no particles of gelatin can be seen.
2. Add the ice and stir slowly until the mixture begins to thicken perceptibly.
3. Remove any remaining ice and then stir in the other ingredients.
4. Chill until congealed in individual molds or ring mold.
5. To serve, unmold by dipping mold quickly in warm water, shaking to loosen, and then inverting onto the serving plate.
6. Garnish with greens.

(Serves four)	
1	small package lemon gelatin
1 c	boiling juice drained from fruit
1/2	tray of ice cubes
1	small can of mandarin oranges, drained
3/4 c	canned pineapple chunks, drained
1	banana, sliced greens to garnish

UNMOLDING GELATIN PRODUCTS

1. Be sure gelatin is set firmly.
2. Remove from refrigerator immediately before unmolding the gelatin.
3. Unmold by a fleeting dip in hot water, quickly followed by a sharp shake to loosen the gelatin. Be careful to avoid letting water actually come in contact with the gelatin.
4. Place a plate inverted on the top of the mold.
5. Quickly flip the plate and gelatin over together. The gelatin should slip easily onto the plate. Be careful not to overheat the gelatin. This causes the pattern of the mold to be indistinct in the unmolded product.
6. Return unmolded gelatin to the refrigerator until ready to serve.

SALAD DRESSING RECIPES

True French Dressing (Temporary Emulsion)

Total Time: 5 minutes

1. Put all ingredients in a container with a tight-fitting lid.
2. Refrigerate.
3. Just before serving, shake vigorously to mix all ingredients thoroughly and form an emulsion.

(Small recipe)

1/4 c	olive oil
1 Tbsp	balsamic vinegar
1 tsp	lemon juice
1/4 tsp	paprika
1/4 tsp	dry mustard
1/4 tsp	salt
1/4 tsp	sugar
dash	black pepper

(Large recipe)

1/2 c	olive oil
2 Tbsp	balsamic vinegar
2 tsp	lemon juice
1/2 tsp	paprika
1/2 tsp	dry mustard
1/2 tsp	salt
1/2 tsp	sugar
1/4 tsp	black pepper

Tomato French Dressing (Semi-Permanent Emulsion)

Total Time: 10 minutes

1. Mince the onion and chop the green pepper.
2. Put all the ingredients in a mixing bowl.
3. Beat slowly with a rotary beater until all ingredients are thoroughly dispersed.
4. Store in the refrigerator.

(Small recipe)

1/2 c	vinegar
1/2 c	olive oil
1/2 c	sugar
1/2 tsp	dry mustard
1/2 tsp	salt
1/2	can condensed tomato soup, undiluted
1/2	medium onion
1/2	green pepper

(Large recipe)

1 c	vinegar
1 c	olive oil
1 c	sugar
1 tsp	dry mustard
1 tsp	salt
1	can condensed tomato soup, undiluted
1	medium onion
1	green pepper

Mayonnaise (Permanent Emulsion)

Total Time: 10 minutes

1. Mix the dry ingredients with the egg yolk and vinegar.
2. Beat well with rotary beater.
3. Add the oil gradually (1 teaspoon at a time), beating after each addition until all the oil is emulsified and no streaks of oil remain.
4. After approximately 1/4 cup oil has been added, the oil can be added in somewhat larger amounts. Continue adding the oil and beating until all the oil has been added. If the emulsion breaks, place an egg yolk in a clean bowl and *very slowly* begin adding the broken emulsion to it, being careful to beat in one addition before adding the next portion.
5. Store in refrigerator in tightly covered container.

(Small recipe)

1/8 tsp	salt
1/4 tsp	sugar
1/2 tsp	dry mustard
dash	cayenne
1	egg yolk
1 Tbsp	vinegar
1/2 c	salad oil

(Large recipe)

1/4 tsp	salt
1/2 tsp	sugar
1 tsp	dry mustard
dash	cayenne
2	egg yolks
2 Tbsp	vinegar
1 c	salad oil

Note: If desired, dressing can be thinned with the addition of vinegar or lemon juice.

Cooked Salad Dressing

Total Time: 15 minutes

1. Mix the dry ingredients together in a 1-quart saucepan, and gradually stir in the water.
2. Bring to a boil, while stirring constantly.
3. Remove from the heat.
4. Add a spoonful of the hot mixture to the beaten egg and quickly stir well.
5. Repeat twice.
6. Stir the egg mixture back into the dressing.
7. Cook over very low heat for 5 minutes while stirring slowly. (Be careful to avoid boiling the mixture.)
8. Remove from heat.
9. Stir in the vinegar and margarine or butter.
10. Cool and store in the refrigerator.

(Small recipe)

2 Tbsp	flour
1/2 tsp	salt
1/2 tsp	dry mustard
2 Tbsp	sugar
3/4 c	water
1/4 c	vinegar
1	egg, beaten
2 Tbsp	margarine or butter

(Large recipe)

1/4 c	flour
1 tsp	salt
1 tsp	dry mustard
1/4 c	sugar
1-1/2 c	water
1/2 c	vinegar
2	eggs, beaten
1/4 c	margarine or butter

Evaluation of Laboratory Products—Salads

Recipe	Notes on Color, Texture, Flavor, or Other Qualities	Comments or Suggestions for Making or Using this Product in the Future

VOCABULARY

Gelatin	Emulsion
Gelation	Temporary emulsion
Collagen	Semi-permanent emulsion
Foam	Permanent emulsion
Sol	Continuous phase
Gel	Interface
Bromelain	Dispersed phase
Proteolytic enzyme	Succulents
Osmosis	

CHAPTER 5

Sugar Cookery

Key Concepts
Crystalline Candy Recipes

Amorphous Candy Recipes
Vocabulary

Yes, there is no doubt that making candy is a sweet job! However, there is much to learn about sugar cookery. A lot is happening while sugar solutions are cooking and cooling. The temperature of boiling candies gets ever higher as water evaporates and the concentration of sugar increases. If caramels or toffee are being made, the color changes as sugar undergoes chemical changes at very high temperatures. The transition from a saturated solution to a supersaturated solution and ultimately to formation of sugar crystals is demonstrated when cooling crystalline candies.

Objectives

1. To demonstrate the direct relationship between boiling temperature and the concentration of a sugar solution.
2. To identify the factors influencing the texture of a crystalline candy.
3. To identify the factors determining whether a candy is crystalline or amorphous.
4. To prepare and evaluate crystalline and amorphous candies of high quality.

KEY CONCEPTS

1. The temperature of a boiling sugar solution rises because water evaporates and causes a decrease in vapor pressure, which means that boiling cannot occur unless more heat energy is added.

2. At very high temperatures, sugar molecules begin to break apart and form smaller compounds that add color and flavor to candies.

3. Crystalline candies contain organized crystalline structures which are influenced by ingredients, rate of heating, final cooking temperature reached, and conditions leading to crystallization.

4. Amorphous candies cannot organize into crystalline areas as they cool because of the high viscosity of their highly concentrated sugar solutions.

CRYSTALLINE CANDY RECIPES

Penuche

Total Time: 45 minutes
Final Temperature: 236°F

(Small recipe)	
3/4 c	sugar
1/2 c	brown sugar
1/3 c	milk
1-1/2 Tbsp	margarine or butter
1/2 tsp	vanilla
1/4 c	chopped nuts

(Large recipe)

1-1/2 c	sugar
1 c	brown sugar
2/3 c	milk
3 Tbsp	margarine or butter
1 tsp	vanilla
1/2 c	chopped nuts

1. Test the accuracy of the thermometer by boiling water and carefully noting the temperature of the actively boiling water. If thermometer does not show that water boils at 212°F, correct the final temperature to which candy is cooked to compensate for the error of the thermometer. For example, if the thermometer reads 210°F (2°F below the expected value), subtract 2°F from the temperature in the recipe to obtain the desired final temperature for the thermometer being used.
2. Put the sugars and milk in a 1-quart saucepan (small recipe) or a 2-quart saucepan (large recipe).
3. Stir slowly while heating to a boil. When the sugar has dissolved, stir only occasionally.
4. Boil the candy to a temperature of 236°F.
5. Remove from the heat and add the margarine, being careful not to stir at all.
6. Cool the candy where it will not be disturbed.
7. While the candy is cooling, grease a shallow pan.
8. Cool until the bottom of the pan feels a bit warm to the hand (110°F). Do not insert a thermometer; the hand test is accurate enough.
9. Add the vanilla and chopped nuts and beat vigorously with a wooden spoon until the thickening candy softens very slightly and loses its gloss.
10. Quickly spread in the pan. Cut into squares.

Note: Penuche typically has a more granular texture than other crystalline candies.

Fudge

Total Time: 45 minutes
Final Temperature: 234°F

1. Test boiling point of water on the thermometer, as described in Penuche, step 1.
2. In a 1-quart (small recipe) or 2-quart (large recipe) saucepan, combine chocolate, sugar, salt, corn syrup, and milk.
3. Stir while slowly heating to boiling.
4. When chocolate has melted and the sugar has dissolved, increase the rate of heating to medium and stir occasionally to keep candy from burning.
5. Continue boiling the candy until it reaches 234°F. Remember to correct for the thermometer if necessary. Just as soon as the candy reaches the correct final temperature, add the butter or margarine and vanilla without stirring, and remove candy from the range.
6. Place the candy in a cool place where it will not be disturbed at all. Avoid touching or moving the candy until the temperature has dropped to about 110°F. The bottom of the pan will feel moderately warm to your hand when the candy reaches 110°F. (This temperature need not be checked with the thermometer; inserting thermometer would start crystallization even if the candy had not cooled sufficiently.)
7. While candy is cooling, grease a shallow pan.
8. Beat vigorously with a wooden spoon until the thickening candy loses its gloss.
9. Quickly spread in the pan. Cut into squares.

(Small recipe)

6 Tbsp	milk
1 oz	unsweetened chocolate[1]
1 c	sugar
	few grains salt
1 tsp	light corn syrup
1 Tbsp	butter or margarine
1/2 tsp	vanilla

(Large recipe)

3/4 c	milk
2 oz	unsweetened chocolate
2 c	sugar
	dash salt
2 tsp	light corn syrup
2 Tbsp	butter or margarine
1 tsp	vanilla

[1]One square of chocolate is equivalent to approximately 3-1/2 tablespoons cocoa plus 1/2 tablespoons butter or margarine.

Fondant

Total Time: 45 minutes
Final Temperature: 238°F

1. Test boiling point of water on thermometer, as described in Penuche recipe, step 1.
2. In a 1-quart (small recipe) or 2-quart (large recipe) saucepan, combine the ingredients.
3. Heat at a medium rate, stirring slowly until the sugar dissolves.
4. Continue boiling until the candy reaches 238°F.
5. Remove from heat and cool without disturbing it.
6. While candy is cooling, grease a platter or jelly roll pan.
7. Cool until the bottom of the pan feels a bit warm to the touch (110°F). Do not insert a thermometer; the hand test is accurate enough.
8. Pour onto a greased platter and begin beating immediately with a wooden spoon until candy becomes firm and loses its gloss.
9. Wash hands with soap; rinse and dry thoroughly. Knead fondant with fingers until perfectly smooth.
10. Wrap tightly in foil to ripen 24 hours. Ripened fondant may be kneaded into after-dinner mints or may be used as the center for stuffed dried fruits or chocolate-dipped candies.

(Small recipe)

1 c	sugar
1 Tbsp	light corn syrup or dash of cream of tartar
1/2 c	water

(Large recipe)

2 c	sugar
2 Tbsp	light corn syrup or 1/8 tsp of cream of tartar
1 c	water

Variations: Knead in any of the following:

1/8 tsp	lemon extract and yellow food coloring
1/8 tsp	orange extract, 1 drop yellow and 1 drop red food coloring
1/8 tsp	rum extract

Divinity

Total Time: 45 minutes
Final Temperature: 261°F

1. Test boiling point of water on thermometer, as described in Penuche recipe, step 1.
2. In a 1-quart (small recipe) or 2-quart (large recipe) saucepan, combine the sugar, corn syrup, water, and salt.
3. Stir slowly while heating the candy to boiling. When the sugar has all dissolved, stir only occasionally.
4. Boil the candy to a temperature of 261°F (263°F in humid or rainy weather). Remove from heat.
5. With electric mixer, beat the egg white until stiff.
6. Add cream of tartar and vanilla, then gradually pour the hot candy syrup into the beaten white while running the mixer on its fastest speed.
7. Continue beating with the electric mixer until the candy is stiff.
8. Drop onto a cookie sheet using two spoons.

(Small recipe)

1 c	sugar
1/4 c	light corn syrup
1/4 c	water
1/8 tsp	salt
1	egg white
1/8 tsp	cream of tartar
1/2 tsp	vanilla

(Large recipe)

2 c	sugar
1/2 c	light corn syrup
1/2 c	water
1/4 tsp	salt
2	egg whites
1/4 tsp	cream of tartar
1 tsp	vanilla

AMORPHOUS CANDY RECIPES

Almond Toffee

Total Time: 2 hours
Final Temperature: 300°F

(Small recipe)	
1/2 c	butter or margarine
2/3 c	sugar
1-1/2 tsp	light corn syrup
2 Tbsp	water
3/4 c	blanched almonds, chopped
6 oz	milk chocolate

1. Test boiling point of water on thermometer, as described in Penuche recipe, step 1.
2. In a 1-quart (small recipe) or 2-quart (large recipe) saucepan, combine the sugar, corn syrup, and water.
3. Stir while melting the margarine or butter and heating the mixture. After the sugar is dissolved, stir continuously to keep the mixture from burning.
4. Boil the candy to a final temperature of 300°F, being careful not to burn any portion of it.
5. Stir in half the almonds and pour onto a greased or Teflon-lined jelly roll pan. Spread into a layer 1/3" thick.
6. Place in freezer to chill. Meanwhile, melt half the milk chocolate over hot water.
7. Remove toffee from freezer and spread melted chocolate over the surface of the candy. Sprinkle with half the remaining almonds, finely chopped.
8. Chill in freezer until chocolate is firm. Meanwhile, melt remaining milk chocolate. Remove from freezer. Flex pan to loosen candy and turn entire sheet of candy over.
9. Spread melted chocolate over the second side and sprinkle with remaining finely chopped almonds.
10. Chill in freezer until chocolate is hard.
11. With a mallet or a knife handle, break the candy into serving-sized pieces.

(Large recipe)

1 c	butter or margarine
1-1/3 c	sugar
1 Tbsp	light corn syrup
3 Tbsp	water
1-1/2 c	blanched almonds, chopped
1 lb	milk chocolate

Caramels

Total Time: 30 minutes
Final Temperature: 260°F, hard caramels; 250°F, chewy caramels

1. Test boiling point of water on thermometer, as described in Penuche recipe, step 1.
2. In a 1-quart (small recipe) or 2-quart (large recipe) saucepan, combine the sugar, corn syrup, margarine or butter, and cream.
3. Stir while bringing to a boil.
4. Stir occasionally while heating the candy to its final temperature.
5. Grease an 80 square pan.
6. Just before pouring out the candy into the pan, stir in the pecans and vanilla.
7. Score the pieces when the candy is still warm, and actually cut them when it has cooled.

(Small recipe)

1/2 c	sugar
7 Tbsp	light corn syrup
1/4 c	margarine or butter
1/2 c	light cream
1/4 c	pecans, broken (optional)
1/4 tsp	vanilla

(Large recipe)

1 c	sugar
7/8 c	light corn syrup
1/2 c	margarine or butter
1 c	light cream
1/2 c	pecans, broken (optional)
1/2 tsp	vanilla

Taffy

Total Time: 45 minutes
Final Temperature: 265°F

1. Test boiling point of water on thermometer, as described in Penuche recipe, step 1.
2. In a 1-quart (small recipe) or 2-quart (large recipe) saucepan, combine all ingredients except the vanilla.
3. Stir slowly while heating the mixture to a boil. Stir occasionally as the candy is boiled to its final temperature of 265°F.
4. Remove from the heat, stir in the vanilla, and pour onto a large, buttered platter.
5. Allow to cool until the taffy can be handled easily without burning the hands.
6. Grease the hands and begin to pull some of the taffy. Pull it into long strands, double it back, and pull again.
7. Keep repeating this process until the candy is very light in color and a bit porous.
8. Twist into a rope about 3/4" in diameter.
9. Cut into pieces with kitchen shears.

(Small recipe)

1 c	sugar
1/4 c	light corn syrup
1/4 c	water
1/8 tsp	cream of tartar
1/2 tsp	vanilla

(Large recipe)

2 c	sugar
1/2 c	light corn syrup
1/2 c	water
1/4 tsp	cream of tartar
1 tsp	vanilla

Peanut Brittle

Total Time: 30 minutes
Final Temperature: 290°F

1. Test boiling point of water on thermometer, as described in Penuche recipe, step 1.
2. In a 1-quart (small recipe) or 2-quart (large recipe) saucepan, combine the first three ingredients.
3. Stir slowly while heating the solution to 240°F.
4. Add the blanched, unroasted peanuts (and a dash of salt, if desired).
5. Continue boiling the candy to a temperature of 290°F, stirring slowly to keep candy from burning.
6. Remove from the heat and stir in butter or margarine and soda.
7. Pour onto a greased or Teflon-coated jelly roll pan.
8. Flex pan to loosen candy.
9. Break into pieces when cool.

(Small recipe)

1 c	sugar
1/2 c	light corn syrup
1/2 c	water
1 c	unroasted peanuts
1 tsp	butter or margarine
1/8 tsp	baking soda

(Large recipe)

2 c	sugar
1 c	light corn syrup
1 c	water
2 c	unroasted peanuts
2 tsp	butter or margarine
1/4 tsp	baking soda

Evaluation of Laboratory Products—Candies

Recipe	Type of Candy	Flavor	Consistency	Texture
Penuche				
Fudge				
Fondant				
Divinity				
Almond Toffee				
Caramels				
Taffy				
Peanut Brittle				

VOCABULARY

Crystalline   Supersaturated solution

Amorphous   Hygroscopic

Inversion   Acid hydrolysis

Saturated solution   Invert sugar

CHAPTER 6

Starch and Cereal Cookery

Objectives

1. To illustrate two techniques suitable for dispersing **starch** in various products.
2. To observe the changes taking place during **gelatinization** of a starch mixture.
3. To compare the thickening ability of various starches.
4. To evaluate the quality of starch pastes and gels.
5. To demonstrate the effect of sugar and/or acid on starch pastes and gels.
6. To prepare and evaluate selected starch-thickened products.

STARCHES AS THICKENING AGENTS

Mastering starch cookery is not difficult, but it does require some careful attention throughout preparation, from mixing through heating. You can save yourself from the difficulty of lumpy gravy, sauces, and other starch-thickened products if you make the effort to eliminate every single lump before you begin to heat the mixture. The other essential technique is to stir uniformly throughout the mixture while gelatinizing the starch at a rate that prevents lumping without developing a sticky character in the starch product. You will find many recipes that involve gelatinizing starch; the techniques you learn in this chapter will be used throughout your career working with food. You will also find that your knowledge of gelatinization is important in preparing pastas and other cereal products that are high in starch.

KEY CONCEPTS

1. Starches from various sources (tapioca, arrow-root, rice, corn, wheat, flour, and dextrinized or browned flour) exhibit differing thickening ability when they are heated sufficiently in the presence of water to undergo gelatinization.

2. The viscosity, appearance, and strength of starch pastes and gels are altered if acid and/or sugar are present during gelatinization.

3. Starch can be dispersed uniformly prior to gelatinization by (1) mixing thoroughly with fluid fat, (2) mixing with cold liquid, or mixing with a large quantity of dry ingredients.

LABORATORY EXPERIMENT

Thickening Power of Various Starches

1. In a 1-quart saucepan, make a starch slurry by very gradually adding the cold water to the starch while stirring with a wooden spoon.
2. As the slurry gets thinner, the water can be added rapidly with stirring.
3. Heat the starch mixture to boiling while stirring carefully all across the bottom and around the sides of the pan. Use a medium heat.
4. As soon as the mixture comes to a boil in the center of the pan, pour the hot starch paste into a beaker. Observe each of the types of starch paste for viscosity and translucency; fill in the accompanying chart.

| 2 Tbsp | starch (e.g., tapioca, arrow-root, rice) or flour, assigned |
| 1 c | cold water |

Effect of Sugar and Acid on Starch Pastes and Gels

Acid-Containing Paste:

1. Stir the starch and acid together thoroughly.
2. Add the water gradually and cook as above.
3. Pour into beaker and compare with other sauces.

2 Tbsp	cornstarch
2 Tbsp	lemon juice or vinegar
14 Tbsp	water

Sugar-containing Paste:

1. Combine ingredients.
2. Cook as described above.
3. Pour into beaker and compare with other sauces.

2 Tbsp	cornstarch
1/4 c	sugar
1 c	water

Viscosity and Appearance of Selected Starch Pastes and Gels

Starch	Viscosity		Appearance
	Hot	Cold	
Tapioca			
Arrowroot			
Rice			
Corn			
Corn plus sugar			
Corn plus acid			
Flour (wheat)			
Browned flour[1]			

[1]Before adding water, heat flour to medium brown in dry skillet while stirring with wooden spoon.

STARCH-THICKENED SAUCES AND PUDDINGS

Objectives

1. To illustrate the use of starch as a thickening agent in sauces and puddings.
2. To demonstrate the use of fat, dry ingredients, and/or cold liquid to disperse starch uniformly.
3. To identify desired characteristics in starch-thickened products.
4. To identify methods for improving the quality of starch-containing products.

White sauces of varying viscosities are used widely in food preparation. Although the final sauces have somewhat different characteristics, they are all made in the same manner. These sauces and their applications are

- thin sauce—cream soups,
- medium sauce—casseroles and creamed vegetables,
- thick sauce—soufflés, and
- very thick sauce—binding agent to hold ingredients together (croquettes).

Various types of fats may be used to make a white sauce. Margarine and butter add both color and flavor to the sauce. A solid vegetable shortening is a suitable fat to use, and it will not alter the color or flavor. Salad oils are easy to use in white sauces because they are already in liquid form, thus eliminating the need to melt the fat. With the exception of olive oil, salad oils do not greatly influence the color or flavor of the finished sauce.

Preparing a Basic White Sauce

1. Preparation of a smooth white sauce begins with thorough distribution of the flour in melted fat or oil.

2. A smooth slurry is maintained as cold milk (or other liquid) is added slowly (carefully stirring to avoid lumps).

3. After the mixture is entirely smooth, it is heated at a moderate rate until it comes to a boil throughout the sauce. Stirring must be done continually and at a rate sufficiently fast to maintain uniform heat throughout. Stirring needs to cover the entire bottom of the pan and around the sides, because these are the areas that receive the heat first. A wooden spoon that is flat across the end is ideal for this purpose because each stroke covers a considerable surface area when the mixture is stirred.

4. The finished sauce should be the desired viscosity (a thick sauce is pictured), and the texture should be completely smooth. Sometimes the fat will begin to separate from the thick and very thick sauces before cooking is completed. This happens when too much water evaporates from the sauce. To remedy this problem, stir a very small amount of water or milk into the sauce. If the fat is still separated, add a little more liquid. Add just enough liquid to unify the sauce.

White Sauce

Total Time: 5 minutes

1. Melt the margarine or butter. Remove from heat.
2. Carefully stir in the flour so that no uncoated flour remains.
3. Add the salt and gradually add the milk while stirring. The milk should be added slowly enough so that the mixture never is lumpy.
4. When all of the milk has been added, begin to heat the sauce over a medium heat. Stir constantly throughout the cooking period. Be careful to stir all parts of the bottom of the pan and all around the sides. Stir rapidly enough so that no lumps form in the thickening sauce.
5. Heat the sauce to boiling.
6. Use immediately. If sauce must be held, cover tightly.

Thin White Sauce (shown below)

1 Tbsp	margarine (or other fat)
1 Tbsp	flour
1/4 tsp	salt
1 c	milk

Medium White Sauce (shown below)

2 Tbsp	margarine (or other fat)
2 Tbsp	flour
1/4 tsp	salt
1 c	milk

Thick White Sauce

3 Tbsp	margarine (or other fat)
3 Tbsp	flour
1/4 tsp	salt
1 c	milk

Very Thick White Sauce

1/4 c	margarine (or other fat)
1/4 c	flour
1/4 tsp	salt
1 c	milk

White Sauces

Type of Sauce	Consistency	Uses
Thin		
Medium		
Thick		
Very Thick		

STARCH-THICKENED PUDDINGS

Vanilla Cornstarch Pudding

Total Time: 10 minutes

1. Thoroughly mix the cornstarch, sugar, and salt.
2. Slowly add the cold milk while stirring to make a smooth slurry.
3. Gradually add the scalded milk.
4. Heat to boiling while stirring constantly across the bottom and around the sides of the pan.
5. Continue to heat the pudding until a path remains when a spoon is pulled through it (see illustration).
6. If pudding has any raw starch flavor, cover and place over boiling water for 5 minutes.
7. Add vanilla and margarine or butter.
8. Pour into custard cups, cover tightly, and chill.

Figure 6.1
When a cornstarch pudding has thickened sufficiently, a spoon drawn through the pudding leaves a path.

(Serves two)

1-1/2 Tbsp	cornstarch
2-2/3 Tbsp	sugar
few grains	salt
1/4 c	milk
3/4 c	scalded milk
1/2 tsp	vanilla
1/2 tsp	margarine or butter

(Serves four)

3 Tbsp	cornstarch
1/3 c	sugar
dash	salt
1/2 c	milk
1-1/2 c	scalded milk
1 tsp	vanilla
1 tsp	margarine or butter

Caramel Pudding

Total Time: 15 minutes

1. Melt the sugar and caramelize it to a medium brown in a small frying pan, stirring it constantly with a wooden spoon.
2. Using a hot pad, carry the frying pan to the sink (being careful not to touch countertops).
3. Immediately add the water.
4. In a 1-quart saucepan, thoroughly mix the cornstarch, sugar, and salt.
5. Gradually stir in the cold milk.
6. Slowly add the scalded milk and caramelized sugar syrup.
7. Heat over medium heat while constantly stirring across the bottom and around the sides of the pan. Bring to a boil and continue cooking until the spoon leaves a path through the pudding. If starchy taste remains, heat over hot water for 5 minutes.
8. Stir in the vanilla and margarine or butter.
9. Pour into custard cups, cover tightly, and chill.

(Serves two)

2 Tbsp	sugar (to caramelize)
3 Tbsp	boiling water
1-1/2 Tbsp	cornstarch
2 Tbsp	sugar
few grains	salt
1/4 c	milk
3/4 c	scalded milk
1/2 tsp	margarine or butter
1/2 tsp	vanilla

(Serves four)

1/4 c	sugar (to caramelize)
1/3 c	boiling water
3 Tbsp	cornstarch
1/4 c	sugar
dash	salt
1/2 c	milk
1-1/2 c	scalded milk
1 tsp	margarine or butter
1 tsp	vanilla

Figure 6.2
A chilled cornstarch pudding sags just a little, but does not collapse or flow if it is unmolded.

Chocolate Cornstarch Pudding

Total Time: 10 minutes

1. Melt the chocolate in the milk as it is being scalded.
2. While the milk is being heated, stir the dry ingredients together.
3. Gradually stir in the cold milk to make a smooth slurry.
4. Add the scalded milk and chocolate.
5. Heat over direct heat, stirring constantly, until mixture boils and a spoon leaves a path in the pudding. If pudding tastes starchy, place over hot water for 5 minutes.
6. Stir in the vanilla and margarine or butter.
7. Pour into custard cups, cover tightly, and chill before serving.

(Serves two)

1-1/3 Tbsp	cornstarch
1/4 c	sugar
few grains	salt
1/4 c	milk
1 oz	(1 square) unsweetened chocolate
3/4 c	scalded milk
1/2 tsp	vanilla
1/2 tsp	margarine or butter

(Serves four)

2-2/3 Tbsp	cornstarch
1/2 c	sugar
dash	salt
1/2 c	milk
2 oz	(2 squares) unsweetened chocolate
1-1/2 c	scalded milk
1 tsp	vanilla
1 tsp	margarine or butter

Orange Tapioca Pudding

Total Time: 25 minutes

1. In a 1-quart saucepan, mix the sugar and tapioca together.
2. Add the salt and orange juice.
3. Let stand 5 minutes to rehydrate the tapioca.
4. Heat to a boil, stirring slowly throughout the mixture.
5. Cover and let the pudding cool 20 minutes.
6. Stir and pour into sherbet glasses to serve.

(Serves two)

1/4 c	sugar
2 Tbsp	quick-cooking tapioca
1-1/4 c	orange juice
	few grains salt

(Serves four)

1/2 c	sugar
1/4 c	quick-cooking tapioca
2-1/2 c	orange juice
	dash salt

Rice Pudding

Total Time: 1 hour and 10 minutes

1. Scald the milk in the top part of a double boiler.
2. When the milk is scalding hot, add the uncooked rice (parboiled is recommended type), sugar, salt, cinnamon, and nutmeg.
3. Place over boiling water and cook until a grain of rice rubbed between the fingers is tender (about 1 hour).
4. Stir occasionally. Keep pan covered when not stirring.
5. During the last 10 minutes of cooking, stir in the raisins and lemon rind.

(Serves two)

1/4 c	uncooked rice
2-1/2 Tbsp	sugar
1/8 tsp	salt
1/8 tsp	cinnamon
1/8 tsp	nutmeg
1-1/4 c	nonfat milk
1/4 c	seedless raisins
1/2 tsp	grated lemon rind

(Serves four)

1/2 c	**uncooked rice**
1/3 c	sugar
1/4 tsp	salt
1/4 tsp	cinnamon
1/4 tsp	nutmeg
2-1/2 c	nonfat milk
1/2 c	seedless raisins
1 tsp	grated lemon rind

Note: Serve warm. A stirred custard adds nutritive value and taste appeal to this simple dessert.

Puddings

Type of Pudding	Appearance	Flavor	Mouth Feel	Consistency
Vanilla cornstarch				
Chocolate cornstarch				
Caramel cornstarch				
Orange tapioca				
Rice				

CEREALS AND PASTAS

Objectives

1. To observe how the processing of cereals influences preparation procedures and cooking times.
2. To compare the physical characteristics and nutritive value of different varieties and types of cooked rices (short grain, long grain, brown, polished, parboiled, minute, and wild rices).
3. To prepare and evaluate the quality of selected pastas.

Cereals are cooked to accomplish two purposes: gelatinize the starch and soften the cellulose. Both of these are achieved by boiling the cereal in water. The amount of water and the cooking time required vary with the type of cereal and the previous treatment of the grain.

To prepare the cooked cereals and pastas, bring the suggested amount of salted water (1 teaspoon salt/quart of water) to a *boil*. Sprinkle the cereal or pasta directly into the boiling water. Granular cereals (cornmeal, farina, cream of wheat) need to be mixed with some cold water before being added to the boiling water if lumps are to be avoided. Specific directions are given in the chart. Stir the product occasionally to keep it from sticking to the bottom of the pan. Cereals are done when thickened and free of a starchy flavor. Pastas are done when just cooked to the point when they can be cut easily, and they no longer have a starchy flavor.

Chart of Cereal Cookery[1]

Type of Cereal	Cups of Water/ Cup of Cereal	Boiling Time (minutes)	Method of Preparing
Granular			
Cream of wheat	5	15	Slurry with cold water. Stir into boiling water.
Quick cream of wheat	5	5	Same as regular cream of wheat.
Cornmeal	4-1/2	5	Same as regular cream of wheat.
Flaked			
Oatmeal	3	5	Sprinkle on boiling water.
Whole			
Polished rice, long or short	2-3/4	20	Sprinkle on boiling water.
Parboiled rice	2-1/2	20	Sprinkle on boiling water.
Basmati rice	1-3/4	20	Add to cold water.
Instant and minute rice	1	—	Add to boiling water.
Brown rice	2-1/2	40	Sprinkle on boiling water.
Minute brown rice	1-1/2	15	Sprinkle on boiling water.
Wild rice	3	60	Sprinkle on boiling water.

[1]Add 1 teaspoon salt to each quart of water.

Chart of Pasta Cookery[1]

Type of Pasta	Quarts of Water/Lb of Pasta	Cooking Time (minutes)[2]
Egg noodles	4	10–15
Macaroni	4	15–20
Spaghetti	6	15–20
Vermicelli	6	8–10

[1]Add 1 teaspoon salt to each quart of water.
[2]Boil just until *al dente* (yielding to gentle pressure).

RECIPES

Penne with Tomatoes, Zucchini, and Basil

Total Time: 20 minutes

1. Boil penne according to package directions. Drain thoroughly.
2. Meanwhile, sauté garlic, zucchini, and tomatoes 2 minutes in the oil.
3. Stir in chopped basil leaves and seasonings.
4. Toss penne with vegetables and top with grated Romano cheese.

(Serves two)

1 c	uncooked penne (or other pasta)
1	garlic clove, peeled and minced
1	yellow zucchini, sliced 1/4" thick
2	Roma tomatoes, seeded and chopped coarsely
1 Tbsp	shredded basil leaves (or pesto)
1/2 tsp	lemon zest
	salt and coarsely ground black pepper to taste
	grated Romano cheese

(Serves four)

2 c	uncooked penne (or other pasta)
2	garlic cloves, peeled and minced
2	yellow zucchini, sliced 1/4" thick
4	Roma tomatoes, seeded and chopped coarsely
2 Tbsp	shredded basil leaves (or pesto)
1 tsp	lemon zest
	salt and coarsely ground black pepper to taste
	grated Romano cheese

Pesto

Total Time: 15 minutes

1. Combine piñon nuts, basil leaves, garlic, and cheeses in a blender. Purée until well blended, stopping occasionally to scrape down with rubber spatula.
2. Slowly add olive oil while continuing to purée.
3. Add pepper to taste and purée until smooth.

(Makes about 1 cup)

1/4 c	piñon nuts
2 c	basil leaves
2	cloves garlic (peeled)
1/2 c	grated Parmesan cheese
2 Tbsp	grated Romano cheese
1/2 c	olive oil
	black pepper, to taste

Note: Pasta fans may wish to make their own pesto, which can be stored in the refrigerator (covered with a layer of olive oil) for up to a month.

Angel Hair Medley

Total Time: 20 minutes

1. Microwave bacon until crisp, covering with paper towel to block spattering. Blot bacon with paper towel, then crumble.
2. Boil angel hair pasta according to package directions. Drain well.
3. Meanwhile, sauté onions and garlic in olive oil until golden brown. Remove and discard garlic.
4. Add dried tomatoes, green pepper, red chili flakes, and half-and-half. Simmer (with some stirring) until heated and desired consistency is reached.
5. Toss sauce with pasta and serve topped with Romano cheese.

(Serves two)

3	slices bacon
1/4 lb	angel hair pasta
2	green onions, sliced thinly
1	garlic clove, crushed
1 Tbsp	olive oil
2 tsp	chopped sun-dried tomato
2 Tbsp	chopped green pepper
1/4 tsp	red chili flakes
1/2 c	half-and-half
	grated Romano cheese

(Serves four)

6	slices bacon
1/2 lb	angel hair pasta
4	green onions, sliced thinly
2	garlic cloves, crushed
2 Tbsp	olive oil
4 tsp	chopped sun-dried tomato
1/4 c	chopped green pepper
1/2 tsp	red chili flakes
1 c	half-and-half
	grated Romano cheese

Wild Rice Casserole

Total Time: 1-1/2 hours
Baking: 375°F for 30 minutes

1. Preheat oven.
2. Gently boil wild rice until tender. Drain.
3. Meanwhile, simmer onions, raisins, mushrooms, carrots, and thyme in chicken bouillon 7 minutes.
4. Stir the vegetables into the wild rice and add enough liquid to moisten the wild rice.
5. Place in casserole dish. Bake at 375°F for 30 minutes.

(Serves two)

1/2 c	wild rice
1 c	water
1/2 c	chopped onions
1/4 c	raisins
3	mushrooms, sliced
1/4 c	carrots, thinly sliced
3/4 tsp	dried thyme
1/2	chicken bouillon cube in 1/2 c water

(Serves four)

1 c	wild rice
2 c	water
1 c	chopped onions
1/2 c	raisins
6	mushrooms, sliced
1/2 c	carrots, thinly sliced
1-1/2 tsp	dried thyme
1	chicken bouillon cube in 1 c water

Noble Noodles

Total Time: 25 minutes

1. Remove skin and bone from chicken and cut into bite-sized pieces.
2. Wash and slice green onions and mushrooms in thin slices.
3. Microwave peppers and broccoli (in a covered dish containing a tablespoon of water) for 2 minutes.
4. Boil noodles according to package directions just to *al dente* stage. Drain well.
5. In a wok or skillet, stir-fry chicken, green onions, and mushrooms in oil olive just until chicken is done. Add the other vegetables and noodles and the seasonings. Stir to blend and continue heating to serving temperature.

(Serves two)

2	chicken breast halves
2	green onions and tops
3	mushrooms
1/2	green pepper, chopped
1/2	red pepper, chopped
1 c	small flowerets of broccoli
1/4 lb	wide noodles
2 Tbsp	olive oil
1/8 tsp	garlic powder
1 tsp	pinch of herbs (basil, rosemary, thyme, oregano, sesame seeds)
1/4 tsp	salt
1/8 tsp	Paprika

(Serves four)

4	chicken breast halves
4	green onions and tops
6	mushrooms
1	green pepper, chopped
1	red pepper, chopped
2 c	small flowerets of broccoli
1/2 lb	wide noodles
3 Tbsp	olive oil
1/4 tsp	garlic powder
2 tsp	pinch of herbs (basil, rosemary, thyme, oregano, sesame seeds)
1/2 tsp	salt
1/4 tsp	Paprika

Pasta Salad

Total Time: 1 hour

1. Cook pasta according to package directions and drain well.
2. Add other ingredients to pasta and blend thoroughly.
3. Chill at least 45 minutes to blend flavors.

(Serves two)

3/4 c	uncooked fusilli (or other pasta)
1 Tbsp	chopped stuffed olives
1/4 c	marinated artichoke hearts
1 Tbsp	green pepper, chopped
1 Tbsp	green onions and tops, chopped
1 Tbsp	parsley, chopped
1/4 tsp	grated lemon rind
1/8 tsp	garlic powder
1/8 tsp	paprika
1-1/2 Tbsp	Italian dressing

(Serves four)

1-1/2 c	uncooked fusilli (or other pasta)
2 Tbsp	chopped stuffed olives
1/2 c	marinated artichoke hearts
2 Tbsp	green pepper, chopped
2 Tbsp	green onions and tops, chopped
2 Tbsp	parsley, chopped
1/2 tsp	grated lemon rind
1/4 tsp	garlic powder
1/4 tsp	paprika
3 Tbsp	Italian dressing

Figure 6.3
Pasta salads can be varied by adding ingredients that provide color, flavor, and textural contrasts.

Dolmas (Stuffed Grape Leaves)

Total Time: 50 minutes
Baking: 325°F for 30 minutes

1. Preheat oven.
2. Brown lamb, onion, and garlic in oil.
3. Stir in tomato sauce, parsley, uncooked rice, salt, and pepper. Simmer 3 minutes.
4. Stir in piñon nuts and currants.
5. Dip grape leaves in hot water to separate before blotting on paper towel and placing shiny side down on cutting board.
6. Put 1 tablespoon of meat mixture near stem end, fold in sides loosely, and roll up loosely to allow rice to expand.
7. Place in oiled, shallow casserole. Weight down rolls with ovenproof plate.
8. Pour boiling water and lemon juice over rolls and cover with foil.
9. Bake at 325°F for 30 minutes. May be served warm or cold.

(Serves two)

2 oz	ground lamb
1/2	medium onion, chopped
1/2	clove garlic, minced
1-1/2 tsp	olive oil
3 Tbsp	tomato sauce
1 Tbsp	parsley, minced
2 Tbsp	long grain rice
	salt and pepper to taste
1 Tbsp	piñon nuts
1 Tbsp	currants
6	preserved grape leaves
1/2 c	boiling water
1-1/2 tsp	lemon juice

(Serves four)

4 oz	ground lamb
1	medium onion, chopped
1	clove garlic, minced
1 Tbsp	olive oil
6 Tbsp	tomato sauce
2 Tbsp	parsley, minced
1/4 c	long grain rice
	salt and pepper to taste
2 Tbsp	piñon nuts
2 Tbsp	currants
12	preserved grape leaves
1 c	boiling water
1 Tbsp	lemon juice

Cracked Wheat Stuffing

Total Time: 20 minutes
Baking: 325°F for 15 minutes

1. Preheat oven.
2. Sauté cracked wheat, onion, and celery in butter.
3. Add salt, pepper, thyme, sage, bouillon cube, raisins, and water.
4. Stir together before baking in 325°F oven for 15 minutes.
5. Stir in nuts.

(Serves two)

1/2 c	cracked wheat
2 Tbsp	chopped onion
2 Tbsp	chopped celery
1 1/2 tsp	butter or margarine
1/8 tsp	salt
	pepper
1/8 tsp	dried thyme
1/8 tsp	sage
1/2	chicken bouillon cube
1/2 c	hot water
2 Tbsp	raisins
2 Tbsp	coarsely chopped walnuts

(Serves four)

1 c	cracked wheat
1/4 c	chopped onion
1/4 c	chopped celery
1 Tbsp	butter or margarine
1/4 tsp	salt
	pepper
1/4 tsp	dried thyme
1/4 tsp	sage
1	chicken bouillon cube
1 c	hot water
1/4 c	raisins
1/4 c	coarsely chopped walnuts

Note: This can be served as a side dish or used as a stuffing for pork chops or Cornish hens.

Evaluation of Laboratory Products—Pastas and Cereals

Recipe	Notes on Color, Texture, Flavor, or Other Qualities	Comments or Suggestions for Making or Using this Product in the Future

VOCABULARY

Slurry	Amylose
Gelatinization	Amylopectin
Dextrinization	Dextrins
Acid hydrolysis	Starch
Syneresis	Endosperm
Starch paste	Bran
Retrogradation	Germ (embryo)
Starch granule	Polysaccharide

CHAPTER 7

Milk and Cheese

Key Concepts
Types of Milk
Recipes

Natural and Process Cheeses
Recipes
Vocabulary

This chapter moves from a focus on carbohydrates and their behaviors during food preparation to quite a different type of food material—protein. Although milk does contain a carbohydrate (lactose) that influences the tendency of milk to scorch when being heated, the milk proteins have unique behavior during cooking. The tendency to boil over because of scum formation and curdling are potential problems in milk cookery. Toughening of cheese and separation of fat when heating cheese products are other results of the high protein content in milk and milk products.

Whenever cooking products containing milk and cheese, remember to keep a careful eye on them and avoid any overheating. The reward will be smooth, highly palatable products. Lack of attention is likely to result in scorching, curdling, and/or tough products, sometimes with fat oozing out. In other words, let the chef beware. The rewards are great—the penalties are dire, including some nasty cleanup problems.

TYPES OF MILK

Objectives

1. To compare the palatability, nutritive value, and cost of various fresh and UHT (ultra high temperature) pasteurized milks available in retail markets.

2. To compare dried milks and canned (evaporated and sweetened condensed) milks with fresh pasteurized milks.

A wide range of fresh and processed milks is available for consumer selection. Fresh, pasteurized milks include whole (usually homogenized), reduced fat (2 percent), low fat or light (1 percent), and nonfat or fat free. Special fluid milks and milk products include sweet acidophilus milk, cultured buttermilk, Lactaid, and yogurt. Imitation milks also are available in some areas. UHT milk is available on store shelves because it has been sterilized and does not require refrigeration until the consumer opens the package. Milks often are dried or canned to reduce bulk and promote shelf life. Canned milks commonly available are evaporated whole milk, evaporated low-fat milk, evaporated nonfat milk, and sweetened condensed milk. Dried milk products (nonfat, low-fat, and whole) are also found in the markets.

To observe and compare the various milks, arrange a display of samples of (1) packages, (2) the milks as contained in the packages, and (3) the milks ready to serve (reconstitute, as necessary, according to package directions). Record the results in the chart.

KEY CONCEPTS

1. Milk contains proteins, which denature and coagulate during heating. Excessive heating causes tightening of the protein coagulum, causing considerable toughening of cheese exposed to very intense heat.

2. Milk proteins coagulate most readily when added acid brings milk closer to the isoelectric point of casein, a major protein.

3. Acids and salts promote the coagulation needed for curd formation in cheese making, but may cause undesirable curdling in smooth product in such items as cream soups.

Comparison of Milk Products

Type of Milk	Palatability Flavor	Color	Viscosity	Nutritive Value/Cup Protein (Grams)	Fat (Grams)	Cost/Qt
Fluid milks						
Whole (homogenized)						
2 percent						
1 percent						
Fat free						
UHT						
Canned milks						
Evaporated						
Evaporated nonfat						
Sweetened condensed						
Dried milks						
Whole						
Low-fat						
Nonfat						

Effect of Added Ingredients

Acid:

1. To each of the milks (reconstituted, where appropriate), add the vinegar.
2. Stir and observe changes in texture and viscosity.
3. Explain the change.

| 2 tbsp | Vinegar |
| 1/2 c | milk |

| 1/4 c | cubed ham |
| 1/4 c | milk |

Salts:

1. Place the cubes of ham in a custard cup, and add 1/4 cup milk.
2. Pour 1/4 cup milk into a second custard cup.
3. Bake both for 1 hour at 350°F. Compare the texture of the sauce in each. What caused the difference?

Objectives

1. To demonstrate the use of thin white sauces as the base for cream soups.
2. To demonstrate a procedure for minimizing curdling when acid is used with milk.
3. To evaluate the quality of cream soups.

RECIPES

Cream of Vegetable Soup

Total Time: 15 minutes

1. In a 1-quart saucepan, combine the oil and flour.
2. Add the salt.
3. Gradually stir in the milk.
4. Heat to boiling, stirring constantly.
5. Add the puréed vegetable.
6. Reheat, if necessary, before serving.

(Serves two)

1/2 c	puréed, cooked vegetable
1-1/2 Tbsp	salad oil
1-1/2 Tbsp	flour
1/4 tsp	salt
1-1/2 c	milk

(Serves four)

1 c	puréed, cooked vegetable
3 Tbsp	salad oil
3 Tbsp	flour
1/2 tsp	salt
3 c	milk

Note: Appropriate puréed fresh or frozen vegetables include spinach, broccoli, onions, celery, and asparagus. For greater variety of texture, vegetables may be chopped, rather than puréed.

Cream of Tomato Soup

Total Time: 15 minutes

1. Simmer the tomatoes and seasonings in a 1-quart covered saucepan for 8 to 10 minutes.
2. Remove bay leaf. Purée tomatoes in blender. Set aside.
3. In a 1-quart saucepan, carefully stir the oil and flour together.
4. Slowly add the milk while stirring.
5. Heat to boiling, stirring constantly.
6. Remove from the heat.
7. Add the strained tomato mixture to the hot white sauce while stirring constantly.
8. If necessary, reheat to serving temperature and serve immediately. Avoid prolonged heating.

Figure 7.1
Vegetables in cream soups can be puréed or chopped to add textural contrast.

(Serves two)

1-1/4 c	canned tomatoes
1	sliced onion
	piece bay leaf
1/4 tsp	salt
dash	white pepper
	few grains garlic powder
1 Tbsp	salad oil
1 Tbsp	flour
1 c	milk

(Serves four)

2-1/2 c	canned tomatoes
2	sliced onions
	piece bay leaf
1/2 tsp	salt
dash	white pepper
	few grains garlic powder
2 Tbsp	salad oil
2 Tbsp	flour
2 c	milk

Cream of Mushroom Soup

Total Time: 15 minutes

1. In a 1-quart saucepan, sauté thinly sliced mushrooms in margarine or butter until mushrooms become slightly translucent. Remove from heat.
2. Stir flour into margarine and mushrooms.
3. Gradually stir in milk and water.
4. Add bouillon and nutmeg.
5. Heat to a boil, stirring constantly.
6. Serve immediately.

(Serves two)

5	fresh mushrooms
1-1/2 Tbsp	margarine or butter
1-1/2 Tbsp	flour
3/4 c	milk
3/4 c	water
1	cube beef bouillon
	dash nutmeg

(Serves four)

10	fresh mushrooms
3 Tbsp	margarine or butter
3 Tbsp	flour
1-1/2 c	milk
1-1/2 c	water
2	cubes beef bouillon
1/8 tsp	nutmeg

Cream of Potato Soup

Total Time: 15 minutes

1. In a 1-quart saucepan, blend the oil and flour.
2. Add the cooked potatoes.
3. Slowly stir in the milk.
4. Add the other ingredients.
5. Heat to boiling while stirring constantly.
6. Serve immediately.

(Serves two)

3/4 c	boiled potatoes, diced
1 Tbsp	salad oil
1/2 tsp	flour
1-1/4 c	milk
1/4 tsp	salt
1 tsp	chopped pimiento

(Serves four)

1-1/2 c	boiled potatoes, diced
2 Tbsp	salad oil
1 tsp	flour
2-1/2 c	milk
1/2 tsp	salt
2 tsp	chopped pimiento

Lemon Cucumber Yogurt Soup

Total Time: 1 hour

1. Combine chicken broth, onion, salt, dill weed, garlic powder, lemon peel, and juice in an electric blender. Blend until smooth.
2. Combine yogurt and sour cream. Add to blender, whirling a few seconds until just blended.
3. Add chopped cucumber; quickly turn blender on and off just to combine. Cucumber will be finely grated but not liquefied.
4. Chill thoroughly (about 50 minutes).
5. Serve in chilled bowls. Garnish with lemon and cucumber slices.

(Serves two)

1/3 c	chicken broth
1-1/2 tsp	finely chopped onion
1/4 tsp	salt
1/4 tsp	dill weed, crushed
few grains	garlic powder
1/2 tsp	grated lemon peel
1 Tbsp	lemon juice
1/3 c	plain yogurt
1/3 c	dairy sour cream
1	small cucumbers, peeled, seeded, and chopped
	lemon and cucumber slices

(Serves four)

2/3 c	chicken broth
1 Tbsp	finely chopped onion
1/2 tsp	salt
1/2 tsp	dill weed, crushed
few grains	garlic powder
1 tsp	grated lemon peel
2 Tbsp	lemon juice
2/3 c	plain yogurt
2/3 c	dairy sour cream
2	small cucumbers, peeled, seeded, and chopped
	lemon and cucumber slices

Baked Custard Espresso

Total Time: 55 minutes
Baking: 325°F for 50 minutes

1. Preheat oven.
2. Scald milk and espresso.
3. Add sugar.
4. Combine egg, salt, vanilla, and sugar.
5. Add scalded milk slowly with stirring.
6. Pour into custard cups and arrange in baking pan. Pour boiling water into the large pan halfway up the depth of the custards.
7. Bake at 325°F until a knife can be inserted halfway between the center and the edge of a custard and come out clean.

(Serves two)

1 c	milk
1-1/2 Tbsp	instant espresso
1	egg, beaten
2 Tbsp	sugar
dash	of salt
1/2 tsp	vanilla

(Serves four)

2 c	milk
3 Tbsp	instant espresso
2	eggs, beaten
1/4 c	sugar
1/8 tsp	salt
1 tsp	vanilla

Lime Pie Classic

Total Time: 55 minutes
Baking: 350°F for 10 minutes; 325°F for 30 minutes

1. Preheat oven.
2. Mix graham cracker crumbs, melted butter or margarine, and sugar together, and press into 8"pie plate to form a crust.
3. Bake at 350°F for 10 minutes.
4. Meanwhile, combine egg yolks, milk, lime juice, and enough green food coloring to tint mixture a delicate green.
5. Pour filling into baked pie shell and return to oven that has been reset to 325°F.
6. Bake 20 minutes while preparing the egg white meringue.
7. Make meringue by beating whites with an electric mixer until foamy. Continue to beat while adding cream of tartar, then gradually add the sugar. Beat until tips just bend over when tested with a spatula.
8. Remove pie from oven and spread meringue on pie. Return to oven and bake until meringue is a pleasing golden brown color on its higher surfaces.

(Makes 18" pie)

Crust:

1-1/4 c	graham cracker crumbs
1/4 c	butter or margarine, melted
2 Tbsp	sugar

Filling:

3	egg yolks
1	14-oz can sweetened condensed milk
1/2 c	lime juice
	green food coloring

Meringue:

3	egg whites
1/4 tsp	cream of tartar
6 Tbsp	sugar

NATURAL AND PROCESS CHEESES

Objectives

1. To demonstrate the differences between natural and process cheeses.
2. To illustrate ways of maintaining high quality when preparing hot dishes using cheeses.

Prepare a display of assorted natural and process cheese. Include a range of flavors and firmness. Note the flavor and texture characteristics of each.

Heat 1/2 cup grated cheddar cheese in a double boiler over boiling water for 30 minutes. Do the same with 1/2 cup process cheese. Compare the results.

Comparison of Cheese Products

Type of Cheese	Texture	Flavor	Comments
Natural cheese			
Process cheese			
Cheddar heated 30 minutes			
Process heated 30 minutes			

RECIPES

Ham Strata

*Total Time: 20 minutes to prepare; refrigeration
3 hours to overnight; 30 to 50 minutes for baking
Baking: 325°F for 30 minutes for small (50 minutes
for large)*

1. Preheat oven.
2. Grease a loaf pan for small or 13 × 9″ baking pan for large recipe.
3. Arrange half of bread on bottom of baking dish; distribute ham, cheese, and shallots evenly over the bread. Place remaining bread on top of the ham/cheese layer.
4. Beat eggs in a bowl; then beat in milk and pepper.
5. Pour egg mixture over bread, cover, and refrigerate for at least 3 hours (overnight is satisfactory).
6. Uncover and bake at 325°F until a knife inserted near center comes out clean. The surface should be golden brown and puffy.

(Serves two)

4	slices bread (crusts trimmed)
1/4 c	chopped ham
1/2 c	shredded sharp cheddar cheese
2 tsp	minced shallots
2	eggs
1 c	milk
	ground black pepper

(Serves four)

8	slices bread (crusts trimmed)
1/2 c	chopped ham
1 c	shredded sharp cheddar cheese
4 tsp	minced shallots
4	eggs
2 c	milk
	ground black pepper

Cheese Rarebit

Total Time: 15 minutes

1. Fry the bacon until crisp. Drain on paper towels.
2. Melt the margarine or butter and combine with flour in a 1-quart saucepan.
3. Add the salt.
4. Gradually stir in the milk.
5. Heat to boiling, stirring constantly.
6. Remove from heat.
7. Stir in cheese and seasonings until cheese is melted. If necessary, place over low heat to completely melt the cheese.
8. Serve at once over toasted English muffin.
9. Garnish with crisp bacon strips.

Figure 7.2
Cheese rarebit garnished with tomato and fresh basil is an appealing, flavorful dish.

(Serves two)

4	slices bacon (optional)
1 Tbsp	margarine or butter
1 Tbsp	flour
dash	salt
1/2 c	milk
1/2 c (2 oz)	grated sharp cheddar cheese
1/4 tsp	dry mustard
dash	paprika
2	English muffins, toasted

(Serves four)

8	slices bacon (optional)
2 Tbsp	margarine or butter
2 Tbsp	flour
1/8 tsp	salt
1 c	milk
1 c (4 oz)	grated sharp cheddar cheese
1/2 tsp	dry mustard
1/8 tsp	paprika
4	English muffins, toasted

Cheese Sticks

Total Time: 25 minutes
Baking: 400°F oven for 15 minutes

1. Preheat oven.
2. Cut the shortening into the flour and salt until shortening is the size of split peas.
3. Stir in the cheese and seeds.
4. While tossing the mixture with a fork, gradually add the water.
5. Mix until the dough holds together.
6. Roll into a rectangle about 1/4″ thick.
7. Cut into strips about 3″ long and 1/3″ wide.
8. Bake at 400°F about 12 minutes until golden brown.

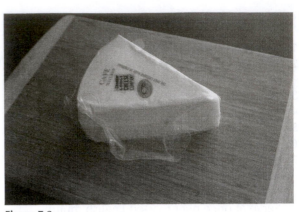

Figure 7.3
Most cheddar cheese is made and aged elsewhere, but this wedge actually was made in Cheddar, England.

(Serves two)

2-2/3 Tbsp	shortening
1/2 c	flour
1/4 tsp	salt
1/4 c	grated sharp cheddar cheese
1 tsp	sesame seeds
1-1/3 Tbsp	water

(Serves four)

1/3 c	shortening
1 c	flour
1/2 tsp	salt
1/2 c	grated sharp cheddar cheese
2 tsp	sesame seeds
2-2/3 Tbsp	water

Quiche Lorraine

Total Time: 55 minutes
Baking: 425°F for 10 minutes; 375°F for 25 minutes

1. Preheat oven.
2. Mix flour and salt.
3. Cut in shortening to the size of rice grains.
4. Slowly add the water while tossing the flour mixture with a fork.
5. Mix the dough into a ball.
6. Divide small recipe into 2 balls and large recipe into 4.
7. Roll out each ball into a circle large enough to fit a tart pan.
8. Fit in pan and make edging. Prick holes with a fork around the side and bottom.
9. Bake at 425°F until lightly browned. Remove from oven and reduce oven heat to 375°F.
10. While the crusts are baking, fry the bacon crisp, drain well, and crumble it.
11. In a mixing bowl, beat the egg, and add the bacon, onion, sour cream, salt, and grated Swiss cheese.
12. Mix well.
13. Pour the filling into the baked crusts; bake at 375°F 25 minutes, or until a knife inserted halfway between the center and edge of the tart comes out clean.
14. Serve hot.

(Serves four)

2 c	flour
1 tsp	salt
2/3 c	shortening
1/3 c	water
4	strips bacon
1/2 c	onion, chopped
2	eggs
1/2 c	dairy sour cream
1/4 tsp	salt
8 oz	Swiss cheese

Figure 7.4
Quiches can be made with many different fillings; many contain a flavorful ripened cheese. The lattice crust adds interest (but also calories).

(Serves two)

1 c	flour
1/2 tsp	salt
1/3 c	shortening
2-2/3 Tbsp	water
2	strips bacon
1/4 c	onion, chopped
1	egg
1/4 c	dairy sour cream
1/8 tsp	salt
4 oz	Swiss cheese

Microwave Quiche

Total Time: 50 minutes
Baking: 425°F for 12 to 15 minutes; Microwaving:
9-1/2 minutes on high, 10 minutes on low, 5 minutes
on browning

1. Preheat oven.
2. Prepare pie crust according to steps 1 through 5 on page xxx. Roll crust to fit a 9" ceramic or glass quiche pan or pie plate.
3. Fit crust in the pan, make edging, and prick holes with a fork around the side and bottom.
4. Bake at 425°F until golden brown (12 to 15 minutes).
5. While crust is baking, cook bacon in microwave oven until crisp (about 6 minutes). Crumble crisp bacon.
6. Combine salt, nutmeg, cayenne, and flour in a glass mixing bowl.
7. Add milk and beaten eggs while stirring to prevent lumping. Add green chilies.
8. Heat this milk mixture in microwave oven on high for 3-1/2 minutes, being sure to stir carefully after 1-1/2 minutes and after 2-1/2 minutes.
9. Meanwhile, line the bottom of the crust with half the bacon bits and grated cheese.
10. Pour the egg mixture into the baked crust and garnish with the other half of the bacon and the green onion.
11. Heat on *low* setting in microwave oven for 10 minutes, followed by 5 minutes in the microwave oven with the browning element, turning once.

(Serves four)

2 c	flour
1 tsp	salt
2/3 c	shortening
1/3 c	water
6	slices bacon
1/4 tsp	salt
1/4 tsp	nutmeg
1/8 tsp	cayenne
1-1/2 Tbsp	flour
1	13-oz can **evaporated milk** (undiluted)
4	eggs, slightly beaten
1 Tbsp	canned green chilies, drained, minced
1-1/4 c	grated Swiss cheese
3	small green onions (including the tops), thinly sliced

Cheese Chowder

Total Time: 20 minutes

1. Add the carrots and celery to the water when the water boils; cover the pan.
2. Boil until tender. Set aside.
3. In a saucepan, sauté the onion in the margarine. Remove from the heat.
4. Stir in the flour and salt.
5. Gradually add the milk and water.
6. Add the bouillon cube and heat to boiling while stirring constantly.
7. Add the cooked vegetables, their cooking water, and cheddar cheese to the white sauce.
8. Stir until cheese melts. If necessary, reheat over low heat to completely melt the cheese.
9. Serve with croutons.

(Serves two)

1/4 c	grated carrots
1/4 c	minced celery
1/2 c	water
1 Tbsp	minced onion
1 Tbsp	margarine or butter
1-1/2 Tbsp	flour
1/4 tsp	salt
3/4 c	milk
3/4 c	water
1/2	cube chicken bouillon
3/4 c (3 oz)	grated sharp cheddar cheese croutons

(Serves four)

1/2 c	grated carrots
1/2 c	minced celery
1 c	water
2 Tbsp	minced onion
2 Tbsp	margarine or butter
3 Tbsp	flour
1/2 tsp	salt
1-1/2 c	milk
1-1/2 c	water
1	cube chicken bouillon
1-1/2 c (6 oz)	grated sharp cheddar cheese croutons

Fondue à la Suisse

Total Time: 10 minutes

1. Place the cheese and the dry ingredients in a bag and shake them together vigorously so that the cheese is completely coated with the dry ingredients.
2. Heat the sauterne in a chafing dish or in a saucepan over low heat.
3. When it begins to steam, gradually add the coated cheese.
4. As the cheese melts, add more until all the cheese has been added.
5. Stir in the kirsch and keep warm over a candle.
6. Provide bite-sized bread cubes and long-handled fondue forks for dipping the bread cubes in the hot fondue mixture.

(Serves two)

1-1/2 c (6 oz)	grated Swiss cheese
dash	garlic powder
1 Tbsp	flour
dash	white pepper
1/4 tsp	salt
10 Tbsp	dry sauterne
1 tsp	kirsch
1/4	loaf French bread, cut in bite-sized cubes

(Serves four)

3 c (12 oz)	grated Swiss cheese
dash	garlic powder
2 Tbsp	flour
1/8 tsp	white pepper
1/2 tsp	salt
1-1/4 c	dry sauterne
2 tsp	kirsch
1/2	loaf French bread, cut in bite-sized cubes

Macaroni and Cheese

Total Time: 1 hour
Baking: 350°F oven for 45 minutes

1. Preheat oven.
2. Bring the water to a boil.
3. Add the macaroni and salt, and continue to boil until the macaroni is white and just tender when cut against the side of the pan with a fork.
4. Drain in a colander.
5. In a 1-quart saucepan, melt the margarine or butter. Remove from heat; stir in the flour and salt, and gradually add the milk.
6. Heat to a boil, stirring constantly. Remove from the heat.
7. Place a layer of macaroni in the bottom of a casserole dish.
8. Pour one-third of the white sauce over the macaroni and sprinkle with one-third of the cheese.
9. Repeat with a second layer of the macaroni, white sauce, and cheese.
10. Top with the remaining third of each item.
11. Generously sprinkle buttered bread crumbs over the entire surface of the casserole.
12. Bake at 350°F for 45 minutes or until bubbling hot.

(Serves two)

1 c	uncooked elbow macaroni
1-1/2 qt	water
1-1/2 tsp	salt
3 Tbsp	margarine or butter
3 Tbsp	flour
1/4 tsp	salt
1-1/2 c	milk
4 oz	grated sharp cheddar cheese
1/4 c	buttered bread crumbs

(Serves four)

2 c	uncooked elbow macaroni
3 qt	water
3 tsp	salt
6 Tbsp	margarine or butter
6 Tbsp	flour
1/2 tsp	salt
3 c	milk
8 oz	grated sharp cheddar cheese
1/2 c	buttered bread crumbs

Pizza

Total Time: 45 minutes
Baking: 425°F oven for 25 minutes

1. Preheat oven.
2. Brown the sausage carefully and drain off all the fat. Set aside.
3. Meanwhile, mix the yeast and flour.
4. Stir in the lukewarm water to make a stiff dough.
5. Add a little more flour if the dough is sticky to handle.
6. Knead dough on lightly floured board for 5 minutes.
7. Roll dough into circle to fit pizza pans. (Large recipe makes two pizzas.)
8. Mix the sauce and seasonings and spread over the dough.
9. Sprinkle sausage and all of the remaining ingredients over the tomato sauce.
10. Bake at 425°F 25 minutes or until cheese is bubbly and dough is crisp.

(Serves four)

1/2 lb	Italian sausage
1/2 tsp	active dry yeast
3 c	flour
14 Tbsp	lukewarm water
24 oz	tomato sauce or pizza sauce
1/2 tsp	oregano
1/4 tsp	thyme
1/2 tsp	salt
1/4 tsp	pepper
1/2 c	canned sliced mushrooms
1/2 c	grated Parmesan cheese
1/2 c	sliced black olives
2 c	grated mozzarella cheese

(Serves two)

1/4 lb	Italian sausage
1/4 tsp	active dry yeast
1-1/2 c	flour
7 Tbsp	lukewarm water
12 oz	tomato sauce or pizza sauce
1/4 tsp	oregano
1/8 tsp	thyme
1/4 tsp	salt
1/8 tsp	pepper
1/4 cup	canned sliced mushrooms
1/4 c	grated Parmesan cheese
1/4 c	sliced black olives
1 c	grated mozzarella cheese

Figure 7.5
Pizza toppings may sometimes include pieces of vegetables, meats, and fruits; however, they always are topped with Italian cheeses, usually Parmesan and mozzarella.

Lasagna

Total Time: 1 hour
Baking: 375°F oven for 30 minutes

1. Preheat oven.
2. Brown the sausage and drain off the fat.
3. Add the other ingredients through the tomato paste.
4. Simmer in a covered 1-quart saucepan for 30 minutes, stirring occasionally.
5. Boil noodles in boiling, salted water until just tender.
6. Mix together the ricotta, mozzarella, and Parmesan cheeses, salt, and pepper.
7. In a loaf pan, arrange a layer of noodles topped with a layer of the cheese and the sauce.
8. Repeat the layering until all ingredients are used, ending with the sauce on top.
9. Bake at 375°F for 30 minutes, or until bubbly.
10. Let stand 5 to 10 minutes, cut in squares, and serve.

(Serves two)

1/4 lb	Italian sausage
dash	garlic powder
1/2 tsp	chopped parsley
1/8 tsp	salt
1/2 c	stewed tomatoes
1/4 c	tomato paste
2 oz	lasagna noodles
3/4 c	ricotta cheese (or cottage cheese)
2 Tbsp	grated Parmesan cheese
1/2 tsp	salt
1/8 tsp	pepper
1/4 lb	grated mozzarella cheese

(Serves four)

1/2 lb	Italian sausage
1/8 tsp	garlic powder
1 tsp	chopped parsley
1/4 tsp	salt
1 c	stewed tomatoes
1/2 c	tomato paste
4 oz	lasagna noodles
1-1/2 c	ricotta cheese (or cottage cheese)
1/4 c	grated Parmesan cheese
1 tsp	salt
1/4 tsp	pepper
1/2 lb	grated mozzarella cheese

Microwave Cheesecake

Total Time: 35 minutes
Microwaving: 4 minutes on high, 4 minutes on low

(Serves eight)

1/4 c	margarine or butter
1 c	graham cracker crumbs
2	eggs, well beaten
1	8-oz package cream cheese (softened in microwave oven)
1-1/2 c	dairy sour cream
1/8 tsp	salt
1 tsp	vanilla
1/8 tsp	almond extract
1/2 c	sugar

1. Melt margarine or butter in a 9" pie plate in microwave oven.
2. Add crumbs and mix thoroughly before pressing the crumbs to conform to the plate.
3. Heat 4 minutes in microwave oven on high.
4. Meanwhile, mix remaining ingredients together in a mixing bowl until smooth.
5. Pour into crust and microwave on low setting for 3 minutes.
6. Rotate dish a quarter turn and microwave on low for a minute or more until the filling sets.
7. Chill thoroughly (several hours, if possible).

Note: May be served with a topping or plain.

Evaluation of Laboratory Products—Milk and Cheese

Recipe	Notes on Color, Texture, Flavor, or Other Qualities	Comments or Suggestions for Making or Using this Product in the Future

VOCABULARY

Natural cheese	Curdling
Process cheese	Protein
Ripened cheese	Lactose
Rennin	Pasteurization
Curd	Evaporated milk
Whey	Condensed milk

CHAPTER 8

Egg Cookery

Egg cookery requires subtlety and attention to get the best possible results. In particular, temperature and time need to be controlled so that the proteins in eggs and egg products are heated to just the right end point.

To illustrate the behavior of eggs in food preparation, you will have opportunities in this chapter to prepare eggs in and out of the shell, as well as use them in recipes where they are combined with other ingredients in different ways. Omelets and soufflés demonstrate the dramatic changes that occur as the result of coagulating eggs. Egg white foams play a significant role in soufflés and are the main component of meringues. Custards are used to illustrate the crucial importance of heating egg proteins to just the correct point to achieve optimum thickening.

KEY CONCEPTS

Eggs contain a variety of proteins and these proteins contribute important functions in food preparation.

1. Because of the variety of proteins in the yolks and whites, careful timing and temperature control are essential to preparing eggs alone or in products containing them.

2. Egg white foams are essential in such products as a fluffy omelet or soufflé.

3. Egg white foams gain optimum stability when they have some acid and/or sugar added to them and when they are beaten to the correct end point, but not overbeaten.

4. French omelets are less tender than fluffy omelets because the protein is concentrated and is not distributed throughout the volume provided by the egg white foam in fluffy omelets.

5. Egg yolks bind the fat in the sauce that is a part of a soufflé and help to keep the sauce distributed in the egg white foam during baking.

6. The thickening provided by egg proteins in custards and other mixtures is effective, but considerably less dramatic than the thickening that occurs when starch is the thickening agent.

7. Overheating of egg proteins causes tightening of the proteins, which results in loss of volume in overbaked soufflés and syneresis and porosity in custards and egg-thickened sauces.

RECIPES (IN THE SHELL)

Objectives

1. To prepare and evaluate soft- and hard-cooked eggs.
2. To study egg quality as revealed by evaluation of hard-cooked eggs.

Soft-Cooked Eggs

Total Time: 8 minutes

1. In a covered saucepan, heat enough water to boiling to just cover the eggs when they are added. As soon as the water boils, reduce the heat to low and add eggs using a slotted spoon to dip each egg in and out of the water once

before depositing in the pan. Simmer the eggs for 3 to 4 minutes. Remove from the water, hold very briefly under cold water, and serve.

eggs

Hard-Cooked Eggs

Total Time: 25 minutes

1. Use the same procedure outlined for soft-cooked eggs, but increase the simmering time to 20 minutes. Then remove the eggs and place them under cold,

running water for several minutes to cool them rapidly.

eggs

RECIPES (OUT OF THE SHELL)

Objectives

1. To compare the quality of fried eggs prepared by two methods.
2. To demonstrate the importance of egg quality in poaching eggs.
3. To prepare and evaluate scrambled eggs, noting carefully the criteria for evaluation.

Fried Eggs—Method 1

Total Time: 5 minutes
(Eggs may be fried by two methods. The first method requires a minimum amount of fat.)

2 tsp	eggs margarine or butter salt pepper

1. Melt just enough margarine or butter in the frying pan to cover the bottom of the skillet.
2. Add the eggs gently and cook over low heat.
3. As soon as the white begins to set, add 1 or 2 teaspoons water and quickly cover the pan.
4. Cook just until the whites are coagulated and the yolk is covered with a thin veil of coagulated white.
5. Season with salt and pepper to serve.

Fried Eggs—Method 2

Total Time: 5 minutes
(The other method for frying eggs uses fat in a large enough quantity to spoon the fat over the eggs.)

2 Tbsp	eggs margarine or butter salt pepper

1. Melt butter in the skillet.
2. While the eggs are frying slowly, baste each yolk frequently with the hot butter to coagulate the white covering the surface of the yolk.
3. Cook until the white is coagulated, and the yolk is covered with a thin layer of coagulated white.
4. Season with salt and pepper to serve.

Poached Eggs

Total Time: 8 minutes

eggs toast salt pepper

1. Fill a saucepan with 2 to 3 inches of water and heat to boiling.
2. Remove from the heat, and very carefully slide egg into the pan.
3. Return to heat and maintain water at simmering, but be careful not to boil it.
4. Poach egg until the white is completely coagulated and the yolk is still fluid.
5. Remove egg from water using a slotted spoon.
6. Serve plain or on buttered toast.
7. Season with salt and pepper.

Scrambled Eggs

Total Time: 7 minutes

1. Melt just enough butter or margarine in frying pan to cover the bottom of the pan.
2. In a small bowl, combine the eggs (which have been broken separately into a small custard cup and transferred to the mixing bowl), milk, and seasonings.
3. Beat slowly with a rotary beater to completely blend the yolk and white. Avoid forming a foam on the mixture.
4. Pour into the frying pan and heat over a medium-low heat to coagulate the egg.
5. Stir occasionally with a narrow spatula or wooden spoon so that the eggs will cook in fairly large pieces without becoming the least bit brown.
6. Cook until all portions are coagulated, but still slightly shiny.

Figure 8.1
Scrambled eggs should be somewhat chunky, barely moist on the surface, and free of any white streaks.

(Serves one)	
2	eggs
2 Tbsp	milk
1/8 tsp	salt
	pepper to taste

(Serves two)

4	eggs
1/4 c	milk
1/4 tsp	salt
	pepper to taste

Objectives

1. To compare French omelets with scrambled eggs.
2. To demonstrate the importance of combining speed with good preparation techniques to make fluffy omelets.
3. To demonstrate the differences in texture and stability of egg white foams made with and without sugar.
4. To identify clearly the characteristics of good French and fluffy omelets and to identify the key techniques needed to prepare them.

French Omelet

Total Time: 12 minutes

1. With a rotary beater gently but thoroughly blend all of the ingredients so there are no unblended portions of yolk and white. Avoid developing any foam.
2. Melt enough margarine or butter to just coat the bottom of the skillet and heat until bubbling, but not brown.
3. Add the egg mixture and cook over medium heat.
4. As the egg begins to coagulate, use a narrow spatula to lift up portions of the omelet and let uncoagulated egg run underneath.
5. Continue lifting only as long as there is uncoagulated egg to fill in.
6. When the egg is all coagulated, but still shiny on the surface, check the bottom of the omelet. If it is not a golden brown, turn up the heat briefly to brown it.
7. Fold omelet in half and transfer to serving platter.

(Serves two)

3	eggs
3 Tbsp	water
1/8 tsp	salt
dash	pepper
	margarine or butter

(Serves four)

6	eggs
6 Tbsp	water
1/4 tsp	salt
1/8 tsp	pepper
	margarine or butter

Note: For variety, cheese, crumbled bacon, minced green onion, or chopped black olives and mushrooms may be added before folding the omelet. Cheese sauce or tomato sauce may be used as a topping for the omelet.

Fluffy Omelet

Total Time: 25 minutes
Baking: 325°F oven for 15 minutes

(Serves two)	
2	eggs
2 Tbsp	water
1/8 tsp	salt
1/4 tsp	cream of tartar
1/2 Tbsp	margarine or butter

(Serves four)

4	eggs
4 Tbsp	water
1/4 tsp	salt
1/2 tsp	cream of tartar
1 Tbsp	margarine or butter

1. Preheat oven.
2. Carefully separate eggs individually over a custard cup, being certain that no yolk is permitted to get into the whites.
3. Beat egg yolks until very thick and lemon colored, preferably using an electric mixer.
4. Wash the beaters to remove all traces of yolk.
5. Beat the whites to the foamy stage.
6. Add the salt, **cream of tartar**, and water to the whites, and continue beating until the peaks just fold over.
7. Begin to melt the margarine or butter in a skillet over low heat so that it is bubbling, but not browned, when the folding of the yolk and white foams is completed.
8. Pour all of the yolk foam down the side of the bowl containing the egg white foam.
9. Gently, but efficiently, use a rubber spatula to fold the yolks into the whites. Folding is done by scraping the spatula down the inside of the bowl farthest away from you. Drag spatula clear across the bottom of the bowl and up the side nearest you. Spread the material on the spatula across the surface of the mixture.
10. Turn the bowl a quarter of a turn and repeat the process.
11. Repeat this process four times (the bowl has now made one complete revolution).
12. On the fifth stroke, pull the spatula only halfway across the bottom of the bowl and then cut up through the middle and spread the mixture across the top of the omelet.
13. Continue this five-stroke cycle until the mixture is entirely homogeneous and no layer remains on the bottom of the bowl.
14. Immediately pour the folded mixture into the bubbling, but not browned, margarine.
15. Heat 30 seconds on medium heat.
16. Immediately transfer the omelet (in its pan) to an oven preheated to 325°F.
17. Bake about 15 minutes until a knife inserted in the center of the omelet comes out clean.
18. Fold the omelet in half and transfer to a serving platter.

Note: Serve with a cheese sauce, Spanish sauce, or other sauce suitable for a main dish.

Lemon Fluffy Omelet

Total Time: 25 minutes
Baking: 325°F oven for 15 minutes

1. Preheat oven.
2. Carefully separate the eggs individually over a custard cup.
3. Beat egg yolks until very thick and lemon colored, preferably using an electric mixer.
4. Thoroughly wash the beaters.
5. Beat the whites to the foamy stage.
6. Add the salt, lemon juice, and water.
7. Continue beating while gradually adding the sugar.
8. Beat until the peaks just bend over.
9. The folding and baking steps of this omelet are the same as for the Fluffy Omelet.

(Serves two)

2	eggs
2 tsp	lemon juice
1-1/3 Tbsp	water
2 Tbsp	sugar
1/8 tsp	salt
1/2 Tbsp	margarine or butter

(Serves four)

4	eggs
1-1/3 Tbsp	lemon juice
2-2/3 Tbsp	water
1/4 c	sugar
1/4 tsp	salt
1 Tbsp	margarine or butter

Note: This is a sweet omelet that makes an excellent dessert when served with Lemon Sauce.

Lemon Sauce

Total Time: 5 minutes

1. Mix the sugar and cornstarch together well with a wooden spoon.
2. Gradually stir in the water.
3. Heat to boiling, while stirring constantly.
4. Remove from heat and stir in the lemon juice and rind.
5. Serve warm over hot omelet.

(Serves two)

1/4 c	sugar
1-1/2 tsp	cornstarch
1/2 c	water
2 tsp	lemon juice
1/2 tsp	grated lemon rind

(Serves four)

1/2 c	sugar
1 Tbsp	cornstarch
1 c	water
1-1/3 Tbsp	lemon juice
1 tsp	grated lemon rind

PRINCIPLES OF PREPARING SOUFFLÉS

Objectives

1. To illustrate the use of a thick white sauce in making a soufflé.

2. To develop an appropriate folding technique for incorporating a sauce into an egg white foam.

3. To evaluate soufflés and identify techniques of preparation that promote high quality in the completed product.

Soufflés are egg foam products that combine the principles of starch cookery with the problems of preparing and utilizing a stable foam. The total preparation involves five key steps:

1. Gelatinization of a starch mixture to yield a smooth, thick white sauce.

2. Combination of the hot starch paste with beaten egg yolks.

3. Formation of a stable egg white foam.

4. Incorporation of the sauce into the egg white foam.

5. Baking of the starch–foam mixture.

Cheese Soufflé

1/4 c	margarine or butter
1/4 c	flour
1/8 tsp	salt
1 c	milk
1/4 lb	grated sharp cheddar cheese
4	eggs (separated, one at a time over a custard cup)
1/2 tsp	cream of tartar

For the most efficient preparation of a soufflé, assemble all ingredients before beginning to prepare the product. Cheese soufflé is used in this series to demonstrate the principles of preparing soufflés. The ingredients are shown above. The necessary utensils, including the soufflé dish, should then be assembled. If a soufflé dish slightly smaller than the necessary size is used, an aluminum foil or paper collar about 1-1/2″ high can be fitted onto the inside lip of the dish.

Before beginning preparation of the white sauce, it is important to begin preheating the oven so that the correct oven temperature will be reached before the soufflé is ready to bake. The oven rack positions should be checked to be certain the top rack is just below the center of the oven and then the oven temperature is set at 325°F. This moderately low oven temperature allows time for the heat to penetrate the center of the soufflé before the outer region is overbaked, yet it is sufficiently hot to set the structure before the sauce begins to drain toward the bottom of the foam.

One means of helping to disperse starch uniformly in a starch-containing product is to blend the starch with melted fat or with an oil. The preparation of the sauce for a soufflé begins with melting the solid fat in a heavy saucepan that will distribute the heat uniformly. Heavy aluminum is a suitable pan material for starch cookery. The margarine or butter should be heated just enough to melt it. Browning is to be avoided because of its influence on the flavor and appearance of the finished sauce.

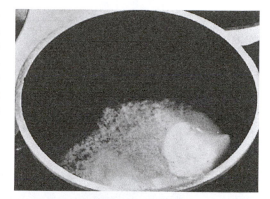

The first ingredients added to the melted margarine or butter are flour and salt. These may be added all at once. A wooden spoon is an excellent choice for stirring these ingredients into the margarine or butter. It is very important to be sure that a smooth paste is formed and that all of the flour is stirred into the margarine. Dry clumps of flour at this point are potential sources of lumps in the finished sauce. The melted margarine or butter is a very effective agent in dispersing the starch granules contained in the flour.

With the pan removed from the heat, cold milk is stirred into the starch–margarine slurry. The milk is added gradually at first with stirring so that the slurry can be thinned smoothly rather than having lumps of thick slurry interspersed with the fluid milk. It is essential that the mixture be perfectly smooth before proceeding to the gelatinization process in the next step. Otherwise, the finished sauce is certain to contain lumps from the dry flour.

As soon as a smooth slurry of the ingredients has been made, the sauce is returned to the heat. As the sauce begins to heat, it is necessary to stir it carefully to ensure uniform heating of all of the starch mixture. A wooden spoon is a very useful utensil because it does not scratch the surfaces of coated pans. It also has the advantage of not becoming hot in the hand during the heating period. Stirring of gelatinizing starch mixtures is an important technique if lump-free sauces are to be made. The starch mixture will be hottest where it comes in contact with the pan. Consequently, continuous stirring is required around the sides of the pan and across the bottom. The heat should be adjusted to a setting that will bring the sauce to a boil in less than 5 minutes, but it should not be so hot that the sauce begins to form lumps or to scorch on the bottom of the pan.

The sauce will be hot all across the bottom as well as around the sides. Good stirring technique will intersperse careful stirring all around the sides with thorough stirring across the bottom of the pan. The technique across the bottom of the pan is comparable to the parallel lines or "push-pull" technique sometimes taught in penmanship. It is very important to be certain that the entire bottom surface is stirred throughout the heating period. A stirring technique featuring a "Figure 8" pattern does not accomplish this, but leaves areas where the mixture will gelatinize unevenly. Unless stirring is done at a moderate rate and throughout the entire mixture, uneven gelatinization will occur and an occasional stirring of an area will simply result in scraping loose gelatinized portions that then become lumps in the finished sauce.

Gelatinization of the sauce will be completed when the entire mixture boils. In a soufflé recipe, this will result in a thick sauce of a sufficient viscosity to leave a very discernible path if the wooden spoon is pulled through the sauce. The viscosity of the sauce is critical to the finished product. Too thin a sauce will tend to drain from the egg white foam before the structure is set, and the soufflé will have a heavy layer in the bottom. Too thick a sauce will not fold well into the egg whites.

Sometimes a sauce may begin to separate at this point, with fat being visible around the edges. This is most likely to occur in the preparation of a chocolate soufflé because of its higher fat content. However, it may happen with any soufflé if the rate of heating the sauce has been extremely slow. Very slow cooking results in excessive evaporation, and the sauce will separate. Although such sauces look very bad, they are remedied easily by stirring in just enough water or milk to reform the smooth sauce. This step must be taken if the sauce separates. Otherwise, fat will continue to ooze from the sauce during the remainder of the soufflé preparation.

When the sauce has reached the correct viscosity, the pan is removed from the heat and the grated cheese is added all at once and stirred into the sauce.

If the sauce is not warm enough to completely melt the cheese, the sauce is returned to a very low heat and stirred slowly as the cheese melts. The cheese must all be melted before proceeding to the next step. Any unmelted cheese at this point will result in pockets of cheese in the finished soufflé. A low heat is used to melt the cheese without causing undue toughening of the protein in the cheese. If the sauce should happen to separate during this process, water or milk should be added as described before. Add only enough liquid to reform the sauce. Excess liquid will make the sauce too thin to remain suspended in the egg white foam.

After the cheese is completely melted and the sauce is of the correct consistency, the pan containing the sauce is set aside, away from the heat. The egg yolks are beaten to mix them thoroughly and to incorporate some air in them. This beating can be done easily with a fork or with an eggbeater. A spoonful of the warm sauce is stirred rapidly into the beaten egg yolks. The sauce must not be in contact with the yolks without stirring because the hot sauce will begin to coagulate the egg yolk protein that it touches, and lumps of unevenly coagulated yolk will be the result.

As soon as the first spoonful of sauce is stirred into the yolks to form a homogeneous mixture, the process is repeated again with another spoonful of the hot sauce. This process is repeated for a total of approximately four cooking spoonfuls of the sauce. Exact measurement of the sauce is not at all important, but efficient stirring as soon as the hot mixture comes in contact with the eggs is essential in this step. This method of combining egg yolk protein with the hot sauce is used as a means of diluting the concentration of the egg yolk protein, thus elevating the coagulation temperature of the protein before the yolks are in contact with a large quantity of the hot sauce.

When approximately 1/4 cup of the hot sauce has been stirred carefully into the yolks to give a smooth and homogenous mixture, the egg yolk–cheese sauce mixture then is ready to be poured back into the main panful of sauce. The yolk–cheese sauce mixture should be poured slowly into the saucepan, and stirring should be done continuously as the yolk mixture is being added. The purpose of this step is to blend the yolks uniformly with the hot mixture and to avoid uneven coagulation of the yolks. When a perfectly homogeneous blending of the yolk–cheese sauce mixture with the white sauce has been completed, the sauce is set aside to wait for the formation of the egg white foam. Note that the entire process of combining the egg yolks with the cheese sauce was done without the addition of any heat. There is no need to coagulate the yolk

proteins at this time. The coagulation will be completed during the baking process.

The egg white foam is a vital part of all soufflés. It is important to be certain that there is absolutely no trace of yolk in the whites or on the beaters that will be used, because any trace of fat will impair formation of the egg white foam. The addition of cream of tartar slows foam formation, making an electric mixer a useful tool.

Cream of tartar is added all at once at the foamy stage. (If a dessert soufflé is being prepared, sugar is added gradually beginning at the foamy stage.) Beating the egg white foam to the correct end point is a critical step in soufflé preparation. The foam should be beaten until the beater can be withdrawn from the mixture to leave peaks that bend over on the end, but that do not fall over. Underbeaten whites will result in a soufflé with smaller volume than optimum and a tougher product. There may also be a tendency toward layering in the bottom. Overbeaten egg whites will not blend readily with the sauce, but will tend to break into chunks. The overfolding that is required to distribute the sauce uniformly will cause a loss of volume in the finished product and consequently a somewhat less tender soufflé. Chunks of egg white are likely to be evident in the baked soufflé if whites are overbeaten.

As soon as the egg whites are beaten to the point where the peaks just bend over, all of the sauce is poured carefully but efficiently down the side of the bowl containing the egg whites. The sauce will collect in the bottom of the bowl with the whites on top. Avoid pouring the sauce on top of the foam because this pushes some of the air out of the foam, and it is the air in the foam that is needed to give maximum volume to the soufflé. All efforts from this point onward are directed toward minimizing the loss of air from the foam. Work should proceed quickly yet gently until the soufflé is in the oven.

Now all of the sauce needs to be folded as efficiently as possible to give a homogenous blending of foam with sauce. A rubber spatula is a useful utensil for efficient folding. Folding is actually a repeating five-step process. The first step is done by running the rubber spatula down the far side of the bowl, scraping across the very bottom of the bowl, dragging the spatula with its load of sauce up the near side of the bowl, and then lightly and gently spreading the sauce across the top of the foam. With a little practice, this folding movement—that is, scraping along the side, across the bottom, up the near side, and across the foam—can be done very efficiently yet gently. The purpose of folding is to bring up the sauce from the bottom of the bowl and distribute it across the foam. The goal is to make a light, completely homogeneous mixture, with no traces of the yellow sauce showing.

When the first folding step has been completed and the sauce spread across the foam, the mixing bowl is rotated one-fourth of a turn or 90°. Then the folding process is repeated by once again scraping the spatula down the far side of the bowl, across the bottom, up the near side, and spreading the sauce across the surface of the foam.

Again, the bowl is rotated 90° and the folding is repeated. The bowl then is rotated another 90° and the folding is repeated. At this point, the folding step has been repeated a total of four times, and the bowl has been rotated 90° before each fold.

After the fourth folding operation, the bowl is rotated 90° to return to its original position. The folding so far has not been involving the center portion of the foam. To incorporate the sauce into the center of the foam, a special folding stroke is done once each time the cycle of four strokes is completed. This special stroke is started in the same way that the other strokes begin; that is, by scraping the spatula carefully down the far side of the bowl. The stroke across the bottom of the bowl proceeds only halfway across. Then the spatula is brought up sideways, bearing its load of sauce through the middle of the foam, and the sauce is spread over the top of the foam.

Following this special stroke, folding again proceeds by scraping down the far side of the bowl and continuing the first folding stroke without rotating the bowl. Then rotation of the bowl continues. Every fifth fold is done by coming up through the middle of the soufflé. Folding needs to be continued just until there is no more sauce remaining on the bottom of the bowl and the soufflé mixture has a homogenous appearance. Overfolding is to be avoided as this merely reduces volume by releasing air from the foam unnecessarily.

As soon as folding has been completed, the soufflé mixture is poured immediately into the dish. The bowl should be held as low as possible and the mixture should be transferred as gently as possible to minimize loss of air from the foam during the transfer. A spatula can be used to expedite the transfer without undue damage to the foam.

When the soufflé has been placed in the baking dish, run a rubber spatula in a circle around the surface of the soufflé at a distance about 1″ to 1-1/2″ from the edge of the dish. This gently breaks the surface of the soufflé and aids in creating a picture-perfect soufflé with an attractive surface when the baked product is served. This circle should be traced very quickly to avoid any delay at this critical point.

The soufflé is placed gently on the top oven rack that has been positioned previously just below the center of the preheated oven. The rack is pushed in, the door is closed, and the time is noted. Most soufflés will need to be baked approximately 55 minutes in a 325°F oven. A timer may be set as a guide to indicate when testing should be done. If possible, the soufflé should be baked in an oven with a window so that the progress of baking can be watched.

There will be very little change in appearance during the initial baking period while the heat is penetrating into the soufflé. The outer region then will begin to rise along the side of the dish, and the surface will begin to brown. As the coagulation temperature of the egg proteins is reached around the edge, the structure will set. However, the inner portion of the soufflé will not yet have reached the coagulation temperature. The air in the soufflé will continue to expand and to stretch the uncoagulated portions. This increase in volume will continue until the protein structure coagulates. It is very important to avoid opening the oven door during the baking process. If cooler air comes in contact with the soufflé, the heated air in the soufflé will be cooled. The result is reduced pressure within the soufflé, and it will begin to fall. Soufflés should not be tested for doneness until the correct amount of time has elapsed because their structure is most delicate just before the protein coagulates.

Prepare for testing the soufflé by having everything set for service of the food. Hot pads and a table knife will be needed for the actual testing. With these items in hand, gently open the oven door and pull the rack out. If the soufflé appears to be shaking considerably, it is not done, and the rack should be returned immediately and the door closed gently. If the soufflé does not shake much, quickly pull out the rack far enough to test the soufflé with the knife. Insert the knife as far as possible vertically in the middle of the soufflé.

Immediately withdraw the knife and check for clinging particles of soufflé. The knife will appear moist, but will not be coated with the soufflé if the soufflé is done. If the soufflé passes this test, serve it immediately. If not, quickly and gently return the soufflé to the oven position and close the door to continue baking. It is important to bake soufflés to the correct degree of doneness. If they are underbaked, they will fall because the protein structure will not be coagulated sufficiently to hold up the weight of the suspended sauce. If the soufflé is baked too long, there will be a shrinking and toughening of the soufflé from the changes in the denatured protein.

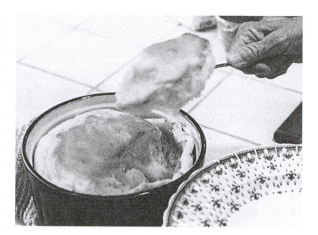

The baked soufflé as it comes from the oven will have its maximum volume. The structure of even a properly baked soufflé is very delicate, and there will be some loss of volume as the cooler air of the room begins to cool the air within the soufflé. The volume then becomes dependent on the strength of the cell walls themselves. A well-prepared soufflé will have a good volume and will also have a pleasingly browned surface. The soufflé should show limited shrinkage when served.

Evaluation of a soufflé requires not only an examination of the total volume achieved and an assessment of the overall external appearance, but it also requires a careful look at the interior cross section of the soufflé. Interior evaluation needs to extend from the upper surface clear to the bottom of the soufflé. In particular, the lower area should be examined for any suggestion of a layer. This layer could be caused by improper beating of the whites, by inadequate folding, by too thin a sauce, or by delayed baking after folding was completed. The cross section should also be reviewed for areas of cheese, which would be caused by failure to melt all of the cheese before adding the yolks. Lumps also should be noted. These might be caused by faulty blending of ingredients in the sauce, by poor stirring techniques while the starch was being gelatinized, or by uneven coagulation of the yolks while the yolks and cheese sauce were being combined.

The other possible problem that can be observed by looking at a cross section of a soufflé is lumps of white. These are caused by overbeating the egg whites. Preparation of a soufflé requires understanding the principles of starch cookery and the formation and use of egg white foams. When attention is paid to the procedures that these require during preparation, a soufflé of high quality can be prepared quickly. A cheese soufflé has been used to demonstrate the principles, but any baked soufflé can be prepared by following these same guidelines.

RECIPES

Cheese Soufflé

Total Time: 65 minutes (small); 75 minutes (large)
Baking: 325°F oven for 45 minutes (small) or
55 minutes (large)

1. Preheat oven.
2. Melt margarine in a 1-quart saucepan.
3. Stir in the flour and salt with a wooden spoon.
4. Gradually stir in the milk to make a slurry.
5. When all the milk is added, return pan to the heat.
6. Stir constantly with wooden spoon while heating to boiling; remove from heat. If fat separates, stir in just enough milk to make a smooth sauce.
7. Add cheese to hot sauce. Heat, if necessary, to melt cheese.
8. While the cheese is melting, beat the egg yolks.
9. Stir a spoonful of the hot sauce into the egg yolks. Be sure to stir immediately to avoid lumps of coagulated egg yolk.
10. Repeat three more times.
11. Then add the egg yolk–cheese sauce mixture back into the remaining sauce while stirring. Cover and set aside.
12. Beat the egg whites to the foamy stage. Add the cream of tartar and continue beating until the peaks just bend over. Be careful to beat to just the right stage.
13. Gently pour the cheese sauce down the side of the bowl containing the beaten egg whites.
14. With a rubber spatula, fold the yolk mixture and whites together completely and efficiently. Remember to (a) drag the spatula down the far side of the bowl, (b) across the bottom, and (c) up the near side; and (d) end the stroke by spreading the sauce from the bottom of the bowl across the upper surface of the whites.
15. Rotate the bowl a quarter of a turn after each stroke.
16. On the fifth stroke, come up through the middle of the mixture.

17. Continue this five-stroke cycle until absolutely no sauce remains in the bottom of the bowl and the entire mass is homogenous.
18. Quickly and gently pour the soufflé mixture into a 1-quart casserole (2-quart soufflé dish for large recipes).
19. With a table knife, trace a circle about an inch from the edge in the upper portion of the soufflé.
20. Place the soufflé on the middle rack of the oven and bake at 325°F for 55 minutes for the large soufflé or 45 minutes for the small one.
21. Test by inserting a knife in the center of the soufflé. It is done when the knife comes out clean. Serve immediately.

(Serves two)

2 Tbsp	margarine or butter
2 Tbsp	flour
1/8 tsp	salt
1/2 c	milk
1/2 c	(1/8 lb) grated sharp cheddar cheese
2	eggs, separated
1/4 tsp	cream of tartar

(Serves four)

1/4 c	margarine or butter
1/4 c	flour
1/4 tsp	salt
1 c	milk
1 c	(1/4 lb) grated sharp cheddar cheese
4	eggs, separated
1/2 tsp	cream of tartar

Broccoli Soufflé

Total Time: 65 minutes (small); 75 minutes (large)
Baking: 325°F oven for 45 minutes (small) or
55 minutes (large)

1. Preheat oven.
2. Put frozen broccoli in boiling salted water, and boil 2 minutes.
3. Drain thoroughly, and chop broccoli very fine. Set aside.
4. Melt margarine or butter in a 1-quart saucepan.
5. Stir in the flour and salt with a wooden spoon.
6. Slowly add the milk, while stirring with a wooden spoon.
7. Return to the heat and bring to boiling while stirring constantly.
8. Remove from the heat.
9. Beat the egg yolks.
10. Add a spoonful of the hot sauce to the egg yolks and stir immediately.
11. Repeat three more times.
12. Pour the egg yolk mixture back into the white sauce, stirring constantly.
13. Add the lemon juice, nutmeg, pimiento, and chopped broccoli to the sauce.
14. Cover and set aside while beating the egg whites.
15. Beat the whites to the foamy stage, add the cream of tartar, and continue beating until the whites just bend over.
16. Fold the white sauce into the egg whites as outlined for the cheese soufflé.
17. Pour into a 3/4-quart soufflé dish (1-1/2-quart for large recipe).
18. Bake in preheated oven at 325°F for 55 minutes (large recipe) or 45 minutes (small recipe) until a knife inserted in the center comes out clean.
19. Serve immediately.

(Serves two)

1/2 package	frozen broccoli
1-1/2 Tbsp	margarine or butter
1-1/2 Tbsp	flour
1/8 tsp	salt
1/2 c	milk
2	eggs, separated
1/2 tsp	lemon juice
few grains	nutmeg
1-1/2 tsp	minced pimiento
1/8 tsp	cream of tartar

(Serves four)

1 package	frozen broccoli
3 Tbsp	margarine or butter
3 Tbsp	flour
1/4 tsp	salt
1 c	milk
4	eggs, separated
1 tsp	lemon juice
Dash	nutmeg
1 Tbsp	minced pimiento
1/4 tsp	cream of tartar

Spoonbread

Total Time: 35 minutes (small); 45 minutes (large)
Baking: 375°F oven for 20 minutes (small) or
30 minutes (large)

(Serves two)	
1/4 c	cornmeal
1 c	milk
2 tsp	margarine or butter
1/4 tsp	salt
1/4 tsp	baking powder
2	eggs, separated
1/4 tsp	cream of tartar

1. Preheat oven.
2. In a saucepan, slowly stir milk into the cornmeal.
3. Heat, while stirring with wooden spoon, until mixture boils and is thick. Remove from the heat.
4. Add the margarine, salt, and baking powder.
5. Beat the egg yolks.
6. Add a spoonful of the hot cornmeal mixture to the yolks and stir.
7. Repeat three more times and then stir the yolk mixture back into the cornmeal.
8. Cover and set aside while beating the whites.
9. Beat the egg whites to the foamy stage. Add cream of tartar and continue beating until the peaks just bend over.
10. Fold the yolk and white mixtures together, as outlined in the cheese soufflé recipe.
11. Pour into a small casserole dish (use 1-1/2-quart casserole for large recipe) and bake in a 375°F oven for 20 minutes (small) to 30 minutes (large), until a knife inserted in the center comes out clean.
12. Serve at once with margarine or butter.

(Serves four)

1/2 c	cornmeal
2 c	milk
1-1/3 Tbsp	margarine or butter
1/2 tsp	salt
1/2 tsp	baking powder
4	eggs, separated
1/2 tsp	cream of tartar

Note: This dish, which may be described as a cornmeal soufflé, is served in place of potatoes.

Chocolate Soufflé

Total Time: 65 minutes (small); 75 minutes (large)
Baking: 325°F oven for 45 minutes (small) or
55 minutes (large)

1. Preheat oven.
2. Melt margarine or butter and chocolate over hot water.
3. Stir in flour and salt, using a wooden spoon.
4. Slowly add the milk while stirring.
5. Place the sauce over direct heat and bring to a boil, stirring constantly.
6. If sauce separates, stir a small amount of water into the sauce. Add just enough water to unite the sauce. Remove from heat.
7. Beat the egg yolks.
8. Add a spoonful of the chocolate sauce to the yolks, and stir it in immediately.
9. Repeat three more times.
10. Pour the yolk mixture back into the chocolate sauce while stirring.
11. Cover and set aside.
12. Beat the egg whites to the foamy stage; add cream of tartar and gradually begin adding the sugar.
13. Beat until the peaks just fold over.
14. Stir the vanilla into the chocolate sauce.
15. Pour the chocolate sauce carefully down the side of the bowl containing the beaten egg whites.
16. Fold as outlined in the procedure for the cheese soufflé.
17. Pour into a small soufflé dish (1-1/2-quart soufflé dish for large recipe) and bake in a 325°F oven for 45 minutes (small) or for 55 minutes (large), until a knife inserted in the center comes out clean.
18. Serve immediately with a large dollop of whipped cream on each portion (optional).

(Serves two)

1-1/2 Tbsp	margarine or butter
1 oz	unsweetened chocolate
2 Tbsp	flour
1/8 tsp	salt
1/2 c	milk
2	eggs, separated
1/4 tsp	cream of tartar
1/4 c	sugar
1/2 tsp	vanilla
	whipped cream

(Serves four)

3 Tbsp	margarine or butter
2 oz	unsweetened chocolate
1/4 c	flour
1/4 tsp	salt
1 c	milk
4	eggs, separated
1/2 tsp	cream of tartar
1/2 c	sugar
1 tsp	vanilla
	whipped cream

Orange Soufflé

Total Time: 1 hour and 30 minutes
Baking: 325°F oven for 1 hour (small) or 70 minutes (large)

1. Preheat oven.
2. Melt the margarine or butter, and stir in the flour and salt, using a wooden spoon. Remove from the heat.
3. Gradually add the milk and stir constantly while heating to boiling. The sauce will be very thick.
4. Remove from the heat and cover.
5. Stir the orange and lemon juices and rinds into the sauce.
6. Beat the egg yolks.
7. Add a spoonful of the white sauce to the yolks and stir.
8. Repeat three more times and then stir the yolk mixture back into the white sauce.
9. Cover while beating the egg whites.
10. Beat the egg whites to the foamy stage; add cream of tartar and gradually begin adding the sugar while beating the whites until the peaks just bend over.
11. Pour the yolk mixture down the side of the bowl containing the whites and fold as outlined in the procedure for cheese soufflé.
12. Pour into a 1-quart casserole (use 2-quart for large recipe).
13. Bake in a preheated oven at 325°F for 1 hour.
14. Test with a knife inserted in the center of the soufflé to be sure it is done before removing from the oven.
15. Serve with lemon sauce (see Lemon Fluffy Omelet) or with whipped cream as soon as it comes from the oven.

(Serves two)

2 Tbsp	margarine or butter
2 Tbsp	flour
1/8 tsp	salt
1/3 c	milk
1-1/2 Tbsp	orange juice
1/2 Tbsp	lemon juice
1/4 tsp	lemon rind, grated
2	eggs, separated
1/4 tsp	cream of tartar
1/4 c	sugar
	lemon sauce or whipped cream

(Serves four)

1/4 c	margarine or butter
1/4 c	flour
1/4 tsp	salt
2/3 c	milk
3 Tbsp	orange juice
1 Tbsp	lemon juice
1/2 tsp	lemon rind, grated
4	eggs, separated
1/2 tsp	cream of tartar
1/2 c	sugar
	lemon sauce or whipped cream

Mocha Mini-Soufflé

Total Time: 30 minutes
Baking: 400°F oven for 10 to 12 minutes

1. Preheat oven.
2. Melt chocolate chips in microwave oven (about 20 seconds) until soft.
3. Meanwhile, beat yolks with coffee briefly.
4. Begin beating egg whites in separate bowl, adding sugar at foamy stage while continuing beating at high speed until soft peaks form.
5. Stir chocolate into yolk mixture and then add all at once to white foam.
6. Lightly fold until no chocolate layer remains and the mixture is homogeneous.
7. Pour into buttered 1/2 cup soufflé dishes (3 for small; 6 for large).
8. Bake at 400°F until top is crisp (about 11 minutes).
9. Dust lightly with sifted powdered sugar to serve.

(Serves three)

3 oz	semisweet chocolate chips
1	egg, separated
1	egg white
2 Tbsp	strong coffee
1-1/2 Tbsp	sugar powdered sugar

(Serves six)

6 oz	semisweet chocolate chips
3	eggs, separated
1	egg white
1/4 c	strong coffee
3 Tbsp	sugar powdered sugar

MERINGUES

Objectives

1. To demonstrate formation of egg white foams using different levels of sugar.
2. To illustrate ways in which soft and hard meringues may be used.
3. To evaluate soft and hard meringues for quality of preparation.

RECIPES

Soft Meringue

Total Time: 20 minutes
Baking: 350°F oven for 12 to 15 minutes

1. Preheat oven.
2. Prepare pie filling or heavy paper (if meringues are being prepared as separate samples).
3. Beat egg white to foamy stage.
4. Add the cream of tartar and gradually begin adding the sugar.
5. Continue beating until all of the sugar is dissolved and the peaks just bend over.
6. Spread gently on pie filling or on baking sheet.
7. Bake in 350°F oven until golden brown.

(Two tart topping)

1	egg white
1/8 tsp	cream of tartar
2 Tbsp	sugar

(1 pie topping)

3	egg whites
1/4 tsp	cream of tartar
6 Tbsp	sugar

Baked Alaska

Total Time: 15 minutes
Baking: 450°F oven for 8 minutes

1. Preheat oven.
2. On a small wooden board, arrange 3″ circles of cake 1/2″ thick.
3. Make **soft meringue**.
4. Place a scoop of ice cream on each cake round.
5. Use a rubber spatula to quickly frost each serving with a thick layer of meringue, being sure to completely cover the ice cream and cake with the meringue.
6. Bake at 450°F until meringue is lightly browned.
7. Serve immediately.

(Serves two)

1	egg white
1/8 tsp	cream of tartar
2 Tbsp	sugar
2	3″ circle cakes
1/2 pt	ice cream

(Serves four)

3	egg whites
1/4 tsp	cream of tartar
6 Tbsp	sugar
4	3″ circle cakes
1 pt	ice cream

Oeufs à la Neige

Total Time: 45 minutes

1. Heat 2″ of water to simmering in a saucepan or deep skillet.
2. Prepare soft meringue and drop by tablespoon into simmering water.
3. At the end of 1 minute, roll the meringue over and finish poaching the second side.
4. Remove with a slotted spoon, and drain on paper towel.
5. Prepare stirred custard (see p. 204) and chill.
6. To serve, put meringues in glass bowl.
7. Add fresh fruit and pour chilled stirred custard to float the meringues.

(Serves two)

Meringue

1	egg white
1/8 tsp	cream of tartar
2 Tbsp	sugar

Stirred Custard

1	egg
	dash salt
2 Tbsp	sugar
1 c	milk, scalded
1/2 tsp	vanilla
1/2 c	fresh fruit

(Serves four)

Meringue

2	egg whites
1/4 tsp	cream of tartar
1/4 c	sugar

Stirred Custard

2	eggs
1/8 tsp	salt
1/4 c	sugar
2 c	milk, scalded
1 tsp	vanilla
1 c	fresh fruit

Figure 8.2
Fluffy poached soft meringue clouds floating on stirred custard and accented with slices of fresh strawberries combine to make a memorable dessert.

Hard Meringue

Total Time: 2 hours and 15 minutes
Baking: 275°F oven for 1 hour

(Serves two)	
2	egg whites
1/8 tsp	cream of tartar
1/2 c	sugar

1. Preheat oven.
2. Using an electric mixer, beat egg whites to foamy stage.
3. Add the cream of tartar and very slowly begin to add the sugar while beating.
4. Continue beating the whites until peaks stand up straight. Finish beating with rotary beater if electric mixer begins to overheat.
5. Line a baking sheet with brown paper and spoon two mounds of meringue for each egg white used.
6. With a rubber spatula, swirl each mound into a shell shaped like a nest.
7. Bake at 275°F for an hour.
8. Turn off oven at end of 1 hour and leave meringue shells in oven to continue baking as oven cools.

(Serves four)

4	egg whites
1/4 tsp	cream of tartar
1 c	sugar

Figure 8.3
Hard meringues serve as sweet, crisp bases for fresh strawberries topped with whipped cream.

Note: Meringue shells may be served with ice cream and/or fruit in the center. Hard meringues can have other ingredients, such as chopped nuts or glazed fruits, added to them before being dropped onto a cookie sheet by the spoonful to make cookies.

Macaroons (Meringue Cookies)

Total Time: 35 minutes
Baking: 325°F oven for 20 minutes

1. Preheat oven.
2. With electric mixer, beat egg whites to the foamy stage; add cream of tartar and vanilla.
3. While beating on high speed, very gradually add sugar.
4. Beat until peaks barely bend over.
5. Fold in coconut and pecans.
6. Drop by teaspoons onto Teflon-lined baking sheet.
7. Bake at 325°F for 20 minutes.

(1 dozen cookies)

1	egg white
1/4 tsp	cream of tartar
1/4 tsp	vanilla
1/4 c	sugar
2/3 c	flaked coconut
3 Tbsp	chopped pecans

(2 dozen cookies)

2	egg whites
1/2 tsp	cream of tartar
1/2 tsp	vanilla
1/2 c	sugar
1-1/3 c	flaked coconut
1/3 c	chopped pecans

EGGS AS THICKENING AGENTS: CUSTARDS AND QUICHE

Objectives

1. To demonstrate the use of egg protein as a thickening agent.
2. To illustrate the influence of agitation on the formation of a gel structure.

(Custard recipes may be made using milks with varying levels of fat and can be compared with results obtained by others in the laboratory.)

RECIPES

Stirred Custard

Total Time: 20 minutes

1. While milk is scalding, combine beaten egg, salt, and sugar.
2. Add the scalded milk slowly into the other ingredients.
3. Strain the mixture.
4. Cook over simmering, not boiling, water while stirring constantly until thick enough to lightly coat a silver spoon.
5. Cool quickly by setting pan in a pan of ice water.
6. Stir in vanilla.

(Serves two)

1	egg, beaten slightly (add an extra egg if thicker product desired)
dash	salt
2 Tbsp	sugar
1 c	milk, scalded
1/2 tsp	vanilla

(Serves four)

2	eggs, beaten slightly (add an extra egg if thicker product desired)
dash	salt
1/4 c	sugar
2 c	milk, scalded
1 tsp	vanilla

Note: Serve chilled over puddings and other desserts. If custard begins to curdle while cooling, beat with rotary beater to help produce a smooth product.

Baked Custard

Total Time: 45 minutes
Baking: 325°F oven for 40 minutes

1. Preheat oven.
2. Follow the recipe for Stirred Custard (p. 204) through first three steps.
3. Stir in vanilla.
4. Pour the strained mixture into custard cups.
5. Sprinkle nutmeg on top of each custard.
6. Put cups in rectangular baking pan, and pour boiling water 1″ deep around the cups.
7. Bake at 325°F for 40 minutes.
8. Test by inserting knife halfway between the center and the edge of the custard. When it comes out clean, the custard is done. The center will still be soft, but it will coagulate from the residual heat in the custard.
9. Serve chilled.

(Serves two)

1	egg, beaten lightly
2 Tbsp	sugar
dash	salt
1 c	milk, scalded
1/2 tsp	vanilla
	nutmeg
	boiling water

(Serves four)

2	eggs, beaten lightly
1/4 c	sugar
1/8 tsp	salt
2 c	milk, scalded
1 tsp	vanilla
	nutmeg
	boiling water

Figure 8.4
Sugar sprinkled generously atop baked custard can be caramelized with a culinary butane torch to transform it into Crème Brûlée.

Note: Baked custards are baked in a pan of hot water to help protect them from the intense heat of the oven. They can be varied through the use of imaginative toppings.

Microwaved Caramel Flan

Total Time: 20 to 25 minutes

1. Microwave sugar and water in glass measuring cup on high 5-1/2 minutes for small (11 minutes for large).
2. Pour into two or four custard cups and cool after swirling up sides of cups.
3. Microwave milk in glass measuring cup on high 2-1/2 minutes for small (5 minutes for large).
4. Combine eggs, sugar, salt, and vanilla; slowly stir in scalded milk.
5. Pour custard into caramel-lined custard cups, cover, and microwave on low 6 minutes for small (12 minutes for large) until set.
6. Chill and unmold.

(Serves two)

1/4 c	water
1/4 c	sugar
	ingredients small Baked Custard (above)

(Serves four)

1/2 c	water
1/2 c	sugar
	ingredients large Baked Custard (above)

Southwestern Quiche

Total Time: 40 minutes (small); 50 minutes (large)
Baking: 350°F oven for 20 minutes (small); 30 minutes (large)

1. Preheat oven.
2. Crumble and brown the sausage until well browned. Drain well.
3. Line shells with chiles and sausage.
4. Combine eggs, milk, cheeses, and seasonings; pour over sausage.
5. Bake at 350°F for 20 to 30 minutes, until golden brown and custard is set halfway between edge and center.
6. Let stand 5 minutes to finish setting before serving.

(Serves two)

2	tart shells, baked
1/3 lb	sausage
2 oz	canned green chiles
2	eggs, lightly beaten
2/3 c	milk
3 Tbsp	grated Swiss cheese
2 Tbsp	grated Parmesan cheese
1/8 tsp	salt
pinch	pepper

(Serves four)

4	tart shells, baked
2/3 lb	sausage
4 oz	canned green chiles
4	eggs, lightly beaten
1-1/3 c	milk
1/3 c	grated Swiss cheese
1/4 c	grated Parmesan cheese
1/4 tsp	salt
dash	pepper

CREAM PUDDINGS

Objectives

1. To demonstrate a technique suitable for combining uncooked egg yolk with hot mixtures without lumping.

2. To evaluate cream puddings and cream pie fillings.

(Pudding recipes may be made using milks with varying levels of fat and can be compared with results obtained by others in the laboratory.)

RECIPES

Vanilla Cream Pudding

Total Time: 15 minutes

1. Combine the ingredients and cook them in the same way as when making a cornstarch pudding.
2. After the pudding is thick enough to leave a path with a spoon, remove from the heat.
3. Beat the egg yolk slightly.
4. Take a spoonful of the hot pudding and stir it rapidly into the egg yolk.
5. Repeat three more times.
6. Immediately stir the egg yolk–pudding mixture back into the pudding.
7. Cook for 5 minutes over boiling water, or else use direct heat controlled so that the pudding does not boil.
8. Stir slowly throughout this period of cooking.
9. Remove from heat, and stir in vanilla and butter.
10. Pour into custard cups or individual serving dishes, cover tightly, and chill.

(Serves two)

1-1/2 Tbsp	cornstarch
2-2/3 Tbsp	sugar
few grains	salt
1/4 c	milk
3/4 c	scalded milk
1	egg yolk
1/2 tsp	vanilla
1/2 tsp	butter or margarine

(Serves four)

3 Tbsp	cornstarch
1/3 c	sugar
dash	salt
1/2 c	milk
1-1/2 c	scalded milk
2	egg yolks
1 tsp	vanilla
1 tsp	butter or margarine

Chocolate Cream Pudding

Total Time: 15 minutes

1. Combine the ingredients (mix cocoa with cornstarch and sugar) in the same way as when making a cornstarch pudding.
2. After the pudding is thick enough to leave a path with a spoon, remove from the heat.
3. Beat the egg yolk slightly.
4. Take a spoonful of the hot pudding and stir it rapidly into the egg yolk.
5. Repeat three more times.
6. Immediately stir the egg yolk–pudding mixture back into the pudding.
7. Cook for 5 minutes over boiling water or use direct heat, controlled so that the pudding does not boil.
8. Stir slowly while the yolk is being coagulated.
9. Remove from heat and stir in vanilla and butter or margarine.
10. Pour into custard cups or individual serving dishes, cover tightly, and chill.

(Serves two)

1-1/3 Tbsp	cornstarch
2-2/3 Tbsp	cocoa
few grains	salt
1/4 c	sugar
1/4 c	milk
3/4 c	scalded milk
1	egg yolk
1/2 tsp	vanilla
1/2 tsp	butter or margarine

(Serves four)

2-2/3 Tbsp	cornstarch
1/3 c	cocoa
dash	salt
1/2 c	sugar
1/2 c	milk
1-1/2 c	scalded milk
2	egg yolks
1 tsp	vanilla
1 tsp	butter or margarine

Butterscotch Cream Pudding

Total Time: 15 minutes

1. Combine the ingredients, and cook them in the same way as when making a cornstarch pudding (see Chapter 6, p. 144).
2. After the pudding is thick enough to leave a path with a spoon, remove from the heat.
3. Beat the egg yolk slightly.
4. Take a spoonful of the hot pudding and stir it rapidly into the egg yolk.
5. Repeat three more times.
6. Immediately stir the egg yolk–pudding mixture back into the pudding.
7. Cook for 5 minutes over boiling water, or else use direct heat controlled so that the pudding does not boil.
8. Stir slowly throughout this period of cooking.
9. Remove from the heat and stir in vanilla and butter or margarine.
10. Pour into custard cups or individual serving dishes, cover tightly, and chill.

(Serves two)

1-1/2 Tbsp	cornstarch
2-2/3 Tbsp	brown sugar
few grains	salt
1/4 c	milk
3/4 c	scalded milk
1	egg yolk
1/2 tsp	vanilla
1-1/2 Tbsp	butter or margarine

(Serves four)

3 Tbsp	cornstarch
1/3 c	brown sugar
dash	salt
1/2 c	milk
1-1/2 c	scalded milk
2	egg yolks
1 tsp	vanilla
3 Tbsp	butter or margarine

Evaluation of Laboratory Products—Eggs

Recipe	Notes on Color, Texture, Flavor, or other Qualities	Comments or Suggestions for Making or Using this Product in the Future

VOCABULARY

Chalazae

Vitelline membrane

Soufflé

Hard meringue

Soft meringue

Cream of tartar

Syneresis

Ferrous sulfide

Coagulation

Denaturation

Ovalbumin

Isoelectric point

Candling

Fluffy omelet

French omelet

CHAPTER 9

Meats, Poultry, and Fish

Objectives

1. To identify primal and retail cuts of beef, veal, pork, and lamb.
2. To select meats according to grading criteria.
3. To prepare cuts of meat by moist or dry heat cookery methods appropriate to the cut.

Meat usually represents the most expensive item in a meal, so consumers are anxious to have the best possible result. Success in meat cookery requires knowledge of meat cuts, the ability to select them, and an understanding of appropriate methods of cooking the various cuts.

SELECTION

Meat preparation begins with selection. Note first that primal cuts of meat have a circular seal indicating that the meat has been inspected by federal inspectors. Then look for the shield-shaped grading stamp. In selecting meat cuts, observe the size of the fibers of the meat, look for the amount of fat in the muscle, and check the proportion of meat to bone. Using the following diagrams of the cuts, begin to study cuts at the market and determine their original location on the carcass. From this knowledge of cuts, decide what method of meat cookery will produce the best result.

KEY CONCEPTS

1. Consumers need knowledge of the various types of meats, poultry, and fish so they can select them wisely in the market, handle them safely during storage, and prepare them for optimum palatability.

   a. Identification of meats, their cuts, and their cooking characteristics will result in wise selections and pleasing meat dishes.

   b. Tender cuts of red meats are best when prepared using dry heat methods (roasting, broiling, pan broiling, pan frying, and deep-fat frying).

   c. Less tender cuts need to be tenderized by a moist heat method, either braising or stewing (cooking in liquid)

2. Fish and poultry are particularly susceptible to spoilage, but red meats also require careful refrigeration and attention to sanitation to avoid contamination and cross-contamination in the kitchen.

3. Careful attention to final temperatures when cooking meats, poultry, and fish is essential to ensure safe products and avoid bacterial, viral, and parasitic infections.

PREPARATION

Meat preparation may be divided into two basic categories: dry heat methods and moist heat methods. Dry heat methods are well suited to preparing tender cuts of meat, but moist heat methods are preferred for less tender cuts of meat or meats with very mild flavors. Dry heat methods include roasting, broiling, pan broiling, pan frying, and deep-fat frying. Braising and stewing are the moist heat methods.

DRY HEAT MEAT COOKERY

Roasting

Roasting is an excellent dry heat method for large, tender cuts of meat from the rib or loin of beef, pork, and lamb. Ham and leg of lamb also are well suited to roasting.

Select a tender cut of meat that is at least 2" thick for roasting. Wipe the cut surfaces of the meat with a damp paper towel. Place the meat on a rack to hold the cut above the drippings (unless the meat contains its own bone rack) and put the meat and rack in a shallow pan. Insert a meat thermometer into the center of the largest muscle, being careful that it does not rest against bone or in fat. Place the meat (uncovered) in the center of the oven. (If foil or some other covering were used, this would trap moisture from the meat and would change the method into a moist heat cookery method.)

Roast at 325°F for small cuts and 300°F for larger roasts until the thermometer indicates the desired internal temperature. For rare beef, this is 145°F; for medium beef, 160°F; and for well done, 170°F. Fresh pork is roasted to at least 160°F to ensure safety from trichinosis. Lamb is roasted to 160°F for those who prefer medium and to 170°F for those who like lamb well done. Timetables for roasting beef, veal, pork, lamb, and turkey are useful in estimating how much time will be required to reach the desired end point, but a thermometer is needed to ascertain that the desired degree of doneness has been reached. Then the meat is removed from the oven and allowed to stand at room temperature for approximately 15 minutes before carving. Roasts are salted as each slice is carved, because flavoring substances barely penetrate the surface of the meat.

Beef Made Easy

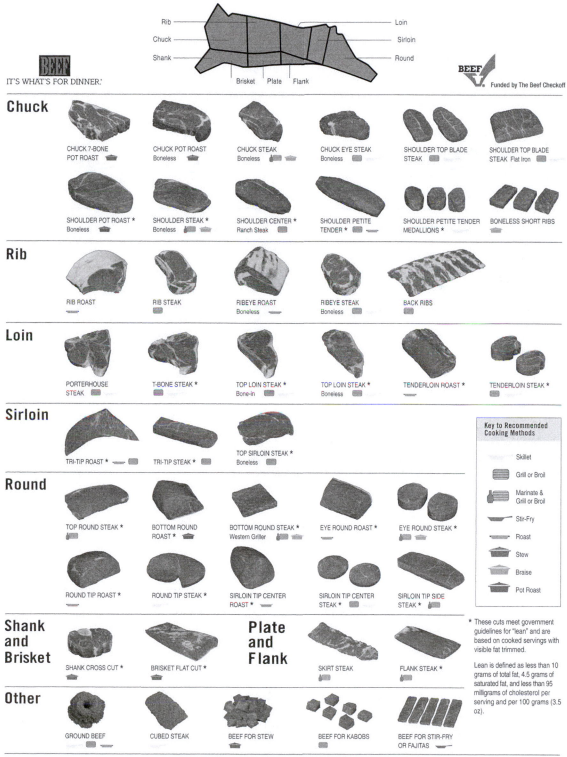

BONE STRUCTURE CHARTS (top to bottom: beef, veal, pork, lamb)

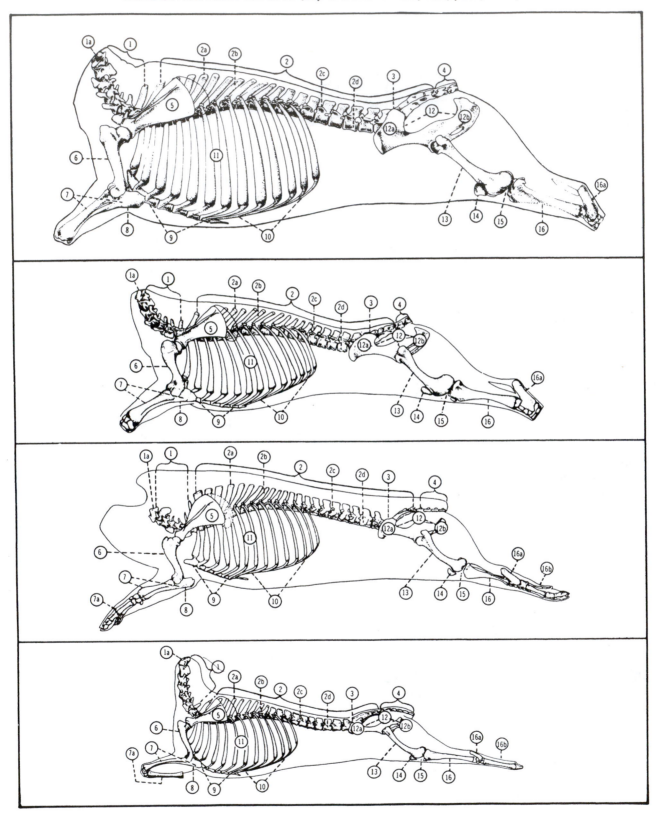

Courtesy of National Cattlemen's Beef Association.

BONE STRUCTURE CHARTS
(on page 214)

    1   Neck bone
    1 a Atlas
    2   Back bone
    2 a Button
    2 b Feather bone
    2 c Finger bone
    3   Slip joint
    4   Tail bone
    5   Blade bone
    6   Arm bone
    7   Fore shank bone(s)
    7 a Fore foot bone(s),
        lower shank
    8   Elbow bone
    9   Breast bone
   10   Rib cartilages
   11   Ribs
   12   Pelvic bone
   12 a Hip bone
   12 b Rump (aitch) bone
   13   Leg (round) bone
   14   Knee cap
   15   Stifle joint
   16   Hind shank bone(s)
   16 a Hock bones
   16 b Hind foot bones,
        lower shank

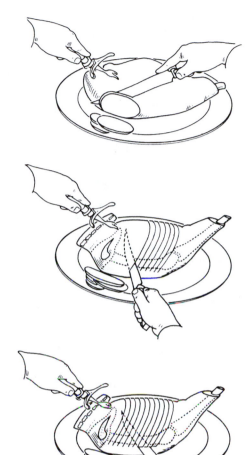

Steps to carve a leg of lamb.

Turkey also is well suited to roasting. A thorough washing of the fowl, both inside and out, is done as soon as the neck and the bag containing the giblets are removed from the cavity. Particular attention needs to be given to scrubbing out the cavity and to removing any traces of feathers in the skin. After the turkey has been washed thoroughly under a stream of water in the sink, it should be drained thoroughly.

Dressing is an optional item in roasting turkey and may be a commercial mix or one prepared using a variety of ingredients. The potential for food spoilage is great if dressing is placed in a turkey several hours in advance of roasting. By far the best practice is to stuff the turkey immediately before beginning to roast the fowl. Stuffing is placed lightly in the body cavity. The turkey now is transferred to a V-shaped rack with the breast down. In this position, it is a simple matter to stuff the neck region of the turkey. This stuffing helps to give the turkey a plump appearance. When lightly stuffed, the flap of skin at the neck is pulled over the dressing and skewered to the back of the bird. The legs are tied together with string.

Figure 9.1
Carving technique for leg of lamb.

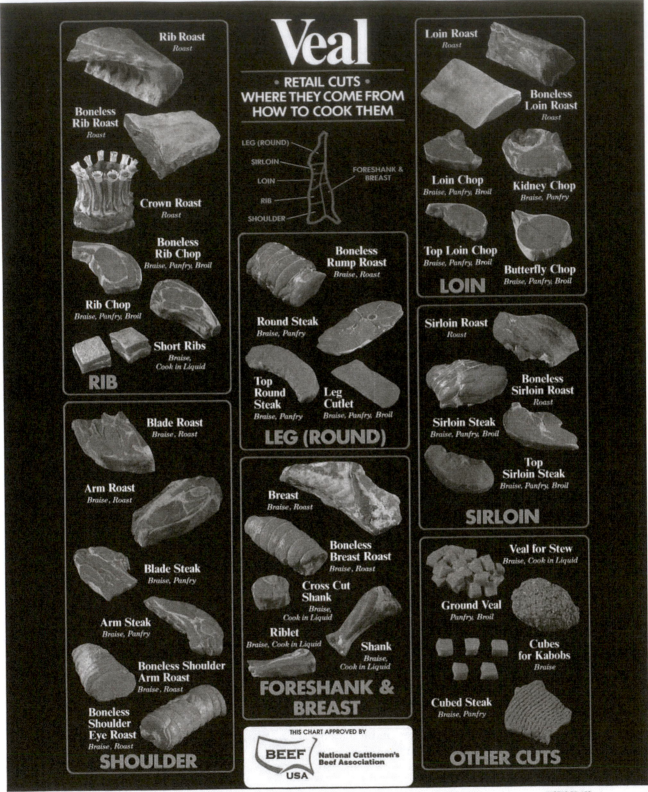

Courtesy of National Cattlemen's Beef Association.

Pork Basics

Be inspired

Shoulder Butt

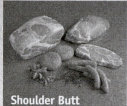

Upper row (l-r):
Bone-in Blade Roast,
Boneless Blade Roast

Lower row (l-r):
Ground Pork,
Sausage, Blade Steak

Picnic Shoulder

Upper row (l-r):
Smoked Picnic,
Arm Picnic Roast

Lower row:
Smoked Hocks

Side

Top:
Spareribs

Bottom:
Slab Bacon, Sliced
Bacon

Leg

Upper row (l-r):
Bone-in Fresh Ham,
Smoked Ham

Lower row (l-r):
Leg Cutlets, Fresh
Boneless Ham Roast

Loin

**Tenderloin &
Canadian-Style Bacon**

Left: Tenderloin
Right: Canadian-Style Bacon

Ribs

Left: Country-Style Ribs
Right: Back Ribs

Roasts

Upper row (l-r):
Center Rib Roast (Rack of Pork),
Bone-in Sirloin Roast
Middle:
Boneless Center Loin Roast
Lower row (l-r):
Boneless Rib End Roast,
Boneless Sirloin Roast

Chops

Upper row (l-r):
Sirloin Chop, Rib Chop,
Loin Chop

Lower row (l-r):
Boneless Rib End Chop,
Boneless Center Loin Chop,
Butterfly Chop

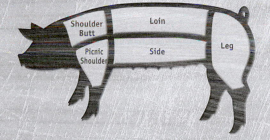

Shoulder Butt | Loin
Picnic Shoulder | Side | Leg

THE MANY SHAPES OF PORK ROASTS

Cut Loose!

When shopping for pork, consider cutting traditional roasts into a variety of different shapes

CHOPS: Dinner, backyard barbecue or gourmet entree

CUBES: Great for kabobs, stew & chili

STRIPS: Super stir fry, fajitas & salads

CUTLETS: Delicious breakfast chops & quick sandwiches

pork ©2007-2011 National Pork Board, Des Moines, IA USA. This message funded by America's Pork Checkoff Program.

www.PorkBeInspired.com

#03342 04/2011

Courtesy of National Pork Board

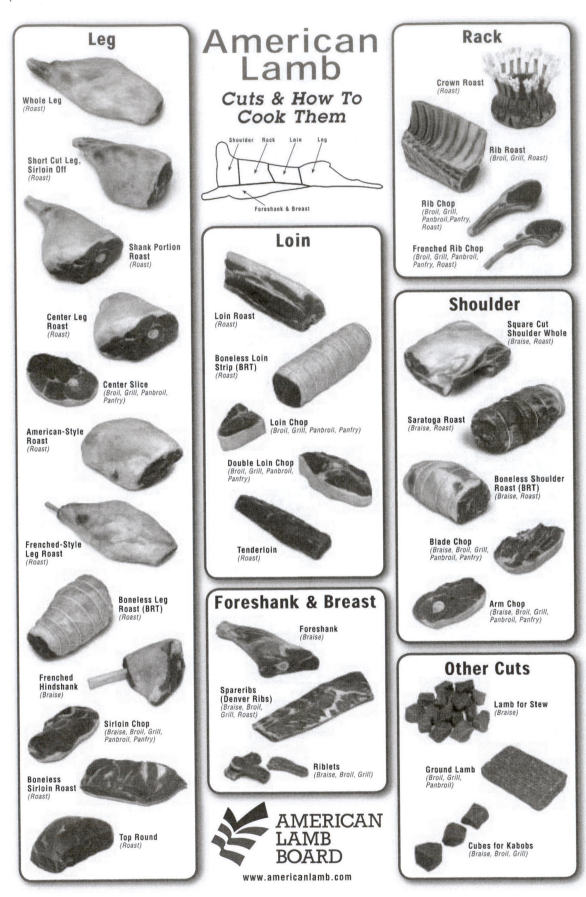

American Lamb
Cuts & How To Cook Them

Leg

Whole Leg
(Roast)

Short Cut Leg, Sirloin Off
(Roast)

Shank Portion Roast
(Roast)

Center Leg Roast
(Roast)

Center Slice
(Broil, Grill, Panbroil, Panfry)

American-Style Roast
(Roast)

Frenched-Style Leg Roast
(Roast)

Boneless Leg Roast (BRT)
(Roast)

Frenched Hindshank
(Braise)

Sirloin Chop
(Braise, Broil, Grill, Panbroil, Panfry)

Boneless Sirloin Roast
(Roast)

Top Round
(Roast)

Loin

Loin Roast
(Roast)

Boneless Loin Strip (BRT)
(Roast)

Loin Chop
(Broil, Grill, Panbroil, Panfry)

Double Loin Chop
(Broil, Grill, Panbroil, Panfry)

Tenderloin
(Roast)

Foreshank & Breast

Foreshank
(Braise)

Spareribs (Denver Ribs)
(Braise, Broil, Grill, Roast)

Riblets
(Braise, Broil, Grill)

Rack

Crown Roast
(Roast)

Rib Roast
(Broil, Grill, Roast)

Rib Chop
(Broil, Grill, Panbroil, Panfry, Roast)

Frenched Rib Chop
(Broil, Grill, Panbroil, Panfry, Roast)

Shoulder

Square Cut Shoulder Whole
(Braise, Roast)

Saratoga Roast
(Braise, Roast)

Boneless Shoulder Roast (BRT)
(Braise, Roast)

Blade Chop
(Braise, Broil, Grill, Panbroil, Panfry)

Arm Chop
(Braise, Broil, Grill, Panbroil, Panfry)

Other Cuts

Lamb for Stew
(Braise)

Ground Lamb
(Broil, Grill, Panbroil)

Cubes for Kabobs
(Braise, Broil, Grill)

Shoulder   Rack   Loin   Leg

Foreshank & Breast

AMERICAN LAMB BOARD
www.americanlamb.com

Courtesy of American Lamb Board

The thermometer is inserted into the stuffing in the main cavity of the bird if the bird is stuffed and adjusted so that it can be read easily while the turkey is roasting. An unstuffed bird is roasted with the thermometer inserted in the inner part of the thigh. (However, thermometers with plastic domes cannot withstand oven heat so need to be read when the turkey is pulled out and the thermometer is read.) The turkey and rack are situated in a shallow pan suitable for catching the drippings, and then the assembly is placed in the oven. The oven rack usually needs to be at the bottom rack position because of the large size of turkeys. The turkey itself should be situated an equal distance from the top and bottom of the oven. The oven is set at 300°F to 325°F and the turkey is roasted until the thermometer indicates 165°F in the dressing or 180°F in the thigh. If roasting only the breast, roast it to an interior temperature of 170°F. If the turkey is roasted breast down, the juices released during roasting will help to baste the breast. If roasted breast side up on a rack,

Figure 9.2

Turkey stuffed with dressing in the cavity and the neck area is placed breast down on a V-shaped rack above a shallow pan for roasting.

the breast may be basted occasionally with margarine or butter. However, it is perfectly appropriate to let turkeys roast without any attention until the fowl is done.

The five tables that follow (pages xxx–xxx) are guides to help in planning the timing of roasts, as well as meats that are broiled, braised, or cooked in liquid.

Approximate Beef Cooking Times °F

Type of Beef	Size	Cooking Method	Cooking Time	Internal Temperature
Rib Roast, bone in	4 to 6 lbs	Roast 325°	23–25 min/lb	145° F and allow to rest at least 3 min
Rib Roast, boneless rolled	4 to 6 lbs	Roast 325°	Add 5–8 min/lb to times above	
Chuck Roast, Brisket	3 to 4 lbs	*Braise 325°	*Braise 325°	
Round or Rump Roast	2-1/2 to 4 lbs	Roast 325°	30–35 min/lb	
Tenderloin, whole	4 to 6 lbs	Roast 425°	45–60 min total	
Steaks	3/4" thick	Broil/Grill	4–5 min per side	
Stew or Shank Cross Cuts	1 to 1-1/2" thick	Cover with liquid; simmer	2 to 3 hrs	
Short Ribs	4" long and 2" thick	*Braise 325°	1-1/2 to 2-1/2 hrs	
Hamburger patties, fresh	4 ounces	Grill, broil or fry	3 to 5 min per side	160°F<

*Braising is roasting or simmering less-tender meats with a small amount of liquid in a tightly covered pan.
Source: U.S.D.A. Food Safety and Inspection Service.

Approximate Veal Cooking Times

Type of Veal	Size	Cooking Method	Cooking Time	Minimum Internal Temperature & Rest Time
Rib Roast	4 to 5 lbs	Roast 325°	25 to 27 min/lb	145°F and allow to rest at least 3 min
Loin	3 to 4 lbs	Roast 325°F	34 to 36 min/lb	
Loin/Rib Chops	1" thick or 8 oz.	Broil/Grill	7 min per side	
Cutlets	1/8" thick	*Pan fry	3 to 4 min	
	1/4" thick		5 to 6 min	
Arm/Blade Steak	3/4" thick 16 oz.	Broil/Grill	7 min per side	145°F and allow to rest at least 3 min
			8 min per side	
Round Steak	1/4" thick	**Braise	30 min	
	1/2" thick		45 min	
Boneless Breast, stuffed	2 to 2.5 lbs	**Braise	1-1/4 to 1-1/2 hrs	
	4 to 4.5 lbs		2 to 2-1/2 hrs	
Cross Cut Shanks	1-1/2" thick	Cover with liquid; simmer	1 to 1-1/4 hrs	145°F and allow to rest at least 3 min
Stew Meat	1 to 1-1/2" cubes / pieces	Cover with liquid: simmer	45 to 60 min	
Ground Patties	1/2" thick, 4 oz.	Broil / Grill / Pan fry	6 to 7 min per side	160°F

*Pan Frying, which is often called "sautéing," is a quick cooking method. Meat is placed in small amount of heated oil and cooked on medium-high heat.

**Braising is roasting or simmering less-tender meats with a small amount of liquid in a tightly covered pan

Source: U.S.D.A. Food Safety and Inspection Service.

Timetable for Cooking Pork

Cut	Roasted (300°F)		Broiled	Braised	Cooked in Liquid	
	(°F)	(min/lb)	(°F)	(min)	(hrs)	(min/lb)
Fresh						
Loin						
Center	145	35				
Whole	145	15				
Ends	145	45				
Shoulder						
Rolled	145	40				
Cushion	145	35				
Boston Butt	145	45				
Leg or ham	145	30				
Chops, steaks					3/4–1	
Spareribs		30–34			1-1/2	30
Pork, ham loaf		30–35				
Smoked						
Ham						
Large	145	15				18–20
Medium	145	18				
Small	145	22				
Half	145	30				25
Ham slice						
1/2"			145	10		
1"			145	16		
Picnic	145	35				
Shoulder butt	145	35				35–45
Bacon				4–5		

[1]A 350°F oven temperature is recommended for fresh pork and 300°F even temperature for smoked pork.

Approximate Lamb Cooking Times °F

Cut of Lamb	Size	Cooking Method	Cooking Time	Minimum Internal Temperature & Rest Time
Lamb Leg, bone in	5 to 7 lbs	Roast 325°	20 to 25 min/lb	
	7 to 9 lbs	Roast 325°	15 to 20 min/lb	
Lamb Leg, boneless, rolled	4 to 7 lbs	Roast 325°	25 to 30 min/lb	145°F and allow to rest for at least 3 min
Shoulder Roast or Shank Leg Half	3 to 4 lbs	Roast 325°	30 to 35 min/lb	
Cubes, for Kabobs	1 to 1-1/2"	Broil/Grill	8 to 12 min	
Ground Lamb Patties	2" thick	Broil/Grill	5 to 8 min	160°F
Chops, Rib, or Loin	1 to 1-1/2" thick	Broil/Grill	7 to 11 min	145°F and allow to rest for at least 3 min
Leg Steaks	3/4" thick	Broil/Grill 4" from heat	14 to 18 min	
Stew Meat, pieces	1 to 1-1/2"	Cover with liquid; simmer	1-1/2 to 2 hrs	145°F and allow to rest for at least 3 min
Shanks	3/4 to 1 lb			
Breast, Rolled	1-1/2 to 2 lb	*Braise 325°	1-1/2 to 2 hrs	

*Braising is roasting or simmering less-tender meats with a small amount of liquid in a tightly covered pan.
Source: U.S.D.A. Food Safety and Inspection Service.

Timetable for Roasting Turkey

Oven Weight (lb)	Oven Temperature (°F)	Cooking Time (min/lb)
8–10	325	20–25
10–14	325	18–20
14–18	300	15–18
18	300	13–15
20	300	13–15

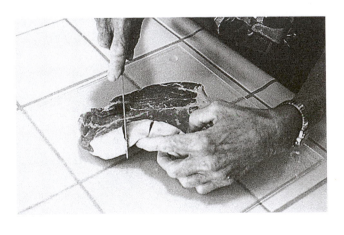

Broiling

Broiling is a direct heat method particularly well suited to meats that are between 1" and 3" thick and are tender. Thinner cuts become too dry when broiled. Thicker cuts tend to char on the surface before the interior is cooked to the desired end point.

To prepare meats for broiling, wipe the surfaces with a damp towel. Use a sharp knife to cut through the fat and connective tissue surrounding the large muscles of steaks. Cuts should be made at 1" intervals to prevent curling of the cut during broiling.

The meat is arranged on a broiler pan with the fat toward the middle of the pan. It is an important safety precaution to use a broiler pan, because the rack is designed to drain the fat away from the meat and protect it from the intense heat of the broiler, thus reducing the risk of a broiler fire.

Position the meat in the broiler so that the top surface of the meat is at least 3 inches from the heat source. If the cut is very thick, move the meat lower in the broiler so there will be more time for the heat to penetrate the meat before the surface becomes too done. Broil the first side of the meat until it is a pleasing brown and the meat is approximately half done. Salt the cooked side, and then turn the meat.

In the event that broiling meat is browning unusually slowly, raise the broiler pan closer to the heat. If the meat is beginning to burn before it has sufficient time to reach the desired interior degree of doneness, the pan should be moved lower in the broiler compartment. Adjustments on rate of broiling are made by moving the meat in relation to the heat rather than adjusting the level of heat, as is done in selecting baking temperatures.

Broil the second side until done. Serve. If the meat being broiled is thick enough, insert a thermometer and broil to the desired doneness. Thinner cuts can be tested by cutting a small incision near the bone. It should not be necessary to turn the meat back to its original position. Proper cooking should occur with only the one turning to expose the second side of the cut.

Charcoal broiling is simply an inverted version of broiling. The rate of broiling is adjusted by moving the rack closer or farther from the coals. Smoke from the hot coals adds flavor. A whole roasting chicken is ideal for barbecuing.

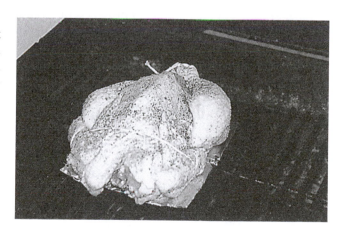

Pan Broiling

Pan broiling is another dry heat method and, consequently, is well suited to many of the same cuts of meat that can be broiled. Pan broiling is particularly good for preparing tender cuts of meat that are less than an inch thick. These thin cuts do not dry out as much when they are pan broiled as when they are broiled.

Preparation of the meat is the same for pan broiling as for broiling. The meat is broiled in a heavy skillet without adding any fat. However, if the skillet is not Teflon coated, it is possible to warm the skillet slightly and then rub the fat side of the meat cut on the hot metal to provide enough fat to keep the meat from sticking. The meat is cooked until the bottom side is a pleasing brown.

Then it is turned over. The cooked surface is salted while the second side is browning. As fat drains from the meat, it is removed from the frying pan so that the meat is pan broiled in an absolute minimum of fat. The meat may be turned as often as needed to cook the meat to the desired doneness without burning the surface.

A thermometer is not used in pan broiling because the cuts used usually are too thin for satisfactory insertion of the thermometer. The important factors in pan broiling are the use of controlled heat, a heavy frying pan, and frequent removal of accumulating fat. Pan-broiled meats are popular because of their slightly reduced fat content when served.

Pan-broiled meats are attractive to serve if the heat has been controlled properly. To achieve a rare pan-broiled steak, a relatively high temperature should be used to brown the outside of the meat quickly before there is sufficient time for the heat to penetrate to the center of the cut. For pork or other cuts that are to be served well done, a somewhat slower rate of heating is preferred to allow time for more uniform heat penetration.

Pan Frying

Thin cuts of meat, such as thin pork chops, thin steaks, and thin lamb chops, are well suited to pan frying. Such cuts can be heated adequately in the center before they become too dark on the outside when pan fried.

There are several similarities between pan broiling and pan frying. Meat is prepared for pan frying by wiping the surface with a dampened paper towel and cutting through the connective tissue to make the meat remain flat during the cooking period. A skillet is used for pan frying, just as it is in pan broiling. Here, however, the two methods become distinctly different. A small amount of fat is melted in the skillet before the meat is added for pan frying. Furthermore, the fat is allowed to collect in the pan during pan frying. The heat should be carefully controlled during pan frying to prevent unnecessary splattering and smoking of the fat. After the meat is browned on the first side, it is turned and the first side is salted. Then the second side is browned. It may be necessary to turn the meat more than once to achieve the desired interior temperature without burning the exterior.

Deep-Fat Frying

A few meats are often prepared by deep-fat frying. To be suitable for deep-fat frying, the cut must be small enough so that it can be cooked through to the center before the outer portion is overcooked. Chicken can be deep-fat fried successfully. Several types of fish and seafood are well suited to deep-fat frying.

The key to successful deep-fat frying is temperature control. The fat must be maintained at 350°F for larger pieces or 375°F for smaller pieces if the food is to be at its best. Too low a temperature results in a very greasy product. Too high a temperature causes the exterior to burn while the interior is still underdone. Fat for deep-fat frying is most effectively maintained at the desired temperature by using a deep-fat fryer or a saucepan on a thermostatically controlled unit.

Foods are prepared for deep-fat frying by first cleaning them carefully. Next, it is very important to dry them, because water causes a great deal of splattering when the food is placed in the hot fat. Only a few pieces can be placed in the deep-fat fryer at one time. Too much food causes a significant drop in the temperature of the fat, and the food will be greasy. When the fat is no longer bubbling right around the edges of the food and the bottom surface is an attractive golden brown, use a slotted spoon or tongs to turn the item over very carefully. Avoid any splashing.

To determine when a deep-fat fried food is done, time it carefully, look at the color of the exterior, and make a small cut into the center to be sure it is done inside. Drain the food on a paper towel and salt it to taste.

The oil used in the deep-fat fryer should be strained each time it is used. By removing extraneous food particles, the useful life of the oil is extended. It is necessary to dispose of the old oil and start with fresh oil when the oil (1) begins to have a strong odor, (2) becomes rather viscous, or (3) starts to smoke at frying temperatures. A deep-fat fried product cannot be any better than the quality of the oil in which it is fried.

RECIPES FOR DRY HEAT MEAT COOKERY

Salmon à la Pesto

Total Time: 20 minutes
Broiling: 10 minutes

1. Preheat oven.
2. Finely chop basil leaves, piñon nuts, and garlic in blender.
3. Slowly pour oil into blender while on purée setting.
4. Stir in cheese, lemon zest, and bread crumbs.
5. Broil salmon steaks on first side 6 minutes before removing from broiler and turning to second side.
6. Spread pesto generously to coat the top surface of the salmon.
7. Continue broiling until salmon flakes when touched with a fork (about 4 minutes).

(Serves two)

1/2 c	basil leaves
1/2 Tbsp	piñon nuts
1/2	garlic clove, minced
1 Tbsp	olive oil
1/2 tsp	grated Parmesan cheese
1/2 tsp	lemon zest
2 Tbsp	bread crumbs
2	salmon steaks

(Serves four)

1 c	basil leaves
1 Tbsp	piñon nuts
1	garlic clove, minced
2 Tbsp	olive oil
1 tsp	grated Parmesan cheese
1 tsp	lemon zest
1/4 c	bread crumbs
4	salmon steaks

Macadamia Sole Rollups

Total Time: 25 minutes
Baking: 325°F for 12 minutes

1. Preheat oven.
2. Sauté mushrooms, garlic, and macadamia nuts in oil about 3 minutes.
3. Place 1-1/2 tbsp of sauté mixture at end of each filet and roll up.
4. Secure each filet roll with a toothpick; place on aluminum foil on baking sheet.
5. Place filets at least 2″ apart on baking sheet.
6. Bake at 325°F until heated through and fish is opaque and flaky (about 12 minutes).
7. Remove toothpick when serving. Garnish with lemon pinwheel.

(Serves two)

1-1/2 Tbsp	chopped mushrooms
1/4 clove	garlic, minced
1-1/2 Tbsp	chopped macadamia nuts
2 tsp	olive oil
2	sole filets
	lemon pinwheels

(Serves four)

3 Tbsp	chopped mushrooms
1/2 clove	garlic, minced
3 Tbsp	chopped macadamia nuts
1 Tbsp	olive oil
4	sole filets
	lemon pinwheels

Baked Halibut

Total Time: 35 minutes
Baking: 325°F for 30 minutes

1. Preheat oven.
2. Arrange fish in a shallow baking dish.
3. Spread the undiluted soup over the fish and sprinkle with the seasonings.
4. Place in a 325°F oven for 30 minutes or until the sauce is bubbling and the fish is hot (or microwave oven: 6 minutes on *high*, 2 minutes on *browning*).
5. Serve with a lemon curl garnish.

(Serves two)

3/4 lb	halibut or other white fish filets
1/2 can	condensed cream of celery soup
1 Tbsp	chopped parsley
dash	poultry seasoning
dash	curry powder
dash	salt dill weed lemon peel garnish

(Serves four)

1-1/2 lb	halibut or other white fish filets
1 can	condensed cream of celery soup
2 Tbsp	chopped parsley
1/8 tsp	poultry seasoning
1/8 tsp	curry powder
1/8 tsp	salt
	dill weed
	lemon peel garnish

Meat Loaf

*Total Time: 1 hour (small recipe); 1 hour and
15 minutes (large recipe)*
Baking: 350°F oven for 45 to 60 minutes

1. Preheat oven.
2. In a small amount of water, boil onion and green pepper together 3 minutes.
3. Drain.
4. Beat egg and combine all ingredients.
5. Mix well and shape into loaf in loaf pan.
6. Spread sauce (below) over unbaked loaf. For microwaving, shape a round loaf in a pie plate.
7. Bake small loaf for 45 minutes at 350°F (or cover and microwave on *high* for 6 minutes); bake large loaf 1 hour at 350°F (or cover and microwave on *high* for 12 minutes). Allow 5 to 10 minutes standing time.

(Serves two)

1/4 c	onion, chopped
1/4	green pepper, chopped
1	egg
1/2 lb	ground chuck
2	soda crackers, rolled into crumbs
1/4 tsp	salt
dash	pepper

(Serves four)

1/2 c	onion, chopped
1/2	green pepper, chopped
2	eggs
1 lb	ground chuck
4	soda crackers, rolled into crumbs
1/2 tsp	salt
1/8 tsp	pepper

Note: Add onion and green pepper uncooked for stronger flavor.

Meat Loaf Sauce

Total Time: 3 minutes

1. Mix the ingredients.

(Serves two)

3 Tbsp	brown sugar
1/4 c	catsup
1/2 tsp	dry mustard
1/4 tsp	lemon juice

(Serves four)

6 Tbsp	brown sugar
1/2 c	catsup
1 tsp	dry mustard
1/2 tsp	lemon juice

Chicken Dijon

Total Time: 45 minutes
Baking: 400°F for 30 minutes

1. Preheat oven.
2. Sauté garlic, onions, and mushrooms in butter in a small skillet until golden brown.
3. Spread surface of chicken breasts heavily with mustard.
4. Place in shallow baking dish and sprinkle with salt, pepper, and poultry seasoning.
5. Spread sour cream on chicken.
6. Bake at 400°F for 15 minutes.
7. Remove briefly from oven to spread vegetables on top before returning to the oven to finish baking (approximately 15 minutes).

(Serves two)

1/2	garlic clove, minced
1-1/2 tsp	thinly sliced green onion
1/8 lb	mushrooms, thinly sliced
2 tsp	butter
1	whole chicken breast, boned, skinned, and split
2 Tbsp	Dijon mustard
	salt and pepper to taste
1/4 tsp	poultry seasoning
1/3 c	sour cream

(Serves four)

1	garlic clove, minced
1 Tbsp	thinly sliced green onion
1/4 lb	mushrooms, thinly sliced
1-1/3 Tbsp	butter
2	whole chicken breasts, boned, skinned, and split
1/4 c	Dijon mustard
	salt and pepper to taste
1/2 tsp	poultry seasoning
2/3 c	sour cream

Deep-Fat Fried Chicken

Total Time: 20 to 40 minutes

1. Preheat the oil in the deep-fat fryer to 350°F while preparing the chicken.
2. Wash the chicken thoroughly.
3. Blot dry with paper towels.
4. Dip each piece of chicken in the batter and then let it drain before putting in the fryer.
5. Fry about three pieces of chicken at a time.
6. Put the chicken in the preheated fat and fry about 10 minutes.
7. Make a small incision to be sure the meat is done next to the bone.
8. Drain on paper towels.
9. Place on baking sheet in 150°F oven to keep warm while frying remainder of chicken.

(Serves two)

3	pieces frying chicken
1/2 c	pancake batter

(Serves four)

6	pieces frying chicken
1 c	pancake batter

Baked Chicken with Coulis

Total Time: 50 minutes
Baking: 350°F oven for 20 minutes; 400°F for
25 minutes

1. Preheat oven.
2. Slice tomatoes in 1/4" slices; mash garlic. Spread in shallow baking dish and bake 20 minutes.
3. Meanwhile, stir mayonnaise, mustard, and herbs together. Spread on chicken breasts heavily before rolling in bread crumbs.
4. Place breaded chicken in shallow baking dish.
5. Bake chicken at 400°F for 25 minutes.
6. Now purée tomatoes and garlic, removing any coarse peels. Stir in the vinegar and olives.
7. Reheat the tomato coulis to serving temperature.
8. Serve chicken on a bed of the hot coulis.

(Serves two)

1 lb	Roma tomatoes
1	clove garlic
1	chicken breast, boneless, skinless, split
2 Tbsp	mayonnaise
2 Tbsp	Dijon mustard
1/2 tsp	pinch of herbs
1/4 tsp	seasoned salt
1/4 cup	fine bread crumbs
1-1/2 tsp	balsamic vinegar
2 Tbsp	sliced black olives

(Serves four)

2 lb	Roma tomatoes
2	cloves garlic
2	chicken breasts, boneless, skinless, split
1/4 c	mayonnaise
1/4 c	Dijon mustard
1 tsp	pinch of herbs
1/2 tsp	seasoned salt
1/2 cup	fine bread crumbs
3 tsp	balsamic vinegar
1/4 c	sliced black olives

Steak with Mushroom Topping

Total Time: 25 minutes

1. Cut edges of steak to prevent curling.
2. Place steak on rack on broiling pan.
3. Position in broiler so top of steak is about 5″ to 6″ from heat. For medium doneness, broil steak about 10 minutes on each side.
4. Turn with tongs.
5. Meanwhile, prepare topping by sautéing the mushrooms and onions 2 minutes.
6. In a mixing bowl, combine cheese and sautéed vegetables.
7. Blend in the bread crumbs.
8. During the last 5 minutes of broiling, spread topping on steak. Continue broiling until cheese melts, approximately 3 to 5 minutes.
9. Serve immediately.

(Serves two)

3/4 lb	sirloin steak, cut 1-1/2″ thick
1 Tbsp	margarine or butter
1/2 c	finely chopped fresh mushrooms
1/4 c	finely chopped green onions
1/3 c	shredded Cheddar cheese
2 Tbsp	seasoned bread crumbs

(Serves four)

1-1/2 lb	sirloin steak, cut 1-1/2″ thick
2 Tbsp	margarine or butter
1 c	finely chopped fresh mushrooms
1/2 c	finely chopped green onions
2/3 c	shredded Cheddar cheese
1/4 c	seasoned bread crumbs

Baby Turkey with Hula Stuffing

Total Time: 3-1/4 to 3-3/4 hours
Baking: 325°F oven for 3 to 3-1/2 hours

1. Preheat oven.
2. Wash turkey thoroughly under running water.
3. Sprinkle turkey inside and out with salt and pepper.
4. In a large bowl, mix dressing, lemon juice and rind, pineapple chunks and juice, melted butter, prunes, and nuts.
5. Stuff hollows in acorn squash.
6. Spoon remaining stuffing into turkey. Sew or skewer the opening.
7. Roast turkey breast down on a V-shaped rack in a shallow, uncovered pan for 2 to 2-1/2 hours or until turkey leg can be moved up and down fairly easily.
8. Place stuffed squash halves into oven with turkey and bake for 1 hour or until squash is pierced easily with a fork.

(Serves six)	
1	turkey, thawed or fresh, 8 to 10 lbs salt and pepper
8 c	dressing mix
	grated rind and juice of 1 lemon
1 can (1 lb 4 oz)	pineapple chunks with juice
1 c	(1/2 lb) margarine or butter, melted
1-1/2 c	chopped pitted prunes
1 c	coarsely broken walnuts, pecans, or macadamia nuts
3	small acorn squash, cut into halves, seeds removed

Fruit-Stuffed Pork Chops

Total Time: 1 hour 10 minutes

1. With a sharp knife, cut a slit about 1-1/2" long in the middle of the side of the pork chops.
2. Extend the cut to make a pocket inside the chops parallel with the meat surfaces.
3. Cut thin slices of apple and stuff the pockets with apple and raisins.
4. Lightly flour the chops.
5. Brown well in a small amount of oil.
6. Add enough water to cover the bottom of the skillet.
7. Reduce the heat and simmer the pork chops in the tightly covered skillet for 1 hour.

(Serves two)	
2	loin pork chops, 1" thick
1/4	tart apple, cored
1/4 c	raisins
2 tsp	salad oil

(Serves four)

4	loin pork chops, 1" thick
1/2	tart apple, cored
1/2 c	raisins
1 Tbsp	salad oil

Note: Moist heat is used to ensure that these thick pork chops will reach a safe interior temperature before they get too dark on the surface.

MOIST HEAT COOKERY METHODS

There are only two basic methods of moist heat meat cookery, yet these two methods provide more variety in flavors than can be achieved by the several dry heat meat cookery methods. The two methods of moist heat meat cookery are braising and stewing (also called cooking in liquid).

Figure 9.3
Pot roast is prepared by braising, a moist heat cookery method suited for less tender cuts of meat because slow cooking converts collagen to gelatin.

Braising

Meat is prepared for braising by first wiping it clean with a damp paper towel. Frequently, it is dipped in flour preparatory to cooking. Sometimes it is dipped in either milk or egg and then in a breading mixture of cracker or bread crumbs. Because less-tender cuts of meat are used for braising, many recipes suggest pounding the meat to break the connective tissue before beginning the actual cooking process.

For the first of the two actual steps of braising, either fat is melted in a skillet or a small amount of oil is poured in. The meat is carefully browned on both sides. The second step is the addition of a small amount of liquid and the simmering of the meat in this liquid for a relatively long period of time. During this second phase of braising, the pan is covered with a tight-fitting lid. Occasionally, it is necessary to check the level of liquid in the pan to be sure that some liquid still remains. If the level drops, more liquid should be added. Meats are braised until they are fork tender. This means that a fork can be inserted and withdrawn from the meat easily.

Braising is a popular method of preparing meats because it is an effective way of making less expensive, less-tender cuts of meat more palatable. It also is an excellent way of introducing a wide variety of flavors to meats.

Stewing (Cooking in Liquid)

The chief difference between braising and stewing is the amount of liquid used. Braising uses only a small amount of liquid, while stewing is done by cooking the meat in enough liquid to cover the cut.

Sometimes meats are browned as the first step in stewing. This is usually done when stew meat is being prepared, but is not commonly done when chicken is being stewed. Next, liquid is added to just cover the meat. The meat is simmered with a cover until the meat is fork tender.

RECIPES FOR MOIST HEAT MEAT COOKERY

Chicken-Fried Steak

Total Time: 1 hour and 10 minutes

1. On a bread board, pound steak until it is half its original thickness.
2. Trim off any areas of fat and connective tissue.
3. Cut into serving-sized pieces.
4. Dip each piece briefly in the mixture of beaten egg and milk and then into the crumbs.
5. Shake gently to remove loose crumbs.
6. Brown each piece in oil to a pleasing brown on both sides.
7. Add salt and pepper after browning the first side.
8. Add just enough water to cover the bottom of the skillet.
9. Cover.
10. Reduce the heat to simmering and cook until meat is fork tender. Total braising time is about 1 hour.

(Serves two)

1/2	round steak, 1/2" thick
1	egg
1 Tbsp	milk
1/2 c	fine bread or cracker crumbs
1 Tbsp	salad oil
	salt and pepper, to taste

(Serves four)

1	round steak, 1/2" thick
2	eggs
2 Tbsp	milk
1 c	fine bread or cracker crumbs
2 Tbsp	salad oil
	salt and pepper, to taste

Coconut-Crowned Chicken

Total Time: 1-1/4 hours
Baking: 350°F oven for 1 hour

1. Preheat oven.
2. Stir salt, pepper, and paprika together before dredging chicken in the mixture.
3. Brown the chicken in olive oil in a skillet.
4. Remove chicken and then sauté onions 2 minutes in the skillet.
5. Add peppers, curry powder, tomatoes, currants, chutney, and wine. Simmer 5 minutes.
6. Add chicken, spooning the vegetables over the chicken before covering and placing in 350°F oven for 40 minutes.
7. Meanwhile, mix melted butter with lime juice, coconut, and almonds.
8. Remove chicken dish from oven to top it with the coconut mixture.
9. Return chicken dish (uncovered) to oven to brown the topping lightly (about 20 minutes.)

(Serves two)

	salt and pepper to taste
2 tsp	paprika
1	whole chicken breast, skinned, boned, and split (or other chicken pieces of choice)
2 Tbsp	olive oil
1	large onion, chopped coarsely
2	garlic clove, minced
1	green bell pepper, strips
1/2	red bell pepper, strips
1/2	yellow bell pepper, strips
2 tsp	curry powder
1 c	canned stewed tomatoes
1/4 c	dried currants
1-1/2 Tbsp	Major Grey chutney
1/4 c	dry red wine
2 Tbsp	melted butter
1-1/2 Tbsp	lime juice
1/2 c	shredded coconut
1/4 c	sliced almonds

(Serves four)

	salt and pepper to taste
4 tsp	paprika
2	whole chicken breasts, skinned, boned, and split (or other chicken pieces of choice)
1/4 c	olive oil
2	large onions, chopped coarsely
2	garlic cloves, minced
1	green bell pepper, strips
1	red bell pepper, strips
1	yellow bell pepper, strips
4 tsp	curry powder
2 c	canned stewed tomatoes
1/2 c	dried currants
3 Tbsp	Major Grey chutney
1/2 c	dry red wine
1/4 c	melted butter or margarine
3 Tbsp	lime juice
1 c	shredded coconut
1/2 c	sliced almonds

Curried Beef Fricassee

Total Time: 45 minutes

1. Sauté curry powder, meat, onions, and salt in oil to brown the meat (about 5 minutes on medium heat).
2. Add potatoes, carrots, bell peppers, raisins, curry powder, and grated ginger and cook 2 minutes.
3. Add tomatoes, bouillon cube, and water. Cover and simmer slowly for 35 minutes.
4. Prepare rice according to package directions 20 minutes before fricassee is done.

(Serves two)

1-1/2 tsp	curry powder
1/2 lb	sirloin tip, cubed
1 c	diced onions
1/4 tsp	salt
1-1/2 c	cubed Red Triumph potatoes, skin on
2 tsp	olive oil
1/2 c	carrots in diagonal slices
1/3 c	red bell pepper, chopped coarsely
1/3 c	raisins
1 Tbsp	curry powder
1-1/2 tsp	grated ginger root
1 c	plum tomatoes, diced
1/2	beef bouillon cube
1/2 c	water
1 c	long grain rice

(Serves four)

1 Tbsp	curry powder
1 lb	sirloin tip, cubed
2 c	diced onions
1/2 tsp	salt
3 c	cubed Red Triumph potatoes, skin on
1 Tbsp	olive oil
1 c	carrots in diagonal slices
2/3 c	red bell pepper, chopped coarsely
2/3 c	raisins
2 Tbsp	curry powder
1 Tbsp	grated ginger root
2 c	plum tomatoes, diced
1	beef bouillon cube
1 c	water
2 c	long grain rice

Coq au Vin

Total Time: 1 hour

1. Coat chicken with flour.
2. Heat oil in a skillet and brown the chicken, shallots, and mushrooms.
3. Remove chicken.
4. Add vegetables and seasonings. Stir while cooking for 2 minutes.
5. Add wine and bouillon. Stir to loosen residue from the pan.
6. Return chicken to pan.
7. Season chicken with salt and pepper before covering pan.
8. Heat on a high simmer for 30 minutes.

(Serves two)

1	chicken breast, split
1 Tbsp	flour
2 tsp	olive oil
1 Tbsp	diced shallots
1/4 lb	small mushrooms
1/2 c	diced Roma tomatoes
1/2 c	diced carrots
1/2 c	celery in diagonal slices
1/2 tsp	dried tarragon
1/2 tsp	dried basil
1/2	bay leaf
1/3 c	dry red wine
1/2	chicken bouillon cube in
1/2 c	hot water
	salt and pepper

(Serves four)

2	chicken breasts, split
2 Tbsp	flour
1 Tbsp	olive oil
2 Tbsp	diced shallots
1/2 lb	small mushrooms
1 c	diced Roma tomatoes
1 c	diced carrots
1 c	celery in diagonal slices
1 tsp	dried tarragon
1 tsp	dried basil
1	bay leaf
2/3 c	dry red wine
1	chicken bouillon cube in
1 c	hot water
	salt and pepper

Lamb Stew

Total Time: 1 hour and 35 minutes

1. Cut meat to bite-sized cubes.
2. Brown the meat well in a small amount of oil.
3. Add enough water to just cover the meat.
4. Put on the lid and simmer 1 hour and 15 minutes.
5. Add the other ingredients and cook until the vegetables are tender.
6. Stir in 1 tablespoon flour thoroughly blended with 1/4 cup water.
7. Stir constantly while heating stew to boiling.
8. Serve.

(Serves two)

1/2 lb	lamb stew meat, breast
2 tsp	salad oil
8	boiling onions
2	small carrots, diced
1/4 c	celery, chopped
2	small potatoes, diced
2	peppercorns
piece	bay leaf
1 Tbsp	flour
1/4 c	water

(Serves four)

1 lb	lamb stew meat, breast
1-1/4 Tbsp	salad oil
16	boiling onions
4	small carrots, diced
1/2 c	celery, chopped
4	small potatoes, diced
4	peppercorns
2 pieces	bay leaf
2 Tbsp	flour
1/2 c	water

Islander's Chicken

Total Time: 1 hour

1. Sprinkle chicken with seasoned salt.
2. Sauté in hot oil until well browned on all sides.
3. Drain excess fat.
4. Drain pineapple and reserve juice for next step.
5. Combine pineapple juice, ginger, orange peel, and honey. Pour over chicken.
6. Cover and simmer 40 minutes or until tender.
7. Remove chicken to a warm serving platter.
8. Mix flour and water together until smooth.
9. Stir into pan drippings, and heat to boiling while stirring.
10. Add pineapple chunks and orange slices. Heat just until fruit is warm.
11. Serve over chicken.

(Serves two)

2–3	chicken legs and thighs
1/2 tsp	seasoned salt
2 tsp	salad oil
1/2 c	pineapple chunks
1/2 tsp	ginger
1 tsp	grated fresh orange peel
3 Tbsp	orange juice
2 Tbsp	honey
1 tsp	flour
1 Tbsp	water
1/2	orange, peeled, sliced into cartwheels

(Serves four)

4–6	chicken legs and thighs
1 tsp	seasoned salt
1 Tbsp	salad oil
1 c	pineapple chunks
1 tsp	ginger
2 tsp	grated fresh orange peel
1/3 c	orange juice
1/4 c	honey
2 tsp	flour
2 Tbsp	water
1	orange, peeled, sliced into cartwheels

Islander's Chicken is featured with orange slices and accented with Chinese pea pods and water chestnuts.

Pot Roast

Total Time: 1-1/2 to 2 hours

1. Lightly flour the meat and brown it well in oil.
2. Salt and pepper are added after the first side is browned.
3. Arrange the onion and lemon on top of the meat.
4. Sprinkle the thyme and marjoram on top.
5. Add just enough water to cover the bottom of the pan.
6. Cover and simmer until fork tender, adding water as needed.
7. Add pared carrots and potatoes the last hour if desired.
8. Total cooking time 1-1/2 to 2 hours.

(Serves two)

1	small chuck roast
2 tsp	salad oil
1/2	medium onion, slices
1/4	lemon, sliced
dash	thyme
dash	Marjoram

(Serves four)

1	average chuck roast
1 Tbsp	salad oil
1	medium onion, slices
1/2	lemon, sliced
1/8 tsp	thyme
1/8 tsp	Marjoram

Figure 9.4
Carving a blade pot roast.

Stuffed Flank Steak

Total Time: 3-1/2 hours

1. Lightly score the flank steak.
2. Mix the remaining ingredients and place in the middle of the flank steak.
3. Roll the flank steak with the dressing in the center.
4. Tie securely with string.
5. Lightly coat the exterior of the flank steak with flour.
6. Brown entire flank steak well in a skillet containing 1 tablespoon oil.
7. Add enough water to just cover the bottom of the skillet and put on the lid.
8. Reduce the heat to simmering and cook until the meat is fork tender.
9. Add more water as necessary.
10. Total cooking time is approximately 3 hours.

(Serves two)

1/2	flank steak
1-1/2	slices dry bread, cubed
1/4	medium onion, chopped
1/4 tsp	salt
pinch	poultry seasoning
1 Tbsp	margarine or butter, melted
1/4	green pepper, chopped
1/2 can	sliced mushrooms
1 Tbsp	salad oil

(Serves four)

1	flank steak
3	slices dry bread, cubed
1/2	medium onion, chopped
1/2 tsp	salt
1/4 tsp	poultry seasoning
2 Tbsp	margarine or butter, melted
1/2	green pepper, chopped
1 can	sliced mushrooms
2 Tbsp	salad oil

Swiss Steak

Total Time: 2 hours and 15 minutes

1. Cut away extra fat and connective tissue.
2. Pound the meat thoroughly with a meat pounder.
3. After lightly flouring it, brown the meat in oil.
4. Season with salt and pepper.
5. Arrange bay leaf and thin slices of onion over the meat and pour the tomatoes on top.
6. If more liquid is needed, add either tomato juice or water.
7. Cover the pan and reduce heat to simmering.
8. Cook until fork tender, adding additional liquid as needed. Allow 2 hours cooking time.

(Serves two)

1/2	round steak
2 tsp	salad oil
piece	bay leaf
1/2	medium onion, sliced
1/2 c	stewed tomatoes

(Serves four)

1	round steak
1 Tbsp	salad oil
piece	bay leaf
1	medium onion, sliced
1 c	stewed tomatoes

Sauerbraten

Total Time: 2 hours and 30 minutes plus 2 days to marinate

1. Put the meat in a bowl just larger than the meat.
2. Make a marinade out of the remaining ingredients and pour over the meat.
3. Cover tightly and place in the refrigerator for two days.
4. Turn the meat occasionally if the marinade does not cover it completely.
5. Take the meat out of the marinade and brown it in oil in a Dutch oven.
6. When the meat has been browned on all sides, add enough of the marinade to cover the bottom of the pan and put on the lid.
7. Simmer until fork tender, adding liquid marinade as needed. Allow 2 hours cooking time.

(Serves two)

	very small rump roast
1 c	vinegar
1 c	water
1	medium onion, sliced
10	whole cloves
2	bay leaves
10	peppercorns
1/4	green pepper, sliced
1 tsp	salt

(Serves four)

	medium rump roast
2 c	vinegar
2 c	water
2	medium onions, sliced
20	whole cloves
4	bay leaves
20	peppercorns
1/2	green pepper, sliced
2 tsp	salt

Fricassee of Veal

Total Time: 1 hour and 15 minutes

1. Trim connective tissue and cut meat into serving-sized pieces.
2. Coat the pieces lightly with flour and brown in oil.
3. Mix the seasonings together and sprinkle over the surface of the meat.
4. Add water to cover the bottom of the pan and put on the lid.
5. Simmer 55 minutes.
6. Add the sour cream and continue simmering for about 5 minutes to warm the sour cream. Serve immediately.

(Serves two)

1/2 lb	thinly cut veal round steak
2 tsp	salad oil
dash	white pepper
dash	salt
1/4 tsp	paprika
dash	cayenne
1/2 c	dairy sour cream

(Serves four)

1 lb	thinly cut veal round steak
1-1/4 Tbsp	salad oil
1/8 tsp	white pepper
1/8 tsp	salt
1/2 tsp	paprika
1/8 tsp	cayenne
1 c	dairy sour cream

Lemon Lamb Shanks

Total Time: 2 hours and 20 minutes

1. Have a butcher "crack" lamb shanks for easier browning.
2. Combine salt, pepper, paprika, and thyme; rub well over all sides of meat.
3. Lightly coat with flour.
4. Place oil in heavy skillet or Dutch oven.
5. Brown shanks very slowly on all sides.
6. Remove from pan.
7. Sauté onions and garlic in remaining oil until limp and transparent.
8. Make a bouquet garni by placing the peppercorns, bay leaf, and parsley in the center of a cheesecloth square. Tie in bundle fashion with clean string.
9. Return shanks to pan; add lemon peel, juice, water, and bouquet garni.
10. Cover tightly, and simmer slowly for about 2 hours or until tender.
11. Baste and turn occasionally during cooking. Add small amounts of water, if necessary.
12. When fork tender, place meat on warm serving platter. Remove bouquet garni and discard.
13. While stirring constantly, add 1 tablespoon flour and 2 tablespoons water and heat until mixture boils and thickens.
14. Pour sauce over lamb shanks; garnish with lemon slices.

(Serves two)

2–3	small lamb shanks
1/4 tsp	salt
1/4 tsp	pepper
1/2 tsp	paprika
1/4 tsp	thyme, crushed
1 Tbsp	flour
1 Tbsp	salad oil
1/2	medium onion, thinly sliced
1 clove	garlic, finely minced
2	whole peppercorns
1	small bay leaf, crushed
1 sprig	parsley
1 Tbsp	grated lemon peel
1/4 c	lemon juice
1/4 c	water
1/2	lemon, thinly sliced

(Serves four)

4–6	small lamb shanks
1/2 tsp	salt
1/2 tsp	pepper
1 tsp	paprika
1/2 tsp	thyme, crushed
2 Tbsp	flour
2 Tbsp	salad oil
1	medium onion, thinly sliced
2 cloves	garlic, finely minced
4	whole peppercorns
2	small bay leaves, crushed
2 sprigs	parsley
2 Tbsp	grated lemon peel
1/2 c	lemon juice
1/2 c	water
1	lemon, thinly sliced

Shrimp with Artichokes

Total time: 30 minutes

1. In olive oil, sauté garlic, red pepper, and celery 2 minutes.
2. Add shrimp and stir while cooking until shrimp are pink.
3. Stir in other ingredients and gently simmer 3 minutes.
4. Serve over rice.

(Serves two)

1 Tbsp	olive oil
1 clove	garlic
1/4	red pepper, chopped
1/4 c	celery, sliced
1/2 pound	peeled, deveined shrimp
1/4 tsp	paprika
1/2 jar	marinated artichoke hearts and liquid
1 tsp	lemon zest
2	plum tomatoes, chopped
1 Tbsp	minced parsley
1/8 tsp	salt
1 Tbsp	minced parsley
1/2 tsp	curry powder
1/2 c	coconut milk
2 c	cooked rice

(Serves four)

2 Tbsp	olive oil
2 cloves	garlic
1/2	red pepper, chopped
1/2 c	celery, sliced
1 pound	peeled, deveined shrimp
1/2 tsp	paprika
1 jar	marinated artichoke hearts and liquid
2 tsp	lemon zest
4	plum tomatoes, chopped
2 Tbsp	minced parsley
1/4 tsp	salt
2 Tbsp	minced parsley
1 tsp	curry powder
1 c	coconut milk
4 c	cooked rice

Evaluation of Laboratory Products—Fruits

Recipe	Notes on Color, Texture, Flavor, or Other Qualities	Comments or Suggestions for Making or Using this Product in the Future

VOCABULARY

Elastin

Collagen

Inspection

Grading

Primal cuts

Dry heat meat cookery

Moist heat meat cookery

Deep-fat frying

Roasting

Pan frying

Pan broiling

Stewing

Braising

CHAPTER 10

Breads

GLUTEN

You are likely to find that making breads of various types is one of the most satisfying and relaxing experiences you will have in preparing food. Creativity is very possible when formulating and shaping breads. The rewards are fairly fast in coming if you are making quick breads; a bit of patience is necessary when making yeast breads because of the need for carbon dioxide formation to leaven them.

In this chapter, you will learn about gluten, the protein complex required for the strong structure needed in various breads. Then you will learn about basic types of quick breads and some variations. The unique aspect of making quality yeast breads is managing temperatures in any part of the preparation where yeast is present to ensure viability of the yeast and the consequent production of carbon dioxide.

By manipulating a simple dough of flour and water, you can develop the gluten of the flour to make gluten balls. Washing of the dough then removes the starch, leaving the protein. In the unbaked gluten ball, the cohesive and elastic nature of gluten can be observed easily. After baking, the structural contribution the denatured gluten makes to baked products can be appreciated. The differences in the gluten of cake and all-purpose flours also are apparent.

Objectives

1. To demonstrate the elastic nature of gluten in its native state.
2. To illustrate the structural characteristics of gluten when denatured by heat.
3. To emphasize the difference in the quantity and quality of gluten in all-purpose and cake flours.

KEY CONCEPTS

1. Gluten, a mixture of proteins in wheat, can be developed into a cohesive, rather elastic complex if some liquid is manipulated with wheat flour; the structure of breads depends heavily on optimal gluten development.

2. Quick breads include biscuits, muffins, popovers, pancakes, waffles, cake doughnuts, and variations of these; all are leavened with steam, and most obtain added volume from baking powder or acids and baking soda.

3. The preparation of yeast breads requires extensive kneading to develop a strong gluten network and care to avoid killing the yeast by exposing to high temperatures.

Gluten Balls—A Basic Demonstration

Total Time: 65 minutes
Baking: 450°F oven for 15 minutes, then 300°F oven for 30 minutes

(1 ball)

1 c   All-purpose or cake flour water

1. Preheat oven.
2. Use either cake flour or all-purpose flour; add just enough water to make a stiff dough.
3. Knead the dough hard for 5 minutes to develop the gluten.
4. Put the ball of dough in a tightly woven cloth and work it under cold running water to wash out the starch. Keep manipulating the dough until the water runs clear and has no trace of milky exudate.
5. Scrape the cream-colored gluten from the cloth with a knife and work into a ball. If patches of white remain, wash the gluten some more to completely remove the starch.
6. Place on a cookie sheet and bake 15 minutes at 450°F in a preheated oven.
7. Turn the temperature down to 300°F and continue baking an additional 30 minutes. With a sharp knife, cut the gluten balls in half and examine the texture.

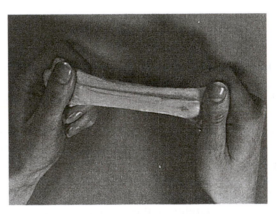

Figure 10.1
Gluten is an elastic protein complex developed when wheat flour and water are manipulated together.

Figure 10.2
Baked cake flour (left) and all-purpose flour (right) gluten balls.

Comparison of Gluten from All-Purpose and Cake Flours

	All-Purpose Flour Gluten Ball	Cake Flour Gluten Ball
Approximate height baked		
Exterior appearance		
Interior appearance		

QUICK BREADS

Objectives

1. To illustrate the effect of mixing methods on the texture and palatability of quick breads.
2. To compare the ingredients used in various quick breads and identify their roles during mixing and baking.
3. To prepare quick breads of high quality, including muffins, biscuits, pancakes, waffles, popovers, doughnuts, and coffee cakes.
4. To apply criteria of quality to evaluation of selected quick breads.

Principles of Preparing Biscuits and Muffins

Quick breads are defined as any breads that are not leavened by yeast. They are termed *quick* because they can be baked quickly rather than having to wait for the action of yeast to leaven the bread. Cake doughnuts, fritters, pancakes, waffles, popovers, many coffee cakes, biscuits, and muffins are classified as quick breads. Air and steam are leavening agents in all of these, but many of them also are leavened by the carbon dioxide, which is generated from baking powder. Popovers are leavened primarily by steam, but muffins, biscuits, pancakes, doughnuts, and most other quick breads rely on baking powder for their primary source of leavening.

Quick breads range in viscosity from the fluid batters of pancakes and popovers, to the thicker batter of muffins, and finally to doughs such as biscuits and doughnuts, which can be handled and cut out before baking or frying. The methods of cooking these batters and doughs vary from one type of quick bread to another.

Doughnuts and fritters are fried in deep fat, while pancakes are baked on a griddle, waffles in a waffle iron, and the other quick breads are baked in an oven.

Biscuits and muffins are typical examples of quick breads, that is, breads that are not leavened by yeast. Like all quick breads, the recipes for biscuits and muffins include all-purpose flour, salt, and liquid (usually milk). In addition to these basic ingredients, biscuits contain baking powder and solid shortening, while muffins are made with melted shortening, eggs, baking powder, and sugar added.

Biscuits

Because the preparation time for mixing biscuits is rather short and proofing or rising time is not required, the oven should be preheating before mixing begins. The oven temperature is set at 425°F. This temperature allows sufficient time for carbon dioxide to be generated from the baking powder to expand the biscuits before the gluten of the flour denatures and loses its extensibility, thus promoting optimum volume. Although this is a high temperature, there is an adequate amount of time during baking to bake the dough throughout before the biscuit surface becomes too brown. At this temperature, the crust browns readily, but there is much less risk of burning than is the case at a higher temperature.

The fat used in biscuits traditionally is a solid fat that is cut into the sifted dry ingredients with a pastry blender or two knives until the pieces are the size of cooked rice grains. The cutting in of fat should be done with a light, tossing motion to avoid packing the dough. At first it will be necessary to scrape the fat from the pastry blender occasionally. The small pieces of fat that are formed by the cutting in of the shortening will melt during baking to help create layering or flakiness in the finished product.

When cutting in of the fat has been completed, a fork is used to make a well in the center of the dry ingredients and the milk is poured in. (This single addition of liquid is in contrast to the very gradual addition of water that is done in making pastry.) By having all of the milk present at one time, this somewhat sticky ratio of milk and flour can be mixed efficiently without developing the gluten excessively.

Efficient and effective mixing of the milk and dry ingredients is done easily with a table fork. Stirring is done with quick, light motions. Attention should be directed toward scraping the edges and the bottom of the bowl while stirring. This helps to get the entire mixture stirred uniformly. In addition, it is necessary to cut through the center of the mass of dough frequently to help moisten all portions of the dough uniformly. Satisfactory mixing should be accomplished in approximately 20 strokes.

Lightly flour a bread board over an area of about 12" square, brushing this entire area well with the hand to rub the flour into the surface of the board. When the board has been floured, push any extra flour to the edge of the floured area, leaving only a very light dusting of flour on the surface. Scrape all of the dough from the bowl onto the floured area in preparation for kneading.

Kneading is done to help finish the uniform mixing of ingredients, to develop the gluten in the flour, and to promote the desired flakiness. The kneading action in making biscuits is much lighter than that used for yeast rolls. Biscuits are kneaded with the fingertips, while rolls are kneaded with a vigorous push with the heel of the hand.

The kneading action is begun by lifting the dough at the far edge. The far edge of the dough is folded over to the near edge. This folding of two layers of dough aids in creating the desired layered or flaky texture of kneaded biscuits.

The kneading action is completed by pressing the near edge of the dough toward the folded rear edge. This action is accomplished using a gentle, light motion with the fingertips of both hands. This gentle, kneading action promotes development of gluten, but is not done vigorously enough to tear the gluten strands.

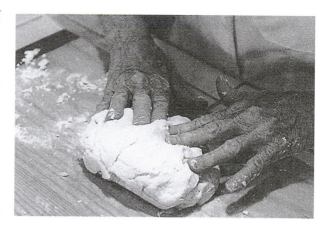

The dough now is turned 90° so that the elongated dough mass is extending away from the person kneading the dough. As the dough is rotated, it may tend to stick to the floured board. If this happens, the dough should be lifted, and a very small amount of flour should be dusted on the kneading area. A minimum of flour should be used on the board to avoid producing a tough, dry biscuit. When the dough has been rotated, the kneading process is repeated by lifting the far edge, folding to the near edge, and pressing lightly toward the fold with the fingertips. Again the dough is rotated 90° and the lifting, folding, and pressing steps are repeated. A smooth rhythm can be developed so that kneading becomes a

quick and effective technique in which the lifting, folding, and pressing of the dough blend into a continuous, fluid motion. During the kneading, the development of the gluten can be felt in the fingertips as the dough becomes somewhat tighter, smoother, and slightly resistant to pressure. An appropriate amount of kneading can be done in 20 strokes or less.

When kneading is completed, use a minimum of flour on the board and roll the dough gently with a lightly floured rolling pin to a uniform thickness of 1/2". If desired, the dough can be rolled thinner to produce crisper biscuits. During the baking period, the biscuits will just about double in height. To obtain a uniform thickness, the pressure on the rolling pin should be lightened near the edge of the dough. Light pressure is used throughout the rolling process to avoid undue stretching and damage to the gluten. This helps to promote the desired flakiness and tenderness.

Use a lightly floured biscuit cutter to cut out the biscuits. The cutting is done by applying a firm, uniform pressure on the cutter handle straight down all the way through the dough. Careful cutting is essential so that the biscuits will be a uniform thickness around the edge. Attention to cutting will help to maintain the shape of biscuits and minimize the tendency to bend over during baking. Biscuits should be cut as close together as possible to obtain the maximum number of biscuits from the first rolling of the dough.

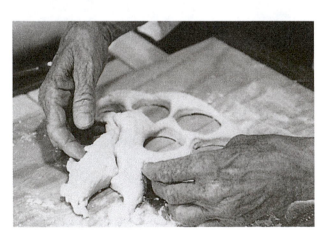

The dough left from the first cutting can be worked into a cohesive mass that can again be rolled and cut. Although biscuits from the second rolling will be a little less attractive and slightly less tender than the first rolling, they still are very satisfactory if the dough has been kneaded and rolled gently.

The cut biscuits are transferred individually from the bread board to a baking sheet. If soft sides are desired, the biscuits should be placed so that their sides touch each other. This arrangement also helps to direct the biscuits up straight so the sides will remain straight as the biscuits rise during baking. For biscuits with crisper sides, arrange the biscuits on the baking sheet with a space of at least 1/2" between biscuits on all sides. Because biscuits rise upward without spreading, this spacing allows the hot oven air to circulate well between the biscuits.

When all of the biscuits are arranged on the baking sheet, they may be brushed with milk on the upper surface. This small amount of liquid aids in dissolving any dry baking powder that may be on the surface. In addition, the protein and lactose contained in the milk aid in developing a pleasing brown color and a slight sheen during baking. Biscuits can be made without brushing them with milk, but their top surface is likely to have small brown flecks of undissolved baking powder, and they will not brown as readily. The use of milk on the surface is strictly a matter of individual preference.

The sheet of biscuits is baked on a central rack position in a 425°F oven for approximately 12 minutes. Biscuits made from dough rolled 1/2" thick are done when their upper surface is a pleasing, medium brown, and they have baked for at least 12 minutes. Thinner biscuits will be done in a slightly shorter time. For the most pleasing results, biscuits should be served hot when they come from the oven.

The evaluation of biscuits begins with an examination of the exterior. The sides of the biscuit should be straight, and the top and bottom should be flat and perpendicular to the sides. If the bottom edge tends to curve upward toward the sides, the dough contained a bit too much liquid in proportion to flour. If the sides are not perpendicular to the top and bottom, the biscuits were cut with uneven pressure on the cutter or the dough was not rolled to a uniform thickness.

The bottom and top surfaces should be evaluated for appearance. They should be a pleasing, medium golden-brown color. Too light a color is an indication of underbaking, either because the oven temperature was too low or the time was too short. Too dark a color may be the result of the oven being too hot or the time too long. If the rack position is too high, the upper surface may fail to brown satisfactorily. Conversely, a very low rack position results in excessive browning or even burning of the bottom crust.

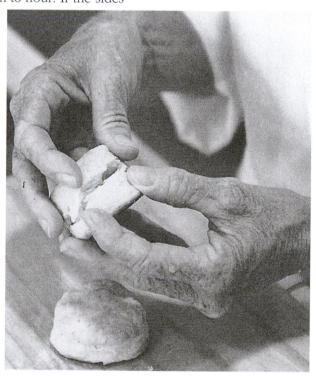

The sides of biscuits provide a clue to the flaky interior. Biscuits that are flaky will exhibit a number of short cracks on the sides. These cracks are caused by the biscuits rising during baking. Correctly kneaded biscuits will have several of these cracks in the sides. Volume also is of interest because a high biscuit implies quality to most people. Biscuits with the correct amount of baking powder and proper mixing should double in volume during baking.

Biscuits, when broken apart, should reveal a flaky interior. This can be judged by rubbing a finger across the exposed interior surface. This motion will begin to peel off layers of the biscuit. In addition to appearance, biscuits are evaluated on the basis of flavor and tenderness. The flavor should be pleasing, with a minimum aftertaste from baking powder and no trace of burning. An excessive amount of double-acting baking powder contributes a metallic aftertaste, a problem not noted if a tartrate baking powder is used. The crust of biscuits should be somewhat crisp, and the crumb should be tender. Tenderness in biscuits is promoted by using an adequate quantity of milk and by avoiding excessive mixing and kneading, either of which would develop the gluten too much.

RECIPES

Biscuits

Total Time: 25 minutes
Baking: 425°F oven for 12 minutes

1. Preheat oven.
2. Sift dry ingredients together in a mixing bowl.
3. Cut in the shortening with a pastry blender until the pieces are about the size of split peas.
4. Make a well in the mixture and pour all the milk in at once. Stir with a fork to mix the dough and moisten all the ingredients.
5. Turn dough out onto a lightly floured bread board.
6. Knead lightly with the fingertips by first lifting the far edge of the dough and folding it over toward you to meet the front edge of the dough.
7. Then press lightly with the fingertips.
8. Turn the dough a quarter of a turn, and knead.
9. Keep repeating this kneading action until the dough has been kneaded at least ten times.
10. With a lightly floured rolling pin, roll out the dough 1/3 to 1/2″ thick (dough will double in height during baking).
11. With a floured, sharp biscuit cutter, cut out the biscuits as close together as possible.
12. Transfer the biscuits to a cookie sheet. For crisp sides, spread the biscuits apart. For soft sides, place the biscuits so that their sides are touching.
13. After cutting all the biscuits possible from the first rolling, rework the dough a little and roll again for a second cutting.
14. Brush the surface of the biscuits lightly with milk if a slightly shiny top is desired.
15. Bake at 425°F for about 12 minutes until the tops are a golden brown. Serve hot.

(Makes 6 biscuits)

1 c	all-purpose flour, sifted
1-1/2 tsp	baking powder
1/4 tsp	salt
3 Tbsp	shortening
6 Tbsp 1/2 tsp	milk

(Makes 12 biscuits)

2 c	all-purpose flour, sifted
1 Tbsp	baking powder
1/2 tsp	salt
1/3 c	shortening
3/4 c	milk

Buttermilk Biscuits

Total Time: 30 minutes
Baking: 425°F oven for 15 minutes

1. Preheat oven.
2. Stir dry ingredients (flour, baking powder, and salt) together in mixing bowl.
3. Cut in shortening with a pastry blender until the pieces are about the size of split peas.
4. Make a well in the ingredients and add the buttermilk. Stir with a fork just until ingredients are all moistened.
5. Flour bread board moderately and turn the dough out onto it.
6. Keep hands floured while lightly kneading the dough until it begins to work together enough to be rolled 1/2″ thick.
7. With a floured biscuit cutter, cut biscuits and arrange on a baking sheet so that they touch each other.
8. Bake at 450°F about 15 minutes until golden brown. Serve hot.

(Makes 6 biscuits)

1 c	all-purpose flour
2 tsp	baking powder
1/8 tsp	salt
3 Tbsp	shortening
1/2 c	buttermilk

(Makes 12 biscuits)

2 c	all-purpose flour
4 tsp	baking powder
1/4 tsp	salt
1/3 c	shortening
1 c	buttermilk

Muffins

The recipe for muffins is different from biscuits in that it contains sugar and eggs. An additional difference is the use of salad oil or melted shortening rather than solid fat. The ratio of liquid to flour in muffins is 1:2—that is, 1 cup liquid to 2 cups of flour. This is a slightly higher ratio of liquid to flour than is found in biscuits.

Muffins, like biscuits, may be baked at 425°F, although they also may be baked successfully at 400°F. The oven should be preheated while the muffins are being mixed. Before beginning to mix the ingredients, the cups in the muffin pan should be greased lightly to facilitate removal of the baked muffins.

The muffin method of mixing, in summary, is a three-step process: (1) mixing of the dry ingredients, (2) mixing of the liquid ingredients, and (3) combining the liquid and dry ingredients to make the finished batter. The first step in this total process is the preparation of the dry ingredients. These are combined by sifting all of them together into a mixing bowl in preparation for incorporation with the liquid ingredients.

Preparation of the liquid ingredients is started by gently beating the egg until it is blended thoroughly, but not foamy. The milk is added to the egg and beaten very gently. Thorough blending of the egg and milk is important. Under-blended egg will cause muffins to have a somewhat waxy quality on the interior and may even result in streaks of egg showing in the baked muffins. The final step in combining liquid ingredients is to stir in the melted shortening.

Make a well in the dry ingredients and pour the liquid mixture into the well. All of the liquid is added at one time to reduce the total amount of mixing. A wooden spoon is a convenient utensil to use for stirring the liquid and dry ingredients together. Stirring needs to be done throughout the mixture as uniformly as possible. Care should be taken to stir in the dry ingredients from the sides and bottom of the mixing bowl. It is also necessary to cut through the batter with the mixing spoon. The objective of the mixing procedure is to moisten all of the dry ingredients without developing the gluten too much. Because the ratio of 1 part liquid to 2 parts flour is very sticky, gluten develops very readily with stirring.

The appearance of muffin batter changes quickly as mixing progresses. At the beginning, there will be many regions where dry ingredients are visible and areas where the liquid is draining from the batter. In these dry regions, the gluten is not yet developing, and the baking powder is not moistened enough to permit the chemical reaction needed to release carbon dioxide for leavening. A muffin batter that still has areas of dry ingredients visible and pools of liquid is under-mixed.

Stirring of muffin batter should be continued until all of the dry and liquid ingredients are blended to the point where no dry areas remain and the liquid is not evident at the edges of the bowl. At this stage of mixing, the batter will still be lumpy. The gluten will be developed sufficiently to provide the necessary structural framework to allow the muffin to expand without falling during baking and to hold the baked muffin together without being excessively crumbly.

Sometimes people overmix muffins because they do not recognize the appearance of properly mixed muffin batter. Muffin batter should not be mixed to the point where it begins to look smooth because the muffins will have a less attractive appearance and will be less tender.

Muffins will have the best appearance if enough batter for a single muffin is placed in a muffin cup at one time. To do this, the mixing spoon is filled with batter by cutting toward the side of the mixing bowl; then a second spoon or spatula is used to scrape the batter gently into the pan. The cup should be filled a little more than half full.

This process is repeated until the batter is gone. The batter should be scooped from the bowl with a minimum amount of manipulation. The practice of scraping down the sides of the bowl and stirring the batter after each spoonful is removed is detrimental to the quality of the batch of muffins. When all of the batter has been spooned into the pans, any spilled batter should be wiped from the pans before baking the muffins.

Muffins are baked approximately 20 minutes until they are a pleasing golden brown. The pan should be positioned on a rack in the center of the oven. If more than one pan is to be baked at the same time, the pans should be at least an inch from the sides, front, and back of the oven and a comparable distance should be allowed between pans. This arrangement is important to avoid blocking the flow of hot oven air needed for satisfactory browning.

To avoid developing a soggy crust, muffins should be removed from the cups after the baked muffins have been taken from the oven. Fresh muffins are best when served while still hot from the oven. However, quick breads (including muffins) can be frozen very successfully. If they are to be frozen, muffins should be cooled to room temperature on a rack before packaging them for freezing.

The exterior of baked muffins clearly reflects the amount of mixing. The surface of under-mixed muffins will be rough and jagged. Specks of dry flour are likely to be in evidence. Correctly mixed muffins have a cauliflower-like top. The surface has softly rounded bumps, the result of adequate gluten development. Batter that has been over-mixed will result in muffins with a very smooth surface, which is similar to the appearance of yeast rolls.

The shape of the upper crust of muffins also is modified by the amount of mixing. Under-mixed muffins are only very slightly rounded, and the volume is small because of the failure of some of the dry baking powder to react. There may be evidence of some liquid draining to the edge of the upper surface. Properly mixed muffins will have a rounded top surface and a greater volume than the under-mixed muffins. With increasing mixing beyond optimum, the rounded contour will change to a humped or peaked shape.

The interior of muffins also reflects the amount of mixing. Under-mixed muffins will not have the gluten developed sufficiently, and they will tend to crumble readily. There also may be evidence of dry flour. Properly mixed muffins will be quite coarse, yet relatively uniform in texture; however, they will crumble just a little. Over-mixed muffins will have some tunnels that extend upward toward the peak. These tunnels are created by pockets of gas expanding upward along strong gluten strands before the protein was denatured during baking. The regions between the tunnels generally will be comprised of comparatively small cells.

In addition to evaluating texture and volume, muffins are rated on the basis of flavor and tenderness. The flavor should be well rounded and pleasing, with no suggestion of any burning. The interior should not have any regions of dry ingredients or any suggestion of waxiness. Muffins should be tender, but they will be just a little bit crumbly.

Figure 10.3
Under-mixed muffin (left) has poor volume and crumbly texture compared with properly mixed muffin (center). The over-mixed muffin (right) has tunnels and a peaked top.

RECIPES

Muffins

Total Time: 30 minutes
Baking: 425°F oven for 20 minutes

(Makes 6 muffins)

1 c	all-purpose flour, sifted
2 Tbsp	sugar
1-1/2 tsp	baking powder
1/4 tsp	salt
1/2	egg
2 Tbsp	salad oil
1/2 c	milk

(Makes 12 muffins)

2 c	all-purpose flour, sifted
1/4 c	sugar
1 Tbsp	baking powder
1/2 tsp	salt
1	egg
1/4 c	salad oil
1 c	milk

1. Preheat oven.
2. Grease the muffin pan.
3. Sift all the dry ingredients into the mixing bowl.
4. In a separate bowl, beat the egg well.
5. Add salad oil and milk to the egg and beat until well blended.
6. Pour the liquid ingredients into the dry ingredients, and mix with a wooden spoon just enough to moisten all the ingredients. The batter will look lumpy, but no dry flour will show.
7. Scoop a spoonful of batter from the mixing bowl. Using a second spoon, push the batter into a greased muffin pan. Be sure to get enough batter at one time to fill muffin cup slightly more than half full.
8. Repeat this procedure until all the muffin batter is used. Avoid stirring the batter when spooning batter from the bowl.
9. Bake in a 425°F oven 20 minutes or until the tops are golden brown.
10. Remove muffins from pan as soon as they are taken from the oven.
11. Serve while hot.

Blueberry Muffins

Total Time: 30 minutes
Baking: 425°F oven for 20 minutes

1. Preheat oven and grease muffin pans.
2. Drain the blueberries thoroughly in a strainer.
3. Sift all the dry ingredients into the mixing bowl.
4. In a separate bowl, beat the egg and stir in the salad oil and milk.
5. Pour the liquid ingredients into the dry ingredients; mix with wooden spoon.
6. Add the blueberries, sprinkle with the sugar, and just barely stir them in.
7. Put the batter in muffin pans and bake at 425°F for 20 to 25 minutes. Serve at once.

(Makes 6 muffins)

1/3 c	blueberries
1 c	all-purpose flour, sifted
2 Tbsp	sugar
1-1/2 tsp	baking powder
1/2 tsp	salt
1/2	egg
1/4 c	milk
2 Tbsp	salad oil
1 tsp	sugar

(Makes 12 muffins)

2/3 c	blueberries
2 c	all-purpose flour, sifted
1/4 c	sugar
1 Tbsp	baking powder
1 tsp	salt
1	egg
1/2 c	milk
1/4 c	salad oil
2 Tbsp	sugar

OTHER QUICK BREAD RECIPES

Popovers

Total Time: 55 minutes
Baking: 425°F oven for 45 minutes

1. Preheat oven.
2. Grease popover pan or custard cups and place in a 425°F oven to preheat while making the batter.
3. Combine all the ingredients and beat until smooth.
4. With the aid of the hot pads, put the hot popover pan on a heat-resistant counter.
5. Quickly pour batter into the hot cups, filling them half full.
6. Immediately bake at 425°F.
7. Bake 40 minutes.
8. Puncture with a cooking fork to let out steam, and bake 5 more minutes.
9. Remove from pan and serve.

(Makes 4 popovers)

1/2 c	all-purpose flour, sifted
1/8 tsp	salt
1/2 c	milk
1	egg

(Makes 8 popovers)

1 c	all-purpose flour, sifted
1/4 tsp	salt
1 c	milk
2	eggs

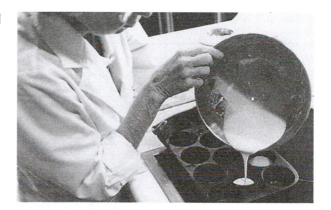

Note: When a popover is broken open (above right) a very large central cavity should be found inside. The walls surrounding the cavity should be rather thin and not doughy. Although the walls will be a bit moist, the general impression is one of crispness and chewiness rather than of sogginess. Failure to achieve the desired cavity may be the result of baking at too low a temperature. A low oven temperature allows heat to penetrate to the interior and begin to coagulate the gluten and egg proteins before enough steam pressure has built up inside to stretch the batter and form the large cavity that is the hallmark of a good popover.

Pancakes

Total Time: 15 minutes

1. Sift the dry ingredients into a mixing bowl.
2. Beat the liquid ingredients together in another bowl, and then pour them into the dry ingredients.
3. Mix with a rotary beater just until the batter is smooth.
4. Bake on a griddle hot enough to make drops of water dance on it.
5. Pour batter from the pitcher to make pancakes the diameter desired. Pour far enough apart so that the sides do not touch.
6. Bake until golden brown on the bottom and the bubbles that form have popped.
7. Flip over and bake the second side to a golden brown.
8. Serve at once, or hold in a 150°F oven with paper towels separating the pancakes.

(Makes 4 pancakes)

10 Tbsp	all-purpose flour, sifted
1 tsp	sugar
1/4 tsp	salt
1-1/2 tsp	baking powder
1/2	egg
1/2 c	milk
1 Tbsp	salad oil

(Makes 8 pancakes)

1-1/4 c	all-purpose flour, sifted
2 tsp	sugar
1/2 tsp	salt
1 Tbsp	baking powder
1	egg
1 c	milk
2 Tbsp	salad oil

Waffles

Total Time: 15 minutes

1. Preheat waffle iron.
2. Sift dry ingredients together in a mixing bowl.
3. Beat egg in another mixing bowl and then beat in the other liquid ingredients.
4. Make a well in the dry ingredients and add all of the liquid ingredients.
5. Beat with a rotary beater just until batter is smooth.
6. Pour batter carefully onto hot waffle iron, being sure to use enough batter just to reach the edge of the iron.
7. Carefully close cover; bake without opening the iron until steam no longer is escaping.
8. Check to be sure that waffle is a pleasing brown. Remove from iron and serve immediately.

(Makes 4 waffles)

1-1/4 c	all-purpose flour, sifted
2 tsp	baking powder
1-1/2 tsp	sugar
1/4 tsp	salt
1	egg
1-1/8 c	milk
1/3 c	salad oil

(Makes 8 waffles)

2-1/2 c	all-purpose flour, sifted
4 tsp	baking powder
1 Tbsp	sugar
1/2 tsp	salt
2	eggs
2-1/4 c	milk
2/3 c	salad oil

Cake Doughnuts

Total Time: 1 hour and 30 minutes
Deep-fat fryer: 375°F for 15 minutes

1. Mix the dry ingredients together.
2. In a separate bowl, beat the eggs well.
3. Stir in the milk and melted shortening.
4. Combine the dry and liquid ingredients, and mix well.
5. Chill dough 1 hour before rolling on a well-floured board.
6. Begin preheating oil in fryer during last 5 minutes of chilling period.
7. Roll dough a little less than 1/2″ thick and cut with a floured doughnut cutter.
8. Use a wide spatula to transfer the doughnuts from the bread board to the deep-fat fryer containing fat preheated to 375°F.
9. Fry on one side until a pleasing golden brown, then turn over and brown the second side.
10. Drain on paper towels.

(Makes 10 doughnuts)

1-3/4 c	all-purpose flour, sifted
6 Tbsp	sugar
1-1/2 tsp	baking powder
1/4 tsp	salt
1/4 tsp	cinnamon
1/4 tsp	nutmeg
1-1/2	eggs
1/4 c	milk
2-2/3 Tbsp	shortening, melted salad oil for fryer

(Makes 20 doughnuts)

3-1/2 c	all-purpose flour, sifted
3/4 c	sugar
1 Tbsp	baking powder
1/2 tsp	salt
1/2 tsp	cinnamon
1/2 tsp	nutmeg
3	eggs
1/2 c	milk
1/3 c	shortening, melted salad oil for fryer

The oil for frying doughnuts should be heated just long enough to bring it to 375°F, the temperature best suited to frying them. Several doughnuts may be fried at one time; there should always be enough surface area in the fryer to permit each one to rise up in a flat position on the surface of the oil. The heat for the deep-fat fryer or kettle should be high enough to maintain the oil at 375°F, with only a very slight drop in temperature when new doughnuts are added for frying. Remove the doughnuts with a chopstick or slotted spoon after they have become a pleasing brown on the second side. Drain them of excess oil by placing them on paper towels.

Evaluation of cake doughnuts begins with the external appearance. They should be a uniform, pleasing brown on both the top and bottom. Ideally, homemade cake doughnuts will be perfectly round, with an open, cylindrical center. Poor exterior color may range from pale (a condition caused by using too low a frying temperature) to very dark. Excessive browning may be the result of too high a frying temperature or too long a time for frying. The doughnuts should be double the volume of the original dough thickness.

The interior of doughnuts should be evaluated for uniformity of cell size and for doneness. Properly mixed doughnuts will have a relatively small and uniform cell size. Sometimes doughnuts may be doughy in the center. This problem usually is caused by using too high a temperature for frying. With too high a temperature, the exterior will become a deceptively pleasing brown before the interior is done.

Excessive moisture in the center also may be caused by rolling the dough so thick that the heat cannot penetrate the doughnut before the exterior browns.

When a doughnut is broken open for evaluation, the amount of oil penetration should be noted. A doughnut that has been fried well at the proper temperature will have only slight evidence of greasiness below the outer surface. If the oil is at too low a temperature during frying, the doughnut will have a greasy crumb. This excess oil will give a doughnut a greasy mouthfeel when it is eaten. This problem is avoided by being sure the oil is maintained at 375°F throughout the frying period and by not overcrowding the oil by frying too many doughnuts at a time. The final evaluation is done by tasting the doughnut. Doughnuts should have a rich, fried flavor without seeming to be greasy and should be a pleasing flavor blend of the ingredients. They also should be tender. Tough doughnuts are caused by too much handling and manipulation of the dough or by working in too much flour.

Coffee Cake

Total Time: 45 to 50 minutes
Baking: 350°F oven for 25 minutes (small) or 35 minutes (large)

1. Preheat oven and grease bottom of pan. Use loaf pan for small recipe and 8" square pan for large one.
2. Cream the shortening, vanilla, and sugar, and then beat in the egg yolk.
3. Sift the dry ingredients together and add by thirds, alternately with milk.
4. Beat egg white with rotary beater until peaks just bend over.
5. Fold into batter.
6. Put half the batter in the pan.
7. Mix the remaining five ingredients together, and sprinkle half of the mixture on the cake batter in the pan.
8. Put the remaining batter on top, and add the other half of the topping.
9. Bake at 350°F until a toothpick inserted in the center comes out clean.

(Makes 1 small coffee cake)

Batter:

2 Tbsp	shortening
1/2 tsp	vanilla
1/2 c	sugar
1	egg, separated
1/8 tsp	salt
3/4 c	all-purpose flour, sifted
1 tsp	baking powder
1/4 c	milk

Topping:

6 Tbsp	brown sugar
1/2 tsp	cinnamon
1-1/2 tsp	flour
1-1/2 tsp	margarine or butter, melted
1/4 c	walnuts, chopped

(Makes 1 large coffee cake)

Batter:

1/4 c	shortening
1 tsp	vanilla
1 c	sugar
2	eggs, separated
1/4 tsp	salt
1-1/2 c	all-purpose flour, sifted
2 tsp	baking powder
1/2 c	milk

Topping:

3/4 c	brown sugar
1 tsp	cinnamon
1 Tbsp	flour
1 Tbsp	margarine or butter, melted
1/2 c	walnuts, chopped

California Cornbread

Total Time: 30 minutes
Baking: 425°F oven for 20 to 25 minutes

1. Preheat oven.
2. Mix dry ingredients in mixing bowl.
3. In another bowl, blend the liquid ingredients.
4. Pour liquid ingredients all at once into a well in the dry ingredients, and stir with a wooden spoon just until all ingredients are moistened.
5. Pour into greased baking pan (loaf pan for small and 8 × 8″ pan for large).
6. Bake in 400°F for 20 to 25 minutes until wooden toothpick inserted in center comes out clean.

(Small recipe)

1/2 c	all-purpose flour
1/2 c	yellow cornmeal
2 Tbsp	sugar
1-1/2 tsp	baking powder
1/8 tsp	salt
1/2 c	whipping cream
2 Tbsp	vegetable oil
2 Tbsp	honey
1	egg, slightly beaten

(Large recipe)

1 c	all-purpose flour
1 c	yellow cornmeal
1/4 c	sugar
1 Tbsp	baking powder
1/4 tsp	salt
1 c	whipping cream
1/4 c	vegetable oil
1/4 c	honey
2	eggs, slightly beaten

Bruschetta

Total Time: 35 minutes
Broiling: 3 minutes each side

1. Preheat oven.
2. Mix tomatoes, basil, oregano, garlic, olive oil, salt, and pepper, and let stand 20 minutes.
3. Brush each side of bread slices with oil.
4. Place bread on baking sheet and broil each side until golden brown, turning once.
5. Distribute tomato mixture uniformly on the toasted bread.
6. Return to broiler briefly just to warm.

(Serves two)

1-1/2	Roma tomatoes (ripe), diced
5	fresh basil leaves, thinly sliced
1/4 tsp	oregano
1/4	garlic clove, minced
1 Tbsp	olive oil
	salt and pepper to taste
2	thick slices crusty Italian bread
2 tsp	olive oil

(Serves four)

3	Roma tomatoes (ripe), diced
10	fresh basil leaves, thinly sliced
1/2 tsp	oregano
1/2	garlic clove, minced
2 Tbsp	olive oil
	salt and pepper to taste
4	thick slices crusty Italian bread
4 tsp	olive oil

Cream Puffs

Total Time: 1 hour
Broiling: 450°F for 15 minutes, then 325°F for 25 minutes

1. Preheat oven.
2. Stir the butter or margarine into the boiling water.
3. As soon as the butter is melted, add the salt and flour all at once.
4. Stir vigorously while continuing to cook the mixture until it forms a ball. Remove from heat.
5. After cooling about 2 minutes, beat in the eggs, adding them one at a time and beating hard to make a smooth mixture.
6. Drop individual puffs on a Teflon-lined jelly roll pan, using about 1 tablespoon of dough for each. Place them at least 3" apart. (Note: Puffs for appetizers are made using only about 1/2 teaspoon of dough.)
7. Bake 15 minutes at 450°F. Reduce heat to 325°F and bake an additional 25 minutes.
8. Cool on a wire rack. Split and fill with ice cream, cream filling, or other desired filling just before serving.

(Makes 6 puffs)

1/2 c	water, boiling
1/4 c	butter or margarine
1/2 c	flour
1/8 tsp	salt
2	eggs

(Makes 12 puffs)

1 c	water, boiling
1/2 c	butter or margarine
1 c	flour
1/4 tsp	salt
4	eggs

Evaluation of Laboratory Products—Quick Breads

Recipe	Notes on Color, Texture, Flavor, or Other Qualities	Comments or Suggestions for Making or Using this Product in the Future

YEAST BREADS

Objectives

1. To observe the differences in the preparation of yeast-leavened and quick breads.
2. To demonstrate the differences in yeast breads resulting from the omission of eggs, sugar, milk, and fats in various selected breads.
3. To prepare yeast breads of high quality and evaluate them according to accepted criteria.

Principles of Preparing Yeast Breads

Yeast breads, in contrast to quick breads, require a relatively long production time to provide sufficient opportunity for carbon dioxide formation by the yeast. The types of yeast breads are numerous, ranging from simple formulas of flour, yeast, and water to rich doughs containing eggs, sugar, salt, milk, and butter, in addition to the flour and yeast. Crusty breads with a chewy, rather tough crumb result when eggs and fat are not included. A softer crust and more tender crumb are produced when the formula is richer. Despite these variations in the characteristics of the end products, the procedures followed in preparing the various yeast breads are basically the same.

Active dry yeast works quickly and well in yeast doughs when the yeast is softened before being incorporated in the dough. The other ingredients can be assembled and measured while the yeast is being hydrated. Yeast is hydrated by stirring the granules into lukewarm water, that is, water at approximately body temperature. The yeast used in breads is *Saccharomyces cerevisiae*, a single-celled plant that produces carbon dioxide from sugar in a dough. This plant will be killed

if subjected to high temperatures, and carbon dioxide will not be produced for leavening. For this reason, temperatures of liquids and doughs in contact with hydrated dry yeast should be monitored and should not exceed 105°F. If the dry yeast is mixed directly with the other dry ingredients, the liquid can be 125°F because the mixture will cool adequately before the yeast is hydrated in the dough.

If milk is used in a yeast bread, it is scalded in a saucepan before being added to other ingredients. The milk is scalded sufficiently when the hot milk clings to the sides of the pan as the pan is tipped. Boiling is not necessary. Originally, scalding was required to kill microorganisms that might be present in raw milk. Even now pasteurized milk is scalded for yeast breads because the hot milk melts the fat to give excellent distribution of fat throughout the dough. This hot liquid also aids in producing a dough sufficiently warm to promote active gas production by the yeast.

While the milk is being scalded and the yeast is hydrating, the next step in the straight dough method is to measure the sugar, salt, and fat into a mixing bowl. Many yeast bread recipes include at least a small amount of sugar to serve as food for the yeast. Without added sugar in the formula, yeast will have only a little sugar

available from the flour in the dough, and gas production will be slow and limited. Increasing the sugar in a bread formula will increase the sweetness of the flavor and also promote tenderness of the bread and browning of the crust. The salt in the formula serves as an inhibitor to yeast growth, thus acting to regulate gas production. Fat in yeast breads promotes tenderness of the crumb and crust. In addition, the flavor is enhanced by fat. If butter or margarine is the fat used, the color of the end product will be more yellow than if other fats are used.

The scalded milk is poured directly into the mixing bowl containing the sugar, salt, and fat. This mixture should be stirred occasionally until the fat is melted. Because the egg is quite cool, the temperature of the mixture will drop, and the egg proteins will not coagulate.

Approximately half a cup of flour is stirred into the mixture. This will result in a very lumpy mixture. The purpose of this small amount of flour is to tie up the fat so that the yeast will not be coated by the fat when the softened yeast is added. There is no need to try to eliminate the lumps of flour at this stage. Subsequent steps will develop a smooth mixture.

The temperature of the mixture needs to be checked at this point to be sure that it is not so hot that the hydrated yeast will be killed when added. The simplest satisfactory way of checking the temperature is to insert a well-washed finger directly into the mixture. Softened yeast can be added immediately if the mixture is approximately body temperature or only very slightly warmer.

If the mixture feels warm or hot, it should be cooled to approximately body temperature before adding the yeast. A thermometer can also be used to check the temperature. The mixture should not be warmer than 105°F when the yeast is added. Higher temperatures kill the yeast and result in a bread dough that will not rise well. At this point, the yeast is added and stirred into the other ingredients.

Then approximately half the flour is added to create a mixture sufficiently viscous to permit vigorous beating. This dough is beaten vigorously for about 3 minutes. During this period, the mixture will become quite smooth and will begin to develop a cohesive quality as a result of gluten development. This is an important step toward achieving the rather tenacious crumb structure needed in breads.

When the gluten has been developed sufficiently, all-purpose flour is added gradually to make a soft dough. As mixing progresses, flour should be mixed throughout the dough by cutting through the dough with a wooden spoon. Unless mixing is done with these cutting strokes, the dough will have many areas in the interior that are very sticky and difficult to manage. Flour should be added just to the point where the entire dough mass can be handled by hand without being sticky. At this point, the dough will be difficult to stir. The actual amount of flour needed varies from one part of the country to another because of the variable nature of the protein contained in flours on the market. For this reason, there is no need to sift and measure flour for yeast breads. The exact amount needed is determined by the handling characteristics of a specific dough.

The dough then is turned out onto a lightly floured board. Additional flour needs to be available to keep the dough from sticking during the kneading process. When the dough is resting on the board, it should be soft enough to sag, but not to flow.

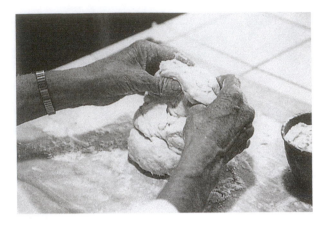

Kneading of yeast dough is designed to develop gluten. Breads need to have a structure strong enough to hold together when butter or margarine, jams, and sandwich fillings are spread on them. This characteristic results when gluten develops to the correct point during kneading. Kneading of yeast doughs is a very vigorous, rhythmic process that is done with the heel of both hands. Each kneading stroke is done by grasping the far edge of the dough, folding it to the front edge, and then pushing away vigorously with the heels of both hands. This stroke turns the dough into an elongated mass.

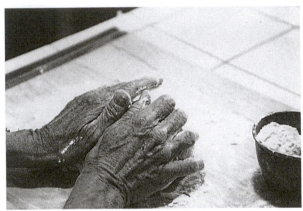

This mass is rotated 90° so that the length of the dough extends away from the operator. The far edge again is folded to meet the front edge, and the dough is pushed vigorously with the heel of both hands. This rotation, folding, and pressing procedure is repeated rapidly and vigorously for 5 minutes or more, until the dough shows blisters under the surface when it is stretched. Kneading should develop into a rhythmic, rapid, and vigorous process. Sufficient gluten development is essential for uniform cell size and adequate cell wall strength in the finished bread. During kneading, more flour may be needed on the board to keep the dough from sticking. However, excess flour should be avoided because too much flour results in a less tender and rather dry product.

When kneading is complete, the dough should be soft, but not sticky. This dough then is ready for the first rising period. Because this first rising usually requires about an hour, the surface of the dough needs to be protected to prevent drying. Protection can be provided by putting a few drops of salad oil in a large bowl, dragging the dough through the oil, and then placing the oiled side of the dough upward in the bowl.

Aluminum foil or a clean towel can be used to provide additional protection from air currents. The bowl then should be placed in a warm place to facilitate yeast growth and carbon dioxide production. Hot places such as an oven with a high pilot light may be so warm that the yeast will be killed; hence such places should be avoided. However, doughs can be placed in the refrigerator or even in the freezer if baking is to be delayed. Doughs will rise very slowly in the refrigerator and not at all in the freezer.

Dough is allowed to rise without disturbance until it has doubled in volume. Under normal room conditions, this first rising will require approximately 1 hour. If this proofing is being done in the refrigerator, between 9 and 12 hours may be required to double the volume. Frozen, unshaped doughs will need to be thawed and then allowed to rise to double their volume. The cooler the actual temperature of the dough, the slower will be the production of carbon dioxide by the yeast. Yeast activity is accelerated by warmer temperatures until temperatures above 105°F are reached.

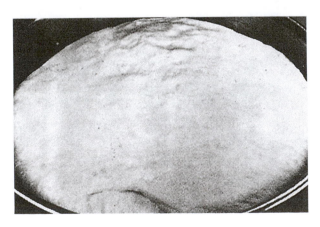

Temperatures higher than this cause permanent damage to the yeast, whereas cool temperatures retard gas production but do not kill the yeast.

The first rising stretches existing gluten strands and expands pockets of carbon dioxide and air. After the dough has doubled, the fist is used to force the extra gas from these pockets and reduce the strain on these stretched strands of gluten. This procedure helps to promote cells of uniform size and to avoid large, coarse cell areas in the bread. It also helps to keep gluten strands from being stretched so far that they break.

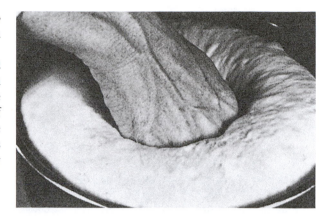

The dough now is ready to be shaped as desired. *Cloverleaf rolls* are shaped by using the thumb and index finger to squeeze small balls of dough from the large dough mass. Three of these balls, each approximately 1/2" in diameter, are placed in each greased cup of a muffin pan. When placing each ball in the cup, be careful to place the rounded, smooth surface upward so that the rough, squeezed region does not show.

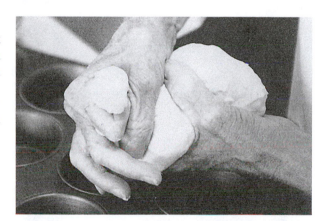

Numerous other shapes can be made from roll doughs. *Bread sticks, bow knot rolls,* and *rosettes* are fashioned by first squeezing off a ball of dough about 1" in diameter. This ball is rolled, either between the hands or by hand on a lightly floured bread board, to make a long, uniform strand of dough about 1/4" in diameter. For *bread sticks,* this strand is placed on an ungreased baking sheet. *Bow knots* are made by tying the strand into a rather loose half knot and placing this on an ungreased baking sheet. To make *rosettes,* the strand is tied into a fairly tight half knot with the ends extending an inch beyond the knot. The end coming from under the knot is stretched up and over the knot and forced down through the center of the roll to hide the end. The other loose end is carried from its position on top of the knot of dough, over the knot, and tucked under the roll.

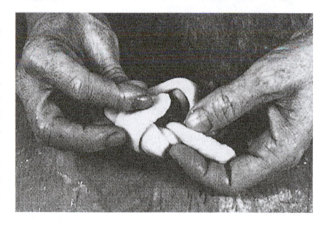

Loaves of bread are made by rolling the dough on a lightly floured board into a rectangle 1/2" thick, with one dimension of the rectangle about 3" greater than the length of the loaf pan in which the bread will be baked. Roll dough into an elongated log.

Press the ends of the dough firmly to seal the roll at each end. Tuck the final 1-1/2" of dough under the roll at each end to make a loaf that just fits the greased loaf pan. Gently fit the dough into the pan with the smooth dough surface on top.

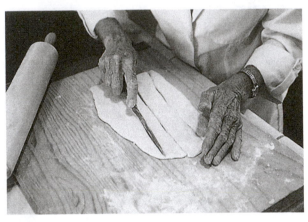

Butterflake or *fantan rolls* are made by rolling half the dough into a rectangle about 1/4" thick, 6" wide, and 12" long. Rolling is done on a lightly floured bread board. Melted butter is spread with a pastry brush over the entire surface of the rectangle. A table knife is used to cut the dough into 6 lengthwise strips, each an inch wide. These strips are stacked, and then rolls are made by cutting through this stacked dough at 1" intervals. The rolls are placed in greased muffin cups with the freshly cut surface turned upward. The dough strips are in a vertical position. Bread sticks, bow knots, cloverleaf rolls, and rosettes usually are made with a basic, simple yeast dough. Butterflake, cinnamon rolls, and coffee rings usually are made from richer doughs with more sugar and fat.

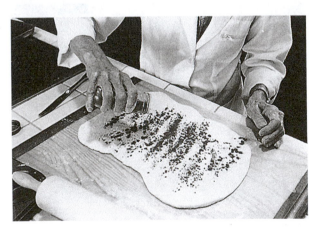

Other variations can also be made using the same rectangular, rolled shape that is used for butterflake rolls. Again, this rectangle is brushed lightly with melted butter. *Cinnamon rolls* are created by sprinkling the entire surface of the rectangle very generously with cinnamon. Because the dough will be more than double in volume in the baked roll, the cinnamon will be covering a much greater volume at that point. Unless cinnamon is shaken on until the dough surface is well covered, the cinnamon flavor may be too delicate for many palates.

Chopped nuts or other optional ingredients also may be added before the rectangle is rolled up. Rolling is done by starting lightly at the far edge to make a log. This log is then sliced at regular intervals, usually an inch wide. The pinwheels of dough may be placed on their sides, either in greased muffin cups or on baking pans. If placed on baking pans, they should be spaced at 1/2" intervals to permit some horizontal expansion.

The same log just described may be transferred in its entirety onto a baking sheet as the first step in fashioning a *coffee ring*. To keep the ring from unrolling, the seam of the roll should be arranged underneath and the ends brought together into a ring and squeezing the ends of the dough to join them firmly. If the diameter of the ring is not uniform, the dough can be manipulated by hand to improve the shape. Kitchen shears are used to cut through the log of dough from the edge to within 1/4" of the inner edge.

This cut is repeated at 1" intervals all around the ring. Each of these segments then is twisted carefully to reveal the pinwheel of dough and cinnamon. As each portion is twisted, it is maneuvered to overlap the preceding segment.

Butterhorns provide an example of rolls made with a dough containing a relatively large proportion of whole egg and margarine or butter. A 4" ball of the dough is rolled on a lightly floured board into a circular shape about 1/4" thick. The circle of dough is brushed lightly with melted margarine or butter.

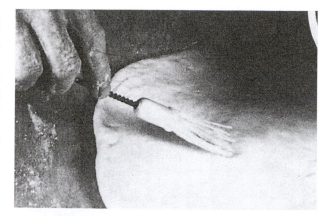

A table knife is used to cut the dough into pie-shaped wedges about 2" wide at the perimeter of the circle. Butterhorns are made by rolling these wedges lightly into their final form. This is done by rolling from the curved edge toward the tip of the dough piece.

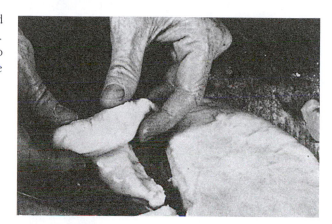

These rolls are placed on an ungreased baking sheet at 2" intervals between rolls. Only about an inch distance needs to be maintained between the ends of the rolls. Each roll should be placed with the tip of the roll extending well underneath the roll dough. Unless this is done, they may unroll during baking.

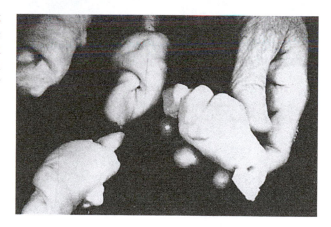

Regardless of the type of dough or the shape of the product, the shaped dough needs to be permitted to rest in a warm place until double in volume. This time the dough is not covered because the slight drying of the surface is not detrimental to the quality of the finished product. In addition, the dough might stick to the covering, and volume would be lost in freeing the roll from the foil. This second rising usually requires about 30 minutes (half as much time as the first rising). For optimum volume and texture in the finished product, it is important to wait until the volume has doubled before baking.

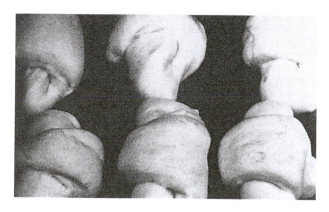

Ten minutes before the shaped rolls have finished doubling their volume again, check to be sure the oven rack is in the center position and preheat the oven. Plain rolls are baked at 425°F, bread at 400°F, and rich rolls at 375°F. Whenever raisins, currants, sweet syrups, and jams are used, the temperature should be 375°F, regardless of the type of dough. Breads containing rich formulas or other additives high in sugar also are baked at 375°F to avoid burning these substances.

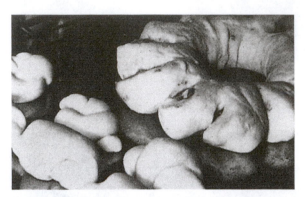

When the dough has doubled, the baking pans are placed in the preheated oven. There should be space between the baking pans and the edges of the oven to permit the circulation needed for good browning of the rolls. Pans should not be placed on a lower rack directly under other pans because the crusts will not brown properly. Rolls are baked for 12 to 15 minutes to a golden brown color if a 425°F oven is used and about 20 minutes if a 375°F oven is used. Bread loaves require about 35 minutes of baking time.

When yeast breads are done, they are removed from the oven and then transferred from the pan to a cooling rack. It is important to remove products from the pans to avoid steaming the crust and producing a soggy product.

Yeast breads are evaluated on the basis of exterior appearance and interior quality. Volume should be just over twice as large as the original dough. Shapes should be neatly executed and of uniform size. The crust is a pleasing, golden brown and slightly crisp rather than soggy. The interior should reveal uniform, medium-sized cells; the structure does not crumble readily when buttered, but still is tender. Excessive fermentation will cause the structure to be too porous and can even result in a fallen, heavy product. Too little volume is caused by inadequate rising time before baking or by killing the yeast during mixing. A dry, tough product results from incorporating too much flour in the dough. (Note: Quick-rise active dry yeast can be used to save preparation time. Follow package directions. When necessary, dough can be shaped immediately after mixing and allowed to rise only one time before baking.)

RECIPES

Rolls

Total Time: approximately 2-1/2 hours
Baking: 425°F or 375°F oven for 12 to 20 minutes

1. Scald the milk until it clings to the sides of the pan.
2. Soften the yeast in the lukewarm water.
3. Meanwhile, put the sugar, salt, and margarine or butter in a mixing bowl, and add the scalded milk.
4. Stir with a wooden spoon to mix the ingredients and melt the margarine or butter.
5. Beat the egg well and add to the milk mixture.
6. Stir in approximately 1/2 cup flour. Add yeast.
7. Check to be sure the mixture is no warmer than 105°F.
8. Add the flour gradually. When about half has been added, beat the dough vigorously for 3 minutes.
9. Continue adding flour to make a soft dough, yet one that can be handled without too much difficulty.
10. Put the dough out onto a floured bread board.
11. Lightly flour hands, and press dough into a ball.
12. Grasp the far side of the dough and fold it over to meet the front edge. Push firmly with the heel of the hand.
13. Rotate the dough a quarter of a turn and repeat the kneading operation. Continue rotating the dough and kneading so that a rhythm develops.
14. Knead about 5 minutes until blisters can be seen just under the surface when the dough is stretched.
15. Put dough in a bowl, and oil the surface.
16. Cover the bowl with aluminum foil and put in a warm place. Allow the dough to rise until doubled in volume (about 1 hour).
17. Punch the dough down with the fist.
18. Pinch the dough in half and shape into rolls.
19. Arrange the rolls on baking pans and put in a warm place for the second rising. Do not cover the rolls.
20. Let rise until doubled in volume (about 45 minutes).
21. During the last 10 minutes, preheat oven to 425°F for plain rolls or 375°F for sweet mixtures or raisins.
22. Bake about 12 minutes if baking at the higher temperature or 20 minutes at the lower one until golden brown.
23. Remove from pans; cool on rack or serve promptly.

(Makes 12 rolls)

6 Tbsp	milk, scalded
1	package active dry yeast
1/4 c	lukewarm water
1-1/2 Tbsp	sugar
1/2 tsp	salt
1-1/2 Tbsp	margarine or butter
1/2	egg
~2 c	unsifted all-purpose flour

(Makes 24 rolls)

3/4 c	milk, scalded
2	packages active dry yeast
1/2 c	lukewarm water
3 Tbsp	sugar
1 tsp	salt
3 Tbsp	margarine or butter
1	egg
~4 c	unsifted all-purpose flour

Butterhorn Rolls

Total Time: approximately 2-1/2 hours
Baking: 425°F oven for 12 minutes

1. Use the same procedure as outlined for rolls (see preceding recipe) to make the dough.
2. When dough is ready to be shaped, roll dough into 1/3" to 1/2" inch thick circles with diameter of approximately 8".
3. With a table knife, cut dough into wedges about 3" wide on the perimeter.
4. Roll the dough from large end to the tip. Arrange on a baking sheet, allowing a couple of inches between rolls.
5. Let rolls double in volume, uncovered.
6. Preheat oven.
7. Bake at 425°F about 12 minutes.
8. Remove from pan to cool.

(Makes 14 rolls)

6 Tbsp	milk, scalded
2 Tbsp	lukewarm water
1	package active dry yeast
1/4 c	sugar
1/2 tsp	salt
1/4 c	margarine or butter
1-1/2	eggs
2-1/2 to 3 c	unsifted all-purpose flour

(Makes 28 rolls)

3/4 c	milk, scalded
1/4 c	lukewarm water
2	packages active dry yeast
1/2 c	sugar
1 tsp	salt
1/2 c	margarine or butter
3	eggs
5–6 c	unsifted all-purpose flour

Swedish Rye Batter Bread

Total Time: approximately 3 hours
Baking: 400°F oven for 30 minutes (small), 40 minutes (large)

1. Heat milk, water, and margarine or butter to 125°F.
2. While heating liquids, combine flours. Then put 1/3 of the flour in mixing bowl with sugar, salt, caraway seed, and dry yeast (not hydrated).
3. Gradually stir in the liquids; beat 2 minutes at medium speed on electric mixer.
4. Stir in enough of the flours to make stiff dough. Use additional all-purpose flour if the flour mixture is inadequate.
5. Cover and set in warm place to double in volume (approximately 40 minutes).
6. Stir dough down. Transfer to greased 1-quart casserole (small) or 1-1/2-quart casserole (large).
7. Set in warm place to double in volume (approximately 20 minutes). Preheat oven to 400°F during last 10 minutes of rising.
8. Bake 30 minutes (small) or 40 minutes (large). Remove from pan and cool on wire rack.

Note: Dough can be kneaded on a mixer with a dough hook.

(Small loaf)

1/2 c	milk
1/2 c	water
1 Tbsp	margarine or butter
1-3/4 to 2 c	unsifted all-purpose flour
3/4 c	unsifted rye flour
2-2/3 Tbsp	dark brown sugar
1 tsp	salt
1/2 tsp	caraway seeds
1	package dry yeast

(Large loaf)

1 c	milk
1 c	water
2 Tbsp	margarine or butter
3-1/2 to 4 c	unsifted all-purpose flour
1-1/2 c	unsifted rye flour
1/3 c	dark brown sugar
2 tsp	salt
1 tsp	caraway seeds
2	packages dry yeast

Cinnamon Pinwheels

Total Time: 2-1/2 hours
Baking: 375°F oven for 20 minutes

1. Heat milk, water, and margarine or butter in saucepan to 125°F.
2. While heating the liquids, mix about 1/3 of the flour, sugar, salt, and dry (not hydrated) yeast in a mixing bowl.
3. Add the hot liquid and mix at medium speed on an electric mixer for 2 minutes.
4. Turn off the mixer to add the eggs and 1/4 cup (1/2 cup for large recipe) of flour. Beat 2 minutes at high speed. Stop the mixer every 30 seconds to scrape bowl with rubber spatula.
5. Stir in (by hand) enough flour to make a dough stiff enough to be kneaded.
6. Knead for 8 minutes before oiling the top of the ball of dough and placing it in a greased bowl.
7. Cover the bowl and place in a warm spot, out of drafts, until dough doubles in volume (about 40 minutes).
8. Punch the dough down and roll into a rectangle 10" × 12" (for large recipe divide dough in half and make two rectangles). Sprinkle with the sugar–cinnamon mixture and roll into a 12" log.
9. Slice log at 1" intervals. On a Teflon-lined baking sheet, arrange on their side to show the pinwheels, leaving a space of approximately 3/4" between rolls.
10. Rub the topping ingredients together in a small bowl until they are crumbly.
11. Sprinkle with the topping and let rise, uncovered, in a warm place until rolls double in volume. Preheat the oven to 375°F about 10 minutes before the dough has doubled.
12. Bake for 20 minutes or until a pleasing golden brown. Cool on a rack.

(12 rolls)

Dough:

1/2 c	milk
6 Tbsp	water
3 Tbsp	margarine or butter
~3-1/2 c	unsifted flour
3 Tbsp	sugar
3/4 tsp	salt
1	package active dry yeast
1-1/2	eggs
1 tsp	ground cinnamon mixed with 2 tbsp sugar

Topping:

2-2/3 Tbsp	flour
2-2/3 Tbsp	brown sugar
1/2 tsp	cinnamon
1-1/2 Tbsp	margarine or butter

(24 rolls)

Dough:

1 c	milk
3/4 c	water
6 Tbsp	margarine or butter
~7 c	unsifted flour
6 Tbsp	sugar
1-1/2 tsp	salt
2	packages active dry yeast
3	eggs
2 tsp	ground cinnamon mixed with 1/4 c sugar

Topping:

1/3 c	flour
1/3 c	brown sugar
1 tsp	cinnamon
3 Tbsp	margarine or butter

Note: Dough may be prepared following the directions for rolls, rather than using steps 1–7 in this recipe. The dough is then shaped and baked according to steps 8–12.

White Bread

Total Time: 2-3/4 hours
Baking: 400°F oven for 35 minutes

1. Scald the milk.
2. Soften the yeast in the lukewarm water while proceeding with the next step.
3. Put the sugar, salt, and margarine or butter in a mixing bowl, and pour the scalded milk in.
4. Stir with wooden spoon to mix the ingredients and melt the margarine or butter.
5. Stir in approximately 1/2 cup flour.
6. Check to be sure the mixture is no warmer than 105°F before adding yeast.
7. Add the flour gradually.
8. When about half has been added, beat the dough vigorously about 3 minutes.
9. Continue adding flour to make a soft dough that can be handled without difficulty on the board.
10. Put the dough out onto a floured bread board.
11. Lightly flour the hands and press the dough into a ball.
12. Grasp the far side of the dough and fold it over to meet the front edge. Push firmly with the heel of the hand.
13. Rotate the dough and fold it over to meet the front edge. Push firmly with the heel of the hand.
14. Continue rotating the dough and kneading so that a rhythm develops. Knead about 5 minutes until blisters can be seen just under the surface when the dough is stretched.
15. Put the kneaded dough in a bowl and lightly grease the surface with oil.
16. Cover the bowl with aluminum foil and put in a warm place. Allow the dough to rise until doubled in volume.
17. Punch the dough down with the fist. Pinch the dough in half if making the large recipe.
18. Roll the dough into a rectangle approximately 1/2" thick with one dimension about 3" longer than the length of the loaf pan.
19. Grasping the dough at one edge, roll it into a log.
20. Press both ends of the dough down firmly. Then tuck the ends under the loaf and place the dough into a lightly greased loaf pan with the smoothest side of the loaf on top. If making the larger recipe, repeat this process with the other half of the dough.
21. Place the shaped bread dough, uncovered, in a warm place until the dough has again doubled in volume.
22. Preheat the oven to 400°F during the last 10 minutes of rising.
23. Bake for approximately 35 minutes. When the loaf comes from the oven, immediately remove the baked bread from the pans and cool on a wire rack to avoid developing a soggy crust.

(1 loaf)

1 c	milk
1	package active dry yeast
2 Tbsp	water, lukewarm
1 Tbsp	sugar
3/4 tsp	salt
1/2 Tbsp	margarine or butter
~3 c	unsifted all-purpose flour

(2 loaves)

2 c	milk
2	packages active dry yeast
1/4 c	water, lukewarm
2 Tbsp	sugar
1-1/2 tsp	salt
1 Tbsp	margarine or butter
~6 c	unsifted all-purpose flour

French Bread

Total Time: 2-1/2 hours
Baking: 375°F oven for 20 minutes

1. Dissolve yeast in 1/4 cup (for 1 loaf) or 1/2 cup (for 2 loaves) lukewarm water.
2. Add remaining measure of water, salt, and 1/3 of the flour.
3. Beat well.
4. Add as much of the remaining flour as can be stirred in with a wooden spoon.
5. Put dough on board and knead in remaining flour.
6. Let rise until double.
7. Punch down and divide in half if making large recipe.
8. Roll dough into 12″ × 15″ rectangle.
9. Roll into a log and seal well.
10. Lightly grease cookie sheet over the area to be covered by the bread; sprinkle cornmeal over the greased area.
11. Place bread on cookie sheet. Score (cut slits in) the bread at an angle every 2-1/2″.
12. Brush the surface with the mixture made by beating egg white and water.
13. Let rise until double in bulk.
14. Preheat the oven to 375°F during the last 10 minutes of rising.
15. Brush again lightly with egg white mixture and bake 20 minutes until golden brown.

(Makes 1 loaf)

1	package active dry yeast
1/4 c	lukewarm water
1 c	lukewarm water
3/4 tsp	salt
3-1/2 c	unsifted all-purpose flour
1-1/2 tsp	cornmeal
1/2	egg white
1-1/2 tsp	water

(Makes 2 loaves)

2	packages active dry yeast
1/2 c	lukewarm water
2 c	lukewarm water
1-1/2 tsp	salt
7 c	unsifted all-purpose flour
1 Tbsp	cornmeal
1	egg white
1 Tbsp	water

Whole Wheat Bread

Total Time: 3 hours
Baking: 375°F oven for 50 minutes

1. Dissolve yeast in lukewarm water.
2. Scald milk, and pour over sugar, salt, molasses, margarine or butter, and honey.
3. Cool to lukewarm before adding yeast, wheat germ, whole wheat flour, and one-third of the all-purpose flour.
4. Beat well with a wooden spoon.
5. Add enough of remaining flour to make a stiff dough.
6. Let rest for 10 minutes before kneading thoroughly (approximately 10 minutes) to make a smooth, elastic dough.
7. Place dough in a bowl, grease the surface, and cover tightly.
8. Let rise until double in volume.
9. Punch down. Divide dough in half if making large recipe.
10. Roll into oblong rectangle about 3" wider than the length of a loaf pan.
11. Roll dough into a log, tucking the ends under to fit the loaf pan.
12. Place in lightly greased loaf pan and let rise, uncovered, until dough doubles.
13. Preheat oven to 375°F during the last 10 minutes rising time.
14. Bake for 50 minutes or until done.
15. Remove from pan and cool.

(Makes 1 loaf)

1	package active dry yeast
1/2 c	lukewarm water
1/2 c	milk
2 Tbsp	brown sugar
1/2 tsp	salt
1-1/2 tsp	molasses
2 Tbsp	margarine or butter
1-1/2 tsp	honey
1/4 c	wheat germ (optional)
1 c	sifted whole wheat flour
~1-1/2 c	unsifted all-purpose flour

(Makes 2 loaves)

2	packages active dry yeast
1 c	lukewarm water
1 c	milk
1/4 c	brown sugar
1 tsp	salt
1 Tbsp	molasses
1/4 c	margarine or butter
1 Tbsp	honey
1/2 c	wheat germ (optional)
2 c	sifted whole wheat flour
~3 c	unsifted all-purpose flour

Croissants

Total Time: 3 hours
Baking: 375°F oven for 25 minutes

1. Cream butter or margarine and flour, and refrigerate (tightly covered).
2. Soften yeast in water.
3. Add sugar, salt, milk, and flour. Blend.
4. Knead dough on floured board, adding flour as needed to make a stiff dough.
5. Let rise 1 hour in covered bowl.
6. Punch dough down and roll into rectangle 1/4" thick.
7. Pat all of flour–butter mixture all over dough to within an inch of the edge.
8. Fold dough in half and roll into a rectangle 1/4" thick.
9. Chill in freezer 15 minutes.
10. Fold each end of dough to center and roll into a rectangle 1/4" thick. Repeat folding and rolling twice.
11. Refrigerate overnight, loosely wrapped, or proceed to shape dough.
12. Roll into a 1/8" thick rectangle.
13. Cut into three squares and cut each square into triangles.
14. Roll triangles, starting from the long end.
15. Place on greased baking sheet.
16. Brush lightly with egg yolk and water mixture.
17. Let rise, uncovered, 1/2 hour; preheat oven to 375°F during last 10 minutes.
18. Bake to golden brown for 20 to 25 minutes.

(Makes 6 croissants)

1/2 c	margarine or butter
1-1/4 Tbsp	all-purpose flour
1	package active dry yeast
1/4 c	lukewarm water
2 tsp	sugar
1/2 tsp	salt
6 Tbsp	milk (lukewarm)
1-1/4 c	unsifted all-purpose flour
1	egg yolk
1 tsp	water

(Makes 12 croissants)

1 c	margarine or butter
2-1/2 Tbsp	all-purpose flour
2	packages active dry yeast
1/2 c	lukewarm water
4 tsp	sugar
1 tsp	salt
3/4 c	milk (lukewarm)
2-1/2 c	unsifted all-purpose flour
2	egg yolks
2 tsp	water

Prune Kolachen

Total Time: 2 hours and 15 minutes
Baking: 375°F oven for 15 minutes

1. Remove yeast from hot roll mix, and stir wheat germ into flour.
2. Soften yeast in lukewarm water.
3. Stir in eggs.
4. Beat in flour mixture.
5. With heels of hands, knead dough vigorously on a floured board until smooth and elastic.
6. Place into a greased bowl, cover with foil, and let rise in a warm place until double in bulk (about 1 hour).
7. Meanwhile, combine filling ingredients, and simmer until thick.
8. Cool quickly to room temperature.
9. Punch dough down when it has doubled; cut into 18 pieces.
10. Pat out dough to 3" rounds and place on greased cookie sheets.
11. Press down center of each round of dough. Fill with cooled filling.
12. Let rise until double in bulk.
13. Bake in a preheated oven for 15 minutes or until richly browned.
14. While buns are baking, mash cream cheese, and beat in honey gradually.
15. Serve buns warm, topped with cream cheese mixture.

(Makes 9 buns)

Dough:

1/2	13.75 oz package hot roll mix
1/4 c	wheat germ
6 Tbsp	lukewarm milk
1	egg, slightly beaten

Filling:

1 c	pitted and chopped dried prunes
1/2	orange (washed and dried), chopped, rind and pulp
1/4 c	sugar
1/2 c	water

Topping:

1/2	Of 3 oz package cream cheese
2 Tbsp	honey

(Makes 18 buns)

Dough:

1	13.75 oz package hot roll mix
1/2 c	wheat germ
3/4 c	lukewarm milk
2	eggs, slightly beaten

Filling:

2 c	pitted and chopped dried prunes
1	orange (washed and dried), chopped, rind and pulp
1/2 c	sugar
1 c	water

Topping:

1	3 oz package cream cheese
1/4 c	honey

Bagels

Total Time: 2 hours
Baking: 450°F oven for 15 minutes

1. Soften yeast in the lukewarm water.
2. In a mixing bowl, combine flour, salt, sugar; then stir in the yeast and water mixture and salad oil.
3. Blend in egg and stir to make soft ball.
4. Knead vigorously on floured board for 10 minutes, adding flour as necessary to make stiff dough.
5. Let rise in covered bowl for an hour.
6. Knead again until smooth and elastic.
7. Pinch off balls of dough 2" in diameter.
8. Roll between palms into ropes 3/4" in diameter and about 6" long.
9. Pinch ends together to form a doughnut-like shape.
10. Preheat oven to 450°F.
11. Drop carefully into boiling mixture of water and sugar.
12. With slotted spoon, turn over each bagel when it surfaces and cook second side 1 minute.
13. Arrange bagels on greased cookie sheet and bake 12 to 15 minutes until golden brown.

(Makes 6 bagels)

1	package active dry yeast
1/2 c	lukewarm water
2 c	unsifted all-purpose flour
3/4 tsp	salt
3/4 tsp	sugar
1 Tbsp	salad oil
1	egg, slightly beaten
1 Tbsp	sugar
1 qt	boiling water

(Makes 12 bagels)

2	packages active dry yeast
1 c	lukewarm water
4 c	unsifted all-purpose flour
1-1/2 tsp	salt
1-1/2 tsp	sugar
2 Tbsp	salad oil
2	eggs, slightly beaten
2 Tbsp	sugar
1 qt	boiling water

Evaluation of Laboratory Products—Yeast Breads

Recipe	Notes on Color, Texture, Flavor, or Other Qualities	Comments or Suggestions for Making or Using this Product in the Future

VOCABULARY

Gluten

Leavening agent

Saccharomyces cerevisiae

Double-acting baking powder

Baking soda

Tartrate baking powder

Quick bread

Biscuit

Roll

Muffins

Carbon dioxide

CHAPTER 11

Cakes and Cookies

Cakes are more delicate than breads because of their ingredients and their proportions; sugar content is considerably higher in cakes than in breads, and the fat content in cakes usually is appreciably higher. These two ingredients interfere with development of the gluten complex during mixing, resulting in tender cakes with good volume. Careful measuring of all ingredients is critical to success, because deviations can easily result in cakes with poor volume or texture.

Be sure to use the exact ingredient specified in the recipe. Cake flour often is used because it has a smaller amount and more delicate gluten that promotes the desired tenderness sought in cakes. Baking soda and baking powder are very different ingredients and cannot be used interchangeably, despite their similar names. Baking soda is an alkaline ingredient that leaves a soapy taste in a cake, a rather yellow color, and poor volume. Baking powder is comprised of an acid ingredient and baking soda; their reaction in a batter produces carbon dioxide that leavens the cake. If a cake recipe specifies baking soda, there also is an acid ingredient such as sour cream to react with the soda. In this type of recipe, your work needs to proceed rapidly to get the cake in the oven before all of the carbon dioxide generated by the reaction of these ingredients escapes from the batter.

KEY CONCEPTS

1. The two basic categories of cakes are foam cakes and shortened cakes.

2. The three types of foam cakes are angel food, sponge, and chiffon.
   a. Much of the volume is the result of a well-prepared egg white and/or egg yolk foam.
   b. Little or no fat is contained in foam cakes.
   c. Foam cakes are cooled inverted to stretch their structure.

3. Shortened cakes differ from foam cakes in fat content and leavening.

   a. Shortened cakes have a fairly high fat content (usually a solid fat that is creamed in), which results in a tender structure that needs to be cooled in an upright position.

   b. Baking powder or other potential source of carbon dioxide is the principal leavening agent in shortened cakes.

4. Compared with cakes, cookie recipes (dropped, molded, bar, and rolled) contain a reduced ratio of liquid to flour and a high proportion of sugar and fat.

FOAM CAKES

Objectives

1. To demonstrate the use of egg white foams in helping to leaven angel food, sponge, and chiffon cakes.

2. To compare the influence of the various ingredients on the volume, tenderness, texture, and palatability of angel food, sponge, and chiffon cakes.

3. To develop the ability to form egg white foams of high quality and to incorporate them successfully in foam-containing cakes.

4. To prepare and evaluate angel food, sponge, and chiffon cakes.

Preparation

Angel food and other foam cakes in tube pans are baked with the oven rack in the next position below the center of the oven. In contrast with sponge and chiffon cakes, which are baked at 325°F, angel food cakes are baked at 375°F. The oven is preheated to minimize loss of air from the foam before heat sets the structure.

Formation of an excellent egg white foam is essential to preparation of any foam cake. Stability of the foam is enhanced by adding the cream of tartar all at once at the foamy stage. Sugar then is added gradually while beating is continued. Unless a mixer with hypocycloidal action is being used, use a clean rubber spatula to continually scrape the egg white foam away from the edge of the bowl. This will help to promote uniform texture throughout the foam.

After the sugar has been added to the whites, beating of the egg white foam is continued on high speed until the foam reaches the right end point when tested by pulling the foam up into a peak with a rubber spatula. For angel food and sponge cakes, the peak should just bend over. A chiffon cake requires a slightly stiffer foam; that is, the peak stands up straight. Be sure to stop the mixer for this test. If the peak is soft, resume beating until the proper stage is reached. The proper extent of beating helps to stabilize the foam and to produce a cake of good volume and relatively fine texture.

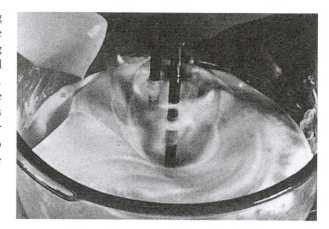

Adequate (but not excessive or rough) folding with a rubber spatula is necessary in foam cakes to blend ingredients. A layer will tend to settle out in chiffon and sponge cakes if folding is inadequate or if baking is delayed.

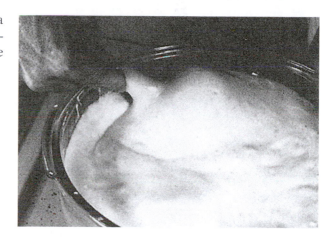

When the baking time has elapsed, foam cakes are tested carefully, using a hot pad to pull the oven rack out gently. If the cake shakes as the shelf is moved, baking should be resumed immediately by pushing the shelf in and quickly closing the oven door. If the cake appears to be set, pull the rack out so that the surface of the cake can be touched lightly with a finger. If the cake is done, the surface will spring back.

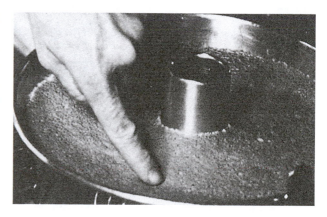

Foam cakes have a rather weak structure when they are hot. By cooling these cakes in an inverted position, the cake hangs suspended in the pan, and the weight of the cake itself pulls the cell walls down in an extended position. This allows the cake structure to be stretched; the cell walls thus are thinner and more tender than they would have been if the cake had been cooled in an upright position. The cake should be cooled to room temperature before being removed from the pan. The structure will then be set sufficiently to withstand the manipulation of the cake.

When the cake has cooled completely, the structure will be strong enough to turn the pan back to its upright position. Use a thin, long-bladed knife to cut around the edges of the cake and free the cake at the outer edge and around the tube.

Lift the cake and the tube portion of the pan out of the cake pan. Still using the slicer, slide the knife along the bottom surface of the pan to cut the cake completely free of the pan. Now the cake is ready for removal from the pan.

Invert a cake plate over the tube of the pan. This plate should be a little larger than the cake so that the cake may be iced or garnished in other ways to make it attractive for service. When the plate is held firmly over the tube, carefully but quickly invert the cake and the plate as single unit. This rapid movement allows the cake to fall gently and without damage onto the plate.

RECIPES

Angel Food Cake

Total Time: 1 hour
Baking: 375°F oven for 25 minutes (loaf) or 35 to 40 minutes (large tube pan)

1. Preheat oven.
2. Sift the flour and sugar together three times.
3. On an electric mixer, beat the egg whites until foamy.
4. Add the salt, vanilla, and cream of tartar.
5. Continue beating while gradually adding the sugar. Beat the egg whites until the peaks just barely bend over.
6. Sift approximately one-fourth of the flour–sugar mixture over the surface of the egg white meringue.
7. With a rubber spatula, efficiently fold the flour into the egg whites, using two five-stroke folding cycles for a total of ten strokes.
8. Sift the second fourth of the flour over the surface of the egg whites and fold ten more strokes.
9. Similarly, add the third and fourth quarters of the flour. Fold ten strokes after the third addition. After the fourth addition, continue folding until all the ingredients are thoroughly blended in the cake.
10. Gently push the batter with the spatula into the ungreased baking pan, and bake (about 25 minutes for the loaf and 35 to 40 minutes for the large cake) in a preheated oven at 375°F until the top springs back when the cake is touched lightly with the finger.
11. Cool inverted, then remove from pan.

(Use loaf pan)

1/3 c	sifted cake flour
4 Tbsp	sugar
1/2 c	(4) egg whites
dash	salt
1/2 tsp	vanilla
1/2 tsp	cream of tartar
4 Tbsp	sugar

(Use 10" tube pan)

1 c	sifted cake flour
3/4 c	sugar
1-1/2 c	(12) egg whites
1/8 tsp	salt
1 tsp	vanilla
1 tsp	cream of tartar
3/4 c	sugar

True Sponge Cake

Total Time: 1 hour and 30 minutes
Baking: 325°F oven for 35 to 40 minutes (small) or
1 hour (large)

1. Preheat oven.
2. With an electric mixer, beat egg yolks until very thick and lemon colored.
3. Add the water and continue beating until yolks pile.
4. Gradually add the sugar and the two extracts. Continue beating until the yolk mixture is thick enough to pile slightly.
5. Sift the salt with the flour. Sift one-fourth of this flour–salt mixture over the yolk mixture and fold in, using two five-stroke folding cycles for a total of ten strokes.
6. Similarly, add the second, third, and fourth quarters of flour. Fold ten strokes after all but the fourth addition. Continue folding after the fourth addition until all the flour is folded in.
7. Wash beater blades well and then use the electric mixer to beat egg whites to the foamy stage.
8. Add the cream of tartar; add sugar gradually while beating.
9. Continue beating until all the sugar is added and the peaks just bend over.
10. Fold the yolk and white mixtures together until completely blended.
11. Use a rubber spatula to push batter gently into ungreased pan.
12. Bake in center of oven preheated to 325°F.
13. Bake until the top springs back when lightly touched with the finger (about 40 minutes for small or 1 hour for large cake).
14. Cool in inverted position; remove from pan.

(Use loaf pan)

2	eggs, separated
2-2/3 Tbsp	water
1/4 c	sugar
1/4 tsp	vanilla
1/4 tsp	lemon extract
1/2 c	sifted cake flour
dash	salt
1/4 c	sugar
1/4 tsp	cream of tartar

(Use 10" tube pan)

6	eggs, separated
1/2 c	water
3/4 c	sugar
1/2 tsp	vanilla
1/2 tsp	lemon extract
1-1/2 c	sifted cake flour
1/4 tsp	salt
3/4 c	sugar
3/4 tsp	cream of tartar

Jelly Roll

Total Time: 35 minutes
Baking: 375°F oven for 12 to 15 minutes

1. Preheat oven.
2. Prepare cake batter, using directions for True Sponge Cake (previous recipe).
3. Bake in a Teflon-lined jelly roll pan or in a jelly roll pan lined with aluminum foil in a preheated oven at 375°F until golden brown and top springs back when touched lightly (about 12 minutes).
4. Immediately cut the cake loose from the sides of the pan and invert onto a dish towel lightly coated with powdered sugar. Remove foil if used.
5. Promptly roll the cake and the towel into a roll, rolling from the short side. Allow to cool in the rolled position.
6. When cool, unroll and spread the cake with the filling. Roll the cake and the filling (being sure to omit the towel).
7. Sprinkle powdered sugar lightly over the top. Refrigerate. (Freeze if filled with ice cream.)
8. Slice into 1" pinwheels and serve with whipped cream, fruit, or other topping.

(1 roll for 10 servings)

Batter:

3	eggs, separated
1/4 c	water
6 Tbsp	sugar
1/4 tsp	vanilla
1/4 tsp	lemon extract
3/4 c	sifted cake flour
1/8 tsp	salt
6 Tbsp	sugar
1/2 tsp	cream of tartar

Filling suggestions:

Ice cream or sherbet, sweetened whipped cream with sliced seasonal fruit (e.g., strawberries), jam

Hawaiian Jelly Roll

Total Times: 45 minutes
Baking: 375°F oven for 20 minutes

(1 roll for 10 servings)	
3-1/2 c	crushed pineapple, drained (reserve syrup)
1/2 c	brown sugar
1/4 c	sifted cake flour
1 tsp	baking powder
1/8 tsp	salt
4	eggs, separated
1/4 c	sugar
1/2 tsp	lemon flavoring
1/4 tsp	cream of tartar
1/2 c	sugar

1. Preheat oven.
2. Prepare 15-1/2" × 10-1/2" × 1" jelly roll pan by spreading well-drained pineapple evenly over the pan and sprinkling with brown sugar.
3. Sift cake flour, baking powder, and salt together.
4. Beat yolks 10 minutes on mixer set at high speed.
5. Gradually beat in 1/4 cup sugar and lemon flavoring.
6. Gently fold (steps 5 and 6 of True Sponge Cake recipe).
7. Wash beater blades in hot soapy water, rinse, and dry before beginning to beat egg whites in a clean bowl.
8. Beat on high speed to the foamy stage and add the cream of tartar.
9. At high speed, beat 15 seconds before gradually adding the remaining sugar. Beat until the peaks just fold over.
10. Gently fold the yolk mixture and whites together until no streaks remain.
11. Using a rubber spatula, gently spread over the pineapple.
12. Bake at 375°F for 20 minutes (until cake springs back when touched).
13. Follow steps 3 through 7 in Jelly Roll recipe.

Pineapple Sauce (optional):

1 Tbsp	sugar
1 Tbsp	cornstarch
3/4 c	reserved pineapple syrup
2 tsp	lemon juice

Optional Pineapple Sauce:

1. Prepare sauce, if desired. Mix sugar and cornstarch in saucepan, stirring thoroughly with wooden spoon.
2. Stir in reserved pineapple syrup until smooth.
3. Place over direct heat and stir constantly until the sauce thickens and boils in the middle of the pan.
4. Remove from heat, stir in lemon juice, and cool.
5. Spoon over individual slices of jelly roll.

Mocha Chiffon Cake

Total Time: 1 hour and 30 minutes
Baking: 325°F oven for 35 minutes (small); 1 hour (large)

1. Preheat oven.
2. Sift the cake flour, sugar, salt, and baking powder in the smaller mixing bowl; make a well in the center.
3. Add coffee crystals, oil, yolks, vanilla, and water to the dry ingredients.
4. Beat until satin smooth on the electric mixer.
5. Stir in the chocolate. Wash beater blades.
6. On an electric mixer, beat egg whites in the larger bowl to foamy stage, and add cream of tartar.
7. Beat at high speed 15 seconds before gradually adding the sugar.
8. Beat whites until the peaks just stand straight, without bending over at all.
9. Pour the batter over the whites and carefully, but efficiently, fold until no fluid remains in the bottom of the bowl and the entire mixture is homogenous. Use the five-stroke folding technique.
10. Scrape batter into ungreased baking pan and bake in a 325°F oven until cake springs back when touched lightly (about 35 minutes for the small or 1 hour for the large cake).
11. Cool inverted, and then remove from pan.

(Use loaf pan)

1-1/8 c	sifted cake flour
1/4 c	sugar
1/2 tsp	salt
1-1/2 tsp	baking powder
2 tsp	freeze-dried coffee
1/4 c	salad oil
2	egg yolks
1/2 tsp	vanilla
6 Tbsp	water
1-1/2 oz	semisweet chocolate, grated
4	egg whites
1/4 tsp	cream of tartar
1/2 c	sugar

(Use 10" tube pan)

2-1/4 c	sifted cake flour
1/2 c	sugar
1 tsp	salt
1 Tbsp	baking powder
4 tsp	freeze-dried coffee
1/2 c	salad oil
4	egg yolks
1 tsp	vanilla
3/4 c	water
3 oz	semisweet chocolate, grated
8	egg whites
1/2 tsp	cream of tartar
1 c	sugar

Burnt-sugar Pecan Chiffon Cake

Total Time: 1 hour and 30 minutes
Baking: 325°F oven for 35 minutes (small); 1 hour (large)

1. Preheat oven.
2. Prepare a burnt-sugar syrup, using the first two ingredients, as follows: Melt the sugar in a heavy skillet while stirring constantly with a wooden spoon; heat and continue stirring until sugar becomes a deep golden brown; immediately carry the skillet to the sink and add boiling water; dissolve the sugar, reheating, if necessary. Measure 3 tablespoons syrup for the loaf or 6 tablespoons for the large cake and set aside. Save the rest for the icing.
3. Sift the cake flour, sugar, baking powder, and salt together into the smaller mixing bowl.
4. Make a well and add the oil, yolks, water, vanilla, and 3 tablespoons (loaf) or 6 tablespoons (tube) of the burnt-sugar syrup from step 1.
5. Beat on an electric mixer until satin smooth. Wash beaters.
6. Beat egg whites in larger bowl to foamy stage, using the electric mixer.
7. Add the cream of tartar and gradually begin adding the sugar.
8. Beat the egg whites until the peaks stand up straight.
9. Pour the batter over the egg whites and sprinkle the nuts over the surface.
10. Fold with a rubber spatula until no fluid remains in the bottom of the bowl and the entire mixture is homogenous.
11. Transfer to ungreased baking pan and immediately start baking.
12. Bake at 325°F until the cake springs back when the surface is lightly touched (about 35 minutes for small and 1 hour for large cake).
13. Cool inverted, then remove from pan.

(Use loaf pan)

3 Tbsp	sugar
1/4 c	water, boiling
1-1/8 c	sifted cake flour
1/4 c	sugar
1-1/2 tsp	baking powder
1/2 tsp	salt
1/4 c	salad oil
2	egg yolks
3 Tbsp	water
1/2 tsp	vanilla
3 Tbsp	burnt-sugar syrup (from step 1)
4	egg whites
1/2 c	sugar
1/4 tsp	cream of tartar
1/2 c	chopped pecans

(Use 10" tube pan)

6 Tbsp	sugar
1/2 c	water, boiling
2-1/4 c	sifted cake flour
1/2 c	sugar
1 Tbsp	baking powder
1 tsp	salt
1/2 c	salad oil
5	egg yolks
6 Tbsp	water
1 tsp	vanilla
6 Tbsp	burnt-sugar syrup (from step 1)
8	egg whites
1 c	sugar
1/2 tsp	cream of tartar
1 c	chopped pecans

Cakes and Cookies   297

Lemon Chiffon Cake

Total Time: 1 hour and 30 minutes
Baking: 325°F oven for 35 minutes (small); 1 hour (large)

1. Preheat oven.
2. Sift cake flour, sugar, salt, and baking powder into smaller mixing bowl; make well in center.
3. Add oil, egg yolks, vanilla, water, and lemon rind. Beat until satin smooth.
4. Wash beater blades. Beat egg whites in the larger mixer bowl to the foamy stage, using electric mixer.
5. Add cream of tartar and begin adding the sugar gradually. Beat until peaks stand up straight.
6. Pour batter over whites. Fold (using five-stroke method) until mixture is homogenous and no fluid is in the bottom.
7. Pour into ungreased pan gently. Bake immediately at 325°F until cake springs back when touched lightly (about 35 minutes for small or 1 hour for large cake).
8. Cool inverted; remove from pan.

(Use loaf pan)

1-1/8 c	sifted cake flour
1/4 c	sugar
1/2 tsp	salt
1-1/2 tsp	baking powder
1/4 c	salad oil
2	egg yolks
1/2 tsp	vanilla
6 Tbsp	water
1 tsp	grated lemon rind
1/4 tsp	cream of tartar
4	egg whites
1/2 c	sugar

(Use 10" tube pan)

2-1/4 c	sifted cake flour
1/2 c	sugar
1 tsp	salt
1 Tbsp	baking powder
1/2 c	salad oil
4	egg yolks
1 tsp	vanilla
3/4 c	water
2 tsp	grated lemon rind
1/2 tsp	cream of tartar
8	egg whites
1 c	sugar

Cocoa Chiffon Cake

Total Time: 1 hour
Baking: 350°F oven for 30 to 35 minutes

1. Preheat oven.
2. In a bowl, stir boiling water into cocoa; cool.
3. Sift cake flour, 6 tablespoons sugar, cinnamon, baking powder, and salt into mixing bowl.
4. Make a well; add salad oil, unbeaten yolks, vanilla, and cooled cocoa mixture.
5. Beat on electric mixer until satin smooth.
6. Wash beater blades. Beat egg whites in clean bowl on electric mixer set at high speed until foamy.
7. Add cream of tartar.
8. Beating at high speed, beat 15 seconds before gradually adding 1/2 cup sugar. Beat until peaks stand up straight.
9. Gently pour the yolk mixture over the whites. Fold (using five-stroke method) until mixture is homogenous and no fluid is in the bottom.
10. Pour into a 9" square, ungreased cake pan lined with wax paper on the bottom.
11. Bake immediately at 350°F for 30 to 35 minutes until cake springs back when touched lightly.
12. Cool inverted; remove from pan while still very slightly warm.

(Serves nine)

3/8 c	boiling water
1/4 c	unsweetened cocoa
7/8 c	sifted cake flour
6 Tbsp	sugar
1/2 tsp	cinnamon
1-1/2 tsp	baking powder
1/4 tsp	salt
1/4 c	salad oil
4	eggs, separated
1/2 tsp	vanilla
1/4 tsp	cream of tartar
1/2 c	sugar

SHORTENED CAKES

Objectives

1. To illustrate various methods of making shortened cakes, including conventional, modified conventional, conventional sponge, muffin, and single-stage methods.
2. To compare the characteristics of cakes made by different methods.
3. To compare differences between foam cakes and shortened cakes.
4. To evaluate quality in shortened cakes.

Shortened cakes may be made by various methods, including the conventional, modified conventional, conventional sponge, muffin, and single-stage methods. The conventional method and its variations have the advantage of producing cakes with excellent texture and of keeping quality, but these methods have the disadvantage of requiring a relatively long mixing period. By comparison, the muffin and single-stage methods are quick to prepare, but the texture will be more porous, and the crumb stales quickly.

The conventional method is used to prepare cakes of high quality. Ingredients for a plain cake prepared by the conventional method are shortening, sugar, vanilla, eggs, cake flour, baking powder, salt, and milk.

The oven rack should be in the center position before pre-heating the oven to 350°F. This moderate oven temperature is appropriate for cakes because there is time for the baking powder in the batter to become activated by oven heat and release carbon dioxide to help stretch out the cell walls and produce a good volume before the protein in the walls coagulates and loses its elasticity.

One way of preparing a cake pan for easy removal of the baked cake is to line the bottom of the pan with wax paper. This is done quickly by placing the pan on top of a sheet of wax paper, tracing a pattern around the edge of the pan with the tip of a pair of scissors, and then cutting out the pattern just inside the traced line. The paper should cover the bottom of the pan, but not curl up the sides. Pans need not be greased. The ungreased sides help the rising cake cling to the sides and pull up. The wax paper is sufficient help in releasing the bottom of the cake from the pan so that greasing is not needed on the bottom either.

Cream the shortening and sugar together, adding the vanilla after all the sugar has been incorporated. Creaming may be done using an electric mixer or a wooden spoon. This is a vigorous process designed to produce an air-in-fat foam. The sugar granules help to trap very small pockets of air in the fat, resulting in a heavy foam that will be of value in producing a cake with a fine texture. Creaming is continued until the foam is comparatively light.

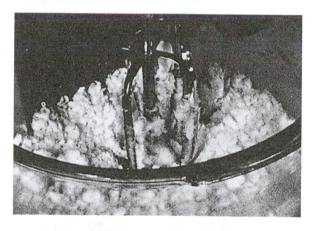

After being beaten well with a rotary egg beater, the eggs are beaten into the fat foam with the aid of either a wooden spoon or an electric mixer. The emulsifying ability of the egg yolk will be an aid in mixing the egg into the foam. This capability also is used later in helping to form an emulsion with milk.

The dry ingredients are sifted together three times as an aid in blending the cake flour, baking powder, and salt thoroughly before the proteins in the flour come into contact with liquid, and gluten development begins. Sifting is of particular importance in helping to distribute the baking powder widely throughout the flour. This is an aid in obtaining uniform leavening in the cake.

The next addition to the egg–fat foam mixture is approximately a third of the dry ingredients. These ingredients are beaten together just until the batter becomes smooth again. The mixture is quite viscous, but there is enough liquid present from the eggs for some gluten development in the flour to occur. This amount of flour gives a mixture that usually will not curdle when some milk is added.

Half the milk is added and stirred in slowly with either an electric mixer or a wooden spoon. When the excess liquid has been blended with the batter, the mixture is beaten again until smooth. Gluten develops reasonably well at this point because of the increased fluidity of the batter. However, the amounts of shortening and sugar in the batter do retard gluten development. The shortening apparently causes the gluten strands to slide by each other with some ease rather than creating a sticky, stretching environment. Sugar, because of its hygroscopic nature, binds some of the liquid, thus impeding gluten development a little.

The second third of the sifted dry ingredients is added and stirred in slowly until all of the flour is incorporated. Again, the mixture is beaten until smooth. Gluten continues to be developed whenever the batter is mixed. Excessive gluten development will produce a tough cake with some tunnels or passages where gas collects during baking and forces its way upward along strands of very well-developed gluten.

The last half of the milk is added to this viscous batter. The milk is stirred in carefully, and the mixture is beaten again. This is a point in the mixing when gluten develops well. Hence, beating is continued only until the batter is smooth.

The final addition of dry ingredients then is made. Again, the flour is stirred in carefully, and the mixture is beaten until smooth. Although the gluten in cake flour is neither as abundant nor as strong as the gluten in all-purpose flour, the mixing described above in this conventional method of making shortened cakes is sufficient to produce a cake that will be tender, yet not crumbly.

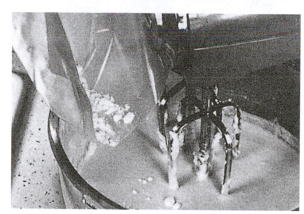

When making a layer cake, pour half the batter into each of the pans that previously were lined with wax paper. Because the cakes will just about double in volume during baking, the pans should be no more than half full. This will produce a cake with a flat surface, one that will not overflow the pan before the structure can set. With the aid of a hot pad, the rack should be pulled out and the cake pans arranged so that air can circulate freely around both pans Layer cakes bake in approximately 30 minutes.

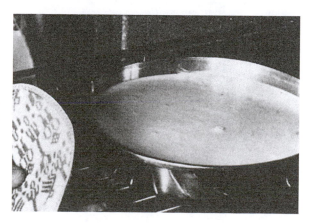

A shortened cake is done when a toothpick can be inserted in the center of the cake and removed without cake clinging to it. This test determines that the protein structure throughout the cake is denatured to the point where it is rigid enough to hold up the cake even when the hot, expanded gases contract and reduce the pressure holding each cell wall in an extended position. If the cake is pulling away from the sides of the pan when the cake is tested, remove the cake at once. This shrinking actually indicates overbaking.

After the cakes have cooled about 5 minutes, they are ready to be removed from the pans. This is done by releasing the cake all the way around the edge with a table knife. Place a cooling rack or plate on top of the layer cake. Invert the cake pan so that the rack is on the bottom, and the cake rests on it. The pan can be removed now while the wax on the paper is still warm and soft. The wax paper layer simply is peeled carefully off the cake.

The muffin method for cakes is basically the same as for making muffins, although more mixing is required to develop the necessary gluten in cakes. The dry ingredients are sifted together in a mixing bowl, and a well is made in the center. Because the shortening will be considered a liquid in this method, it must be liquefied by melting before being combined with the other liquids and beaten eggs. All of the liquid is poured at one time into the dry ingredients, and the batter is beaten for 2 minutes to develop a smooth batter and develop the gluten. The finished batter is baked in the conventional way.

A single-stage cake is made with the aid of an electric mixer because the first part of the mixing forms quite a stiff batter that is hard to mix by hand. All the dry ingredients, flavorings, shortening, and 2/3 cup milk are put in the mixer's large bowl and beaten at medium speed for 2 minutes. Preparation of the batter for a cake made by the single-stage method is completed by adding the remaining 1/3 cup milk and 4 egg yolks, and then beating for 2 more minutes at medium speed. The batter is poured into two 8" layer cake pans and baked at 350°F for 30 minutes.

Adjustments for Altitude

Ingredient Modification	3,000 FT	5,000 FT	7,000 FT
For each teaspoon baking powder, *reduce*	1/8 tsp	1/8–1/4 tsp	1/4 tsp
For each cup sugar, *reduce*	0–1 Tbsp	0–2 Tbsp	1–3 Tbsp
For each cup of liquid, *increase*	1–2 Tbsp	2–4 Tbsp	3–4 Tbsp

RECIPES

Plain Cake (Conventional Method)

Total Time: 45 minutes
Baking: 350°F oven for 30 minutes

1. Preheat oven.
2. Prepare cake pan(s) by tracing a pattern around the pan onto wax paper, using a scissors' tip.
3. Cut out the pattern and fit the wax paper into the pan, being sure that the paper fits the bottom but does not go up the side at all. Do not grease the pan(s).
4. If available, use an electric mixer to cream shortening and sugar until light and fluffy.
5. Add vanilla and well-beaten egg; beat well.
6. Sift the dry ingredients together three times.
7. Add one-third of the dry ingredients to the creamed mixture and beat briefly.
8. Add half of the milk and beat briefly.
9. Add the second third of the dry ingredients, the last half of the milk, and the final third of the dry ingredients, beating after each addition.
10. Pour into pan(s) and bake for 30 minutes at 350°F.
11. Test for doneness by inserting a toothpick in the center of the cake. When it comes out clean, the cake is done. The cake is over-baked if it is pulling away from the sides of the pan.
12. Cool in pan (upright) on rack for 5 minutes.
13. Cut around the edge of the cake with a sharp knife.
14. Invert layer onto a plate and peel off wax paper.

(Makes one 8″ layer)

1/4 c	shortening
1/2 c	sugar
1/2 tsp	vanilla
1	egg
1 c	sifted cake flour
1 tsp	baking powder
1/4 tsp	salt
1/2 c	milk

(Makes two 8″ layers)

1/2 c	shortening
1 c	sugar
1 tsp	vanilla
2	eggs
2 c	sifted cake flour
2 tsp	baking powder
1/2 tsp	salt
1 c	milk

Chocolate Cake (Modified Conventional Method)

Total Time: 45 minutes
Baking: 350°F oven for 30 minutes

1. Preheat oven.
2. Prepare cake pan(s) as for plain cake.
3. Melt the chocolate over hot water and set aside to cool.
4. Cream the butter or margarine with the sugar (use an electric mixer, if available).
5. Beat in the vanilla and beaten egg yolks.
6. Stir in the melted chocolate.
7. Sift the cake flour, soda, and salt together.
8. Add one-third of the dry ingredients and beat with the electric mixer until completely blended.
9. Add half the water and beat.
10. Add the second third of the dry ingredients, the last half of the water, and the final third of the dry ingredients, beating after each addition.
11. Use a rotary egg beater to beat the egg whites until the peaks just bend over.
12. With the aid of a rubber spatula, gently transfer the foam to the top of the batter. Fold gently and quickly with the spatula just until completely blended, using the five-stroke folding cycle.
13. Pour into round cake pan(s) and bake for 30 minutes at 350°F until a toothpick inserted in the center comes out clean.
14. Cool 5 minutes upright on the rack.
15. Cut around the edge of the cake with sharp knife.
16. Invert a plate over the pan; quickly flip the cake and plate. Remove pan and wax paper.

(Makes one 9″ layer)

1 oz	unsweetened chocolate
1/3 c	butter or margarine
14 Tbsp	sugar
1	egg, separated
1/2 tsp	vanilla
1-1/4 c	sifted cake flour
5/8 tsp	baking powder
1/4 tsp	salt
10 Tbsp	water

(Makes two 9″ layers)

2 oz	unsweetened chocolate
2/3 c	butter or margarine
1-3/4 c	sugar
2	eggs, separated
1 tsp	vanilla
2-1/2 c	sifted cake flour
1-1/4 tsp	baking powder
1/2 tsp	salt
1-1/4 c	water

White Cake (Conventional Sponge or Meringue Method)

Total Time: 40 minutes
Baking: 375°F oven for 20 minutes

1. Preheat oven.
2. Prepare cake pan(s) as for plain cake.
3. If available, use an electric mixer to cream the shortening, sugar, and vanilla together until light and fluffy.
4. Sift flour, baking powder, and salt together.
5. Add one-third of the dry ingredients to the creamed mixture and beat with an electric mixer.
6. Add one-half of the milk and beat.
7. Add the second third of the dry ingredients, the last half of the milk, and the remaining third of the dry ingredients, beating after each addition.
8. Wash the beater blades of the mixer thoroughly before using to beat the egg whites to the foamy stage.
9. Gradually add the sugar while beating the whites until the peaks just bend over.
10. Transfer all of the egg white foam to the cake batter at once; use a rubber spatula to gently fold whites into batter until no traces of whites remain.
11. Pour into 9" round cake pan(s) and bake at 375°F.
12. Place gently on a rack and cool 5 minutes.
13. Cut around the edge of the cake with a sharp knife.
14. Invert a plate over the pan; quickly flip the cake and plate. Remove pan and wax paper.

(Makes one 9" layer)

6 Tbsp	shortening
6 Tbsp	sugar
3/4 tsp	vanilla
1-1/8 c	sifted cake flour
1-1/2 tsp	baking powder
1/2 tsp	salt
1/2 c	milk
2	egg whites
6 Tbsp	sugar

(Makes two 9" layers)

3/4 c	shortening
3/4 c	sugar
1-1/2 tsp	vanilla
2-1/4 c	sifted cake flour
1 Tbsp	baking powder
1 tsp	salt
1 c	milk
5	egg whites
3/4 c	sugar

Gingerbread (Muffin Method)

Total Time: 45 to 55 minutes
Baking: 375°F oven for 35 to 45 minutes

1. Preheat oven.
2. Prepare cake pan(s) by lightly greasing the bottom, but not the sides.
3. Sift flour, brown sugar, cinnamon, ginger, soda, and salt together into a mixing bowl, and make a well in the center. Set aside.
4. Melt the shortening.
5. Mix the molasses and hot water.
6. Stir in the beaten egg.
7. Pour the liquid ingredients into the dry ingredients, all at once.
8. Mix well to make a smooth batter.
9. Pour the batter into the pan, and bake 35 to 45 minutes at 375°F, until a toothpick inserted in the center comes out clean.
10. Place pan on rack to cool. Leave gingerbread in pan for easy service and storage.

(Makes one 8″ square cake pan)

1-1/2 c	sifted all-purpose flour
1/2 c	brown sugar
1 tsp	cinnamon
1 tsp	ginger
1 tsp	soda
1/8 tsp	salt
1/2 c	shortening
1/2 c	molasses
2/3 c	hot water
1	egg, beaten

(Makes one 13″ × 9-1/2″ rectangular cake pan)

3 c	sifted all-purpose flour
1 c	brown sugar
2 tsp	cinnamon
2 tsp	ginger
2 tsp	soda
1/4 tsp	salt
1 c	shortening
1 c	molasses
1-1/3 c	hot water
2	eggs, beaten

Golden Yolk Cake (Single-Stage Method)

Total Time: 45 minutes
Baking: 350°F oven for 30 minutes

1. Preheat oven.
2. Prepare cake pan(s) by using scissors' tip to trace a pattern around the pan onto wax paper. Cut out the pattern and fit the wax paper into the pan(s), being sure that the paper fits the bottom of the pan and does not go up the sides at all. Do not grease the pan(s).
3. Sift the flour, sugar, baking powder, and salt into the mixing bowl.
4. Add the shortening, two-thirds of the milk, the extract, and grated rind, and beat at medium speed on an electric mixer for 2 minutes.
5. Add the last third of the milk and the egg yolks, and beat 2 more minutes at medium speed.
6. Pour into cake pan(s) and bake for 30 minutes at 350°F, until a toothpick comes out clean.
7. Place gently on a rack and cool 5 minutes.
8. Cut around the edge of the cake with a sharp knife.
9. Invert a plate over the pan; quickly flip the cake and plate while holding firmly.
10. Remove the pan and wax paper.

(Makes one 8" layer)

1 c	sifted cake flour
2/3 c	sugar
1-1/2 tsp	baking powder
3/8 tsp	salt
2-2/3 Tbsp	shortening (room temperature)
1/3 c	milk
1/8 tsp	lemon extract
1/2 tsp	grated lemon rind
2-2/3 Tbsp	milk
2	egg yolks

(Makes two 8" layers)

2 c	sifted cake flour
1-1/3 c	sugar
1 Tbsp	baking powder
3/4 tsp	salt
1/3 c	shortening (room temperature)
2/3 c	milk
1/4 tsp	lemon extract
1 tsp	grated lemon rind
1/3 c	milk
4	egg yolks

Homey Gingerbread

Total Time: 1 hour
Baking: 350°F oven for 35 to 40 minutes

1. Preheat oven.
2. Lightly grease an 8" square pan.
3. Cream shortening and sugar until light and fluffy, using electric mixer.
4. Add egg and molasses.
5. Sift the dry ingredients together before adding one-third of the dry ingredients to the molasses mixture. Beat in.
6. Add half of the boiling water, beating 30 seconds.
7. Add the second third of the dry ingredients and beat in.
8. Add the last half of the boiling water, beating 30 seconds.
9. Add the final third of the dry ingredients and beat just until smooth.
10. Pour into cake pan and bake 35 to 40 minutes (until toothpick inserted in center comes out clean).

(Serves eight)

1/2 c	shortening
1/2 c	sugar
1	egg
1/2 c	molasses
1-1/2 c	sifted all-purpose flour
1/4 tsp	salt
3/4 tsp	baking soda
1/2 tsp	ground ginger
1/2 tsp	cinnamon
1/2 c	boiling water

Prune Banana Cake

Total Time: 1 hour
Baking: 350°F oven for 30 minutes (small); 35 to 40 minutes (large)

1. Simmer prunes 10 minutes in water to cover.
2. Preheat oven.
3. Grease the bottom of the pan.
4. Sift dry ingredients into large mixing bowl.
5. Add shortening, milk, and vanilla.
6. Mash bananas and add to mixture. Beat at medium speed for 2 minutes.
7. Add eggs; beat 2 minutes.
8. Chop prunes; add prunes and walnuts to batter, stirring in by hand.
9. Pour into baking pan. Bake at 350°F until toothpick inserted in center comes out clean (30 minutes for small and 35 to 40 minutes for large).

(Makes 8″ × 8″ cake)

1/2 c	stewed prunes
1 c	sifted cake flour
3/4 tsp	baking powder
1/2 tsp	soda
1/2 tsp	salt
2/3 c	sugar
1/4 c	shortening
2 Tbsp	milk
1/2 tsp	vanilla
1/2 c	mashed bananas
1	egg
1/4 c	chopped walnuts

(Makes 9″ × 13″ cake)

1 c	stewed prunes
2 c	sifted cake flour
1-1/2 tsp	baking powder
1 tsp	soda
1 tsp	salt
1-1/3 c	sugar
1/2 c	shortening
1/4 c	milk
1 tsp	vanilla
1 c	mashed bananas
2	eggs
1/2 c	chopped walnuts

Spice Cake

Total Time: 40 minutes
Baking: 350°F oven for 20 to 25 minutes

1. Preheat oven.
2. Prepare pan(s) as for plain cake.
3. Cream fat, spices, and sugars until light.
4. Beat in the eggs.
5. Sift together the flour, baking powder, and salt. Add a fourth of this to the mixing bowl; stir 35 strokes.
6. Add a third of the milk; stir 15 strokes.
7. Continue adding flour by fourths and milk by thirds, stirring 35 strokes after flour additions and 15 strokes after milk additions.
8. Stir 140 strokes after last addition.
9. Pour into pan(s) and bake 20 to 25 minutes until toothpick inserted in center comes out clean.
10. Cool upright on rack 5 minutes.
11. With a sharp knife, cut around the edge of the cake to loosen it.
12. Place a plate over the cake, invert the cake, and remove the wax paper.

(Makes 8″ × 8″ cake)

1/4 c	shortening
1/2 tsp	ground cloves
1/2 tsp	nutmeg
1/2 tsp	cinnamon
1/4 c	brown sugar
1/2 c	granulated sugar
1-1/2	eggs
1 c 2 Tbsp	sifted cake flour
1-1/2 tsp	baking powder
1/4 tsp	salt
1/2 c	milk

(Makes 9″ × 13″ cake)

1/2 c	shortening
1 tsp	ground cloves
1 tsp	nutmeg
1 tsp	cinnamon
1/2 c	brown sugar
1 c	granulated sugar
3	eggs
2-1/4 c	sifted cake flour
1 Tbsp	baking powder
1/2 tsp	salt
1 c	milk

Pound Cake

Total Time: 1 hour and 15 minutes (small); 1 hour and 35 minutes (large)
Baking: 350°F oven for 1 hour (small); 1 hour 20 minutes (large)

1. Preheat oven.
2. Grease the bottom of the pan.
3. Cream sugar, shortening, margarine or butter, and lemon rind on an electric mixer until fluffy.
4. Slowly beat in the milk, beating until mixture is smooth.
5. Sift the dry ingredients together and add to the mixing bowl.
6. Beat 2 minutes on an electric mixer (use setting for beating cakes.)
7. Add one-third of the egg and beat for a minute.
8. Add the second and third portions of egg, beating one minute after each addition. Bake in loaf pan at 300°F for about 1 hour for small or 1 hour 20 minutes for large cake (until a toothpick inserted in the center comes out clean).

(Makes 8-1/2″ × 4-1/2″ × 3″ loaf pan)

10 Tbsp	sugar
2-2/3 Tbsp	shortening
2-2/3 Tbsp	margarine or butter
1/2 tsp	grated lemon rind
5 Tbsp	milk
1-1/8 c	sifted cake flour
1/2 tsp	salt
3/4 tsp	baking powder
1-1/2	eggs

(Makes 9-1/2″ × 5-1/2″ × 3″ loaf pan)

1-1/4 c	sugar
1/3 c	shortening
1/3 c	margarine or butter
1 tsp	grated lemon rind
2/3 c	milk
2-1/4 c	sifted cake flour
1 tsp	salt
1-1/2 tsp	baking powder
3	eggs, separated

Poppy Seed Bundt Cake

Total Time: 1 hour and 15 minutes
Baking: 350°F oven for 1 hour or until done

1. Preheat oven.
2. Spray 3-quart bundt pan (or tube pan) with no-stick cooking spray.
3. Cream butter and 1 cup sugar on electric mixer until fluffy.
4. Add poppy seed filling and blend.
5. Beat in egg yolks, one at a time, with the mixer running.
6. Blend in the sour cream and vanilla.
7. Stir flour, baking soda, and salt together before gradually adding to poppy seed mixture; beat until blended.
8. In clean bowl and with clean beaters, beat egg whites to the foamy stage, using electric mixer. Gradually add 1/4 cup sugar while continuing to beat on high speed. Beat until peaks just bend over.
9. Add whites to batter by carefully folding until mixture is homogenous.
10. Transfer batter to baking pan and bake 1 hour until a toothpick inserted in center comes out clean.
11. Cool upright 10 minutes before removing from pan.

(Serves 16)	
1 c	butter or margarine
1 c	sugar
1	can poppy seed filling (generally found with kosher foods in grocery store)
4	eggs, separated
1 c	sour cream
1 tsp	vanilla
2-1/2 c	all-purpose flour
1 tsp	baking soda
1 tsp	salt
1/2 c	sugar

ICING RECIPES

Figure 11.1
To ice a cake, first dust off the crumbs. Then apply the filling or icing on the top of the bottom layer.

Figure 11.2
Position the second layer, then swirl the icing on the sides of the cake.

Figure 11.3
Finally, apply the icing artistically to the top surface of the cake.

Marshmallow Frosting

1. Beat egg whites and salt on electric mixer and gradually add sugar while continuing to beat on high speed.
2. When peaks form, begin adding the corn syrup very slowly while continuing beating on high speed.
3. Beat until firmly peaked before adding vanilla.

(Icing for two layers)

1/4 tsp	salt
2	egg whites
1/4 c	sugar
3/4 c	light corn syrup
1-1/4 tsp	vanilla

Never Fail Icing

1. Cream the butter or margarine until soft.
2. Add the sugar, vanilla, and milk.
3. Beat with an electric mixer, slowly at first, until the mixture is light and creamy.
4. If necessary, gradually add more milk to achieve the desired spreading consistency. Food coloring can be used to vary the color, as desired.

(Icing for one layer)

2 Tbsp	butter or margarine
2-1/4 c	powdered sugar, sifted
1/2 tsp	vanilla
1-1/2 Tbsp	milk

(Icing for two layers)

1/4 c	butter or margarine
4-1/2 c	powdered sugar, sifted
1 tsp	vanilla
3 Tbsp	milk

Note: This icing may be varied by adding grated lemon rind, grated orange rind, or 2 ounces of melted chocolate chips. Icing may be used between layers; jams, marmalade, or cream puddings also make suitable fillings. If a cream pudding filling is used, the cake must be refrigerated to avoid growth of harmful levels of microorganisms.

Seven-Minute Frosting

1. Beat egg white, sugar, cream of tartar, water, and salt in the top of a double boiler, using an electric mixer at top speed.
2. After one minute, cook over boiling water while continuing to beat with the mixer. Continue cooking and beating the mixture until firm enough to hold peaks.
3. Remove from heat, beat in the vanilla, and beat until thick enough to spread well.

(Icing for one layer)

1	egg white
3/4 c	sugar
1/8 tsp	cream of tartar
6 Tbsp	water
3/4 tsp	vanilla
few grains	salt

(Icing for two layers)

2	egg whites
1-1/2 c	sugar
1/4 tsp	cream of tartar
1/3 c	water
1-1/2 tsp	vanilla
Dash	salt

Note: Be careful to observe if the mixer motor is overheating. Some mixers, especially the portable electric mixers, are not powerful enough to maintain the prolonged period of maximum operation without overheating.

Nutty Coconut Frosting

1. Stir ingredients together and spread evenly over the surface of the cake.
2. Place cake at lowest position in broiler compartment and broil until the frosting bubbles and coconut begins to brown.
3. Watch carefully to avoid burning the coconut.

(Icing for two layers)

1/3 c	margarine or butter
2/3 c	brown sugar
1/4 c	milk
1 c	shredded coconut
1/2 c	chopped walnuts

COOKIES

Objectives

1. To observe the effect of a lower ratio of liquid in cookies compared with cakes.
2. To demonstrate differences between dropped, bar, molded, and rolled cookies.

Cookies are popular to make because they usually are enjoyed, regardless of the skill of the baker. Most have a heavy, dense crumb, which is in sharp contrast to the expected light texture of cakes. Therefore, bakers need not be concerned about cookies falling. High levels of fat (butter, margarine, or shortening) and sugar are often used in cookie recipes to create a crisp texture after baking. Recipes included in this chapter provide examples of dropped cookies (Oatmeal Cookies), molded cookies (Sands, Cranberry-Coconut Chews, Quick Sugar Cookies), bar cookies (Lemon Squares, Three-Layer Bars), and rolled cookies (Rolled Gingerbread Cookies).

RECIPES

Oatmeal Cookies

Total Time: 45 minutes
Baking: 325°F oven for 8 to 12 minutes

1. Preheat oven.
2. Cream shortening and sugars.
3. Beat in eggs and vanilla.
4. Sift salt, soda, and flour together.
5. Add sifted dry ingredients and oatmeal; mix.
6. Add nuts and raisins and stir to mix completely.
7. Drop by teaspoons onto cookie sheet.
8. Bake in 325°F oven until somewhat browned (8 to 12 minutes).
9. Remove from cookie sheet to cool on rack or paper towel.

1 c	shortening
1 c	brown sugar
1 c	granulated sugar
2	eggs (or 4 yolks)
1 tsp	vanilla
1 tsp	salt
1 tsp	soda
1-1/2 c	flour
3 c	oatmeal
1/2 c	chopped walnuts
1-1/2 c	raisins

Sands

Total Time: 30 minutes
Baking: 350°F oven for 15 minutes

1. Preheat oven.
2. Cream butter, sugar, and vanilla.
3. Add remaining ingredients.
4. Roll into 1" balls and place about an inch apart on a cookie sheet.
5. Bake about 15 minutes, until just before they start to brown.
6. Remove from cookie sheet and roll each ball in confectioners' sugar while still warm.

1 c	butter
1/2 c	confectioners' sugar
1 tsp	vanilla
pinch	salt
2 c	flour
2 c	chopped pecans

Cranberry-Coconut Chews

Total Time: 45 minutes
Baking: 350°F oven for 11 to 15 minutes

1. Preheat oven.
2. Cream butter, sugar, grated orange rind, and vanilla together.
3. Beat in the egg.
4. Add flour, baking powder, and salt and mix thoroughly on low speed of mixer.
5. Stir in the cranberries and coconut until well mixed.
6. Roll into 1" balls and place 2" apart on a cookie sheet.
7. Bake 11 to 15 minutes until cookies just begin to brown.

1-1/2 c	butter
2 c	sugar
1 Tbsp	orange zest
2 tsp	vanilla
1	egg
3-1/4 c	flour
1 tsp	baking powder
1/4 tsp	salt
1-1/2 c	dried cranberries
1-1/2 c	flaked coconut

Quick Sugar Cookies

Total Time: 30 minutes
Baking: 350°F oven for 6 to 8 minutes

2 c	butter
2 c	sugar
1 Tbsp	vanilla
1 tsp	baking soda
1 Tbsp	vinegar
4 c	flour

1. Preheat oven.
2. Cream butter and sugar together for 5 minutes with mixer on high speed.
3. Add vanilla and baking soda dissolved in the vinegar.
4. Mix in flour, 1 cup at a time.
5. Roll into 1" balls and place 2" apart on a cookie sheet.
6. Spray bottom of a glass (preferably one with a pretty pattern on the bottom) with cooking spray and dip in granulated sugar.
7. Press each cookie with the bottom of the glass to imprint the pattern and flatten the cookie to a thickness of about 1/4". (Repeat step 6 before pressing each cookie.)
8. Bake at 350°F for 6 to 8 minutes until golden in color and just beginning to brown.

Lemon Squares

Total Time: 50 minutes
Baking: 350°F oven for 30 minutes

1/2 c	butter
1 c	flour
1 tsp	baking powder
1	egg
4	egg yolks (or 2 eggs)
2 Tbsp	butter
1 c	sugar
2 tsp	lemon zest
1/4 c	lemon juice
1	egg
3/4 c	sugar
2 c	grated coconut

1. Preheat oven.
2. Mix butter, flour, baking powder, and egg together.
3. Press into a uniform layer in the bottom of a 9" square baking pan.
4. Mix together the beaten yolks, butter, sugar, lemon zest, and juice.
5. Stir constantly while heating in the top of a double boiler over boiling water until thickened.
6. Spread uniformly over the bottom layer.
7. Beat egg well with the sugar and add coconut.
8. Spread evenly as a topping.
9. Bake at 350°F for 30 minutes.

Three-Layer Cookies

Total Time: 50 minutes
Baking: 375°F oven for 5 minutes + 20 minutes

1/2 c	butter
1 c	flour
1-1/2 c	brown sugar
1 tsp	vanilla
2 eggs	beaten
2 Tbsp	flour
1/4 tsp	baking powder
Pinch	salt
1/2 c	chopped pecans
1/2 c	flaked coconut
1-1/2 c	confectioners' sugar
1 tsp	vanilla
2 Tbsp	buttermilk

1. Preheat oven.
2. Work butter and flour together until smooth and press into a flat layer in a pan 8" square.
3. Bake at 375°F about 5 minutes until a light brown.
4. Mix sugar, vanilla, and beaten eggs.
5. Sift flour, baking powder, and salt together before stirring into the egg mixture.
6. Stir in the pecans and coconut.
7. Spread over first layer and bake 20 minutes at 375°F.
8. Beat together confectioners' sugar, vanilla, butter, and enough milk to make a smooth icing that can be spread.
9. Spread icing on the cookies after they have cooled.
10. Cut in bars or squares.

Rolled Gingerbread Cookies

Total Time: 40 minutes
Baking: 350°F oven for 12 to 15 minutes

3 Tbsp	butter-flavored shortening
3/4 c	molasses
1/2 c	brown sugar
1/3 c	water
3 c	flour
1 tsp	soda
1/2 tsp	salt
1/2 tsp	ground ginger
1/2 tsp	allspice
1/2 tsp	ground cloves
1/2 tsp	cinnamon

1. Preheat oven.
2. Cream the shortening, molasses, and brown sugar together thoroughly before mixing in the water.
3. Sift the dry ingredients and spices together before mixing them into the dough.
4. Roll on a floured board to a thickness of about 1/3". Dip cookie cutter in flour before cutting out individual cookies and transferring them to a cookie sheet.
5. Bake at 350°F about 12 minutes or until no print shows when a cookie is touched lightly.
6. Remove from baking sheet to a rack to cool, being careful not to damage the outline of cookies while they are warm.

Evaluation of Laboratory Products—Cakes and Cookies

Recipe	Notes on Color, Texture, Flavor, or Other Qualities	Comments or Suggestions for Making or Using this Product in the Future

VOCABULARY

Angel food cake	Muffin method
Chiffon cake	Single-stage method
Sponge cake	Bar cookies
Shortened cake	Dropped cookies
Conventional method	Molded cookies
Modified conventional method	Rolled cookies
Conventional sponge method	

CHAPTER 12

Pies

Objectives

1. To prepare pie crust of high quality.
2. To develop knowledge of techniques needed to make pies and pastry of high quality.
3. To identify and apply standards of quality to the preparation and evaluation of one- and two-crust pies.
4. To illustrate the methods needed to optimize protein and starch cookery in pie fillings.

When you look at the recipe for pastry, you probably will think that it is simple to put only four ingredients together and end up with a great pie crust. Actually, it is easy to make wonderfully tender and flaky pie crust—after you have learned how to manipulate the fat, flour, and water into a thin crust that you arrange attractively in a pie pan. All it takes is knowledge and practice.

KEY CONCEPTS

1. Gluten needs to be developed in pastry by very limited mixing after the water is added.
   a. Too much water and/or too much mixing will develop the gluten too much and result in a tough crust.
   b. With too little water and/or too little mixing, pastry is difficult to handle and will tend to fall apart because of inadequate gluten development.

2. The cutting of fat into particles contributes flakiness to pastry, but reduces the tenderizing effect that could be achieved if the fat were spread thinly throughout.

ONE-CRUST PIES

Principles of Preparing One-Crust Pies

Check to be sure that the oven rack is positioned in the center of the oven before beginning to preheat the oven. Then heat the oven to 425°F.

The ingredients for a pie crust are very simple: all-purpose flour, salt, shortening, and water. Margarine or butter should not be substituted for shortening in this recipe because both of these fats contain water as well as fat, and the resulting crust will be tough. The substitution of oil is not recommended because oil promotes a mealy rather than a flaky texture in the finished product.

The ingredients are combined by first stirring the salt thoroughly into the flour, using a table fork for mixing. This blends the salt flavoring throughout the crust uniformly. The fat is cut into the flour–salt mixture with the aid of a pastry blender. A light, tossing motion is used to facilitate cutting the shortening into discrete, small flour-coated pieces. The shortening that collects on the wires should be scraped off frequently to avoid having large particles of fat remaining when the rest of the fat has reached the correct size. Cutting in of the shortening continues until the pieces are generally about the size of split peas. Some particles will be a bit smaller than this, while others will be a bit larger. This variation in size is appropriate in helping to develop the desired flaky character of the crust.

Water is added in a dropwise fashion at a very slow rate. While the water is being added a drop at a time, the mixture is tossed with a fork. Addition of the drops of water needs to be spread throughout the bowl so that all parts of the dough are moistened equally. The mixing action is done very gently as the water is being added to avoid unnecessary gluten development.

When all of the water has been added, the dough is stirred into a ball. A table fork can be used in a mashing motion to help form a cohesive dough without developing the gluten extensively. Mixing is done only until the dough holds together.

The dough is turned out onto a piece of wax paper. Then the wax paper–wrapped ball of dough is worked very quickly and lightly with the hands until the dough holds together well. This operation needs to be done quickly and lightly to avoid the excessive gluten development that will occur when a warm dough is manipulated. The heat from the hands is sufficient to warm the dough unless the step is done quickly.

Let the dough rest in the wax paper while rubbing a light coating of flour into a pastry cloth. The cloth will feel like suede when the correct amount of flour has been rubbed in. Then the rolling pin covered with its stocking is rolled over the floured cloth to flour the sock. Avoid using more than the minimum amount of flour because the crust will pick up dough from the cloth and sock during rolling. The result will be a less tender crust.

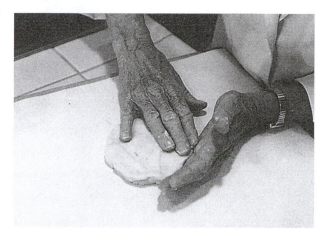

Now place half of the large ball of dough on the cloth. Use the left hand as a guide and flatten the half ball of dough into a flat, circular shape in preparation for rolling. When shaping this disk of dough, strive to develop a circular shape that is free from cracks around the edges. This will make the rolling of the crust quite simple because the dough will already have the basic shape desired.

Roll the flattened disk of dough into a crust large enough to be fitted into the pie plate and to extend at least over the lip of the pie plate. The sock-covered rolling pin should be moved with light, gentle strokes over the dough. Quick, long strokes that lift toward the edge of the dough will permit efficient rolling of the crust to a uniform thickness throughout and will not stretch the gluten unduly. Heavy stretching strokes will tend to tear the gluten strands in the dough and will also promote a less tender crust.

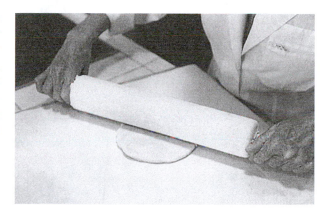

Hold the pie plate over the crust when rolling is apparently completed. Be sure that the crust is large enough to fit down into the plate and to extend to the outer edge of the lip of the plate. This requires that the circular crust must be at least 1-1/2" larger at its narrowest dimension than is the pie plate being used.

Quickly test the crust at several points to see if the crust is a uniform thickness throughout. When the crust is touched with a firm thump of the index finger, only a slight impression of the finger should show in the crust. If the crust is too thick in some areas, roll lightly in those regions until the correct thickness has been achieved. Avoid rolling any areas too thin. There is no satisfactory way of correcting too thin a crust because any rerolling that might be needed to correct the error will cause the crust to become tough.

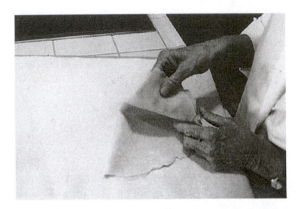

To aid in transferring the crust from the cloth to the pie plate without stretching or tearing the dough, gently fold the dough in half and then in half again. This gives a small enough package of dough to be able to handle it easily without risk of tearing.

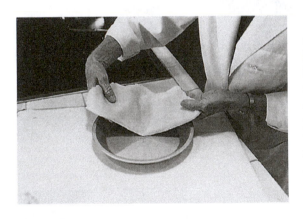

Very carefully unfold the dough into the pie plate, being sure to let the dough rest on the bottom of the plate as much as possible. When the dough is unfolded and resting loosely in the plate, hold the edge of the dough loosely in the left hand and use the right hand to help ease the dough against the edge and bottom of the plate, being particularly careful to have the crust fit into the junction between the side and bottom of the pan. The weight of the dough itself should be the main means of getting the crust to fit into the junction. The right hand is used only to ease, not to stretch the dough into place; stretched dough shrinks and pulls away from the plate when it is baking and makes the pie less attractive and more difficult to serve.

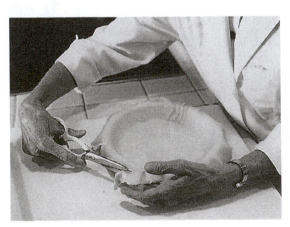

Use a pair of kitchen shears to trim the crust 1/2" beyond the edge of the pie plate. This needs to be done carefully as an aid in achieving a pie with a rim of uniform thickness. The scraps from trimming the crust are put aside.

On the far side of the pie plate, fold the overhanging crust under and stand the crust upright on the flat rim of the pie plate. This operation is continued all the way around the edge of the pie.

The edge of the pie may be trimmed in a variety of ways to suit individual preference. One attractive yet simple edging is done by using the thumb and index finger of the right hand as a pattern and the index finger of the left hand as a press. To do this, the right-hand thumb and index finger are placed on the rim of the pie plate. The left index finger is placed just opposite these fingers on the inside of the crust and pressed firmly toward the pinched pattern made by the right hand. This leaves a sharp point of crust as a design in the edge of the pie. Then the right hand is moved so that the thumb is immediately adjacent to the edge of the point just made. The left index finger is positioned inside the crust opposite the right hand, and a second point is pressed into the rim. This process is repeated continuously around the edge of the pie to make an even, sharp-point trim that rests on the lip of the pie plate all the way around the pie.

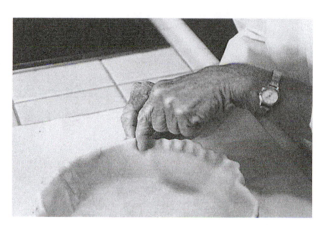

One-crust pies, such as meringue pies, are made using a baked, rather than an unbaked, pie crust. Pie crusts baked without a filling will tend to blister badly and form large air pockets unless they are pricked before being baked. To avoid these problems, unfilled pie crusts can be pricked with a table fork in a number of places. It is important to prick at frequent intervals all the way around the circle where the bottom and sides of the pan are joined. Be sure to prick all the way through the crust. This will keep the crust from forming large blisters and pulling away from the plate.

The fork also should be used to prick frequent holes all around the sides of the pastry shell.

In addition, many holes need to be pricked across the bottom of the crust so that the crust will lie flat during baking. These holes, of course, are not pricked if a filling is to be poured into an unbaked crust because the filling will run through the holes and cause the crust to stick to the pan.

The unfilled pie crust is baked in a 425°F oven for about 12 minutes until the crust is a pleasing, golden brown all over. If any portion of the crust begins to get dark, it will be necessary to stop baking the crust. Uneven browning is an indication of uneven thickness in the pastry itself and suggests the need for more careful rolling techniques when preparing a crust another time. If a meringue pie is being prepared, turn the oven thermostat to 350°F when the baked crust is removed from the oven.

PASTRY RECIPES

Pastry for One-Crust Pies

Total Time: 25 minutes
Baking: 425°F oven for 12 to 15 minutes

1. Preheat oven.
2. With a fork, stir the flour and salt together.
3. Add the shortening all at once and cut into pieces the size of split peas, using a pastry blender.
4. Toss the dough with a fork, while adding the water slowly in drops all over the dough.
5. Press dough together with a fork to form a ball.
6. Turn dough out onto a piece of wax paper. Pick up the paper and quickly press firmly into a ball with the hands.
7. Flour a pastry cloth and sock until they feel like suede.
8. Put the ball of dough on the cloth and work into a round, flat pancake shape by pressing down with the right hand and using the left hand as a guide to curve the edge of the dough. (If making the tart recipe, divide the dough approximately in half before beginning to handle the dough.)
9. Roll with a rolling pin covered with a lightly floured pastry sock.
10. Roll the dough into a circle about 1/8" thick and large enough to extend 1/2" beyond the edge of the pie plate.
11. Fold the rolled dough in half and then into quarters.
12. Gently pick up the dough and fit it into the pie plate.
13. Ease the pastry into the pie plate, being sure that it fits snugly along the bottom and sides.
14. With kitchen shears, trim the pastry 1/3" beyond the edge of the pie plate. Turn the edge under and make a fluted trim that rests on the lip of the pie plate. Puncture holes with a fork all around the side and across the bottom of the crust if the crust is being baked unfilled. Bake at 425°F about 12 minutes until the crust is a pleasing golden brown.

(Makes 2 tart shells)	
1 c	flour, sifted
1/4 tsp	salt
1/3 c	shortening
2-2/3 Tbsp	water

(Makes 1 9" pie shell)

1 c	flour, sifted
1/4 tsp	salt
1/3 c	shortening
2-2/3 Tbsp	water

Oil Pastry (for 1-crust pie)

1. Stir flour and salt together.
2. Add oil and water all at once and stir with a fork until mixed.
3. Roll out between two pieces of wax paper.

(pastry for 2 1-crust tarts)

1 c	flour
1/2 tsp	salt
1/4 c	oil
2-2/3 Tbsp	water

(pastry for 1 9″ 1-crust pie)

1 c	flour
1/2 tsp	salt
1/4 c	oil
2-2/3 Tbsp	water

Custard and Custard Type Fillings

Custard and custard-type pie fillings are prepared at this point and poured into the baked crust; pecan pie filling is poured into the partially baked crust. Custard and pumpkin pie fillings are prepared in basically the same way. These fillings are thickened with the coagulating egg during the baking process, but are very fluid before baking. Therefore, the fillings should be poured into the partially baked crust and then baked immediately for 8 minutes at 425°F to avoid soaking the crust. Then the oven thermostat is turned down to 325°F to finish coagulating the filling. If the edge of the crust begins to get too dark, cover it with aluminum foil.

Custard pies are baked until a table knife can be inserted in the filling halfway between the center and edge of the pie and can be removed with its surface showing clean, although slightly moist. The filling will be soft enough to shake just a bit when the pie is moved, but the residual heat in the filling will be just sufficient to finish coagulating the egg proteins in the center of the pie filling. If baking is allowed to continue until the knife comes out clean from the center of the pie, the filling will be over-baked.

An over-baked custard filling will be porous and exhibit syneresis (liquid draining from the filling), and the crust will become soggy. A properly baked custard pie will be firm enough to hold its shape when cut after it is allowed to cool. The crust will be flaky and tender, but will not be soggy. Pies with egg in the filling should be stored in the refrigerator as soon as they have cooled to avoid the possibility of food poisoning, such as staphylococcal or salmonella infections.

CUSTARD AND CUSTARD TYPE PIE RECIPES

Pecan Pie

Total Time: 1 hour and 10 minutes
Baking: 425°F oven 4 minutes, then 325°F 30 minutes,
tarts; 425°F oven 8 minutes, then 325°F 45 minutes, pie

1. Preheat oven.
2. Prepare pastry and bake 5 minutes (see pastry recipes on p. 328).
3. Beat the egg(s).
4. Add the sugars, salt, corn syrup, and vanilla.
5. Beat with rotary beater until well blended.
6. Stir in the pecans.
7. Pour into the partially baked pie shell.
8. Bake for 8 minutes at 425°F.
9. Then reduce heat to 325°F about 30 minutes for tarts and about 45 minutes for pie until a knife inserted halfway between the center and the edge comes out clean.
10. Cool on rack until room temperature; refrigerate promptly until served.

(Makes 2 tarts)

	pastry for 2 tarts (see p. 328)
1	egg
1/4 c	light brown sugar
1 tsp	sugar
dash	salt
1/3 c	light corn syrup
1/4 tsp	vanilla
1/3 c	pecan halves

(Makes 1 9" pie)

	pastry for 9" pie (see p. 328)
3	eggs
3/4 c	light brown sugar
1 Tbsp	sugar
1/8 tsp	salt
1 c	light corn syrup
1 tsp	vanilla
1 c	pecan halvesr

Pumpkin Pie

Total Time: 55 minutes
Baking: 425°F oven 4 minutes then 325°F 15 minutes,
tarts; 425°F oven 8 minutes then 325°F 25 minutes, pie

1. Preheat oven.
2. Prepare pastry and bake 5 minutes (see pastry recipes on p. 328).
3. Scald the milk.
4. Beat the egg(s) with a rotary beater.
5. Stir in the pumpkin, salt, sugars, and spices.
6. Quickly stir in the hot milk.
7. Pour into the partially baked pie shell.
8. Bake for 4 minutes (for tarts) or 8 minutes (for pie) at 425°F.
9. Reduce heat to 325°F for 15 minutes (tarts) or 25 minutes (pie) until knife inserted halfway between the center and the edge comes out clean.
10. Cool on a rack until room temperature; refrigerate immediately until served.

(Makes 2 tarts)

	pastry for 2 tarts (see p. 328)
10 Tbsp	milk, scalded
1	egg
10 Tbsp	canned pumpkin
1/8 tsp	salt
1/4 c	sugar
1 Tbsp	brown sugar
1/2 tsp	cinnamon
1/8 tsp	ground cloves
1/8 tsp	nutmeg
1/8 tsp	ginger
1/8 tsp	allspice

(Makes 1 9" pie)

	pastry for 9" pie (see p. 328)
1-1/4 c	milk, scalded
2	eggs
1-1/4 c	canned pumpkin
1/4 tsp	salt
1/2 c	sugar
2 Tbsp	brown sugar
1 tsp	cinnamon
1/4 tsp	ground cloves
1/4 tsp	nutmeg
1/4 tsp	ginger
1/4 tsp	allspice

Custard Pie

Total Time: 1 hour
Baking: 425°F oven 4 minutes then 325°F 15 minutes, tarts; 425°F oven 8 minutes then 325°F 25 minutes, pie

1. Preheat oven.
2. Prepare pastry and bake 5 minutes (see pastry recipes on p. 328).
3. Scald the milk.
4. Beat the eggs slowly to completely blend the yolk and white without making a foam.
5. Stir in the other ingredients including the hot milk. Blend completely and then pour into partially baked pastry shell.
6. Sprinkle with nutmeg.
7. Bake at 425°F for 8 minutes (see note below).
8. Reduce heat to 325°F for about 15 minutes (tarts) or 25 minutes (pie) until knife inserted halfway between the center and the edge comes out clean.
9. Cool on rack until room temperature; refrigerate promptly until served.

(Makes 2 tarts)

	pastry for 2 tarts (see p. 328)
2/3 c	milk, scalded
1	egg
3 Tbsp	sugar
dash	salt
1/4 tsp	vanilla
2 drops	almond extract nutmeg

(Makes 1 9" pie)

	pastry for 9" pie (see p. 328)
3	eggs
1/2 c	sugar
1/4 tsp	salt
2 c	milk, scalded
3/4 tsp	vanilla
1/8 tsp	almond extract nutmeg

Note: This pie filling may be prepared by baking the pastry in a glass pie plate, then pouring in the filling, covering loosely with plastic wrap, and microwaving for 13 to 15 minutes to coagulate the filling at low setting.

Meringue Pie

The filling for meringue pies begins with preparation of a gelatinized starch mixture. A lemon meringue pie filling is made by stirring together cornstarch, sugar, and salt until the starch is blended thoroughly with the other dry ingredients. Then water can be added slowly while stirring with a wooden spoon. A smooth slurry should be formed before applying any heat to this mixture.

Place the pan over direct heat and stir continuously with a wooden spoon while bringing the mixture to a boil. Continue heating until the spoon leaves a path across the bottom of the pan and the mixture appears to be relatively translucent. In fillings using flour and/or milk, the translucent appearance will be difficult to detect, so the viscosity will be the guide to use. Remove the thickened filling from the heat.

Beat egg yolks with a table fork until blended. Stir approximately a tablespoonful of the hot starch mixture into the yolks, being sure to avoid letting any of the hot mixture come in contact with the yolks without being stirred in thoroughly. This is very important if lumps in the yolk are to be avoided. When the first spoonful has been blended completely, repeat the process with a second spoonful. Continue with a third and finally a fourth spoonful of the hot starch paste. This procedure is used to dilute the egg yolk protein and raise the temperature at which coagulation will take place in the total mixture. As a result of the higher coagulation temperature, there will be less likelihood of developing lumps of egg yolk in the pie filling.

Now the diluted egg mixture is ready to be added to the hot starch paste. The hot starch paste should be stirred efficiently with a wooden spoon while the egg yolk mixture is poured slowly into the hot paste. The total mixture should be stirred with a wooden spoon until no streaks of yolk or starch paste remain in the mixture.

The mixture then is returned to the heat by placing either overboiling water or on the simmer setting of a temperature-controlled range unit and stirred very slowly for five minutes while becoming slightly thicker and less glossy. It must not be overheated after the egg has been added because the egg yolk will curdle, but complete coagulation of the egg yolk is essential. Incomplete coagulation of the yolk results in a pie filling that is quite thin when served, even though it may have appeared to be thick before the egg was added. When the yolk has thickened, the starch–yolk mixture is removed from the heat.

The final step in preparing the filling for a lemon meringue pie is the addition of lemon juice, grated lemon rind, and margarine or butter. The acidic lemon is added after the starch has been gelatinized and the egg yolk protein has been coagulated to avoid the acid hydrolysis that would result in less than optimum thickening of the filling. By adding the lemon after cooking of the filling is completed, hydrolytic breakdown to smaller, more soluble molecules is prevented. All meringue pie fillings except banana cream pie are covered at this point to help keep the filling warm while the meringue is being prepared. Banana cream pie filling is allowed to cool so that it will not be hot enough to cook the bananas when the pie is assembled.

Just as soon as the filling is completed, egg whites are beaten on an electric mixer until the whites reach the foamy stage, when cream of tartar and the first tablespoon of sugar are added. The mixer is set at high speed, and the remaining sugar is added gradually, a tablespoonful at a time.

Beating is continued until the correct stage is reached. To test the extent of beating, stop the mixer. Use a rubber spatula to pull some of the egg white foam up into a peak. Lift the spatula up slowly so the true character of the foam will show. When tested in this way, the egg white foam will form peaks that just barely bend over.

Assemble the pie by pouring the filling into the baked crust. Gently scrape all of the meringue from the bowl onto the surface of the pie with the aid of a rubber spatula.

Use the spatula to spread the meringue gently all the way to the edge of the pie and to seal the meringue into each point of the edging. It is important to seal the meringue to the crust in this way to help avoid having the meringue pull away from the edge during the baking. When the edge is sealed all the way around, swirl an attractive design in the meringue with the aid of the spatula, being careful to prevent any peaks in the meringue. Peaks need to be avoided because they will get too dark before the rest of the meringue bakes enough to coagulate the egg white protein.

Immediately place the pie in the oven that has been set at 350°F. Bake the meringue until the surface is a pleasing golden brown. The valleys in the meringue design will still be rather white when the upper surfaces are appropriately browned. Remove the pie from the oven at this time and cool it at room temperature until the pan can be handled comfortably without hot pads. Store the pie in the refrigerator until serving time.

A meringue pie is evaluated on the basis of the crust, the filling, and the meringue. The crust should be crisp, tender, flaky, and a pleasing golden brown. The filling should be firm enough to be cut easily, but should soften almost imperceptibly along the cut edge when served cold. The texture of the filling should be smooth, and there should be a light rather than a pasty feeling on the tongue.

The meringue is evaluated on its volume, general appearance, ease of cutting, and stability. A good meringue will be a pleasing golden brown on the higher surfaces and only very slightly brown in the valleys; the volume will be excellent. A fresh, properly baked meringue will cut without clinging to the knife. There should be virtually no liquid collecting between the meringue and the filling. The use of a hot filling is an aid in avoiding this problem because the filling helps to coagulate the egg white proteins in the lower part of the meringue, thus minimizing drainage from the meringue.

MERINGUE AND CREAM PIE RECIPES

Lemon Meringue Pie

Total Time: 1 hour
Baking: 425°F oven 12 to 15 minutes, pastry; 350°F oven 12 to 15 minutes, meringue

1. Preheat oven.
2. Prepare and bake the pie crust. Then reduce oven to 350°F.
3. With a wooden spoon, mix the cornstarch, sugar, and salt together thoroughly in a 1-quart saucepan.
4. Add the water gradually while stirring.
5. Continue to stir; heat to boiling, being careful to stir all across the bottom and around the sides of the pan.
6. Remove from heat and stir a spoonful of the hot filling into the beaten egg yolk.
7. Repeat three more times, then stir the yolk mixture back into the filling.
8. Place mixture over boiling water and cook for 5 minutes or until filling thickens slightly and loses its gloss. (Direct heat may be used if the heat never rises to the point where the filling boils.) Stir slowly while coagulating the egg yolk.
9. Remove from the heat and stir in the butter, lemon juice, and lemon rind. Cover and set aside.
10. With an electric mixer, beat the egg white to the foamy stage.
11. Add the cream of tartar.
12. Pour the filling into the baked pie shell(s).
13. Top with the meringue; use a rubber spatula to seal the meringue carefully to the edge of the crust all the way around.
14. Swirl the top of the meringue without drawing up peaks.
15. Bake at 350°F 12 to 15 minutes or until golden brown.
16. Chill at least 2 hours before serving and keep in refrigerated storage until served to avoid possible growth of microorganisms.

(Makes 2 tarts)

	pastry for 2 tarts (see p. 328)
3 Tbsp	cornstarch
3/4 c	sugar
1/8 tsp	salt
3/4 c	water
1	egg yolk, beaten
2 tsp	butter or margarine
3 Tbsp	lemon juice
1/2 tsp	grated lemon rind
1	egg white
2 Tbsp	sugar
1/8 tsp	cream of tartar

(Makes 1 9" pie)

	pastry for 9" pie (see p. 328)
6 Tbsp	cornstarch
1-1/2 c	sugar
1/4 tsp	salt
1-1/4 c	water
3	egg yolks, beaten
1-1/2 Tbsp	butter or margarine
6 Tbsp	lemon juice
1 tsp	grated lemon rind
3	egg whites
6 Tbsp	sugar
1/4 tsp	cream of tartar

Coconut Cream Pie

Total Time: 1 hour
Baking: 425°F oven 12 to 15 minutes, pastry; 350°F oven 12 to 15 minutes, meringue

1. Preheat oven.
2. Prepare and bake the pie crust. Then reduce oven to 350°F.
3. With a wooden spoon, mix the flour, sugar, and salt together in a 1-quart saucepan.
4. Slowly add the milk while stirring. Stir constantly while heating the mixture to a boil.
5. Continue boiling until a spoon leaves a path in the mixture.
6. Remove from the heat and stir a spoonful of the hot filling into the beaten yolk.
7. Repeat three more times and then stir the yolk mixture back into the filling.
8. Place the mixture over boiling water and cook for 5 minutes or until the mixture thickens slightly and loses its gloss. (Direct heat may be used if the heat never rises to the point where filling boils.) Stir slowly while coagulating the egg yolk.
9. Add margarine or butter and vanilla. Cover pan to help retain heat while making meringue.
10. With an electric mixer, beat the egg white to the foamy stage and add the cream of tartar.
11. Beating at high speed, beat 15 seconds before gradually adding the sugar. Beat until peaks just fold over.
12. Stir the shredded coconut into the filling.
13. Pour the filling into the baked pie crust.
14. Pile the meringue on the filling and spread it carefully over the surface of the pie. Use a rubber spatula to press the meringue firmly against all edges of the pastry. Then make a circular swirl in the meringue to give some contrast without developing peaks that will burn before other portions are baked.
15. Bake the meringue in a 350°F oven for 12 to 15 minutes or until a golden brown.
16. Chill at least 2 hours before serving and keep pie in refrigerated storage until consumed to avoid possible growth of microorganisms.

(Makes 2 tarts)

	pastry for 2 tarts (p. 328)
2-2/3 Tbsp	flour, sifted
1/3 c	sugar
1/8 tsp	salt
1 c	milk
1	egg yolk
1/2 tsp	margarine or butter
1/2 tsp	vanilla
1	egg white
1/8 tsp	cream of tartar
2 Tbsp	sugar
1/2 c	shredded coconut

(Makes 1 9" pie)

	pastry for 9" pie (p. 328)
1/3 c	flour, sifted
2/3 c	sugar
1/4 tsp	salt
2 c	milk
3	egg yolks
1 tsp	margarine or butter
1 tsp	vanilla
3	egg whites
1/4 tsp	cream of tartar
6 Tbsp	sugar
1 c	shredded coconut

Banana Cream Pie

Total Time: 1 hour
Baking: 425°F oven 12 to 15 minutes, pastry; 350°F oven 12 to 15 minutes, meringue

1. Preheat oven.
2. Prepare and bake the pie crust. Then reduce oven to 350°F.
3. With a wooden spoon, mix flour, sugar, and salt together in a 1-quart saucepan and gradually stir in the milk.
4. Heat to boiling while stirring constantly.
5. Remove from the heat and stir a spoonful of the hot filling into the beaten yolk.
6. Repeat three more times.
7. Pour the yolk mixture back into the filling as the filling is being stirred.
8. Cook the filling over boiling water for 5 minutes or until the mixture thickens slightly and loses its gloss. (Direct heat may be used if the heat never rises to the point where the filling boils.) Stir slowly while coagulating the yolk.
9. Remove from the heat, stir in the vanilla and margarine or butter, cover, and cool the filling by placing pan in ice.
10. When the filling has cooled to about 100°F, begin to make the meringue.
11. With an electric mixer, beat the egg whites to the foamy stage.
12. Add the cream of tartar.
13. Beating at high speed, beat 15 seconds before gradually adding the sugar. Beat until peaks just fold over.
14. Slice the bananas in the pie crust.
15. Pour in the filling.
16. Spread the meringue on top.
17. Use a rubber spatula to seal the meringue to the crust and swirl the meringue surface without pulling up high peaks.
18. Bake at 350°F for 12 to 15 minutes or until the meringue is a golden brown.
19. Chill at least 2 hours before serving and keep in refrigerated storage until served to avoid possible growth of microorganisms.

(Makes 2 tarts)

	pastry for 2 tarts (p. 328)
2-2/3 Tbsp	flour, sifted
1/3 c	sugar
1/8 tsp	salt
1 c	milk
1	egg yolk, beaten
1/2 tsp	margarine or butter
1/2 tsp	vanilla
1	egg white
2 Tbsp	sugar
1/8 tsp	cream of tartar
1	banana

(Makes one 9" pie)

	pastry for 9" pie (p. 328)
1/3 c	flour, sifted
2/3 c	sugar
1/4 tsp	salt
2 c	milk
3	egg yolks, beaten
1 tsp	margarine or butter
1 tsp	vanilla
3	egg whites
6 Tbsp	sugar
1/4 tsp	cream of tartar
3	bananas

Note: Other cream pies may be made by using the recipes from the Cream Puddings section in Chapter 8 (p. 207) as the filling in a baked crust and topping with a meringue. Use the meringue recipe for the banana cream pie. Sometimes whipped cream is used in place of meringue as the topping for a cream pie.

CHIFFON PIE RECIPES

Lemon Chiffon Pie

Total Time: 1 hour
Baking: 425°F oven 12 to 15 minutes

1. Preheat oven.
2. Prepare and bake pastry (see pastry recipes on p. 328).
3. In a double boiler, soften the gelatin in the cold water.
4. Stir in the first measure of sugar, the lemon juice, and the beaten egg yolks.
5. Stir while heating over boiling water until mixture thickens enough to pile.
6. Add the lemon rind.
7. Chill until mixture begins to congeal.
8. With an electric mixer, quickly beat the egg whites to the foamy stage.
9. Gradually add the remaining measure of sugar while continuing beating.
10. Beat until the peaks just bend over when the beater is withdrawn.
11. Fold the gelatin mixture into the beaten whites thoroughly, but gently.
12. Pile into the baked pie shell.
13. Chill in the refrigerator. Garnish with whipped cream.

(Makes 2 tarts)

	Pastry for 2 tarts (p. 328)
1/2	envelope unflavored gelatin
3 Tbsp	cold water
1/4 c	sugar
1/4 c	lemon juice
2	eggs, separated
1 tsp	grated lemon rind
1/4 c	sugar
	whipped cream for garnish

(Makes 1 9" pie)

	pastry for 9" pie (p. 328)
1	envelope unflavored gelatin
1/3 c	cold water
1/2 c	sugar
1/2 c	lemon juice
4	eggs, separated
2 tsp	grated lemon rind
1/2 c	sugar
	whipped cream for garnish

Eggnog Chiffon Pie

Total Time: 1 hour
Baking: 425°F oven 12 to 15 minutes

1. Preheat oven.
2. Prepare and bake pastry (see pastry recipes on p. 328).
3. Soften the gelatin in cold water.
4. Combine the beaten yolks, hydrated gelatin, first measure of sugar, salt, and warm water in the top of a double boiler.
5. Cook over boiling water, stirring constantly, until mixture thickens.
6. Chill until partially congealed.
7. With an electric mixer, beat the egg whites to the foamy stage, then gradually add the remaining sugar while beating until the peaks of the whites just bend over.
8. Add the nutmeg and flavorings and blend.
9. Fold the first mixture into the egg whites gently, but thoroughly, using a rubber spatula.
10. Pile into the pie shell and chill.
11. Garnish with whipped cream and almonds.

(Makes 2 tarts)

	pastry for 2 tarts (p. 328)
1/2	envelope unflavored gelatin
2 Tbsp	cold water
2	egg yolks, beaten
1/4 c	sugar
1/8 tsp	salt
1/4 c	warm water
1/4 c	sugar
2	egg whites
1/8 tsp	nutmeg
1 tsp	rum flavoring
1/8 tsp	almond extract
1/2 c	whipping cream
1/4 c	slivered almonds, toasted

(Makes 1 9″ pie)

	pastry for 9″ pie (p. 328)
1	envelope unflavored gelatin
1/4 c	cold water
4	egg yolks, beaten
1/2 c	sugar
1/4 tsp	salt
1/2 c	warm water
1/2 c	sugar
4	egg whites
1/4 tsp	nutmeg
2 tsp	rum flavoring
1/4 tsp	almond extract
1 c	whipping cream
1/2 c	slivered almonds, toasted

Note: Chiffon pies can be made with a variety of pie shells. The fillings should be uniform and should have a light, airy texture with no obvious pieces of gelatin. They should be tender and easy to cut. For best results, chiffon pies should be served the same day they are made.

TWO-CRUST PIES

Principles of Preparing Two-Crust Pies

Although the dough is prepared the same for one- and two-crust pies, the treatment in the pan is different. Two-crust pies are made by trimming the bottom crust even with the edge of the pan.

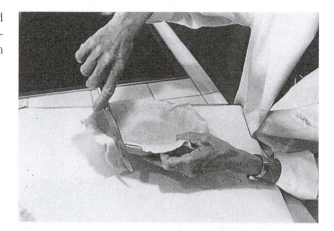

The top crust is rolled and folded into quarters, ready for placement on the filling.

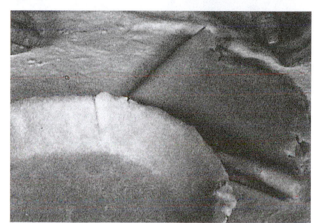

Then the filling is prepared. This avoids having the filling sitting in the unbaked crust while the second crust is rolled, thus reducing the likelihood of a soggy bottom crust. Fresh fruits such as apples need to be arranged as compactly as possible to help minimize the shrinkage of the filling during baking. Unless care is taken to do this and to position the top crust gently but firmly on the fruit, the fruit filling may shrink during baking and leave the top crust suspended an inch or more above the fruit. This makes the baked pie difficult to serve. If canned or frozen fruits are used for the filling, there will be essentially no shrinkage of the filling.

The top crust is unfolded to a semicircle and arranged over the nearest half of the pie before unfolding the other half of the crust over the remainder of the pie. Gently press the top crust to the bottom crust around the lip of the pie plate.

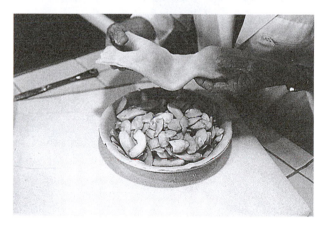

Use kitchen shears to trim the top crust 1/2" beyond the lip of the plate. This trimming should be done carefully and uniformly.

Finish assembling the crusts by turning the extension of the upper crust under the portion of the lower crust that is resting on the lip of the plate. This operation, in essence, makes a sandwich, with the bottom crust serving as the sandwich filling that is encased in two layers of the upper crust. This technique effectively seals the pie filling into the pie crusts and reduces the possibility of overflow.

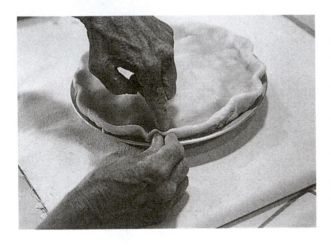

To improve the appearance of the pie and strengthen the seal of the filling, an edge trim is used. A simple edge trim is done by placing the index finger and thumb of the right hand right next to the crust on the lip of the pie plate and then pressing the crust between the fingers into a sharp point with the aid of the index finger of the left hand. This process is repeated all the way around the edge of the pie, being sure to place the thumb of the right hand just to the right of the previous point. It is important to pinch the dough into sharp points so that the pattern will show distinctly after baking. The dough will tend to soften and straighten out a bit during baking.

Use a sharp knife to cut steam vents in the top crust of the pie. These steam vents can be an attractive design that enhances the appearance of the pie while serving their utilitarian function of releasing steam from the hot filling during baking. These vents should be primarily in the center of the pie and ideally extend no closer than within 1-1/2" of the edge of the pie. This helps to keep the boiling filling from running over. Be sure that the steam vents are large enough to remain open during the entire baking period. Vents less than 1/4" long tend to seal over while the pie is baking. When steam cannot escape from the filling, the top crust will become soggy.

Some people prefer the appearance of the baked crust if the crust has been dusted with a bit of granulated sugar or brushed with a light glaze of milk before baking. If desired, this treatment is applied at this point.

For a lattice crust, the bottom crust is trimmed 1/2" beyond the edge of the pie plate, using kitchen shears. After the filling is added, the lattice strips are placed in position and trimmed even with the edge of the bottom crust. Then the lower crust is folded up and over the edge of the lattice strips before the edge is fluted.

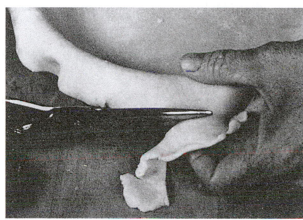

TWO-CRUST PIES RECIPES

Pastry for Two-Crust Pie

1. Mix the flour and salt with a fork.
2. Use a pastry blender to cut in the shortening efficiently until it is the size of split peas.
3. Toss the pastry lightly with a fork as the water is added dropwise throughout the pastry.
4. Press together with a fork.
5. Turn dough out onto wax paper and press it firmly into a ball.
6. Divide the dough (in halves for large recipe, in quarters for small).
7. On a lightly floured pastry cloth, shape one of the pieces of dough into a round shape.
8. Press it into a disk.
9. Put a floured stocking on the rolling pin and roll out the first crust.
10. When it is 1/8″ thick and large enough to fit the pan, fold the dough in half and then in quarters.
11. Pick it up and transfer it to the pie plate.
12. Unfold it carefully and fit it gently into the pie plate.
13. Use a table knife to trim the edge of the crust along the edge of the pie plate.
14. Roll the second crust in the same manner.
15. Fold it in quarters and set aside until the pie is assembled. If tarts are being made, repeat the process for the other tart.

(pastry for 2 two-crust tarts)

2 c	flour
1/2 tsp	salt
2/3 c	shortening
1/3 c	water

(pastry for 1 9″ two-crust pie)

2 c	flour
1/2 tsp	salt
2/3 c	shortening
1/3 c	water

Apple Pie

Total Time: 1 hour
Baking: 400°F oven 25 minutes for tarts; 35 minutes for pie

1. Preheat oven.
2. Prepare crust recipe for two-crust pie (see pastry recipe, p. 344).
3. Pare and core the apples. Slice very thin.
4. In a mixing bowl, mix the sugar, cornstarch, and cinnamon; stir the apples in so the slices are well coated.
5. Arrange the apples in the bottom pie crust, pressing them down gently to help pack them.
6. Sprinkle the lemon juice over the apples.
7. Dot filling with small pieces of butter or margarine.
8. Unfold the top crust over the filling and center it on the pie.
9. Press the edges so they conform to the lip of the pie plate.
10. With kitchen shears, trim the top crust 1/2" beyond the lip of the plate.
11. Turn the extension of the upper crust under the lower crust on the lip of the plate.
12. Flute the edge of the pie.
13. Use a paring knife to cut an artistic design to serve as a steam vent in the middle of the pie.
14. Sprinkle the top with some sugar. Bake at 400°F until the filling begins to bubble and the crust is a pleasing golden brown (about 25 minutes for tarts or 35 minutes for pie).

(Makes 2 two-crust tarts)

	pastry for 2 two-crust tarts (p. 344)
2	pippins or other tart apples
1/2 c	sugar
1 Tbsp	cornstarch
1/2 tsp	cinnamon
1 tsp	lemon juice
1-1/2 tsp	margarine or butter

(Makes one 9" two-crust pie)

	pastry for 1 two-crust pie (p. 344)
5	pippins or other tart apples
1 c	sugar
2 Tbsp	cornstarch
1 tsp	cinnamon
2 tsp	lemon juice
1 Tbsp	margarine or butter

Note: Fresh peaches or pears may be substituted for apples. One teaspoon (large recipe) grated lemon rind (1/2 teaspoon for small recipe) may be added with the cinnamon.

Rhubarb Pie (lattice top)

Total Time: 50 minutes
Baking: 400°F oven 25 minutes for tarts; 35 minutes for pie

1. Preheat oven.
2. Prepare crust recipe for two-crust pie (see pastry recipe, p. 344). When fitting the bottom crust, let the pastry extend 1/2" beyond the lip of the pie plate.
3. Roll out the top crust and use a pastry wheel to cut strips for making a lattice top.
4. In a mixing bowl, mix sugar, flour, and grated orange rind together, and stir in the rhubarb.
5. Place in the bottom crust and dot filling with small pieces of margarine or butter.
6. Weave the strips of lattice across the top of the pie. For a quick lattice, lay all the strips across in one direction and then put the other strips on top of them at right angles without actually weaving the strips.
7. Press the end of the lattice strips firmly to the lower crust along the lip of the pie plate.
8. With kitchen shears, trim the strips even with the lower crust.
9. Fold the lower crust up over the strips and stand the edge of the crust up along the lip of the pie plate.
10. Flute the edge. Bake at 400°F until the filling is bubbling and the crust is a golden brown (about 25 minutes for tarts or 35 minutes for pie).

(Makes 2 two-crust tarts)

	pastry for 2 two-crust tarts (p. 344)
1-1/2 c	fresh rhubarb, washed and cut in 1/2" pieces
1/2 c	sugar
1/2 tsp	grated orange rind
1-1/2 Tbsp	flour
1-1/2	Tsp margarine or butter

(Makes 1 9" two-crust pie)

	pastry for 1 two-crust pie (p. 344)
3 c	fresh rhubarb, washed and cut in 1/2" pieces
1 c	sugar
1 tsp	grated orange rind
3 Tbsp	flour
1 Tbsp	margarine or butter

Canned Cherry Pie

Total Time: 1 hour
*Baking: 400°F oven 30 minutes for tarts; 40 minutes
for pie*

1. Preheat oven.
2. Prepare crust recipe for two-crust pie (see pastry recipe, p. 344).
3. In a saucepan, mix half of the sugar and cornstarch together and gradually stir in the cherry juice.
4. Heat to boiling while stirring constantly with a wooden spoon.
5. Cook until thick and clear.
6. Remove from heat.
7. Add the other half of sugar, cherries, margarine or butter, and almond extract. If desired, tint with red food coloring.
8. Put filling in pie crust and fit the top crust as described in the recipe for apple pie.
9. Bake at 400°F until the filling is bubbling, and the crust is golden brown.

(Makes 2 two-crust tarts)

	pastry for 2 two-crust tarts (p. 344)
1/2 c	sugar
2 Tbsp	cornstarch
1/3 c	cherry juice
1-1/2 c	canned cherries, well drained
1 tsp	margarine or butter
2	drops almond extract red food coloring (optional)

(Makes 1 9" two-crust pie)

	pastry for 1 two-crust pie (p. 344)
1 c	sugar
1/4 c	cornstarch
2/3 c	cherry juice
3 c	canned cherries, well drained
2 tsp	margarine or butter
4	drops almond extract red food coloring (optional)

Canned Peach Pie

Total Time: 1 hour
Baking: 400°F oven 30 minutes for tarts; 40 minutes for pie

1. Preheat oven.
2. Prepare crust recipe for two-crust pie (see pastry recipe, p. 344).
3. In a saucepan, mix the sugar and cornstarch together; gradually stir in the measured juice.
4. Heat to boiling while stirring constantly with wooden spoon.
5. Cook until thick and clear. Remove from heat.
6. Add the drained peaches, cinnamon, almond extract, and margarine or butter.
7. Pour filling into pie crust, and fit the top crust as described in the recipe for apple pie.
8. Bake at 400°F until the filling is bubbling and the crust is golden brown.

(Makes 2 two-crust tarts)

	pastry for 2 two-crust tarts (p. 344)
1/4 c	sugar
2 Tbsp	cornstarch
1/3 c	peach juice
1	1lb can sliced peaches, well drained
1/4 tsp	cinnamon
2	drops almond extract
1 tsp	margarine or butter

(Makes 1 9″ two-crust pie)

	pastry for 1 two-crust pie (p. 344)
1/2 c	sugar
1/4 c	cornstarch
2/3 c	peach juice
2	1 lb cans sliced peaches, well drained
1/2 tsp	cinnamon
1/8 tsp	almond extract
2 tsp	margarine or butter

Evaluation of Laboratory Products—Pies

Recipe	Notes on Color, Texture, Flavor, or Other Qualities	Comments or Suggestions for Making or Using this Product in the Future

VOCABULARY

Flakiness

Gel

Mealiness

Shortening power of fats

CHAPTER 13

Beverages

Tea and coffee provide the background fabric for many meetings and social occasions. The way in which these two classic and universal beverages are served may differ widely from country to country and even within parts of a country, but they still serve as classic symbols of hospitality. You will find that entertaining is easier if you are able to prepare and serve them. After you master the basics, you can explore the many variations that currently are available to add variety and interest to your meals. You will also learn to make cocoa and hot chocolate in this chapter.

Objectives

1. To prepare beverages of high quality, including tea, coffee, cocoa, and hot chocolate.

2. To evaluate the beverages according to accepted criteria.

3. To identify differences in beverages created using different equipment and/or ingredients.

KEY CONCEPTS

1. The color, aroma, and flavor of tea are determined by the treatment of the leaves.
   a. Green tea is made from unfermented leaves, resulting in a pale green, somewhat astringent beverage with a light aroma.
   b. Oolong tea leaves have been fermented a bit and yield a moderately golden brown beverage with a mild flavor and pleasing aroma.
   c. Black tea is made from leaves that have been allowed to ferment longer than oolong, producing a beverage that has a fairly deep golden brown color, a full flavor, and a satisfying brisk character.

2. Coffee beans are roasted to varying degrees to suit preferences around the world before they are ground and brewed to make the beverage.
   a. Roasting develops flavors, but grinding leads to gradual loss of aromatic and flavor compounds as well as detrimental oxidation of the oils in the beans over long storage.
   b. Coffee most commonly is made by the drip method today, although percolator coffee also is brewed; drip (dripolator) coffee is usually a bit fuller in flavor and less bitter than percolator coffee.

3. Cocoa and hot chocolate are brewed from cocoa or chocolate made from the nibs obtained from the cacao pods.
   a. Preparation of either cocoa or hot chocolate requires gelatinization of the starch that is present.
   b. Care must be taken when making cocoa or hot chocolate to avoid scorching the milk and to minimize scum formation.

Figure 13.1
Tea grown in the hills in Sri Lanka is a major crop and is shipped to ports around the world.

TEA RECIPES

Hot Tea

Total Time: 6 minutes

1. Fill teapot with hot water to preheat the pot.
2. Heat water to boiling in a 1-quart covered saucepan.
3. Pour the hot water out of the teapot.
4. Place either the tea leaves enclosed in a tea ball or the tea bags in the empty teapot.
5. Pour the freshly boiled water over the tea leaves and cover the teapot.
6. Steep for 3 minutes, remove the leaves, and serve the beverage.

(Serves two)

2 tsp	tea leaves or 2 tea bags
1-1/2 c	boiling water

(Serves four)

4 tsp	tea leaves or 4 tea bags
3 c	boiling water

Note: To compare the characteristics of green, oolong, and black teas and some of their variations, prepare the tea beverages according to the above procedure.

Iced Tea

Total Time: 7 minutes

1. Prepare tea infusion as above.
2. After tea infusion has been steeped 3 minutes, remove the tea leaves and pour the beverage over ice.

(Serves two)

2 tsp	tea leaves or 2 tea bags
3/4 c	boiling water
8	ice cubes

(Serves four)

4 tsp	tea leaves or 2 tea bags
1-1/2 c	boiling water
16	ice cubes

Criteria for Evaluation

Hot and iced teas should be sparklingly clear with no film on the surface. Color, aroma, and flavor should be pleasing and characteristic of the type of tea selected. Black tea will be amber colored, full flavored, and not bitter, and the aroma will be pleasing. Green tea will be a pale yellow green and the aroma will be delicate. Oolong is intermediate between these two.

COFFEE RECIPES

Dripolator

Total Time: 18 minutes

1. Heat water to boiling in a 1-quart covered saucepan.
2. Measure drip grind coffee into the basket and assemble the dripolator. (If desired, line the bottom of the basket with filter paper before adding the coffee.)
3. Pour the freshly boiled water into the upper container and cover.
4. When all the water has dripped through, remove the upper container and basket of grounds.
5. Place the lid on the lower pot and serve the beverage.

(Serves two)

4 Tbsp	drip grind coffee (use less if weaker beverage desired)
1-1/2 c	water

(Serves four)

8 Tbsp	drip grind coffee (use less, if weaker beverage desired)
3 c	water

Note: Automatic dripolators are used very commonly for brewing dripolator coffee and are available with various features. Follow the manufacturer's directions for using a specific dripolator. However, regular dripolators are also used by many. The directions above are for using this type of dripolator.

Figure 13.2
Coffee bean cherries are harvested, dried, and the seeds (called coffee beans) inside are roasted before being ground to make the beverage.

Figure 13.3
Coffee beans are roasted by a woman in the highlands of Ethiopia, the region where coffee originated.

Percolator

Total Time: 6 minutes

1. Place water in the percolator and put regular grind coffee in the basket. Assemble the basket and its cover on the stem, place in the percolator, and put the lid on.
2. Heat on high temperature setting until the beverage begins to percolate. Adjust the heat somewhat lower to maintain a steady, but not vigorous percolation.
3. Percolate for 3 minutes. (Use longer time if stronger, more bitter beverage is preferred.)
4. Remove from heat and take out the basket containing the grounds and the stem. Serve the beverage.

(Serves two)

| 4 Tbsp | regular grind coffee (use less if weaker beverage is desired) |
| 1-1/2 c | water (use cold water for automatic pots) |

(Serves four)

| 8 Tbsp | regular grind coffee (use less, if weaker beverage is desired) |
| 3 c | water (use cold water for automatic pots) |

Note: Follow the manufacturer's directions if using an automatic percolator. If using a nonautomatic percolator, follow the directions above.

Criteria for Evaluation

A quality cup of coffee will be flavorful and free of bitterness, dark and clean, relatively free of sediment, with only a suggestion of a fat film.

Evaluation of Laboratory Products—Coffee

Recipe	Appearance	Aroma	Flavor
Dripolator coffee			
Percolator coffee			

COCOA AND HOT CHOCOLATE RECIPES

Cocoa

Total Time: 5 minutes

1. Mix the sugar, cocoa, and salt together.
2. Add the water and heat to boiling while stirring constantly.
3. Add the milk and heat to simmering while stirring slowly.
4. With a rotary beater, beat briefly.
5. Serve steaming hot.

(Serves two)

1-1/2 Tbsp	sugar
1-1/2 Tbsp	cocoa
1/4 c	water
trace	salt
1-1/4 c	milk

(Serves four)

3 Tbsp	sugar
3 Tbsp	cocoa
1/2 c	water
dash	salt
2-1/2 c	milk

Hot Chocolate

Total Time: 5 minutes

1. Melt chocolate in water to which sugar and salt have been added.
2. Heat to boiling.
3. Add milk gradually and heat to serving temperature.
4. Beat the hot chocolate briefly with a rotary beater.
5. Serve steaming hot.

(Serves two)

1	square unsweetened chocolate
1/2 c	water
2 Tbsp	sugar
trace	salt
1-1/2 c	milk

(Serves four)

2	squares unsweetened chocolate
1 c	water
4 Tbsp	sugar
dash	salt
3 c	milk

Figure 13.4
Pods from the cacao tree; the nibs inside are fermented and ground before ultimately becoming chocolate.

Criteria for Evaluation

Hot chocolate or cocoa should be a pleasing, delicate chocolate flavor, with no trace of scorching. There should not be a scum or a sediment.

Evaluation of Laboratory Products—Cocoa and Hot Chocolate

Recipe	Appearance	Aroma	Flavor
Hot chocolate			
Cocoa			

VOCABULARY

Oolong tea	Caffeine
Green tea	Caffeol
Black tea	Theine
Polyphenols	Tannins
Astringent	Scum formation

CHAPTER 14

Food Preservation

Key Concepts	Jams and Jellies
Canning Recipes	Recipes
Freezing	Vocabulary

Objectives

1. To demonstrate the preservation of foods by use of the following techniques: heat processing, freezing, drying, and addition of sugar and/or acid.

2. To identify the differences in the safe processing of canned fruits and vegetables and the reasons for these differences.

3. To illustrate the advantages and limitations of preserving foods by various techniques.

Food can be preserved at home by canning, freezing, drying, pickling with acid, and preserving with sugar or salt. The method used most commonly today is freezing because of its speed and convenience (especially for preserving leftovers). Commercial food companies include these techniques as well as irradiation or other techniques that require more sophisticated equipment than is available in the home. In this chapter, you will find a few recipes for preserving food at home. If you happen to live in an area where you have access to produce at good prices when the various crops are in season, you may find that food preservation is a task that you will enjoy and that will be cost effective. However, many people today have limited free time and little access to economical produce buys; for them, food preservation at home probably is not feasible.

KEY CONCEPTS

1. Food to be preserved should be of high quality so that the end product can be of sufficient quality to justify the time and energy spent in preserving it.

2. Food preservation requires use of some method for stopping or greatly retarding growth of microorganisms and chemical reactions within the food. For example, high temperatures or very low ones effectively preserve food by killing or greatly retarding microorganisms and halting biochemical processes.

3. Preservation makes it possible to safely store excess food supplies through to times when a particular food may be scarce or less abundant.

CANNING RECIPES

Apples

Water bath time: 20 minutes

(Makes 1 quart)	
1-1/2 lb	Rome Beauty, Winesap, or Jonathan apples
1-1/2 c	sugar
2 c	water
1/2 tsp	ascorbic acid

1. Wash jars in hot, soapy water and rinse thoroughly in very hot water. Be sure to use only glass canning jars in good condition.
2. Combine the water and sugar and heat to simmering.
3. Keep warm and covered while paring, coring, and slicing apples.
4. Hold sliced apples in water containing a small amount of lemon juice until all the apples are sliced and ready for canning.
5. Place the apple slices in the hot syrup, and boil gently for 5 minutes.
6. Fill jars with hot apples; be sure to leave 1/2" headspace.
7. Pour the boiling syrup over the fruit until the jar is filled to 1/2" from the top of the jar.
8. Run a rubber spatula around the inside of the jar to release all air bubbles that may be trapped by the fruit. Put on the lid, following the directions for the type of cap being used. (Dome caps are prepared by tightening the metal band and zinc caps are tightened with a new rubber ring and then loosened slightly.)
9. Place the jars on a rack in a boiling water bath and boil actively for 20 minutes.
10. The water level should be maintained at 1" to 2" above the tops of the jars throughout the processing period.
11. Remove jars from the canner and cool slowly for half a day. Be sure to tighten zinc caps slowly as soon as the jars are removed from the water bath.
12. After the jars are cooled completely, check the seal. The center of the cap is pulled downward if the seal is good. Remove metal bands if using dome caps.

(Makes 16 quarts)

1	bushel Rome Beauty, Winesap, or Jonathan apples
9 c	sugar
12 c	water
4 tsp	ascorbic acid

Peaches

Water bath time: 30 minutes

1. Wash jars in hot, soapy water and rinse thoroughly in very hot water. Be sure to use only glass canning jars in good condition.
2. Combine the water and sugar and heat to simmering.
3. Keep warm in a covered saucepan while preparing the peaches.
4. Wash the peaches before blanching them in boiling water for 30 seconds to loosen their skins.
5. Immediately after blanching, dip peaches in cold water.
6. Quickly peel the peaches, cut them in half, and remove the pit and red fibers surrounding the seed.
7. Place peaches in water containing lemon juice or ascorbic acid to prevent discoloration.
8. Pack each peach half, pit side down.
9. Pour hot syrup over peaches. Fruit and syrup should be at least 1/2″ below the top of the jar.
10. Use a rubber spatula to release bubbles of air from the jar.
11. Cap as described in the procedure for canning apples and process for 30 minutes, as described above.

(Makes 1 quart)

2 lb	peaches, freestone
1 c	sugar
1 c	water
1/4 tsp	ascorbic acid or lemon juice

(Makes 10 quarts)

1 lug	peaches, freestone
8 c	sugar
8 c	water
2-1/2 tsp	ascorbic acid or lemon juice

Pears

Water bath time: 25 minutes

1. Wash jars in hot, soapy water and rinse thoroughly in very hot water. Be sure to use only glass canning jars in good condition.
2. Prepare the syrup as described for peaches.
3. Wash, pare, and quarter the pears.
4. Hold in water containing lemon juice.
5. Add pear quarters to the syrup and boil gently 5 minutes.
6. Pack immediately.
7. Pour hot syrup over the fruit, being sure to leave 1/2″ headspace for both the fruit and the syrup.
8. Put the jars on a rack in the water bath, which is half filled with boiling water.
9. Maintain the water level 1″ to 2″ above the top of the jars during the 25-minute boiling period.
10. Cool and check the seal as described above.

(Makes 1 quart)

2 lb	pears
2/3 c	sugar
1-1/2 c	water
1/4 tsp	lemon juice

(Makes 15 quarts)

16 lb	pears
6 c	sugar
12 c	water
3-3/4 tsp	lemon juice

Green Beans

Pressure cooker time: 20 minutes at 10 pounds for pints; 25 minutes at 10 pounds for quarts

1. Wash jars in hot, soapy water and rinse thoroughly in very hot water. Be sure to use only glass canning jars in good condition.
2. Wash beans, break off ends, and cut or leave whole.
3. Boil in salted water for 5 minutes.
4. Pack jar loosely, leaving 1″ headspace for vegetable and liquid.
5. Process according to pressure cooker information. Add 20 additional minutes if using a pressure saucepan.
6. Place jars on rack, leaving space between.
7. Exhaust air from cooker (about 10 minutes).
8. Regulate heat to maintain pressure. Gauge will jiggle several times each minute. (Read directions for pressure device.)
9. Process the length of time indicated.
10. Let cooker return to room temperature before starting to remove jars.
11. Let cool, as above, and check seals.

(Makes 1 pint)

1 lb	green beans
2 c	water
1/2 tsp	salt

(Makes 2 pints)

2 lb	green beans
4 c	water
1 tsp	salt

Beet Pickles

Water bath time: 30 minutes

1. Wash jars in hot, soapy water and rinse thoroughly in very hot water. Be sure to use only glass canning jars in good condition.
2. Wash beets and cut off tops, but leave stems and tap root.
3. Put beets in pan of boiling water to just cover the vegetable; boil until tender.
4. Peel and slice the beets into slices about 1/4″ thick.
5. Meanwhile, simmer all of the other ingredients in a covered saucepan for 10 minutes.
6. Pack beets and add hot, spiced liquid after the cinnamon and cloves have been removed.
7. Leave 1/2″ headspace for the beets and the juice. Process as described above for 30 minutes.

(Makes 1 pint)

1/3 c	sugar
7/8 c	distilled vinegar
1/4 c	water
1/4 tsp	salt
1/2 tsp	pickling spices
2	whole cloves
1/3	stick cinnamon
2 c	sliced, cooked beets

(Makes 3 pints)

1 c	sugar
2-3/4 c	distilled vinegar
3/4 c	water
3/4 tsp	salt
1-1/2 tsp	pickling spices
6	whole cloves
1	stick cinnamon
6 c	sliced, cooked beets

Dill Pickles

Water bath time: 15 minutes

1. Wash jars in hot, soapy water and rinse thoroughly in very hot water. Be sure to use only glass canning jars in good condition.
2. Tie the spices in cheesecloth and simmer in a covered saucepan with the sugar, salt, water, and vinegar for 15 minutes.
3. Cut the cucumbers in halves or spears and pack into jars.
4. Remove spices from the salt brine.
5. Heat the brine to boiling and pour over the cucumbers.
6. Put a sprig of dill weed in each jar.
7. Leave 1/4" headspace in each jar.
8. Heat for 15 minutes in a boiling water bath as described above.

(Makes 1 pint)

6	medium cucumbers
3-1/2 tsp	salt
1/2 c	vinegar
1/2 c	water
1-1/2 tsp	mixed pickling spices
1-1/2 Tbsp	sugar
	sprig dry dill

(Makes 4 pints)

24	medium cucumbers
4-1/3 Tbsp	salt
2-1/4 c	vinegar
1-1/4 c	water
2 Tbsp	mixed pickling spices
6 Tbsp	sugar
4	sprigs dry dill

Peach Pickles

Water bath time: 10 minutes

1. Wash jars in hot, soapy water and rinse thoroughly in very hot water. Be sure to use only glass canning jars in good condition.
2. Wash the peaches and place in boiling water for 30 seconds to loosen skin.
3. Peel the peaches and place them in water containing lemon juice.
4. Combine the vinegar, water, sugar, and cinnamon; bring to boiling.
5. Place a clove in each peach and put the peaches in the boiling liquid.
6. Continue boiling until the peaches are heated through.
7. Put the peaches in glass jars.
8. Pour the boiling syrup over the peaches, leaving 1/4" headspace.
9. Process as described above for 10 minutes.

(Makes 1 pint)

1 c	white vinegar
1 c	water
1/4 tsp	lemon juice
1 c	granulated sugar
1-1/2	sticks cinnamon
4	whole cloves
4	small peaches

(Makes 6 pints)

2 c	white vinegar
2 c	water
1 tsp	lemon juice
2 c	granulated sugar
3	sticks cinnamon
24	whole cloves
24	small peaches

FREEZING

Broccoli

Thoroughly wash fresh broccoli to remove all dirt and possible insects. Trim the leaves from the stalk and cut the stalk where it begins to be slightly woody. If stalks are large, split in quarters lengthwise. Place in a perforated basket and immerse in a large kettle of rapidly boiling water for 3 minutes (blanch 4 minutes if preparation is being done at 4,000 feet elevation or higher). Immediately transfer the blanched broccoli into a large kettle of ice water for 3 to 4 minutes. Package the drained broccoli in plastic or other relatively airtight containers. Pack tightly with an absolute minimum of air space. Label the container with the contents and the date of processing. Put in freezer immediately.

Asparagus

Wash asparagus very carefully to remove all traces of sand and dirt. Trim asparagus stalks to remove woody portion of the stalk. Leave in spears or cut into 100 segments. Blanch in a large kettle of rapidly boiling water for 2 to 4 minutes, depending upon the thickness of the stalk. Chill a comparable length of time in a large kettle of ice water. Package, label, and store as suggested for broccoli.

Spinach

Wash spinach thoroughly in a sinkful of cold water to remove all sand. Break off the ends of the stems and any bruised leaves. Blanch the spinach in a large kettle of rapidly boiling water for 2 minutes. Immediately plunge into a large kettle of ice water for 2 minutes. Package, label, and store as suggested for broccoli.

Corn

Remove the husk, being careful to clean away the silks. Wash well. Blanch 4 minutes if corn is to be frozen off the cob and 8 minutes if it is to be left on the cob. Chill in ice water for the same length of time as the blanching period. Cut corn from cob, if desired. Package, label, and store as suggested for broccoli.

Green Beans

Wash thoroughly. Cut off the ends and cut as desired or leave whole. Blanch 3 minutes in a large kettle of rapidly boiling water and chill 3 minutes in ice water. Package, label, and store as suggested for broccoli.

Strawberries

Wash berries well and look them over carefully. Cut away any soft or bruised spots. Pull off the caps. If desired, slice strawberries. Spread 2 cups of fruit in a shallow pan and sprinkle 6 tablespoons of sugar over the fruit. Stir very carefully until all of the fruit is coated with sugar and the sugar has dissolved to make a syrup over the fruit. Pack carefully into a plastic container or other relatively airtight package. Label with the contents and the date of processing. Freeze at once.

Peaches

First prepare sugar syrup by heating together 1-1/2 cups of sugar and 2 cups of water until the sugar is completely dissolved. Stir in 1/4 teaspoon ascorbic acid and thoroughly chill the syrup before using it with fruits. Wash peaches well. Dip peaches in boiling water for 30 seconds to loosen the skin. Peel the peaches and cut away any bruised or spoiled portions. Cut in half, remove pit, and slice, if desired. Put 1/2 cup of sugar syrup in a plastic container. Fill the container with the sliced fruit and pour enough sugar syrup over the fruit to completely cover the fruit. Avoid any delay from the time the fruit is peeled until the peaches are covered with the syrup so that discoloration of the peaches does not occur. The syrup prevents the browning that occurs as a result of oxidation. Seal the fruit tightly, label, and freeze immediately.

Pears

Prepare syrup as outlined for freezing peaches. Wash and peel pears. Cut pears into halves, quarters, or slices and package as indicated for peaches.

Pineapple

Cut pineapple into slices, spears, or cubes, as desired. Put fruit carefully into plastic container. Seal, label, and freeze promptly.

JAMS AND JELLIES

Before beginning to make jams and jellies, wash the jars carefully in soapy water and rinse them well with scalding water. Melt paraffin carefully in a double boiler. Keep the heat relatively low, but be sure the paraffin is fluid when needed. Be very careful to avoid splashing hot paraffin. Paraffin, when carelessly handled, presents a serious fire and burn hazard.

RECIPES

Freezer Strawberry Jam

Total time: 25 minutes

1. Wash jars well and rinse thoroughly in very hot water.
2. Wash the strawberries well. Remove the caps and cut away any spoiled or bruised areas.
3. Crush the fruit well.
4. Combine the fruit, sugar, and lemon juice, and let sit 20 minutes.
5. Heat the powdered **pectin** and water together until it boils and continue to boil 1 minute. If liquid pectin is used, omit water and do not heat the pectin.
6. Combine the liquid pectin or the rehydrated powdered pectin with the fruit–sugar mixture and stir for 3 minutes.
7. Pour into jars and cover tightly. Store in refrigerator for a maximum of three weeks, or in the freezer for longer storage.

(Makes 3 jelly jars)

2 c	fresh strawberries
2 c	sugar
1 Tbsp	lemon juice
1/4 bottle	liquid pectin
or	
1/2 package	powdered pectin
6 Tbsp	water (omit if using liquid pectin)

(Makes 6 jelly jars)

4 c	fresh strawberries
4 c	sugar
2 Tbsp	lemon juice
1/2 bottle	liquid pectin
or	
1 package	powdered pectin
3/4 c	water (omit if using liquid pectin)

Frozen Strawberry Jam

Total time: 10 minutes

1. Wash jars well and rinse thoroughly in very hot water.
2. Thaw berries to room temperature.
3. Stir in the sugar completely. Be sure there is no gritty feeling remaining. If necessary to dissolve all the sugar, warm the berries slightly.
4. Stir in the pectin very thoroughly.
5. Pour into jars.
6. Store in the refrigerator in tightly covered jars for a maximum of six weeks.

(Makes 3 jelly jars)

10 ounces	frozen strawberries
1-2/3 c	sugar
1/4 bottle	liquid pectin
1 tsp	lemon juice

(Makes 6 jelly jars)

20 ounces	frozen strawberries
3-1/3 c	sugar
1/2 bottle	liquid pectin
2 tsp	lemon juice

Rhubarb Marmalade

Total time: 10 minutes

1. Wash jars well and rinse thoroughly in very hot water.
2. Thinly slice the well-washed rhubarb, leaving it unpeeled.
3. Heat water and rhubarb to simmering in a covered saucepan; simmer until tender (about 1 minute).
4. Put 3 cups of fruit (6 cups for the large recipe) into large saucepan.
5. Stir in the sugar.
6. Bring quickly to a boil and boil hard for 1 minute.
7. Remove from heat.
8. Stir in the liquid pectin thoroughly so that it is well mixed with the fruit.
9. Stir and skim the mixture for 5 minutes to remove all traces of foam.
10. Put into jelly glasses and cover immediately with about 1/4" of melted paraffin.

(Makes 5 jelly jars)

1-1/2 lb	rhubarb
2 Tbsp	shredded orange rind
3/4 c	water
1/2 bottle	liquid pectin
5-1/2 c	sugar
	paraffin

(Makes 10 jelly jars)

3 lb	rhubarb
4 Tbsp	shredded orange rind
1-1/2 c	water
1 bottle	liquid pectin
11 c	sugar
	paraffin

Orange Marmalade

Total time: 45 minutes

1. Wash jars well and rinse thoroughly in very hot water.
2. With a sharp knife, cut the skin on the oranges and lemons into quarters and peel the fruit. Remove about half of the albedo (white portion of the skin).
3. Slice the remaining rind into very thin slices or shavings.
4. Add the water and soda.
5. Simmer in a covered saucepan for 20 minutes, stirring occasionally.
6. Meanwhile, remove the seeds from the fruit and cut the pulp into small pieces.
7. Add the pulp to the cooked rind, and continue simmering for 10 minutes.
8. Place 3 cups of this mixture (6 cups for large recipe) in a very large saucepan and stir in the sugar.
9. Heat over high heat to a rolling boil and boil 1 minute, stirring constantly.
10. Remove from the heat and immediately stir in the liquid pectin thoroughly.
11. Alternately, skim off the foam and stir the mixture for 7 minutes.
12. Put in jelly glasses.
13. Cover immediately with 1/4" of melted paraffin.

(Makes 6 jelly jars)

3	navel oranges
2	lemons
1/8 tsp	baking soda
1-1/2 c	water
5 c	sugar
1/2 bottle	liquid pectin
	paraffin

(Makes 12 jelly jars)

6	navel oranges
4	lemons
1/4 tsp	baking soda
3 c	water
10 c	sugar
1 bottle	liquid pectin
	paraffin

Blueberry Jam

Total time: 10 minutes

1. Wash jars well and rinse thoroughly in very hot water.
2. Crush the berries and stir in the pectin.
3. Add the lemon juice and heat quickly to a boil while stirring slowly.
4. Stir in the sugar, and continue stirring the mixture while it boils actively for 1 minute.
5. Remove from the heat. Skim off the foam.
6. Alternately, stir and skim off the foam for 5 minutes before pouring into jars.
7. Seal immediately with melted paraffin about 1/4" thick.

(Makes 5 jelly jars)

2 c	blueberries, fresh or frozen
1 Tbsp	lemon juice
2 c	sugar
1/2 box	powdered pectin
	paraffin

(Makes 9 jelly jars)

4 c	blueberries, fresh or frozen
2 Tbsp	lemon juice
4 c	sugar
1 box	powdered pectin
	paraffin

Grape Jelly

Total time: 8 minutes

1. Wash jars well and rinse thoroughly in very hot water.
2. Heat the juice and sugar to a boil.
3. Stir in the liquid pectin and boil 1 minute, stirring continuously.
4. Remove from heat.
5. While cooling for 2 minutes, skim off the foam.
6. Pour into jelly glasses.
7. Immediately pour 1/4" of melted paraffin over the jars of jelly.

(Makes 6 jelly jars)

2 c	bottled grape juice
3-2/3 c	sugar
1/2 bottle	liquid pectin

(Makes 12 jelly jars)

4 c	bottled grape juice
7 c	sugar
1 bottle	liquid pectin

Apple Jelly

Total time: 25 minutes

1. Wash jars well and rinse thoroughly in very hot water.
2. Quarter unpeeled apples and remove the stem and flower ends of each piece. Chop the quarters into small pieces. Be sure to leave in the core.
3. Put the apple pieces and the water into a kettle and quickly bring to a boil.
4. Simmer fruit 10 minutes.
5. Use a potato masher to crush the fruit and continue simmering.
6. Line a colander with two layers of cheesecloth.
7. Pour the fruit into the colander; catch the juice.
8. Measure 5 cups (10 cups for large) of the juice and combine with the sugar in a large saucepan.
9. Stir constantly while heating to a boil.
10. Stir in the pectin.
11. Heat again to boiling.
12. Boil for 1 minute while stirring.
13. Remove from heat, skim off the foam, and pour into jelly glasses.
14. Cover with a layer of melted paraffin 1/4" thick.

(Makes 4 jelly jars)

4 lb	tart, ripe apples
6-1/2 c	water
7-1/2 c	sugar
1/2 bottle	liquid pectin
	paraffin

(Makes 9 jelly jars)

8 lb	tart, ripe apples
13 c	water
15 c	sugar
1 bottle	liquid pectin
	paraffin

Raspberry-Pear Jam (with Fresh Berries)

Total time: 15 minutes

1. Wash jars well and rinse thoroughly in very hot water.
2. Quarter, core, and finely chop pears; mash on the cutting board with fork and *pack* to measure.
3. Wash and pick over raspberries and *pack* into measuring cup.
4. Combine fruits, lemon juice, and pectin in the kettle; bring to a boil.
5. Boil 1 minute, stirring.
6. Add sugar all at once and cook, stirring, until it returns to a boil.
7. Boil vigorously 1 minute.
8. Remove from heat; stir and skim for about 5 minutes to cool slightly and remove foam on top.
9. Pour into hot sterilized jars; seal at once with melted paraffin.

(Makes 3 jars)

3	fresh Bartlett pears (2 c mashed)
2/3 c	fresh raspberries (packed firmly)
1-1/2 Tbsp	lemon or lime juice
1/2 package	powdered fruit pectin
1-3/4 c	sugar
	paraffin

(Makes 7 jars)

6–8	fresh Bartlett pears (4 c mashed)
1-1/3 c	fresh raspberries (packed firmly)
3 Tbsp	lemon or lime juice
1 package	powdered fruit pectin
3-1/2 c	sugar
	paraffin

Raspberry-Pear Jam (with Frozen Berries)

Total time: 15 minutes

1. Wash jars well and rinse thoroughly in very hot water.
2. Halve, core, and chop pears.
3. Combine all ingredients except pectin in kettle; bring to boil and boil vigorously 1 minute.
4. Remove from heat, stir in pectin and stir, skimming off foam, for 5 minutes.
5. Pour into hot sterilized jars; seal at once with melted paraffin.

(Makes 4 jars)

1-1/2 lb	fresh Bartlett pears (3 c mashed)
1/2 package (5 oz)	frozen raspberries thawed, undrained
3-3/4 c	sugar
dash	salt
2 Tbsp	lemon juice
1-1/2 tsp	grated orange rind
1/4 bottle	liquid pectin
	paraffin

(Makes 9 jars)

3 lb	fresh Bartlett pears (6 c mashed)
1 package (10 oz)	frozen raspberries thawed, undrained
7-1/2 c	sugar
1/8 tsp	salt
1/4 c	lemon juice
1 Tbsp	grated orange rind
1/2 bottle	liquid pectin
	paraffin

Fruit Leather

Total time: 9 hours
Baking: 150°F

1. Grind fruits together until very fine.
2. Sprinkle a circle of powdered sugar (about 13″ in diameter) on a bread board.
3. Place 1/3 of the fruit (1/6 for the large recipe) on the powdered sugar.
4. Coat with the sugar and roll into a circle about 1/8″ thick.
5. Place on baking sheet and bake until leather-like (8–9 hours).
6. Roll in plastic wrap when cool.
7. Store in refrigerator in a plastic bag.

(Makes 3 sheets)

1/4 lb	dried prunes, pitted
1/4 lb	dried peaches
1/2 lb	dried apricots
1 c	powdered sugar

(Makes 6 sheets)

1/2 lb	dried prunes, pitted
1/2 lb	dried peaches
1 lb	dried apricots
2 c	powdered sugar

Note: Fruit leathers are interesting novelty items. They are of particular interest when planning food for camping trips.

Evaluation of Laboratory Products—Preserved Foods

Recipe	Notes on Color, Texture, Flavor, or Other Qualities	Comments or Suggestions for Making or Using this Product in the Future

VOCABULARY

Pectin	*Salmonella*
Pectic acid	Molds
Pectinic acid	Jams
Protopectin	Jelly
Botulism	Freezer burn

CHAPTER 15

Meal Management

Key Concepts
Aspects of Planning
   Nutrition
   Aesthetics

Time
Cost
Suggested Activities

Objectives

1. To integrate principles of food preparation into daily and individual meal preparation and planning.
2. To plan nutritionally adequate meals that meet economic parameters while also meeting specific food preferences and cultural patterns.
3. To develop time plans for selected menus and to evaluate time management.
4. To evaluate meal planning, food buying, preparation, and service of selected meals.

The preceding chapters have provided the basic knowledge necessary to prepare all parts of a meal. The trick is to plan the entire meal so that it meets nutritional needs while also being pleasing to eat without requiring too much time, energy, and money. There really is a great deal to coordinate when planning and preparing meals.

This chapter provides the chance to begin to put knowledge of food preparation to good use. The challenge of managing meals can be satisfying and rewarding. Recipes in previous chapters can serve as the springboard to creative menus. There are many other resources that may also be explored to help stretch creativity in meal planning.

KEY CONCEPTS

1. Meals need to be planned to provide the recommended intake of nutrients in a way that is pleasing to eat and that fits your lifestyle.

2. Menus can be evaluated on the basis of the nutritive value, sensory satisfaction (flavor, color, aroma, and texture), and cost (time, energy, and money).

ASPECTS OF PLANNING

A good meal requires sound planning of time and budget as well as knowledge of preparing specific foods. Success requires using knowledge of nutrition, managing resources, applying food science and practical skills of food preparation, and utilizing aesthetic and psychological principles. The following laboratory experiences provide the format needed to illustrate all aspects of good meal management.

Nutrition

The total plan of the day's menu should be developed carefully to provide the daily menu balance recommended in MyPlate to meet daily need for nutrients and calories. Visit the MyPlate website (http://www.choosemyplate.gov/) for suggestions.

Suggested amounts of foods from the various food groups daily for a 2000-calorie diet include the following:

Grains, 6.2 ounces (3.8 whole grains, 2.4 refined grains)

Vegetables, 2.6 cups

Fruits, 2.1 cups

Dairy, 3.1 cups

Protein foods, 5.7 ounces (including 8.8 ounces of seafood during a week)

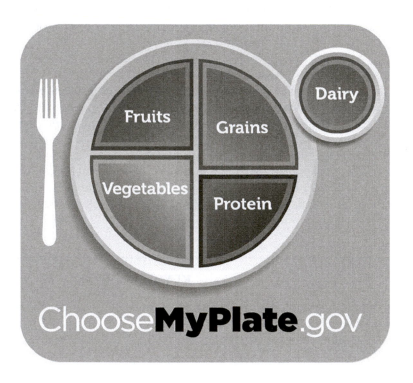

For most people it is important to include a good source of ascorbic acid at breakfast. To ensure good nutrition to start the day right, include an egg or other good protein source along with a glass of milk and some cereal or toast. Lunch and dinner should be planned to round out the recommended balance from all the groups of MyPlate, plus enough additional food for satisfaction and energy.

Aesthetics

Plan the foods in the menu for optimum color, texture, appearance, and flavor appeal. With the menu and the occasion in mind, select the table setting and service to fit the situation. Think carefully about the total setting for the meal so that it is pleasing to the eye, mind, and palate.

Time

A well-planned time schedule is essential when first learning to coordinate an entire meal. Time needed for setting the table, preparing foods for cooking, and serving the food all should be a part of the schedule. This takes careful thought if all the details are arranged so that the meal is served on time.

Cost

Money management can be learned by planning meals using grocery ads to meet the cost limitations. For the most experience, plan a meal and then see what variations might be made to adjust the basic plan to a low-, medium-, or high-cost meal. If possible, do the actual purchasing of food at the grocery store.

Efficient and economical food buying and preparation are boons to everyone with responsibilities for meal preparation. Many types of information are available to today's consumers to aid them in these tasks. The following listings are provided for convenience when shopping for and preparing food.

Equivalent Measures

1 Tbsp	= 3 tsp
1 fl oz	= 2 Tbsp
1/4 c	= 4 Tbsp
1 c	= 16 Tbsp or 8 fl oz
1 pt	= 2 c
1 qt	= 2 pt or 4 c
1 gal	= 4 qt or 8 pt or 16 c

Equivalent Weights

1 oz	= 28.35 g
1 lb	= 16 oz or 453.6 g
1 kg	= 2.21 lb

Substitutions

1 c nonfat milk	= 1 c minus 1 Tbsp of water + 1/3 c instant nonfat dry milk
1 c buttermilk	= 1 c yogurt
1 c milk	= 1 c buttermilk + 1/2 tsp soda + 1 tsp butter; reduce baking powder by 1 tsp in batters and doughs
1 c sour milk or buttermilk	= 1 Tbsp lemon juice or vinegar + milk to equal 1 c
1 Tbsp cornstarch	= 2 Tbsp flour
1 c cake flour	= 1 c 2 Tbsp all-purpose flour
1 package active dry yeast (1 oz)	= 1 Tbsp active dry yeast
1 package active dry yeast (1 oz)	= 1 cake compressed yeast
1 tsp baking powder	= 1/4 tsp baking soda + 3/4 tsp cream of tartar
1 tsp baking powder	= 1/4 tsp baking soda + 1/3 c molasses
1 tsp baking powder	= 1/4 tsp baking soda + 1/2 c sour milk
1 oz unsweetened chocolate	= 3 Tbsp cocoa (unsweetened) + 1 Tbsp margarine or butter

Approximate Yield Equivalents

1 c whipping cream	= 2 c whipped
1 lb butter or margarine	= 2 c
1 lb cheese	= 4 c grated cheese
1 lb all-purpose flour	= 4 c
1 c rice	= 1-2/3 c cooked rice
1 c bulgur	= 2-3/4 c cooked bulgur
1 c macaroni or spaghetti	= 2-1/4 c cooked pasta
1 c noodles	= 1-1/4 c cooked noodles
1 yolk	= 1 Tbsp
1 white	= 2-1/2 Tbsp
1 lb granulated sugar	= 3 c
1 lb brown sugar	= 2-1/4 c
1 lb nuts	= 3–4 c, depending on type of nuts
1 lb ground coffee	= 5 c
1 lb coffee	= 40–50 c prepared beverage
1 lb soda crackers	= 5 c medium fine crumbs
1 lb graham crackers	= 4-1/3 c crumbs

Common Container Sizes

Container (Industry Term)	Consumer Description		~ Cups	Principal Products
	~ Net Wt/Fl oz (Check Label)			
8 oz	8 oz		1	Fruits, vegetables, specialties for small families (2 servings)
Picnic	10-1/2–12 oz		1-1/4	Mainly condensed soups. Some fruits, vegetables, meat, fish, specialties (2–3 servings)
12 oz (vac)	12 oz		1-1/2	Principally for vacuum pack corn (3–4 servings)
No. 300	14–16 oz (14 oz to 1 lb)		1-3/4	Pork and beans, baked beans, meat products, cranberry sauce, blueberries, specialties (3–4 servings)
No. 303	16–17 oz (1 lb to 1 lb 1 oz)		2	Principal size for fruits and vegetables. Some meat products, ready-to-serve soups, specialties (4 servings)
No. 2	20 oz or 18 fl oz (1 lb 4 oz or 1 pt 2 fl oz)		2-1/2	Juices, ready-to-serve soups, some specialties, pineapple, apple slices. No longer in popular use for most fruits and vegetables (5 servings)
No. 2-1/2	27–29 oz (1 lb 11 oz to 1 lb 13 oz)		3-1/2	Fruits, some vegetables (pumpkin, sauerkraut, spinach and other greens, tomatoes) (5–7 servings)
No. 3 cyl or 46 fl oz	51 oz or 46 fl oz (3 lb 3 oz or 1 qt 14 fl oz)		5-3/4	Fruit and vegetable juices, pork and beans. Institutional size for condensed soups, some vegetables (10–12 servings)
No. 10	6-1/2 lb–7 lb 5 oz		12–13	Institutional size for fruits, vegetables, and some other foods (25 servings)
Other				Meats, poultry, fish, and seafood are advertised and sold almost entirely under weight terminology

SUGGESTED ACTIVITIES

1. Using the forms that follow, plan the meals for a day for a family of four.
2. Prepare one of the meals and evaluate the following:
   a. time plan
   b. the cost of the meal
   c. the accuracy of the market order
   d. the quality of the prepared food
   e. the table setting
   f. the service

Breakfast Menu

Time Schedule	Table Setting
Prepreparation:	Cloth or mats:
Day of meal:	Dishes:
Type of service:	Silverware:
Serving time:	Glassware:
	Accessories:
	Sketch of place setting:

Market Order—Breakfast

Food	Quantity	Unit Price	Total Cost
Dairy products			
Meat, fish, poultry, eggs			
Fresh produce			
Canned and frozen foods			
Bread and cereals			
Fats and oils			
Miscellaneous			

Total cost of meal: _____

Cost per person: _____

Lunch Menu

Time Schedule	**Table Setting**
Prepreparation:	Cloth or mats:
Day of meal:	Dishes:
Type of service:	Silverware:
Serving time:	Glassware:
	Accessories:
	Sketch of place setting:

Market Order—Lunch

Food	Quantity	Unit Price	Total Cost
Dairy products			
Meat, fish, poultry, eggs			
Fresh produce			
Canned and frozen foods			
Bread and cereals			
Fats and oils			
Miscellaneous			

Total cost of meal: _____

Cost per person: _____

Dinner Menu

Time Schedule	Table Setting
Prepreparation:	Cloth or mats:
Day of meal:	Dishes:
Type of service:	Silverware:
Serving time:	Glassware:
	Accessories:
	Sketch of place setting:

Market Order—Dinner

Food	Quantity	Unit Price	Total Cost
Dairy products			
Meat, fish, poultry, eggs			
Fresh produce			
Canned and frozen foods			
Bread and cereals			
Fats and oils			
Miscellaneous			

Total cost of meal: _____

Cost per person: _____

Complete the following chart with the menus used for breakfast, lunch, and dinner and evaluate the nutritional adequacy of the menus. If shortages exist in particular categories, suggest ways in which the menus could be improved.

Summary Chart of Sample Day's Menus

Food Group	Menu Item	Servings Recommended	Actual	Adequacy
Grains		6 oz		
Vegetables		2.6 cups		
Fruits		2.1 cups		
Milk		3.1		
Meat and beans		5.6 oz		
Oils		7.2 tsp		

Recommendations:

APPENDIX A

The Metric System

The metric system has been the means of weighing and measuring in Europe and most other parts of the world for a very long time. However, the United States has based its recipes (and most of its industry) on cups and pounds, not liters and kilograms. Length is stated in inches and yards, not in meters; temperature is in Fahrenheit, not in Celsius.

These differences in weighing and measuring systems sound rather unimportant, yet they are the source of many problems in international trade. Because of the economic and trade difficulties arising from these differences, the United States several years ago legislated to convert to the metric system over a 10-year period. Large investments were made in industry and in education to prepare for this crucial change. However, the momentum for making the change gradually was lost during the transition period.

Despite the fact that consumers in the United States have not converted to metrics, professionals do need to be able to interpret units of weights and measures in the metric system, for the technical and industrial world exists today in an international setting and the language of that setting is the metric system.

The language of technical laboratories where research and development are done in food companies also is metric. Food technologists and other scientists working in these competitive laboratories must be totally familiar with the metric system and able to work with it. They also must be able to convert recipes into consumer language, our present system of weights and measures.

The metric system is not a fact of life in U.S. homes, but the ability to convert to and from it is essential to food professionals. They also need to be functional in the metric system itself. Although it is a logical system based on units of ten, knowledge of the prefixes and the basic measures of weights, volumes, and lengths of the metric system is essential. The key information for application to the food industry, including temperature conversion, is presented below.

The prefixes for the units that are used commonly in food preparation are as follows:

kilo $= 1,000$ $= 10^3$

centi $= 1/100$ $= 10^{-2}$

milli $= 1/1,000$ $= 10^{-3}$

KEY CONCEPTS

1. The metric system is the common system for expressing volume, weight, and temperature in most countries today.

2. Knowledge of a few basic equivalencies and terminology will make conversion between metric and household units comparatively easy.

Conversions can be made readily if the following equivalencies are known:

Weights:

1 kilogram (kg) = 2.2 pounds (lb)

1 lb = 454 grams (g)

Volumes:

1 liter (l) = 1.06 quarts

1 cup = 236 milliliters (ml)

Lengths:

1 meter (m) = 39.37 inches (in)

1 inch = 2.54 centimeters (cm)

The formulae for converting temperature are as follows:

$$°C = 5/9(°F - 32)$$
$$°F = (9/5 \ °C) + 32$$

Calculate the following equivalencies:

1-1/2 c	=	_____	ml
472 ml	=	_____	c
3.3 lb	=	_____	kg
5 kg	=	_____	lb
9 in	=	_____	cm
25 cm	=	_____	in
300°F	=	_____	°C
400°F	=	_____	°C
220°C	=	_____	°F
100°C	=	_____	°F
190°C	=	_____	°F

Examples of a recipe for coffee cake in both the metric and standard systems are presented on the next page. Note particularly the use of the *temperature scales* in the two versions, the *pan sizes,* and the designations of *ingredient amounts.*

Blueberry Coffee Cake

Metric:	
125 ml	sugar
125 ml	shortening
1	large egg
500 ml	sifted flour
10 ml	baking powder
1 ml	salt
125 ml	milk
500 ml	blueberries, well drained
125 ml	brown sugar
125 ml	flour
3 ml	cinnamon
30 ml	margarine, melted

Standard:	
1/2 c	sugar
1/2 c	shortening
1	medium egg
2 c	flour
2 tsp	baking powder
1/4 tsp	salt
1/2 c	milk
2 c	blueberries, well drained
1/2 c	brown sugar
1/2 c	flour
1/2 tsp	cinnamon
2 Tbsp	margarine, melted

Oven: 175°C

1. Preheat oven.
2. Cream the shortening and sugar until light and fluffy.
3. Beat in the well-beaten egg.
4. Sift the dry ingredients together. Add a third of the dry ingredients to the creamed mixture, and stir.
5. Add half the milk and stir.
6. Repeat with the remaining thirds of dry ingredients alternately with the other half of the milk.
7. Pour into a well-greased pan. Metric: 20 cm × 30 cm.
8. Put blueberries over surface of the batter.
9. Combine brown sugar, flour, cinnamon, and melted margarine, and sprinkle over the blueberries.
10. Bake at 175°C for 35 to 45 minutes until a toothpick inserted in the center comes out clean.

Oven: 350°F

1. Same as metric.
2. Same as metric.
3. Same as metric.
4. Same as metric.
5. Same as metric.
6. Same as metric.
7. Pour into a well-greased pan. Standard: 8″×12″.
8. Same as metric.
9. Same as metric.
10. Bake at 350°F for 35 to 45 minutes until a toothpick inserted in the center comes out clean.

INDEX